# Financing Institutions of Higher Education

NBER

NATIONAL BUREAU *of* ECONOMIC RESEARCH

**National Bureau of Economic Research**

**Conference Report**

NBER
NATIONAL BUREAU *of* ECONOMIC RESEARCH

# Financing Institutions of Higher Education

Edited by **John Y. Campbell and Kaye Husbands Fealing**

**The University of Chicago Press**

Chicago and London

The University of Chicago Press, Chicago 60637
The University of Chicago Press, Ltd., London

Published 2026
Printed in the United States of America

35 34 33 32 31 30 29 28 27 26 1 2 3 4 5

ISBN-13: 978-0-226-84481-7 (cloth)
ISBN-13: 978-0-226-84482-4 (ebook)
DOI: https://doi.org/10.7208/chicago/9780226844824.001.0001

Library of Congress Cataloging-in-Publication Data

Names: Campbell, John Y., editor. | Fealing, Kaye Husbands, editor.
Title: Financing institutions of higher education / edited by John Y. Campbell and Kaye Husbands Fealing.
Other titles: National Bureau of Economic Research conference report.
Description: Chicago : The University of Chicago Press, 2026. | Series: National Bureau of Economic Research conference report | Papers from a conference held 2024 in Cambridge, Mass. | Includes bibliographical references and index.
Identifiers: LCCN 2025029930 | ISBN 9780226844817 (cloth) | ISBN 9780226844824 (ebook)
Subjects: LCSH: Universities and colleges—United States—Finance—Congresses. | Education, Higher—Economic aspects—United States—Congresses. | LCGFT: Conference papers and proceedings.
Classification: LCC LB2342 .F563 2026
LC record available at https://lccn.loc.gov/2025029930

⊚ This paper meets the requirements of ANSI/NISO Z39.48-1992 (Permanence of Paper).

Authorized Representative for EU General Product Safety Regulation (GPSR) queries: **Easy Access System Europe**—Mustamäe tee 50, 10621 Tallinn, Estonia, gpsr.requests@easproject.com
Any other queries: https://press.uchicago.edu/press/contact.html

## Relation of the Directors to the Work and Publications of the NBER

1. The object of the NBER is to ascertain and present to the economics profession, and to the public more generally, important economic facts and their interpretation in a scientific manner without policy recommendations. The Board of Directors is charged with the responsibility of ensuring that the work of the NBER is carried on in strict conformity with this object.

2. The President shall establish an internal review process to ensure that book manuscripts proposed for publication DO NOT contain policy recommendations. This shall apply both to the proceedings of conferences and to manuscripts by a single author or by one or more co-authors but shall not apply to authors of comments at NBER conferences who are not NBER affiliates.

3. No book manuscript reporting research shall be published by the NBER until the President has sent to each member of the Board a notice that a manuscript is recommended for publication and that in the President's opinion it is suitable for publication in accordance with the above principles of the NBER. Such notification will include a table of contents and an abstract or summary of the manuscript's content, a list of contributors if applicable, and a response form for use by Directors who desire a copy of the manuscript for review. Each manuscript shall contain a summary drawing attention to the nature and treatment of the problem studied and the main conclusions reached.

4. No volume shall be published until forty-five days have elapsed from the above notification of intention to publish it. During this period a copy shall be sent to any Director requesting it, and if any Director objects to publication on the grounds that the manuscript contains policy recommendations, the objection will be presented to the author(s) or editor(s). In case of dispute, all members of the Board shall be notified, and the President shall appoint an ad hoc committee of the Board to decide the matter; thirty days additional shall be granted for this purpose.

5. The President shall present annually to the Board a report describing the internal manuscript review process, any objections made by Directors before publication or by anyone after publication, any disputes about such matters, and how they were handled.

6. Publications of the NBER issued for informational purposes concerning the work of the Bureau, or issued to inform the public of the activities at the Bureau, including but not limited to the NBER Digest and Reporter, shall be consistent with the object stated in paragraph 1. They shall contain a specific disclaimer noting that they have not passed through the review procedures required in this resolution. The Executive Committee of the Board is charged with the review of all such publications from time to time.

7. NBER working papers and manuscripts distributed on the Bureau's web site are not deemed to be publications for the purpose of this resolution, but they shall be consistent with the object stated in paragraph 1. Working papers shall contain a specific disclaimer noting that they have not passed through the review procedures required in this resolution. The NBER's web site shall contain a similar disclaimer. The President shall establish an internal review process to ensure that the working papers and the web site do not contain policy recommendations, and shall report annually to the Board on this process and any concerns raised in connection with it.

8. Unless otherwise determined by the Board or exempted by the terms of paragraphs 6 and 7, a copy of this resolution shall be printed in each NBER publication as described in paragraph 2 above.

# Contents

# Acknowledgments

This project was made possible by a generous research grant from the Alfred P. Sloan Foundation. We are very grateful to Daniel Goroff, a vice president and program director at the Foundation, for his interest in the issues examined in this volume, and for his engagement and support. The project drew together higher education administrators and researchers from many subfields within economics who share a common interest in the financing of colleges and universities. The papers in this volume were presented and discussed at a research conference in Cambridge, Massachusetts, in April 2024.

We acknowledge the thoughtful input of Nikki Edgecombe, Benjamin Hermalin, Marie Mora, and Christina Paxson, who served as an advisory committee at the outset of this project. Many NBER staff members also contributed in important ways to the project's success. Jim Poterba, the NBER's President, has been an enthusiastic supporter; he helped turn informal conversations into a formal research plan. Denis Healy and Abbie Murrell were superb grant managers and served as liaisons between the NBER and the Sloan Foundation. The NBER conference staff, especially Tricia Stillwell, executed the meeting logistics with great efficiency. Helena Fitz-Patrick did a terrific job of managing the production process for this volume and has provided superb editorial assistance. Monica Novoa, a graduate student at Georgia Tech, gave outstanding assistance with background research for the introduction and curated the data appendix. Two anonymous reviewers provided comments and suggestions on the manuscript; we are very grateful for their input. The staff of the University of Chicago Press, especially Chad Zimmerman, were extremely helpful throughout the publication process.

# Introduction

John Y. Campbell and Kaye Husbands Fealing

In fall 2023, more than 18 million students were enrolled in degree-granting colleges and universities, about three-quarters of them in public institutions (Welding 2024). In 2022, about 62 percent of US high school graduates enrolled in college, and 36 percent of the US population aged 25 and above had a bachelor's degree or higher (Talbott 2024). Despite recent downward trends, the reach of higher education has expanded greatly in recent decades. In 1960, only 8 percent of the over-25 US population had college degrees.

The higher education sector contributes to the creativity, economic competitiveness, and resiliency of the US economy. Tertiary education is a key factor in upward economic mobility of individuals who seek undergraduate and graduate degrees from community colleges, four-year colleges and universities, and of those in the workforce who seek upskilling and reskilling training to keep up with rapidly changing technologies. Although the measurement of the economic return to higher education, in the form of increased earnings, raises many subtle issues, summarized for example in a recent review by Lovenheim and Smith (2022), Cecchetti and Schoenholtz (2019) suggest that a plausible estimate is that the median real return to a private or out-of-state public education is around 8 percent, while the reduced tuition of an in-state public education implies an even higher median real return around 10 percent. These returns are extremely high relative to those available in financial markets with comparable risk.

John Y. Campbell is the Morton L. and Carole S. Olshan Professor of Economics at Harvard University, and a research associate of the National Bureau of Economic Research.

Kaye Husbands Fealing is a professor in the Jimmy and Rosalynn Carter School of Public Policy at the Georgia Institute of Technology.

For acknowledgments, sources of research support, and disclosure of the authors' material financial relationships, if any, please see https://www.nber.org/books-and-chapters/financing-institutions-higher-education/introduction-financing-institutions-higher-education.

Institutions of higher education also have important effects on the economies where they are located. Valero and Van Reenen (2019) estimate that internationally, a 10 percent increase in the number of universities in a region is associated with an increase in regional GDP of 0.4 percent, with positive spillover effects to neighboring regions as well.

There is wide variation in the financial circumstances facing different types of institutions and the students they serve. However, for several parts of the higher education sector, the basic financial model has been under increasing stress for the last two decades. Institutions have faced rising costs and difficulty in securing commensurate revenue growth. These costs are passed on to students attending these institutions and may appear prohibitive to some prospective students. This makes it difficult for institutions of higher education to diversify their student bodies to educate more students from families with limited financial means. In a recent study, Wilson et al. (2021) analyzed how public universities' diversity and inclusion units managed budget allocations in response to the recent economic downturn due to the coronavirus pandemic. The authors concluded that when diversity and inclusion efforts are a strategic priority for the institution, this is reflected in the budget structure and should be manageable even during fiscal uncertainty, like a global pandemic.

In 2019–20, public four-year colleges and universities received roughly 38 percent of their revenues from federal and state governments, down more than 6 percentage points from the share in 2007–08 (National Center for Education Statistics 2021, table 333.10). The other sources of funds for public colleges and universities include self-supporting operations, net tuition and fees, private gifts, investment revenue and endowment income, and local government support. State funds provided to academic institutions are used to support four primary activities: general operations; research, agriculture, and medical programs; financial aid; and non-credit and continuing education (State Higher Education Executive Officers Association—SHEEOA—2021).

Private schools, as well as some public research universities, rely heavily on private philanthropy to cover costs that are not supported by student tuition, state support, or sponsored research. Philanthropic giving has remained strong at the most selective private schools. Growing wealth inequality has increased the resources of the wealthiest donors, many of whom appreciate both the social value of higher education—which has contributed to the emergence of many newer fortunes—and the long-term favorable publicity that named gifts to universities can provide. However, to the extent that private philanthropy takes the form of endowment gifts rather than current-use gifts, schools can spend only the investment income on the gifts and not the principal. The difficulty for universities is that the safe real interest rate, and hence the investment income generated by a conservative investment strategy, declined considerably during the first two decades of this century (Campbell and Sigalov 2022).

A low-return environment presents endowment-dependent institutions with a difficult choice. They can ignore the problem, in which case their endowment value will likely decline in real terms, forcing future reductions in spending; they can cut the spending rate today; or they can seek to increase return by taking more risk. The last reaction, sometimes known as "reaching for yield," is documented by Campbell and Sigalov (2022), who present a theoretical analysis of its motivation.

One investment strategy that many larger endowments have followed is to diversify broadly across asset classes, reducing allocations to US stocks and bonds and increasing allocations to international markets, commodities, real estate, hedge funds, and particularly private equity. This strategy, sometimes called the "Yale model" because it was pioneered by the university's endowment manager, David Swensen, in the late 1980s, has the potential to improve returns while limiting the additional risk that is taken on. However, diversified Yale-model endowments are still exposed to large common shocks affecting all asset classes, such as the global financial crisis in 2008–09, and there are concerns, raised for example by Stafford (2022), that risks in private equity are understated because these investments are not promptly marked to market. The illiquidity of private equity can also cause problems for universities that seek to draw on their endowments during downturns.

A key question for endowment-dependent institutions is how they should react to unexpected endowment returns that can be highly volatile from one year to the next. Unusually good returns trigger a debate between those who would like to smooth benefits over time, either by increasing current spending gradually or by capital spending on infrastructure and renovations, and those who would like to use a windfall to meet core educational objectives such as expanding access. Unusually poor returns trigger an even more intense debate between those who would like to take time to adapt to reduced resources and those who argue with Winston Churchill that one should "never let a good crisis go to waste," and that the university should take the opportunity of financial stringency to cut activities that are less successful or of lower priority to the institution.

These issues were particularly salient during the global financial crisis in 2008–09, and again during the coronavirus pandemic in 2020–21. Importantly, these recent downturns occurred at a time when inflation was low, and hence universities were unable to adjust by constraining nominal wage growth and allowing real wages to fall, a strategy that many followed during the high-inflation 1970s. Commonfund Higher Education Price Index® (HEPI) data show that costs for colleges and universities rose 1.9 percent in FY2020 and 2.7 percent in FY2021. The five-year average HEPI inflation rate for the 2016–2021 period was 2.6 percent. Within the index there are some more volatile components, notably utilities, which saw a 15.0 percent cost increase in FY2021 versus a 15.7 percent decline in FY2020.

The higher inflation experienced since 2021 presents both challenges and opportunities for universities. Comparative research on the experience of higher education institutions during periods of low and high inflation would be especially useful in providing guidance for this new economic setting. If colleges and universities are able to raise nominal tuition prices, while holding down wage growth, their financial profile may brighten. For institutions that are constrained by the need for legislative approval of tuition increases, however, higher inflation may be a challenge that further stresses finances.

The COVID-19 pandemic disrupted cash flows but also coincided with some of the strongest financial returns on record for many large college and university endowments. The impact of the pandemic and its aftermath varies substantially across institutions. Some schools, particularly in the community college sector, have experienced cost pressures and enrollment declines in response to a tight labor market. On the other hand strong financial returns after the pandemic—34 percent at Harvard, 40 percent at Yale, and an extraordinary 65 percent at Washington University in St. Louis—have provided new financial flexibility for institutions fortunate enough to have such resources (Bauman 2022). These institutions account for a relatively small share of enrollment but are widely followed in the media and other outlets.

Given this backdrop of demographic and institutional challenges, the goal of this conference volume is to understand changes in decision-making by students, families, and financial managers of institutions as they face financial challenges in US higher education sector. Such challenges include the stagnating number of college-age domestic students, geographic mismatch of growing populations and thriving colleges and universities, financial pressures stemming from the coronavirus pandemic, growing student debt burdens and sticker prices that deter prospective applicants, conflicting objectives among those who have fiduciary responsibilities for these institutions, and low expected returns in capital markets. There are also opportunities on the horizon to increase access to education among diverse and distributed populations, and to reimagine the use of financial instruments and organizational structures to improve performance in the sector. The volume aims to promote an exchange of ideas among higher education administrators, consultants, and scholars. It draws together insights from financial and organizational economics, public finance, and industrial organization, as well as the economics of education.

## Paper Summaries

Some of the questions addressed in this conference volume include:

1. Affordability, access, and impacts on sustainability of various types of institutions of higher education: How will the gradual decline in the size of domestic cohorts of 18-year-olds affect the financing of the higher education sector?

2. Management strategies of financial assets and liabilities of universities, given uncertainties related to endowments and debt: How will endowment-dependent institutions adjust to unexpected positive or negative shocks in capital markets, and handle low prospective asset returns? Are there ways to make university budgets more flexible to accommodate these shocks? Given the difficulties that universities face in adjusting their operations rapidly, what is the right model for long-term economic planning in institutions of higher education?

3. Financing community colleges and minority serving institutions (MSIs): How have universities and colleges incorporated diversity and inclusion goals in financial frameworks? What are the prospects of developing new revenue sources that can increase access to higher education for students from a broad spectrum of experiences and geographies? What are the actual and perceived barriers to entry to institutions of higher education that reimagining financial models and organizational structures could solve? What does it take to broaden access to higher education, what does it cost institutionally, and how can those costs be managed?

The papers in the volume are organized into three broad groups that address these questions. The volume also includes several written discussions of the papers as well as written remarks by three academic leaders who participated in an informative panel session. In addition, many other participants attended the two meetings associated with this project, and made valuable comments and suggestions that improved the papers.

The first group of papers looks at tuition revenue, the most obvious source of income for an educational institution but one with doubtful growth prospects in the coming years. A challenge for the higher education sector is that enrollment has declined considerably since its peak in 2010. A paper by Jacob Vigdor, "The Ebbing Tide: How Will Higher Education Adapt to Demographic Change?" reports a decline in enrollment from 2010 to 2022 of 2.7 million students, about 12 percent of the 22 million students enrolled at the peak. Vigdor asks to what extent this decline is driven by demographic trends and other exogenous forces, and to what extent it can be offset by policy changes available to colleges and universities.

At the aggregate level, the period from 2010 to 2022 saw a 5 percent decline in the number of 18-year-olds in the United States, so that declining enrollment might appear unsurprising in this environment. However, Vigdor points out that the number of 18-year-olds declined far more, by almost 25 percent, during the period from 1981 to 1991, and during that time enrollment growth was positive albeit slower than it had been in earlier decades. Universities and colleges at that time were able to sustain growth by increasing the share of 18-year-olds who went to college and lowering their dropout rates, as well as by expanding graduate degrees and recruiting international students.

To understand the different experience in the 2010–2022 period, Vigdor performs a cross-sectional analysis for an important type of institution: public schools offering four-year degrees. He shows that for these institutions, state-level demographic trends are strong predictors of enrollment changes in 2010–2022. The demographic effects are strongest for baccalaureate colleges that award only bachelor's degrees, and weakest for flagship research universities with R1 status. Enrollment declines are also stronger among commuter schools without on-campus housing, historically Black colleges and universities (HBCUs), and institutions with lower grant revenue. It appears that the measures schools took in earlier decades to resist demographic forces have no longer proved effective.

Looking into the future, Vigdor combines demographic projections with the estimated enrollment model to forecast an overall enrollment decline of almost 13 percent in public four-year institutions between 2021 and 2033. Enrollment projections are much more favorable for R1 universities but much worse for baccalaureate colleges, whose enrollment is projected to decline by over 25 percent. These trends will be challenging to manage as the most affected schools have negligible endowments, limited grant revenue, and little ability to raise tuition. In recent years state and local governments have increased transfers per student for schools experiencing enrollment declines, but there are political constraints on the extent of this type of support.

Francisca Antman, the discussant of Vigdor's paper, emphasizes that demographic projections can be enhanced by performing them separately for different racial and ethnic groups, given that these groups have different propensities to attend college. Antman also highlights the strong shift in student demand away from humanities and toward engineering and scientific fields, which have implications for resource allocation within universities as well as for the prospects of smaller schools that may be less equipped to offer the majors that are most in demand.

A paper by Peter Hinrichs, "How Much Can Families Afford to Pay for College?" turns attention to the resources families have available to pay college tuition bills. Hinrichs uses the federal government's concept of Expected Family Contribution (EFC), as calculated on the Free Application for Federal Student Aid (FAFSA) form. The EFC combines student and parental income and assets, excluding housing and retirement accounts, and then applies a graduated contribution rate (analogous to a progressive tax rate) to estimate the amount that a family can reasonably pay for college. Using survey data on enrolled undergraduates over the period 1996–2020, Hinrichs finds that the EFC was relatively stable in real terms from 1996 until 2012 and increased thereafter, with the increase being concentrated in the top quartile of family incomes, among White and Asian households, and among households with college degrees—all of these patterns reflecting trends in the distribution of income and wealth rather than any important changes in the methodology used to calculate the EFC.

Hinrichs compares these trends in the EFC with the average cost of attendance (COA) at the colleges attended by the students in the survey. COA reflects the "full sticker price," the maximum cost that any student could be charged by a college. COA has grown faster than EFC, so financial need, defined as the gap between COA and EFC, has also increased—although less strongly among households in the top quartile of income.

This does not necessarily mean that households are under greater financial stress, however, because as Hinrichs's discussant, Phillip Levine, emphasizes, few students—even those with top-quartile family income—actually pay the COA. Tuition discounts are widespread, and the COA may have risen as fast as it has precisely because colleges are willing to charge high prices to a few particularly wealthy students in order to keep costs down for other families. But such a strategy can raise only limited revenue for schools given the small number of COA-paying students.

Another contribution of Hinrichs's paper is to show how the EFC would change under various possible changes in the methodology used to calculate it. Including home equity in the EFC calculation of wealth would penalize Hispanic households and help Asian households relative to White and Black households, while including retirement accounts would penalize White and Asian households and help Black and Hispanic households.

A paper by Robert Kelchen, Dubravka Ritter, and Douglas Webber, "Predicting College Closures and Financial Distress," asks how operational and financial data, including data on enrollments and tuition revenue, can be used to forecast the closure of colleges. The focus is on private colleges, both non-profit and for-profit, since public institutions very rarely close although they may be merged. (Mergers and consolidations are excluded from the focus of the paper because of challenges in measuring these events.)

While rich data on college operations and finances are available in the US Department of Education's Integrated Postsecondary Education Data System (IPEDS), many variables have incomplete coverage, and this is a particular problem for measures of debt, assets, and leverage. To handle this, the paper argues for the use of a machine learning classification algorithm, XGBoost, that can handle missing data and nonlinearly transform available predictors and interact them with one another. The performance of XGBoost compares favorably with more traditional prediction methods: specifically, with OLS estimation of linear probability models using continuous predictors, a subset of continuous predictors selected using least absolute shrinkage and selection (LASSO), or discretized (binned) predictors that can include dummies for variables that are expected to be missing.

The authors find substantial predictability in college closures. As one measure of this, among colleges with complete data, 83 out of the 100 observations with the highest XGBoost-predicted closure probabilities actually closed within three years. The most important variables contributing to this predictive ability are growth rates of operating variables such as revenue, tuition, enrollment, and staff, along with failures to meet federal accountability metrics.

The paper uses the XGBoost model to forecast what may happen in the future under alternative enrollment scenarios. Using 2019 as a pre-COVID baseline, the enrollment declines that occurred in 2019–2023 already imply an additional institution closing each year. A onetime decline of 15 percent in enrollment relative to 2019 would create a wave of over 70 closures and ongoing closures of an additional five institutions per year. While the precise numbers depend on the particular model used and scenarios considered, it is clear that demographic trends are likely to put a significant number of colleges and universities under significant financial stress. Closures also have the potential to adversely affect the local economies surrounding closed colleges, a topic the paper highlights as a priority for future research.

A second group of papers focuses on the financial assets and liabilities of universities, specifically endowments and debts.

Christopher Avery, Ronald Ehrenberg, Catharine Hill, and Douglas Webber's paper, "Endowment Spending Rules," takes a comprehensive look at the financial decisions of private, non-profit institutions that report endowment information on IRS Form 990. The paper focuses on 187 colleges and universities with the highest 2021 endowments per student and tracks these institutions using available data between 2008–09 and 2021–22. During this period investment returns on these endowments were strong, above 7 percent in nominal terms, and were supplemented by contributions above 3 percent of endowment value. Average payout rates from endowments were about 5 percent, and inflation in the higher education price index (HEPI) averaged about 2.5 percent.

Observed spending data can be used to estimate the parameters of spending rules relating endowment distributions to lagged endowment values and lagged spending. The authors obtain estimates that are broadly in line with institutions' statements about their payout rules, although they do show that schools spend new contributions relatively rapidly, consistent with the idea that they aim to demonstrate to donors near-term mission impact from the gifts they receive.

The paper emphasizes the importance of quasi-endowment funds, also known as "funds functioning as endowment," which are unrestricted funds invested alongside true endowment funds. Endowment distributions do not represent actual spending if the distributions are reinvested as quasi-endowment. The paper shows that net spending that adjusts for quasi-endowment accumulation is more volatile, as a fraction of initial endowment, than conventional measures of endowment distributions. The paper also shows that colleges and universities have built up their quasi-endowments alongside their endowments during the period of strong investment returns in the early part of this century. While this could be criticized as "hoarding" funds, it could be justified if schools are taking the time to plan large new initiatives or if they are building reserves in anticipation of future financial challenges.

Jeffrey Brown, the paper's discussant, questions whether endowment spending and asset allocation decisions can be justified as the outcome of a university's intertemporal optimization problem. Standard theory would for example imply that universities should match assets and liabilities and should use endowment assets to hedge the risks in their other sources of income; yet there is little evidence that this occurs. Brown suggests instead that principal-agent problems are important. As one example, Brown cites the finding of his earlier research (Brown et al. 2014) that university leaders are reluctant to allow endowment values to fall below the level that prevailed when they took office.

A paper by John Campbell, Jeremy Stein, and Alex Wu, "Economic Budgeting for Endowment-Dependent Universities," develops a framework to analyze a university's financial position using an intertemporal budgeting approach. The approach, designed for universities with substantial financial assets, forecasts university operating revenues and costs over the infinite future, calculates the present value of those operating obligations, and then compares the value of the obligations to the value of the university's wealth.

This approach differs from standard university budgeting procedures, which typically focus on a single year and use generally accepted accounting principles (GAAP) to calculate an annual budget surplus or deficit. A GAAP budget is misleading from the perspective of an economist interested in the university's intertemporal budget constraint, because it mixes financial flows with the real-side revenues and expenses that reflect the physical economics of the university. For example, distributions from the endowment and proceeds from new debt issuance are both treated as forms of revenue. However, these sources of revenue simply transfer a pool of fixed resources from the future to the present—higher endowment spending today leads to lower endowment spending in the future, and debt issuance today requires debt repayment in the future. There is no distinction in a GAAP budget between these sources of revenue and other sources, such as increased tuition income, which improve the university's long-run financial position.

In contrast to the conventional budgeting method, the intertemporal approach fully separates real and financial flows. The real operating economics of the university are captured in the present value of the net expenditures, which have nothing to do with debt issuance, interest expense, or endowment payouts. And financial resources are fully captured by the current value of the endowment in excess of debt obligations. The difference between the present value of operating obligations and wealth is the present-value shortfall of the university.

The authors illustrate their approach using data from the Harvard Faculty of Arts and Sciences (FAS) as of June 30, 2023. For the first few years through 2028 they have granular FAS cash-flow forecasts, and they assume constant growth rates for subsequent years. These cash-flows are discounted at a real interest rate of 5 percent, consistent with the assumption that Harvard's endowment is able to earn a 5 percent real rate of return in expectation. These procedures imply that FAS has a present-value shortfall of $6.54 billion, corresponding to an annualized structural deficit of $327 million or about 20 percent of the 2023 operating costs of the FAS. This negative finding contrasts with modest positive GAAP surpluses reported by the FAS in recent years. It highlights the fact that a large endowment—almost $18 billion for the FAS—is not available to fund new spending if the institution is already using it to pay for operating expenses.

Antoinette Schoar, the paper's discussant, highlights the danger that an intertemporal budgeting approach can be misused by manipulating assumptions about distant future cash-flow growth rates to disguise a university's true financial position. Schoar also discusses the responses of universities to short-term GAAP deficits and questions whether these responses are optimal.

In "The Role of Debt in Financing Higher Education," Matteo Binfarè and Kyle Zimmerschied turn attention to the use of debt by both public and private non-profit four-year universities. They combine municipal bond data from Refinitiv with financial and operating data on universities from IPEDS over a long sample period from 1985 to 2022. They compare tax-exempt and taxable issuance, the former having lower yields and the latter—increasingly popular since the 2008–09 Great Recession—allowing greater flexibility in the use of bond proceeds. A substantial fraction of bond issuance is associated with refinancing given the prolonged decline in interest rates over their sample period. However, public universities in particular increased their leverage substantially during the 2000s and the early 2010s, with some reversal in recent years.

Binfarè and Zimmerschied also track changes in credit ratings for issuers and bonds over time, observing that university credit quality has remained stable over time, with an increasing number of schools being rated, while the average credit quality of bonds declined after the Great Recession when municipal bond insurance became unavailable or exorbitantly expensive. AAA bonds have accounted for less than 10 percent of recent issuance, as compared with about 50 percent before the Great Recession.

Comparing bond yields across issuers and controlling for a wide variety of issuer and bond characteristics, the authors find that public universities issue bonds at slightly lower yields than private universities must pay.

The authors also relate university leverage to the composition of revenue and expenses. Public universities that receive a lower share of their revenue from state and federal government support tend to have higher leverage, and schools with high reliance on long-term debt tend to spend heavily on student services and dormitory capacity. This pattern is consistent with the view that debt is used to finance fixed assets, particularly when direct state support is not available for this purpose.

The discussant of this paper, Daniel Bergstresser, emphasizes that public-private partnerships, in which universities sign lease contracts with private developers, are an increasingly common alternative way for schools to finance the provision of fixed assets such as dormitories, parking garages, and even classrooms and offices. Understanding such novel forms of leverage is an interesting task for future research.

A third group of papers in this volume focuses attention on community colleges and minority serving institutions (MSIs) that provide higher education to traditionally underserved populations. Such institutions are particularly important as the higher education sector seeks to increase the fraction of Americans who earn college degrees and to realize the ideals of diversity, equity, and inclusion.

Nikki Edgecombe, Elise Swanson, Thomas Brock, Maria Cormier, Christopher Avery, and Carmen Huynh provide an overview of the community college sector in "Financing Community Colleges: Current Landscape and Future Directions." They delineate the scale of the sector (almost 1,000 community colleges enrolling over one-third of all US undergraduates) and highlight the attractions of low tuition and convenient local access to lower-income and minority students.

The financing problem for community colleges is that tuition can only be kept low if the colleges receive public support, particularly from states but sometimes from local governments as well. (Federal funding is generally modest for these institutions.) The heart of the paper is a detailed comparison of the systems by which this support is allocated in six states—California, Michigan, New York, Ohio, Tennessee, and Texas—that account for almost half of all community college students in the United States. These states vary widely in the proportion of state support provided (highest in Tennessee at 52 percent, lowest in Michigan and Texas at 22 percent), the proportion of local support (highest in Texas at 36 percent, lowest in Tennessee at 1 percent, and the reliance on tuition and fees (highest in Tennessee at 43 percent, lowest in California at 13 percent). They also vary in the extent to which they tie state support to student enrollments or to educational outcomes. The paper highlights the importance of allocating funds in a way that takes account of the varying educational challenges that each community college faces, for example with regard to the level of services its students require to succeed.

The authors also discuss the relatively flexible federal funding that was provided to community colleges during the COVID-19 pandemic by the Higher Education Emergency Relief (HEER) fund. Community colleges used these funds to offset lost tuition revenue, assist students with food, housing, and mental health needs, and invest in information technology to offer online education. Importantly, funds were allocated in a way that recognized the greater needs of schools enrolling larger numbers of low-income students receiving Pell grants. The paper suggests that lessons learned from this experience can be valuable for states in the post-pandemic environment.

The two final papers in the volume examine in detail two barriers to college enrollment that particularly affect lower-income and minority students: distance to school, and the level of tuition before discounts (sticker price).

Riley Acton, Kalena Cortes, and Camila Morales, in "Distance to Opportunity: Higher Education Deserts and College Enrollment Choices," use administrative data from Texas to explore how the distance to the nearest two-year and four-year schools (from the high schools that students attended, used as proxies for their home locations) affects students' decisions whether to attend college and if so whether to go to a two-year school or a four-year school.

Setting the stage, the authors show that students in rural south and west Texas, who are disproportionately White and Hispanic, must often contend with much greater distances to the nearest schools than students in east Texas and particularly the densely populated Texas Triangle, who are disproportionately Black and Asian. These distances are associated with reduced probabilities of college attendance, but the effects are heterogeneous across income levels, race, and ethnicity. Specifically, White and higher-income students who live far from the nearest two-year college tend to respond by attending a four-year college, whereas Black, Hispanic, and lower-income students tend to respond by not going to any college at all. (The distinction between higher- and lower-income students is measured by whether students qualify for lunch subsidies or other public assistance.) These differences in responses to distance, rather than differences in distance itself, are important for understanding racial and economic disparities in four-year college enrollment propensities.

The paper also explores nonlinear effects of distance, with special attention to "college deserts," areas that are more than 30 miles away from the nearest two- or four-year college. Living in a two-year college desert has a negligible effect on college attendance for White and higher-income students, but lowers the probability of college enrollment by as much as 12 percentage points for Black, Hispanic, and lower-income students. The paper uses these estimates to simulate the effects of closing specific community colleges, finding for example that two-year colleges in Hispanic areas of Texas are particularly important for sustaining overall enrollment levels in Texas public colleges.

Zachary Bleemer, the discussant of this paper, emphasizes that while distance and the response to distance are important for understanding four-year college enrollment, they do not appear to contribute importantly to the gaps by income and race in the overall propensity to attend college (including both two-year and four-year colleges). Bleemer calls for further research on the causal effects of college openings and closings, and for analysis of distance effects on students' choice of college majors.

In "Examining the Effects of Tuition Reset Policies on Enrollment and Institutional Finances at Minority Serving Institutions," James Dean Ward, Daniel Corral, and Catharine Hill ask whether minority students are particularly susceptible to "sticker shock," in which the level of full tuition and fees deters students from applying and enrolling even if schools are willing to offer tuition discounts. To respond to this problem, some minority serving institutions (MSIs) have used tuition resets, defined as cutting their sticker prices by at least 5 percent.

The paper provides a general overview of minority serving institutions and of the strategy of tuition resets. The core of the paper is a difference-in-difference estimation that compares outcomes for tuition-resetting MSIs with outcomes for a matched control group of non-resetting MSIs. Importantly, the sample includes both public and private MSIs. The paper finds that tuition resets do not increase the number of applications to a school, possibly because some potential applicants interpret low tuition as a sign of low quality, a negative effect that may offset positive effects on other applicants who prioritize affordability. However, private MSIs (which typically have higher initial tuition levels) do experience growth in enrollments, including enrollments of Pell grant recipients, and growth in tuition revenue. Overall, these findings suggest that lower-income minority students are particularly vulnerable to sticker shock that may be ameliorated by resetting tuition; but schools should beware of reputational side effects of tuition resets, which may outweigh their benefits particularly for public MSIs.

Bridget Long, the discussant of this paper, stresses the importance of the topic but emphasizes the need to make finer distinctions between different types of MSIs, for example with regard to selectivity and the degree of commitment to serving minority students. She also calls for more research on the drivers of tuition policy and the relative importance of schools' financial circumstances, potential student population, and the competitive environment they face.

The volume also includes written remarks by three senior academic leaders based on a panel discussion at the conference.

Benjamin Hermalin, currently the Provost of the University of California at Berkeley, clarifies the long-term financial challenges facing California's flagship research university. He highlights Berkeley's dependence on state funding and the decline in the real value of that funding over the last 20 years, even as the size of Berkeley's student body has increased and the share of out-of-state students, who make high tuition payments, has declined. On the cost side, Hermalin emphasizes the financial costs of regulatory compliance, efforts to expand educational opportunities to a broader range of students, and competition to recruit faculty in the face of high living costs in the Bay Area. He argues that until now Berkeley has responded by limiting new initiatives and deferring maintenance expenditures, but that these responses, while expedient in the short term, are inadequate in the long term. In the future Berkeley may need to concentrate its spending on core educational and research activities, while cutting non-core spending and improving its productivity through the use of technology.

Robert Brown, who retired as president of Boston University in 2023, makes the case for an approach to university financial management that he calls Strategy Centered Management (SCM). By contrast with Responsibility Centered Management (RCM), a common management approach since the 1970s, which decentralizes budgetary authority to various academic units within a university, SCM centralizes control of core revenues and expenses and allows the central administration of the university to use operational surpluses to build reserves, which can be reinvested in new strategic initiatives. Brown argues that this approach better reflects the current academic environment in which both student interests and the most exciting research opportunities are interdisciplinary. He cites Boston University's new Faculty of Computing and Data Sciences as an example of the institutional creativity that SCM makes possible.

Lisa Lynch, former Dean of the Heller School for Social Policy and Management at Brandeis University, and former Provost and Interim President of the university, explores trends in the workforce of higher education. She highlights that since 2011, there has been a reversal of a previous trend to hire more part-time faculty. The share of full-time faculty, which was 50 percent in 2011, had risen to 56 percent by 2022. However, many of these full-time faculty are contract faculty rather than tenured or tenure-track faculty. Retirements of tenured faculty stimulated by the COVID-19 pandemic may have accelerated this shift in faculty composition.

Full-time staff are also vitally important to the functioning of higher education and account for 45 percent of its workforce. The hot labor market of the last few years has driven up staff compensation costs and increased turnover. A challenge for institutions of higher education is that many staff express a strong desire to work remotely, but this can be difficult to reconcile with the creation of a vibrant on-campus community.

Lynch discusses the increase in collective bargaining and strike activity by both faculty and students over the past decade, arguing that this is a natural response to the precarity of contract faculty employment and to the financial pressures experienced by graduate students. She predicts further conflict related to unionization efforts by student athletes.

The contributions to this volume explore the financing of higher education by students and the institutions that serve them, drawing on insights from financial economics and industrial organization and complementing a rich literature on the economics of higher education grounded in labor economics. Within this focus on individual and institutional financial decision-making, several important topics deserve further exploration. While the volume highlights the importance of broadening access to higher education and the factors that influence the attendance decisions of diverse students, a more systematic exploration of the institutional costs of diversity, equity, and inclusion and the strategies available to schools to manage these costs would be valuable. Also, the papers in the volume focus on financial management strategies, taking operational structures such as faculty tenure and educational technology as given. Operational reforms, for example to the delivery of classroom education or the provision of student services, are not considered. An important task for future research is to understand the educational, labor market, and financial implications of changing operational models in higher education. We hope that the work presented in *Financing Institutions of Higher Education* will be a useful starting point for research that addresses these issues.

## Appendix: Data Summary

### *Financing Institutions of Higher Education*

The table below details the data sets used in the papers in this volume. They include:[1]

- National Postsecondary Student Aid Study (NPSAS)
- Panel Study of Income Dynamics (PSID)
- Integrated Postsecondary Education Data System (IPEDS) (UnitID, Revenue by Source, and Higher Education Emergency Relief Funds [HEERF])
- College Scorecard (Closed School Weekly Reports, and Heightened Cash Monitoring [HCM] Level 2)
- Postsecondary Education Participants System (PEPS)
- US Bureau of Economic Analysis (population and income per capita at the county level)
- IRS 990 Tax Filings (Schedule D)
- Institutional Financial Data
- Municipal Bond Issuances
- Coincident Index (Philadelphia Federal Reserve Bank)
- Accelerating Recovery in Community Colleges Network (ARCC) (Interviews with College Administrators)
- Texas Education Authority (TEA)
- Common Core of Data (CCD) by the National Center for Education Statistics in the Institute for Education Science (NCES)
- Texas Higher Education Coordinating Board (THECB)
- The American Association of Community Colleges (AACC)
- Texas Association of Community Colleges (TACC)
- Minority Serving Institutions (MSI) Data Project

1. In addition, other specialized data sets were not used in this volume's papers but also provide helpful information to study the finances of higher education: Common Data Set (CDS); College Board (Trends in College Pricing Report); Higher Education General Information Survey (HEGIS) Series (the predecessor to IPEDS); and College and Beyond II (CBII). Some states have made institutional data available, for example for the City University of New York (CUNY).

**Table IA.1**

| Title | Authors | Data Sources |
|---|---|---|
| **The Ebbing Tide: How Will Higher Education Adapt to Demographic Change?** | **Jacob L. Vigdor**, *University of Washington and NBER* | 1) **Integrated Postsecondary Education Data System (IPEDS):** The analysis uses IPEDS data on enrollment and institutional characteristics restricted to public institutions offering 4-year degrees. The data span 1984 to 2022, but most analyses of cross-sectional variation examine the change in log enrollment between fall 2010 and fall 2022 as they necessarily exclude institutions that closed over the intervening period.<br>https://nces.ed.gov/ipeds/ |
| **How Much Can Families Afford to Pay for College?** | **Peter Hinrichs**, *Federal Reserve Bank of Cleveland* | 1) **National Postsecondary Student Aid Study (NPSAS)**: Used to document Expected Family Contribution (EFC) from the Free Application for Federal Student Aid (FAFSA). Note: EFC is being replaced with the Student Aid Index (SAI) beginning in the 2024–25 cycle, but many of the same principles carry over to this newer measure.<br>https://nces.ed.gov/datalab |
| | | 2) **Panel Study of Income Dynamics (PSID)**: Used to calculate alternative measures of the ability to pay for college.<br>https://psidonline.isr.umich.edu/default.aspx |
| **Predicting College Closures and Financial Distress** | **Robert Kelchen**, University of Tennessee–Knoxville<br>**Dubravka Ritter**, Federal Reserve Bank of Philadelphia<br>**Douglas A. Webber**, Board of Governors of the Federal Reserve | 1) **Integrated Postsecondary Education Data System (IPEDS): UnitID:** Used to obtain information on the historical features of colleges and universities (organizational structure, location, and finances) and on the characteristics of their students and staff primarily from 2002 to 2023. IPEDS: data are collected annually on the academic year calendar for each UnitID (IPEDS ID for an individual institution).<br>https://nces.ed.gov/ipeds/ |
| | | 2) **College Scorecard:** Used the predominant degree from College Scorecard and supplement with Carnegie classifications where available to classify institutions (2 or 4 year, private or public, non-profit, or for-profit)<br>https://collegescorecard.ed.gov/ |
| | | 3) **Postsecondary Education Participants System (PEPS) Closed School Weekly Reports:** From the Federal Student Aid (FSA). This database classifies institutions based on their Office of Postsecondary Education identification number (OPEID), which is based on the unit of analysis under which a program participation agreement is entered upon with the Department of Education (Office of Federal Student Aid 2017). The sample of institutions in the PEPS data is restricted to those where the main campus (FSA OPEID ending in "00"), as opposed to a branch/satellite campus, closed.<br>https://fsapartners.ed.gov/home/ |
| | | 4) **College Scorecard Heightened Cash Monitoring (HCM) Level 2:** The College Scorecard data on colleges placed on Heightened Cash Monitoring (HCM) level 2 is used to flag institutions perceived by sector observers to be in precarious financial condition. HCM level 2 is the most serious level of federal monitoring that requires a college to get reimbursed after the fact for federal financial aid disbursed to students instead of receiving those funds in advance.<br>https://collegescorecard.ed.gov/ |

| | | |
|---|---|---|
| | | 5) **US Bureau of Economic Analysis:** To collect population and income per capita received by residents at the county level, from 1967 to 2022.<br>https://www.bea.gov/ |
| **Endowment Spending Rules** | **Christopher Avery,** *Harvard University and NBER*<br>**Ronald G. Ehrenberg**, *Cornell University and NBER*<br>**Catharine Hill,** *Ithaka S+R*<br>**Douglas A. Webber,** *Federal Reserve Board* | 1) **IRS 990 Tax Filings, Schedule D:** Data reported by private, nonprofit colleges and universities from 2008–09 to 2021–22. 2008–09 was the first year that colleges filed Schedule D as part of their 990 tax returns. Schedule D reports endowment levels along with revenues (1. Investment returns; 2. Contributions) and (3. Grants and scholarships; 4. Administrative costs; 5. Other costs).<br>https://www.irs.gov/forms-pubs/about-form-990 |
| **Economic Budgeting for Endowment-Dependent Universities** | **John Y. Campbell**, *Harvard University and NBER*<br>**Jeremy C. Stein**, *Harvard University and NBER*<br>**Alex A. Wu**, *Harvard University* | 1) **Institutional Data from Harvard's Faculty of Arts and Sciences (FAS):** Multi-year financial plans were used to forecast cash flows over an infinite horizon.<br>Note: this paper presents an alternative framework that discounts cash flow forecasts over the infinite future and compares the present value of operating obligations to the value of the university's endowment net of any debt it has issued. |
| **The Role of Debt in Financing Higher Education** | **Matteo Binfarè**, *University of Missouri*<br>**Kyle Zimmerschied**, *University of Missouri* | 1) **Municipal Bond Issuances:** Municipal bond issuances and US higher education institutions that report to the Integrated Postsecondary Education Data System (IPEDS). Municipal bond issuances were obtained from Refinitiv's SDC Platinum. A unique list of municipal bond issuers and beneficiaries of proceeds (in cases of debt issued on behalf of higher education institutions) was hand-matched with the universe of IPEDS reporting organizations by a bond's beneficiary and then by a bond's issuers. The sample was restricted to bond issuances from academic years 1985 to 2022.<br>https://www.lseg.com/en/data-analytics/products/sdc-platinum-financial-securities |
| | | 2) **Integrated Postsecondary Education Data System (IPEDS):** Data on the financial position and operations of US four-year public and private not-for-profit universities comes. These data were merged, including relevant university controls from 1985 to 2022, into an issuance panel. The analysis was restricted in this setting to data from 2001 to 2022.<br>https://nces.ed.gov/ipeds/ |
| | | 3) **Coincident Index:** This is a measure of a state's economic activity and unemployment rates from the Philadelphia Federal Reserve Bank. Additionally, to control the underlying state distress risk, data were obtained from S&P global on ratings changes at the state level.<br>https://www.philadelphiafed.org/surveys-and-data/regional-economic-analysis/state-coincident-indexes |

*(continued)*

**Table IA.1** **(cont.)**

| Title | Authors | Data Sources |
|---|---|---|
| **Financing Community Colleges: Current Landscape and Future Directions** | **Nikki Edgecombe**, *Columbia University*<br>**Elise Swanson**, *Harvard University*<br>**Thomas Brock**, *Columbia University*<br>**Maria Cormier**, *Columbia University*<br>**Christopher Avery**, *Harvard University and NBER*<br>**Carmen Huynh**, *Columbia University* | 1) **Revenue by Source:** Data on community college revenue per full-time equivalent (FTE) student were obtained from the Integrated Postsecondary Education Data System (IPEDS), and used to represent the proportion of revenue per FTE student by source and state in 2019.<br>https://nces.ed.gov/ipeds/ |
| | | 2) **State Funding Formulas:** From existing literature, specifically Lingo et al. (2021, 2023). These data were used to characterize the funding formulas within the focal states as traditional, incentive, and hybrid.<br>https://static1.squarespace.com/static/5d9f9fae6a122515ee074363/t/6446df7a981da30ef202a70c/1682366330568/ISBrief_TheLandscapeofStateFundingFormulas_PublicCollegesUniversities_April2023.pdf |
| | | 3) **Higher Education Emergency Relief Funds (HEERF):** Data on HEER funding on a per full-time equivalent (FTE) basis were obtained from the Integrated Postsecondary Education Data System (IPEDS). The data were used to examine how institutions used federal relief funds, what groups of students they targeted for assistance, and what types of assistance they felt were most important to retaining and helping students advance.<br>https://nces.ed.gov/ipeds/ |
| | | 4) **Interviews with College Administrators:** To examine how institutions used HEERF funds utilization. Interview data were collected in the summer of 2023 as part of the Accelerating Recovery in Community Colleges Network (ARCC) analysis of federal relief efforts for the Community College Research Center (CCRC)'s project on community college finance. |
| **Distance to Opportunity: Higher Education Deserts and College Enrollment Choices** | **Riley K. Acton**, *Miami University*<br>**Kalena Cortes**, *Texas A&M University and NBER*<br>**Camila Morales**, *University of Texas at Dallas* | 1) **Longitudinal records from the Texas Education Authority (TEA):** Records on K-12 school enrollment and high school graduation. Student-level data from the UT Dallas Education Research Center (ERC).<br>https://tsp.utdallas.edu/ut-dallas-education-research-center/ |
| | | 2) **Longitudinal records from Texas Higher Education Coordinating Board (THECB):** Student-level records containing information on student enrollment in all Texas public two-year and four-year postsecondary institutions.<br>https://www.highered.texas.gov/ |

| | | |
|---|---|---|
| | | 3) **Common Core of Data (CCD) by the National Center for Education Statistics in the Institute for Education Science (NCES):** Comprehensive, annual, national database of all public elementary and secondary schools and school districts. The data were used to observe a high school's latitude and longitude, urbanicity, overall student enrollment, student-teacher ratio, charter, magnet, and eligibility for Title I.<br>https://nces.ed.gov/ccd/ |
| | | 4) **Texas Higher Education Coordinating Board (THECB), the American Association of Community Colleges (AACC), and the Texas Association of Community Colleges (TACC):** The latitudes and longitudes of all colleges reported on these data sets were merged to create measures of distance between all Texas high schools and their nearest postsecondary higher education institutions.<br>https://nces.ed.gov/ipeds/ |
| **Examining the Effects of Tuition Reset Policies on Enrollment and Institutional Finances at Minority Serving Institutions** | **James Dean Ward**, *Ithaka S+R*<br>**Daniel Corral**, *University of Toronto*<br>**Catharine Hill**, *Ithaka S+R* | 1) **Integrated Postsecondary Education Data System (IPEDS) Institutional Enrollment and Finances:** A panel data set from 2003 through 2021 of 2,966 public and private institutions was used to estimate the relationship between a tuition reset and institutional outcomes.<br>https://nces.ed.gov/ipeds/ |
| | | 2) **Minority Serving Institutions (MSI) Data Project:** Classification data from the MSI compiled by Nguyen et al. (2023) were used to obtain estimates and calculations specific to MSI institutions.<br>https://www.msidata.org/ |
| | **Panel Discussions: Financial Management Challenges in Higher Education** | |
| **The Finances of a Public Flagship University** | **Benjamin E. Hermalin,** University of California | 1) **Institutional Financial Data for the Fiscal Year FY 2022–23:**<br>https://controller.berkeley.edu/accounting-andcontrols/financial-reporting/uc-berkeley-financial-reports-unaudited. |
| **Strategy-Centered Leadership and Financial Management Is Needed in Research Universities** | **Robert A. Brown,** Boston University | 1) **Secondary and Institutional Data:** Statistics about Higher Education. |
| **Financial Management Challenges in Higher Education** | **Lisa M. Lynch,** Brandeis University and NBER | 1) **Secondary Data:** Statistics about the Higher Education labor market from secondary sources. |

## References

Bauman, Dan. 2022. "Booming Endowments Draw Broad Demands." *Chronicle of Higher Education* February 18: 60–62.
Brown, Jeffrey R., and Caroline Hoxby, editors. 2015. *How the Financial Crisis and Great Recession Affected Higher Education*. Chicago: University of Chicago Press.
Brown, Jeffrey R., Stephen G. Dimmock, Jun-Koo Kang, and Scott J. Weisbenner. 2014. "How University Endowments Respond to Financial Market Shocks: Evidence and Implications." *American Economic Review* 104(3): 931–62.
Campbell, John Y. 2012. "Investing and Spending: The Twin Challenges of University Endowment Management." In *Forum Futures 2012*. Cambridge, MA: Forum for the Future of Higher Education, 32–40.
Campbell, John Y., and Roman Sigalov. 2022. "Portfolio Choice with Sustainable Spending: A Model of Reaching for Yield." *Journal of Financial Economics* 143(1): 188–206.
Cecchetti, Stephen, and Kermit Schoenholtz. 2019. "Should Students Borrow?" MON€¥ $ BAN£ING, September 16. https://www.moneyandbanking.com/commentary/2019/9/14/should-students-borrow.
Lovenheim, Michael, and Jonathan Smith. 2022. "Returns to Different Postsecondary Investments: Institution Type, Academic Programs, and Credentials." NBER Working Paper No. 29933. Cambridge, MA: National Bureau of Economic Research.
National Center for Education Statistics. 2021. *Digest of Educational Statistics, 2021*.
Stafford, Erik. 2022. "Replicating Private Equity with Value Investing, Homemade Leverage, and Hold-to-Maturity Accounting." *Review of Financial Studies* 35(1): 299–342.
State Higher Education Executive Officers Association (SHEEOA). 2021. "State Higher Education Finance." FY2020. https://shef.sheeo.org/.
Talbott, Tyler. 2024. "The Percentage of Americans with College Degrees in 2024." College Transitions, August 14. https://www.collegetransitions.com/blog/percentage-of-americans-with-college-degrees/.
Valero, Anna, and John Van Reenen. 2019. "The Economic Impact of Universities: Evidence from across the Globe." *Economics of Education Review* 68: 53–67.
Welding, Lyss. 2024. "College Enrollment Statistics in the US." Best Colleges, February 7. https://www.bestcolleges.com/research/college-enrollment-statistics/.
Wilson, Jeffery L., Gerron Scott, and Reginald Stroble. 2021. "Prioritizing Campus Diversity Budgets: DEI Funding Has Mostly Survived the Post Pandemic Cuts." *Planning for Higher Education*. 49(4):22–28.

# 1

# The Ebbing Tide
## How Will Higher Education Adapt to Demographic Change?

Jacob L. Vigdor

## 1.1 Introduction

In the fall of 2010, American institutions of higher education enrolled just under 22 million students. As figure 1.1 shows, this tally reflected a period of incredible growth over the prior few decades. While the period between the mid-1950s and mid-1970s witnessed the fastest growth, attributable largely to the baby boom generation, a second enrollment boom occurred just after the turn of the 21st century. Between 1999 and 2010, a period when the size of the traditional college-age population increased by about a tenth, American colleges and universities increased enrollment by over 40 percent.

The past decade has seen this trend reverse. By fall 2022 enrollment had dropped 2.7 million from its 2010 peak, or roughly 12 percent. Figure 1.1 shows that the majority of this decline occurred before the onset of the COVID-19 pandemic, though trends have clearly continued from 2020 onwards (Harris et al. 2024). As we will see below, this decline has been uneven across institutions. Prestigious, research-intensive universities categorized as Carnegie R1 institutions counted 13 percent more students in fall 2022 than they enrolled in fall 2010. Less research-intensive colleges awarding bachelor's and master's degrees enrolled 7.5 percent fewer students over the same time period. Associate's degree–granting institutions including community colleges witnessed a precipitous 28 percent drop. The drop in enrollment has been most severe at those institutions most dependent on

Jacob L. Vigdor is professor of public policy and governance at the University of Washington, and a research associate of the National Bureau of Economic Research.

For acknowledgments, sources of research support, and disclosure of the author's material financial relationships, if any, please see https://www.nber.org/books-and-chapters/financing-institutions-higher-education/ebbing-tide-how-will-higher-education-adapt-demographic-change.

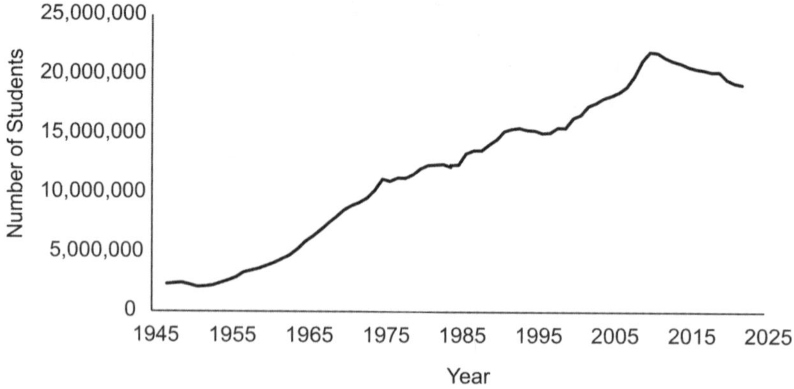


**Fig. 1.1 Postsecondary enrollment in the United States, 1947–2022**
Source: IPEDS, US Department of Education.

tuition revenue relative to research grants and endowment income, as well as the institutions most commonly associated with providing opportunity to first-generation students and other under-represented groups. For many public institutions, increased state subsidies have filled revenue gaps, raising questions of long-term sustainability.

To some extent, the drop in enrollment can be associated with demographic trends. According to the Current Population Survey, the number of 18-year-olds in spring 2022 was about 5 percent smaller than the tally in spring 2010. If shrinking enrollments are a function of declining cohort sizes, the future appears bleak. Figure 1.2, which tracks the number of 18-year-olds in the March CPS from 1962 to 2022, and then projects forward with the size of each age cohort as of 2022, augurs sustained declines in birth cohort size, with a noticeable turning point around 2027 and pronounced declines to come in the mid-2030s.

Demography is certainly not perfectly correlated with demographic destiny. Figure 1.2 shows that the number of 18-year-olds in March 1991 was some 20 percent lower than it had been a decade earlier, reflecting the so-called "baby bust." Figure 1.1 shows that this translated to no more than a 3 percent enrollment drop in the mid-1990s.

In light of this observation, it's fair to ask: to what extent can the recent decline in enrollment be attributed to demographic trends? If so, what might we forecast regarding the fortunes of academic institutions over the coming 10–15 years, particularly those most dependent on tuition revenue? How might institutions respond, particularly in light of evidence that enrollments withstood demographic challenges a generation ago?

This paper assesses these questions using data from the Integrated Postsecondary Education Data System (IPEDS) spanning the years 1984–2022. Analysis of cross-sectional variation in enrollment trends between 2010

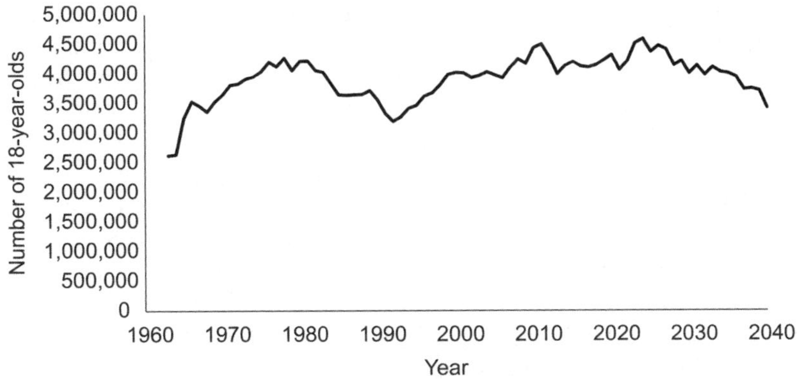


**Fig. 1.2 Number of 18-year-olds, 1962–2040 (projected 2023–2040)**
Source: March CPS. Projections 2023–2040 based on age cohorts under 18 in March 2022, and abstract from changes due to net migration or mortality.

and 2022 confirms that simple state-level demographic projections, namely the ratio of the 5–9-year-old population to the 18–22-year-old population in 2010, strongly predict enrollment changes. Point estimates suggest that master's-granting regional colleges and universities are approximately three times more responsive, and colleges awarding only bachelor's degrees five times more responsive, to demographic change than R1 flagship institutions. The period of enrollment decline coincides with a "flip" in short-run growth dynamics. Before 2010, the smallest institutions at all Carnegie classifications tended to post the fastest year-over-year growth. Afterward, smaller institutions shrank the fastest.

The model of dynamics in the 2010–2022 time period can be used to forecast enrollment trends over the next decade. Forecasts indicate continued divergence in enrollment trends across institutions, with research-intensive flagship R1 universities predicted to continue growth, with a few exceptions concentrated in Rust Belt states, and master's- and baccalaureate-level institutions facing decline, with exceptions concentrated in a few Sun Belt states.

Universities and colleges exhibit economies of scale, with large fixed personnel and physical plant costs along with modest marginal costs. When institutions with limited endowment funds and little in the way of grant and contract revenue shrink, they can attempt to cover costs by raising tuition or relying more heavily on government subsidies. Data point clearly to the latter strategy, which avoids the prospect of higher tuition revenue per student leading to further enrollment declines. But increased per-student subsidies to operate smaller institutions might not be sustainable in the long run.

This paper concludes by considering the options available to institutions in the face of the coming "demographic cliff." If anything, the demographic trends of the 1980s and early 1990s appear more severe than those projected to occur in the next two decades, and institutions managed to avoid severe enrollment losses. In that era, higher education benefited from increased matriculation rates among high school graduates, new programs for part-time students, and the expansion of postgraduate education. There is still room for improvement in matriculation rates, as well as degree completion rates—although improvements taking the form of reducing time-to-degree might have the perverse effect of reducing enrollment. In theory, shortfalls of domestic students could be offset by recruiting more from abroad, however the less-selective institutions experiencing the most severe enrollment declines have seldom been magnets for international enrollment. Likewise, the strategy of expanding postgraduate programming faces the challenge that many master's-level programs have themselves faced enrollment declines in recent years. Appealing to part-time or non-traditional students might work well for those institutions in large urban areas with a large pool of potential working students, but not as well for colleges in smaller college towns.

There have been isolated cases of colleges closing or consolidating over the past decade, and absent significant departures from trend more will arrive in the next 15 years. Closing institutions entails difficult trade-offs between access and efficiency, and the elimination of what may be the largest employer in many communities will face significant political opposition. Fortunately, the demographic projections for the immediate future are favorable, with a small "baby blip" about to enter the college-going years. Planning undertaken over the next few years may spell the difference between survival and closure for many institutions.

## 1.2 Long-Run Trends in Postsecondary Enrollment

Between 1947 and 2010, the trajectory of postsecondary enrollment in the United States can be characterized as alternating between periods of stasis and growth. The start date for this time series obscures the impact of the G.I. Bill, which substantially increased enrollment and attainment for eligible cohorts (Bound and Turner 2002). The initial years depicted in figure 1.1 show little to no trend in enrollment, with the period of the Korean War (1950–1953) coinciding with a modest decline at a time when roughly two-thirds of postsecondary students were male.

The decade following the conclusion of the Korean War, a period when the earliest members of the baby boom generation were not yet college-going age, saw postsecondary enrollment double. Enrollment doubled again in the ten years between 1963 and 1973. While the arrival of the baby boom cohort on college campuses helps explain this period of unprecedented growth, the expansion of enrollment goes well beyond what might be explained by demographics alone. The size of the 18-year-old cohort, depicted in figure 1.2, rose about 50 percent between 1963 and 1973.

The 20-year boom in enrollment was accommodated disproportionately by the establishment and expansion of public institutions. As late as 1951, there were more students enrolled in private than public institutions in the United States. By 1973, there were 3.4 public postsecondary enrollees for every private college student. Private college enrollment doubled between 1953 and 1973; public college enrollment sextupled. Most of this expansion was accommodated by increasing the size of existing institutions rather than creating new ones; as late as 1985, the median postsecondary student attended an institution founded in 1919. Only a third attended an institution founded later than 1953. The divergence of growth trajectories between private and public institutions coincides with divergence in selectivity; between the early 1960s and the early 1970s elite four-year colleges institutions became more selective, the median institution became somewhat less selective, and the least selective institutions witnessed a marked decrease in mean student standardized test percentiles (Hoxby 2009).

Enrollment growth slowed considerably after 1973, a deceleration that can be at least partially explained by demographic trends. As figure 1.2 shows, 18-year-old cohort sizes continued to grow through the early 1980s, but at a much slower rate. The 1981 cohort attained a local maximum that would not be eclipsed for another 27 years; over the following decade the number of 18-year-olds in the United States fell by nearly a quarter.

It is remarkable, in this context, that postsecondary enrollment continued to grow during the 1980s. Institutions reacted to declining undergraduate enrollments by expanding other types of degree offerings. Between 1984 and 1994, the number of four-year institutions offering post-baccalaureate programming expanded by 155 (18 percent). In fall 1984, there were 468,189 full-time graduate students in the United States. A dozen years later there were 1,016,395. The number of part-time graduate students expanded by roughly 400,000 over the same time period. American institutions expanded international student enrollments as well, by roughly 140,000 between 1984 and 1996. Altogether, these sources of growth can account for roughly a million extra students. But the undergraduate student headcount expanded by about 1.5 million during the same time period. The story of product and customer base expansion is thus secondary in this era: American universities continued expanding by attracting a greater share of traditional college-age youth and exhibiting greater success in shepherding them to degree completion.

Between 1965 and 1982, the percentage of high school graduates enrolling in college fluctuated in a narrow range around 50 percent, never falling below 46 percent and exceeding 55 percent once. After 1982, this ratio steadily rose to a local maximum of 67 percent in 1997.[1] While modern longitudinal data

1. Source: National Center for Education Statistics, *Digest of Education Statistics*. See https://nces.ed.gov/programs/digest/d99/d99t187.asp.

**Table 1.1** **Enrollment by sector at five points in time**

| Institution type | 1984 | 1992 | 1996 | 2010 | 2022 |
|---|---|---|---|---|---|
| Private R1 | 603,933 | 633,938 | 630,508 | 759,187 | 870,039 |
| Public R1 | 2,311,009 | 2,497,761 | 2,451,059 | 2,972,467 | 3,286,311 |
| Doctoral | 991,936 | 1,097,082 | 1,097,383 | 1,446,532 | 1,379,991 |
| Master's I | 2,478,156 | 2,902,290 | 2,888,556 | 3,753,501 | 3,517,312 |
| Master's II | 209,131 | 262,676 | 260,341 | 404,205 | 328,024 |
| Baccalaureate | 824,691 | 965,916 | 993,259 | 1,388,226 | 1,140,716 |
| Associate's | 4,071,452 | 5,549,637 | 5,408,278 | 8,923,255 | 5,948,058 |

on six-year degree completion rates did not exist prior to the late 1990s, available evidence points to maintained or improved degree completion rates over this time period. The number of bachelor's degrees awarded in the 1980/81 academic year equaled 7.7 percent of fall 1980 enrollment. The number of degrees awarded in the 1995/96 academic year, following a period of expanded matriculation rates and outsize growth of postbaccalaureate enrollment, was 7.6 percent of fall 1995 enrollment.[2]

During the two decades of more modest growth, public institutions continued to expand more rapidly than private ones. By 1992, there were 3.67 public students for every private enrollee. Enrollment gains were also concentrated among less selective two- and four-year institutions. As table 1.1 shows, private R1 institutions saw enrollments increase 5 percent between 1984 and 1992. Public R1 flagships expanded enrollment just 8 percent. Master's-granting regional public institutions increased enrollment by 17 percent, and associate's-granting public community and technical colleges by 35 percent.

Cohort size reached a local minimum in 1992, the 3.2 million 18-year-olds that year being both the lowest number recorded since 1964 and a low the United States is not projected to reach again through at least 2040. It is certainly not a coincidence that the period between 1993 and 1996 represents the first sustained loss in postsecondary enrollment in the postwar era. These enrollment losses were modest, less than 3 percent overall, and spread broadly across institutions, with declines recorded in sectors ranging from private R1 institutions to community colleges.

Both cohort size and enrollment rebounded over the next 15 years, to the high points recorded around 2010. The rates of increase for the two time series were closely linked; enrollment grew 42 percent between 1992 and 2010 while the size of the 18-year-old cohort grew 39 percent. While research-intensive institutions showed higher growth rates in this time period, on the order of 20 percent, master's-level institutions and community colleges

2. Source: National Center for Education Statistics, *Digest of Education Statistics*. See https://nces.ed.gov/programs/digest/d23/tables/dt23_322.10.asp.

continued to grow faster. Notably, the for-profit college sector expanded significantly, with fall 2010 enrollment more than four times the level recorded in 1996.

It is important to note the increasingly strong tie between demography and enrollment. The latter grew at twice the rate of the former as the baby boom cohort reached college age through the 1960s. Stagnation in cohort size in the 1980s coincided with continued, albeit modest, growth in enrollment. The tie between population and enrollment appears strong in the 1990s.

This historical context places more recent trends in stark perspective. Over 62 years between 1947 and 2010, postsecondary enrollment endured a year-over-year decline just six times, and in no more than three consecutive years. Since 2010, enrollment has declined for 12 consecutive years. In the longest episode of decline prior to 2010, enrollment declines applied broadly across higher education institutions. Since 2010, the most prestigious research-intensive institutions have bucked the trend while the least-selective, most tuition-dependent sectors have borne the brunt of decline. And importantly, while the decline in enrollment coincides with a drop in college-going cohort size, demographics alone appear insufficient to explain the trend. The number of 18-year-olds in the United States fell by about 5 percent between 2010 and 2022. Postsecondary enrollment fell by 12.5 percent.

## 1.3 Understanding the Decline in Enrollment

Standard human capital theory posits that individual educational decisions are based on the expected rate of return (Becker 1964). The expected rate of return is in turn a function of several factors, including the up-front cost of attendance, the expected labor market returns to knowledge gained and credentials earned, and the probability that attendance results in that attainment. Whereas canonical economic models assume rationality of expectation formation, the adolescents making key human capital investments may be myopic or poorly informed. Expectations may be influenced by social or political arguments as much as economic data.

This basic economic framework, augmented to consider cognitive or political influences on expectations formation, could help explain why college enrollment has posted a steady decline over the past decade or more. This section will review the data and evidence on a series of factors implicated in this framework.

### 1.3.1 Does Rising Cost of Attendance Explain Declining Enrollment?

A variety of evidence links college costs, and rising costs, to lower enrollment. Panel data analyses suggest an elasticity of public college enrollment with respect to tuition of roughly –0.1 (Hemelt and Marcotte 2011). Quasi-experimental methods exploiting financial aid eligibility and the introduc-

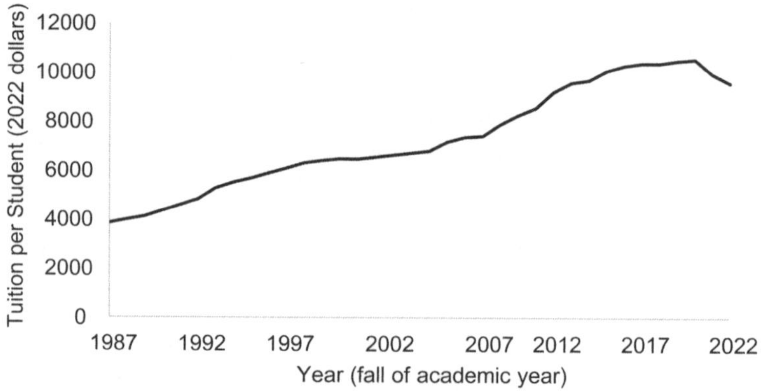


**Fig. 1.3 Real tuition revenue per student 1987–2022**
Source: IPEDS. Inflation adjustment uses CPI-U.

tion of tuition at previously tuition-free institutions yield more mixed evidence (Hansen 1983; Dynarski 2000; Seftor and Turner 2002; Dynarski 2003; Abraham and Clark 2006; Cornwell et al. 2006; Kane 2007; Goodman 2008; Hübner 2012). The effectiveness of financial aid assistance interventions also point to a strong role for financial barriers in determining enrollment outcomes (Bettinger et al. 2012; Dynarski et al. 2021).

List tuition prices at both private and public institutions have risen faster than inflation for decades. Actual trends in the cost of attending college are also influenced by financial aid, which has also tended to expand over time (Gordon and Hedlund 2022). Figure 1.3 tracks the inflation-adjusted amount of tuition revenue per student at a set of about 500 public four-year institutions between 1987 and 2022.[3] Tuition payments per student reached an inflation-adjusted maximum in 2020, at just over $10,500 2022 dollars per year. This represents a 27 percent increase in real costs per student over the preceding decade. If we accept a tuition-enrollment elasticity of −0.1, these increased real costs of attendance would explain roughly one-fifth of the observed decline in enrollment since 2010.

Extending the time series complicates inference. Inflation-adjusted tuition per student also increased 27 percent in the decade between 2000 and 2010, a period that saw the highest enrollment growth since the 1970s. While the net price of college clearly increased in the period of declining enrollment, there's no evidence to indicate that 2010 represents an inflection point in that time series. Attendance costs alone would appear to explain at most a fraction, and perhaps none, of the decline in enrollment.

3. Dollar values are converted to September 2022 dollars using the Consumer Price Index. Statistics are weighted by total enrollment.

### 1.3.2 Have Returns to College Education Declined?

A 2020 review of returns to college education concluded that they are generally increasing over time (Gunderson and Oreopoulos 2020). Evidence also points to a widening gradient between college graduates with varying majors, suggesting the returns to specific skills imparted by some types of college education, but not others, are increasing (Altonji et al. 2016). There is some evidence of a declining skill gradient in post-pandemic labor market data (Autor et al. 2023), but the period of declining enrollment precedes the arrival of COVID-19 by a decade.

While it is conceivable that increased earnings in jobs requiring lower education levels may explain some portion of the decline in enrollment in the most recent data, there have been no studies identifying an inflection point in the returns to college education around 2010.

All this said, the immediate opportunity cost to attending college was relatively low during the Great Recession, with annual average unemployment rates above 9 percent in both 2009 and 2010. The sharp rise in enrollment seen immediately before 2010 coincides with the onset of the Great Recession, and evidence indicates that unemployed adults took advantage of recession-era extensions to unemployment insurance benefits to enroll in educational programs (Barr and Turner 2015). Unemployment declined monotonically after 2010 until the onset of the COVID-19 pandemic in 2020. Hillman and Orians (2013) estimate increases in community college enrollment of 1.1–3.3 percent with every percentage point increase in the unemployment rate; by this measure the 6 percentage point nationwide drop in unemployment between 2010 and 2022 would appear sufficient to explain the entirety of the decline in enrollment.

### 1.3.3 Has the Risk of Non-Completion Increased?

The literature on returns to education has long recognized "sheepskin effects," the notion that most of the benefit from attending college accrues upon earning a degree rather than gradually over the course of attendance (Hungerford and Solon 1987; Jaeger and Page 1996). Were the probability of completion to exogenously decline over time, a rational agent would become less likely to invest in higher education even if the returns to a degree remained constant.

Figure 1.4, based on IPEDS data, confirms that six-year completion rates for first-time full-time students at four-year institutions trended steadily upward between the entering cohorts of 2000 and 2014 (see Denning et al. 2022).[4] If anything, completion rates have accelerated, rising 3.8 percentage

4. Denning et al (2022) attribute rising completion rates to grade inflation and the general tendency for higher completion rates among students with higher GPA.

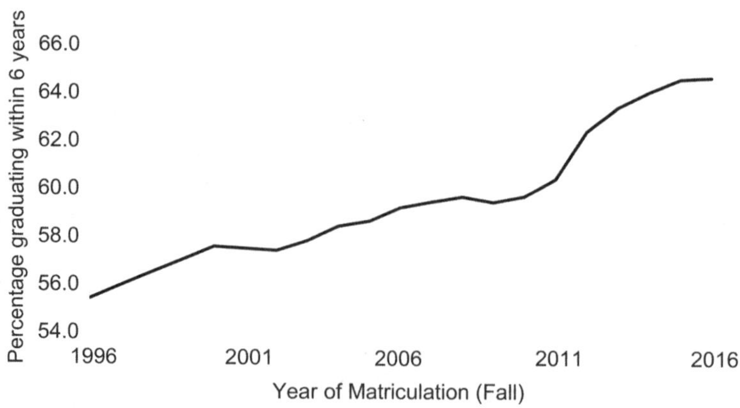


**Fig. 1.4 Six-year completion rates, all four-year institutions**
Source: IPEDS.

points between the cohorts of 2010 and 2014 after increasing just 2.4 percentage points over the prior decade. Available data on completion stops almost exactly when the COVID-19 pandemic sets in, so post-2020 declines in completion or matriculation rates could help explain some of the most recent enrollment data points, but the completion rate data point to greater enrollment in the period after 2010, not less.

### 1.3.4 Have Prospective Students Become More Short-Sighted?

The decision to attend college brings short-term costs, in the form of tuition and the opportunity cost of attendance, paired with longer-term benefits. Adolescents may be ill equipped to make this decision given the nature of brain development and a tendency to over-discount the future. In theory, increasing myopia among prospective students could drive a trend toward lower enrollment.

While there is some evidence to suggest an increase in the prevalence of youth anxiety coincident with the enrollment decline (Parodi et al. 2022), there has not been a broad analysis of measures of future orientation. In general, had myopic decision-making become more prevalent over time, we might expect a variety of risk behaviors, for which short-term rewards are offset by potential longer-term costs, to increase. In fact, most developed countries have exhibited long-run declines in adolescent youth behaviors, a trend attributed to the decline in "unstructured face-to-face time with friends," an antecedent to the peer influence thought to drive many such behaviors (Ball et al. 2023).

It is conceivable that the effect of declining peer interaction time on negative behaviors could also exert a similar, though opposite-signed, impact on positive behaviors such as college-going. The evidence base on this question is scant.

### 1.3.5 Political Polarization and Higher Education

In the United States, political conservatism has recently become associated with skepticism toward higher education. An October 2022 Pew Research Center poll found just one-third of respondents identifying as Republican or leaning Republican held a positive view of colleges and universities, against 72 percent of Democrats or individuals leaning Democrat. Evidence indicates that this partisan gap has widened over time (Houston 2024). Republican-controlled state legislatures have introduced measures to weaken tenure protections, roll back diversity, equity, and inclusion initiatives, and more directly intervene in matters of curriculum and institutional leadership.

Increased skepticism toward higher education could influence matriculation decisions. While there have been a number of studies seeking to study whether college attendance affects political orientation (e.g., Campbell and Horowitz 2016), the reverse association has not been a topic of analysis. Political variables will enter into the analysis below.

### 1.3.6 Returning to Demographics

Figure 1.2 shows a peak in the 18-year-old population occurring around 2010, with a second peak projected to occur within the next two years, followed by an extended decline through 2040. The number of 18-year-olds in the United States is a function of the number of live births, infant and child mortality, and migration.

Generally speaking, the number of 18-year-olds as estimated by the March CPS tracks the number of births 19 calendar years prior closely ($r = 0.86$ in data from 1962 through 2022). Cohorts born prior to the 1960s generally show net out-migration, consistent with that era's restrictions on immigration. Among cohorts born after the mid-1960s, the number of 18-year-olds consistently exceeds the number of lagged births, reflecting a combination of more lenient immigration policy and the entry of hundreds of thousands of youths now participating in the DACA program.

The drop in the number of 18-year-olds between 2010 and the most recent cohorts coincides with a decline and rise in number of births between 1990 and 2007. Cohort sizes have also been impacted by relatively slow migration rates. The birth cohorts of 1978 through 1982 saw their numbers increased by over 300,000 each by the time they reached age 18. A similar phenomenon occurred in the cohorts of 1991 and 1992. Since that time, however, the estimated augmentation-by-immigration has only exceeded 300,000 once. This is consistent with other data pointing to a general slowdown in immigration after the Great Recession.

To the extent that demographics have played a significant role in driving college enrollment trends, the future appears bleak. There were just under 3.8 million births in the United States in 2018, half a million fewer than in

2007 and the lowest tally since 1986. The trend has only continued further downward. Even if changes in migration policy bring an additional 300,000 youth into these cohorts, as occurred in the 1978–1982 cohorts, the projected number of 18-year-olds in 2040 will be lower than any figure observed since the mid-1990s.

Shrinking cohort size may have both a direct and indirect effect on enrollment. The direct effect occurs because there are fewer students of typical college-going age. The indirect effect may occur through the effect of demographics on the labor market (Vigdor 2023). As the share of young adults in the labor market increases, the wages of occupations that rely on physical fortitude more than education and experience may increase, reducing the returns to education. The possibility of an indirect effect is consistent with the observation that the ratio of first-time first-year college students to persons age 18 has declined in recent years, from an estimated 76 percent in 2010 to 68 percent in 2022.

The data analysis below studies the connection between demographics and enrollment more directly, while also shedding some light on other mechanisms discussed above.

## 1.4 Data and Methods

This descriptive analysis uses information on enrollment and other institutional characteristics drawn from the IPEDS data, which cover all postsecondary institutions, public and private, for-profit and non-profit. Attention will be restricted to public institutions offering four-year degrees, which provide more detailed financial information to IPEDS.

The dependent variable of interest is based on the institution's report of the total number of degree-seeking students enrolled as of an official fall reporting date, commonly October 15. This is a headcount enrollment measure, weighting full- and part-time students equivalently, and including both undergraduate and post-baccalaureate enrollment. Most analyses below examine the change in log enrollment between fall 2010 and fall 2022. These analyses necessarily exclude those institutions that ceased to exist over the intervening period. The raw count of four-year institutions in the IPEDS data dropped by 69 between 2010 and 2022, on a base of just under 1,400.

Explanatory variables include basic institutional characteristics: whether the institution operates a medical school, is considered a Morrill land grant institution, whether it is coded as a Historically Black College or University (HBCU), and whether it offers on-campus housing. Institutions are further divided into seven categories on the basis of their Carnegie classification in 2010. Three expenditure variables capture the essential characteristics of finance: the percent of revenues from tuition, federal grants and contracts, and state or local appropriations. The log of initial enrollment is included in

**Table 1.2** **Summary statistics for analysis sample**

| Variable | Mean (Standard Deviation) |
|---|---|
| Δln(enrollment) 2010–2022 ($n = 485$) | −0.096 (0.289) |
| Historically Black College or University | 0.076 |
| Medical School | 0.132 |
| Land Grant Institution | 0.134 |
| On-campus housing | 0.886 |
| Tuition share of revenue | 0.256 (0.106) |
| State/local allocation share of revenue | 0.277 (0.103) |
| Federal grant/contract share of revenue | 0.066 (0.065) |
| ln(2010 enrollment) | 9.161 (0.876) |
| ln(county population) | 12.15 (1.419) |
| ln(CBSA population) ($n = 468$) | 13.07 (1.799) |
| ln(state population) | 15.69 (0.938) |
| County ratio of 5–9 to 18–21-year-olds | 0.878 (0.342) |
| CBSA ratio of 5–9 to 18–21-year-olds ($n = 468$) | 0.968 (0.329) |
| State ratio of 5–9 to 18–21-year-olds | 1.133 (0.102) |
| Percent of county voters supporting Obama in 2008 | 0.535 (0.141) |
| Percent of state voters supporting Obama in 2008 | 0.509 (0.087) |

Note: $n = 499$ except as noted.

some specifications to examine whether growth trajectories varied by initial institution size. A series of variables captures potentially relevant demographic characteristics: the log of 2010 population in the county, core-based statistical area (CBSA), and state where the institution is located, as well as the ratio of 5–9-year-olds to 18–21-year-olds at the same three geographic levels, also as captured in the 2010 Census.[5]

Table 1.2 presents unweighted summary statistics for the just under 500 institutions in the analysis sample. The typical institution saw enrollment decline between 2010 and 2022, consistent with the broad patterns documented above. The sample includes several historically black colleges and universities, land grant institutions, and 66 institutions that operate medical schools, indicating a financial model more reliant on patient revenues. Institutions are quite heterogeneous with respect to size and sources of revenue. Perhaps importantly, they tend to be located in counties and core-based statistical areas with less favorable demographic trends than the surrounding state. This may reflect higher housing costs in college towns, or lower fertility among more-educated adults. Institutions also tend to be located in counties that were more favorably inclined toward Barack Obama than their surrounding states as of the 2008 election.

5. As the numerator of this ratio includes five distinct ages and the denominator four, a ratio of 1.2 would indicate a uniform age distribution within this range. The population-weighted average county-level ratio is 1.215.

In addition to models examining "long changes" in enrollment between 2010 and 2022, a series of models examines short-term dynamics in enrollment, segmenting institutions by Carnegie classification and time period. These models will help explore the extent to which decline has tended to affect larger or smaller institutions, and either equilibrium or fulcrum points at which enrollment trends diverge.

## 1.5 Results

Table 1.3 shows the results of specifications analyzing variation in enrollment growth across institutions between fall 2010 and fall 2022. The first

**Table 1.3 Correlates of enrollment trends, public four-year institutions**

| Independent variable | Dependent variable: Δln(enrollment) 2010–2022 | | | |
|---|---|---|---|---|
| *Carnegie classification (R1 omitted)* | | | | |
| Doctoral | −0.175 (0.045) | −0.130 (0.053) | −0.113 (0.051) | −0.109 (0.051) |
| Master's I | −0.198 (0.034) | −0.121 (0.051) | −0.113 (0.050) | −0.110 (0.050) |
| Master's II | −0.317 (0.067) | −0.191 (0.081) | −0.163 (0.081) | −0.150 (0.081) |
| Liberal Arts College | −0.207 (0.065) | −0.049 (0.086) | −0.107 (0.089) | −0.066 (0.091) |
| Baccalaureate | −0.277 (0.050) | −0.109 (0.074) | −0.112 (0.075) | −0.136 (0.075) |
| Baccalaureate/Assoc. | −0.369 (0.082) | −0.190 (0.098) | −0.189 (0.096) | −0.204 (0.097) |
| HBCU | — | −0.035 (0.053) | −0.080 (0.055) | −0.061 (0.057) |
| Has medical school | — | −0.033 (0.048) | −0.018 (0.047) | −0.0002 (0.05) |
| Land−grant institution | — | 0.024 (0.045) | 0.101 (0.046) | 0.084 (0.047) |
| Has on−campus housing | — | 0.119 (0.042) | 0.129 (0.043) | 0.085 (0.046) |
| ln(2010 enrollment) | — | 0.066 (0.022) | 0.013 (0.028) | 0.002 (0.028) |
| ln(2010 county pop.) | — | — | 0.050 (0.021) | 0.073 (0.023) |
| ln(2010 CBSA pop.) | — | — | −0.011 (0.014) | 0.004 (0.015) |
| ln(2010 state pop.) | — | — | 0.035 (0.017) | 0.025 (0.017) |
| *Ratio of 5–9-year-olds to 18–21-year-olds* | | | | |
| County | — | — | −0.122 (0.088) | −0.192 (0.090) |
| CBSA | — | — | 0.121 (0.091) | 0.099 (0.092) |
| State | — | — | 0.569 (0.141) | 0.476 (0.148) |
| *Share of 2008 Presidential vote to Obama* | | | | |
| County | — | — | — | −0.430 (0.129) |
| State | — | — | — | −0.232 (0.210) |
| Intercept term | 0.080 (0.029) | 0.198 (0.148) | −1.94 (0.304) | −1.56 (0.313) |
| *N* | 485 | 485 | 458 | 447 |
| $R^2$ | 0.106 | 0.138 | 0.225 | 0.245 |

Note: Standard errors in parentheses. Institutions not located in Core-Based Statistical Areas excluded from the third and fourth specifications. Institutions not linked to jurisdictions reporting 2008 voting results excluded from the final specification.

specification includes only a set of binary indicators for Carnegie classification, with R1 institutions the omitted category. The constant term shows that R1 institutions saw an average log enrollment increase of 0.08 over this time period. Every other category saw significant declines. The greatest declines pertained to institutions categorized as "Master's Institutions II" and "Baccalaureate/Associate's." Carnegie classification alone explains about 10 percent of the institutional variation in enrollment growth.

The second specification adds a basic set of institutional characteristics, including indicator variables for whether the institution is an HBCU; is a land grant institution; offers on-campus housing; or has a medical school, as well as measures of the share of revenue derived from tuition, direct transfers from state or local government, and federal grants. A lagged enrollment measure rounds out the controls.

These controls contribute modestly to the model's explanatory power ($R^2 = 0.15$) but help to explain much of the variation across Carnegie classifications. Coefficients on the Carnegie indicators are no more than half the magnitude of the first specification. Only two institutional characteristic controls yield statistically significant coefficients. Colleges that offer housing posted more positive enrollment trends, as did colleges of larger initial size. This pattern of divergence will be explored at greater depth in table 1.5 below.

A number of additional controls linger around the margins of statistical significance; HBCUs, institutions with medical schools, and institutions more dependent on tuition revenue all saw more negative trends, while institutions with more grant revenue grew at higher rates. Each of these coefficients posts a $p$-value of 0.2 or less.

The third model adds a series of demographic controls. The sample size is reduced slightly, as institutions not located in a core-based statistical area are excluded. The six demographic controls boast more than twice the marginal impact on explanatory power of the eight institutional characteristics added to the second model, and in several cases further reduce the magnitude of the Carnegie classification coefficients—none of which remain statistically significant at the 5 percent level. Institutions in more populous counties and states posted significantly higher enrollment trends, with effects of comparable magnitudes at the two geographic levels. And a basic measure of the state-level age distribution, the ratio of 5–9-year-olds to 18–21-year-olds in the 2010 census, shows the strongest relationship with enrollment trends of any variable in the model ($t = 3.81$, $p < 0.001$). The magnitude of the effect indicates that a 10 percent increase in the number of 5–9-year-olds relative to 18–21-year-olds, equivalent to a one standard deviation change, predicts a 0.054 more positive trend in log enrollment.

It is interesting to note that state-level age distribution trends are more salient than more localized measures. If anything, institutions with a surplus of 5–9-year-olds in their county population witnessed more negative enroll-

**Table 1.4 Heterogeneous effects of demographic variables**

| Variable | Main effect | Carnegie Master's Interaction | Carnegie Baccalaureate Interaction |
|---|---|---|---|
| ln(2010 county pop.) | 0.103<br>(0.037) | −0.045<br>(0.036) | 0.013<br>(0.043) |
| *Ratio of 5–9-year-olds to 18–21-year-olds* | | | |
| County | −0.314<br>(0.137) | 0.199<br>(0.130) | −0.076<br>(0.220) |
| State | 0.168<br>(0.240) | 0.378<br>(0.285) | 0.722<br>(0.414) |

Note: Standard errors in parentheses. All coefficients derived from a single specification, with controls as shown in the rightmost column in table 1.3. Dependent variable is Δln(enrollment) 2010–2022.

$n = 447$

$r^2 = 0.285$

ment trends, holding state ratios constant. Among other things, a burgeoning local population may make it more difficult for institutions to expand.

The final model in table 1.3 adds election return information from the 2008 presidential race. Although only county-level election returns significantly predict enrollment trends, both county- and state-level data discount the theory that enrollment trends reflect growing conservative disdain for higher education. Other things equal, enrollment trends were lower in counties that exhibited greater support for Barack Obama in the 2008 election. To be clear, this is not a direct test of the hypothesis, as the decline in enrollment in "blue" counties might well reflect a decreased willingness of more conservative families to send their children to school in those counties. But a disdain for exposing children to liberal college towns is somewhat distinct from a disdain for higher education in general. Although the county-level vote share variable is strongly significant, its addition has a relatively modest impact on model fit. Demographic variables continue to exert strong predictive power.[6]

As noted above, less-research-intensive institutions have shown more negative enrollment trends in the period since 2010. Table 1.4 investigates

6. While, as noted above, estimates of the responsiveness of enrollment to unemployment suggest that recovery from the Great Recession can explain much if not all of the decline in enrollment nationally, addition of state-level unemployment rates to the models reported in table 1.3, as well as table 1.4 below, consistently attribute no significant impact to institution-level enrollment patterns. It is possible that community college enrollments are more responsive to unemployment rate changes than the public four-year institutions studied here. It is also possible that jurisdictions with higher unemployment rates were less likely to adopt policies that encouraged the unemployed to enroll in school (Barr and Turner 2015).

whether these differential trends can be explained by differential sensitivity to demographics. The coefficients presented are derived from a single OLS regression model, employing the same control variables as the final model presented in Table 1.3. The specification here adds a series of interaction terms between county population, the county ratio of 5–9-year-olds to 18–21 year-olds, and the state level age ratio, and Carnegie classification indicators. The Carnegie classifications are collapsed here, with one indicator for what in 2010 were termed "master's-level" institutions, and a second for baccalaureate institutions.

While these interaction terms are generally not statistically significant, the magnitudes are noteworthy. Point estimates suggest that the state-level age ratio, a strong predictor of enrollment trends in table 1.3, has a relatively modest impact among the most research-intensive institutions. The coefficient is less than half the magnitude here. Interaction terms point to a much stronger effect among less research-intensive institutions. Among master's-granting institutions, point estimates suggest a sensitivity to age trends nearly three times that of doctorate-granting institutions. Baccalaureate institutions are more than four times more sensitive to age trends, with an interaction term statistically significant at the 10 percent level.

To summarize the evidence to this point, the declines in enrollment after 2010 were concentrated in less research-intensive institutions, a phenomenon partially explained by their differential characteristics. Commuter campuses without housing, HBCUs, and institutions receiving less grant revenue all consistently show more negative trends. Demographic patterns, most significantly state-level forecasts of relative cohort size as well as local population, have significant explanatory value. Less research-intensive institutions, particularly those without graduate programs, show some evidence of greater sensitivity to trends in cohort size.

While initial enrollment appears as a significant predictor in some of the long difference specifications, in more complete models estimated impacts fall closer to zero. Nonetheless, there are particular concerns that institutions might enter a form of "death spiral," where enrollment losses lead to reductions in tuition revenue, which in turn lead to expenditure cuts, which may then spur additional enrollment losses as academic programs are eliminated. From another perspective, modern institutions of higher education enjoy some degree of scale economy, with larger enrollments permitting a wider array of specialized course and program offerings. Below some critical value, those economies of scale might rapidly erode, placing an institution at risk of consolidation or closure.

Table 1.5 explores this subject by providing results from a series of short-term regression analyses, where the change in log enrollment from one year to the next is modeled as a function of lagged enrollment. If enrollment is a mean reverting process, where smaller institutions trend upward and larger

**Table 1.5** **Short-run dynamics by Carnegie classification and time period**

| DV: Δln(enrollment) | R1/Doctoral | Master's | Baccalaureate | Associate's |
|---|---|---|---|---|
| *2000–2005* | | | | |
| Intercept | 0.100 | 0.074 | 0.132 | 0.188 |
| | (0.020) | (0.017) | (0.025) | (0.016) |
| Lagged ln(enrollment) | −0.008 | −0.006 | −0.015 | −0.020 |
| | (0.002) | (0.002) | (0.003) | (0.002) |
| *2005–2010* | | | | |
| Intercept | 0.003 | 0.093 | 0.047 | 0.124 |
| | (0.016) | (0.028) | (0.020) | (0.012) |
| Lagged ln(enrollment) | 0.001 | −0.009 | −0.004 | −0.011 |
| | (0.002) | (0.003) | (0.003) | (0.002) |
| *2010–2015* | | | | |
| Intercept | −0.032 | −0.027 | 0.026 | −0.163 |
| | (0.015) | (0.017) | (0.019) | (0.013) |
| Lagged ln(enrollment) | 0.004 | 0.003 | −0.004 | 0.016 |
| | (0.002) | (0.002) | (0.003) | (0.002) |
| *2015–2020* | | | | |
| Intercept | −0.077 | −0.190 | −0.031 | −0.202 |
| | (0.013) | (0.026) | (0.019) | (0.014) |
| Lagged ln(enrollment) | 0.008 | 0.021 | 0.002 | 0.021 |
| | (0.001) | (0.003) | (0.003) | (0.002) |
| *2020–2022* | | | | |
| Intercept | −0.061 | −0.050 | 0.011 | −0.056 |
| | (0.021) | (0.020) | (0.029) | (0.018) |
| Lagged ln(enrollment) | 0.006 | 0.002 | −0.005 | 0.002 |
| | (0.002) | (0.002) | (0.004) | (0.002) |

Note: Standard errors in parentheses.

ones downward, we might expect a positive intercept and negative slope in these regressions. If enrollment is instead a divergent process, where smaller institutions lose economies of scale while larger ones gain, we might expect the opposite pattern.

Table 1.5 divides the period since 2000 into five periods, including three in the critical period of enrollment losses since 2010. The final period tracks enrollment from fall 2020 forward, the pandemic- and post-pandemic eras. It further stratifies the analysis by Carnegie classification, using the same simplified three-tier distinctions utilized in table 1.4.

Across all tiers of institutions, there is a significant shift from the earliest time period analyzed here to the post-2010 era. Among the most research-intensive institutions, for example, dynamics in the period between 2000 and 2005 show a form of mean reversion, with the smallest institutions tending to exhibit higher growth rates. After 2010, the pattern has flipped, growth now positively associated with initial size. In the 2015–2019 time period, the model implies negative predicted growth at institutions with an initial size below 10,470 students. Several R1 institutions fell below this threshold as of 2015.[7] The pattern continues to hold in the most recent data.

A similar phenomenon is evident among master's-level institutions. These show a pattern of mean reversion through 2009, no statistically significant relationship between lagged enrollment and growth between 2010 and 2014, and then strong evidence of divergence between 2015 and 2019. The fulcrum point dividing institutions predicted to decline from those predicted to grow rests around an initial enrollment of 9,720. In the post-pandemic period, these institutions exhibited negative growth more uniformly.[8]

Baccalaureate institutions similarly show evidence of mean-reverting growth patterns in the 2000–2004 period, transitioning to a divergence pattern after 2015. Point estimates imply negative growth at essentially all institutions in the tier between 2015 and 2019, followed by some degree of stabilization after 2020.

The final set of estimates in table 1.5 examines associate's-granting institutions such as community colleges. These institutions, too, show a shift in dynamics over time. Growth relates negatively to initial size between 2000 and 2009, then flips to the opposite pattern after 2010. Point estimates for the 2015–2019 period indicate a fulcrum point at enrollment around 16,600.

In general, then, these results point to a pattern of smaller institutions bearing the brunt of short-run enrollment declines, most notably in the period between 2015 and 2019. Universities offering graduate degrees were at the greatest risk of enrollment declines during this period if their initial enrollment fell below roughly 10,000 students; community colleges tended to shrink even with enrollments somewhat greater than this level. Should these patterns re-emerge in the post-pandemic era, they intimate significant concerns regarding loss of scale economies at relatively small institutions.

## 1.6 Implications

The broad declines in college enrollment since 2010 exhibit a significant cross-sectional relationship with state and local baseline demographic conditions, and have disproportionately affected less research-intensive public institutions. There are two important implications to discuss, one regarding finance and the other regarding the prognosis for the future.

From a financial perspective, the most-affected institutions typically do not manage large extramural grant portfolios and do not have significant endowments. They rely significantly on tuition revenue and direct allocations

7. Specifically, Cal Tech, Claremont Graduate University, Catholic University, Howard, Brandeis, Princeton, CUNY Graduate Center, RPI, Teacher's College, Yeshiva, Lehigh, Brown, and Rice.

8. Point estimates suggest that predicted enrollment growth in the 2020–2022 period would be negative except at institutions with initial enrollment above 1.2 billion.

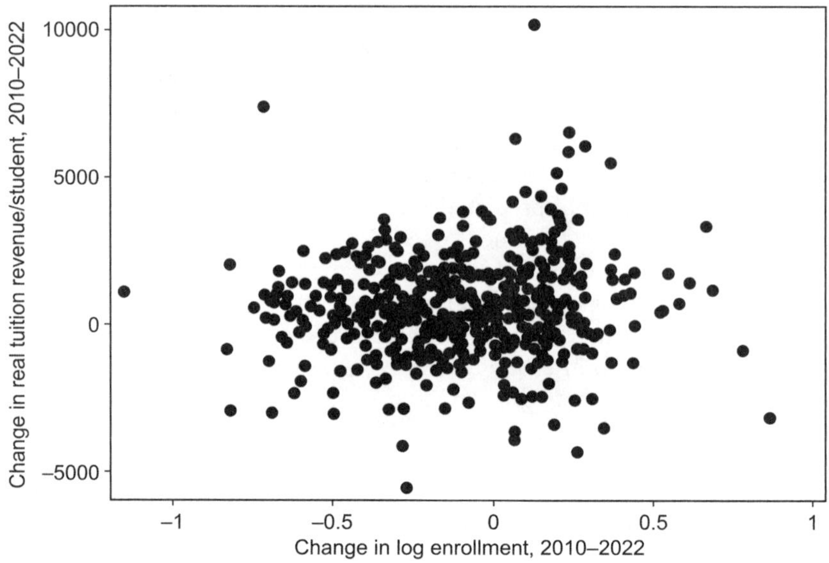


**Fig. 1.5 Change in real tuition revenue per student, inflation-adjusted 2022 dollars, 2010–2022**
Source: IPEDS.

from state and local government. To the extent these institutions exhibit economies of scale, declining enrollment should increase their per-student expenditures. Were these increased expenditures to be covered by raising tuition, the higher costs might exacerbate enrollment declines. Covering higher per-student costs with government transfers avoids this potential vicious cycle, but raises questions about long-term viability.

Figures 1.5 and 1.6 show that enrollment changes between 2010 and 2022, for public institutions offering four-year degrees, are much more highly correlated with per-student government transfers ($r = -0.40$) than per-student tuition revenue ($r = 0.07$). States have, in general, stepped in to shore up the finances of institutions experiencing enrollment declines, while exhibiting a tendency to reduce per-student subsidies to institutions with stable or increasing enrollment. Given the substantial fixed costs of shutting down an institution, and the option value of retaining one should enrollment trends reverse, this may be a sensible short-run reaction. In the longer run, states may face difficult decisions regarding whether it is worthwhile to fund higher per-student operating subsidies with a system of institutions below their intended capacity.

And projections point to continued declines in enrollment below 2010 capacity. The regression model represented in table 1.4 can be used to make out-of-sample predictions. Every variable controlled for in that regression can be replicated as late as fall 2021, with demographic data updated from

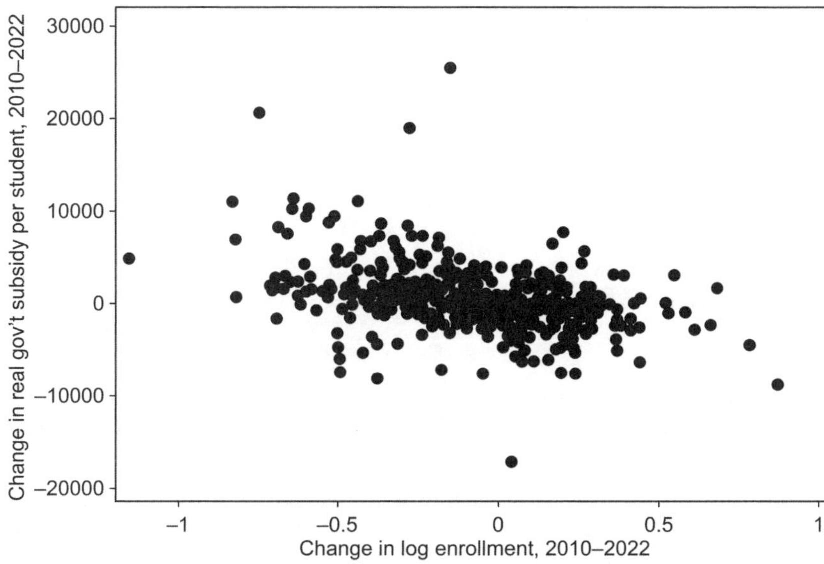


**Fig. 1.6 Change in real government subsidy per student, inflation-adjusted 2022 dollars, 2010–2022**
Source: IPEDS.

the 2020 Census. The resulting predicted values indicate forecasted changes in enrollment over a 12-year period to roughly 2033, based in part on the number of 5–9-year-olds in 2020 who would be expected to be of college-going age at that later time.

This exercise should be taken with a grain of salt. Predictions will hold if the model determining enrollments between 2010 and 2022 continues to accurately describe patterns in the future. Evidence in table 1.5 above indicates that enrollment dynamics are not necessarily stable, and past performance may not guarantee future results. Nonetheless, the estimates provide a sense of how changing demographics may impact institutions in the coming years.

Table 1.6 presents summary information regarding these predictions, stratified by Carnegie classification and presented alongside information on actual changes in enrollment observed over the 2010–2022 time period. Overall, in this sample of 450 institutions, log enrollment dropped by an unweighted mean of 0.089 between 2010 and 2022. Predictions based on the 2010–2022 model suggest accelerated decline through 2033, with a mean decline of 0.126.

The R1 institutions, which were largely immune from enrollment declines over the past decade, will continue to exhibit such immunity as a group—although table 1A.1, which provides a comprehensive list of predicted enrollment changes for these 450 institutions, suggests that several are at

**Table 1.6 Summary of projections**

| Institution category | Mean Δln(enrollment) 2010–2022 | Mean projected Δln(enrollment) 2021–2033 |
|---|---|---|
| Overall ($n$ = 450) | −0.089 | −0.126 |
| R1 Research-intensive ($n$ = 90) | 0.080 | 0.065 |
| Doctoral ($n$ = 60) | −0.086 | −0.093 |
| Master's I ($n$ = 220) | −0.116 | −0.163 |
| Master's II ($n$ = 18) | −0.223 | −0.254 |
| Baccalaureate ($n$ = 62) | −0.202 | −0.263 |

risk of shrinking enrollment. Where log enrollment averaged an increase of 0.08 in the recent past, the model forecasts a slightly more modest 0.06 increase going forward.

For the next tier of less research-intensive doctorate-granting institutions, the future is projected to closely resemble the recent past, with a −0.086 realized decline in log enrollment followed by a −0.093 predicted decline. More significant acceleration is forecast for master's-level institutions. The set of 220 Master's 1 institutions, nearly half the public universities in the sample, collectively averaged a −0.116 decline in log enrollment between 2010 and 2022; the projected trend is −0.163. The small set of Master's II institutions, which fared much worse in the recent interval, is projected to experience a steeper decline as well. And finally, the set of 62 public baccalaureate institutions is projected to experience the most severe worsening in trend, with average log enrollment predicted to decline by −0.263. The worsening trends are driven in large part by changing demographics, with the ratio of 5–9-year-olds in 2020 falling well below the equivalent value in 2010.

How will American higher education adapt to the changes wrought by declining birthrates? As a baseline, consider the evidence in figure 1.6. Absent other intervention, shrinking institutions will require increasing per-student subsidies to operate, unless they impose tuition increases that would threaten to further erode headcount. There are four categories of intervention that might offset or reverse demography-driven trends, and a fifth intervention that would reduce operational subsidies by ceasing to operate some institutions.

### 1.6.1 Intervention Type 1: Improving Matriculation

As noted above, postsecondary institutions overcame the "baby bust" in part by moving matriculation rates from the 50 percent range in the early 1980s to as high as 67 percent in 1997. Since that high water mark, matriculation rates have fluctuated, reaching an all-time high of 70 percent in 2009. The period of declining enrollment has also been a period of declining matriculation rates. In fall 2021 and 2022, the matriculation rate stood at 61.8 percent and 62 percent respectively, the first incidence of two consecutive years below 62 percent since 1994 and 1995, in the midst of the baby-bust ramp-up. With roughly three million high school graduates each year, improving the matriculation rate back to its high point could yield an additional 240,000 college students per cohort.

There are strong evidence-based strategies for improving matriculation rates. Helping families navigate the financial aid system and the uncertainties of college admissions has been shown to have an impact (Bettinger et al. 2012; Dynarski et al. 2021). Offering access to college-level coursework in high school has also been shown to raise matriculation rates—as well as credential attainment rates (Edmunds et al. 2017). Nationwide, numerous states have undertaken policy interventions to smooth the transition to college, such as eliminating tuition at community colleges, requiring students to complete the FAFSA as a condition of high school graduation, and expanding opportunities for taking college courses in high school.

It is somewhat disheartening to understand that this evidence, and these implemented interventions, have taken place in an environment of declining matriculation rates. These rates dropped discretely with the onset of the pandemic, from 66.2 percent in 2019 to 62.7 percent in 2022. They may recover. The 70 percent high water mark was nearly equaled in 2018, when the rate hit 69.1 percent. With continued efforts to implement evidence-based strategies, some portion of the projected enrollment decline could be reasonably offset.

### 1.6.2 Intervention Type 2: Improve Persistence

Among students who began study at a four-year institution in the fall of 2015, 64.6 percent had earned a bachelor's degree from that institution within six years.[9] This ratio is the highest recorded since the necessary longitudinal data began being reported in the late 1990s. Nonetheless, there are at least in theory enrollment gains to be made by reducing the rate at which students who begin a degree withdraw. And many of the interventions proven effective at increasing matriculation—financial aid navigation, access to college-level material in high school—have also shown promise in improving completion rates.

For several reasons, improved completion statistics may not necessarily yield benefits to institutions or society. Achieving higher completion rates by imposing lower standards for degree completion may help institutions

9. Data from the National Student Clearinghouse, which allows the tracking of students who transfer across institutions, show an overall six-year degree completion rate of 69 percent for students in the 2015 entry cohort who begin at public four-year institutions, and 78.3 percent for those who begin at private non-profit four-year institutions. The National Student Clearinghouse has made data available for the entering cohorts of 2016 and 2017, which exhibit slight declines from these levels. See https://nscresearchcenter.org/completing-college/.

keep students enrolled, but may not yield much benefit in the form of human capital accumulation (Denning et al. 2022). And interventions that succeed in reducing the time it takes students to complete a degree—roughly one-third of four-year degree completers take more than four years to do so—may be helpful to students while on net reducing headcount at postsecondary institutions.

### 1.6.3 Intervention Type 3: Increase International Enrollment

Foreign student enrollment expanded during the "baby bust" years. By fall 2015, over one million non-immigrant student visa holders were enrolled at American institutions, an increase of more than 300,000 over the number recorded five years earlier. Clearly, in the early years of the enrollment decline institutions turned to foreign students to keep their numbers up. The number of foreign students declined after 2015, reaching a low of 914,095 in the pandemic-affected fall of 2020 and since picking back up to 948,519.

In theory, admitting more foreign students to study in the United States could help institutions make up for the decline in US-born students. Relatedly, a broader relaxation of immigration policy could bring more future college students into the country. These could be thought of as distinct interventions.

Raising the number of foreign student visas may accomplish little for the less research-intensive institutions likely to face the greatest risk of enrollment decline. In the 2022–23 academic year, over 5,000 students of Chinese nationality enrolled at the University of Washington, a public flagship R1 institution in a large cosmopolitan city. Washington State University, itself an R1 institution, but a land grant institution located in a smaller town, enrolled just 246. The state's four public master's- and baccalaureate-level institutions enrolled a grand total of zero. The nation's most research-intensive institutions offer educational opportunities that may be difficult to replicate elsewhere in the world. The case for matriculating at a less research-intensive institution in a foreign country may be more difficult.

Additionally, the strategy of attracting more foreign nationals is complicated by the fact that birth rates in most other nations are falling just as fast, if not faster, than in the United States. With fewer students competing for scarce admission slots to elite domestic institutions, the number of students expressing interest in going abroad for study might well decline.

The potential impact of family-based migration on college enrollment is quite different. To continue considering the experience of the state of Washington, immigration has significantly increased the proportion of Evergreen state residents reporting Hispanic or Latino ethnicity, from 2.9 percent in 1980 to 14.5 percent in 2022. Students reporting this ethnicity are distributed much more evenly across the state relative to foreign nationals on student visas, reflecting in part their distribution in more agricultural regions of the state and the effect of their socioeconomic disadvantage on the likelihood of admission to more-selective campuses. Where the University of Washington accounts for over 95 percent of the public four-year enrollment of Chinese nationals in the United States, two-thirds of the state's Hispanic or Latino public college students are enrolled at other institutions.

This said, the prospects for reforms to immigration policy that bring more lower-income families with young children to the United States within the next few years seem dim to say the least. An alternative strategy would be to raise the caps many states impose on out-of-state enrollment at their flagship institutions, which are most likely to attract foreign applications, redirecting in-state students to the less research-intensive institutions with spare capacity.

### 1.6.4 Intervention Type 4: Increasing Offerings For "Non-Traditional" Students

Universities navigated the "baby bust" in part by creating new opportunities for students other than 18-year-old high school graduates pursuing full-time study. Between 1984 and 1996, part-time undergraduate enrollment rose 58 percent, more than twice the rate of growth in full-time enrollment. Graduate enrollment rose 84 percent. Creating more opportunities for non-traditional students to return to school, whether for conventional degree programs or other types of skill acquisition or even pure consumption value, might help some institutions offset enrollment declines.

The strategy of expanding alternative degree or program offerings faces some of the same challenges as increasing traditional student enrollment. Some common postbaccalaureate degree programs have themselves been experiencing enrollment declines. In fall 2023, just under 38,000 college graduates enrolled as first-year law students, falling below 40,000 for the 10th out of the past 11 years. Law school first-year enrollment had exceeded 40,000 every year from 1978 to 2012. While the number of doctorates awarded has trended upward over the past decade, fields including education, the humanities, and arts are on downward trends. Graduate business enrollments have trended downward in recent years.

A more general concern about product innovation strategies once again pertains to the nature of the institutions at greatest risk for significant enrollment declines. These institutions have traditionally focused on undergraduate instruction, and would need to make significant infrastructure investments to begin offering, for example, graduate business degrees. Part-time non-traditional students will, by default, be more common in more populated metropolitan areas. Local community colleges without residential facilities may be more adaptable to their needs than institutions in less-populated counties that have historically offered full-time instruction to students in residence.

### 1.6.5 Intervention Type 5: Closure

Edinboro University of Pennsylvania was founded as a school for training teachers, a normal school, in 1857. It is one of hundreds of institutions nationwide that can claim similar origins. Like many, it was not originally a public institution but was purchased by the state of Pennsylvania in 1914. It was located in the small town of Edinboro, which claimed fewer than 1,000 residents at the time the state purchased the school, just south of Erie in the northwestern corner of the state. Edinboro University reached an all-time peak enrollment of 8,642 in fall 2010. Over the next decade that student headcount would steadily decline, to the point where just 4,043 students arrived for class in the fall of 2021. State appropriations to support operations increased, from $4,054 per student to $7,646 in inflation-adjusted 2023 dollars.

That would be the last class of students to attend Edinboro University. Before the 2022/23 school year began, the state of Pennsylvania consolidated the institution, along with two other public universities, into Pennsylvania Western University. By consolidating rather than closing the institution, the state preserves access to education for those students in the northwestern corner of the state, as well as jobs for those employed there.

Closing a campus is politically difficult, and rare. Given broad enrollment trends there are likely few buyers for the physical plant of an aging multi-building campus. State legislators may not be warm to the notion of eliminating jobs in their districts. Proximity to college has been associated with higher rates of enrollment and earnings (Card 1993). Consolidation may permit institutions to economize on certain inputs into educational production, but when the consolidated institutions are beyond a simple commuting distance it may be difficult to reap significant benefits without requiring some students to, for example, take remote biology classes from a satellite campus because the biology department at their location was shut down.

The potential downside of maintaining a fixed number of public colleges in the face of persistent enrollment declines is either rising public subsidy or declining college quality. The returns to proximity for some students may be more than offset if the nearby college ceases to offer programs or reduces course availability. And many campuses at risk of closure are in sparsely populated areas, where the cost of reduced proximity would be borne by a relative few.

It is conceivable that states with particularly negative enrollment trends, including those where the overall population is declining due to outmigration, might address the political difficulty of shuttering campuses by appointing special commissions to study and propose closures that could not be legislatively amended, similar to the procedure of base realignment and closure implemented by the US military to reduce the number of installations between 1988 and 2005.

## 1.7 Conclusion

Demography is not necessarily destiny. American higher education has withstood declines in cohort size much greater than that projected to occur over the next 15 years, increasing enrollment in the process. This was accomplished primarily by converting a greater share of high school graduates to undergraduate students, easing the path for part-time enrollees, and expanding graduate program offerings. Each of these possible interventions remains available to colleges and universities today. But each of them has been available since 2010, and they have not been sufficient to offset what appears by standards of either the past or future to be a modest decline in cohort size.

The cross-sectional evidence presented in this paper links institutional fates over the post-2010 period to patterns of state and local demographics. Generally speaking, the colleges that saw the greatest enrollment declines were in states where the raw number of youth available to educate was forecast to decline the most as of 2010. And projections based on this measure indicate that enrollment trends may well worsen over the next decade. The institutions at greatest risk of decline are those least well positioned to expand graduate enrollment or attract foreign students.

The pattern apparent in recent data, whereby public flagship institutions have expanded enrollment even as their sibling regional universities have declined, is a political choice. Legislatures could, in theory, impose stricter limits on growth and reserve fewer flagship seats for in-state students. While such measures could help bolster enrollments at regional universities, preserving access in what might become underserved corners of states, they would likely face public backlash.

To some extent, the decline in enrollment may reflect improved wages in jobs available to inexperienced workers, which in turn may be a function of changing demographics (Vigdor 2023). Future technological change may play a significant role in determining whether a higher share of high school graduates continues on to college. If that change is skill biased, as many have argued it was for much of the latter half of the 20th century, matriculation rates may resume the upward trend they exhibited at that time. If, on the other hand, artificial intelligence reduces demand for occupations that have traditionally required college-acquired intelligence, the projections developed here might understate future enrollment losses.

# Appendix

**Table 1A.1 Enrollment projections for public four-year institutions, 2021–2033**

*PANEL A: Carnegie R1 (Research Intensive Doctoral)*

| Institution Name | Fall 2021 enrollment | Δln(enrollment) 2010–2022 | Projected Δln(enrollment) 2021–2033 |
|---|---|---|---|
| Arizona State University Campus Immersion | 77,881 | 0.128 | 0.274 |
| Auburn University | 31,526 | 0.236 | 0.070 |
| Binghamton University | 18,055 | 0.207 | −0.003 |
| CUNY Graduate School and University Center | 9,017 | 0.282 | −0.011 |
| Clemson University | 27,341 | 0.381 | 0.241 |
| Colorado State University−Fort Collins | 32,586 | 0.102 | 0.130 |
| Florida International University | 56,664 | 0.276 | 0.208 |
| Florida State University | 45,130 | 0.089 | 0.092 |
| Georgia Institute of Technology−Main Campus | 43,859 | 0.782 | 0.384 |
| Georgia State University | 36,973 | 0.147 | 0.108 |
| Indiana University−Bloomington | 45,328 | 0.102 | −0.050 |
| Iowa State University | 30,708 | 0.044 | 0.024 |
| Kansas State University | 20,229 | −0.179 | 0.075 |
| Kent State University at Kent | 26,597 | −0.028 | 0.021 |
| Louisiana State University and Agricultural & Mechanical College | 35,912 | 0.238 | 0.129 |
| Michigan State University | 49,659 | 0.063 | 0.062 |
| Mississippi State University | 23,086 | 0.142 | 0.014 |
| New Mexico State University−Main Campus | 13,904 | −0.265 | 0.014 |
| North Carolina State University at Raleigh | 36,831 | 0.065 | 0.115 |
| Northern Illinois University | 16,234 | −0.421 | −0.038 |
| Ohio State University−Main Campus | 61,677 | 0.077 | 0.134 |
| Ohio University−Main Campus | 24,797 | −0.039 | −0.187 |
| Oklahoma State University−Main Campus | 24,577 | 0.070 | 0.083 |
| Old Dominion University | 23,494 | −0.057 | −0.021 |
| Oregon State University | 33,193 | 0.367 | 0.003 |
| Purdue University−Main Campus | 50,344 | 0.227 | 0.065 |
| Rutgers University−New Brunswick | 50,804 | 0.263 | 0.163 |
| SUNY at Albany | 17,075 | −0.056 | 0.043 |
| Southern Illinois University−Carbondale | 11,266 | −0.590 | −0.194 |
| Stony Brook University | 26,608 | 0.054 | 0.182 |
| Texas A&M University−College Station | 72,530 | 0.410 | 0.320 |
| Texas Tech University | 40,542 | 0.244 | 0.190 |
| The University of Alabama | 38,316 | 0.249 | 0.097 |
| The University of Tennessee–Knoxville | 31,701 | 0.109 | 0.177 |
| The University of Texas at Arlington | 45,949 | 0.287 | 0.247 |
| The University of Texas at Austin | 51,991 | 0.023 | 0.170 |
| University at Buffalo | 32,332 | 0.098 | 0.068 |
| University of Alabama at Birmingham | 22,289 | 0.210 | 0.074 |
| University of Arizona | 48,274 | 0.234 | 0.209 |
| University of Arkansas | 29,068 | 0.368 | 0.167 |
| University of Cincinnati−Main Campus | 40,329 | 0.243 | 0.071 |
| University of Colorado Boulder | 39,000 | 0.191 | 0.113 |
| University of Connecticut | 26,876 | 0.057 | 0.016 |

**Table 1A.1 (cont.)**

| Institution Name | Fall 2021 enrollment | Δln(enrollment) 2010–2022 | Projected Δln(enrollment) 2021–2033 |
|---|---|---|---|
| University of Florida | 55,781 | 0.103 | 0.176 |
| University of Georgia | 40,118 | 0.158 | 0.039 |
| University of Hawaii at Manoa | 19,098 | −0.064 | 0.040 |
| University of Houston | 47,031 | 0.187 | 0.335 |
| University of Idaho | 11,303 | −0.067 | −0.066 |
| University of Illinois Chicago | 34,199 | 0.192 | 0.141 |
| University of Illinois Urbana-Champaign | 56,607 | 0.261 | 0.112 |
| University of Iowa | 29,909 | 0.017 | −0.109 |
| University of Kansas | 26,780 | −0.072 | −0.049 |
| University of Kentucky | 30,390 | 0.152 | 0.113 |
| University of Louisville | 22,140 | 0.036 | 0.008 |
| University of Maine | 12,657 | 0.062 | −0.033 |
| University of Maryland−Baltimore County | 13,638 | 0.082 | 0.088 |
| University of Maryland−College Park | 41,272 | 0.080 | 0.016 |
| University of Massachusetts−Amherst | 32,045 | 0.156 | −0.001 |
| University of Memphis | 21,622 | −0.023 | −0.014 |
| University of Michigan−Ann Arbor | 50,278 | 0.200 | 0.016 |
| University of Minnesota−Twin Cities | 52,376 | 0.061 | 0.131 |
| University of Mississippi | 21,203 | 0.266 | −0.068 |
| University of Missouri−Columbia | 31,401 | −0.033 | 0.040 |
| University of Nebraska−Lincoln | 24,431 | −0.033 | 0.132 |
| University of Nevada−Reno | 21,034 | 0.169 | 0.102 |
| University of New Hampshire−Main Campus | 14,001 | −0.079 | −0.023 |
| University of New Mexico−Main Campus | 22,139 | −0.268 | 0.010 |
| University of North Carolina at Chapel Hill | 31,641 | 0.076 | 0.042 |
| University of North Texas | 42,441 | 0.210 | 0.183 |
| University of Oklahoma−Norman Campus | 28,042 | 0.067 | 0.209 |
| University of Oregon | 22,257 | −0.008 | 0.011 |
| University of Rhode Island | 17,511 | 0.070 | −0.003 |
| University of South Carolina−Columbia | 35,471 | 0.186 | 0.007 |
| University of South Florida | 49,708 | 0.204 | 0.191 |
| University of Southern Mississippi | 14,146 | −0.154 | 0.022 |
| University of Toledo | 16,979 | −0.395 | −0.126 |
| University of Utah | 34,464 | 0.120 | 0.123 |
| University of Vermont | 13,826 | 0.039 | −0.178 |
| University of Virginia−Main Campus | 26,005 | 0.067 | −0.120 |
| University of Washington−Seattle Campus | 52,434 | 0.209 | 0.114 |
| University of Wisconsin−Madison | 47,016 | 0.149 | 0.075 |
| University of Wisconsin−Milwaukee | 23,829 | −0.295 | −0.031 |
| University of Wyoming | 11,479 | −0.151 | −0.011 |
| Utah State University | 27,426 | 0.529 | 0.288 |
| Virginia Commonwealth University | 28,594 | −0.131 | −0.072 |
| Virginia Polytechnic Institute and State University | 37,279 | 0.208 | 0.063 |
| Washington State University | 29,843 | 0.046 | 0.000 |
| Wayne State University | 24,919 | −0.288 | −0.027 |
| West Virginia University | 25,474 | −0.169 | −0.027 |
| Western Michigan University | 18,266 | −0.387 | −0.110 |

*(continued)*

**Table 1A.1 (cont.)**

*PANEL B: Carnegie R2 (Doctoral)*

| Institution Name | Fall 2021 enrollment | Δln(enrollment) 2010–2022 | Projected Δln(enrollment) 2021–2033 |
|---|---|---|---|
| Alabama A & M University | 5,969 | 0.033 | 0.079 |
| Ball State University | 20,319 | −0.110 | −0.168 |
| Bowling Green State University−Main Campus | 17,645 | −0.045 | −0.115 |
| Central Michigan University | 15,424 | −0.665 | −0.292 |
| Cleveland State University | 15,308 | −0.189 | −0.113 |
| East Carolina University | 28,021 | −0.023 | −0.168 |
| East Tennessee State University | 13,303 | −0.103 | −0.067 |
| Florida Atlantic University | 30,155 | 0.046 | −0.014 |
| George Mason University | 38,628 | 0.182 | −0.056 |
| Idaho State University | 12,135 | −0.019 | −0.263 |
| Illinois State University | 20,233 | −0.022 | −0.097 |
| Indiana State University | 9,459 | −0.283 | −0.189 |
| Indiana University of Pennsylvania−Main Campus | 9,298 | −0.540 | −0.183 |
| Indiana University−Purdue University−Indianapolis | 27,690 | −0.163 | −0.026 |
| Jackson State University | 7,080 | −0.229 | −0.238 |
| Louisiana Tech University | 11,037 | −0.080 | −0.140 |
| Miami University−Oxford | 19,264 | 0.089 | 0.031 |
| Michigan Technological University | 7,008 | 0.013 | −0.180 |
| Middle Tennessee State University | 21,568 | −0.274 | −0.036 |
| Missouri University of Science and Technology | 7,241 | −0.018 | −0.146 |
| Montana State University | 16,788 | 0.243 | 0.000 |
| New Jersey Institute of Technology | 11,901 | 0.322 | −0.047 |
| North Dakota State University−Main Campus | 12,461 | −0.163 | −0.123 |
| Northern Arizona University | 28,711 | 0.109 | −0.094 |
| Oakland University | 17,170 | −0.168 | −0.160 |
| Portland State University | 22,858 | −0.260 | −0.241 |
| Rutgers University−Newark | 12,168 | −0.068 | −0.169 |
| SUNY College of Environmental Science and Forestry | 2,012 | −0.305 | −0.060 |
| San Diego State University | 36,484 | 0.248 | 0.135 |
| South Carolina State University | 2,374 | −0.499 | −0.248 |
| South Dakota State University | 11,465 | −0.124 | −0.194 |
| Tennessee State University | 8,077 | 0.032 | −0.002 |
| Texas A&M University−Commerce | 11,504 | 0.047 | −0.025 |
| Texas A&M University−Kingsville | 6,405 | −0.462 | −0.219 |
| Texas Southern University | 7,524 | −0.102 | 0.118 |
| Texas Woman's University | 16,338 | 0.118 | 0.101 |
| The University of Montana | 10,106 | −0.452 | −0.162 |
| The University of Texas at Dallas | 29,696 | 0.611 | 0.127 |
| The University of Texas at El Paso | 24,003 | 0.077 | 0.025 |
| University of Akron Main Campus | 14,498 | −0.699 | −0.156 |
| University of Alabama in Huntsville | 9,636 | 0.193 | 0.231 |
| University of Arkansas at Little Rock | 8,295 | −0.475 | −0.115 |

**Table 1A.1 (cont.)**

| Institution Name | Fall 2021 enrollment | Δln(enrollment) 2010–2022 | Projected Δln(enrollment) 2021–2033 |
|---|---|---|---|
| University of Central Florida | 70,310 | 0.197 | 0.101 |
| University of Colorado Denver/Anschutz Medical Campus | 24,267 | −0.015 | −0.154 |
| University of Louisiana at Lafayette | 16,225 | −0.097 | −0.066 |
| University of Maryland, Baltimore | 7,244 | 0.088 | −0.085 |
| University of Massachusetts–Boston | 15,637 | 0.009 | −0.156 |
| University of Massachusetts–Lowell | 17,597 | 0.154 | −0.051 |
| University of Missouri–Kansas City | 16,003 | 0.029 | −0.096 |
| University of Missouri–St Louis | 15,189 | −0.101 | −0.074 |
| University of Nevada–Las Vegas | 30,679 | 0.084 | −0.037 |
| University of New Orleans | 7,953 | −0.461 | −0.198 |
| University of North Carolina at Greensboro | 19,038 | −0.043 | −0.005 |
| University of North Dakota | 13,772 | −0.023 | −0.203 |
| University of Northern Colorado | 10,348 | −0.329 | −0.183 |
| University of South Alabama | 13,992 | −0.095 | −0.117 |
| University of South Dakota | 9,464 | −0.029 | −0.368 |
| Wichita State University | 15,394 | 0.107 | 0.067 |
| William & Mary | 9,517 | 0.188 | −0.218 |
| Wright State University–Main Campus | 10,295 | −0.645 | −0.072 |

*PANEL C: Carnegie Master's I*

| Institution Name | Fall 2021 enrollment | Δln(enrollment) 2010–2022 | Projected Δln(enrollment) 2021–2033 |
|---|---|---|---|
| Alabama State University | 3,964 | −0.399 | −0.200 |
| Albany State University | 6,297 | 0.308 | −0.314 |
| Angelo State University | 10,826 | 0.436 | 0.004 |
| Appalachian State University | 20,641 | 0.171 | −0.234 |
| Arkansas State University | 12,863 | −0.017 | −0.053 |
| Arkansas Tech University | 9,640 | −0.038 | −0.062 |
| Auburn University at Montgomery | 5,068 | −0.130 | −0.243 |
| Austin Peay State University | 9,609 | −0.140 | −0.114 |
| Boise State University | 25,794 | 0.267 | 0.021 |
| Bowie State University | 6,308 | 0.118 | −0.248 |
| Bridgewater State University | 9,942 | −0.154 | −0.264 |
| CUNY Bernard M Baruch College | 19,969 | 0.151 | −0.269 |
| CUNY Brooklyn College | 15,938 | −0.175 | −0.233 |
| CUNY City College | 15,031 | −0.062 | −0.245 |
| CUNY Hunter College | 24,099 | 0.025 | −0.143 |
| CUNY Lehman College | 14,392 | 0.072 | −0.277 |
| CUNY Queens College | 18,772 | −0.207 | −0.181 |
| California Polytechnic State University–San Luis Obispo | 22,231 | 0.181 | −0.140 |
| California State Polytechnic University–Humboldt | 5,908 | −0.271 | −0.221 |

(*continued*)

Table 1A.1 (cont.)

| Institution Name | Fall 2021 enrollment | Δln(enrollment) 2010–2022 | Projected Δln(enrollment) 2021–2033 |
|---|---|---|---|
| California State Polytechnic University–Pomona | 29,456 | 0.282 | 0.033 |
| California State University–Bakersfield | 10,972 | 0.195 | 0.009 |
| California State University–Chico | 15,702 | −0.120 | −0.125 |
| California State University–Dominguez Hills | 17,837 | 0.170 | 0.036 |
| California State University–East Bay | 15,189 | 0.059 | −0.140 |
| California State University–Fresno | 25,047 | 0.137 | −0.021 |
| California State University–Fullerton | 40,738 | 0.126 | 0.079 |
| California State University–Long Beach | 40,190 | 0.154 | 0.034 |
| California State University–Los Angeles | 27,513 | 0.273 | 0.050 |
| California State University–Northridge | 40,108 | 0.063 | 0.040 |
| California State University–Sacramento | 32,498 | 0.163 | −0.058 |
| California State University–San Bernardino | 19,514 | 0.189 | 0.025 |
| California State University–San Marcos | 16,255 | 0.441 | 0.014 |
| California State University–Stanislaus | 10,481 | 0.201 | −0.050 |
| Cameron University | 3,470 | −0.616 | −0.106 |
| Central Connecticut State University | 9,653 | −0.276 | −0.280 |
| Central Washington University | 10,176 | −0.227 | −0.144 |
| Cheyney University of Pennsylvania | 642 | −0.822 | −0.151 |
| Chicago State University | 2,366 | −1.155 | −0.041 |
| Citadel Military College of South Carolina | 3,693 | 0.090 | −0.165 |
| College of Charleston | 10,941 | −0.058 | −0.201 |
| College of Staten Island CUNY | 11,793 | −0.304 | −0.153 |
| Colorado State University Pueblo | 6,110 | −0.109 | −0.110 |
| Columbus State University | 7,898 | −0.104 | −0.231 |
| Coppin State University | 2,101 | −0.639 | −0.310 |
| Delaware State University | 5,200 | 0.439 | −0.279 |
| Delta State University | 2,727 | −0.526 | −0.356 |
| East Central University | 3,350 | −0.374 | −0.119 |
| East Stroudsburg University of Pennsylvania | 5,129 | −0.362 | −0.290 |
| Eastern Connecticut State University | 4,319 | −0.317 | −0.351 |
| Eastern Illinois University | 8,608 | −0.272 | −0.198 |
| Eastern Kentucky University | 13,984 | −0.145 | −0.050 |
| Eastern Michigan University | 15,340 | −0.519 | −0.258 |
| Eastern New Mexico University–Main Campus | 4,991 | 0.006 | −0.251 |
| Eastern Washington University | 10,892 | −0.056 | 0.020 |
| Emporia State University | 5,615 | −0.162 | −0.262 |
| Fayetteville State University | 6,748 | 0.160 | −0.267 |
| Fitchburg State University | 6,674 | −0.033 | −0.244 |
| Florida Agricultural and Mechanical University | 9,000 | −0.366 | −0.131 |
| Florida Gulf Coast University | 15,909 | 0.284 | −0.014 |
| Fort Hays State University | 14,102 | 0.086 | −0.202 |
| Fort Valley State University | 2,923 | −0.358 | −0.289 |
| Framingham State University | 4,495 | −0.370 | −0.195 |
| Francis Marion University | 3,923 | 0.003 | −0.215 |
| Frostburg State University | 4,452 | −0.296 | −0.145 |
| Georgia College & State University | 6,763 | −0.065 | −0.285 |
| Georgia Southern University | 27,076 | 0.258 | −0.144 |
| Georgia Southwestern State University | 3,157 | 0.011 | −0.305 |

**Table 1A.1** (cont.)

| Institution Name | Fall 2021 enrollment | Δln(enrollment) 2010–2022 | Projected Δln(enrollment) 2021–2033 |
|---|---|---|---|
| Governors State University | 4,395 | −0.246 | −0.160 |
| Grambling State University | 5,270 | 0.013 | −0.221 |
| Grand Valley State University | 22,406 | −0.125 | −0.069 |
| Henderson State University | 2,919 | −0.387 | −0.225 |
| Indiana University−Northwest | 3,460 | −0.624 | −0.273 |
| Indiana University−South Bend | 4,449 | −0.686 | −0.263 |
| Indiana University−Southeast | 4,051 | −0.670 | −0.277 |
| Jacksonville State University | 9,540 | 0.013 | −0.141 |
| James Madison University | 22,166 | 0.134 | −0.263 |
| Kean University | 12,759 | −0.213 | −0.164 |
| Kutztown University of Pennsylvania | 7,673 | −0.362 | −0.177 |
| Lamar University | 16,320 | 0.155 | −0.090 |
| Lincoln University | 1,794 | −0.603 | −0.193 |
| Louisiana State University−Shreveport | 8,881 | 0.662 | −0.287 |
| Marshall University | 11,023 | −0.283 | −0.162 |
| McNeese State University | 6,454 | −0.361 | −0.034 |
| Midwestern State University | 5,797 | −0.105 | 0.008 |
| Millersville University of Pennsylvania | 7,191 | −0.253 | −0.131 |
| Minnesota State University Moorhead | 5,088 | −0.476 | −0.224 |
| Minnesota State University−Mankato | 14,576 | −0.056 | −0.217 |
| Minot State University | 2,836 | −0.331 | −0.208 |
| Missouri State University−Springfield | 22,925 | 0.096 | −0.025 |
| Montana State University Billings | 4,114 | 0.064 | −0.164 |
| Montclair State University | 20,744 | 0.169 | −0.111 |
| Morgan State University | 8,469 | 0.154 | −0.276 |
| Murray State University | 9,414 | −0.094 | −0.157 |
| New Jersey City University | 6,918 | −0.264 | −0.200 |
| New Mexico Highlands University | 2,645 | −0.337 | −0.437 |
| Nicholls State University | 6,225 | −0.185 | −0.052 |
| Norfolk State University | 5,458 | −0.186 | −0.274 |
| North Carolina A & T State University | 13,322 | 0.223 | −0.128 |
| North Carolina Central University | 7,953 | −0.135 | −0.364 |
| Northeastern Illinois University | 6,440 | −0.713 | −0.104 |
| Northeastern State University | 7,025 | −0.355 | −0.202 |
| Northern Kentucky University | 15,979 | 0.005 | −0.126 |
| Northern Michigan University | 7,214 | −0.301 | −0.328 |
| Northern State University | 3,340 | 0.044 | −0.220 |
| Northwest Missouri State University | 7,870 | 0.175 | −0.263 |
| Northwestern State University of Louisiana | 10,735 | 0.016 | −0.234 |
| Pittsburg State University | 6,017 | −0.197 | −0.248 |
| Plymouth State University | 4,224 | −0.410 | −0.417 |
| Prairie View A & M University | 9,400 | 0.031 | −0.032 |
| Purdue University Fort Wayne | 8,298 | −0.448 | −0.118 |
| Radford University | 8,998 | −0.154 | −0.303 |
| Rhode Island College | 6,331 | −0.459 | −0.362 |
| Rowan University | 19,052 | 0.547 | −0.146 |
| Rutgers University−Camden | 6,569 | −0.032 | −0.188 |
| SUNY Brockport | 6,991 | −0.290 | −0.133 |

*(continued)*

**Table 1A.1** **(cont.)**

| Institution Name | Fall 2021 enrollment | Δln(enrollment) 2010–2022 | Projected Δln(enrollment) 2021–2033 |
|---|---|---|---|
| SUNY Buffalo State | 7,173 | −0.656 | −0.108 |
| SUNY College at Geneseo | 4,535 | −0.303 | −0.178 |
| SUNY College at Oswego | 7,058 | −0.184 | −0.212 |
| SUNY College at Plattsburgh | 4,738 | −0.364 | −0.297 |
| SUNY College at Potsdam | 2,607 | −0.598 | −0.252 |
| SUNY Cortland | 6,658 | −0.095 | −0.305 |
| SUNY Empire State College | 9,462 | −0.242 | −0.316 |
| SUNY Oneonta | 5,918 | −0.098 | −0.256 |
| SUNY Polytechnic Institute | 2,850 | 0.008 | −0.082 |
| SUNY at Fredonia | 3,764 | −0.503 | −0.217 |
| Saginaw Valley State University | 7,523 | −0.399 | −0.263 |
| Saint Cloud State University | 10,774 | −0.582 | −0.100 |
| Salem State University | 7,131 | −0.424 | −0.267 |
| Salisbury University | 7,570 | −0.165 | −0.158 |
| Sam Houston State University | 21,612 | 0.217 | −0.109 |
| San Francisco State University | 26,899 | −0.162 | −0.177 |
| San Jose State University | 37,133 | 0.207 | −0.107 |
| Shippensburg University of Pennsylvania | 5,667 | −0.478 | −0.100 |
| Slippery Rock University of Pennsylvania | 8,405 | −0.074 | −0.152 |
| Sonoma State University | 7,371 | −0.235 | −0.181 |
| Southeast Missouri State University | 9,851 | −0.106 | −0.118 |
| Southeastern Louisiana University | 13,456 | −0.130 | −0.043 |
| Southeastern Oklahoma State University | 5,420 | 0.273 | −0.133 |
| Southern Arkansas University Main Campus | 4,434 | 0.410 | −0.167 |
| Southern Connecticut State University | 8,788 | −0.297 | −0.244 |
| Southern Illinois University−Edwardsville | 13,010 | −0.121 | −0.145 |
| Southern Oregon University | 5,179 | −0.213 | −0.191 |
| Southern University and A & M College | 8,317 | 0.176 | −0.009 |
| Southwestern Oklahoma State University | 4,648 | −0.096 | −0.137 |
| State University of New York at New Paltz | 7,075 | −0.107 | −0.256 |
| Stephen F Austin State University | 12,000 | −0.134 | −0.065 |
| Tarleton State University | 13,995 | 0.237 | −0.005 |
| Tennessee Technological University | 9,840 | −0.153 | −0.059 |
| Texas A&M International University | 8,455 | 0.216 | −0.144 |
| Texas A&M University−Corpus Christi | 10,762 | 0.072 | 0.016 |
| Texas A&M University−Texarkana | 2,112 | 0.052 | −0.116 |
| Texas Southmost College | 7,527 | −0.689 | 0.048 |
| Texas State University | 37,864 | 0.159 | 0.036 |
| The College of New Jersey | 7,589 | 0.070 | −0.236 |
| The University of Tennessee–Chattanooga | 11,457 | 0.046 | −0.042 |
| The University of Tennessee–Martin | 6,712 | −0.209 | −0.148 |
| The University of Texas Permian Basin | 5,534 | 0.364 | 0.041 |
| The University of Texas Rio Grande Valley | 31,940 | 0.521 | −0.066 |
| The University of Texas at San Antonio | 34,734 | 0.128 | 0.122 |
| The University of Texas at Tyler | 9,687 | 0.364 | 0.094 |
| The University of West Florida | 13,288 | 0.153 | −0.002 |
| Towson University | 20,856 | −0.098 | −0.084 |
| Troy University | 14,901 | −0.694 | −0.168 |

**Table 1A.1** **(cont.)**

| Institution Name | Fall 2021 enrollment | Δln(enrollment) 2010–2022 | Projected Δln(enrollment) 2021–2033 |
|---|---|---|---|
| Truman State University | 4,225 | −0.421 | −0.240 |
| University of Alaska Anchorage | 10,845 | −0.551 | 0.012 |
| University of Baltimore | 3,710 | −0.682 | −0.315 |
| University of Central Arkansas | 10,105 | −0.144 | −0.032 |
| University of Central Missouri | 10,530 | 0.025 | −0.205 |
| University of Central Oklahoma | 13,250 | −0.334 | −0.006 |
| University of Colorado Colorado Springs | 12,031 | 0.160 | −0.022 |
| University of Houston−Clear Lake | 9,279 | 0.056 | 0.088 |
| University of Houston−Victoria | 4,189 | −0.009 | −0.091 |
| University of Illinois Springfield | 3,944 | −0.209 | −0.159 |
| University of Louisiana at Monroe | 8,718 | −0.047 | −0.081 |
| University of Maryland Eastern Shore | 2,384 | −0.589 | −0.225 |
| University of Maryland Global Campus | 55,323 | 0.344 | −0.381 |
| University of Massachusetts−Dartmouth | 7,717 | −0.235 | −0.288 |
| University of Michigan−Dearborn | 8,331 | −0.045 | −0.277 |
| University of Michigan−Flint | 6,418 | −0.307 | −0.326 |
| University of Minnesota−Duluth | 9,884 | −0.193 | −0.227 |
| University of Montevallo | 2,625 | −0.163 | 0.071 |
| University of Nebraska at Kearney | 6,275 | −0.111 | −0.094 |
| University of Nebraska at Omaha | 15,328 | 0.026 | −0.029 |
| University of North Alabama | 8,526 | 0.310 | −0.049 |
| University of North Carolina Wilmington | 18,030 | 0.311 | −0.132 |
| University of North Carolina at Charlotte | 30,448 | 0.165 | −0.083 |
| University of North Carolina at Pembroke | 8,318 | 0.099 | −0.234 |
| University of North Florida | 16,594 | 0.016 | 0.030 |
| University of Northern Iowa | 9,217 | −0.389 | −0.236 |
| University of Southern Indiana | 9,756 | −0.154 | −0.160 |
| University of Southern Maine | 7,996 | −0.241 | −0.272 |
| University of West Georgia | 12,687 | 0.053 | −0.067 |
| University of Wisconsin−Eau Claire | 10,569 | −0.122 | −0.257 |
| University of Wisconsin−La Crosse | 10,337 | 0.014 | −0.207 |
| University of Wisconsin−Oshkosh | 14,142 | 0.006 | −0.195 |
| University of Wisconsin−Platteville | 6,773 | −0.201 | −0.325 |
| University of Wisconsin−River Falls | 5,394 | −0.285 | −0.200 |
| University of Wisconsin−Stevens Point | 8,129 | −0.176 | −0.309 |
| University of Wisconsin−Stout | 7,695 | −0.255 | −0.302 |
| University of Wisconsin−Superior | 2,613 | −0.052 | −0.340 |
| University of Wisconsin−Whitewater | 11,446 | −0.042 | −0.217 |
| University of the District of Columbia | 3,476 | −0.434 | −0.546 |
| Valdosta State University | 11,557 | −0.234 | −0.171 |
| Virginia State University | 4,300 | −0.192 | −0.126 |
| Washburn University | 5,657 | −0.281 | −0.180 |
| West Chester University of Pennsylvania | 17,614 | 0.176 | −0.183 |
| West Texas A&M University | 9,602 | 0.165 | 0.082 |
| Western Carolina University | 11,877 | 0.213 | −0.229 |
| Western Connecticut State University | 4,802 | −0.399 | −0.251 |
| Western Illinois University | 7,455 | −0.499 | −0.241 |

*(continued)*

**Table 1A.1 (cont.)**

| Institution Name | Fall 2021 enrollment | Δln(enrollment) 2010–2022 | Projected Δln(enrollment) 2021–2033 |
|---|---|---|---|
| Western Kentucky University | 16,750 | −0.237 | −0.097 |
| Western New Mexico University | 3,013 | −0.037 | −0.328 |
| Western Oregon University | 4,029 | −0.507 | −0.174 |
| Western Washington University | 15,125 | −0.016 | −0.133 |
| Westfield State University | 5,013 | −0.224 | −0.344 |
| William Paterson University of New Jersey | 9,369 | −0.223 | −0.127 |
| Winona State University | 6,545 | −0.338 | −0.249 |
| Winthrop University | 5,174 | −0.241 | −0.117 |
| Worcester State University | 5,417 | −0.072 | −0.261 |
| Youngstown State University | 11,298 | −0.309 | −0.210 |

*PANEL D: Carnegie Master's II*

| Institution Name | Fall 2021 enrollment | Δln(enrollment) 2010–2022 | Projected Δln(enrollment) 2021–2033 |
|---|---|---|---|
| Bemidji State University | 4,279 | −0.286 | −0.286 |
| Eastern Oregon University | 2,825 | −0.436 | −0.285 |
| Ferris State University | 10,361 | −0.356 | −0.345 |
| Keene State College | 3,100 | −0.620 | −0.483 |
| Kentucky State University | 2,279 | −0.502 | −0.110 |
| Lake Superior State University | 1,812 | −0.475 | −0.349 |
| Lander University | 3,825 | 0.309 | −0.251 |
| Metropolitan State University | 6,914 | −0.213 | −0.229 |
| Mississippi University for Women | 2,477 | −0.101 | −0.335 |
| SUNY at Purchase College | 3,522 | −0.270 | −0.182 |
| Savannah State University | 3,385 | −0.326 | −0.183 |
| Southern University at New Orleans | 2,106 | −0.484 | −0.275 |
| Southern Utah University | 13,611 | 0.580 | −0.080 |
| Thomas Edison State University | 9,721 | −0.820 | −0.383 |
| University of Mary Washington | 3,956 | −0.326 | −0.313 |
| University of Wisconsin–Green Bay | 9,780 | 0.369 | −0.233 |
| University of Wisconsin–Parkside | 4,132 | −0.268 | −0.232 |
| Weber State University | 29,774 | 0.218 | −0.020 |

*PANEL E: Carnegie Baccalaureate Institutions*

| Institution Name | Fall 2021 enrollment | Δln(enrollment) 2010–2022 | Projected Δln(enrollment) 2021–2033 |
|---|---|---|---|
| Athens State University | 2,794 | −0.224 | −0.259 |
| Black Hills State University | 3,539 | −0.321 | −0.166 |
| Bluefield State College | 1,358 | −0.457 | −0.452 |
| California State University–Monterey Bay | 7,503 | 0.386 | −0.140 |
| Central State University | 6,044 | 0.865 | 0.039 |
| Charter Oak State College | 1,618 | −0.352 | −0.342 |

**Table 1A.1** (cont.)

| Institution Name | Fall 2021 enrollment | Δln(enrollment) 2010–2022 | Projected Δln(enrollment) 2021–2033 |
|---|---|---|---|
| Christopher Newport University | 4,584 | −0.075 | −0.176 |
| Clayton State University | 6,817 | −0.122 | −0.486 |
| Coastal Carolina University | 10,473 | 0.172 | −0.027 |
| Colorado Mesa University | 8,907 | 0.091 | −0.046 |
| Concord University | 1,749 | −0.479 | −0.293 |
| CUNY Medgar Evers College | 4,134 | −0.642 | −0.213 |
| CUNY New York City College of Technology | 14,277 | −0.161 | −0.271 |
| CUNY York College | 7,027 | −0.193 | −0.131 |
| Dickinson State University | 1,415 | −0.594 | −0.555 |
| Elizabeth City State University | 2,054 | −0.431 | −0.500 |
| Fairmont State University | 3,562 | −0.297 | −0.373 |
| Farmingdale State College | 9,348 | 0.306 | −0.017 |
| Fashion Institute of Technology | 8,150 | −0.246 | −0.149 |
| Fort Lewis College | 3,567 | −0.125 | −0.189 |
| Granite State College | 1,692 | −0.234 | −0.477 |
| Indiana University–East | 3,111 | −0.102 | −0.428 |
| Indiana University–Kokomo | 2,995 | −0.088 | −0.459 |
| Langston University | 1,960 | −0.384 | −0.170 |
| Lewis–Clark State College | 3,710 | −0.193 | −0.271 |
| Massachusetts College of Liberal Arts | 994 | −0.744 | −0.456 |
| Metropolitan State University of Denver | 17,678 | −0.343 | −0.279 |
| Mississippi Valley State University | 2,064 | −0.339 | −0.644 |
| Missouri Southern State University | 4,352 | −0.337 | −0.138 |
| Missouri Western State University | 4,395 | −0.415 | −0.301 |
| New College of Florida | 659 | −0.151 | −0.012 |
| Ohio State University–Lima Campus | 874 | −0.626 | −0.429 |
| Ohio State University–Mansfield Campus | 954 | −0.529 | −0.385 |
| Ohio State University–Marion Campus | 1,047 | −0.702 | −0.568 |
| Ohio State University–Newark Campus | 2,730 | −0.124 | −0.275 |
| Oklahoma Panhandle State University | 1,294 | −0.110 | −0.309 |
| Ramapo College of New Jersey | 5,732 | −0.092 | −0.031 |
| Shawnee State University | 3,216 | −0.328 | −0.215 |
| Shepherd University | 3,015 | −0.269 | −0.365 |
| Southwest Minnesota State University | 6,986 | 0.047 | −0.429 |
| St. Mary's College of Maryland | 1,544 | −0.283 | −0.193 |
| Stockton University | 9,352 | 0.142 | −0.043 |
| SUNY College at Old Westbury | 4,381 | −0.020 | −0.014 |
| SUNY College of Agriculture and Technology at Cobleskill | 1,820 | −0.364 | −0.398 |
| The Evergreen State College | 2,116 | −0.831 | −0.095 |
| University of Arkansas at Pine Bluff | 2,670 | −0.362 | −0.221 |
| University of Hawaii at Hilo | 3,243 | −0.315 | −0.244 |
| University of Hawaii–West Oahu | 3,008 | 0.683 | −0.069 |
| University of Houston–Downtown | 15,077 | 0.097 | 0.246 |
| University of Maine at Augusta | 4,422 | −0.240 | −0.536 |
| University of Minnesota–Crookston | 2,304 | −0.093 | −0.478 |

(*continued*)

**Table 1A.1 (cont.)**

| Institution Name | Fall 2021 enrollment | Δln(enrollment) 2010–2022 | Projected Δln(enrollment) 2021–2033 |
|---|---|---|---|
| University of New Hampshire at Manchester | 664 | −0.714 | −0.543 |
| University of North Carolina at Asheville | 3,233 | −0.308 | −0.149 |
| University of Science and Arts of Oklahoma | 849 | −0.237 | −0.188 |
| University of South Carolina Aiken | 3,869 | 0.166 | −0.226 |
| University of South Carolina–Upstate | 5,438 | −0.111 | −0.160 |
| University of Virginia's College at Wise | 1,814 | −0.155 | −0.237 |
| Utah Valley University | 41,262 | 0.277 | 0.058 |
| West Liberty University | 2,291 | −0.168 | −0.339 |
| West Virginia State University | 3,415 | 0.171 | −0.323 |
| West Virginia University at Parkersburg | 2,346 | −0.665 | −0.559 |
| Winston-Salem State University | 5,226 | −0.236 | −0.238 |

## References

Abraham, K., and M. Clark. 2006. "Financial Aid and Students' College Decisions: Evidence from the District of Columbia Tuition Assistance Grant Program." *Journal of Human Resources* 41: 578–610.

Altonji, J., L. Kahn, and J. Speer. 2016. "Cashier or Consultant? Entry Labor Market Conditions, Field of Study, and Career Success." *Journal of Labor Economics* 34: S361–S401.

Autor, D., A. Dube, and A. McGrew. 2023. "The Unexpected Compression: Competition at Work in the Labor Market." NBER Working Paper No. 31010. Cambridge, MA: National Bureau of Economic Research.

Ball, J., R. Grucza, M. Livingston, T. ter Bogt, C. Currie, and M. de Looze. 2023. "The Great Decline in Adolescent Risk Behaviours: Unitary Trend, Separate Trends, or Cascade?" *Social Science & Medicine* 317.

Barr, A., and S. Turner. 2015. "Out of Work and into School: Labor Market Policies and College Enrollment during the Great Recession." *Journal of Public Economics* 124: 63–73.

Becker, Gary S. 1964. *Human Capital: A Theoretical and Empirical Analysis with Special Reference to Education.* New York: National Bureau of Economic Research.

Bettinger, E., B. Long, P. Oreopoulos, and L. Sanbonmatsu. 2012. "The Role of Application Assistance and Information in College Decisions: Results from the H&R Block FAFSA Experiment." *Quarterly Journal of Economics* 127: 1205–1242.

Bound, J., and S. Turner. 2002. "Going to War and Going to College: Did World War II and the G.I. Bill Increase Educational Attainment for Returning Veterans?" *Journal of Labor Economics* 20: 784–815.

Campbell, C., and J. Horowitz. 2016. "Does College Influence Sociopolitical Attitudes?" *Sociology of Education* 89: 40–58.

Card, D. 1993. "Using Geographic Variation in College Proximity to Estimate the Return to Schooling." NBER Working Paper No. 4483. Cambridge, MA: National Bureau of Economic Research.

Cornwell, C., D. Mustard, and D. Sridhar. 2006. "The Enrollment Effects of Merit-Based Financial Aid: Evidence from Georgia's HOPE Scholarship." *Journal of Labor Economics* 24: 761–86.

Denning, J., E. Eide, K. Mumford, R. Patterson, and M. Warnick. 2022. "Why Have College Completion Rates Increased?" *American Economic Journal: Applied Economics* 14: 1–29.

Dynarski, S. 2000. "Hope for Whom? Financial Aid for the Middle Class and Its Impact on College Attendance." *National Tax Journal* 53: 629–61.

Dynarski, S. 2003. "Does Aid Matter? Measuring the Effect of Student Aid on College Attendance and Completion." *American Economic Review* 93: 279–88.

Dynarski, S., C. Libassi, K. Michelmore, and S. Owen. 2021. "Closing the Gap: The Effect of Reducing Complexity and Uncertainty in College Pricing on the Choices of Low-Income Students." *American Economic Review* 111: 1721–1756.

Edmunds, J., F. Unlu, E. Glennie, L. Bernstein, L. Fesler, J. Furey, and N. Arshavsky. 2017. "Smoothing the Transition to Postsecondary Education: The Impact of the Early College Model." *Journal of Research on Educational Effectiveness* 10: 297–325.

Goodman, J. 2008. "Who Merits Financial Aid? Massachusetts' Adams Scholarship." *Journal of Public Economics* 92: 2121–2131.

Gordon, G., and A. Hedlund. 2022. "Accounting for Tuition Increases Across U.S. Colleges." Unpublished manuscript.

Gunderson, M., and P. Oreopoulos. 2020. "Chapter 3—Returns to Education in Developed Countries." In *The Economics of Education: A Comprehensive Overview*, edited by S. Bradley and C. Green. Academic Press.

Hansen, W. L. 1983. "The Impact of Student Financial Aid on Access." In *The Crisis in Higher Education*, edited by J. Froomkin. New York: Academy of Political Science.

Harris, D., F. Chen, R. Martin, A. Bernhardt, C. Marsicano, and P. von Hippel. 2024. "The Effects of the COVID-19 Pandemic on Educational Attainment." *RSF: The Russell Sage Foundation Journal of the Social Sciences* 10: 152–80.

Hemelt, S., and D. Marcotte. 2011. "The Impact of Tuition Increases on Enrollment at Public Colleges and Universities." *Educational Evaluation and Policy Analysis* 33: 435–57.

Hillman, N., and E. Orians. 2013. "Community Colleges and Labor Market Conditions: How Does Enrollment Demand Change Relative to Local Unemployment Rates?" *Research in Higher Education* 54: 765–80.

Houston, D. 2024. "Polarization, Partisan Sorting, and the Politics of Education." *American Education Research Journal* preprint.

Hoxby, C. 2009. "The Changing Selectivity of American Colleges." *Journal of Economic Perspectives* 23: 95–118.

Hübner, M. 2012. "Do Tuition Fees Affect Enrollment Behavior? Evidence from a 'Natural Experiment' in Germany." *Economics of Education Review* 31: 949–60.

Hungerford, T., and G. Solon. 1987. "Sheepskin Effects in the Returns to Education." *Review of Economics and Statistics* 69: 175–77.

Jaeger, D., and M. Page. 1996. "Degrees Matter: New Evidence on Sheepskin Effects in the Returns to Education." *Review of Economics and Statistics* 78: 733–40.

Kane, T. 2007. "Evaluating the impact of the D.C. Tuition Assistance Grant program." *Journal of Human Resources* 42: 555–82.

Parodi, K., M. Holt, J. Green, M. Porche, B. Koenig, and Z. Xuan. 2022. "Time Trends and Disparities in Anxiety among Adolescents, 2012–2018." *Social Psychiatry and Psychiatric Epidemiology* 57: 127–37.
Seftor, N., and S. Turner. 2002. "Back to School: Federal Student Aid Policy and Adult College Enrollment." *Journal of Human Resources* 37: 336–52.
Vigdor, J. 2023. "Was It Demography All Along? Population Dynamics and Economic Inequality." Unpublished manuscript.

## **Comment** Francisca M. Antman

Much discussion has surrounded precipitous declines in college enrollments forecast to hit institutions of higher education in the coming years due to falling birth rates (Bauman 2024). Yet despite the considerable attention paid to this potentially transformative event, relatively few concrete estimates have been produced to predict how higher education may be transformed on a broad scale.[1] In this environment, college and university administrators will read Jacob L. Vigdor's "The Ebbing Tide: How Will Higher Education Adapt to Demographic Change?" with great interest as they weigh the potential impacts of the so-called "demographic cliff" on their campuses specifically (Boeckenstedt 2022).

Vigdor begins by considering possible explanations for the decline in college enrollments in recent years, finding notable support for the explanation grounded in the economic recovery from the Great Recession which can match both the timing of the national drop in enrollments and the magnitude of the decline. This makes sense from a basic labor economics perspective: As employment prospects in the broader labor market improve, opportunity costs of college attendance rise, and thus college-age individuals are more likely to opt out of college enrollment. Nevertheless, on the local level, Vigdor notes that state-level unemployment rates cannot explain the variation in the drop in enrollment across institutions over time.

Local demographics, however, seem to be closely linked with institutional enrollment changes, particularly for bachelor's-only and master's-granting regional institutions, which appear to be more vulnerable to demographic changes compared with larger R1 institutions which are expected to continue to grow. Thus, Vigdor's analysis predicts diverging enrollment trends for most R1 institutions and other colleges and universities into the future,

Francisca M. Antman is professor of economics at the University of Colorado Boulder
I thank Sheng Qu for excellent research assistance and participants at the 2024 NBER conference on Financing Higher Education for useful feedback. For acknowledgments, sources of research support, and disclosure of the author's material financial relationships, if any, please see https://www.nber.org/books-and-chapters/financing-institutions-higher-education/comment-ebbing-tide-how-will-higher-education-adapt-demographic-change-antman.

1. An important exception is Grawe (2018), which builds projected estimates at the regional level and by institution type but does not provide forecasts at the institutional level.

and he is able to report projected changes in enrollments for institutions in the sample which will be of great value to college administrators. Vigdor then discusses interventions which might help colleges and universities address enrollment declines. Admittedly, many of these interventions have been well-known throughout the most recent enrollment declines, and thus it is hard to see how these will serve as a significant means of altering the dynamics to avoid institutional closures for those institutions at greatest risk.[2] This in turn raises questions about the students who may lose access to a local college or university as a result and face increased barriers to college attendance as distance to school rises (Wozniak 2018).

While Vigdor's article is an important step in the right direction toward quantifying specific impacts on institutions and thus helping universities prepare for coming challenges, his analysis does not fully capture the seismic changes occurring in demographics and higher education in important ways that limit the utility of this exercise. In this short piece, I point out a couple of missing pieces that could be brought to bear on the important question of institutional survival to suggest ways in which future research could expand on Vigdor's approach to provide a more complete picture of demographic change in the United States, how it might impact colleges and universities, and thus how institutions might respond in more creative ways to adapt and continue to serve their critical missions.

First, demographic change has not been evenly distributed. Vigdor's analysis leverages geographical variation in population declines but ignores important changes in the US population by race and ethnicity which are also likely to affect college enrollments.[3] As many other studies have shown, rates of college attendance differ quite significantly across demographic and socioeconomic groups (e.g., see Grawe 2018, chapter 9). To the extent that racial and ethnic minorities are more likely to face greater barriers to college matriculation and completion (e.g., fewer financial resources), and may be less likely to have other forms of capital which can inhibit college enrollment (e.g., having parents who went to college), relying solely on changes in age-specific headcounts is likely to miss important impacts on institutional enrollment projections.

To illustrate the importance of incorporating race/ethnicity and gender into the demographic components of the model, figure 1C.1 describes the percentage of undergraduate enrollment at four-year postsecondary institutions by race and gender. In it, we see that the share of non-Hispanic White men and women (noted on the right axis) has been steadily declining for several decades whereas the share of Black men and women (noted on the left

2. The parallels with K-12 school closures, also driven by demographic change, are strong here (Grose 2023), and future research should consider their implications in tandem.

3. US Census predictions anticipate that the share of children who are non-Hispanic White will decline to about one-third by 2060, from more than one-half of children in 2016 (Vespa et al. 2020).

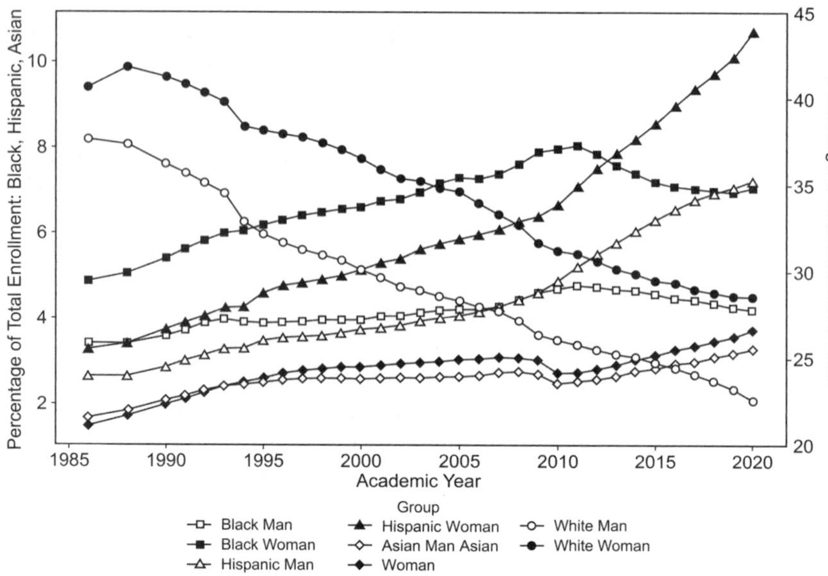


**Fig. 1C.1 Percentage of undergraduate enrollment at four-year postsecondary institutions by race and gender, 1986–2020**

Note: Data sourced from harmonized version of Integrated Postsecondary Education Data System (IPEDS 2024).

axis) began to decline relatively recently, after 2011, around the same point of declining enrollments which Vigdor emphasizes. In contrast, Hispanic men and women (noted on the left axis) have generally increased their share of college enrollments, and Hispanic women's share of college enrollment has risen especially dramatically since 2010. The enrollments of Asian men and women have also increased since 2010, though they constitute a much smaller share of overall college enrollments (noted on the left axis). Women have higher college enrollment in all race/ethnicity groupings, and gender gaps in college enrollment have generally risen over time as fewer men have enrolled in college, especially at four-year institutions (Fry 2023).

Incorporating changes in the population by race/ethnicity and gender into the model to develop a more nuanced measure of demand for college, such as the one built by Grawe (2018), which weights headcount estimates of students of various demographic profiles by the probability of college attendance for those students, would be a significant improvement to the analysis and thus would likely yield more useful forecasts. Moreover, it would give us a clearer understanding of the link between a broader definition of demographics and college enrollment. To the extent that there are important demographic differences in ability to pay for college, such estimates could also shed light on financial challenges likely to hit institutions which support

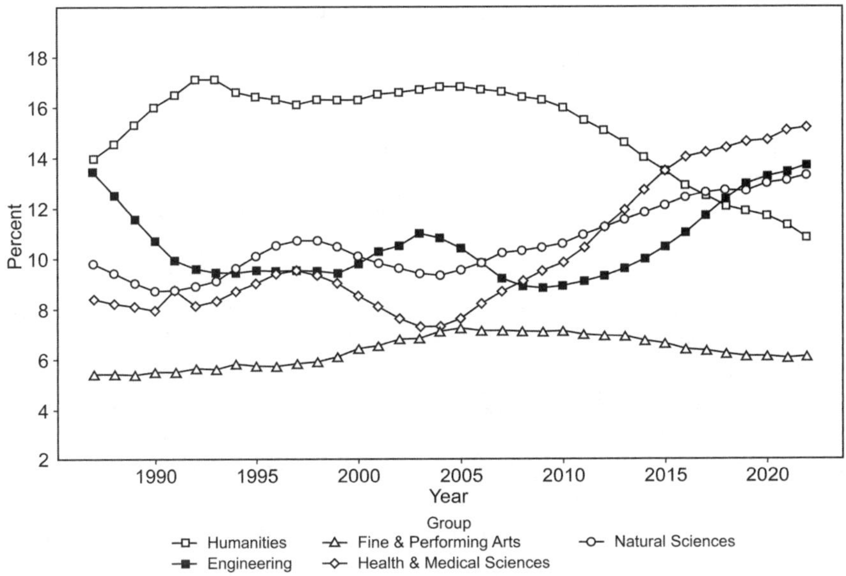


**Fig. 1C.2 Shares of all bachelor's degrees awarded in selected academic fields, 1987—2022**

Note: Data sourced from American Academy of Arts and Sciences (2024).

students who may be interested in enrolling in college, but who may lack the resources to pay for it.

The second profound shift in higher education which would benefit from incorporation into a model of projected enrollment changes is also a major topic of discussion in higher education, namely, the shift away from humanities majors and toward engineering and science degrees (Anderson 2023). To illustrate this shift, figure 1C.2 presents the shares of all bachelor's degrees awarded in selected academic fields. In it, we see that humanities degrees have declined steadily just as health and medical sciences degrees and natural science degrees have increased since around 2005. Engineering degrees began to steadily increase around 2010, around the same time as fine and performing arts degrees began to decline, which is also around the same time of the turning point in college enrollments which Vigdor emphasizes in his study.

Changes in demand for college majors may stem from the same sources which brought about the decline in national enrollments and may all be related to a greater focus on the labor market return to a college degree and specifically to the returns to college major. Some institutions may be better situated to transition into serving new STEM majors, which may require not only faculties with different skill sets but also costly infrastructure and investment, which not all institutions may be able to provide. Incorporating the capacity of institutions to offer the types of majors that are of greater interest to students into a model of enrollment changes will also help us understand which institutions will survive going forward. Moreover, greater focus on these issues will also shed light on how enrollment shifts across majors may predict difficult changes within institutions (e.g., program closures in low-demand disciplines) that may be masked by a relatively rosy picture of continued growth in overall enrollment at most R1 institutions.

In this short comment, I have highlighted only two critical factors that should be considered in a model aimed at understanding changes in college enrollment that will shape the future of higher education. More broadly, incorporating more nuanced measures of demand for institutions of higher education and their programs of study into a model of enrollment changes would be a useful extension of Vigdor's noteworthy contribution in "The Ebbing Tide: How Will Higher Education Adapt to Demographic Change?" A better understanding of the forces underlying changes in demand for higher education will help administrators and public officials adapt to changes on the horizon to ensure that colleges and universities are able to fulfill their missions and provide accessible higher education to all.

## References

American Academy of Arts and Sciences. 2024. "Humanities Indictors." Accessed on July 22, 2024. https://www.amacad.org/humanities-indicators/higher-education/bachelors-degrees-humanities#31600.

Anderson, Nick. 2023. "College Is Remade as Tech Majors Surge and Humanities Dwindle." *Washington Post*, May 20. Accessed on April 4, 2024. https://www.washingtonpost.com/education/2023/05/19/college-majors-computer-science-humanities/.

Bauman, Dan. 2024. "Colleges Were Already Bracing for an 'Enrollment Cliff.' Now There Might be a Second One." *Chronicle of Higher Education*, February 7. Accessed July 31, 2024. https://www.chronicle.com/article/colleges-were-already-bracing-for-an-enrollment-cliff-now-there-might-be-a-second-one.

Boeckenstedt, Jon. 2022. "Will Your College Survive the Demographic Cliff?" *Chronicle of Higher Education*, March 22. Accessed July 31, 2024. https://www.chronicle.com/article/will-your-college-survive-the-demographic-cliff.

Fry, Richard. 2023. "Fewer Young Men Are in College, Especially at 4-year Schools." *Pew Research Center*, December 18. Accessed on April 4, 2024. https://www.pewresearch.org/short-reads/2023/12/18/fewer-young-men-are-in-college-especially-at-4-year-schools/.

Grawe, Nathan D. 2018. *Demographics and the Demand for Higher Education*. Johns Hopkins University Press.

Integrated Postsecondary Education Data System (IPEDS). 2024. Education Data Portal (Version 0.21.0), Urban Institute. Accessed July 22, 2024. https://educationdata.urban.org/documentation/, made available under the ODC Attribution License.

Grose, Jessica. 2023. "Soon We Won't Have Enough Kids to Fill Our Schools. That's a Problem." *New York Times*, June 14. Accessed on July 31, 2024. https://www.nytimes.com/2023/06/14/opinion/declining-enrollment.html.

Vespa, Jonathan, Lauren Medina, and David M. Armstrong. 2020. "Demographic Turning Points for the United States: Population Projections for 2020 to 2060." US Census Bureau. Accessed on April 4, 2024. https://www.census.gov/content/dam/Census/library/publications/2020/demo/p25-1144.pdf.

Wozniak, Abigail. 2018. "Going Away to College? School Distance as a Barrier to Higher Education." *Econofact*, March 22. Accessed on July 31, 2024. https://econofact.org/going-away-to-college-school-distance-as-a-barrier-to-higher-education.

2

# How Much Can Families Afford to Pay for College?

Peter Hinrichs

## 2.1 Introduction

Research consistently finds that college is a worthwhile investment for many people and that a college degree leads to important benefits, both pecuniary and nonpecuniary (Barrow and Malamud 2015; Oreopoulos and Salvanes 2011; Oreopoulos and Petronijevic 2013; Smith et al. 2020; Zimmerman 2014). However, there are racial and socioeconomic gaps in college attendance and completion (Bailey and Dynarski 2011; Chetty et al. 2014; Reber and Smith 2023). There is also concern that many are unable to afford to attend college (Council of Economic Advisers 2023; Levine 2022; National Collegiate Attainment Network n.d.). If people are deterred from attending college because they cannot afford to do so, or because they perceive that they cannot afford to do so, this could result in unfulfilled potential and lost productivity. And if this unaffordability, whether real or imagined, is related to race, ethnicity, or family background, the result could be an increase in inequality.

This chapter studies families' capacity to pay for college in the United

Peter Hinrichs is a research fellow at the W. E. Upjohn Institute for Employment Research.

I thank Zachary Bleemer, John Campbell, Ben Jones, Phillip Levine, Bruce Sacerdote, and Christopher Taber; conference participants at the NBER Financing Higher Education conference, the 2024 University of Wisconsin Institute for Research on Poverty Summer Research Workshop, and the 2024 Association for Education Finance and Policy conference; and seminar participants at Northeastern University and the W.E. Upjohn Institute for Employment Research for helpful comments and discussions. For acknowledgments, sources of research support, and disclosure of the author's material financial relationships, if any, please see https://www.nber.org/books-and-chapters/financing-institutions-higher-education/how-much-can-families-afford-pay-college.

States, focusing on changes over time and differences by race and socioeconomic status. Although my focus is on the families that make up the demand side of higher education, this information is also relevant to the colleges and universities on the supply side. The relationship between race, socioeconomic status, and ability to pay sheds light on the challenges colleges face as they seek to diversify their student bodies, given the changing income distribution and racial composition of the US population. If we wish to draw more people into college, knowing how much they would be able to pay could help determine how much extra support they would need from the government, universities, and private sources. Perhaps on an even more basic level, if students are asked to pay more than they can afford, they may have to forgo educational opportunities that would have been valuable or else take part in these opportunities at the cost of creating financial hardship for themselves. Studying whether students are paying more than they can afford involves comparing how much students can afford to pay for college to how much they actually pay. The latter is somewhat more straightforward, whereas the former is more nebulous.

The empirical analysis in this chapter has two components. First, I use data from the National Postsecondary Student Aid Study (NPSAS) to document changes over time in the Expected Family Contribution (EFC) from the Free Application for Federal Student Aid (FAFSA), focusing on differences between racial and socioeconomic groups. The EFC is a basic measure of ability to pay that is calculated by the federal government and is used by many colleges. Although the EFC was replaced with the Student Aid Index (SAI) beginning in 2024–2025, many of the same principles carry over to this newer measure. The results suggest that the EFC has been rising over time, and that this has been driven primarily by families in the upper quartile of the income distribution.

Second, I use data from the Panel Study of Income Dynamics (PSID) to calculate alternative measures of the ability to pay for college. In particular, I make various assumptions about the percentage of a family's wealth that is available to pay for college, as well as whether home equity and retirement savings are included in available wealth. I find that it is possible to alter the distribution of who pays what amount by changing details of the EFC calculation, but the extent of this depends on details of the implementation.

The next section of this chapter discusses in more detail why a family's ability to pay for college might matter. After that, I review prior research related to paying for college. I then describe two important recent events related to college pricing: first, the redesigned FAFSA, and, second, the ongoing antitrust litigation involving financial aid at elite private universities. I then turn to the empirical work, beginning with a discussion of the data and continuing with results on the changes in the EFC over time and the simulations of alternative measures of the ability to pay. The final section offers a conclusion.

## 2.2 Why Might Ability to Pay Matter?

One might question whether family resources actually matter for college attendance decisions. After all, the United States has a large and robust financial aid system in which various levels of government, higher education institutions, and private organizations supply a variety of loans and grants to college students and their parents. Moreover, many colleges are committed to meeting a student's full financial need. So why would a family's available resources matter?

One reason a family's resources might matter is that a number of colleges actually do take the ability to pay into account in admissions decisions. Thus, a greater ability to pay may expand a potential college student's choice set and have a very direct effect on college access.

Second, even if a college does not take ability to pay into account in admissions decisions, it still might not offer financial aid packages that meet the full financial need of every admitted student. This could result in different financial aid packages and different prices for a student at different colleges, which could affect a student's choice of which college to attend.

Third, even colleges that meet full financial need may make different calculations of how much a student is able to pay and how much financial aid the student needs. For example, many colleges use the CSS Profile, a supplemental financial aid form that allows universities to ask customized questions about a family's finances. If two colleges are asking different questions and using different information about family resources, it is natural that they may arrive at different conclusions about how much a family will be able to pay and how much financial aid a student needs.[1]

Fourth, even if colleges were to meet each student's full financial need and calculate need in the exact same way, they might differ in the mix of loans versus grants. Receiving a financial aid package that is heavy on loans that need to be repaid is less desirable than receiving a package that is heavy on grants that do not need to be repaid.[2]

Fifth, even if a college would offer a very generous financial aid package to a student, the student might not necessarily be aware of this before applying. Financial aid offers are generally not given until a student has been admitted to a university, and so the perception that a college is too expensive may deter students from applying in the first place.[3]

1. In addition to variation across methodologies at a given point in time, the methodologies have also changed over time. Lumina Foundation and Institute for Higher Education Policy (n.d.) traces the history of need analysis formulas from the first such formula at Harvard University in the 1950s to the Pell Grant formula in the 1970s and the creation of the FAFSA in the 1990s.

2. The mix of loans vs. grants might affect educational and career choices as well. For example, Hampole (2024) finds that universal no-loans policies at colleges result in students selecting majors that are associated with low earnings earlier in their careers but high earnings later on.

3. The issue of college pricing transparency is discussed in detail in Levine (2022, chap. 4). Many of the other points in this section are made in Levine (2022, chap. 1).

In addition, even if a family is able to pay for college, that family may not necessarily be willing to do so. Some families may be averse to taking out loans, and students who come from families with fewer resources may be less willing to borrow, because their families might be less able to help them in the event that they run into difficulty repaying.[4]

All of these reasons suggest that family resources might affect whether a student attends college, and which college the student attends. These decisions are highly consequential, given both the earnings advantage associated with higher education, noted earlier, and the earnings differences across colleges (Chetty et al. 2023; Cohodes and Goodman 2014; Hoekstra 2009).

Moreover, even in cases for which a family's resources do not affect a student's college choice, college tuition can still strain the student's and family's finances before, during, and after the time the student is in college. Covering a large amount for college tuition may make it more difficult to finance major purchases such as a home or an automobile or to save for retirement.

Even apart from the impacts on students, the amount of money that families can afford to pay has direct implications for the finances of universities and governments. To the extent that students demonstrate greater need, colleges and governments may need to contribute a larger share. Knowing how much students can afford to pay can help colleges decide on their pricing strategies and assist with financial planning. That knowledge might also help governments formulate financial aid policies.

Colleges have an interest in enrolling more first-generation students and also in diversifying their student bodies along a variety of dimensions, including race and socioeconomic status, and they may be able to use financial aid policy to do so. And financial aid policy may become even more important following the Supreme Court's ruling limiting the use of race-based affirmative action in *Students for Fair Admissions, Inc. v. President and Fellows of Harvard College*. This ruling will make it more difficult for colleges to diversify their student bodies through admissions policies, so they may thus attempt to do so by offering greater financial aid across the board. Earlier research on affirmative action, which primarily studied statewide affirmative action bans, suggests that the challenge may be compounded by the new ruling. This research finds that affirmative action leads underrepresented minority students to "cascade down" from highly selective higher education institutions to somewhat less selective ones (Arcidiacono 2005; Bleemer 2022; Hinrichs 2012; Long 2004b). In light of this, the result of the Supreme Court affirmative action ruling might be a shift of underrepresented minority students from universities with greater resources and more

4. One caveat is that there are some cases in which loans are forgiven. Although the Supreme Court invalidated a large-scale loan forgiveness proposal in *Biden et al. v. Nebraska et al.*, smaller and more targeted loan forgiveness programs remain.

generous financial aid policies to those with fewer resources and less generous financial aid policies.

## 2.3 Prior Research

### 2.3.1 Direct Evidence on Families' Ability to Pay and How Families Finance Higher Education

A relatively small amount of research directly studies how much families can afford to pay for college, how paying for college affects households' balance sheets, and how families save for college. Levine (2022, chap. 5) acknowledges the difficulty of defining "affordability" but assumes that a student should be able to contribute their EFC, as well as an additional $5,500 from a student loan and $2,500 earned by working. Based on this definition, college is unaffordable for a high percentage of people, although private institutions with large endowments are actually more affordable than other institutions because of their more generous financial aid policies. Souleles (2000) uses data from the Consumer Expenditure Survey from 1980 through 1993 to study the relationship between expenditures to pay for college and other expenditures. He generally finds that other expenditures do not fall at the time that families are paying for college. This consumption smoothing suggests that households do a good job of planning in advance for college expenditures. Li et al. (2023) study saving for college using 529 savings plans. They find that many people invest suboptimally in the sense that they could earn higher returns by investing in a 529 savings plan from a different state.

### 2.3.2 Financial Aid and Student Debt

Compared to the dearth of research on families' capacity to pay for college, the body of research on college financial aid is voluminous. Dynarski et al. (2023) summarize research on the effects of college financial aid on enrollment, persistence, and other outcomes. A general finding is that financial aid programs can lead to better outcomes for students, but that the details of the particular financial aid program matter in accomplishing this. For example, to the extent that the application process is burdensome or that families are unaware of their eligibility, financial aid programs may be ineffective. Moreover, if a financial aid program incentivizes students to attend lower-quality institutions, then it might even have negative effects on students, as found by Cohodes and Goodman (2014).

A recent paper about the overall financial aid system by Levine and Ritter (2024) is highly relevant for the PSID simulations I conduct in this chapter. The authors note that the Expected Family Contribution calculation ignores home equity and retirement savings, assets that White people disproportionately hold relative to Black people and Hispanic people. As a result, the financial aid system creates an implicit subsidy that disproportionately benefits White people.

There is also a fair amount of research on student loan debt. Yannelis and Tracey (2022) summarize this work.[5] One general finding is that students who attend for-profit institutions have worse repayment outcomes on average. But, beyond that, many of the effects of student loan debt are ambiguous in theory and heterogeneous in practice. For example, debt overhang could make it difficult to obtain financing to buy a home. On the other hand, student loans can provide liquidity that can free up resources to, for example, make a down payment on a home.

### 2.3.3 Credit Constraints and the Relationship Between Family Resources and College Attendance

A general question related to college affordability is whether credit constraints hinder people from attending college. One set of research either directly estimates a structural model or uses the predictions of a theoretical model to formulate a test for credit constraints. An example of this work is Cameron and Taber (2004), which does not find evidence that credit constraints affect schooling decisions. Two additional papers add nuance to this finding: Brown et al. (2012) find that credit constraints are important for certain families in which parents underinvest in their children but not for other families. Caucutt and Lochner (2020) find that credit constraints at one particular point in time do not have much effect, but because of dynamic complementarities, relaxing credit constraints at multiple points in a person's life may have an impact.[6]

A second set of research on credit constraints uses natural experiments to study the impacts of income, wealth, and easier access to credit.[7] Sun and Yannelis (2016) exploit variation in bank deregulation across US states over time in order to estimate the effects of easier credit, finding that easier credit increases college enrollment. Manoli and Turner (2018) use a regression kink design with the Earned Income Tax Credit (EITC) formula and find that tax refunds lead to increases in college enrollment. Bastian and Michelmore (2018) find that greater exposure to the EITC as a teenager is associated with a higher chance of graduating from college. One paper that

5. Also see the collection of papers on the topic in Hershbein and Hollenbeck (2015).

6. Additional examples of research on credit constraints include Belley and Lochner (2007); Carneiro and Heckman (2002); Cowan (2016); Hanushek et al. (2014); Johnson (2013); Keane and Wolpin (2001); and Lochner and Monge-Naranjo (2011). Lochner and Monge-Naranjo (2012) provide a review.

7. Certain research does not fall into either category. For example, Stinebrickner and Stinebrickner (2008) survey students at Berea College in order to estimate which students are credit constrained. They find that credit-constrained students are more likely to drop out of college. Using the RAND American Life Panel, Ringo (2019) finds that children whose parents have low credit scores are less likely to attend and graduate from college.

finds somewhat different results is that of Bulman et al. (2021), who use data on lottery winners and find that young people are not deterred from attending college because of limited parental resources. Hilger (2016) finds that parental layoffs have only a small negative effect on whether the children of the affected parents enroll in college, whereas Pan and Ost (2014) find a much larger negative effect.

Additional evidence comes from research on the impacts of housing wealth on college enrollment. Lovenheim (2011) finds that higher parental home equity results in higher college enrollment for college-aged children, while Johnson (2020) finds that increases in parental wealth induced by housing price shocks result in a higher probability that children graduate from college. Lovenheim and Reynolds (2013) find that greater parental housing wealth increases the propensity of children to attend a public flagship university, decreases their propensity to attend a community college, and has little effect on their propensity to attend a four-year private institution, relative to a flagship public four-year institution. On the other hand, Hotz et al. (2018) do not find much impact of parental home equity on an index of college quality, although the results are somewhat imprecise. Lastly, a paper by Amromin et al. (2016) gives direct evidence on how families finance higher education. Their paper finds that falling home prices result in higher student loan debt and a lower reliance on home equity in paying for college.

### 2.3.4 Implicit Taxes on Income and Wealth

The financial aid system imposes implicit taxes on income and wealth. Although this is not a tax in the literal sense of being a mandatory contribution to the government, it functions similarly to a tax, in that higher income and wealth can reduce the amount of financial aid offered by colleges. Thus, in some sense, the financial aid dollars that families would have received if they had lower incomes and lower wealth are "taken away" by universities or the government. So, just as having a higher income can result in a higher tax bill, it can also result in a higher tuition bill.

The implicit financial aid tax potentially has an important effect on how much families can afford to pay for college. If people are saving more and earning more, then they should be able to pay more for college. On the other hand, if they are discouraged from saving or working due to the implicit financial aid tax, then they may not be able to pay as much. And even if this implicit financial aid tax affects the labor supply and savings decisions of only those families with relatively high levels of income and wealth, the amount that such families pay for college can have implications for how much financial aid is available for families with a lower ability to pay.

The general issues surrounding the implicit financial aid tax are laid out by Case and McPherson (1986) and Edlin (1993), although the authors of these two works emphasize different issues. Edlin (1993) stresses the high level of the tax. The implicit tax on incomes is levied on top of the usual federal and state taxes; the tax on wealth can apply for a number of years in a row, as long as a family has children in college receiving financial aid; and not only are assets, in essence, taxed, but the income received from them is taxed as well. All of these reasons suggest that the implicit taxes may create serious disincentives for savings and labor supply.

On the other hand, Case and McPherson (1986) argue that the disincentives might only be relevant for a relatively small group of families whose children attend expensive colleges. In other families, if the children even attend college at all, they may not receive any financial aid, or they may not receive the full amount of financial aid they need. In that case, an extra dollar of income could fully be used to pay tuition and might not crowd out financial aid. Also, the temporary nature of the financial aid tax means that the disincentive effects on labor supply are smaller than if the tax were permanent. In addition, parents may not understand the incentives to reduce labor supply and assets—in which case the disincentives may not have any effect.

Feldstein (1995) brings these ideas to the data, using the 1986 Survey of Consumer Finances. He finds that families facing higher implicit tax rates do indeed have a lower level of assets. Babiarz and Yilmazer (2009), Kim (1997), and Reyes (2008) find that the implicit financial aid tax leads families to shift assets toward retirement savings accounts, which are untaxed. Dick et al. (2003) run simulations using data from the 1986–1987 and 1995–1996 NPSAS. Their results indicate that the savings disincentives embedded in the financial aid system cause an inefficiency that is modest relative to the size of the overall economy but fairly large for particular families. Moreover, Long (2004a) argues that it is difficult for a family to forecast what its implicit financial aid tax rate will be.[8] He finds that the estimated effects on asset accumulation of this tax are sensitive to which assumptions are made, but that the estimated effects are small when making the assumptions that he considers to be the most plausible. Monks (2004) finds similar results. And although most studies focus on the parents of dependent students, Darolia (2017) focuses on independent students, who may face the same disincentives. However, he finds no evidence that such students reduce their earnings in response to their incentives.

Gebbia (2023) uses the full set of FAFSA applicants from California from 2010 through 2021, along with two quasi-experimental research designs, to study the effects of the financial aid tax rates on taxable income. One of the research designs is based on an unexpected change in the year of income

8. Dick and Edlin (1997) use data from the 1997 NPSAS to study how large the implicit tax rates actually are. Because colleges do not all meet every student's full financial need, an extra dollar of income may not reduce a financial aid offer by as much as it increases the EFC. Thus, implicit tax rates cannot be calculated directly from the EFC formula. Nonetheless, Dick and Edlin (1997) still find that, in practice, increases in income and assets lead to fairly sizable reductions in financial aid offers, implying a fairly high implicit tax rate.

used to calculate the EFC, and the other is based on variation across families in the number of children they have in college at the same time. Gebbia (2023) finds that middle-income families have an elasticity of taxable income of 0.10.

Finally, although most research focuses on the negative incentives of the means-tested financial aid system, Fan et al. (2021) focus on a potential benefit. In particular, the fact that families receive greater financial aid if they have lower incomes and wealth but lower financial aid if they have higher incomes and wealth means that the financial aid system provides a type of income and wealth insurance. Fan et al. (2021) simulate a model of this and find that the insurance value of financial aid is large.

## 2.4 Background Information

### 2.4.1 Changes to the Free Application for Federal Student Aid and the Expected Family Contribution

The Free Application for Federal Student Aid (FAFSA) is administered by the federal government and is the primary application form for student financial aid in the United States. Students and their families provide information on income, wealth, and family structure, and then a formula is used to give an indication of how much the families might be able to pay for college.

Some aspects of this formula changed beginning with the 2024–2025 school year as a result of the FAFSA Simplification Act. As a matter of terminology, the name of the output of the formula changed from "Expected Family Contribution" to "Student Aid Index."[9] A more substantive change is that families with multiple children in college at the same time will now be expected to contribute more than they did previously. In particular, the EFC formula had a step at the end of the section for the parents' contribution that divided by the number of children enrolled in college, but that step has been eliminated for the Student Aid Index calculation. Another change is that the EFC had a minimum value of $0, but the SAI can be as low as −$1,500. In principle, this change may allow colleges to make finer distinctions among students with a low ability to pay.

There have been challenges with the rollout of the new FAFSA that have led to financial aid offers being delayed, and it remains to be seen what the impacts of the new FAFSA and the new SAI calculation will be in the future after these challenges are resolved. In general, though, with the exception of the aforementioned changes, the overall structure of the EFC calculation has remained quite similar for many years. There are three branches:

9. Despite this change in terminology, I generally use the two terms interchangeably in this chapter.

one for dependent students, one for independent students with their own dependents, and one for independent students without dependents.[10] Each branch uses a formula in order to produce the EFC.

For dependent students, who are the focus of the empirical work in this chapter, there is a parent component of the calculation and a student component of the calculation. Students are expected to contribute 50 percent of their own income above an allowance level, as well as 20 percent of their assets. For the parents, loosely, 12 percent of their assets are added to their income above an allowance level to form a quantity called the "adjusted available income." The amount that parents are expected to contribute from this quantity is determined by a graduated tax with six different implicit tax rates that range from 22 percent to 47 percent.

For independent students without their own dependents, the structure is similar to the student part of the contribution for dependent students, except that a spouse's income and assets are included in the calculation and the allowances are calculated somewhat differently. For independent students with their own dependents, the structure is similar to the parents' part of the calculation for dependent students, except that a spouse's income and assets are included and only 7 percent of assets are added to income to form the adjusted available income.

A criticism of the FAFSA and EFC is that they exclude housing wealth and retirement savings from the calculation, which may in some cases give a distorted view of a family's true ability to pay. As noted earlier, some colleges supplement the FAFSA with the College Board's CSS Profile, which does ask about housing wealth, retirement savings, and other more detailed financial information.[11] However, the exact ways in which this information is used are not publicly available. On the other hand, the EFC formula from the FAFSA is publicly available, the EFC is directly included as a variable in the NPSAS data that I use, and I am able to estimate the EFC using income and wealth data in the PSID.

### 2.4.2 Litigation Surrounding Financial Aid

A recent lawsuit has the potential to substantially impact college pricing and financial aid, especially among highly selective private institutions. In 2022, a set of former students filed a lawsuit against 16 such institutions, alleging that the universities conspired to raise the price of college attendance by colluding on financial aid offers.[12] The institutions were members

10. There are a variety of criteria that make someone an independent student for financial aid purposes, including being at least 24 years of age by January 1 of the relevant school year, being married, being in the military, or having children to support.

11. A list of colleges using this form can be found at https://profile.collegeboard.org/ppi/participatingInstitutions.aspx.

12. The 16 universities are Brown University, California Institute of Technology, University of Chicago, Columbia University, Cornell University, Dartmouth College, Duke University, Emory University, Georgetown University, Massachusetts Institute of Technology, North-

of a now-dissolved group called the 568 Presidents Group, which met regularly to discuss and coordinate on financial aid policy.[13] According to the universities, they were cooperating to ensure that financial aid dollars were targeted to needy students rather than being used to compete for top students that did not have as much financial need. The universities argue that this cooperation was allowed under Section 568 of the Improving America's Schools Act of 1994, which carved out an antitrust exemption for universities to formulate shared general financial aid principles, as long as all the universities involved admitted students on a need-blind basis.

The plaintiffs in this case, which has been known by several names, including *Carbone et al. v. Brown University et al.* and *Henry et al. v. Brown University et al.*, argue that the universities do not all admit students on a need-blind basis and are thus ineligible for the antitrust exemption because, among other reasons, they consider ability to pay when admitting students from the wait-list, give admissions preferences to students from wealthy families that have made or may make large donations to the university, and practice "enrollment management" that integrates admissions and financial aid decisions.

Beginning with the University of Chicago, a number of the universities have agreed to settle the case. However, others remain as defendants. It is not yet clear what the ultimate outcome of this case will be. However, it could become more difficult for highly selective institutions to coordinate on financial aid, which could lead to more price competition but also potentially less financial aid for students with financial need.

## 2.5 Data

### 2.5.1 National Postsecondary Student Aid Study

The National Postsecondary Student Aid Study (NPSAS) is conducted by the National Center for Education Statistics in the US Department of Education. NPSAS uses a random sample of students that, when apply-

western University, University of Notre Dame, University of Pennsylvania, Rice University, Vanderbilt University, and Yale University. The lawsuit has since expanded to include Johns Hopkins University.

13. The 568 Presidents Group followed an earlier group called the Overlap Group, a group of selective institutions that cooperated more specifically on financial aid offers for individual students. In 1991, the US Department of Justice sued the eight Ivy League institutions and the Massachusetts Institute of Technology (MIT), which were all members of this group, alleging a conspiracy on financial aid policy. The Ivy League institutions agreed to settle the case, but MIT went to trial in 1992. MIT lost at the district court level, but in 1993 the circuit court reversed the decision and remanded the case back to the district court. MIT then settled the case. See Carlton et al. (1995) and Masten (1995) for more information about this case. Meanwhile, the Higher Education Act of 1992 permitted some amount of cooperation on financial aid, and this gave way to Section 568 of the Improving America's Schools Act of 1994, from which the 568 Presidents Group took its name.

ing appropriate weights, is intended to be representative of all US college students enrolled at institutions that participate in federal financial aid programs.[14] The NPSAS data include background information on the students in the sample, as well as highly detailed information on financial aid. The data come from a student survey, as well as from administrative sources. NPSAS also includes a survey of graduate students, but I use data only from the undergraduate survey. And although a restricted-use version of NPSAS is available to researchers, I analyze publicly available NPSAS data using PowerStats on the NCES DataLab (https://nces.ed.gov/datalab).

NPSAS began in 1987 and has generally been conducted every three or four years.[15] In particular, NPSAS has been conducted in 1987, 1990, 1993, 1996, 2000, 2004, 2008, 2012, 2016, and 2020.[16] I begin my NPSAS analysis with the 1996 wave because certain variables I rely on are unavailable in earlier waves. Also, there are differences in the calculation of financial need over time, but the methodology for calculating the EFC is fairly stable over the time period I study.

Even though I do not use the full range of NPSAS data, the time span and frequency still allow for meaningful comparisons over time. Additional features of the NPSAS include its large sample size and its EFC variable, which is taken directly from administrative records when possible. A disadvantage of NPSAS relative to the PSID is that the data on family income and sources of wealth are not as detailed in NPSAS. An additional caveat is that the NPSAS sample only contains data only for people who are already enrolled in college. If someone has been deterred from attending college because of the perception that college is unaffordable, this person would not be represented in the data.

In my analysis of the NPSAS data, I limit the sample to full-time full-year dependent students who are between the ages of 18 and 22 and are US citizens. Additionally, I limit the sample to students enrolled at four-year institutions in the 50 states and the District of Columbia. Some years of NPSAS involve a small number of students enrolled at institutions in Puerto Rico, but these students are dropped from my analysis. Finally, all analyses use weights provided in the data, and I convert dollar values to 2023 dollars using the Consumer Price Index Retroactive Series (R-CPI-U-RS).

Neither limiting the sample to US citizens nor excluding institutions in Puerto Rico changes the results very much at all. The other restrictions I make can change the results somewhat, but I impose these restrictions in order to focus attention on "traditional" college students. Although non-

14. NPSAS excludes the US service academies because those institutions have a special funding model.

15. NPSAS uses the second calendar year in a school year to refer to that school year. Thus, the 1987 NPSAS covers the 1986–1987 school year.

16. There is also a 2018 NPSAS that I do not use. This wave of NPSAS contains information from administrative sources only.

traditional students are certainly worthy of study as well, they may face a different set of issues in financing higher education.

### 2.5.2 Panel Study of Income Dynamics

The Panel Study of Income Dynamics (PSID) is a comprehensive survey that includes information on demographics, education, income, wealth, and more. The PSID began in 1968. Data were initially collected each year, but, beginning in 1997, data have only been collected every other year. The most recent data available as of this writing are from 2021. Unlike the NPSAS, which is a pooled cross section, the PSID is a panel that follows the same families over time. In particular, the PSID began in 1968 with a sample of 1,872 low-income families and 2,930 families that are nationally representative. It includes descendants of these families, as well as new members who joined the families through marriage.

The PSID is particularly well suited for the simulations I conduct in this chapter because, at least in recent years, it provides detailed financial information as well as information on college attendance. The PSID sample size can be small when limiting the sample to subgroups, but Black families are well represented in the PSID due to the initial sample design, which involved a large number of low-income families. Asian families and Hispanic families are also fairly well represented due to occasional refresher samples of immigrants to the United States.

The PSID contains both individual-level data and family-level data. Some of the PSID data I use come from the Transition into Adulthood Supplement (TAS), a supplement that has been conducted every other year beginning in 2005 and contains detailed information on young adults in the sample. I limit the PSID sample to persons aged 18 through 22 who are enrolled in college according to either the Transition into Adulthood Supplement (odd years from 2005 through 2019) or the individual-level section of the standard PSID (odd years from 2005 through 2021). I link individual-level data for students to data from the student's mother's family using the PSID parent identification file. The wealth and income data I use are for this same family, and the race data are based on the race of the head of this family. As with my analysis of NPSAS data, I report PSID results using the provided weights, and I convert dollar amounts to 2023 dollars using the Consumer Price Index Retroactive Series (R-CPI-U-RS).

## 2.6 Trends in the Expected Family Contribution

I begin the empirical work by using the NPSAS to show how the FAFSA EFC and related variables change over time and differ by demographic group. Studying the EFC gives a first pass at the question of how much we might expect families to be able to pay for college.

Figure 2.1 shows changes over time in the mean EFC, broken down by

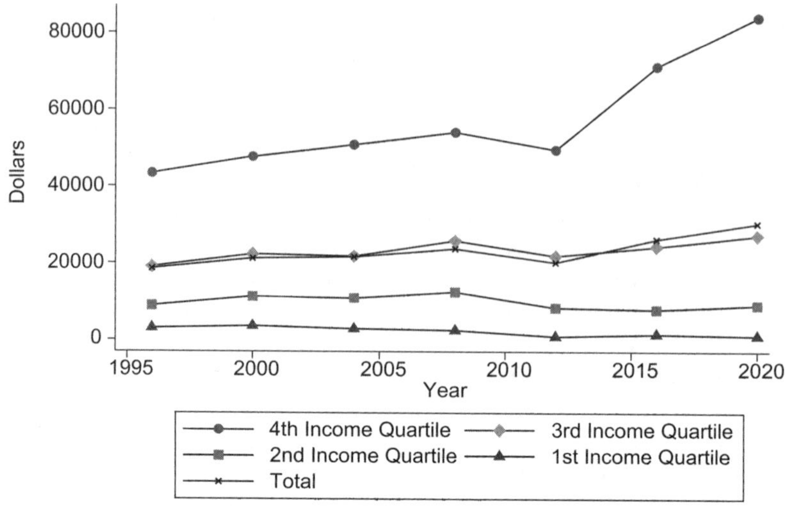


**Fig. 2.1 Mean Expected Family Contribution by family income quartile for each year**

Note: This figure shows the mean Expected Family Contribution (EFC) by family income quartile for each year using data from the National Postsecondary Student Aid Study (NPSAS). The sample consists of full-time full-year dependent students between the ages of 18 and 22 who are US citizens and are enrolled at four-year institutions in the 50 states and DC. The figure uses NPSAS weights and reports results in 2023 dollars using the Consumer Price Index Retroactive Series (R-CPI-U-RS).

family income quartile. After being fairly stable for a number of years, the average EFC rose substantially between 2012 and 2020. The figure shows that the increase was concentrated in the top income quartile.

Changes over time in the EFC can come about for two reasons: (1) changes in the inputs to the EFC formula, and (2) changes to the formula itself. The EFC formula, though, has been remarkably stable over time. For example, the implicit tax rates of 22 percent through 47 percent on parental adjusted available income have been the same for many years, although the income thresholds have changed gradually over time as incomes and prices have risen throughout the economy. However, families with incomes below a certain threshold automatically receive an EFC of 0, and this threshold has occasionally changed quite sharply from one year to the next. For example, there was a large increase in the cutoff from $20,000 in 2008–2009 to $30,000 in 2009–2010, making more families eligible for the automatic zero EFC. On the other hand, the threshold fell from $32,000 in 2012–2013 to $24,000 in 2013–2014, making fewer families eligible for the automatic zero EFC. Nevertheless, this change likely does not explain the increase in the average EFC between 2012 and 2020, since the increase seems to have been driven by families in the upper income quartile rather than families with incomes that would qualify them for a zero EFC.

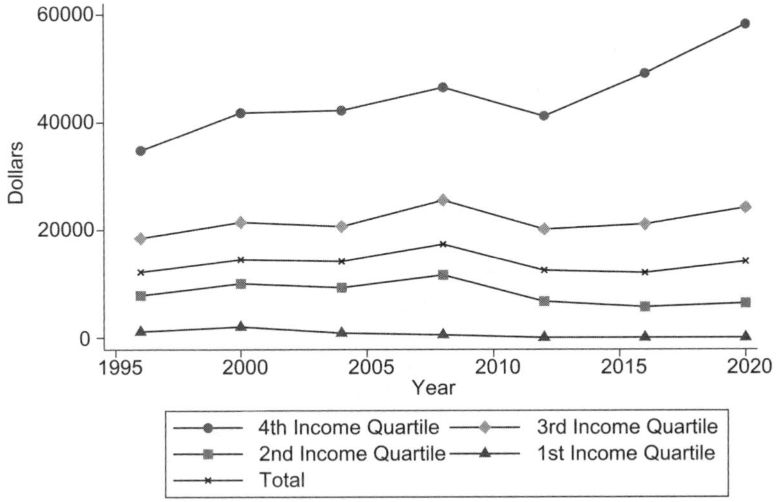


**Fig. 2.2 Median Expected Family Contribution by family income quartile for each year**

Note: This figure shows the median Expected Family Contribution (EFC) by family income quartile for each year using data from the National Postsecondary Student Aid Study (NPSAS). The sample consists of full-time full-year dependent students between the ages of 18 and 22 who are US citizens and are enrolled at four-year institutions in the 50 states and DC. The figure uses NPSAS weights and reports results in 2023 dollars using the Consumer Price Index Retroactive Series (R-CPI-U-RS).

There is another change to the EFC, though, that may explain the recent increase in the EFC for the top income quartile. As noted in the NPSAS documentation, "Beginning with the 2014–15 academic year, the FAFSA EFC field included six digits rather than five, increasing the maximum possible value of EFC from $99,999 to $999,999." This change in the EFC formula does not imply that the results in figure 2.1 show the EFC incorrectly, but they do call into question whether the large increase in the EFC from 2012 to 2020 represents an actual increase in the ability to pay. There could potentially be a small share of families with extremely high EFCs in 2016 and 2020 that pull the mean EFC up substantially in those years.

One way to gain some insight into the issue is by examining the median EFC. The median is robust to taking above-median values like $99,999 and making them even larger. Figure 2.2 shows changes in the median EFC over time by income quartile. When comparing figure 2.2 to figure 2.1, it is clear that the overall median EFC is lower than the overall mean, and that the median EFC for the top income quartile is lower than the mean in any given year. However, the median EFC for the top income quartile has risen substantially from 2012 to 2020, just as the mean has. This suggests that the large increase in the mean observed in figure 2.1 in recent years is not merely an artifact of the shift from a five-digit EFC to a six-digit EFC, but rather

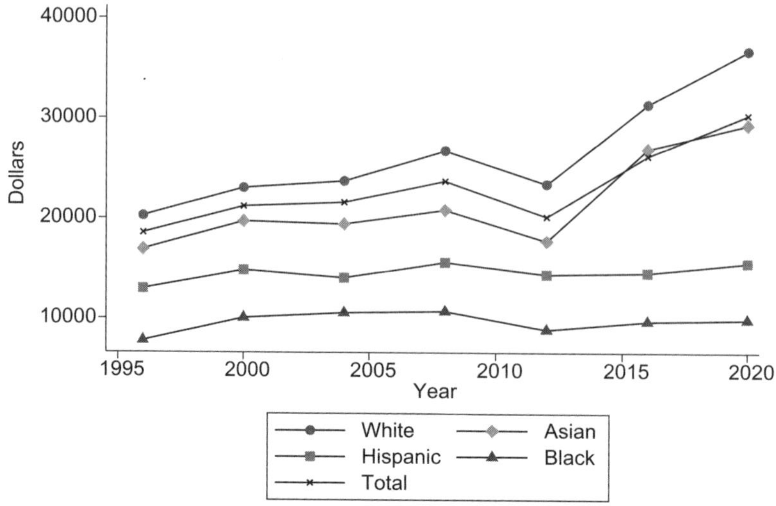


**Fig. 2.3 Mean Expected Family Contribution by racial or ethnic group for each year**
Note: This figure shows the mean Expected Family Contribution (EFC) by racial or ethnic group for each year using data from the National Postsecondary Student Aid Study (NPSAS). The sample consists of full-time full-year dependent students between the ages of 18 and 22 who are US citizens and are enrolled at four-year institutions in the 50 states and DC. The figure uses NPSAS weights and reports results in 2023 dollars using the Consumer Price Index Retroactive Series (R-CPI-U-RS).

is related to a change in the population distributions of income and wealth, which are the key inputs to the EFC formula.

Figure 2.3, which focuses on changes in the mean EFC by racial or ethnic group over time, shows results that are in line with those from figure 2.1. At a given point in time, the average EFC for White students is higher than that for Hispanic students, which in turn is higher than that for Black students. White students and Asian students were particularly affected by an increase in EFC between 2012 and 2020.

Figure 2.4 shows the distribution of EFC by race in 2020. This distribution is interesting in that it has a substantial mass at 0 but also an extremely long right tail. The bar graph representation in figure 2.4 obscures the right tail somewhat, but it does show that 36.3 percent of Black students had an EFC of zero, compared to 8.6 percent of White students. On the other hand, 12.7 percent of White students had an EFC larger than $70,000, while only 2.3 percent of Black students had an EFC of that level.

Figure 2.5 shows changes in the mean EFC over time by parental education level. The results mirror those of figures 2.1 and 2.3. At a given point in time, students with more educated parents have higher EFCs on average. For first-generation college students, or those for whom neither parent completed college, the EFC has been relatively stable over time and has even fallen by a small amount in recent years. For students who have a parent that

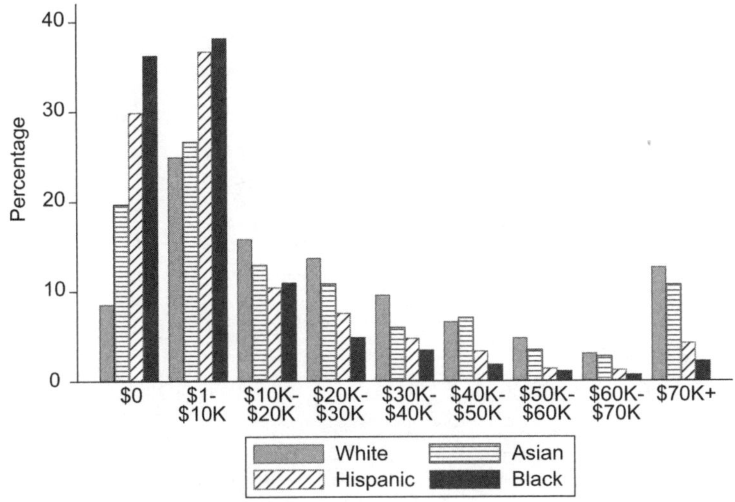


**Fig. 2.4 Distribution of Expected Family Contribution by racial or ethnic group in 2020**

Note: This figure shows the distribution of Expected Family Contribution (EFC) by racial or ethnic group in 2020 using data from the National Postsecondary Student Aid Study (NPSAS). The sample consists of full-time full-year dependent students between the ages of 18 and 22 who are US citizens and are enrolled at four-year institutions in the 50 states and DC. The figure uses NPSAS weights and reports results in 2023 dollars using the Consumer Price Index Retroactive Series (R-CPI-U-RS).

completed a bachelor's degree or an advanced degree, the average EFC rose substantially between 2012 and 2020.

In studying whether college is affordable, the amount that families can afford to pay is a key part of the equation. The other part of the equation is the amount that it actually costs to attend college. Figure 2.6 uses NPSAS data to show the overall mean cost of attendance, or the "budget," by racial group. The cost of attendance includes tuition and fees, housing, food, transportation, and other necessary expenses. The figure shows that the cost of attendance has been rising for all groups, even after adjusting for overall inflation. Although not shown here, the figures by family income and parental education reveal similar patterns.

A limitation of using the cost of attendance as a measure of how much a student would have to pay in order to attend college is that, as Levine (2024) notes, relatively few students pay the full sticker price for tuition. Thus, the cost of attendance is not in itself a clear measure of how much a student would need to pay in order to attend college. Moreover, the cost of attendance is based on the college a student actually attends, and a student may be able to attend college at a lower cost by enrolling in a less expensive college. In addition, the cost of attendance is generally not the true cost to a college of providing a student with an education either, since students at many universities are subsidized by university endowments in a way that

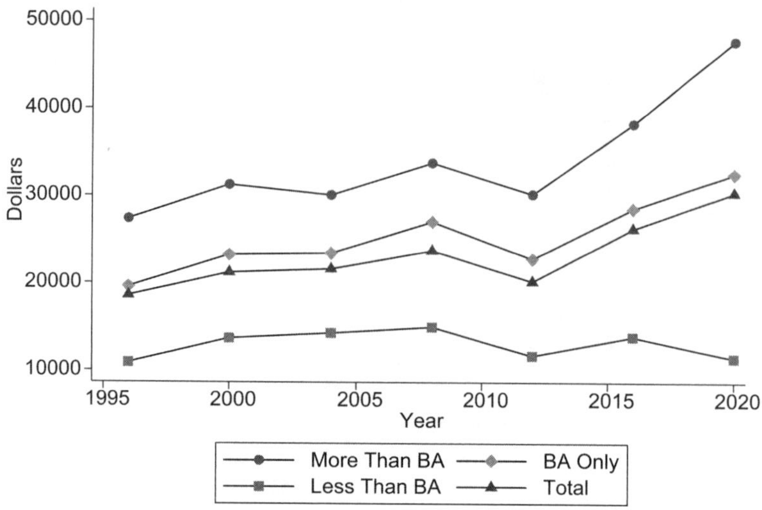


**Fig. 2.5 Mean Expected Family Contribution by parental education level for each year**

Note: This figure shows the mean Expected Family Contribution (EFC) by parental education level for each year using data from the National Postsecondary Student Aid Study (NPSAS). The sample consists of full-time full-year dependent students between the ages of 18 and 22 who are US citizens and are enrolled at four-year institutions in the 50 states and DC. The figure uses NPSAS weights and reports results in 2023 dollars using the Consumer Price Index Retroactive Series (R-CPI-U-RS).

never shows up in tuition (Hoxby 2009). However, the cost of attendance is still potentially somewhat useful because it represents the maximum amount a family would have to pay to attend a given college.[17]

I next turn to financial need. Mathematically,

$$Need = \max\{COA - EFC, 0\},$$

in which COA is the cost of attendance and EFC is the Expected Family Contribution. In other words, need is generally the difference between the cost of attendance and the Expected Family Contribution, although students with an Expected Family Contribution greater than the cost of attendance have no financial need.

Figure 2.7 shows that financial need has been rising over time for each income quartile. Figure 2.8, which focuses on race and ethnicity, shows similar results. Interestingly, Asian students have higher need on average

17. As a hypothetical example to consider why the cost of attendance may or may not be a useful concept, suppose a college increased its tuition but gave students offsetting grants. In this case, the cost of attendance can increase without any meaningful change in how much students are paying or how much colleges are receiving. However, if the college does not give additional grant aid to each student in the amount of the tuition increase, then this increase in tuition would represent a meaningful change for at least some students. In particular, the students would need to either pay more from their own resources, take out loans, or receive more grant aid from elsewhere.

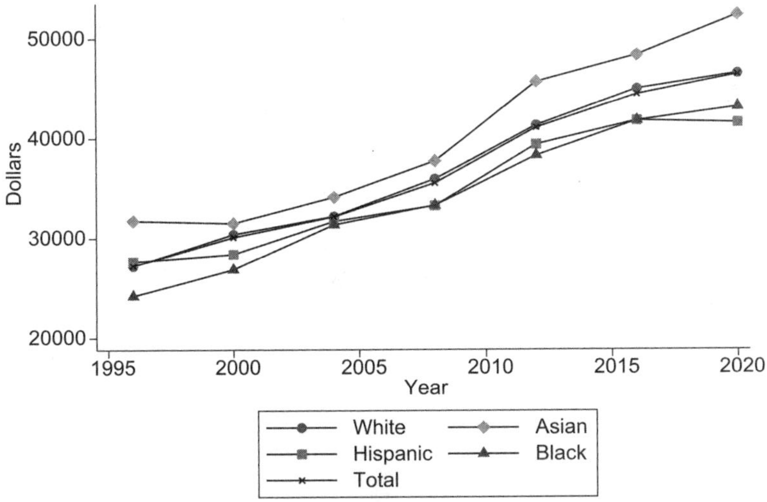


**Fig. 2.6 Mean cost of attendance by racial or ethnic group for each year**

Note: This figure shows the mean cost of attendance by racial or ethnic group for each year using data from the National Postsecondary Student Aid Study (NPSAS). The sample consists of full-time full-year dependent students between the ages of 18 and 22 who are US citizens and are enrolled at four-year institutions in the 50 states and DC. The figure uses NPSAS weights and reports results in 2023 dollars using the Consumer Price Index Retroactive Series (R-CPI-U-RS).

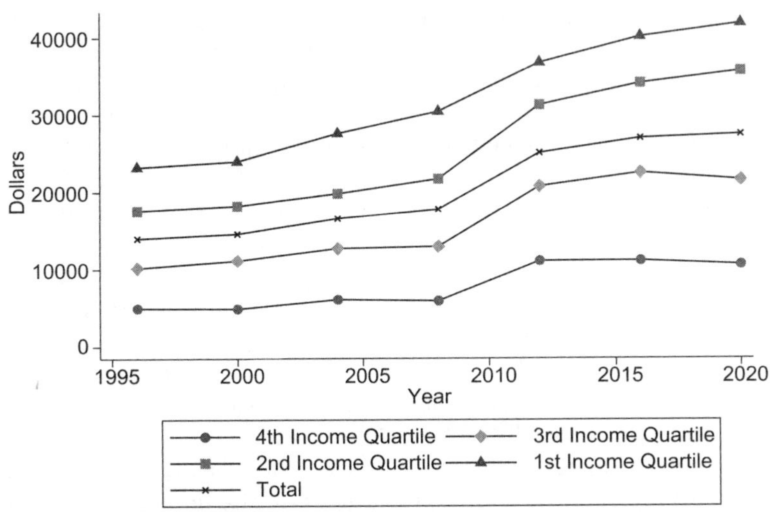


**Fig. 2.7 Mean financial need by family income quartile for each year**

Note: This figure shows the mean financial need by family income quartile for each year using data from the National Postsecondary Student Aid Study (NPSAS). The sample consists of full-time full-year dependent students between the ages of 18 and 22 who are US citizens and are enrolled at four-year institutions in the 50 states and DC. The figure uses NPSAS weights and reports results in 2023 dollars using the Consumer Price Index Retroactive Series (R-CPI-U-RS).

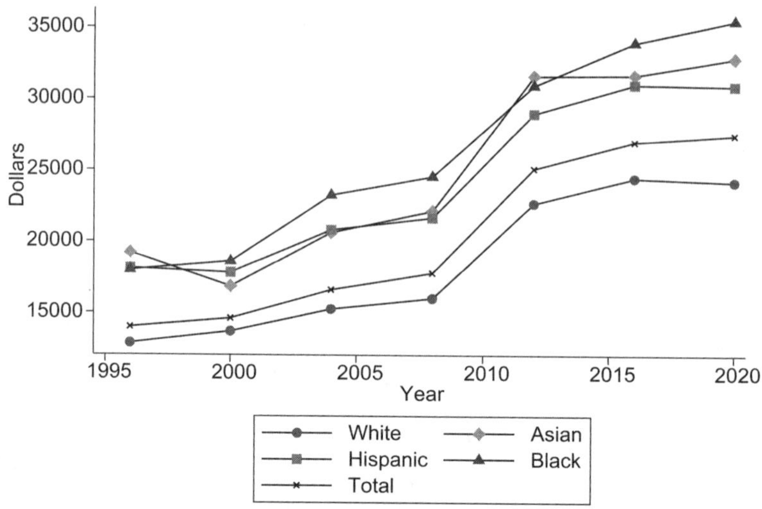


**Fig. 2.8 Mean financial need by racial or ethnic group for each year**

Note: This figure shows the mean financial need by racial or ethnic group for each year using data from the National Postsecondary Student Aid Study (NPSAS). The sample consists of full-time full-year dependent students between the ages of 18 and 22 who are US citizens and are enrolled at four-year institutions in the 50 states and DC. The figure uses NPSAS weights and reports results in 2023 dollars using the Consumer Price Index Retroactive Series (R-CPI-U-RS).

than Hispanic students in most years even though figure 2.3 also shows that they have higher EFCs. The explanation for this can be found in figure 2.6, which shows that Asian students attend more expensive colleges on average. And compared to White students, Asian students have lower EFCs but also attend more expensive colleges, resulting in the fairly large gap in financial need between White students and Asian students shown in figure 2.8.

Figure 2.9 shows the distribution of financial need by racial or ethnic group. A fairly large share of White students has no financial need, while the share of Black students with no financial need is much lower. A fairly large share of students in each racial or ethnic group has more than $50,000 of need. Lastly, figure 2.10 shows the mean financial need by parental education level and suggests that financial need has risen over time for each group, but has leveled off in recent years for families with parents who have more education.

Students do not generally pay the full cost of attendance. Rather, many students receive financial aid. The net price is a measure of how much a student must pay to attend college after accounting for financial aid.[18] Mathematically, we have

18. Although the net price as written includes the cost of attendance, this measure is arguably a decent measure of how much students actually pay to attend college. To continue the hypothetical example from footnote 17: if a college increased tuition but gave grants to each student that completely offset the tuition increase, then the cost of attendance may rise but the net price would be unchanged. This is a desirable feature of the net price.

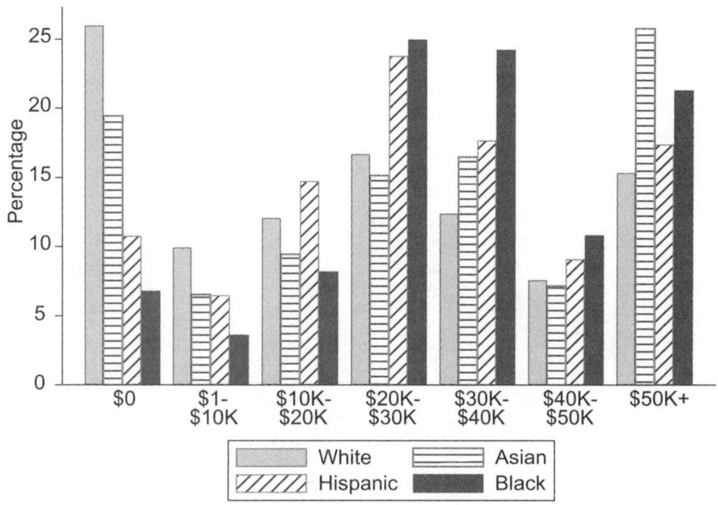


**Fig. 2.9 Distribution of financial need by racial or ethnic group in 2020**

Note: This figure shows the distribution of financial need by racial or ethnic group in 2020 using data from the National Postsecondary Student Aid Study (NPSAS). The sample consists of full-time full-year dependent students between the ages of 18 and 22 who are US citizens and are enrolled at four-year institutions in the 50 states and DC. The figure uses NPSAS weights and reports results in 2023 dollars using the Consumer Price Index Retroactive Series (R-CPI-U-RS).

$$NetPrice = COA - \text{Aid}.$$

Moreover, family incomes have risen over time. Comparing changes in the net price to changes in family incomes gives a sense of whether college has become more or less affordable over time. Looking at changes over time in the percentage of income people are paying for college is particularly useful, because the precise meaning of whether a college is "affordable" or "unaffordable" in the absolute sense is subjective, but the meaning of relative affordability arguably is clearer.[19]

Figure 2.11 shows how the net price as a percentage of income has evolved over time. The results suggest that the net price paid after grants as a percentage of income has risen in recent years, especially for students from families with lower incomes. Thus, college has become somewhat more expensive in a relative sense, although perhaps not as much as one might think by

19. For example, suppose someone is able to attend college only by exhausting nearly all of their income and existing wealth and also taking out a sizable loan. That person may be able to afford college in the sense that it technically satisfies their budget constraint, but in the colloquial sense most people would probably consider college to be unaffordable under those circumstances. However, if attending college used to require paying 30 percent of income but now requires 40 percent, then college has become less affordable in a relative sense. And additional evidence suggesting that the exact ability to pay is difficult to define comes from the fact that different methodologies (e.g., the FAFSA Expected Family Contribution and the results from the CSS Profile) can come up with different estimates, as well as the fact that a given methodology can change over time (e.g., the elimination of the sibling discount with the FAFSA).

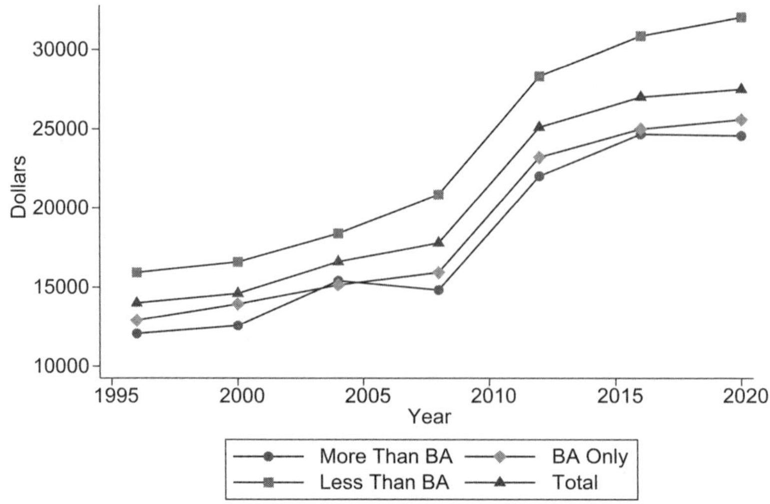


**Fig. 2.10 Mean financial need by parental education level for each year**

Note: This figure shows the mean financial need by parental education level for each year using data from the National Postsecondary Student Aid Study (NPSAS). The sample consists of full-time full-year dependent students between the ages of 18 and 22 who are US citizens and are enrolled at four-year institutions in the 50 states and DC. The figure uses NPSAS weights and reports results in 2023 dollars using the Consumer Price Index Retroactive Series (R-CPI-U-RS).

looking at the increases in the cost of attendance shown in figure 2.6. An important caveat, though, is that changes over time in figure 2.11 can be a result of composition effects. For example, if more people from families with extremely low incomes are attending college over time, then the average college student from the lowest income quartile in 2020 may be poorer than the average college student from the lowest income quartile earlier in the sample period.

## 2.7 Alternative Measures of the Ability to Pay

Thus far, I have given estimates of families' ability to pay under the existing EFC formula. But what would happen if that formula were changed? The existing formula makes particular assumptions about how much families should be able to pay for college out of their income and wealth, as well as which forms of wealth are "fair game" and which are not. But in principle, we could imagine Congress making different choices about the EFC formula, or even colleges making different financial aid choices from what they currently do.

This section uses data from the PSID to study the effects of several potential changes to the EFC formula, including changing the percentage of wealth that is considered available and treating home equity and retirement

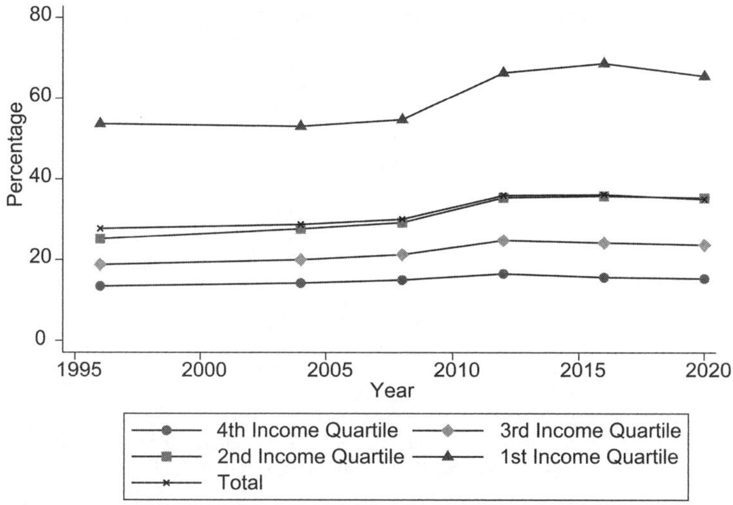


**Fig. 2.11 Mean net price after grants as a percentage of income by family income quartile for each year**

Note: This figure shows the mean net price after grants as a percentage of income by family income quartile for each year using data from the National Postsecondary Student Aid Study (NPSAS). The sample consists of full-time full-year dependent students between the ages of 18 and 22 who are US citizens and are enrolled at four-year institutions in the 50 states and DC. The figure uses NPSAS weights and reports results in 2023 dollars using the Consumer Price Index Retroactive Series (R-CPI-U-RS).

savings as available wealth. Changing the formula may have implications for the amount of tuition revenue colleges receive from their students, as well as distributional consequences in terms of how much different types of students pay for college.

To begin, table 2.1 shows summary statistics for the sample. The table shows that there is both income inequality and wealth inequality. White families and Asian families have, on average, higher incomes and higher wealth than Black families and Hispanic families. They also have more of each of the three types of wealth shown in the table: (1) home equity, (2) retirement savings, and (3) all other wealth. However, the extent of the inequality depends on which measure we look at. The bottom of the table shows that White families have a substantially higher share of their wealth invested in retirement accounts than any other group, while White families in the sample have the same share of their wealth in home equity as Black families do and a lower share than Hispanic families do. The average White family has a wealth-to-income ratio of 4.45, while the average Black family has a ratio of 1.48.[20] These differences suggest that the relative implicit tax

20. The fact that the wealth gap is larger than the income gap has been documented by others, including Aliprantis et al. (2023) and Barsky et al. (2002).

**Table 2.1** **Sample means from the Panel Study of Income Dynamics**

| Variable | White | Black | Hispanic | Asian |
|---|---|---|---|---|
| Income | 199,295 | 89,472 | 95,033 | 176,025 |
| Wealth | 689,341 | 123,454 | 179,078 | 576,377 |
| Home Equity | 239,541 | 54,379 | 111,944 | 258,792 |
| Retirement Savings | 120,808 | 13,507 | 21,615 | 110,641 |
| All Other Wealth | 328,993 | 55,568 | 45,518 | 206,944 |
| Ratios | | | | |
| Home Equity to Wealth | 0.51 | 0.51 | 0.63 | 0.39 |
| Retirement Savings to Wealth | 0.13 | 0.04 | 0.04 | 0.07 |
| Wealth to Income | 4.45 | 1.48 | 1.72 | 3.46 |

Note: This table shows the means of variables by racial or ethnic group for odd years from 2005 through 2021 in the Panel Study of Income Dynamics. The sample consists of college students between the ages of 18 and 22. The bottom three rows of the table show means of ratios, rather than ratios of means. The table uses PSID weights and reports results in 2023 dollars using the Consumer Price Index Retroactive Series (R-CPI-U-RS).

rates on income and wealth, as well as which types of wealth are taxed and which are not, may have distributional consequences.

Table 2.2 shows the results of my EFC simulations. The table shows overall results, as well as results broken down by racial or ethnic group. The top row of Panel A shows results from the 2020 NPSAS that come primarily from administrative records and were previously shown in figure 2.1. This top row provides a basis to help gauge whether the simulation in the second row is reasonable.

The second row of Panel A shows the mean EFC by racial or ethnic group from my simulation. The simulation uses the six tax rates and the adjusted available income cutoffs for those tax rates in effect for 2020–2021, and it incorporates an automatic zero EFC for people with an income below \$26,000. I assume allowances against income based on a 20 percent federal income tax, 4 percent state income tax, 8 percent Social Security tax, and \$28,000 income protection allowance. I also assume that the average college student has 0.5 siblings currently enrolled in college, an assumption that seems reasonable based on results from NPSAS.[21]

Apart from the fact that I use a simple approximation to a more complicated formula, there are other reasons for which there might be a disparity between the top two rows of the table, though, including sampling variability, measurement error, and differences in the definition of the income and wealth variables between the PSID and the FAFSA. But even with this in

21. Although this captures the general tenor of the EFC calculation, there are certainly limitations. For example, while on the one hand I assume that everyone is a dependent student, on the other hand I ignore the student part of the EFC calculation. Also, while the parameter values I assume may be reasonable in general, it would be possible to obtain better approximations by using additional data.

**Table 2.2** **Results of Expected Family Contribution simulations**

| Simulation | White | Black | Hispanic | Asian | Overall |
|---|---|---|---|---|---|
| *A. Target and Simulation Results* | | | | | |
| 2020 EFC from NPSAS | 36,777 | 9,907 | 15,587 | 29,398 | 30,377 |
| Simulated from PSID | 39,706 | 9,559 | 9,393 | 31,759 | 30,061 |
| *B. Counterfactual Policies—Not Revenue Neutral* | | | | | |
| Consider 16% of Wealth Available | 43,795 | 10,224 | 9,925 | 34,320 | 32,986 |
| Consider 8% of Wealth Available | 35,622 | 8,900 | 8,864 | 29,199 | 27,141 |
| Include Home Equity | 46,314 | 10,884 | 12,564 | 39,463 | 35,457 |
| Include Retirement Savings | 42,520 | 9,858 | 10,079 | 34,271 | 32,178 |
| Include Home Equity and Retirement Savings | 53,000 | 11,684 | 13,649 | 44,324 | 40,303 |
| *C. Counterfactual Policies—Revenue Neutral* | | | | | |
| Consider 16% of Wealth Available | 39,970 | 9,201 | 8,907 | 31,317 | 30,061 |
| Consider 8% of Wealth Available | 39,393 | 9,986 | 9,968 | 32,280 | 30,061 |
| Include Home Equity | 39,373 | 9,015 | 10,390 | 33,552 | 30,061 |
| Include Retirement Savings | 39,764 | 9,124 | 9,318 | 32,052 | 30,061 |
| Include Home Equity and Retirement Savings | 39,723 | 8,332 | 9,716 | 33,211 | 30,061 |

Note: This table shows simulated values of the mean Expected Family Contribution (EFC) by racial or ethnic group under various hypothetical changes to the EFC formula. The first row of Panel A shows results from figure 2.3 giving mean values of the EFC by racial or ethnic group from the National Postsecondary Student Aid Study (NPSAS) in 2020. The second row of Panel A uses data from the Panel Study of Income Dynamics (PSID) from 2005 through 2021 to simulate the EFC. See the text for details of the simulation. Panel B uses the PSID data to conduct five counterfactual simulations that change various features of the EFC formula. Panel C is identical to Panel B except that each simulation involves an offsetting change that shifts up or down the six EFC implicit tax rates by the same amount in order to maintain the overall average EFC shown in the second row of Panel A.

mind, comparing the two rows in Panel A suggests that the approximation is quite reasonable. I overestimate EFCs somewhat for White students and Asian students, underestimate them substantially for Hispanic students, and am quite close for Black students and overall. This is consistent with the results of Dynarski and Scott-Clayton (2006), who find that it is possible to predict EFCs quite well using just a small number of variables.

Panel B considers potential changes to the formula. The first two involve changes to the percentage of wealth that is considered available. Students sometimes attend colleges that do not meet their full financial "need" (i.e., the difference between the total cost of attending the college and the Expected Family Contribution), which suggests that at least some people can actually afford to pay more than the EFC.

The first counterfactual simulation shows what would happen if we considered 16 percent of wealth to be available rather than 12 percent. Note that this does not mean that families are expected to pay 16 percent of their wealth, but rather that 16 percent of their wealth is added to their income and then run through the nonlinear implicit tax schedule. The result of doing this is an increase in the EFC and potentially more revenue for colleges, with the average EFC rising from $30,061 to $32,986. Each racial or ethnic group shown on the table also pays more on average, but in the levels they pay the increase is larger for White families and Asian families.

The next row shows what would happen if we considered only 8 percent of wealth to be available. In this case, there is a drop in the EFC and potentially less revenue for colleges, with the average EFC falling to $27,141. Each group pays less, but in the levels paid, the decrease is larger for White families and Asian families.

The other three counterfactual simulations in Panel B involve including forms of wealth that are not currently taken into account. The first of these involves home equity, the second involves retirement savings, and the third involves both home equity and retirement savings. Each of these simulations increases the mean EFC for each group, although the extent of the increase depends on the simulation and the group. In the levels paid, the increases are larger for White families and Asian families. And if there were a choice between including home equity and including retirement savings, including home equity would lead to a larger increase in EFCs.

Panel C is identical to Panel B except that it considers "revenue neutral" changes, which change one aspect of the formula but also make an offsetting change to keep the average EFC the same as it was in the baseline simulation. The offsetting change involves shifting all six tax EFC implicit rates down additively by the same level, in a way that maintains the same overall mean EFC shown in the baseline simulation in the second row of Panel A.[22] These simulations change the distribution of the EFC across racial groups, although the effects are generally not large. For White families, the mean EFC changes by no more than a couple of hundred dollars in any of the simulations. Interestingly, in the simulation that includes home equity in available wealth without also including retirement savings, the average EFC for White families actually falls. In this simulation, the mean EFC rises for Hispanic families and Asian families. This reflects the high fraction of wealth in home equity for Hispanic families and the high overall level of home equity for Asian families, shown in table 2.1. If we included both home equity and retirement savings as available wealth, the mean EFC for White families would be very similar to its baseline value, the mean EFC for Black families would fall, and the mean EFC for Hispanic families and Asian families would rise.

The analysis here is a static analysis that studies the immediate effects of

22. In results not shown here, I have also examined what would happen if the offsetting changes involved multiplying all six rates by the same factor. The results are generally similar to the results from the additive offsetting change.

an unanticipated change in the financial aid formula. The analysis does not take into account changes in labor supply or savings decisions in response to the new implicit tax rates. However, there are two reasons why this first approximation may still be useful. First, based on earlier research, it is unclear that families actually will adjust their behavior by a large amount in response to new financial aid rules. Second, there is precedent for the federal government changing financial aid rules without giving families time to fully respond. A somewhat trivial example of this is that the recent elimination of the EFC discount for having multiple children in college at the same time happened long after birth spacings of those children had been determined. But perhaps a more relevant example is that, beginning with the 2016–2017 school year, there was a shift back of one year in the year of income that was to be reported on the FAFSA. The 2016–2017 FAFSA used 2015 income, and, rather than using 2016 income, the 2017–2018 FAFSA used 2015 income as well. This change was announced in September 2015, which did not provide families with very much time to adjust their income in advance of completing the 2017–2018 FAFSA.

In the longer run, though, students and parents might adjust their labor supply or savings decisions. If that happens, then EFCs, as well as the amount that governments and universities would need to contribute in order to meet students' full financial need, could differ from the estimates shown in these simulations. If there were changes to the EFC formula, colleges might even adjust their pricing strategies, and there might be effects on students' enrollment patterns.

## 2.8 Conclusion

If the current trends keep on into the future, then we can expect the cost of college to continue to rise. Household incomes and financial aid may rise as well, but it remains to be seen whether they will keep pace with the cost of attendance. If they do not, then we may see more families being asked to pay more than they can really afford, which might lead to their children forgoing college or else choosing to attend college at the cost of creating financial hardship. We may, however, expect higher-income families to be able to pay higher amounts for college over time, which could allow for more redistribution in the form of financial aid to lower-income families. Nevertheless, recent events, such as the Supreme Court's 2023 affirmative action ruling, the ongoing litigation involving financial aid at highly selective private institutions, and the FAFSA Simplification Act, have the potential to reshape the financial aid landscape and alter the trajectory we're currently on.

The results in this chapter are also potentially informative about the effects of possible future changes to the FAFSA. These results suggest that it is possible to change both the level and the distribution of financial aid expenditures by changing details of the EFC calculation, although the extent of this would depend on implementation details. A change to the formula can have a larger impact if it does not come along with offsetting changes.

## References

Aliprantis, Dionissi, Daniel R. Carroll, and Eric R. Young. 2023. "The Dynamics of the Racial Wealth Gap." Unpublished Working Paper.

Amromin, Gene, Janice Eberly, and John Mondragon. 2016. "The Housing Crisis and the Rise in Student Loans." Unpublished Working Paper.

Arcidiacono, Peter. 2005. "Affirmative Action in Higher Education: How Do Admission and Financial Aid Rules Affect Future Earnings?" *Econometrica* 73(5): 1477–1524. doi:10.1111/j.1468–0262.2005.00627.x.

Babiarz, Patryk, and Tansel Yilmazer. 2009. "The Impact of College Financial Aid Rules on Household Portfolio Choice." *National Tax Journal* 62(4): 635–55. doi:10.17310/ntj.2009.4.03.

Bailey, Martha J., and Susan M. Dynarski. 2011. "Inequality in Postsecondary Education." In *Whither Opportunity? Rising Inequality, Schools, and Children's Life Chances*, edited by Greg J. Duncan and Richard J. Murnane, 117–32. New York: Russell Sage Foundation.

Barrow, Lisa, and Ofer Malamud. 2015. "Is College a Worthwhile Investment?" *Annual Review of Economics* 7: 519–55. doi:10.1146/annurev-economics-080614–115510.

Barsky, Robert, John Bound, Kerwin Ko' Charles, and Joseph P. Lupton. 2002. "Accounting for the Black–White Wealth Gap." *Journal of the American Statistical Association* 97(459): 663–73. doi:10.1198/016214502388618401.

Bastian, Jacob, and Katherine Michelmore. 2018. "The Long-Term Impact of the Earned Income Tax Credit on Children's Education and Employment Outcomes." *Journal of Labor Economics* 36(4): 1127–163. doi:10.1086/697477.

Belley, Philippe, and Lance Lochner. 2007. "The Changing Role of Family Income and Ability in Determining Educational Achievement." *Journal of Human Capital* 1(1): 37–89. doi:10.1086/524674.

Bleemer, Zachary. 2022. "Affirmative Action, Mismatch, and Economic Mobility after California's Proposition 209." *Quarterly Journal of Economics* 137(1): 115–60. doi:10.1093/qje/qjab027.

Brown, Meta, John Karl Scholz, and Ananth Seshadri. 2012. "A New Test of Borrowing Constraints for Education." *Review of Economic Studies* 79(2): 511–38. doi:10.1093/restud/rdr032.

Bulman, George, Robert Fairlie, Sarena Goodman, and Adam Isen. 2021. "Parental Resources and College Attendance: Evidence from Lottery Wins." *American Economic Review* 111(4): 1201–40. doi:10.1257/aer.20171272.

Cameron, Stephen V., and Christopher Taber. 2004. "Estimation of Educational Borrowing Constraints Using Returns to Schooling." *Journal of Political Economy* 112(1): 132–82. doi:10.1086/379937.

Carlton, Dennis W., Gustavo E. Bamberger, and Roy J. Epstein. 1995. "Antitrust and Higher Education: Was There a Conspiracy to Restrict Financial Aid?" *RAND Journal of Economics* 26(1): 131–47.

Carneiro, Pedro, and James J. Heckman. 2002. "The Evidence on Credit Constraints in Post-Secondary Schooling." *Economic Journal* 112(482): 705–34. doi:10.1111/1468-0297.00075.

Case, Karl E., and Michael S. McPherson. 1986. "Does Need-Based Student Aid Discourage Saving for College?" The Washington Office of the College Board.

Caucutt, Elizabeth M., and Lance Lochner. 2020. "Early and Late Human Capital Investments, Borrowing Constraints, and the Family." *Journal of Political Economy* 128(3): 1065–1147. doi:10.1086/704759.

Chetty, Raj, David J. Deming, and John N. Friedman. 2023. "Diversifying Society's Leaders? The Determinants and Causal Effects of Admission to Highly Selective Private Colleges." NBER Working Paper No. 31492. Cambridge, MA: National Bureau of Economic Research.

Chetty, Raj, Nathaniel Hendren, Patrick Kline, and Emmanuel Saez. 2014. "Where Is the Land of Opportunity? The Geography of Intergenerational Mobility in the United States." *Quarterly Journal of Economics* 129(4): 1553–1623. doi:10.1093/qje/qju022.

Cohodes, Sarah R., and Joshua S. Goodman. 2014. "Merit Aid, College Quality, and College Completion: Massachusetts' Adams Scholarship as an In-Kind Subsidy." *American Economic Journal: Applied Economics* 6(4): 251–85. doi:10.1257/app.6.4.251.

Council of Economic Advisers. 2023. *Economic Report of the President*. Washington: US Government Publishing Office.

Cowan, Benjamin W. 2016. "Testing for Educational Credit Constraints Using Heterogeneity in Individual Time Preferences." *Journal of Labor Economics* 34(2): 363–402. doi:10.1086/683644.

Darolia, Rajeev. 2017. "Assessing the College Financial Aid Work Penalty." *Journal of Higher Education* 88(3): 350–75. doi:10.1080/00221546.2016.1271696.

Dick, Andrew W., and Aaron S. Edlin. 1997. "The Implicit Taxes from College Financial Aid." *Journal of Public Economics* 65(3): 295–322. doi:10.1016/S0047-2727(97)00018-2.

Dick, Andrew W., Aaron S. Edlin, and Eric R. Emch. 2003. "The Savings Impact of College Financial Aid." *Contributions in Economic Analysis & Policy* 2(1): 1–29. doi:10.2202/1538-0645.1044.

Dynarski, Susan, Lindsay Page, and Judith Scott-Clayton. 2023. "College Costs, Financial Aid, and Student Decisions." In *Handbook of the Economics of Education*, vol. 7, edited by Eric A. Hanushek, Stephen Machin, and Ludger Woessmann, 227–85. Amsterdam and Oxford: Elsevier. doi:10.1016/bs.hesedu.2023.03.006.

Dynarski, Susan M., and Judith E. Scott-Clayton. 2006. "The Cost of Complexity in Federal Student Aid: Lessons from Optimal Tax Theory and Behavioral Economics." *National Tax Journal* 59(2): 319–56. doi:10.17310/ntj.2006.2.07.

Edlin, Aaron S. 1993. "Is College Financial Aid Equitable and Efficient?" *Journal of Economic Perspectives* 7(2): 143–58. doi:10.1257/jep.7.2.143.

Fan, Kristy, Tyler J. Fisher, and Andrew A. Samwick. 2021. "The Insurance Value of Financial Aid." NBER Working Paper No. 28669. Cambridge, MA: National Bureau of Economic Research.

Feldstein, Martin. 1995. "College Scholarship Rules and Private Saving." *American Economic Review* 85(3): 552–66.

Gebbia, Nick. 2023. "Misperception and Income Response to Means-Tested Programs: Evidence from the College Financial Aid Implicit Tax." Unpublished Working Paper.

Hampole, Menaka V. 2024. "Financial Frictions and Human Capital Investments." Unpublished Working Paper.

Hanushek, Eric A., Charles Ka Yui Leung, and Kuzey Yilmaz. 2014. "Borrowing Constraints, College Aid, and Intergenerational Mobility." *Journal of Human Capital* 8(1): 1–41. doi:10.1086/675501.

Hershbein, Brad, and Kevin M. Hollenbeck. 2015. *Student Loans and the Dynamics of Debt*. Kalamazoo, MI: W.E. Upjohn Institute for Employment Research.

Hilger, Nathaniel G. 2016. "Parental Job Loss and Children's Long-Term Outcomes: Evidence from 7 Million Fathers' Layoffs." *American Economic Journal: Applied Economics* 8(3): 247–83. doi:10.1257/app.20150295.

Hinrichs, Peter. 2012. "The Effects of Affirmative Action Bans on College Enrollment, Educational Attainment, and the Demographic Composition of Universities." *Review of Economics and Statistics* 94(3): 712–22. doi:10.1162/REST a 00170.

Hoekstra, Mark. 2009. "The Effect of Attending the Flagship State University on Earnings: A Discontinuity-Based Approach." *Review of Economics and Statistics* 91(4): 717–24. doi:10.1162/rest.91.4.717.

Hotz, V. Joseph, Emily E. Wiemers, Joshua Rasmussen, and Kate Maxwell Koegel. 2018. "The Role of Parental Wealth and Income in Financing Children's College Attendance and Its Consequences." NBER Working Paper No. 25144. Cambridge, MA: National Bureau of Economic Research.

Hoxby, Caroline M. 2009. "The Changing Selectivity of American Colleges." *Journal of Economic Perspectives* 23(4): 95–118. doi:10.1257/jep.23.4.95.

Johnson, Matthew T. 2013. "Borrowing Constraints, College Enrollment, and Delayed Entry." *Journal of Labor Economics* 31(4): 669–725. doi:10.1086/669964.

Johnson, Rucker C. 2020. "The Impact of Parental Wealth on College Degree Attainment: Evidence from the Housing Boom and Bust." *AEA Papers and Proceedings* 110: 405–10. doi:10.1257/pandp.20201110.

Keane, Michael P., and Kenneth I. Wolpin. 2001. "The Effect of Parental Transfers and Borrowing Constraints on Educational Attainment." *International Economic Review* 42(4): 1051–1103. doi:10.1111/1468-2354.00146.

Kim, Taejong. 1997. *College Financial Aid and Family Saving*. PhD diss., Massachusetts Institute of Technology.

Levine, Phillip. 2024. "Ignore the Sticker Price: How Have College Prices Really Changed?" The Brookings Institution.

Levine, Phillip B. 2022. *A Problem of Fit: How the Complexity of College Pricing Hurts Students—and Universities*. Chicago: University of Chicago Press.

Levine, Phillip B., and Dubravka Ritter. 2024. "The Racial Wealth Gap, Financial Aid, and College Access." *Journal of Policy Analysis and Management* 43(2): 555–81. doi:10.1002/pam.22550.

Li, James J., Olivia S. Mitchell, and Christina Zhu. 2023. "Household Investment in 529 College Savings Plans and Information Processing Frictions." NBER Working Paper No. 30848. Cambridge, MA: National Bureau of Economic Research.

Lochner, Lance, and Alexander Monge-Naranjo. 2012. "Credit Constraints in Education." *Annual Review of Economics* 4: 225–56. doi:10.1146/annurev-economics-080511-110920.

Lochner, Lance J., and Alexander Monge-Naranjo. 2011. "The Nature of Credit Constraints and Human Capital." *American Economic Review* 101(6): 2487–2529. doi:10.1257/aer.101.6.2487.

Long, Mark. 2004a. "The Impact of Asset-Tested College Financial Aid on Household Savings." *Journal of Public Economics* 88(1–2): 63–88. doi:10.1016/S0047-2727(02)00136-6.

Long, Mark C. 2004b. "Race and College Admissions: An Alternative to Affirmative Action?" *Review of Economics and Statistics* 86(4): 1020–1033. doi:10.1162/0034653043125211.

Lovenheim, Michael F. 2011. "The Effect of Liquid Housing Wealth on College Enrollment." *Journal of Labor Economics* 29(4): 741–71. doi:10.1086/660775.

Lovenheim, Michael F., and C. Lockwood Reynolds. 2013. "The Effect of Housing Wealth on College Choice: Evidence from the Housing Boom." *Journal of Human Resources* 48(1): 1–35. doi:10.3368/jhr.48.1.1.

Lumina Foundation and Institute for Higher Education Policy. n.d. "Form & Formula: How the Federal Government Distributes Aid to Students" (Viewing Guide).

Manoli, Day, and Nicholas Turner. 2018. "Cash-on-Hand and College Enrollment: Evidence from Population Tax Data and the Earned Income Tax Credit." *American Economic Journal: Economic Policy* 10(2): 242–71. doi:10.1257/pol.20160298.

Masten, Scott E. 1995. "Old School Ties: Financial Aid Coordination and the Governance of Higher Education." *Journal of Economic Behavior & Organization* 28(1): 23–47. doi:10.1016/0167–2681(95)00018–7.

Monks, James. 2004. "An Empirical Examination of the Impact of College Financial Aid on Family Savings." *National Tax Journal* 57(2.1): 189–207. doi:10.17310/ntj.2004.2.03.

National Collegiate Attainment Network. n.d. "The Growing Gap: Public Higher Education's Lack of Affordability for Pell Grant Recipients." https://www.ncan.org/page/Affordability.

Oreopoulos, Philip, and Uros Petronijevic. 2013. "Making College Worth It: A Review of the Returns to Higher Education." *Future of Children* 23(1): 41–65. doi:10.1353/foc.2013.0001.

Oreopoulos, Philip, and Kjell G. Salvanes. 2011. "Priceless: The Nonpecuniary Benefits of Schooling." *Journal of Economic Perspectives* 25(1): 159–84. doi:10.1257/jep.25.1.159.

Pan, Weixiang, and Ben Ost. 2014. "The Impact of Parental Layoff on Higher Education Investment." *Economics of Education Review* 42: 53–63. doi:10.1016/j.econedurev.2014.06.006.

Reber, Sarah, and Ember Smith. 2023. "College Enrollment Disparities: Understanding the Role of Academic Preparation." The Brookings Institution.

Reyes, Jessica Wolpaw. 2008. "College Financial Aid Rules and the Allocation of Savings." *Education Economics* 16(2): 167–89. doi:10.1080/09645290701383605.

Ringo, Daniel. 2019. "Parental Credit Constraints and Child College Attendance." *Education Finance and Policy* 14(4): 548–71. doi:10.1162/edfp a 00259.

Smith, Jonathan, Joshua Goodman, and Michael Hurwitz. 2020. "The Economic Impact of Access to Public Four-Year Colleges." NBER Working Paper No. 27177. Cambridge, MA: National Bureau of Economic Research.

Souleles, Nicholas S. 2000. "College Tuition and Household Savings and Consumption." *Journal of Public Economics* 77(2): 185–207. doi:10.1016/S0047–2727(99)00068–7.

Stinebrickner, Ralph, and Todd Stinebrickner. 2008. "The Effect of Credit Constraints on the College Drop-Out Decision: A Direct Approach Using a New Panel Study." *American Economic Review* 98(5): 2163–84. doi:10.1257/aer.98.5.2163.

Sun, Stephen Teng, and Constantine Yannelis. 2016. "Credit Constraints and Demand for Higher Education: Evidence from Financial Deregulation." *Review of Economics and Statistics* 98(1): 12–24. doi:10.1162/REST a 00558.

Yannelis, Constantine, and Greg Tracey. 2022. "Student Loans and Borrower Outcomes." *Annual Review of Financial Economics* 14: 167–86. doi:10.1146/annurev-financial-111720–092601.

Zimmerman, Seth D. 2014. "The Returns to College Admission for Academically Marginal Students." *Journal of Labor Economics* 32(4): 711–54. doi:10.1086/676661.

## Comment Phillip Levine

Let's be honest. The system of paying for college in the United States is unbelievably complicated. Prospective students are forced to make college-going decisions with limited and potentially incorrect information. College officials have difficulty communicating to prospective students how much they can expect to pay. And policymakers, whose views determine the public's role in the system, often express views that indicate they don't really understand it. All of this occurs in a context of considerable dismay regarding the rising cost of college.

"How Much Can Families Afford to Pay for College?" by Peter Hinrichs attempts to shed some light on the issue, focusing specifically on college affordability. What are students expected to pay? How does that compare to the amount they are asked to pay? How has that changed over time? How does affordability differ for different groups of students? And are there tweaks to the system that may make it more equitable? In the present environment, all of these are interesting and relevant questions.

This paper does a nice job of documenting what we know within the structure of our current financial aid system. The first part of the analysis (following a substantive review of related past research) focuses on how much students and their families can afford to pay for college. The focus rests on dependent students whose parents would be expected to help them pay for college. The author carefully explains the process determining how this amount is calculated.

He makes one point that cannot be stressed enough. There is no definitive method of translating a family's financial resources into a figure indicating how much that family can afford to pay for college. The process is, by nature, arbitrary. Nonetheless, a financial aid system needs such a figure to guide aid determination. In the United States, FAFSA is that system and the "Expected Family Contribution" (EFC—recently renamed the "Student Aid Index," or SAI) is the result. In theory, that amount represents how much the family can "afford" to pay.

This analysis reports a series of statistics regarding the EFC, including its trend over time for students with different family incomes, in different race/ethnicity categories, and parental education. In general, EFC has risen over time, particularly for higher-income students, White students, and students of more educated parents. The author indicates that none of this is related to changes in the financial aid system, which was largely stable over the period of the analysis. Although not highlighted, the real culprit is the trend

Phillip Levine is the Katharine Coman and A. Barton Hepburn Professor of Economics at Wellesley College, and a research associate of the National Bureau of Economic Research.

For acknowledgments, sources of research support, and disclosure of the author's material financial relationships, if any, please see https://www.nber.org/books-and-chapters/financing-institutions-higher-education/comment-how-much-can-families-afford-pay-college-levine.

in income and wealth inequality (Stone et al. 2020; Horowitz et al. 2020). As those at the tops of those distributions pull away from others, their EFC will rise. They can afford to pay more for college. That is what the system was designed to do.

The true gauge of affordability, though, is how the amount students are expected to pay for college relates to what it actually costs them. The next section of the paper addresses that issue. I'll be honest. A pet peeve of mine is the use of the measure, cost of attendance, as an indicator of the amount that institutions charge. The author references my research on this point (Levine 2024). The cost of attendance (COA) is a figure that the federal government requires institutions to report. It includes the full cost of tuition, food and housing, books and supplies, travel, and other living expenses. But most students, including those from high-income/wealth families, pay less than the full COA.

The problem is that there needs to be an upper bound representing the most a student could pay at an institution to determine how much financial assistance the student needs to help them pay to attend. This concept is labeled *financial need*. If the COA were a reasonable measure of that upper bound, then measuring financial need as COA—EFC would be appropriate. Since so few students pay the COA, it is not.

The problem is that there is no alternative, easily available measure of that upper bound. The author has no choice other than to rely on COA in his analysis. But as I have shown, the gap between COA and the actual upper bound on what students pay has been growing over time. That calls into question the results of any analysis that calculates financial need based on COA. This analysis has that problem. It is the best the author can do, but it is a caveat that the reader should fully incorporate in interpreting those results.

The final part of the analysis transitions from how the financial system is designed to think about the consequences of different design. In particular, the author focuses on the sensitivity of college pricing by race and ethnicity as a function of different "tax rates" on income and wealth. The author does a nice job of explaining what he means by these tax rates. As income and wealth rise, the amount of financial aid potentially available falls. It could lead to greater college costs, and that is akin to a tax.

Along with changing tax rates, he also considers the impact of changing what forms of wealth "count." In the current system, housing wealth and retirement savings are not measures of wealth that are used to determine how much a student can afford to pay. The parents of two students can have the same income, but one may have greater levels of wealth in these forms. They would have the same EFC, though, despite the difference in their financial resources. This creates an inequity in the system.

It is difficult to avoid creating inequities in designing systems like this, but in this case, it creates a systematic inequity by race and ethnicity. Since White households hold considerably more wealth in these (and other) forms than

Black and Hispanic households, paying for college is harder for these underrepresented groups. Aside from varying tax rates, the author examines how college costs would change by race/ethnicity if these forms of assets were simply included in the calculation of wealth that is taxed.

Perhaps not surprisingly, the results indicate that a large tax change in the tax rate on wealth or the inclusion/exclusion of entire categories of wealth (i.e., home equity and retirement savings) has a substantive effect for White families on the calculation of how much students can afford to pay—the EFC. These families are the ones that hold the largest amount of wealth. For instance, counting home equity and retirement savings alone, with no change in tax rates, would increase the EFC of White families by $13,000, on average. On the other hand, a revenue-neutral change that counted these assets but lowered tax rates on income so that the average EFC across the entire population remained constant, would have little impact on the EFC that White families would face.

Black families, though, would see meaningful reductions in their EFC from such a revenue-neutral change. For them, including home equity and retirement savings in the current system would only increase their EFC by around $2,000, on average, because their holdings of these assets are more limited. On the other hand, lowering their tax rates to generate revenue neutrality across the population would reduce their EFC by over $1,000 relative to the current system.

Yet these results represent averages by race and ethnicity. But the distribution of income and assets matters a lot in calculations like these. The biggest impact of such a policy change would occur among middle- to upper-middle-income families. Lower-income families typically have low levels of assets as well, so they always face a low EFC. Higher-income families would face large changes in their EFC by such policy changes, but they largely won't matter because they are unlikely to be eligible for financial aid anyway. In my coauthored past work (Levine and Ritter 2024), we show that families with incomes in the $75,000 to $125,000 range and those in the $125,000 to $200,000 range are the ones who are most affected by the failure to count these forms of wealth.

My guess is that if the author's simulations were narrowed to this segment of the income distribution, the impact on EFC would likely be larger. It's also likely to be the case that such an analysis is hampered by the small sample size of students by race/ethnicity and family income to conduct such an analysis in the available data. That said, I think it is important to keep in mind that in evaluating the magnitude of the simulated impacts, they are likely to be potentially considerably larger for the relevant slice of the population.

One of the underlying messages of this paper is that even when a skilled economist applies his tools to the best available data, it is difficult to assess the affordability of our higher education system. Imagine how hard it must be for the students and the families themselves. If there is no other takeaway from this paper, it is the limited transparency in how colleges set and communicate their prices.

## References

Horowitz, Juliana Menasce, Ruth Igielnik, And Rakesh Kochhar. 2020. *Trends in Income and Wealth Inequality*. Report, Pew Research Center, January 9. https://www.pewresearch.org/social-trends/2020/01/09/trends-in-income-and-wealth-inequality/.

Levine, Phillip. 2024. "Ignore the Sticker Price: How Have College Prices Really Changed?" Brookings Institution, April 12. https://www.brookings.edu/articles/ignore-the-sticker-price-how-have-college-prices-really-changed/.

Levine, Phillip B., and Dubravka Ritter. 2024. "The Racial Wealth Gap, Financial Aid, and College Access." *Journal of Policy Analysis and Management* 43(2): 555–81.

Stone, Chad, Danilo Trisi, Arloc Sherman, and Jennifer Beltrán. 2020. *A Guide to Statistics on Historical Trends in Income Inequality*. Report, Center for Budget and Policy Priorities, updated December 11, 2024. https://www.cbpp.org/research/poverty-and-inequality/a-guide-to-statistics-on-historical-trends-in-income-inequality.

# 3

# Predicting College Closures and Financial Distress

Robert Kelchen, Dubravka Ritter,
and Douglas A. Webber

## 3.1 Introduction

College closures, mergers, and other forms of financial distress can have profound effects not only on students and employees of the affected institutions but also on local economics—particularly in areas where the institution of postsecondary education serves as an anchor of local economic activity. The postsecondary education sector is facing serious financial headwinds, both due to long-term trends and to the post-pandemic recovery. For this reason, measuring and predicting financial distress for these institutions is more important than ever. Yet this endeavor is difficult owing to the complexity of their financial structures and the limited availability of suitable data.

One key challenge is declines in enrollment, as the number of students enrolled in degree-granting colleges and universities fell by 15 percent from 2010 to 2021 (National Center for Education Statistics 2023). Enrollment declines were particularly stark during the height of the pandemic, as individuals chose to participate in a strong labor market over taking classes that were primarily offered online, but participation in higher education was already falling prior to the pandemic. This trend might have finally reversed

Robert Kelchen is professor and head of the Department of Educational Leadership and Policy Studies at the University of Tennessee, Knoxville.

Dubravka Ritter is a special advisor, higher education finance at the Consumer Finance Institute at the Federal Reserve Bank of Philadelphia.

Douglas A. Webber is a principal economist in the Consumer and Community Research Section of the Board of Governors of the Federal Reserve.

For acknowledgments, sources of research support, and disclosure of the authors' material financial relationships, if any, please see https://www.nber.org/books-and-chapters/financing-institutions-higher-education/predicting-college-closures-and-financial-distress.

during the fall 2023 semester, which saw the first across-the-board increase in enrollment in many years (National Student Clearinghouse Research Center 2024).

Part of these recent enrollment declines is frequently blamed on what is referred to as the "demographic cliff" in higher education, or the decline in the number of high school graduates in parts of the country that is spreading across more states (Bransberger et al. 2020; Grawe 2018). This has undoubtedly contributed to enrollment declines and explains a sizable portion of the observed enrollment trends. The effect is amplified by low graduation rates and the declining share of high schoolers enrolling in college immediately after graduation, which has fallen from 70 percent to 62 percent over the last decade (National Center for Education Statistics 2023). This decline, which also began before the pandemic, could reflect growing skepticism among the public about the value of higher education (e.g., Brenan 2023).

The other primary source of students—adult learners—has also seen substantial declines over the last decade. The enrollment of adult learners has traditionally been countercyclical, as potential students seek out community colleges and broad-access private institutions when recessions hit (Barr and Turner 2015; Hillman and Orians 2013). The number of students over the age of 25 has fallen by nearly half since the Great Recession (authors' calculations using Integrated Postsecondary Education Data System data), meaning that colleges do not have as large an alternative market of students to consider when the labor market is strong.

Growing competition for students, along with an increasing number of states limiting the tuition-setting authority of public colleges (Kelchen and Pingel 2024), has limited institutions' ability to increase tuition revenue from existing students. Listed prices for tuition and fees have increased at or below the rate of inflation since 2018 following decades of substantial real increases (Ma and Pender 2023). Tuition discount rates have steadily risen over time, surpassing 50 percent at private nonprofit colleges in 2022 (National Association of College and University Business Officers 2023). At the same time, operating costs have also risen quickly owing to the pandemic-era inflationary shock and a longer trend of rising benefits expenses (Commonfund Institute 2023).

These financial pressures on higher education have elevated financial distress—up to and including closures—as a major higher education policy issue. While there have been predictions of a wave of closures for the last decade (e.g., Eide 2018; Horn 2018), most colleges survived the pandemic thanks to timely federal support and emergency actions taken to freeze or reduce personnel costs (Natow 2021). However, the withdrawal of pandemic-era federal funding, along with existing stressors, likely resulted in an increase in closures during 2023 (Sanchez 2024) and into 2024. There has also been a wave of colleges declaring financial exigency, eliminating academic programs and employees in an effort to cut costs and to avoid potential closures (Ambrose and Nietzel 2024). Even flagship universities such as West Virginia University and Pennsylvania State University have pursued sizable reductions in the number of academic programs as they face budget deficits (Burke 2024; Povich 2023).

Considerable attention has been given to the plight of students attending colleges that close, as it negatively affects the likelihood of students eventually earning a credential (Burns et al. 2023). But the potential effects of closures and significant budget cuts can also spill over into the broader communities, as colleges often serve as anchor institutions—economic and cultural engines of their local communities (Birch et al. 2013; Harris and Holley 2016). Research on the effects of mass layoffs in other sectors has found declines in total regional employment as some workers either move to a new region or drop out of the labor market entirely (Celli et al. 2023; Foote et al. 2019).

In this study, we combine rich data on higher education institutions' students, staff, and financial circumstances with county-level data on economic activity to explore various forms of fiscal challenges—including full closure—facing institutions of postsecondary education. We focus most closely on strong predictors of closures as the most extreme form of financial distress and one that both college administrators and sector regulators spend considerable resources preventing and addressing. More specifically, we answer the following research questions:

1) To what extent can college financial distress (substantial downsizing or closures) be predicted based on institutional characteristics, enrollment/staff metrics, financial indicators, and local economic conditions in preceding years?

2) What types of institutions may be at risk of financial distress in the future based on reasonable scenarios of enrollment changes and broader economic conditions?

We assemble the most comprehensive data set to date on the characteristics of closed institutions compared with institutions that did not close. This paper begins with an extensive description of what is known and unknown about these colleges. The current monitoring solution to predicting the financial distress and closure of institutions—at least at the federal level—is to provide straightforward and intuitive financial performance metrics that are correlated with closure. These federal performance metrics represent helpful but suboptimal measures for purposes of predicting closures for two reasons: data availability and predictive accuracy. We document a high degree of missing data among colleges that eventually close, show that this is a key impediment to identifying institutions at risk of closure, and also show how modern machine learning algorithms can provide a concrete solution to this problem. These same algorithms greatly improve the predictive accuracy even for institutions with complete data but can only deliver on their predictive accuracy promises if used judiciously and with the full set of available data instead of selected (key) metrics.

For instance, consider three distinct models predicting closure: (1) an OLS model that includes only federal accountability metrics combined with sector and year controls; (2) an OLS model that includes a broader set of financial data and other controls in binned form (to accommodate missing values); and (3) a machine learning model that has the capability of addressing missing data while utilizing the maximum number of variables. To provide but one illustration of improvement in predictive accuracy analysts can expect with carefully employed machine learning methods, consider the 100 institutions with the highest predicted closure probabilities according to each model. Some 47 percent of the 100 institutions with the highest predicted likelihood of closing actually closed within three years using the federal metrics model, whereas 61 percent of institutions actually closed within three years using the OLS model with additional binned controls and 84 percent of institutions actually closed within three years using the machine learning model. We further illustrate the benefits of using our models and data to assess closure predictions in more local geographic areas, like states, while urging analysts to carefully consider measures of predictive accuracy before doing so. Finally, we also provide some back-of-the-envelope calculations showing the range of possible future increases in closures if predictions about the severity of the so-called "demographic cliff" are realized.

## 3.2 Postsecondary Education Landscape and Fiscal Challenges

In this section, we motivate our study by reviewing the history of financial distress and college closures, as well as consider extant research on factors associated with college closures. We then discuss the relationship between postsecondary education, the labor market, and regional economic growth; examine the role that colleges and universities play as anchor institutions in their local communities; and summarize the current landscape of postsecondary education revenue and expenditure sources.

### 3.2.1 Financial Distress and College Closures

Financial challenges have long played an important role in the history of American postsecondary education. For example, Harvard was able to continue operating in the 1640s and 1650s through fundraising one-quarter of a bushel of corn ("colledge corne") from each local family (Curti and Nash 1965). While college closures have a long history in America (Tewksbury 1932), many colleges are resilient and manage to avoid closure against difficult odds. An analysis of nearly 500 private nonprofit colleges that were identified as having limited resources in 1972 found that nearly 85 percent of the institutions continued to operate in some form four decades later (Tarrant et al. 2018). Public higher education systems, in particular, rarely suffer closures because of local and state financial support, but they do sometimes face mergers and consolidations (which are more difficult to observe and outside the scope of the present study, but a fruitful area for future research).

A number of analysts and consulting firms have identified factors that they view as being indicative of college closures without empirically testing their accuracy (e.g., Denneen and Dretler 2012; Parthenon-EY 2017; Zemsky et al. 2020). There is much less research that examines factors associated with a higher risk of closure using econometric or statistical frameworks. Institutional characteristics that are related to closure in statistical analyses include being a Historically Black College or University (HBCU) or a women's college, while being an urban college reduces the likelihood of closure (Britton et al. 2023; Zapp and Dahmen 2023). Financial characteristics associated with closures include lower faculty salaries, lower tuition, smaller endowments, and higher shares of instructional spending (Bates and Santerre 2000; Britton et al. 2023; Porter and Ramirez 2009). Yet many of the factors identified in these studies are not necessarily causing colleges financial distress in and of themselves but rather are correlated with institutional characteristics and financial indicators predictive of institutional financial distress.

We take inspiration for our study from Kelchen (2020), who used linear probability models to predict college closures within two and four years separately for private nonprofit and for-profit institutions. Some of the key variables associated with closures in that study included declines in enrollment, increases in the tuition discount rate, a decline in endowment values, and triggering the Department of Education's monitoring metrics for Title IV eligibility: failing the federal financial responsibility test or being on the more serious level 2 of heightened cash monitoring. While models in Kelchen (2020) were able to identify colleges at the highest risk of closures, only a small fraction of the riskiest institutions closed in the short term.

### 3.2.2 Postsecondary Education, the Labor Market, and Economic Growth

While postsecondary education serves numerous purposes, including personal growth, fostering civic engagement, and advancing society, students and policymakers often focus on colleges' role in preparing students for the labor market. Students rate economic factors among the most important reasons for going to college (e.g., Stolzenberg et al. 2020), and a growing number of states explicitly tie public funding for higher education to workforce-related metrics (Kelchen et al. 2024b). And the sizable economic returns for college completers—albeit with significant variation by field of study, student ability, and the price tag of the credential—highlight the importance of higher education in the labor market (Webber 2016; Zhang et al. 2024).

A sizable body of research shows a strong relationship between the availability of higher education opportunities in a local community and economic health, emphasizing the importance of colleges as anchor institutions along with medical institutions (e.g., Birch et al. 2013; Harkavy and Zuckerman 1999; Harker et al. 2022; Harris and Holley 2016). Much of the relationship is due to increased employment because many graduates (particularly at less selective colleges) stay in the area (Conzelmann et al. 2023) and because of the service-related jobs that are associated with having colleges in the area (Lee 2019). The presence of colleges leads to higher levels of educational attainment and employment in human capital-intensive industries, more patents, increased economic mobility, and increased local economic output (Andrews 2023; Carlino and Hunt 2009; Howard et al. 2022; Lehnert et al. 2024; Russell and Andrews 2022; Russell et al. 2022).

It is also important to emphasize that colleges serve as more than economic engines of local communities. Particularly in more rural and isolated areas, higher education institutions have the potential to function as the cultural hub of communities by supporting civic engagement, the arts, and providing entertainment and educational opportunities (Ashley et al. 2023; Howard 2014). An important activity of many colleges is noncredit courses, which can serve to develop individuals' skills for the labor market or to simply promote lifelong learning (Arena 2013; Xu and Ran 2020). The proximity to colleges has even been a factor in the retirement decisions of some Americans, as they seek out a stimulating environment in their golden years (Smith et al. 2014).

Put together, colleges have the ability to attract individuals to local communities and to better the overall quality of life. For those reasons, struggles of higher education institutions—through closures or cutbacks caused by severe financial distress—are of particular interest to college leaders, researchers, policymakers, and others. They also represent a large part of the motivation behind our analysis to examine the factors associated with closures or severe declines in institutional health.

### 3.2.3 College Funding Metrics and Patterns

The American postsecondary education system today consists of approximately 6,000 colleges and universities that receive federal financial aid under Title IV of the federal Higher Education Act. There is also a substantial number of very small colleges, particularly in the for-profit sector, that operate without receiving federal financial aid (e.g., Cellini and Goldin 2014) and are outside the scope of this chapter because of a lack of available data. As an industry, American higher education directly produces approximately $700 billion in expenditures, enrolls nearly 25 million students, and has approximately 3 million employees. In the following section, we discuss key revenue and expenditure categories and the implications for institutional finances.

**Table 3.1 Revenues by institutional sector, 2021–2022**

| | Public | | Private nonprofit | | Private for-profit | |
|---|---|---|---|---|---|---|
| | $ | % | $ | % | $ | % |
| **Total revenue** | **460.97** | **100.0** | **220.42** | **100.0** | **18.06** | **100.0** |
| Tuition and fees | 79.84 | 17.3 | 81.62 | 37.0 | 16.66 | 92.3 |
| Appropriations | 102.17 | 22.2 | 1.36 | 0.6 | 0.03 | 0.2 |
| Grants and contracts | 66.27 | 14.4 | 39.75 | 18.0 | 0.40 | 2.2 |
| Auxiliary enterprises | 28.00 | 6.1 | 17.91 | 8.1 | 0.11 | 0.6 |
| Hospitals | 66.86 | 14.5 | 39.43 | 17.9 | 0.00 | 0.0 |
| Investment revenue | −11.32 | −2.5 | −26.40 | −12.0 | 0.04 | 0.2 |
| Gifts | 11.66 | 2.5 | 26.40 | 12.0 | 0.00 | 0.0 |
| Other | 117.48 | 25.5 | 40.36 | 18.3 | 0.82 | 4.5 |

Source: IPEDS Data Explorer, Table 5, 2021–2022.

Note: Values are in billions of dollars. Approximately $15 billion in revenues from 17 FASB-reporting public institutions is excluded from this table.

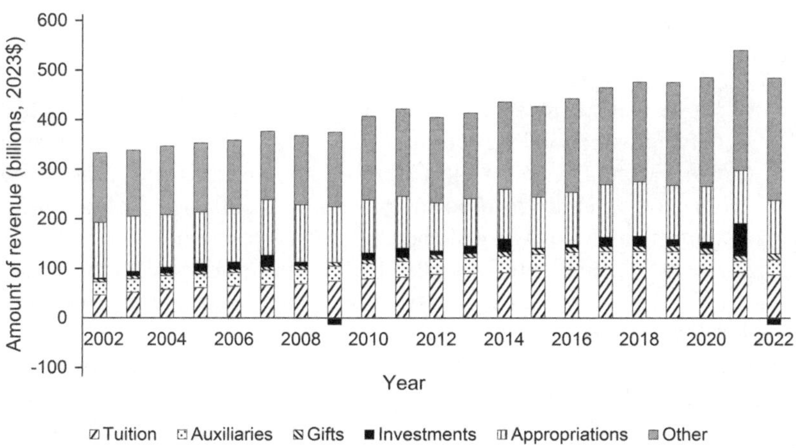


**Fig. 3.1a Trends in sources of college revenues, public institutions, 2002–2022**
Source: Authors' calculations based on IPEDS data, 2002–2022.

### *3.2.3.1 Revenues*

Table 3.1 highlights key revenue categories by institutional sector from the most recent year comprehensive data (Integrated Postsecondary Education Data System, or IPEDS) are available, the 2021–22 academic year. Owing to both the business cycle and the pandemic, this year is not necessarily representative of a "typical" year in each category, e.g., investment revenue. We discuss each revenue category individually in this section, as well as provide historical trends to put the 2021–2022 figures into perspective.

Figures 3.1a–3.1c depict trends in key revenue categories by institutional sector from 2002 to 2022. Figure 3.1a considers public colleges and universi-

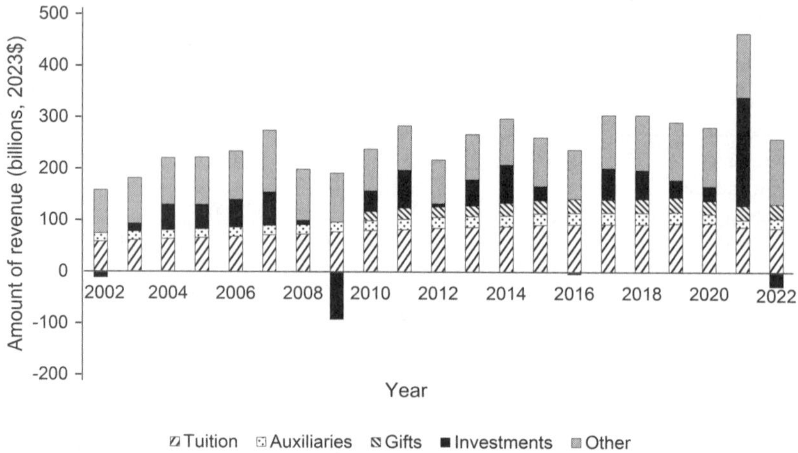


**Fig. 3.1b Trends in sources of college revenues, private nonprofit institutions, 2002–2022**

Source: Authors' calculations based on IPEDS data, 2002–2022.

ties and shows a clear upward trend in inflation-adjusted revenue, with the total increasing from $333 billion in 2002 to $472 billion in 2022. Revenue from tuition, auxiliaries, and gifts steadily increased during most of the panel. However, revenue from both tuition and auxiliaries declined in real terms beginning in 2020 owing to the COVID-19 pandemic and enrollment declines. Investment revenue is generally a modest portion of total revenue and is highly dependent on stock market performance, while appropriations dipped following the Great Recession before recovering.

Figure 3.1b is for private nonprofit colleges, with gift revenue only being available separate from grants and contracts beginning in 2010. Total revenue in this sector over time has been highly dependent on investment returns, with real revenue falling by half from 2008 to 2009 and again from 2021 to 2022. However, the long-term trend has been toward increased revenues for the sector. Other variables have been more consistent, with tuition and auxiliary revenue generally following the same path as public institutions. Gift revenue is about twice as high compared with public colleges, while investment returns are far more influential owing to a relatively small number of colleges with massive endowments.

Finally, figure 3.1c shows two key trends about the finances of for-profit colleges. The first is that for-profit colleges have consistently derived approximately 90 percent of their funding from tuition and fees over the past two decades. Second, revenue tripled from $15 billion to $46 billion from 2002 to 2011 as the for-profit sector grew dramatically. Following enrollment declines and the collapse of some large for-profit chains, total revenue fell to just over $20 billion by 2018.

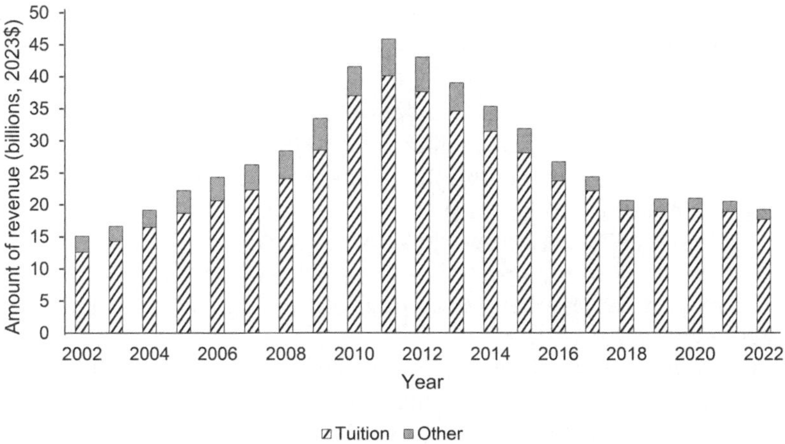


**Fig. 3.1c Trends in sources of college revenues, private for-profit institutions, 2002–2022**
Source: Authors' calculations based on IPEDS data, 2002–2022.

*3.2.3.1.1 Tuition Revenue*

The most important revenue source for private nonprofit and for-profit colleges, and the second most important primary revenue source for public colleges, is revenue from tuition and fees. Between the early 1970s and mid-2010s, listed real tuition and fee rates more than tripled at public and private nonprofit colleges, as strong demand for higher education allowed colleges to continue increasing their prices. But since 2018, tuition increases have consistently been below the rate of inflation (Ma and Pender 2023), and tuition discount rates have continued to rise (National Association of College and University Business Officers 2023), contrary to public perception of skyrocketing college prices.

Public universities can face particularly challenging situations because a majority of states explicitly restrict how much institutions can increase tuition (Kelchen and Pingel 2024), and legislatures and governors can pressure colleges to limit tuition increases even without a formal tuition control mechanism being in place (Kelchen 2018). This has led public universities to prioritize recruiting and enrolling out-of-state students (Jaquette and Curs 2016), although these efforts often fail to generate additional revenue for colleges (Kelchen 2021). At selective public universities, these efforts to recruit out-of-state students have crowded out in-state students—particularly underrepresented minority students (Curs and Jaquette 2017; Jaquette et al. 2016).

*3.2.3.1.2 Government Appropriations*

The single most important source of revenue for public institutions is appropriations, which primarily consist of local and state funding to support general operations. At least some community colleges in nearly 30 states receive local funding, which makes up roughly 21 percent of total revenue for community colleges in those states (Ortagus et al. 2020). State support for public higher education is much larger (approximately $106 billion in fiscal year 2022, compared with $12 billion in local funding) and is spread across two-year and four-year institutions (Kunkle and Laderman 2023). There is a strong relationship between state funding and improved completion rates and post-college outcomes alike (Chakrabarti et al. 2020). However, the mechanism used to allocate funding (such as by enrollment or performance) matters far less than the amount of funding (Kelchen et al. 2024a; Ortagus et al. 2020).

States allocate approximately 90 percent of support for public higher education to institutions, with financial aid to students—a category that is rapidly growing—making up the remainder of support (Kunkle and Laderman 2023). State funding for public higher education is highly volatile, with implications both for students and colleges (Delaney 2023). Much of this volatility is driven by higher education's function as a balancing wheel in state budgets (Delaney and Doyle 2018; Hovey 1999), as states make sharp cuts in appropriations during recessions in order to fund other priorities that do not have alternative revenue sources such as tuition. This leaves public colleges, particularly those that have been heavily reliant on state funding, especially vulnerable to declines in resources and tuition increases as enrollment increases during recessionary periods of reduced state funding (Barr and Turner 2013; Rosinger et al. 2022). Research by Webber (2017) has also shown a relationship between state funding cuts and tuition increases, although tuition increases only backfill a portion of lost appropriations.

*3.2.3.1.3 Research and Hospital Revenue*

For a relatively small number of large public and private nonprofit universities, research (represented primarily through grants and contracts) and hospitals make up a majority of total revenue reported to the US Department of Education. An example of this is the University of Michigan at Ann Arbor, which generated $5.6 billion in hospital revenue and $1.3 billion in grants and contracts in fiscal year 2022, compared with $1.4 billion in tuition revenue (authors' calculations using IPEDS data). Only 89 universities contributed to the nearly $67 billion in hospital revenue, as not all university-connected hospitals report financials in conjunction with universities.

Research funding is distributed across a larger group of institutions, although the vast majority of dollars flows to the 146 institutions that are designated as Research I universities in the Carnegie classifications. Research grants and contracts frequently come with indirect cost allowances that help fund the infrastructures of personnel and facilities that are needed to support a research enterprise. These indirect cost rates tend to be higher for grants received from federal agencies compared with nonprofit foundations, creating strong pressures to seek federal research funds (Graddy-Reed et al. 2021).

*3.2.3.1.4 Auxiliary Enterprise Revenue*

Auxiliary enterprises consist of activities that are not directly tied to instruction, research, and student services. Some of these activities, such as housing, food service, and parking, are typically expected to break even or potentially help support other campus activities through generating a profit. Other activities, such as athletics, may be allowed to operate at a loss in order to help achieve other institutional priorities. Auxiliary revenues reflect a modest share of overall revenue across higher education but are particularly important at residential liberal arts colleges and large research universities with sizable on-campus populations and prominent intercollegiate athletics programs.

Because housing, dining, and parking generate consistent revenue streams, a growing number of public universities have sought capital to upgrade their facilities in these areas. This can take the form of issuing bonds to finance improvements (Denison et al. 2014) or through using public-private partnerships that leverage private capital to make improvements and then lease the assets back to universities (McClure et al. 2017; Storms et al. 2017). Private universities typically issue bonds on their own, which helps explain debt burdens that are higher among private than public institutions because some debt associated with public universities is held outside of balance sheets (Ward et al. 2022).

The vast majority of revenue from intercollegiate athletics comes from the approximately 360 universities in Division I of the National Collegiate Athletic Association (NCAA), and much of this revenue is concentrated among the approximately 60 institutions in the most powerful athletic conferences. Forty-nine public universities brought in more than $100 million in athletics revenue in the 2021–22 fiscal year (USA Today 2024), but many Division I institutions still rely on student fees and institutional contributions to fund athletics. Total student fees for athletics are in excess of $1 billion per year and can exceed $2,000 per student per year at some universities (Enright et al. 2020). Meanwhile, smaller institutions view athletics as a way to recruit tuition-paying students who want to continue their athletic careers and thus are willing to operate athletics with little direct revenue (Knox 2023).

*3.2.3.1.5 Investment and Gift Revenue*

Like research and hospital revenue, the vast majority of support from private donors is concentrated in a small number of colleges. Just 136 colleges or university systems in the United States had endowments of more than $1 billion in fiscal year 2023, but they account for more than 80 percent of all endowment assets in American higher education. Going further, 5 institutions held 25 percent of all endowment assets, and 25 institutions held half of all assets (Redd 2024). Private institutions are far more reliant on endowments and investment income than public institutions, as private institutions hold the majority of assets and tend to have smaller student bodies to support (Baum and Lee 2018).

A college's endowment does not consist of one single piggy bank that leaders can use in any way they see fit. Rather, endowments are made up of numerous accounts that frequently have restrictions placed on their usage by donors. Common categories for giving include student financial aid, funding the building and maintenance of facilities, and supporting faculty positions. Institutional leadership can petition a court to remove restrictions in the case of financial distress (e.g., Moody 2024), but those efforts tend to be expensive to undertake and can damage relationships with donors. In general, colleges are expected to spend approximately 4 percent to 5 percent of a rolling average value of the endowment each year. This is below the long-term rate of return, which allows endowments to keep growing (American Council on Education 2014). It also helps smooth out year-over-year changes in the value of the endowment, which have been considerable over the last decade.

### *3.2.3.2 Expenditures*

One of the key challenges facing colleges and universities is that operating costs have increased faster than general inflation for decades, driven by rising expenses for health insurance and administrative support (Commonfund Institute 2023). To provide an extreme example of rising costs, the University of Delaware announced in early 2024 a freeze on all nonessential spending, in large part owing to skyrocketing health insurance costs driven by the popular weight loss drug Ozempic (Greene 2024; Owens 2024). This is a particular concern for public institutions, which often have limited control over benefits costs compared with private institutions.

Postsecondary education suffers from Baumol's (1967) cost disease as an industry that relies on highly educated labor and is unable to incorporate technological efficiencies as well as many other fields have done; this has explained the majority of rising operating costs over time (Archibald and Feldman 2008). However, Bowen's rule, in which colleges seek to raise as much money as possible in order to spend it on educationally worthwhile pursuits, likely also plays a role in rising expenditures as institutions try to keep up with their peers (Bowen 1980; Kolpin and Stater 2024).

As a labor-intensive industry, expenses related to personnel are by far the single largest expenditure category in most institutions' budgets. While the share of faculty members who are tenured or are on the tenure track has steadily declined over time (Colby 2023), even a move to contingent faculty does not eliminate the need for individuals to teach classes. The two other

**Table 3.2** **Expenses by institutional sector, 2021–22**

| | Public | | Private nonprofit | | Private for-profit | |
|---|---|---|---|---|---|---|
| | $ | % | $ | % | $ | % |
| **Total expenses** | **439.79** | **100.0** | **246.08** | **100.0** | **15.80** | **100.0** |
| Instruction | 116.14 | 26.4 | 68.48 | 27.8 | 4.77 | 30.2 |
| Research | 44.64 | 10.2 | 26.66 | 10.8 | 0.01 | 0.1 |
| Academic support | 34.49 | 7.8 | 20.84 | 8.5 | 1.54 | 9.7 |
| Student services | 24.00 | 5.5 | 21.14 | 8.6 | 3.07 | 19.4 |
| Institutional support | 40.93 | 9.3 | 30.51 | 12.4 | 4.99 | 31.6 |
| Auxiliary enterprises | 33.51 | 7.6 | 18.18 | 7.4 | 0.22 | 1.4 |
| Hospitals | 64.33 | 14.6 | 39.81 | 16.2 | 0.00 | 0.0 |
| Other | 81.74 | 18.6 | 20.45 | 8.3 | 1.21 | 7.7 |

Source: IPEDS Data Explorer, Table 5, 2021–2022.

Note: Values are in billions of dollars. Approximately $15 billion in expenditures from 17 FASB-reporting public institutions is excluded from this table.

primary drivers of institutional expenses are maintaining facilities and debt service. Both these categories also tend to be difficult to change in the short or medium term, as there is often little ability to sell off assets that are on an existing college campus and bonds are often paid off over a period of several decades. As a result, it is difficult for colleges to make meaningful reductions to budgets without eliminating a broad range of academic programs.

Table 3.2 highlights key functional expenses by institutional sector in the 2021–22 academic year. More money was spent on instruction than any single other category across both public and private nonprofit institutions, but this only included between 26 percent and 30 percent of all spending. This low share of spending on instruction often raises concerns regarding so-called administrative bloat, which is a rare argument that unites faculty members, with advocates from across the ideological spectrum (e.g., American Council of Trustees and Alumni 2021; Ginsberg 2011; Whistle and Erickson 2019).

The construction of the instructional expenditures category in IPEDS is relatively narrow, excluding key functions such as advising (classified under academic support), student services, and information technology (which can fall under multiple functional categories, depending on how an institution allocates expenses). These three categories represent just under one-fourth of all spending at public institutions but 60 percent of spending at for-profit colleges. Research has shown that spending in these areas has been shown to significantly improve student outcomes (Griffith and Rask 2016; Webber and Ehrenberg 2010). Spending on other categories, such as research, auxiliary enterprises, and hospitals, tends to be more closely aligned with the associated revenue categories and is less driven by tuition dollars and state appropriations.

## 3.3 Data Sources

### 3.3.1 Institutional Characteristics (IPEDS and College Scorecard)

We obtain information on the historical features of colleges and universities (organizational structure, location, and finances) and on the characteristics of their students and staff primarily from the Department of Education's Integrated Postsecondary Education Data System (IPEDS) data. The panel we assemble spans from 2002 to 2022 and is based on data that are collected annually on the academic year calendar for each UnitID (an IPEDS ID for an individual institution). Some of the IPEDS data we collect are available prior to 2002, but data elements collected frequently changed during the 1990s and are missing for a large share of institutions either because the institution's sector was not asked a particular module or because reporting was optional for the type of institution in a particular year. We focus on institutions in the 50 states and Washington, DC in this analysis.

We use the predominant degree from the College Scorecard and IPEDS to classify institutions into public two-year (or less), public four-year (or more), private nonprofit two-year (or less), private nonprofit four-year (or more), private for-profit two-year (or less), and private for-profit four-year (or more). Considering the predominant degree classification better reflects the institutions' focus, since the highest degree offered would often classify community colleges that offer a single, small BA program as four-year institutions. About one-fifth of colleges are missing information on the predominant degree level variable, so we supplement with Carnegie classifications where available and count the rest as two-year colleges (confirmed by visual inspection of the data for the missing predominant degree level).

The rich IPEDS data include hundreds of variables, with many of them only available for certain institution types or enrollment/revenue thresholds. We consider a range of variables that could potentially be associated with college closures based on prior research, economic theory, and our experiences in the field of higher education finance. The main variables drawn from IPEDS that are of focus for this study include:

- Enrollment: total enrollment; change in enrollment; share full-time enrollment; share undergraduate enrollment
- Staff: total staff; change in staff; share full-time staff; share instructional staff
- Revenues: total revenue; change in revenue; shares of revenue from tuition, auxiliary enterprises, investments, and gifts/grants/contracts
- Expenses: total expenses; percent change in expenses; shares of expenses on instruction, scholarships, interest, depreciation, and salaries
- Assets and debt: Unrestricted net assets; debt; endowment

- Derived financial metrics: operating margin; change in operating margin; days cash on hand (liquidity); change in days cash on hand; earnings before interest, debt, and amortization (EBIDA); debt to EBIDA; debt to assets (leverage); change in debt to assets
- Other derived measures: 10 percent decline in revenue relative to high in the last five years; persistent negative operating margin (at least three of the past five years); 10 percent decline in enrollment relative to high in the last five years; 5 percent or more decline in enrollment each year for the last three years

We adjust financial values such as total revenue, assets, and debt into 2023 dollars using the Consumer Price Index but leave year-over-year percent change metrics as nominal values. For variables with skewed distributions in our analyses (generally, dollar values and measure of students/staff counts), we use logs of nominal values, and winsorize outliers at the 2.5 percent level.

As mentioned previously, most data fields have considerable coverage. That said, data are missing for a variety of reasons, both idiosyncratic and systematic. For example, institutions that only grant certificates frequently do not report detailed asset or other financial data. Given the low risk of bias due to a correlation between the (systematically) missing values and likelihood of closure after conditioning on covariates such as sector or degree level, we include indicators for reasons data are missing (e.g., an institution type such that detailed financial data are unavailable) in certain models in order to maximize sample size; we discuss this process in more detail in the next section. The variables most susceptible to missing values are virtually all measures of debt, assets, and leverage.

In addition to the enumerated variables, the IPEDS data contain a wealth of institutional, financial, student, and staff fields that we consider potentially marginally informative for purposes of predicting financial distress of institutions of higher education. When possible, we assess how much incremental explanatory value these metrics hold, but the covariates selected above are expected to be and empirically are the relatively stronger predictors.

### 3.3.2 College Closures (PEPS)

To consider college closures in the context of this study, we draw on the Closed School Weekly Reports from the Federal Student Aid's (FSA's) Postsecondary Education Participants System (PEPS) database. FSA data classify institutions based on their Office of Postsecondary Education identification number (OPEID), which is based on the unit of analysis under which a program participation agreement is entered upon with the Department of Education (Office of Federal Student Aid 2024). We restrict the sample of institutions in the PEPS data to those where the main campus (FSA OPEID ending in "00"), as opposed to a branch/satellite campus, closed.[1] We made this decision because colleges frequently close branch campuses that may only offer one or two programs of study; fully 90 percent of closures in PEPS in the 2010s were of branch campuses.[2] The PEPS data include a precise date of closure as reported by the US Department of Education, which can be months or even years after the closure was initially announced. A small number of colleges closed, reopened, and then closed again during the period of analysis, but we considered the first closure only in our analyses. PEPS data as of the writing of this paper were only available through November 2023, so 2023 is an incomplete year of data.

Combining data at the IPEDS UnitID and the FSA OPEID levels is a complex endeavor as the relationship between the two classifications is not one-to-one. College and university systems often operate under the same program participation agreement with the FSA, and thus all report data together under what is often called a "parent-child" agreement (Jaquette and Parra 2016). However, seemingly similar university systems differ in whether institutions report separately or jointly to the FSA. For example, Indiana University and University of Wisconsin campuses report separately, while Ohio State University and Rutgers University report as systems. Further complicating this data merge is that colleges that share the same program participation agreement can report certain IPEDS data elements (such as finance and completions) at the OPEID level while reporting other elements (such as enrollment and staffing) at the UnitID level (National Center for Education Statistics 2024).

We meticulously aggregate all our data to the OPEID level to reduce this complication, although it comes at the expense of focusing on only main campus closures. If there are two- year and four-year institutions within the same OPEID, we consider the resulting overall institution to be a four-year college. This results in a final analytic sample of 8,633 institutions that operated and were eligible to receive federal financial aid at some point during the panel; more than one in ten closed during our sample period, as we will show below. We were unable to match 55 closures in the PEPS data to IPEDS UnitIDs, with all but nine of those non-matches occurring between

1. Some colleges have hundreds of branches listed in PEPS, and PEPS creates a new OPEID by adding 10, 20, 30, or 40 to the original OPEID. In about 10 cases, this new OPEID had a branch campus ending in 00, but we dropped those observations because they are not main campuses. An example is OPEID 10224300, which is Central Michigan University's former branch campus at Schoolcraft College.

2. An example of this is Georgia's Piedmont College, which closed 32 branch campuses in 2020 alone. All these campuses were in local school buildings. A similar dynamic occurred at Oregon's Concordia University, which closed its main campus in 2020. However, it closed multiple branch campuses in area school buildings in 2014, which was near the peak of its enrollment and years before any financial challenges. Additionally, there are no data available on the size of these branch campuses or their financial characteristics.

1996 and 1998. These relatively few institutions are therefore excluded from our analyses.

### 3.3.3 Federal Accountability Metrics and County Characteristics

To flag institutions perceived by sector observers to be in precarious financial condition, we use the College Scorecard data on colleges placed on Heightened Cash Monitoring (HCM) level 2, the most serious level of federal monitoring that requires a college to get reimbursed after the fact for federal financial aid disbursed to students instead of receiving those funds in advance. In other words, HCM2 places scrutiny on each student's aid package to minimize the risk of lost funds to taxpayers (Office of Federal Student Aid 2024). We also use data from Federal Student Aid on whether private colleges failed the government's Financial Responsibility Composite (FRC) score, which places colleges on HCM level 1.

Cohort default rates (CDRs) are another accountability tool available to the federal government and represent the share of an institution's student loan borrowers who are in default. Historically, CDRs have tended to flag many low-value programs (especially in the private sector) somewhat accurately but retain relatively less value from a prediction perspective going forward. This is due to the availability of increasingly generous reduced payment plans (including automatic enrollment in case of 90+ days late payments) and debt cancellation available to federal student loan borrowers. These recent policy changes are likely to dramatically reduce default rates to a point where they are no longer informative. Although we collected CDR data, we exclude this metric from our analyses, given that the most likely context for a real-life application of our methodology is predictions of future college financial distress based on most recent data.

We also collect measures of population and income per capita received by local residents at the county level from 1967 to 2022 from the US Bureau of Economic Analysis. Finally, we collect estimates of the poverty rate at the county level from the Small Area Income and Poverty Estimates survey from the US Census Bureau for 1997–2022. The county-level unemployment rate is obtained from the Bureau of Labor Statistics' Local Area Unemployment Statistics program for 1990–2022.

### 3.3.4 Analytical Sample—Closure Predictions

Table 3A.1 shows summary statistics of the analytic panel, divided between observations with closed colleges (using data from two years prior to closure) and observations for colleges that never closed during our sample period of 2002–2023. Colleges that closed were smaller, more tuition-driven, and saw larger declines in enrollment and revenue than colleges that remained open. For example, more than one-fourth of colleges that closed posted operating losses in at least three of the five years prior to closure. This was twice the rate of colleges that remained open. However, there is a substantial overlap in the distributions of variables between open and closed colleges, highlighting the need for multivariate predictions.

Figure 3.2 highlights the number of colleges that closed in each year from 1996 to 2023, broken down by institutional type and level based on the predominant degree offered. As the previous literature shows, the majority of institutions that closed were for-profit two-year colleges with relatively few students. Table 3.3 shows the number of colleges that ever existed and/or closed during our panel by institutional type and level. Overall, a total of 1,671 colleges closed during the period of analysis, with the number of closures peaking from 2016 to 2018.

A striking fact emerges from our data: Public institutions hardly ever

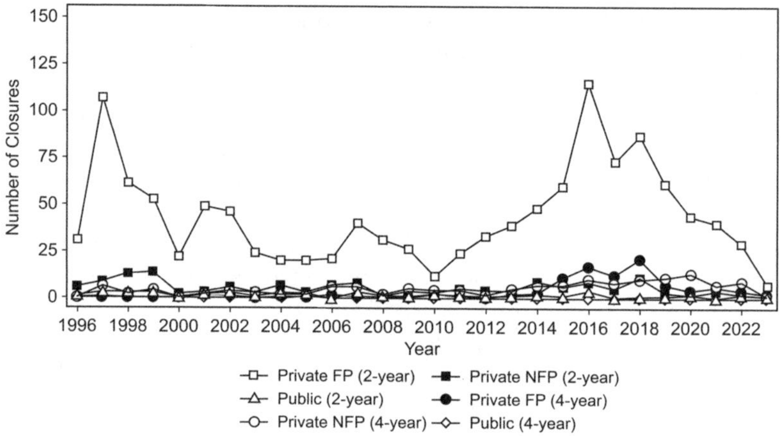


**Fig. 3.2 Number of closed institutions by institution type and year, 1996–2023**
Source: Authors' calculations based on IPEDS, PEPS Closed School Reports, and College Scorecard, 1996–2023.

**Table 3.3 Number of institutions that ever closed, by institution type, 1996–2023**

| Sector | Number of institutions | Number of closures | Closure rate |
|---|---|---|---|
| Public 4-year | 850 | 2 | 0.2% |
| Public 2-year | 1,682 | 45 | 2.7% |
| For-profit 4-year | 473 | 100 | 21.1% |
| For-profit 2-year | 3,732 | 1,222 | 32.7% |
| Nonprofit 4-year | 2,002 | 142 | 7.1% |
| Nonprofit 2-year | 732 | 152 | 20.8% |
| **Total** | **8,633** | **1,661** | **19.2%** |

Source: Authors' calculations based on PEPS Closed School Reports and College Scorecard, 1996–2023.

Note: A small number of colleges changed sectors during the panel, and they are reported in both sectors.

close. Only two four-year public institutions (one tribal college and one graduate health sciences–focused institution) closed during the panel, and nearly all the 45 two-year public institutions that closed were career and technical centers run by local school districts. This shows that despite challenging operational metrics, public institutions under financial pressure tend to remain open, particularly if there is a dearth of public education options in the local area. If more drastic measures are required to address financial distress among public institutions, more often than not, it will be mergers or consolidations that are presented as the remedy, not closure. This is in part because closing a public college is a deeply political decision, similar to closing a military base. As a result, less drastic steps are typically taken that preserve an educational option in the local community. In future work, we hope to collect data on these mergers and consolidations, but they are not available for the present study. As a result, we focus our closure-related analyses on private institutions; however, we consider public institutions when estimating the likelihood of facing significant financial distress.

The vast majority of closures have been among private for-profit colleges, which is intuitive because for-profit colleges are much more likely to exit the marketplace if they do not see the opportunity to make a profit in the future. They are, as Deming et al. (2012) famously posed, nimble critters. Nearly three-fourths of closures in the data set are two-year for-profit colleges, and almost one-third of the 3,732 institutions observed in this sector closed at some point between 1996 and 2023. On the other hand, while private nonprofit four-year colleges get the lion's share of attention regarding college closures, closure rates are relatively modest (just over 7 percent during this time period).

Table 3.4 shows the share of colleges in operation by sector in 1996 that were still in operation in 2006, 2016, and 2023, as this highlights the longevity (or lack thereof) of colleges that were in the panel in the very beginning. Nearly 40 percent of the two-year for-profit colleges open in 1996 closed

**Table 3.4** **Trends in closures by institution type among colleges open in 1996**

| Sector | Open in 1996 | Closed by 2006 | Closed by 2016 | Closed by 2023 |
|---|---|---|---|---|
| Public 4-year | 778 | 0.3% | 0.3% | 0.3% |
| Public 2-year | 1,389 | 1.1% | 1.6% | 1.9% |
| For-profit 4-year | 332 | 1.8% | 10.8% | 24.1% |
| For-profit 2-year | 2,339 | 17.5% | 29.4% | 38.3% |
| Nonprofit 4-year | 1,715 | 1.7% | 4.3% | 7.3% |
| Nonprofit 2-year | 548 | 10.9% | 18.1% | 21.2% |
| **Total** | **6,411** | **8.1%** | **12.7%** | **19.4%** |

Source: Authors' calculations based on PEPS Closed School Reports and College Scorecard, 1996–2023.

Note: A small number of colleges changed sectors during the panel, and they are reported in both sectors.

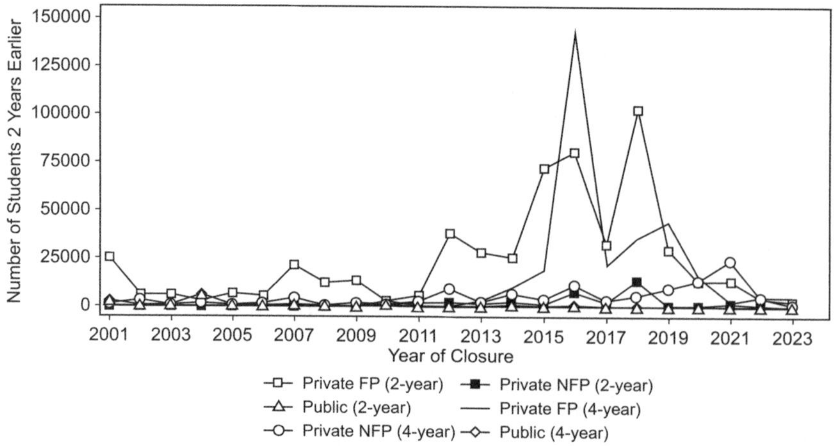


**Fig. 3.3 Number of students enrolled in closed institutions two years prior to closure, by institution type and year, 2001–2023**

Source: Authors' calculations based on IPEDS, PEPS Closed School Reports, and College Scorecard, 2001–2023.

by 2023, with many of them closing in the late 1990s. Most of the closures among four-year for-profits closed in the 2010s and early 2020s, while closures in the nonprofit sector were relatively more evenly distributed over time.

Figure 3.3 shows the number of students affected by college closures each year between 2001 and 2023 by institution classification. Median full-time equivalent (FTE) enrollment two years prior to closure (for example, 2017–18 enrollment for a 2019 closure) was 219 students at nonprofit colleges and 162 students at for-profit colleges. Most colleges in the sample were small, with median enrollment among nonprofit colleges being 1,015 students and just 192 students at for-profit colleges, such that closed schools are somewhat smaller than average (but not dramatically so). However, a few prominent closures in the for-profit sector (such as the Art Institutes and ITT Tech) resulted in just over 1 million students during our panel who attended colleges that closed two years later. The vast majority of students affected by closures were enrolled in the 2010s.

Figure 3.4 plots the number of staff affected by college closures each year by institution classification, again using staff data from two years prior to the closure date. Again, the vast majority of colleges that closed had relatively few employees. The median for-profit college that closed had 20 employees, compared with 48 employees at the typical private nonprofit college. Yet there were approximately 100,000 employees across all affected institutions between 2003 and 2023, with about 70 percent of affected employees working at for-profit colleges. Just over 200 closures had more than 100 employees, reflecting a potentially sizable impact on the local economy.

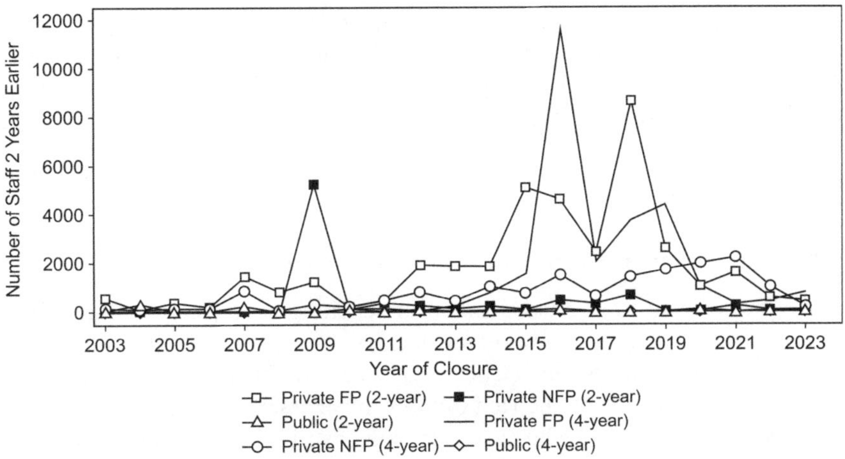


**Fig. 3.4 Number of staff employed by closed institutions two years prior to closure, by institution type and year, 2003–2023**

Source: Authors' calculations based on IPEDS, PEPS Closed School Reports, and College Scorecard, 2001–2023.

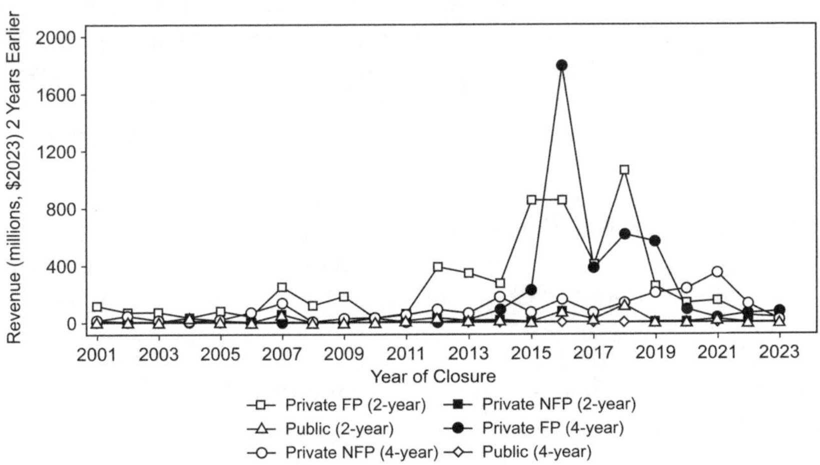


**Fig. 3.5 Total revenue at closed institutions two years prior to closure, by institution type and year, 2001–2023**

Source: Authors' calculations based on IPEDS, PEPS Closed School Reports, and College Scorecard, 2001–2023.

Finally, figure 3.5 examines the total revenue generated by institutions that closed two years later. The median total revenue was $2.18 million two years prior to closure, with the median nonprofit college having total revenue of $5.06 million, and the median for-profit college having total revenue of $1.84 million. Nearly one-fifth of all closed colleges generated at least $10 million in revenue two years before closing, and the total amount of revenue generated by closing colleges exceeded $13 billion over the last two decades. Again, the large for-profit college closures explain the substantial revenue values in the mid-to-late 2010s.

## 3.4 Methodology

### 3.4.1 Identifying Predictors of Financial Distress

We implement a supervised machine learning classification algorithm using a distributed gradient boosting decision tree methodology, and specifically the XGBoost algorithm (Chen and Guestrin 2016). We do this in order to make the most out of the rich data we have assembled and because the IPEDS data that form the basis of our panel exhibit considerable gaps. Our work builds on the analysis in Kelchen (2020), which examined the extent to which institutional and local economic conditions two years or four years earlier were associated with a college closing in a given year.

Classification algorithms such as XGBoost are designed to handle large amounts of incomplete data and are capable of incorporating complex interactions and nonlinear relationships. They are thus likely to be better suited for predicting rare events like college closures or financial distress compared with traditional linear probability estimation or compared with extant score-based accountability metrics (we directly test this hypothesis below).[3] XGBoost is particularly well suited for predictive analytics and builds upon traditional gradient boosting methods while introducing several enhancements that make it particularly efficient and tractable compared with other machine learning algorithms. Because public institutions rarely close, we restrict our sample to private colleges and universities and consider the time period between 2001 and 2023, when the majority of our preferred covariates have at least some coverage.

We then compare the performances of the XGBoost algorithm to several alternative models. First, we estimate a linear probability model using continuous controls consistent with the equation:

$$Y_{it} = \alpha + \beta X_{i,t-2} + \gamma X_{i,t-n} \ldots + \delta W_i \ldots + \theta_t + \varepsilon_{it}, \quad (1)$$

where $Y_{it}$ is an outcome variable denoting either closure or a measure of financial distress (10 percent enrollment decline relative to five-year high, 10 percent revenue decline relative to five- year high, three consecutive years of a negative operating margin, or Heightened Cash Monitoring Level 2 status) as of time $t$. $X_{i,t-n}$ represent lags of varying lengths of time-varying

3. For simplicity, much of the discussion in this section references closures, but we estimate our models for the full set of derived outcome variables enumerated previously. The modeling choices and the proposed principles for using/interpreting the model output translate for all the other metrics of financial distress, as well.

institutional characteristics (e.g., revenue, enrollment), $W_i$ represents time-invariant institutional characteristics (e.g., sector or predominant degree level), and $\theta_t$ represents year fixed effects.

To increase the number of colleges for which we can generate predicted probabilities (in other words, to increase the sample size), we produce a series of least absolute shrinkage and selection operator (LASSO) estimates for each of our outcome variables as part of a data-driven covariate selection process. The LASSO procedure allows us to focus our attention on the set of covariates that produces the smallest out-of-sample mean squared error of the predictions, which allows us to reduce the dimensionality of the prediction problem while simultaneously identifying the strongest predictors of financial distress for colleges. This is important, given the high prevalence of missing values in our data. To put it differently, we can reduce the number of covariates in the linear probability models, which allows us to use more observations and therefore produce predictions of financial distress for more institutions. Once we identify the optimal set of covariates for our sample using the LASSO procedure, we then estimate equation (1) using standard OLS regression.

We also estimate a linear probability model using binned versions of the continuous controls. We do so because we are necessarily restricted to the sample with non-missing covariates if we use continuous values and because linear relationships between the likelihood of closures and measures such as enrollment, staff, or revenue are not necessarily reasonable to assume. With binned controls, we can include observations in "expected missing" bins for each covariate when the field in question is expected to be missing; for example, if a particular institution type was not fielded a particular module in a given year. To put it differently, we can derive predicted closure probabilities for institution-year observations with one or more expected missing values in our sample, which is important in our setting, given that some two-thirds of institution-year observations have at least one expected missing value among covariates most likely to be predictive of closures. We refer to the larger sample (which includes one or more covariates with missing values for a given institution-year) as the "full sample" and to the smaller sample where each covariate is populated for each institution-year as the "non-missing sample."

For an alternative version of the XGBoost algorithm, we also include richer covariates, including additional lags of variables included in the model and a host of additional institutional characteristics that did not rise high enough in the priority list for the limited controls (either continuous or binned) models but might be helpful for increasing predictive accuracy for XGBoost. One set of these additional variables includes lags of county-level covariates (poverty rate, unemployment rate, log of population, and income per capita) to ascertain whether the local economic environment might be contributing to college financial distress.

To compare the performance of these predictive models, we split our observations into 75 percent training data and 25 percent evaluation data, then estimate the different models on the two described samples of our training data. This results in a total of six model-data pairs, which we can then compare in terms of goodness-of-fit measures (such as the area under the curve, or AUC, considering acceptable true positive rates, or TPR, and false positive rates, or FPR).[4]

The model-data pairs are:

A. Linear probability model using select continuous variables—non-missing sample

B. Linear probability model with LASSO selection using select continuous variables—non-missing sample

C. Linear probability model using select binned variables—full sample

D. Gradient boosting algorithm using select binned variables—full sample

E. Gradient boosting algorithm using select continuous variables—full sample

F. Gradient boosting algorithm using all continuous variables—full sample

In theory, each subsequent model could improve upon predictive ability, either by improving accuracy conditional on sample (e.g., E → F) or by improving sample size and therefore the set of institutions for which prediction can be generated (e.g., A → B).

### 3.4.2 Assessing Potential Screening Models for Detecting Closures

The focus of this analysis is on predicting college closures, rather than causally identifying the effect of particular covariates on the probability of closure. For this reason, we focus much of the discussion on the predictive accuracy of the models, rather than the direction or magnitude of individual coefficients. That said, we also analyze our model output to ascertain feature importance and identify covariates that contribute most to predictive accuracy, while cautioning the reader that prediction models that do not take into account causation are inherently unstable. Analysts should take care to monitor model performance carefully, especially with respect to evolution over time.

We use the predicted probabilities of closure from the models to derive metrics of predictive precision. This allows us to examine the relationship between model choice and the accuracy of closure predictions, and to con-

4. The AUC is the area under the ROC curve, which is created by plotting the true positive rate (TPR) against the false positive rate (FPR) at various thresholds. The ROC curve compares the models' TPR and FPR to a random assignment. A higher AUC implies that the model is more successful at correctly classifying the binary outcome. An AUC of 0.5 essentially means that the model is no better than random chance, while models with AUCs in excess of 0.8 or 0.9 are considered highly effective at correctly classifying the outcome.

sider ways in which predictions like ours can be interpreted and used for monitoring the higher education sector. This includes both the possibility of false positive and of false negative predictions when transforming predicted probabilities into binary classifiers.

The output from our models can be used in at least two commonly accepted ways. First, the predicted probabilities can be used in their continuous form to consider relative risks, including by rank-ordering institutions. The predicted probabilities serve a "distance to default" sort of purpose, similar to the FRC score calculated by the Department of Education, which may be particularly helpful in sorting institutions into "zones of danger," as well as in monitoring risk of financial distress over time. They can also be used to prioritize additional data collection or examination, along the lines of Internal Revenue Service audits; an economical auditor will know to stratify their examinations, selecting higher shares of institutions with higher predicted risk and no institutions with very low predicted risk.

Second, the predictions can be translated into binary classifiers, akin to government metrics such as HCM2, meant to serve as a warning sign for institutions that could be at risk. For any such metric, there is a trade-off between false positives (institutions included in the list that will not ultimately close) and false negatives (institutions at moderate risk of closure that are not placed on the list). In illustrative examples, we show how the models estimated in this paper can be used in conjunction with threshold selection methodologies in ways that perform better than currently used metrics of financial risk. To formalize this, we estimate both XGBoost and linear probability models using the two key federal accountability metrics—HCM2 and the FRC score—and compare the predictions from these models to predictions from our preferred full models with the richest controls. These estimates can serve as a useful benchmark for the predictive accuracy of our models.

### 3.4.3 Simulating Changes in Closures

With a model predicting college closures in hand, we can use the estimated coefficients to simulate aggregate predicted closures under different potential fiscal paths for institutions of higher education. In other words, what types of institutions may be at risk of financial distress in the future given reasonable and extreme scenarios on enrollment, revenue, and expense trends? Still on the horizon for many schools is the so-called "demographic cliff," which might see overall higher education enrollment drop by as much as 15 percent from 2025 to 2029. These effects would be concentrated locally and regionally based on declines in college-age populations resulting from changes in migration and fertility rates, such that some institutions of higher education (e.g., those in the Northeast and Midwest) could see even larger downturns, while others (e.g., those serving Hispanic students) would be largely unaffected.

To start, we use 2019 as a baseline, and estimate the change (increase) in closures suggested by our estimated coefficients for the following scenarios:

a) The enrollment declines institutions have experienced since 2019 persist into the future (with no recovery or further decline), or

b) The predicted "demographic cliff" style (e.g., Grawe 2018) aggregate enrollment declines of 15 percent from 2025 to 2029 come to pass, considering two potential manifestations:

a. A onetime 15 percent drop in enrollment, with no further declines but a permanently lower level of enrollment, and
b. An annual enrollment decline such that the aggregate enrollment decline reaches 15 percent by 2029.

We make certain assumptions to approximate a more realistic scenario, since it is unlikely that enrollment would change in isolation. Instead, we assume that revenues and expenses scale with enrollment, and that institutions maintain the same revenue and expense shares when this occurs. This likely results in a conservative estimate of the number of closures because of the presence of fixed costs such as facilities and tenured faculty at many institutions.

## 3.5 Results—Predictive Accuracy

### 3.5.1 Closures Predictions—Overall Accuracy

Consistent with our methodology discussion in the previous section, we estimate linear probability (including classic OLS and LASSO-informed OLS) and XGBoost models with different sets of controls: selected continuous covariates, selected binned covariates, and a full set of available covariates. We do so for two samples: 2002–2023 (full sample) and for 2006–2020 (sample for which federal accountability metrics are more consistently available). We define our closure outcome in two ways: as "closed in year *t*" and as "closed within three years of year *t*." The two measures are complementary; one can imagine circumstances in which predicting the specific year of closure may be desirable, but "closing soon" may be sufficient in others. Ex ante, we suspect that our models may perform better in predicting closures that are coming "soon" without being required to predict the specific year of those closures as well.

Again, owing to missing values, sample sizes vary considerably, being by far the lowest for the linear probability models with continuous covariates and no help from LASSO. We compare AUC metrics for each of the models, samples, covariates, and outcome measures we consider in table 3.5, below, in order to arrive at our preferred model. For all specifications other than "All Controls," we use two-year and three-year lags of all time-variant control variables, which we identify as the optimal number of lags based on a

**Table 3.5** **Predictive accuracy for linear regression and XGBoost models, 2002–2021**

| | | | Closure (point in time) | | | Closure (within 3 yrs) | | |
|---|---|---|---|---|---|---|---|---|
| Sample | Model | Controls | Predicted Closures | AUC | Sample Size | Predicted Closures | AUC | Sample Size |
| 2002–2023 | Linear Probability | Select Continuous | 16 | 78.7% | 2,990 | 32 | 81.8% | 2,062 |
| | Linear Probability—LASSO | Select Continuous | 35 | 83.4% | 3,415 | 59 | 84.4% | 2,353 |
| | Linear Probability | Select Binned | 327 | 75.6% | 20,596 | 1,172 | 76.2% | 18,073 |
| | XGBoost | Select Binned | 267 | 76.9% | 20,596 | 1,073 | 80.6% | 18,073 |
| | XGBoost | Select Continuous | 253 | 80.6% | 20,596 | 1,060 | 82.8% | 18,073 |
| | XGBoost | All | 231 | 81.8% | 20,596 | 1,023 | 86.8% | 18,073 |
| 2006–2020 | Linear Probability | Federal Metrics | 158 | 76.5% | 10,331 | 586 | 78.8% | 9,107 |
| | XGBoost | Federal Metrics | 257 | 77.4% | 16,800 | 978 | 79.5% | 14,240 |
| | Linear Probability | Select Continuous | 16 | 78.7% | 2,990 | 32 | 81.8% | 2,062 |
| | Linear Probability—LASSO | Select Continuous | 35 | 83.3% | 3,414 | 59 | 84.4% | 2,352 |
| | Linear Probability | Select Binned | 291 | 75.6% | 16,800 | 1,037 | 77.4% | 14,240 |
| | XGBoost | Select Binned | 234 | 78.5% | 16,800 | 940 | 82.2% | 14,240 |
| | XGBoost | Select Continuous | 219 | 81.5% | 16,800 | 930 | 83.7% | 14,240 |
| | XGBoost | All | 197 | 83.1% | 16,800 | 893 | 88.6% | 14,240 |

Source: Authors' calculations based on IPEDS, PEPS Closed School Reports, College Scorecard, Federal Student Aid, US Bureau of Economic Analysis, US Census Bureau, and US Bureau of Labor Statistics data, 2002–2023.

Note: Models estimated or trained on 75 percent of institution-year observations. Predictions and area under the curve (AUC) reported for remaining evaluation observations (25 percent). Closure is measured both as point-in-time (closed in given year) and in a three-year window (closed within three years of current year). There were 342 actual closures (1,091 within three years) in the 2002–2021 sample and 305 (945 within three years) in the 2006–2020 sample.

comparison of AUCs for models with increasingly larger numbers of lags of the same set of covariates. Once we bring in a fuller set of covariates in "All Controls," we allow up to five lags in the XGBoost model; the linear probability models perform quite poorly for this larger set of covariates, so we omit those results from the table.

As shown in table 3.5, with AUCs approaching or in excess of 80 percent, most of the models can be considered highly predictive, especially on more well-populated data. But the XGBoost model outperforms the linear probability models consistently on the evaluation data set (25 percent of observations). This can be surmised using the combined objectives of predictive accuracy (informed by the AUC) and the ability to consider a fuller set of institutions (informed by the sample size). To illustrate this, it is instructive to follow the progression of predicted closures and AUCs across the rows of the upper panel of table 3.5, which use the full 2002–2023 sample.

Beginning with the linear probability model using continuous controls, the sample size is only 2,990 institution-year observations, which represents only 15 percent of the available sample, owing to the prevalence of the missing data. So, although the AUC is a respectable 78.7 percent, the model predicts only 16 closures because it is unable to generate predictions for the vast majority of institutions. In the next row, we employ the LASSO procedure to restrict the number of covariates to only the most predictive ones, still using continuous controls like in the previous specification. This increases the sample size slightly, improves the AUC to a magnitude comparable to the XGBoost models (83.4 percent), and increases the number of predicted closures to 35, yet this is still far from the actual number of closed institutions of 335 in the evaluation data set. Finally, when we use binned controls that include a category for expected missing values for each covariate, we are able to consider most institution-year observations using OLS (20,596, because some observations still get dropped owing to unexpected missing values), such that the model predicts a more on-target 327 closures. However, the predictive accuracy drops to 75.6 percent, meaning that the model discriminates less well because of the implicit imputation inherent in using the binning method. We also note that the OLS-based AUCs are more unstable and vary more than XGBoost AUCs—often significantly outperforming XGBoost, even with the use of LASSO—with relatively minor changes in the sample period.

In the row that follows, we show that using the XGBoost model on the same binned controls as the OLS improves predictive accuracy to an AUC of 76.9 percent and allows us to consider the full sample of 20,596 institution-year observations in the evaluation data. For that same sample, XGBoost does even better using continuous versions of the binned controls (an AUC of 80.6 percent), and better still using the fullest available set of covariates including fourth and fifth lags, county controls, institutional features, and even richer financial metrics (an AUC of 81.8 percent).

In other words, the missing data in our assembled institution-level data set are costly in terms of predictive power, but the machine learning model can account for the missing data much more effectively than a linear probability model. Conditional on targeting the same AUC of about 79–80 percent, there are benefits to using XGBoost compared with binned OLS because researchers can estimate closure probabilities for the full sample of institutions, thereby considering institutions with and without missing data. In other words, machine learning compared with linear probability models can buy researchers either accuracy (a higher AUC for same sample relative to linear probability) or reliability when some of the data are missing (the same AUC on a larger sample of institutions). The trade-off is that these methods can be rather data intensive and may require more training for the analyst, which may limit their use in certain contexts.

Also, in the upper panel of table 3.5, we provide comparable estimates considering "closed within three years" as the closure outcome variable in the last three columns. As before, the relative performance of XGBoost compared with linear probability using the various forms of our covariates is unchanged relative to the point-in-time definition of closure. The peak predictive accuracy we can achieve is considerably better using this definition of "closure," reaching an AUC of 86.8 percent in our preferred specification with the richest controls. For simplicity of interpretation, we focus on the predicted probability of closure at a point in time in some of the following sections, while generally preferring a definition of closure with a longer time window because of its promising improvement in predictive performance.

To benchmark our models against existing methods, in the lower panel of table 3.5, we provide estimates of predicted number of closures and AUCs for the same models as before, but considering the 2006–2020 period, when we have better coverage for the key federal accountability metrics. This allows us to estimate both XGBoost and linear probability models using the two key federal accountability metrics—HCM2 and the FRC score—as key predictors, along with sector and year fixed effects. We can then compare the predictions from these models to predictions from our preferred full models with the richest controls, using the federal metrics models as a useful benchmark for the predictive power of our own models. In the first two rows of the bottom panel of table 3.5, we show that XGBoost outperforms OLS even on the model with federal metrics, both in terms of AUCs and in terms of number of institutions with predictions (and therefore total number of predicted closures), and especially for the definition of closure as "closed within three years."

With an AUC of 88.6 percent, the XGBoost with the richest controls significantly outperforms even the 79.5 percent AUC of the XGBoost on the federal metrics. That said, we note that the FRC score does have predictive power, even controlling for all the richest financial, student, and staff data. But as a stand-alone measure, it significantly underperforms the full

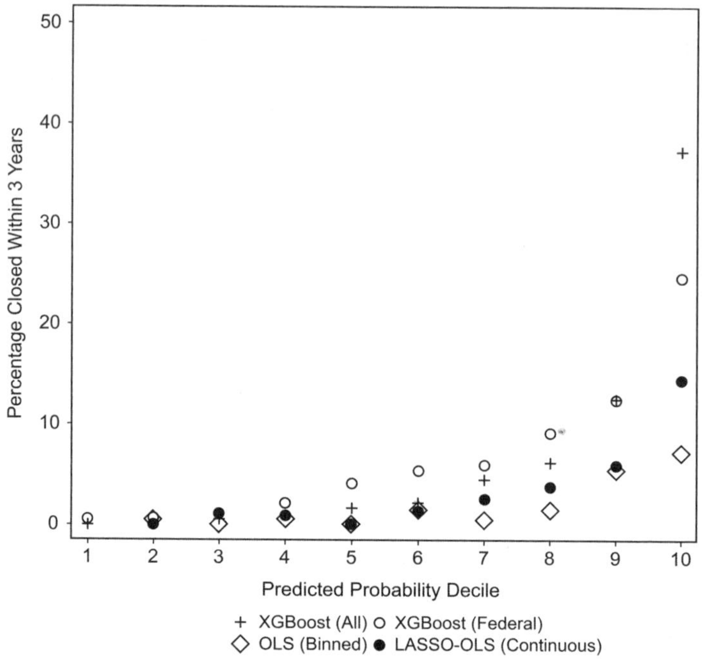


**Fig. 3.6a Relationship between predicted and actual closures, share institutions closed by prediction decile, 2006–2021**

Source: Authors' calculations based on IPEDS, PEPS Closed School Reports, College Scorecard, Federal Student Aid, US Bureau of Economic Analysis, US Census Bureau, and US Bureau of Labor Statistics data, 2002–2023.

machine learning model. What is more, the FRC score's usefulness is limited in the broader context of predicting severe financial distress for all institutions since it is only available for private colleges, while our preferred models can be easily estimated for all institutions. Finally, because they are designed as a point-in-time measure, the federal metrics do not benefit from the alternate definition of closure (within three years), while the XGBoost model performs much better with the alternate closure definition on the better populated 2006–2020 data than on the 2002–2023 data. Reassuringly, our preferred model is most predictive for institutions whose closures are likely to be more impactful to their local economies, namely larger institutions (featuring near-perfect predictive accuracy for institutions with more than 5,000 students) and four-year institutions.

Next, we turn to an analysis of actual and predicted closure probabilities in figures 3.6a–3.6b, sorting our predicted values for each model into deciles. We present the share of institutions that actually closed within three years by prediction decile in figure 3.6a. As expected, given our relatively high AUCs, the share of institutions that actually closed increases with the predicted

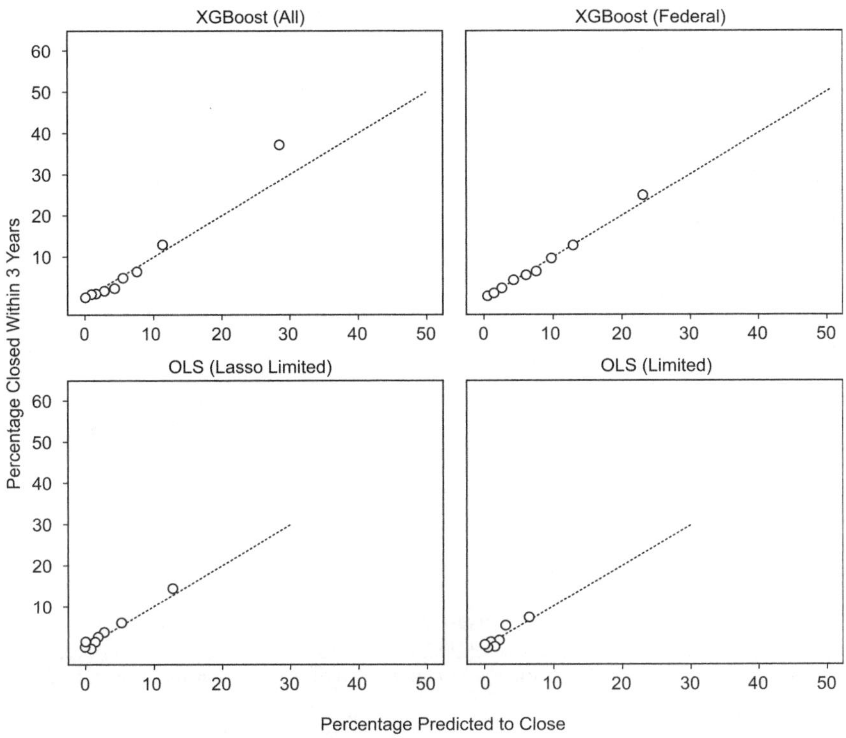


**Fig. 3.6b Relationship between predicted and actual closures, actual v. predicted closures for each prediction decile, 2006–2021**

Source: Authors' calculations based on IPEDS, PEPS Closed School Reports, College Scorecard, Federal Student Aid, US Bureau of Economic Analysis, US Census Bureau, and US Bureau of Labor Statistics data, 2002–2023.

Note: Dashed line represents the line where share of institutions predicted to close within three years would equal share actually closed within that time period.

probability decile, reaching a high of 34 percent of institutions closed in the top decile for the XGBoost model with all controls. The XGBoost model with federal metrics and the binned OLS model follow somewhat behind, while the LASSO OLS model performs rather poorly along this dimension. Then in figure 3.6b, we give a sense of the alignment between predicted and actual closures with the share of institutions that actually closed within three years against the share predicted to close in each of our models, for each model's prediction deciles. Once more, XGBoost significantly outperforms the other models. In fact, the model does especially well among the riskiest institutions (not shown in the figures). Some 84 percent of the 100 institutions with the highest predicted probability of closure actually closed within three years, compared with 47 percent for the federal metrics model and 61 percent for OLS with binned controls.

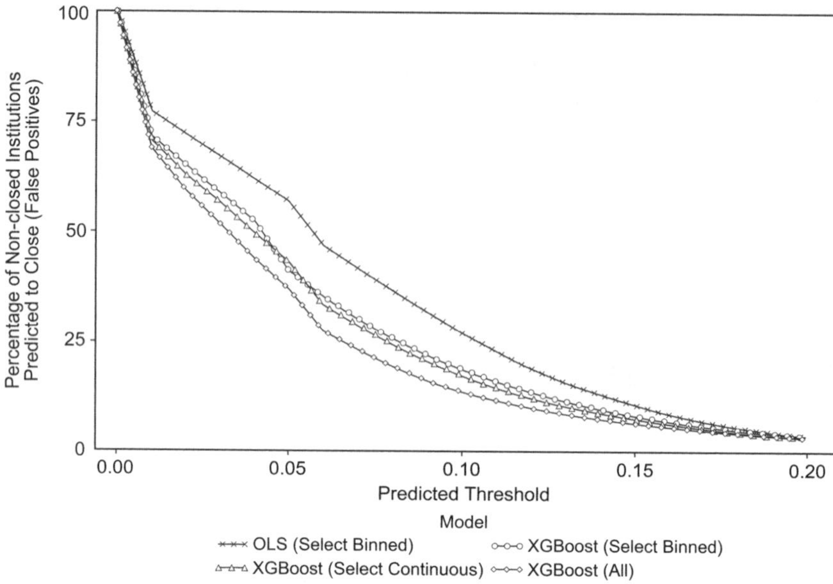


**Fig. 3.7a False positive rates for closure predictions, by model, 2002–2023**
Source: Authors' calculations based on IPEDS, PEPS Closed School Reports, College Scorecard, Federal Student Aid, US Bureau of Economic Analysis, US Census Bureau, and US Bureau of Labor Statistics data, 2002–2023.

Next, we consider the performance of our models under simple binary sorting mechanisms, displaying the implied false positive/negative rates conditional on a chosen threshold of "predicted closure." In other words, we show the false positive/negative rates based on the threshold at which an institution would be predicted to close for each of the models in figures 3.7a–3.7b, below. All models have relatively low false positive rates, even at low thresholds, although the XGBoost false positive rates are a little lower (figure 3.7a). Yet figure 3.7b shows that false negative rates, conversely, are quite high, even at low thresholds. This is because the distributions of predicted probabilities are skewed strongly to the left, as shown in figure 3.8. This is to be expected, given that closure is a rather rare event.

Consistent with our AUC measures, the machine learning model has lower false negative rates at moderate thresholds, as shown in figure 3.7b. This is because the right tail of the distribution of predicted closure probabilities is thicker and longer for this model relative to any of the three linear probability models. The sector-specific predicted closure probability distributions, included in figures 3A.1a–3A.1d, show that the improvement in accuracy in the right tail for the machine learning model comes predominantly from more accurately predicting closures of for-profit institutions. This is partially an artifact of the larger share of true positives that come from this segment, yet it might be an appealing feature for regulatory or accrediting agencies.

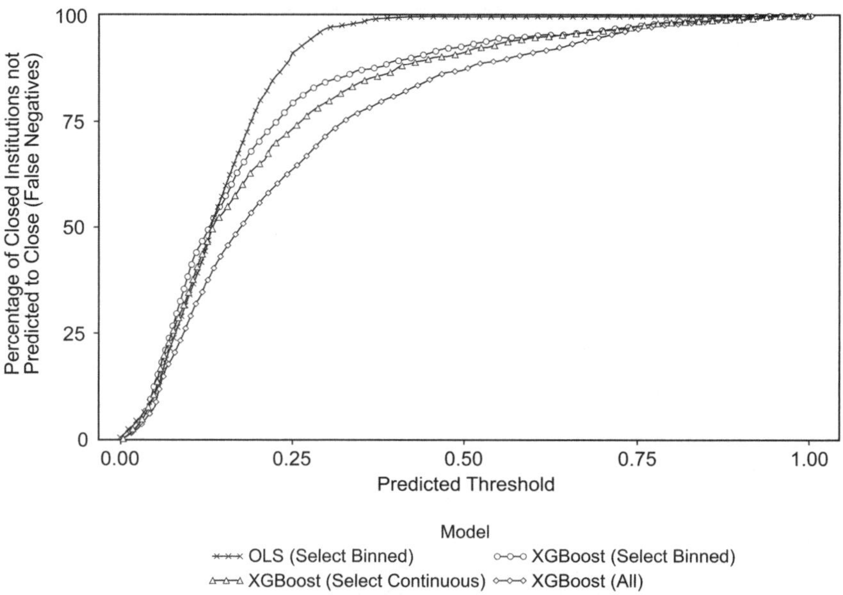


**Fig. 3.7b False negative rates for closure predictions, by model, 2002–2023**
Source: Authors' calculations based on IPEDS, PEPS Closed School Reports, College Scorecard, Federal Student Aid, US Bureau of Economic Analysis, US Census Bureau, and US Bureau of Labor Statistics data, 2002–2023.

Overall, the XGBoost algorithm performs considerably better in predicting institutions with very high probabilities of closure. To provide further insights regarding the accuracy of the models, we compare the ability of multiple models to correctly predict closures in the cases that were viewed as having the highest likelihood of closure within three years. Restricting our attention to the subset of the evaluation data sets for which there are complete data (over 16,000 institution-year observations), 83 of the 100 observations with the highest predicted closure probabilities and 278 of the 500 observations with the highest predicted closure probabilities from the XGBoost model with all available controls closed within three years. Meanwhile, our OLS models with binned controls had insufficient data to estimate data on 1,240 observations (including 79 closures) and only saw 46 of the 100 highest predictions and 177 of the 500 highest predictions closed within three years.

### 3.5.2 Feature Importance Across Models

As noted above, the majority of our analysis focuses on predictive power and accuracy of the overall models. This is done for two related reasons. First, without a causal research design, the interpretation of individual coefficients is correlational, at best. Second, the fact that many variables are highly correlated with one another, and in many cases are functions of one

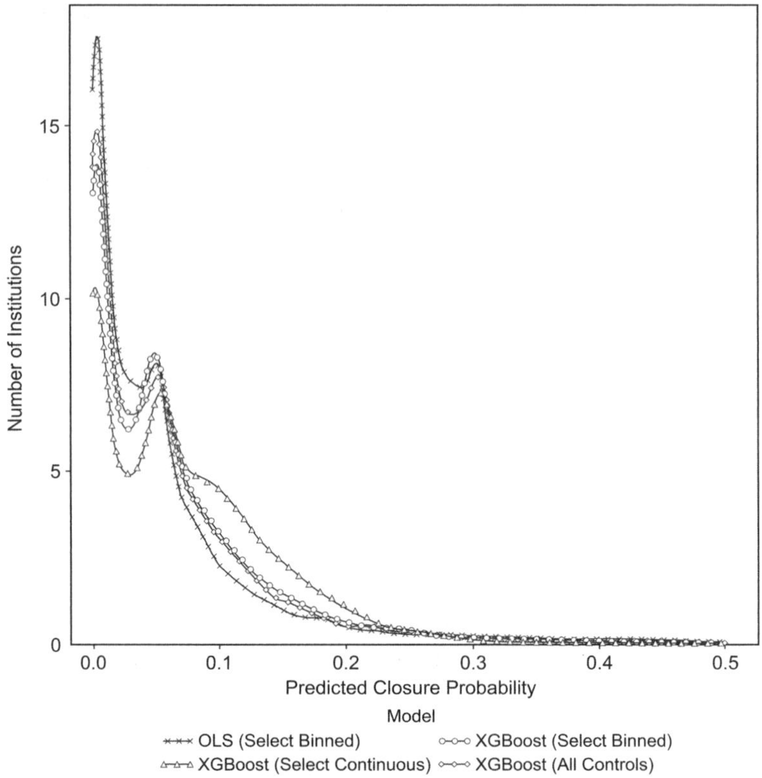


**Fig. 3.8 Distribution of predicted closure probabilities by model, 2002–2023**

Source: Authors' calculations based on IPEDS, PEPS Closed School Reports, College Scorecard, Federal Student Aid, US Bureau of Economic Analysis, US Census Bureau, and US Bureau of Labor Statistics data, 2002–2023.

Note: Lines represent kernel density functions, concentrating on the portion of the distribution where the vast majority of the institutions' predicted closure probabilities (predicted closure probability of 0.5 or less) lie.

another, makes any interpretation of magnitude very difficult. For instance, the Financial Responsibility Composite Score is a function of a number of different financial metrics. These metrics are either directly or indirectly in our models (or at least at risk of being selected by the LASSO procedure). These metrics themselves are then functions of other key variables such as enrollment and the recent change in enrollment. In other words, it is difficult to interpret even the magnitude of any given coefficient because it is nonsensical to discuss the partial effect (e.g., holding all other variables constant), when that cannot conceivably happen in most cases. Having these various classes of variables in the model is still very important for predictive reasons, particularly because nonlinearity is of outsized importance for predicting rare and extreme events such as the closure of an institution.

However, while the magnitude of coefficients is difficult (in the case of OLS) or impossible (in the case of some machine learning models) to quantify, this does not mean that we cannot provide evidence on the relative importance of different covariates. Table 3.6 presents measures of relative importance for variables in five of the predictive models on which we focused. For each of the three XGBoost models, relative importance is measured by the gain in predictive power from models that include the variable compared with models that do not include it, averaged over every version of each model estimated. For the two OLS models presented in table 3.6, variables are ranked based on their *p*-values, and standardized coefficients are included.[5]

While we don't want to focus on any given variable for the reasons discussed above, there are still some broad takeaway messages from table 3.6 that may be useful for researchers and policymakers. First, reassuringly, the variables that should have a strong theoretical impact on the likelihood of closure (e.g., measures of financial distress) are well represented across all models. Second, particularly for the XGBoost models, variables measuring ratios of financial metrics and those measuring changes in covariates are generally more important than those measuring the level of those covariates. This is an intuitive finding, and it argues for the inclusion of recent trajectory as an important metric that should be considered by monitoring agencies in addition to absolute levels, but it is not currently part of federal accountability policy.

Comparing the classes of variables that are identified as influential in the XGBoost compared with OLS models, we can again find support for the utility of machine learning methodology in predicting closures. First, year fixed effects are much more important predictors in the OLS models; our preferred models do not include year fixed effects because of their limited utility in this context.[6] Nevertheless, we estimated our models with year fixed effects (not shown) and found them to be marginal contributors to predictive accuracy only for the linear models but not predictive in the machine learning models. For the XGBoost models, which allow for more complex interactions and nonlinear relationships, it is the underlying metrics (e.g., financial conditions) that are of greater relative importance. In OLS models, it is more common for the model to imply "there is something about a particular year that is important, but we don't know what it is," while machine learning models can better identify which underlying metrics are actually important. That said, even XGBoost models indicate that a portion of closure propensity for private nonprofit four-year institutions cannot be captured very well

5. For the most part, the variables with the strongest p-values also happen to be those with the highest standardized coefficients in the OLS models.

6. In any predictive model, future time fixed effects (e.g., the knowledge of whether a given year had many or few aggregate closures, all else equal) are unknown. To put it differently, year effects may be useful in predicting past closures but not future ones.

**Table 3.6** **Key predictors of closure and contribution to prediction, select models, 2002–2021**

| XGBoost Models | | | | | |
|---|---|---|---|---|---|
| XGBoost (All Controls) | | XGBoost (Continuous) | | XGBoost (Binned) | |
| Covariate | Gain | Covariate | Gain | Covariate | Gain |
| L2 FRC Score | 4.0% | L3 Enroll % change | 4.0% | L2 Enroll % change 1stQ | 3.2% |
| L2 Enroll % change | 2.4% | L2 OP Margin | 4.0% | L3 Revenue % GGC 1stQ | 2.6% |
| L2 Total EAP % change | 2.1% | L2 Enroll % change | 3.9% | L3 Enroll % change 1stQ | 2.5% |
| L3 Enroll % change | 2.0% | L2 Total EAP % change | 3.9% | L2 Revenue % GGC 1stQ | 2.1% |
| L2 Revenue % change | 1.9% | L2 EAP % Instruction | 3.8% | L2 Salaries % Staff 1stQ | 2.0% |
| L4 Revenue % change | 1.8% | L2 Revenue % change | 3.6% | L2 DCOH 3rdQ | 2.0% |
| PNFP 4yr | 1.8% | L3 Revenue % change | 3.3% | L2 Total EAP % change 1stQ | 1.9% |
| L2 Staff Total | 1.7% | PNFP 4yr | 2.9% | L3 Revenue % change 1stQ | 1.8% |
| L3 Revenue % change | 1.6% | L2 Expenses % Instruction | 2.7% | L2 Revenue % change 1stQ | 1.7% |
| L2 EAP % Instruction | 1.6% | L2 EAP % ft | 2.6% | L2 Expenses % Interest 1stQ | 1.4% |
| L2 Salaries % Staff | 1.6% | L3 OP Margin | 2.6% | L3 Total EAP % change 1stQ | 1.4% |
| L2 OP Margin | 1.5% | L2 Revenue % Tuition | 2.5% | L2 Log Unrestricted Assets 4thQ | 1.4% |
| L2 Log Unrestricted Assets | 1.5% | L3 Expenses % Instruction | 2.4% | L3 OP Margin 3rdQ | 1.3% |
| L3 FRC Score | 1.3% | L2 Log Unrestricted Assets | 2.4% | L2 DCOH 1stQ | 1.2% |
| L5 Revenue % GGC | 1.2% | L3 Revenue % Tuition | 2.4% | L3 EAP % ft 1stQ | 1.1% |
| L2 DCOH | 1.1% | L3 Total EAP % change | 2.3% | L2 Debt to Assets 1stQ | 1.1% |
| L2 Revenue % Tuition | 1.1% | L3 EAP % Instruction | 2.3% | L2 OP Margin 1stQ | 1.1% |
| L4 Expenses % Instruction | 1.1% | L2 Log Enroll 12mo | 2.0% | L2 Revenue % Tuition 4thQ | 1.0% |
| L2 Expenses % Instruction | 1.1% | L3 Log expenses | 2.0% | L2 EAP % ft 1stQ | 1.0% |

| Linear Probability Models | | | | | |
|---|---|---|---|---|---|
| OLS (Binned) | | | OLS—Lasso (Continuous) | | |
| Variable | Standardized Coeff. | *P*-Value | Variable | Standardized Coeff. | *P*-Value |
| L2 EAP % Instruction 4thQ | 0.8% | 0.00 | L2 DCOH | −4.8% | 0.00 |
| L2 DCOH 1stQ | −1.1% | 0.00 | L3 DCOH | 4.5% | 0.00 |
| L2 EAP % Instruction 3rdQ | 0.7% | 0.00 | L3 Enroll % change | −0.5% | 0.00 |
| L2 Deprec. % Expenses 1stQ | 0.7% | 0.00 | L2 Log expenses | −10.2% | 0.00 |
| L2 Log Unrestricted Assets 1stQ | −2.7% | 0.00 | L2 Expenses % Instruction | −1.3% | 0.00 |
| L3 Log Unrestricted Assets 1stQ | 2.7% | 0.00 | L3 Log expenses | 9.7% | 0.00 |
| L2 Debt to Assets 1stQ | 2.9% | 0.00 | L3 Expenses % Instruction | 1.0% | 0.00 |
| L2 EAP % Instruction 2ndQ | 0.6% | 0.00 | L2 HCM2 indicator | 0.4% | 0.00 |
| L2 Log Unrestricted Assets 4thQ | 1.2% | 0.00 | L2 Five % Enroll 3yr | 0.4% | 0.00 |
| L3 Debt to Assets 1stQ | −2.6% | 0.00 | L3 Five % Enroll 3yr | 0.4% | 0.00 |
| L3 Deprec. % Expenses 1stQ | −0.7% | 0.00 | L2 Total EAP % change | 0.3% | 0.02 |
| L2 Log Unrestricted Assets 3rdQ | 0.8% | 0.00 | L3 HCM2 indicator | 0.3% | 0.03 |
| L3 DCOH 1stQ | 0.7% | 0.00 | L3 Ten % Revenue 5yr | 0.2% | 0.05 |
| L2 EAP % Instruction 1stQ | 0.5% | 0.00 | L3 DBT asst PP change | 0.2% | 0.05 |
| L2 DCOH 2ndQ | −0.5% | 0.00 | L2 Revenue % Tuition | 0.6% | 0.06 |
| L2 Log Unrestricted Assets 2ndQ | 0.7% | 0.00 | L3 Revenue % Tuition | −0.6% | 0.06 |
| L3 Revenue % auxiliary 1stQ | 0.9% | 0.00 | L2 Log EBITDA | 0.6% | 0.08 |
| L3 Deprec. % Expenses 2ndQ | −0.5% | 0.00 | L3 DCOH change | 0.2% | 0.09 |
| L3 OP Margin PP change 1stQ | 0.5% | 0.00 | L3 Ten % Enroll 5yr | −0.2% | 0.15 |

Source: Authors' calculations based on IPEDS, PEPS Closed School Reports, College Scorecard, Federal Student Aid, US Bureau of Economic Analysis, US Census Bureau, and US Bureau of Labor Statistics data, 2002–2023.

Note: Key predictors identified from models where closure is defined as within three years of evaluation year.

by the observables.[7] This speaks to idiosyncratic, unobservable factors—like governance—likely having a role in closures of these institutions. On the other hand, the machine learning models—especially those with the richest covariates—generally perform quite well in explaining financial distress among for-profit institutions using available historical data. Importantly, this increase in performance is due to richer institution-level covariates and not county-level controls; county-level covariates appear quite low in the feature importance lists for the XGBoost model with the richest controls. XGBoost models omitting those county-level controls perform just as well as those considered in table 3.5.

We note that these key predictors are intended to be illustrative and should not be used outside of this methodology with the expectation of comparable predictive accuracy. They are helpful in understanding the qualitative differences between the models and the performance improvements machine learning methodologies brings to the table by using a longer time series of richer data with a more flexible estimation. In other words, the improvements in predictive power we present are only possible because we (1) assembled a long time series, (2) collected and synchronized a large number of variables, and (3) used a machine learning model. We recognize that this combination of data and methodological choices renders our methodology more complex and time-consuming to adopt compared with focusing on a small number of commonly used metrics.

### 3.5.3 Closure Predictions—Targeting Annual Closures

Next, we consider the potential performance of a screening mechanism targeting the predicted number of closures (i.e., the sum of predicted closure probabilities) comparable in magnitude with the actual number of closures. In other words, with the predicted probabilities in hand, what would happen if we selected the "optimal" screening method for detecting institutions likely to close by selecting the optimal prediction threshold such that we predict approximately the correct number of closures in our evaluation data set (again, the 25 percent of data withheld from the training models)? Since closure is such a low-probability event, setting the target threshold low enough to only predict the relatively few closures that actually occur implies rates of false positives and true negatives that leave much to be desired. Of the actual closures in the 2002–2023 evaluation data set, the XGBoost model predicts very few institutions accurately, and the binned linear probability

7. For the most recent years of data, the CARES Act funding to colleges and universities affected smaller PNFP four-year institutions in particular, so the sector dummy is likely picking up some of the effect of that funding on financial solvency of smaller institutions. This might mean that enrollment changes are a better harbinger of doom for those types of institutions than financials because financials effectively have an error term incorporated in certain circumstances.

model even fewer; the remaining institutions flagged as "likely to close" based on the implied threshold are all false positives.

Because of the missing data, the linear probability model with binned covariates detects only 35 closed institutions, or some 1 in 10 closures in the evaluation data set. The false positive rate appears relatively low only because the models are unable to provide any prediction for the vast majority of institutions, including the vast majority of institutions that closed. This exercise illustrates a key feature of prediction models on low-probability outcomes: They are not terribly good at *simultaneously* predicting the correct number of closures and predicting the timing of those few closures very accurately.

### 3.5.4 Closures Predictions—Targeting True Positive Rates

To illustrate the predictive capabilities of the models, we use each of them in a simple screening methodology based on a target true positive rate. We consider: What would be the true/false positive/negative rates if, for each model, we selected the threshold such that we detect *at least* 50 percent, 60 percent, 70 percent, or 80 percent of true positives?[8] In other words, how many institutions would a regulatory or accrediting agency have to monitor in order to "catch" most of the real closures? As we discussed previously, the predicted closure probabilities our models output can be used in a variety of ways, including many more complex than what we consider here. For example, an economical auditor will know to rank order institutions and then select the share to audit in a stratified manner, sampling a higher share of institutions with higher predicted closure probabilities. We are not suggesting that the exercise we conduct here is in any way prescriptive as to the optimal screening technology, but rather illustrative of the trade-offs between the models and the clear improvement in performance of the XGBoost model with all controls.

The results of this illustrative example are presented in table 3.7. The clear trade-off between the target true positive rate and the false positive rate with a prediction algorithm that has any power to discriminate, as ours do, is evident here. The false positive rate (the percent of total institutions that did not close but were predicted to close) for the best-performing model, XGBoost, ranges from 12 percent in the full sample with a true positive rate of 51 percent, to 51 percent when the true positive rate is 92 percent. In other words, a regulator would have to screen only one-tenth of institutions in order to detect half of true closures, but a full half of institutions in order to detect 92 percent of true closures—even for institutions with (some) missing data.

8. In our application, targeting a true positive rate of 90 percent would cause the optimal threshold to be close to 0, such that nearly 100 percent of institutions that did not close to be predicted to close, so we omit the results for brevity.

**Table 3.7** **Predictive power based on target true positive rate, by model, 2002–2021**

| | | | Closures | | Non-Closures | | | | True Positives | | | False Negatives | | | False Positives | | | Closures w/ No Prediction | |
|---|---|---|---|---|---|---|---|---|---|---|---|---|---|---|---|---|---|---|---|
| Sample | Model | Controls | In Sample | Total | In Sample | Total | Target % of True Positives In Sample | Implied Threshold | # | % in Sample | % of Total | # | % in Sample | % of Total | # | % in Sample | % of Total | # | % of Total |
| 2006–2020 | XGBoost | Federal Metrics | 305 | 305 | 16,495 | 16,495 | 50% | 0.027 | 155 | 51% | 51% | 150 | 49% | 49% | 2,771 | 17% | 17% | 0 | 0% |
| 2002–2023 | OLS | Select Binned | 342 | 342 | 20,254 | 20,254 | 50% | 0.034 | 174 | 51% | 51% | 168 | 49% | 49% | 2,981 | 15% | 15% | 0 | 0% |
| 2002–2023 | XGBoost | Select Continuous | 342 | 342 | 20,254 | 20,254 | 50% | 0.026 | 171 | 50% | 50% | 171 | 50% | 50% | 2,188 | 11% | 11% | 0 | 0% |
| 2002–2023 | XGBoost | All | 342 | 342 | 20,254 | 20,254 | 50% | 0.021 | 174 | 51% | 51% | 168 | 49% | 49% | 2,397 | 12% | 12% | 0 | 0% |
| 2002–2023 | OLS LASSO | Select Continuous | 26 | 342 | 3,389 | 20,254 | 50% | 0.057 | 13 | 50% | 4% | 13 | 50% | 4% | 89 | 3% | 0% | 316 | 92% |
| 2006–2020 | XGBoost | Federal Metrics | 305 | 305 | 16,495 | 16,495 | 60% | 0.02 | 186 | 61% | 61% | 119 | 39% | 39% | 3,996 | 24% | 24% | 0 | 0% |
| 2002–2023 | OLS | Select Binned | 342 | 342 | 20,254 | 20,254 | 60% | 0.027 | 213 | 62% | 62% | 129 | 38% | 38% | 4,317 | 21% | 21% | 0 | 0% |
| 2002–2023 | XGBoost | Select Continuous | 342 | 342 | 20,254 | 20,254 | 60% | 0.018 | 206 | 60% | 60% | 136 | 40% | 40% | 3,472 | 17% | 17% | 0 | 0% |
| 2002–2023 | XGBoost | All | 342 | 342 | 20,254 | 20,254 | 60% | 0.016 | 207 | 61% | 61% | 135 | 39% | 39% | 3,310 | 16% | 16% | 0 | 0% |
| 2002–2023 | OLS LASSO | Select Continuous | 26 | 342 | 3,389 | 20,254 | 60% | 0.028 | 16 | 62% | 5% | 10 | 38% | 3% | 399 | 12% | 2% | 316 | 92% |
| 2006–2020 | XGBoost | Federal Metrics | 305 | 305 | 16,495 | 16,495 | 70% | 0.017 | 224 | 73% | 73% | 81 | 27% | 27% | 5,115 | 31% | 31% | 0 | 0% |
| 2002–2023 | OLS | Select Binned | 342 | 342 | 20,254 | 20,254 | 70% | 0.018 | 243 | 71% | 71% | 99 | 29% | 29% | 6,749 | 33% | 33% | 0 | 0% |
| 2002–2023 | XGBoost | Select Continuous | 342 | 342 | 20,254 | 20,254 | 70% | 0.015 | 240 | 70% | 70% | 102 | 30% | 30% | 5,754 | 28% | 28% | 0 | 0% |
| 2002–2023 | XGBoost | All | 342 | 342 | 20,254 | 20,254 | 70% | 0.013 | 248 | 73% | 73% | 94 | 27% | 27% | 5,593 | 28% | 28% | 0 | 0% |
| 2002–2023 | OLS LASSO | Select Continuous | 26 | 342 | 3,389 | 20,254 | 70% | 0.015 | 19 | 73% | 6% | 7 | 27% | 2% | 719 | 21% | 4% | 316 | 92% |
| 2006–2020 | XGBoost | Federal Metrics | 305 | 305 | 16,495 | 16,495 | 80% | 0.013 | 247 | 81% | 81% | 58 | 19% | 19% | 6,596 | 40% | 40% | 0 | 0% |
| 2002–2023 | OLS | Select Binned | 342 | 342 | 20,254 | 20,254 | 80% | 0.01 | 299 | 87% | 87% | 43 | 13% | 13% | 12,070 | 60% | 60% | 0 | 0% |
| 2002–2023 | XGBoost | Select Continuous | 342 | 342 | 20,254 | 20,254 | 80% | 0.009 | 288 | 84% | 84% | 54 | 16% | 16% | 8,444 | 42% | 42% | 0 | 0% |
| 2002–2023 | XGBoost | All | 342 | 342 | 20,254 | 20,254 | 80% | 0.01 | 279 | 82% | 82% | 63 | 18% | 18% | 6,720 | 33% | 33% | 0 | 0% |
| 2002–2023 | OLS LASSO | Select Continuous | 26 | 342 | 3,389 | 20,254 | 80% | 0.008 | 21 | 81% | 6% | 5 | 19% | 1% | 1,103 | 33% | 5% | 316 | 92% |
| 2006–2020 | XGBoost | Federal Metrics | 305 | 305 | 16,495 | 16,495 | 90% | 0.007 | 277 | 91% | 91% | 28 | 9% | 9% | 9,097 | 55% | 55% | 0 | 0% |
| 2002–2023 | OLS | Select Binned | 342 | 342 | 20,254 | 20,254 | 90% | 0.006 | 308 | 90% | 90% | 34 | 10% | 10% | 13,564 | 67% | 67% | 0 | 0% |
| 2002–2023 | XGBoost | Select Continuous | 342 | 342 | 20,254 | 20,254 | 90% | 0.006 | 312 | 91% | 91% | 30 | 9% | 9% | 10,437 | 52% | 52% | 0 | 0% |
| 2002–2023 | XGBoost | All | 342 | 342 | 20,254 | 20,254 | 90% | 0.005 | 315 | 92% | 92% | 27 | 8% | 8% | 10,299 | 51% | 51% | 0 | 0% |
| 2002–2023 | OLS LASSO | Select Continuous | 26 | 342 | 3,389 | 20,254 | 90% | 0 | 26 | 100% | 8% | 0 | 0% | 0% | 3,389 | 100% | 17% | 316 | 92% |

Source: Authors' calculations based on IPEDS, PEPS Closed School Reports, College Scorecard, Federal Student Aid, US Bureau of Economic Analysis, US Census Bureau, and US Bureau of Labor Statistics data, 2002–2023.
Note: Models estimated or trained on 75 percent of institution-year observations; predictions reported for remaining 25 percent of observations. Closure is measured within three years of evaluation year.

Screening about one-third of institutions (a false positive rate of 33 percent) with XGBoost would detect over 80 percent of true closures (a true positive rate of 82 percent), and so forth.

While the binned OLS model appears to have generally similar false positive rates to XGBoost, this is the case only because it is unable to produce any prediction at all for 18 percent of institutions owing to unexpected missing values. And XGBoost with the full set of controls consistently outperforms the model with federal metrics, especially at higher target thresholds for true positives. For example, if a regulator wanted to detect 90 percent or more closures, the model with all controls would have a false positive rate of 51 percent and the federal metrics model 55 percent. Finally, using the LASSO OLS produces clearly inferior results in this exercise. Because the model cannot provide a prediction of any kind for the 92 percent of observations with at least one missing covariate, the calculated false positive rates out of the full sample are misleadingly low. In fact, the upper bound on a true positive rate is 8 percent, even if screening all the 2,950 institutions in the relevant sample.

To summarize, table 3.7 suggests that lower false positive rates (in other words, fewer institutions requiring screening for a given true positive rate) using the target threshold method are associated with (a) the full sample compared with the non-missing sample, and (b) the XGBoost algorithm compared with the linear probability models, and (c) the full available metrics compared with the federal metrics.

### 3.5.5 Case Studies of College Closures

To provide some context for our predictions, we examined a few case studies using the results from our models predicting closure within the next three years. The XGBoost models predicted an average likelihood of closure of about 0.058, while the linear regression models predicted an average likelihood of about 0.068.

Our first case study is Birmingham-Southern College, which closed after the spring 2024 semester following years of very public financial stress and a failed effort to get a bond from the state of Alabama (Korn 2024). None of the models accurately reflected the risk that the college faced, with the closure probability being at the median of private nonprofit colleges. This could be because it did not have concerns with federal accountability metrics and had a relatively strong balance sheet owing to its historic endowment, even as net operating losses were common. This reinforces the limitation of the models in accurately predicting idiosyncratic closures of private nonprofit four-year institutions, where unobservable (to the researcher) governance and specialized reasons leading to closure are concealed by financial performance that does not necessarily give rise to concerns.

On the other hand, the models strongly predicted the closure of Judson College in Alabama in 2021. Our XGBoost models had predicted probabilities of as high as 0.25 in 2019 and 0.29 in 2020, including being rated as the seventh most likely private nonprofit college to close in 2020. Meanwhile, closure probabilities in the XGBoost models using only federal data remained below average. Closure risks in the OLS models also remained near or below the sample average for Judson, although some years were not calculable owing to missing data (highlighting the value of XGBoost models). Overall, 52 of the 100 riskiest private nonprofit observations and 120 of the 500 predicted as most likely to close in the XGBoost models closed within three years. Only 70 of the other 7,034 observations closed, suggesting that focusing on the riskiest cases would capture most closures, even if some recent closures such as Birmingham-Southern, Iowa Wesleyan, and the University of the Arts would be missed.

The models generally had stronger predictive power in the for-profit sector. An example is the Marinello School of Beauty chain, which closed in 2016. Between 2011 and 2016, the predicted probability of closure rose from nearly the sample mean to over 0.50, while there was generally too much missing data to generate a closure prediction using OLS models. Similar successful flagging of closures using XGBoost models while frequently having insufficient data for OLS predictions occurred at Everest Colleges (closed in 2017) and the Art Institutes (closed in 2018). Overall, the XGBoost models correctly identified 84 of the riskiest 100 observations and 266 of the riskiest 500 observations as closing within three years, while the closure rate among observations outside of the top 500 was about 7 percent.

### 3.5.6 Predicting Closures in Smaller Geographic Areas

While producing national-level estimates of predicted closures is a worthwhile exercise, it may be in the interest of regional, state, and other authorities to monitor closures more locally. To do this effectively, the analyst must be sure to assess the predictive accuracy of the model(s) in the specific geographic area studied. To illustrate the potential benefits—and to warn of potential pitfalls—associated with predicting college closures at subnational levels, we use our predicted closure probabilities to assess predictive accuracy of our preferred model for each of the states in the United States. In figure 3.9, below, we display the AUCs at the state level, calculated from a model that pools observations across states. We note that the state-level AUC values range from effectively a coin toss (an AUC of 51 percent in Montana) to near-perfection predictions (an AUC of 99 percent in Connecticut). Of the states with at least one closure during our sample period that are included in figure 3.9 (i.e., for which it is possible to test the model's accuracy), about two-thirds have an AUC in excess of 70 percent, which is generally considered strong. Those states with the weakest AUCs are typically either quite small (so it is difficult to achieve predictive accuracy for sample size reasons) or have particularly idiosyncratic private higher edu-

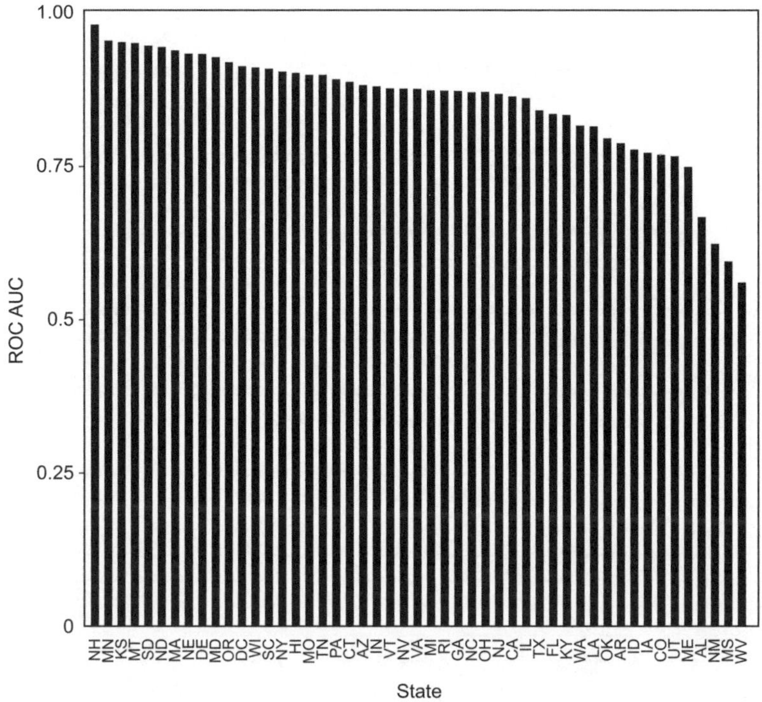


**Fig. 3.9 Predictive accuracy by state, preferred model, 2002–2021**

Source: Authors' calculations based on IPEDS, PEPS Closed School Reports, College Scorecard, Federal Student Aid, US Bureau of Economic Analysis, US Census Bureau, and US Bureau of Labor Statistics data, 2002–2023.

Note: Model is our preferred specification (XGBoost model with all controls) from table 3.5. Model is trained on 75 percent of institution-year observations; predictions calculated for remaining 25 percent of observations. Closure is measured within three years of evaluation year. ROC AUC represents the Area Under the [Relative Operating Characteristic] Curve.

cation environments (e.g., Wisconsin). Comparable methodology could be used—again, with appropriate precautions and after carefully evaluating the predictive power of the models for the selected sample—to study specific sub-sectors or institutions of special interest.

To further illustrate the potential usefulness of our methodology for state-level closure predictions, we compare time-specific measures of actual closures and predicted closures (calculated as a sum of college-level predicted probabilities in each state and year) in figure 3.10. Not surprisingly, our predictions match actual closures best in states with higher AUCs and perform reasonably well in nearly all states with large numbers of closures (e.g., California, Florida, Illinois, Missouri, New York, Pennsylvania, Tennessee, Texas). Notably, our model predicted an increase in closures within

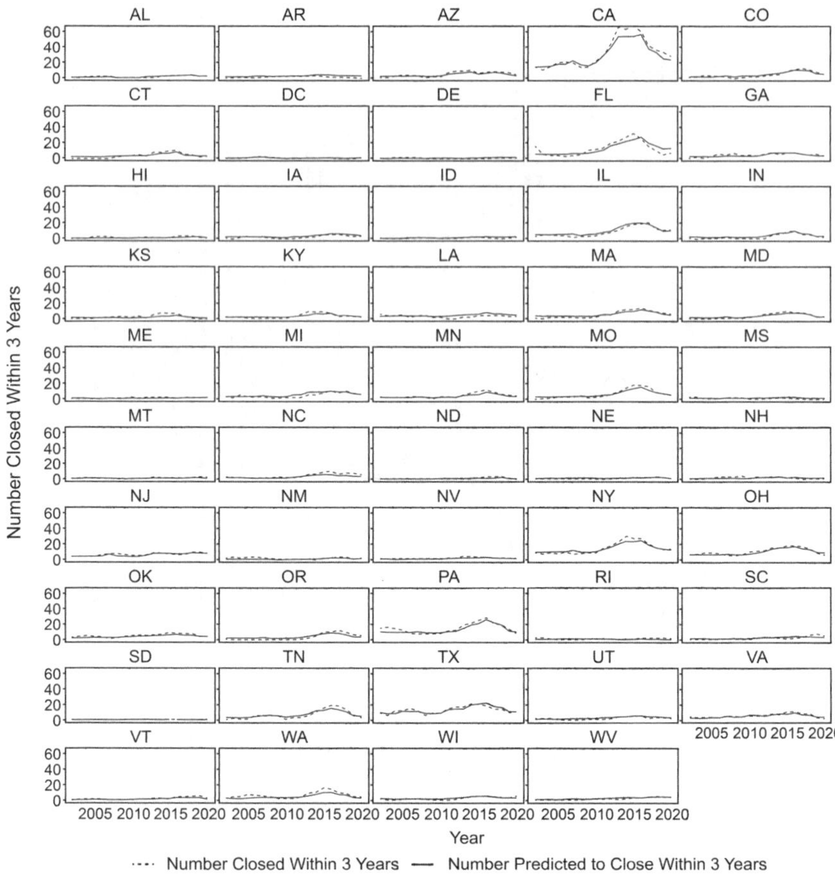


**Fig. 3.10 Actual v. predicted closures by state, preferred model, 2002–2021**

Source: Authors' calculations based on IPEDS, PEPS Closed School Reports, College Scorecard, Federal Student Aid, US Bureau of Economic Analysis, US Census Bureau, and US Bureau of Labor Statistics data, 2002–2023.

Note: Model is our preferred specification (XGBoost model with all controls) from table 3.5. Model is trained on 75 percent of institution-year observations; predictions calculated for remaining 25 percent of observations. Closure is measured within three years of evaluation year.

three years in the post-pandemic period, which is consistent with the recently observed uptick in the number of institutions announcing or considering closure or other severe fiscal measures.

Theoretically, analysts could develop predictive models that are specific to a particular segment or geography, assuming data availability and sample sizes allow such a pursuit. We note that our prior caution regarding using college-and-year level predicted probabilities to identify *individual institutions* at risk of closure remains, even if the model is developed specifically for a particular segment or local area. In most cases, the majority of institutions with elevated predicted probabilities for closure represent false negatives.

## 3.6 Simulated Increases in Closures Due to Potential Enrollment Changes

In addition to using model output to identify institutions at risk of closure, we can also simulate the impact of recent and projected future enrollment declines. For simplicity and interpretability, we do so using the continuous covariates OLS model using LASSO-determined optimal controls (including enrollment). The parameters from this model are scaled up to the most recent population of all private nonprofit and for-profit colleges. In other words, we are making the assumption that no public institutions will (be allowed to) close. Table 3.8 presents the predicted number of students, faculty, staff, and expenses that would be predicted to be affected by the continuous LASSO model, should these additional closures occur.

Using 2019 as a baseline (to avoid contamination by COVID-19 induced disruptions), if the enrollment declines that colleges have experienced since then persisted into the future (no recovery or further decline), column (1) shows that we can expect to see an additional 1.0 closures per year (an increase of 2 percent over the average annual closures). To assess how the demographic cliff might impact closures, we consider two types of potential enrollment changes—a onetime 15 percent drop (with permanently lower enrollment), presented in column (2), and a "downward-sloping hill" of enrollment in column (3). In other words, under the last scenario, enrollments would decline gradually over time as large, older cohorts of students are successively replaced by smaller, younger cohorts. This process may take a decade or more to fully play out in reality, but we consider a worst-case scenario of it materializing over five years in our analysis. The thought exercise we conduct here with respect to the prospective enrollment changes due to external factors such as the demographic cliff is how many additional

**Table 3.8** **Predicted additional annual closures under selected scenarios, 2019**

| | 2019 Enrollment Patterns Continue (1) | Demographic Cliff (one-time, worst-case) (2) | Demographic Cliff (annual, worst-case) (3) |
|---|---|---|---|
| Institutions | 1.0 | 80 | 4.6 |
| Students | 1,263 | 101,040 | 7,337 |
| Staff | 261 | 20,880 | 1,200 |
| Expenses | \$15.4m | \$1,231m | \$70.8m |

Source: Authors' calculations based on IPEDS, PEPS Closed School Reports, and College Scorecard, 2002–2023.

Note: Predictions are based on the outlined scenarios and predictions from the continuous OLS model with LASSO-selected covariates, scaled up to the full sample of private institutions in the IPEDS data.

*annual* closures we might expect once the demographic changes have fully phased in; the cumulative effect would represent a multiple of these additional annual closures.

Assuming the worst-case scenario predictions come to pass from the upcoming demographic cliff (or a 15 percent decline in enrollment), there could be as many as 80 (142 percent of the average annual closures) additional closures. On the other hand, a gradual decrease in enrollment equivalent to the demographic cliff would result in a predicted annual increase in the rate of closures of 4.6 (an increase of 8.1 percent over the average annual closures). Looking instead at a measure of severe financial distress (not reported), such as a persistently negative operating margin, the analogous numbers would be an addition 21 institutions annually if current trends persist, and an additional 99 under the worst-case predictions following the demographic cliff.

These simulations point to the precarious potential situation facing postsecondary education in the coming years, especially if the demographic cliff materializes in a moderate to severe fashion. While some of these estimated increases might seem small at the national level, they would be significant for the handful of localities predicted to experience college closures in a given year. It is important to reiterate that most institutions that close are somewhat smaller than average, with the median closed school enrolling a student body of about 1,389 full-time equivalent students several years prior to closure, although the distribution is skewed. This means that, even if our projections are accurate, many (if not all) of these additional predicted closures are unlikely to be institutions known outside of their local communities or states, yet their closures could be quite disruptive to those communities. Some institutions can be considered significant employers even in small and medium-size communities, and often act as anchor institutions in those communities.

Even ignoring the potential negative effects due to reduced training capacity in a county that loses a college, the immediate employment effects as a share of the labor force might be large. This includes not only the loss in employment coming directly from the college but also the immediate spillovers from establishments that provide goods/services to schools (most notably, retail, health care, and food services). Moreover, most students work while attending college, so any working students who are either attracted to or kept from leaving the community because of the presence of the educational institution will also contribute to local economic effects.

### 3.7 Discussion

Colleges and universities are facing unprecedented fiscal challenges in today's economic climate. The cost of education is rising, while many colleges have faced enrollment challenges over the last decade. The COVID-19 pandemic did not directly result in the anticipated increase in college closures because of a timely and substantial influx of federal funds. However, the resulting enrollment decline and period of relatively high inflation has exacerbated many institutions' liquidity, and even solvency, concerns. Moreover, many funding streams—exemplified, perhaps, by federal financial aid—are active areas of public policy and administration. Yet the precursors to colleges' fiscal challenges are an understudied area in higher education finance, even as the economic importance of institutions of higher education has grown significantly over the past century as college attendance rates have steadily climbed.

Our study contributes to this literature by examining the extent to which college financial distress—exemplified, in its most severe form, by full institution closures—can be predicted in advance based on publicly available data. We assemble the most comprehensive data set to date on the characteristics of colleges and universities, including dates of operation, institutional setting, student body, staff, and finance data from 2002 to 2023. We provide an extensive description of what is known and unknown about closed colleges compared with institutions that did not close. Then we develop a series of predictive models of severe financial distress for colleges and universities, incorporating a range of predictors, from operational revenue and expense patterns, to sources of revenue, to metrics of liquidity and leverage, to declining enrollment patterns, to prior signs of significant financial strain. Our preferred model using modern tools of machine learning significantly outperforms models based on existing federal accountability metrics, as well as linear probability models with richer covariates. We highlight the significant concern of missing data that can render more traditional estimation methods less effective than machine learning algorithms, which accommodate missing data more flexibly than even elaborate binning or other linear imputation methods.

We then use our predictions to document our estimated increase in the likelihood of future closures due to commonly predicted scenarios. In particular, we focus on enrollment declines—both temporary, such as those that arose during the COVID-19 pandemic, and systemic, like those resulting from predicted future demographic changes—that are often accompanied by fiscal challenges and represent one of the strongest explanatory variables in our predictive models. We conclude that the demographic cliff is predicted to significantly increase the number of institutions at risk of severe financial distress, including closure.

As future research, it would be valuable to estimate the impact of college closures and severe financial stress on county-level measures of employment and wages, and population. This would be an important addition to the literature because of the role that higher education institutions, particularly in the nonprofit sector, play as anchor institutions in the local community. We are particularly interested in the effect of these college-induced disruptions on temporary or permanent reallocations of human capital and employment within and across local and regional economic areas.

We caution that our earlier emphasis on negative effects of college financial distress and closures should not be taken to suggest that regulators or localities should seek to prevent college closures. A comprehensive welfare analysis is likely to show that institutions of higher education (and particularly those in the for-profit sector) do not close randomly or without cause. If these institutions are unable to produce outcomes that students, employers, or society at large find valuable, then they should not be artificially sustained by governments absent significant evidence of significant positive externalities. Indeed, extending the existence of an educational institution destined for failure may actually compound the locality's fiscal problems if the college is never able to survive on its own.

While our predictive models of college financial distress and closure may not be able to accurately predict the eventual failure of each individual institution, they are certainly effective at capturing the riskiest institutions. For example, of the 100 institutions with the highest predicted probability of closure for our preferred model, 84 percent of colleges actually closed within three years. The methods we outline may also be useful to various levels of government preparing for sector-level disruptions and their subsequent economic fallout, but we caution that our data and models should be used cautiously for more localized geographic areas (the state level or smaller), with due attention paid to metrics of predictive accuracy like AUCs and false/negative rates for the specific area studied. Indeed, our results suggest that local communities may be able to anticipate and prepare for labor market and infrastructure disruptions if an increase in aggregate college closings appears imminent and be prepared to use whatever levers available to support affected community members and businesses during the transition.

**Disclaimer:** The views expressed here are those of the authors and do not necessarily reflect the views of the Board of Governors of the Federal Reserve, the Federal Reserve Bank of Philadelphia, or the Federal Reserve System. No statements here should be treated as legal advice. We thank John Campbell, Julia Cheney, Robert Hunt, and Jeff Larimore for helpful comments. We also gratefully acknowledge excellent research support by Akash Banerjee and Jacob Goldsmith. All remaining errors are our own.

# Appendix

**Table 3A.1** **Descriptive statistics, 2002–2023**

| | | Never-Closed Institutions | | | Closed Institutions (2 yrs Earlier) | | |
|---|---|---|---|---|---|---|---|
| Covariate Type | Covariate | Mean | Median | % w/ Data | Mean | Median | % w/ Data |
| Accountability Metrics | Heightened Cash Monitoring (Level 2) | 1% | No | 100% | 1% | No | 100% |
| | Financial responsibility composite score | 2.3 | 2.5 | 37% | 1.8 | 2.0 | 5% |
| Financial Performance | Operating margin | 4.1% | 9.2% | 79% | −44.8% | 3.0% | 10% |
| | Persistently negative operating margin | 15.7% | No | 69% | 35.5% | No | 28% |
| | YOY change, operating margin | 0% | 0% | 77% | −2% | 0% | 10% |
| | Days cash on hand (DCOH) | 170.3 | 11.4 | 100% | 10.1 | 0.0 | 100% |
| | YOY change, DCOH | −339% | 0% | 99% | −2158% | 0% | 100% |
| | Debt ($mil) | 94.9 | 5.4 | 59% | 2.3 | 0.0 | 4% |
| | EBIDA ($mil) | 19.0 | 1.7 | 79% | 0.2 | 0.0 | 10% |
| | Debt to EBIDA | −123.2 | 0.9 | 54% | −4.6 | 0.0 | 4% |
| | Debt to assets | 2399.7 | 0.0 | 75% | 0.0 | 0.0 | 12% |
| | YOY change, debt to assets | −1% | 0% | 74% | −2% | 0% | 12% |
| | Unrestricted net assets ($mil) | 72.2 | 2.1 | 93% | 2.7 | 0.0 | 16% |
| Revenue | Total revenue ($mil) | 138.8 | 23.3 | 93% | 6.1 | 1.5 | 16% |
| | YOY change, total revenue | 5% | 2% | 92% | −13% | −2% | 16% |
| | Revenue 10% lower than 5-year high | 40% | No | 92% | 86% | Yes | 16% |
| | Tuition/total revenue | 48% | 45% | 93% | 77% | 86% | 16% |
| | Auxiliary/total revenue | 7% | 4% | 75% | 3% | 0% | 8% |
| | Investment revenue/total revenue | 3% | 0% | 93% | 1% | 0% | 16% |
| | Gifts, grants, contracts/total revenue | 4% | 0% | 82% | 1% | 0% | 16% |
| Expenses | Total expenses ($mil) | 130.5 | 22.6 | 93% | 6.5 | 1.5 | 16% |
| | Instructional/total expenses | 40% | 37% | 93% | 45% | 38% | 16% |
| | Scholarships/total expenses | 16% | 13% | 93% | 6% | 0% | 16% |
| | Interest/total expenses | 1% | 1% | 79% | 1% | 0% | 10% |
| | Depreciation/total expenses | 5% | 5% | 79% | 3% | 2% | 10% |

*(continued)*

**Table 3A.1 (cont.)**

| | | Never-Closed Institutions | | | Closed Institutions (2 yrs Earlier) | | |
|---|---|---|---|---|---|---|---|
| Covariate Type | Covariate | Mean | Median | % w/ Data | Mean | Median | % w/ Data |
| Staff | Total staff | 689.0 | 195.0 | 94% | 33.7 | 11.0 | 18% |
| | YOY change, total staff | 3% | 1% | 91% | −8% | 0% | 18% |
| | Instructional/total staff | 50% | 50% | 89% | 52% | 50% | 13% |
| | Full-time/total staff | 66% | 68% | 94% | 75% | 77% | 17% |
| Enrollment | Total enrollment (12-month) | 5190.0 | 1257.0 | 95% | 214.2 | 0.0 | 99% |
| | YOY change, 12-month enrollment | 3% | 0% | 92% | −38% | −58% | 94% |
| | Undergraduate/total enrollment | 87% | 100% | 93% | 97% | 100% | 44% |
| | Enrollment 10% lower than 5-year high | 41% | 0% | 94% | 93% | 100% | 99% |
| | 3 consecutive years of >5% enrollment drops | 3% | 0% | 94% | 21% | 0% | 93% |
| County Controls | Population (mil) | 1.1 | 0.4 | 92% | 1.5 | 0.8 | 96% |
| | Personal income per capita ($) | 46670.8 | 42450.0 | 92% | 52095.9 | 47541.0 | 96% |
| | Unemployment rate | 1% | 0% | 95% | 0% | 0.1 | 99% |
| | Poverty rate | 15% | 14% | 93% | 14% | 0.1 | 97% |
| | # of Observations | | | 110,559 | | | 1,263 |

Source: Authors' calculations based on IPEDS, PEPS Closed School Reports, College Scorecard, Federal Student Aid, US Bureau of Economic Analysis, US Census Bureau, and US Bureau of Labor Statistics data, 2002–2023.

Note: Number of observations reflects the 2002–2023 sample; many covariates are missing at much lower rates for the subsample used for some of the analysis (2006–2020). Examples include the financial responsibility composite score and financial data. Never-closed institutions are included in the sample each year they reported being in operation. The 1,263 closed institutions are observed once, two years before closure, because the data are predominantly missing in the year of actual closure.

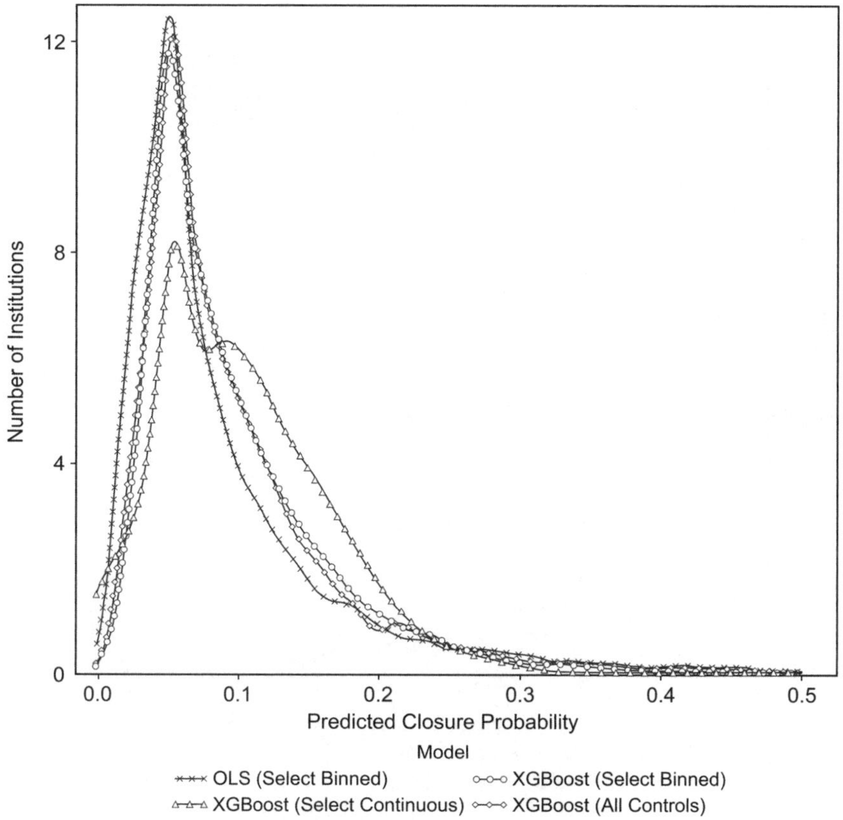


**Fig. 3A.1a Distributions of closure predictions by model, private for-profit two-year, 2002–2023**

Source: Authors' calculations based on IPEDS, PEPS Closed School Reports, College Scorecard, Federal Student Aid, US Bureau of Economic Analysis, US Census Bureau, and US Bureau of Labor Statistics data, 1996–2023.

Note: Models estimated or trained on 75 percent of institution-year observations; distribution of predicted values reported for remaining evaluation observations (25 percent).

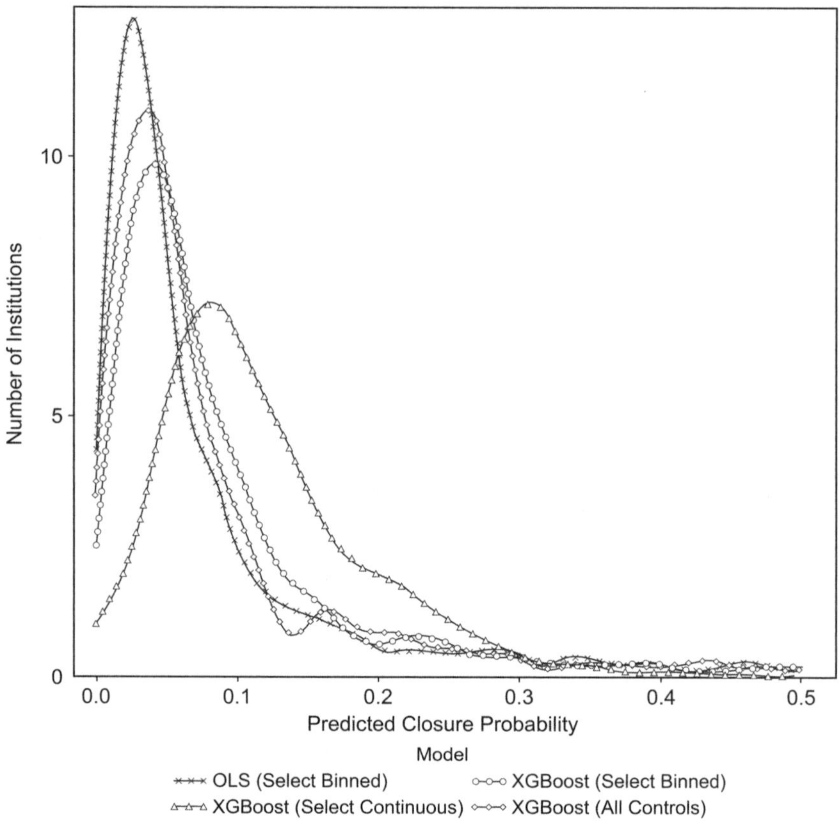


**Fig. 3A.1b Distributions of closure predictions by model, private for-profit four-year, 2002–2023**

Source: Authors' calculations based on IPEDS, PEPS Closed School Reports, College Scorecard, Federal Student Aid, US Bureau of Economic Analysis, US Census Bureau, and US Bureau of Labor Statistics data, 1996–2023.

Note: Models estimated or trained on 75 percent of institution-year observations; distribution of predicted values reported for remaining evaluation observations (25 percent).

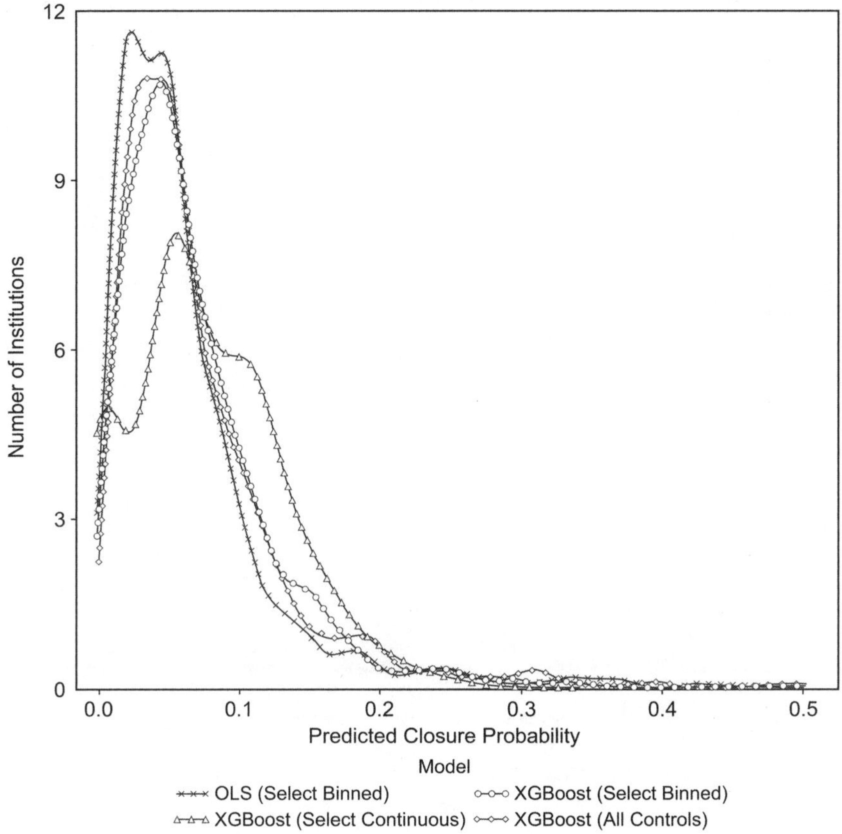


**Fig. 3A.1c Distributions of closure predictions by model, private nonprofit two-year, 2002–2023**

Source: Authors' calculations based on IPEDS, PEPS Closed School Reports, College Scorecard, Federal Student Aid, US Bureau of Economic Analysis, US Census Bureau, and US Bureau of Labor Statistics data, 1996–2023.

Note: Models estimated or trained on 75 percent of institution-year observations; distribution of predicted values reported for remaining evaluation observations (25 percent).

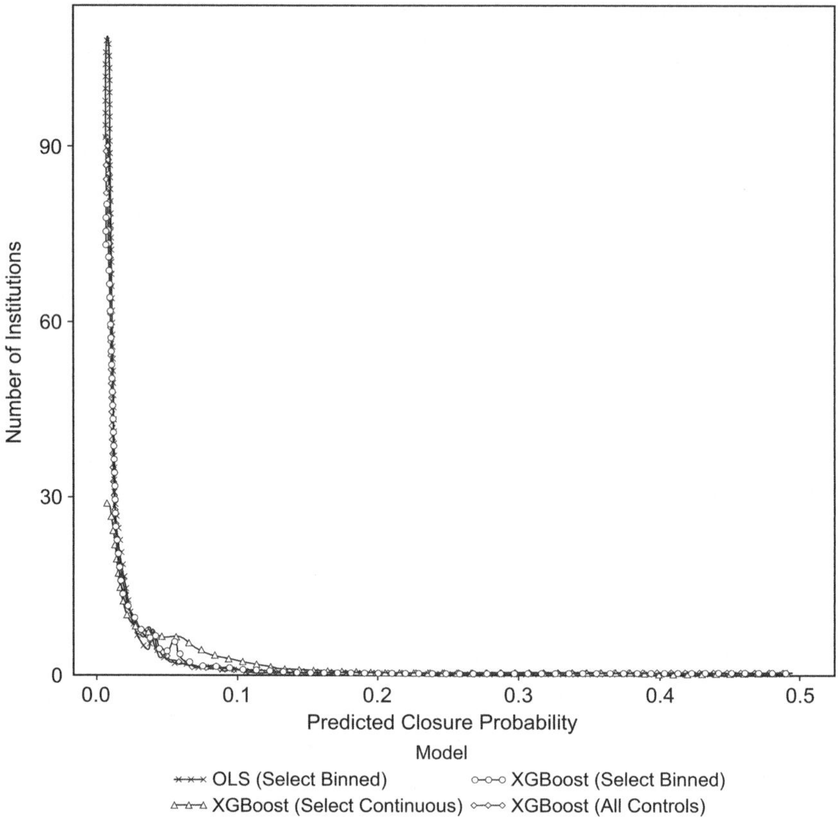


**Fig. 3A.1d Distributions of closure predictions by model, private nonprofit four-year, 2002–2023**

Source: Authors' calculations based on IPEDS, PEPS Closed School Reports, College Scorecard, Federal Student Aid, US Bureau of Economic Analysis, US Census Bureau, and US Bureau of Labor Statistics data, 1996–2023.

Note: Models estimated or trained on 75 percent of institution-year observations; distribution of predicted values reported for remaining evaluation observations (25 percent).

## References

Ambrose, C. M., and M. T. Nietzel. 2024. *Colleges on the Brink: The Case for Financial Exigency.* Rowman and Littlefield.

American Council of Trustees and Alumni. 2021. *The Cost of Excess: Why Colleges and Universities Must Control Runaway Spending.* Washington, DC: American Council of Trustees and Alumni.

American Council on Education. 2014. *Understanding College and University Endowments.* Washington, DC: American Council on Education.

Andrews, M. J. 2023. "How Do Institutions of Higher Education Affect Local Invention? Evidence from the Establishment of US Colleges." *American Economic Journal: Economic Policy* 15(2): 1–41. https://doi.org/10.1257/pol.20200320.

Archibald, R. B., and D. H. Feldman. 2008. "Explaining Increases in Higher Education Costs." *Journal of Higher Education* 79(3): 268–95. https://doi.org/10.1080/00221546.2008.11772099.

Arena, M. L. 2013. "The Crisis in Credit and the Rise of Non-Credit." *Innovative Higher Education* 38: 369–81. https://doi.org/10.1007/s10755-012-9249-5.

Ashley, A., C. G. Loh, L. Durham, R. Kim, and K. Bubb. 2023. "Identifying Plan Perceptions: Higher Education Institutions as Arts and Cultural Anchors." *Urban Affairs Review* 59(5): 1496–1529. https://doi.org/10.1177/10780874221108103.

Barr, A., and S. E. Turner. 2013. "Expanding Enrollments and Contracting State Budgets: The Effect of the Great Recession on Higher Education." *ANNALS of the American Academy of Political and Social Science* 650(1): 168–93. https://psycnet.apa.org/doi/10.1177/0002716213500035.

Barr, A., and S. Turner. 2015. "Out of Work and into School: Labor Market Policies and College Enrollment during the Great Recession." *Journal of Public Economics* 124: 63–73. https://doi.org/10.1016/j.jpubeco.2014.12.009.

Bates, L. J., and R. E. Santerre. 2000. "A Time Series Analysis of Private College Closures and Mergers." *Review of Industrial Organization* 17: 267–76. https://doi.org/10.1023/A:1007898402967.

Baum, S., and V. Lee. 2018. *Understanding Endowments.* Urban Institute.

Baumol, W. J. 1967. "Macroeconomics of Unbalanced Growth: The Anatomy of Urban Crisis." *American Economic Review* 57(3): 415–26. https://www.jstor.org/stable/1812111.

Birch, E., D. C. Perry, and H. L. Taylor, Jr. 2013. "Universities as Anchor Institutions." *Journal of Higher Education Outreach and Engagement* 17(3): 7–15.

Bowen, H. R. 1980. *The Costs of Higher Education: How Much Do Colleges and Universities Spend per Student and How Much Should They Spend?* Jossey-Bass.

Bransberger, P., C. Falkenstern, and P. Lane. 2020. *Knocking at the College Door: Projections of High School Graduates.* Western Interstate Commission for Higher Education.

Brenan, M. 2023. "Americans' Confidence in Higher Education Down Sharply." Gallup, July 11. https://news.gallup.com/poll/508352/americans-confidence-higher-education-down-sharply.aspx.

Britton, T., R. M. Rall, and F. Commodore. 2023. "The Keys to Endurance: An Investigation of the Institutional Factors Related to the Persistence of Historically Black Colleges and Universities." *Journal of Higher Education* 94(3): 310–32. https://doi.org/10.1080/00221546.2022.2082786.

Burke, L. 2024. "Penn State Plans Nearly $100M in Cuts for FY26 budget." *Higher Ed Dive*, January 24. https://www.highereddive.com/news/penn-state-cuts-budget-2026/705542/.

Burns, R., L. Brown, K. Heckert, D. Weeden, H. S. Kim, B. Randolph, A. Pevitz, S. Karamarkovich, and J. Causey. 2023. *A Dream Derailed? Investigating the Impacts of College Closures on Student Outcomes.* State Higher Education Executive Officers Association.

Carlino, G., and R. Hunt. 2009. "What Explains the Quantity and Quality of Local Inventive Activity?" *Brookings Papers on Economic Activity* 2009: 65–123.

Celli, V., A. Cerqua, and G. Pellegrini. 2023. "The Long-Term Effects of Mass Layoffs: Do Local Economies (Ever) Recover?" *Journal of Economic Geography* 23(5): 1121–144. https://doi.org/10.1093/jeg/lbad012.

Cellini, S. R., and C. Goldin. 2014. "Does Federal Student Aid Raise Tuition? New Evidence on For-Profit Colleges." *American Economic Journal: Economic Policy* 6(4): 174–206. https://doi.org/10.1257/pol.6.4.174.

Chakrabarti, R., N. Gorton, and M. F. Lovenheim. 2020. *State Investment in Higher Education: Effects on Human Capital Formation, Student Debt, and Long-Term Financial Outcomes of Students.* Federal Reserve Bank of New York Staff Reports 941.

Chen, T., and C. Guestrin. 2016. "XGBoost: A Scalable Tree Boosting System." In *Proceedings of the 22nd ACM SIGKDD International Conference on Knowledge Discovery and Data Mining*, 785–94. Association for Computing Machinery. https://doi.org/10.1145/2939672.2939785

Colby, G. 2023. *Data Snapshot: Tenure and Contingency in US Higher Education.* American Association of University Professors.

Commonfund Institute. 2023. *Commonfund Higher Education Price Index*. Wilton, CT: Commonfund Institute.

Conzelmann, J. G., S. W. Hemelt, B. J. Hershbein, S. Martin, A. Simon, and K. M. Stange. 2023. "Grads on the Go: Measuring College-Specific Labor Markets for Graduates." *Journal of Policy Analysis and Management* 00: 1–22. https://doi.org/10.1002/pam.22553.

Curs, B. R., and O. Jaquette. 2017. "Crowded Out? The Effect of Nonresident Enrollment on Resident Access to Public Research Universities." *Educational Evaluation and Policy Analysis* 39(4): 644–69. https://doi.org/10.3102/0162373717704719.

Curti, M., and R. Nash. 1965. *Philanthropy in the Shaping of American Higher Education*. Rutgers University Press.

Delaney, J. A., ed. 2023. *Volatility in State Spending for Higher Education*. American Educational Research Association.

Delaney, J. A., and W. R. Doyle. 2018. "Patterns and Volatility in State Funding for Higher Education, 1951–2006." *Teachers College Record* 120(6): 1–42. https://doi.org/10.1177/016146811812000605.

Deming, D. J., C. Goldin, and L. F. Katz. 2012. "The For-Profit Postsecondary School Sector: Nimble Critters or Agile Predators?" *Journal of Economic Perspectives* 26(1): 139–64. https://doi.org/10.1257/jep.26.1.139.

Denison, D., J. Fowles, and M. J. Moody. 2014. "Borrowing for College: A Comparison of Long-Term Debt Financing between Public and Private, Nonprofit Institutions of Higher Education." *Public Budgeting and Finance* 34(2): 84–104. https://doi.org/10.1111/pbaf.12034.

Denneen, J., and T. Dretler. 2012. *The Financially Sustainable University.* Bain and Company.

Eide, S. 2018. "Private Colleges in Peril." *Education Next* 18(4): 34–41. https://www.educationnext.org/private-colleges-peril-financial-pressures-declining-enrollment-closures/.

Enright, M., A. W. Lehren, and J. Longoria. 2020. "Hidden Figures: College Students May Be Paying Thousands in Athletic Fees and Not Know It." *NBC News*, March 8. https://www.nbcnews.com/news/education/hidden-figures-college-students-may-be-paying-thousands-athletic-fees-n1145171.

Foote, A., M. Grosz, and A. Stevens. 2019. "Locate Your Nearest Exit: Mass Layoffs and Local Labor Market Response." *ILR Review* 72(1): 101–26. https://doi.org/10.1177/0019793917753095.

Ginsberg, B. 2011. *The Fall of the Faculty: The Rise of the All-Administrative University and Why It Matters*. Oxford University Press.

Graddy-Reed, A., M. Feldman, J. Bercovitz, and W. S. Langford. 2021. "The Distribution of Indirect Cost Recovery in Academic Research." *Science and Public Policy* 48(3): 364–86. https://doi.org/10.1093/scipol/scab004.

Grawe, N. D. 2018. *Demographics and the Demand for Higher Education.* Johns Hopkins University Press.

Greene, S. 2024. "University of Delaware Issues Hiring Freeze, Cites Rising Health Care Costs." *WDEL*, February 7. https://www.wdel.com/news/university-of-delaware-issues-hiring-freeze-cites-rising-health-care-costs/article_ad710c74-c63b-11ee-ae84-8b2eab190c36.html.
Griffith, A. L., and K. N. Rask. 2016. "The Effect of Institutional Expenditures on Employment Outcomes and Earnings." *Economic Inquiry* 54(4): 1931–1945. https://doi.org/10.1111/ecin.12336.
Harkavy, I., and H. Zuckerman. 1999. *Eds and Meds: Cities' Hidden Assets*. Brookings Institution.
Harker, P. T., D. Diamond, and D. Reed. 2022. *Anchor Impact: Understanding the Role of Higher Education and Hospitals in Regional Economies*. Federal Reserve Bank of Philadelphia.
Harris, M. S., and K. Holley. 2016. "Universities as Anchor Institutions: Economic and Social Potential for Urban Development." In *Higher Education: Handbook of Theory and Research*, volume 31, edited by M. B. Paulsen, 393–439. Springer.
Hillman, N. W., and E. L. Orians. 2013. "Community Colleges and Labor Market Conditions: How Does Enrollment Demand Change Relative to Local Unemployment Rates?" *Research in Higher Education* 54: 765–80. https://doi.org/10.1007/s11162-013-9294-7.
Horn, M. B. 2018. "Will Half of All Colleges Really Close in the Next Decade?" *Christensen Institute*, December 13. https://www.christenseninstitute.org/blog/will-half-of-all-colleges-really- close-in-the-next-decade/.
Hovey, H. A. 1999. *State Spending for Higher Education in the Next Decade: The Battle to Sustain Current Support.* California State Policy Research, Inc.
Howard, G., R. Weinstein, and Y. Yang. 2022. "Do Universities Improve Local Economic Resilience?" *Review of Economics and Statistics.* https://doi.org/10.1162/rest_a_01212.
Howard, T. 2014. "How Communities Can Make the Most of Their Anchor Institutions." *Governing*, January 9. https://www.governing.com/gov-institute/voices/col-communities-local-government-anchor-institutions-democracy-collaborative-dashboard.html.
Jaquette, O., and B. R. Curs. 2016. "Creating the Out-of-State University: Do Public Universities Increase Nonresident Freshman Enrollment in Response to Declining State Appropriations?" *Research in Higher Education* 56(6): 535–65. https://doi.org/10.1007/s11162-015-9362-2.
Jaquette, O., B. R. Curs, and J. R. Posselt. 2016. "Tuition Rich, Mission Poor: Nonresident Enrollment Growth and the Socioeconomic and Racial Composition of Public Research Universities." *Journal of Higher Education* 87(5): 635–73. https://doi.org/10.1080/00221546.2016.11777417.
Jaquette, O., and E. Parra. 2016. "The Problem with the Delta Cost Project Database." *Research in Higher Education* 57(5): 630–51.
Kelchen, R. 2018. *Higher Education Accountability*. Johns Hopkins University Press.
Kelchen, R. 2020. *Examining the Feasibility of Empirically Predicting College Closures.* Brookings Institution.
Kelchen, R. 2021. "An Exploration of Nonresident Student Enrollment and Institutional Finances at Public Universities." *Journal of Postsecondary Student Success* 1(1): 81–105. https://doi.org/10.33009/fsop_jpss121539.
Kelchen, R., J. Ortagus, K. Rosinger, D. Baker, and M. Lingo. 2024a. "The Relationships between State Higher Education Funding Strategies and College Access and Success." *Educational Researcher* 53(2): 100–110. https://doi.org/10.3102/0013189X231208964.
Kelchen, R., J. Ortagus, K. Rosinger, and A. Cassell. 2024b. "Investing in the Work-

force: The Impact of Performance-Based Funding on Student Earnings Outcomes." *Journal of Higher Education* 95(2): 172–99. https://doi.org/10.1080/00221546.2023.2171201.

Kelchen, R., and S. Pingel. 2024. "Examining the Effects of Tuition Controls on Student Enrollment." *Research in Higher Education* 65: 70–91. https://doi.org/10.1007/s11162-023-09748-5.

Knox, L. 2023. "Seeking an Enrollment Hail Mary, Small Colleges Look to Athletics." *Inside Higher Ed*, December 4. https://www.insidehighered.com/news/admissions/traditional-age/2023/12/04/small-colleges-bet-new-sports-boost-enrollment.

Kolpin, V., and M. Stater. 2024. "The Perverse Equilibrium Effects of State and Federal Student Aid in Higher Education." *Journal of Economic Behavior and Organization* 217: 679–91. https://doi.org/10.1016/j.jebo.2023.11.022.

Korn, M. 2024. "This Private College Has Been on Its Deathbed—for 15 Years." *Wall Street Journal*, January 20. https://www.wsj.com/us-news/education/birmingham-southern-college-alabama-aef0fcb7.

Kunkle, K., and S. Laderman. 2023. *State Higher Education Finance: FY2022*. State Higher Education Executive Officers Association.

Lee, J. 2019. "The Local Economic Impact of a Large Research University: Evidence from UC Merced." *Economic Inquiry* 57(1): 316–32. https://doi.org/10.1111/ecin.12734.

Lehnert, P., M. Dell, U. Backes-Gellner, and E. Bettinger. 2024. *The Effect of Post-secondary Educational Institutions on Local Economies: A Birds-Eye View*. Swiss Leading House Economics of Education Working Paper No. 210.

Ma, J., and M. Pender. 2023. *Trends in College Pricing and Student Aid 2023*. College Board.

McClure, K. R., A. J. Ryder, and J. M. DeVita. 2017. "Public-Private Partnerships in College Student Housing: Lessons from Three Institutions." *Journal of College and University Student Housing* 43(2): 72–93.

Moody, J. 2024. "Judge Allows Webster to Lift Endowment Restrictions." *Inside Higher Ed*, March 4. https://www.insidehighered.com/news/quick-takes/2024/03/04/judge-allows-webster-lift-endowment-restrictions.

National Association of College and University Business Officers. 2023. *2022 NACUBO Tuition Discounting Study*. Washington, DC: National Association of College and University Business Officers.

National Center for Education Statistics. 2023. *The Condition of Education*. US Department of Education.

National Center for Education Statistics. 2024. *2024–25 Survey Materials*.

National Student Clearinghouse Research Center. 2024. *Current Term Enrollment Estimates: Fall 2023*. January 24. https://nscresearchcenter.org/current-term-enrollment-estimates/.

Natow, R. S. 2021. "Why Haven't More Colleges Closed?" *Chronicle of Higher Education*, March 1. https://www.chronicle.com/article/why-havent-more-colleges-closed.

Office of Federal Student Aid. 2024. *2024–25 Federal Student Aid handbook*. US Department of Education.

Ortagus, J., R. Kelchen, K. Rosinger, and N. Voorhees. 2020. "Performance-Based Funding in American Higher Education: A Systematic Synthesis of the Intended and Unintended Consequences." *Educational Evaluation and Policy Analysis* 42(4): 520–50. https://doi.org/10.3102/0162373720953128.

Owens, J. 2024. "Cost of Weight-Loss Drugs for State Employees Hits Taxpayers." *Delaware Live*, February 2. https://delawarelive.com/cost-of-weight-loss-drugs-hits-taxpayers/.

EY Parthenon. 2017. *Strength in Numbers: Strategies for Collaborating for a New Era in Higher Education. Ernst & Young LLP.*

Porter, S. R., and T. J. Ramirez. 2009. *Why Do Colleges Fail? An Analysis of College and University Closings and Mergers, 1975–2005.* Working paper.

Povich, E. S. 2023. "Flagship Public Universities Likely to Cut More Humanities, Staff—Especially in Rural Areas." *Stateline*, December 15. https://stateline.org/2023/12/15/flagship-public-universities-likely-to-cut-more-humanities-staff-especially-in-rural-states/.

Redd, K. 2024. *2023 NACUBO-Commonfund Study of Endowments.* National Association of College and University Business Officers.

Rosinger, K., R. Kelchen, D. J. Baker, J. Ortagus, and M. D. Lingo. 2022. "State Higher Education Funding during COVID-19: Lessons from Prior Recessions and Implications for Equity." *AERA Open* 8. https://doi.org/10.1177/23328584221091277.

Russell, L. C., and M. J. Andrews. 2022. *Not the Great Equalizer? Local Economic Mobility and Inequality Effects for the Establishment of U.S. Universities.* EdWorkingPaper No. 22–634.

Russell, L. C., L. Yu, and M. J. Andrews. 2022. "Higher Education and Local Educational Attainment: Evidence from the Establishment of U.S. Colleges." *Review of Economics and Statistics.* https://doi.org/10.1162/rest_a_01214.

Sanchez, O. 2024. "Experts Predicted Dozens of Colleges Would Close in 2023—and They Were Right." *Hechinger Report*, January 12. https://hechingerreport.org/experts-predicted-dozens-of-colleges-would-close-in-2023-and-they-were-right/.

Smith, E. K., E. K. Rozek, and K. D. Moore. 2014. "Creating SPOTs for Successful Aging: Strengthening the Case for Developing University-Based Retirement Communities Using Social-Physical Place over Time Theory. *Journal of Housing for the Elderly* 28(1): 21–40. https://doi.org/10.1080/02763893.2013.858091.

Stolzenberg, E. B., M. C. Aragon, E. Romo, V. Couch, D. McLennan, M. K. Eagan, and N. Kang. 2020. *The American Freshman: National Norms Fall 2019.* Higher Education Research Institute, University of California, Los Angeles.

Storms, K., S. E. Miller, and B. Hall. 2017. "P4: The Role of Planning in Successful Public-Private Partnerships (P3s)." *Planning for Higher Education* 45(3): 1–13.

Tarrant, M., N. Bray, and S. Katsinas. 2018. "The Invisible Colleges Revisited: An Empirical Review." *Journal of Higher Education* 89(3): 341–67. https://doi.org/10.1080/00221546.2017.1390971.

Tewksbury, D. G. 1932. *The Founding of American Colleges and Universities before the Civil War, with Particular Reference to the Religious Influences Bearing Upon the College Movement.* Teachers College, Columbia University.

*USA Today*. 2024. "NCAA Finances: Revenue and Expenses by School." March 14. https://sports.usatoday.com/ncaa/finances.

Ward, J. D., M. Haynes, and S. Gusakova. 2022. *Borrowing During a Time of Crisis: Examining Institutional Debt During the Great Recession and COVID-19.* Ithaka S+R. https://doi.org/10.18665/sr.317442.

Webber, D. A. 2016. "Are College Costs Worth It? How Ability, Major, and Debt Affect the Returns to Schooling." *Economics of Education Review* 53: 296–310. https://doi.org/10.1016/j.econedurev.2016.04.007.

Webber, D. A. 2017. "State Divestment and Tuition at Public Institutions." *Economics of Education Review* 60: 1–4. https://doi.org/10.1016/j.econedurev.2017.07.007.

Webber, D. A., and R. G. Ehrenberg. 2010. "Do Expenditures Other than Instructional Expenditures Affect Graduation and Persistence Rates in American Higher Education?" *Economics of Education Review* 29(6): 947–58. https://doi.org/10.1016/j.econedurev.2010.04.006.

Whistle, W., and L. Erickson. 2019. *Using Instructional Spending to Test for Value in Higher Ed.* Third Way, April 18. https://www.thirdway.org/memo/using-instructional-spending-to-test-for-value-in-higher-ed.

Xu, D., and F. X. Ran. 2020. "Noncredit Enrollment in Community College: Students, Course Enrollments, and Academic Outcomes." *Community College Review* 48(1): 77–101. https://doi.org/10.1177/0091552119876039.

Zapp, M., and C. Dahmen. 2023. "Live and (Let) Die—Shifting Legitimacies and Organizational Mortality in American Higher Education, 1944–2018." *Social Problems.* https://doi.org/10.1093/socpro/spad001.

Zemsky, R., S. Shaman, and S. C. Baldridge. 2020. *The College Stress Test: Tracking Institutional Futures Across a Crowded Market.* Johns Hopkins University Press.

Zhang, L., X. Liu, and Y. Hu. 2024. "Degrees of Return: Estimating Internal Rates of Return for College Majors Using Quantile Regression." *American Educational Research Journal.* https://doi.org/10.3102/00028312241231512.

# 4 Endowment Spending Rules

Christopher Avery, Ronald Ehrenberg, Catharine Hill, and Douglas A. Webber

## 4.1 Introduction

We study historical endowment spending by colleges in the United States, focusing on how those institutions respond to fluctuations in the size of their endowment. Using data reported by private, non-profit colleges and universities (IRS 990 tax filings, including Schedule D) we explore spending from endowments and the extent to which institutions follow specific rules or exercise greater discretion. Our data allow us to estimate the spending rules followed by institutions and examine deviations from these rules and what might explain them. Institutions can deviate from their spending rules by distributing an amount from the endowment that differs from the amount called for by their rule. These differences may result in greater or less smoothing than the rule implies and may also be asymmetric in response to increases and decreases in returns or to other variables. It is also the case that distributing resources from the endowment to units on campus may not actually lead to increased spending, because these units may not actually spend them

Christopher Avery is the Roy E. Larsen Professor of Public Policy at Harvard Kennedy School, and a research associate of the National Bureau of Economic Research.

Ronald Ehrenberg is the Irving M. Ives Professor of Industrial and Labor Relations and Economics at Cornell University, a Stephen H. Weiss Presidential Fellow, and a research associate of the National Bureau of Economic Research.

Catharine Hill is managing director of Ithaka S+R.

Douglas A. Webber is a principal economist in the Consumer and Community Research Section of the Board of Governors of the Federal Reserve.

We are grateful to Jeff Brown, John Campbell, and seminar participants for comments and to Helen Krieger for research assistance. The views expressed here are those of the authors and do not necessarily reflect the views of the Board of Governors of the Federal Reserve or the Federal Reserve System. For acknowledgments, sources of research support, and disclosure of the authors' material financial relationships, if any, please see https://www.nber.org/books-and-chapters/financing-institutions-higher-education/endowment-spending-rules.

but accumulate them as reserves, or these distributions may substitute for otherwise unrestricted funds, which can then be saved. Actual spending from the endowment depends on this as well as the amount distributed.

The IRS 990 data allow us to gain insight into the importance of this behavior by examining the behavior of discretionary reinvestment in the endowment in the form of funds functioning as endowment, also known as quasi-endowment. We estimate the spending rules of institutions looking at actual distributions but then also take into account funds returning to the endowment in the form of funds functioning as endowment (FFE), to get an estimate of "net spending" from the endowment over time. By netting out changes in the endowment in the form of funds functioning as endowment, we can examine the true net spending from the endowment, with the change in funds functioning affecting the actual distribution from the endowment.

Our paper is distinguished from previous studies of endowment spending both because of the nature and time period of our analysis. Previous studies (such as K. Brown and Tiu 2013; J. Brown et al. 2014; Bulman 2022) primarily utilized a combination of IPEDS and NACUBO (National Association of College and University Business Officers) survey data. The NACUBO data are self-reported and do not include all institutions with endowments, although both private and public institutions participate. By rule, our data are comprehensive, and since they consist of official tax filings, it is presumably more accurate than the survey data compiled by NACUBO. Recent papers by Dahiya and Yermack (2021) and Lo et al. (2019) use 990 filings to analyze returns and spending for a broader set of non-profit organizations but do not focus on colleges or other subgroups of those organizations.

Our paper is distinct from two other active strains of the literature in objective as our primary goal is to use tax filings to reconstruct the spending rules used by universities, and to examine whether these rules actually lead to spending. One other set of papers studies university asset allocation with an eye toward assessing whether they are choosing optimal risk levels in their investments (see, e.g., Dimmock 2012; Blanchett 2014; Gilbert and Hrdlicka 2015; Ang et al. 2018; Campbell and Sigalov 2022; Cejnek et al. 2023). Similarly, Filosa (2023) considers endowment levels and spending relative to university debt levels. A second set of papers considers the implications of sustainability on optimal spending from an endowment (Brown and Scholz 2019; Dybvig and Qin 2021; Campbell and Martin 2023). Our paper is mostly closely related to Halem et al. (2022), who assess the interaction between stated spending rules and current asset allocations for Harvard, MIT, Stanford, and Yale and project the trajectories of their endowment levels across a variety of different scenarios.[1]

Our paper makes the following contributions to the literature. Anecdot-

1. Cejnek et al. (2014) provide a broader survey of past research on university endowments, while Chambers et al. (2020) study endowment spending of 12 institutions over a longer period of 75 years.

ally, many faculty appear to have a poor understanding of both what is possible (e.g., restricted vs. unrestricted spending) and what the long-term drawbacks are to increased endowment spending. On the other hand, institutions often lack transparency in the manner in which they spend their endowment, even when they state an explicit endowment spending rule. Money is fungible, and endowment spending nominally directed toward financial aid may not functionally be spent on that category if money from a different institutional source is reduced. In order to shed some light on the above questions, we first empirically estimate the spending rules for each school in our sample. Using a small set of assumptions and a simple empirical model, we are able to closely (within 10 percent) approximate the spending rules of 80 percent of the sample. We examine deviations in distributions from the estimated spending rules, to see if there are systematic changes in distributions that shed light on the actual management of endowment spending. Finally, we also examine the impact of institutions investing in quasi-endowment or funds functioning as endowment as a way of estimating "net spending" from endowments, netting out from distributions any reinvestment in the endowment through funds functioning as endowment, which is essentially an offset to the distribution resulting from the original spending rule. Notably, we find that both investment returns and contributions are positively associated with the quasi-endowment, suggesting that institutions are strategically managing their budgets to increase flexibility in the long run.

The paper proceeds as follows. Section 4.2 provides formal definitions and conceptual background on university endowments and endowment spending. Section 4.3 describes the data and the sample of institutions that we study. Section 4.4 provides descriptive statistics. Section 4.5 analyzes the properties of the spending rules adopted by many colleges. Section 4.6 presents the results of simulations designed to reverse engineer the specific spending rules utilized by each of the colleges. Section 4.7 discusses the relationship between changes in funds functioning as endowment and the spending rules of institutions, to examine the actual net spending from the endowment. Section 4.7 also examines the relationship between endowment distributions and spending in the operating budget on several categories of expenditures. Section 4.8 analyzes changes in different types of spending over time by these institutions. Section 4.9 concludes.

## 4.2 Conceptual Discussion of Endowments

Endowments consist of restricted and unrestricted funds. The restricted portion usually comprises about two-thirds of the entire endowment and can only be spent for predesignated purposes. From the institution's perspective, unrestricted funds are the most valuable, as they can be allocated to the areas of greatest need. However, money is fungible, and restricted funds can often replace/free up other sources of funding. For instance, a newly endowed faculty line can replace a planned future additional line to a given department (or could replace a retiring faculty member whose salary was paid from the general fund).

At the core, an endowment brings value to an institution in two main ways. First, the strategic endowment spending can provide insurance. Since many institutions are heavily dependent on tuition to fund operations, an unexpected drop in enrollment could necessitate layoffs even if that decline is anticipated to be transitory. One potential way that trustees could use the endowment then would be to distribute more during bad times but distribute less during good times, thus mitigating the need for layoffs in response to revenue declines. It is tricky to enact this type of strategic spending because investment returns can fluctuate considerably from year to year, and further that negative shocks may pertain to both tuition revenues and investment returns. On the other hand, it is no secret that academic budgets can become bloated over time. An alternative approach is to use downturns as a way to right-size budgets, which might be termed the "never waste a good crisis" strategy (J. Brown et al. 2014).

Second, the endowment can fund projects that advance the mission of the school. A challenge is for a university to determine whether to use endowment funds in the present or to use the endowment as a savings vehicle to promote future spending opportunities. These options are in conflict because spending an additional dollar today means that this dollar and its investment return cannot be spent on future students.

Figure 4.1 compares undiscounted cumulative expenditures for a future-oriented (4 percent payout) and a present-oriented spending rule (6 percent payout rate) for a hypothetical institution with a $1 billion endowment and

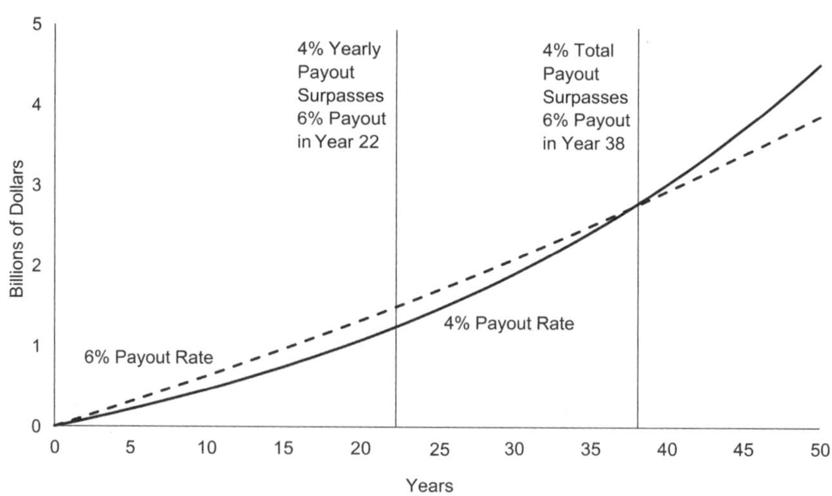


**Fig. 4.1 Total endowment spending for a hypothetical institution**

7 percent annual return on investments. Although spending is initially higher with the higher yearly payout rule, the alternative lower payout increases the ongoing endowment balance. The vertical bars represent two key points in time where the lower rate yields higher payouts than the higher one. First, in year 22, annual endowment spending with the 4 percent rule exceeds that of the 6 percent rule (as additional investment returns now outweigh the higher proportional spending). Second, in year 38, cumulative lifetime spending from the endowment with the 4 percent rule exceeds that from the 6 percent rule. This highlights a central tension that trustee boards face.

Spending rules only explain a small part of the evolution of endowments over time. They are designed to sustain the real value of endowment gifts, so that the activity to which the gift is restricted can be supported financially in perpetuity, but endowment spending accounts for only a small part of total institutional spending. To the extent that growth in the total endowment is the outcome of an institution's maximizing some objective function over time, the endowment needs to be evaluated within the overall finances of the institution.

## 4.3 Data and the Sample

Our sample period begins in 2008–2009, which is the first year that colleges filed Schedule D, as part of their 990 tax returns and continues to 2021–2022, the most recent fiscal year for which colleges have filed returns. Schedule D is essential to our analysis because it reports endowment levels along with revenues or additions to the endowment (1. investment returns; 2. contributions to the endowment) and distributions or costs (3. grants and scholarships; 4. administrative costs; 5. other costs) in a cleaner fashion than in previous 990 returns. This sample period is of interest because it includes a prolonged positive period from the end of the Great Recession to the start of the pandemic as well as the unexpectedly positive year for stock market investment returns during the first full fiscal year of the pandemic in 2020–21. At the same time, this sample period has limitations, and in particular, we are unable to study the reaction of colleges to downturns (the focus of J. Brown et al. 2014), as the two primary negative years for endowment returns occurred during the first (2008–09) and last (2021–22) years of this period.

Our sample of four-year institutions includes the 187 private, non-profit colleges and universities with highest endowments per full-time equivalent (FTE) student in 2021. We excluded public institutions because they are not required to file 990 tax returns. We also excluded three institutions that would otherwise qualify for our sample: (1) Salem College because its returns combine the financial information for a college and an associated high school; (2–3) Cedarville University and Earlham College, whose 990 forms include one year with a large negative value for "Other expenditures" in line 1e of the 990 form, as that entry disrupts our ability to assess their spending rules.

College 990 filings are public information and are collected and made b If "Yes," explain the arrangement in Part XIII. Check here if the explanation has been provided in Part XIII . . . .

**Part V Endowment Funds.**
Complete if the organization answered "Yes" on Form 990, Part IV, line 10.

| | | (a) Current year | (b) Prior year | (c) Two years back | (d) Three years back | (e) Four years back |
|---|---|---|---|---|---|---|
| 1a | Beginning of year balance . . . | 4,300,531,130 | 2,920,494,006 | 2,834,560,524 | 2,730,457,710 | 2,582,167,326 |
| b | Contributions . . . . . . . . | 27,637,614 | 22,710,434 | 40,108,241 | 36,374,365 | 9,539,445 |
| c | Net investment earnings, gains, and losses . . . . . . . . . . | -366,559,937 | 1,558,216,605 | 241,101,788 | 266,451,383 | 318,881,870 |
| d | Grants or scholarships . . . . | 31,438,697 | 29,170,697 | 29,175,071 | 27,017,069 | 25,705,466 |
| e | Other expenditures for facilities and programs . . . . . . . . . | 123,858,319 | 107,047,350 | 113,544,782 | 126,559,026 | 113,534,651 |
| f | Administrative expenses . . . . | 47,499,119 | 64,671,868 | 52,556,694 | 45,146,839 | 40,890,814 |
| g | End of year balance . . . . . | 3,758,812,672 | 4,300,531,130 | 2,920,494,006 | 2,834,560,524 | 2,730,457,710 |

2 Provide the estimated percentage of the current year end balance (line 1g, column (a)) held as:
a Board designated or quasi-endowment ▶ 25.680 %
b Permanent endowment ▶ 74.320 %
c Term endowment ▶ %
The percentages in lines 2a, 2b, and 2c should equal 100%.

**Fig. 4.2 2021–2022 Schedule D form 990 filing from Amherst College**

available by ProPublica and other organizations. We used data files compiled by the Federal Reserve Board for 9 of the 14 years in the sample period and filled out the data set by manual entry of data found on the ProPublica website. We checked the data for all anomalies and corrected a number of errors in either initial data entry or in the original 990 files.[2] Our data include 14 years of 990 filings for each of the colleges in the sample with the single exception of the filing for one year for Illinois Wesleyan where the publicly available version of the 990 file is incomplete. We added data compiled from the Integrated Postsecondary Education Data System (IPEDS) for these 187 institutions for this sample period.

Figure 4.2 presents a snapshot of the relevant portion of the Amherst College 2021–2022 Schedule D form. The entries in lines 1b and 1c represent inflows or endowment revenues. The entries in lines 1d, 1e, and 1f represent distributions or endowment payouts. By accounting rule, the balance at the end of the year is determined by initial balance adjusted for the difference of yearly revenues and distributions or payouts:

$$\text{End Balance (1g)} = \text{Starting Balance (1a)}$$
$$+ \text{Inflows (1b, 1c)}—\text{Distributions (1d, 1e, 1f)}$$

Line 2a in Schedule D reports the current percentage of the endowment designated as "Funds Functioning as Endowment," which is sometimes described as "quasi-endowment." This is essentially another version of savings; increases in the corresponding value from year to year in this category

2. In many cases, an error in the initial data entry by a college was straightforward to correct because the college fixed the error in reports provided in subsequent years. As shown in the Schedule D provided for Amherst, each filing provides information from the current year and four most recent years. Except in cases of obvious mistakes, we use the report for a given year for each year's filing rather than the information provided for that year in subsequent 990 filings, primarily because the Federal Reserve Board files only contain entries for the current year.

**Table 4.1** **Subgroups of colleges by initial endowment levels**

| GROUP 1 | GROUP 2 | GROUP 3 | GROUP 4 | GROUP 5 |
|---|---|---|---|---|
| Ivy League | Amherst | Bowdoin | American | Belmont |
| Chicago | Baylor | Brandeis | Babson | Bennington |
| Duke | Boston College | Carleton | Bates | Univ. of Dallas |
| Emory | Boston U | Davidson | Fordham | Elon |
| Johns Hopkins | Cal Tech | Haverford | Franklin Marshall | Emerson |
| MIT | Carnegie Mellon | Macalester | Gonzaga | Endicott |
| Northwestern | Case Western | Middlebury | Lewis and Clark | Evansville |
| Notre Dame | George Wash. | Northeastern | Loyola Marymt. | Hampshire |
| NYU | Smith | Oberlin | Marquette | Knox |
| Pittsburgh | Swarthmore | RPI | Providence | Lake Forest |
| Rice | TCU | Syracuse | Quinnipiac | Millsaps |
| Stanford | Tufts | Vanderbilt | Reed | Mt. St. Mary's |
| USC | Tulane | Vassar | St. Lawrence | Sarah Lawrence |
| Vanderbilt | Wellesley | Wake Forest | Tulsa | Thomas Aquinas |
| Washington U | Williams | Wesleyan | Villanova | Westmont |
| **22 colleges** | **24 colleges** | **34 colleges** | **78 colleges** | **29 colleges** |
| START BALANCE $2 \times 10^9$ or more | START BALANCE $1 \times 10^9$ to $2 \times 10^9$ | START BALANCE $5 \times 10^8$ to $1 \times 10^9$ | START BALANCE $1 \times 10^8$ to $5 \times 10^8$ | START BALANCE 0 to $10^8$ |

may be indicative of hoarding, whereby the college payout or other sources of revenue, such as a surplus in the operating budget, are saved and invested in the endowment at the discretion of the board of trustees. We divide the sample of colleges into five groups based on their initial endowment values at the start of the sample period, July 1, 2008. Table 4.1 provides the criteria for each of these groups as well as a selection of colleges from each group.

## 4.4 Descriptive Statistics for Endowment Returns

The 15 or so years since the end of the Great Recession have provided an unusual period of nearly consistently positive stock returns and minimal inflation. As suggested by Ehrenberg (2000), figure 4.3 compares yearly endowment returns to the percentage change in the Higher Education Price Index (HEPI) compiled by the Commonfund Institute during the sample period.

As shown in table 4.2, the universities in our sample accrued average endowment revenues at a yearly rate of 10.5 percent, which was well more than their yearly average endowment spending of 5.1 percent. There was relatively little difference in nominal yearly endowment growth by size of initial endowment: increases in endowment for colleges in each group outpaced increases in the HEPI by at least an average of 2.35 percentage points per year over the sample period.

Table 4.3 divides the sample period into four subperiods. During the first

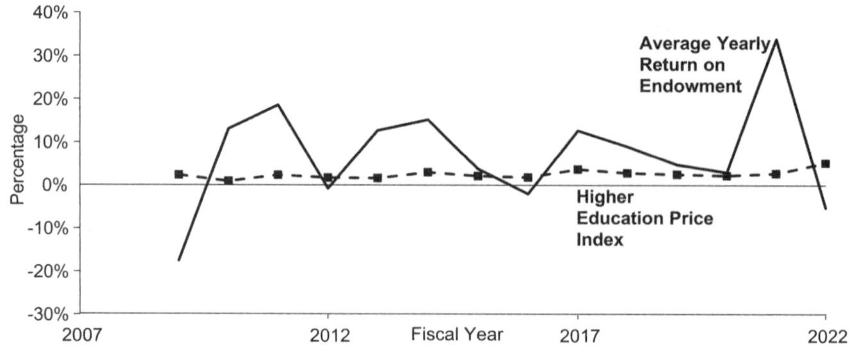


**Fig. 4.3 Endowment returns and inflation: 2008–09 to 2021–22**

**Table 4.2 Average yearly revenues and distributions as % of endowment**

| | All | Group 1 | Group 2 | Group 3 | Group 4 | Group 5 |
|---|---|---|---|---|---|---|
| Invest Return | 7.28% | 8.74% | 7.77% | 7.43% | 7.04% | 6.23% |
| Contributions | 3.27% | 3.00% | 2.32% | 2.46% | 3.14% | 5.54% |
| Grants | 1.60% | 1.03% | 1.35% | 1.79% | 1.79% | 1.54% |
| Other Cost | 3.16% | 3.82% | 3.50% | 3.02% | 2.87% | 3.35% |
| Admin Cost | 0.30% | 0.27% | 0.35% | 0.32% | 0.35% | 0.14% |
| Revenues | 10.54% | 11.74% | 10.09% | 9.89% | 10.18% | 11.77% |
| Total Cost | 5.07% | 5.12% | 5.19% | 5.13% | 5.00% | 5.03% |
| Change in HEPI | 2.48% | 2.48% | 2.48% | 2.48% | 2.48% | 2.48% |

**Table 4.3 Cumulative change in endowment by time period**

| | Group 1 | Group 2 | Group 3 | Group 4 | Group 5 |
|---|---|---|---|---|---|
| 2008–09 to 2012–13 | −1.75% | −4.72% | −3.91% | −2.13% | 10.33% |
| 2012–13 to 2016–17 | 25.74% | 18.12% | 20.73% | 25.07% | 43.81% |
| 2016–17 to 2020–21 | 32.67% | 22.14% | 20.18% | 20.43% | 28.98% |
| 2020–21 to 2021–22 | 31.20% | 29.70% | 24.92% | 22.20% | 12.48% |
| July 2008 to June 2022 | 116.12% | 82.39% | 75.98% | 84.31% | 134.25% |
| Initial Balance 2009 | $8.17 B | $1.38 B | $676 M | $248 M | $51.4 M |
| | (8.09 B) | (303 M) | (101 M) | (94.4 M) | (26.9 M) |
| End Balance 2022 | $16.2 B | $2.51 B | $1.19 B | $451 M | $105 M |
| | (12.9 B) | (781 M) | (339 M) | (224 M) | (81.1 M) |
| # of Institutions | 22 | 24 | 34 | 78 | 29 |

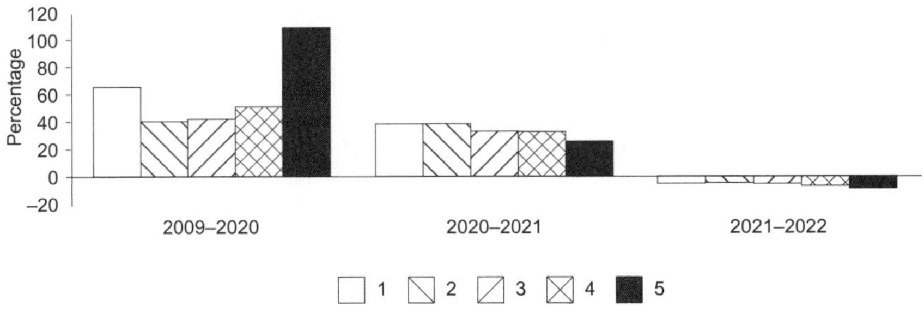


**Fig. 4.4 Endowment changes by group and year of colleges in groups 1–5**

four years from 2008–09 to 2011–12, these colleges were still recovering from the Great Recession; with most using the initial period of stock market recovery to recoup losses from 2008–09. In the next two sets of four years, colleges in each group expanded their endowments despite somewhat lower return years in 2015–16 and 2019–20. Finally, colleges in each group benefited from the extraordinary positive stock market year of 2020–21 though this was followed by average losses in 2021–22.

In all, on a nominal basis, the colleges in each group doubled or nearly doubled their average endowment levels during the sample period. Figure 4.4 highlights the extraordinary nature of the conditions in 2021–22. After the colleges in Group 1 increased their endowment levels by an average of 60 percent from January 2008 to December 2020, they further increased their endowments by an average of nearly 40 percent in 2020–2021. There was considerable positive correlation between endowment size and investment return in that year: colleges in Group 1 had investment gains of more than 40 percent of endowment levels by comparison to investment gains of 33 percent to 38 percent for colleges in Groups 2 to 4 and 25 percent for colleges in Group 5 for that year.

Figure 4.5 compares the change in distributions from the endowments reported in Schedule D, once again highlighting the last two years of the sample period.[3] On a percentage basis, the institutions in the sample increased their endowment distributions at a faster rate than inflation for 2008–09 to 2019–20. With the exception of colleges in Group 5, the colleges in the sample increased average yearly payouts by an average of nearly 50 percent during the first 12 years of the sample from 2008–09 to 2019–20 above inflation.

The colleges in Group 5 increased distributions by the greatest proportional amount in 2020–21, the unusually positive year for investments, then had a

3. We exclude Willamette University (in group 4) from the computations for figure 4.5 because it reported substantial grants for most years and 0 expenditures on grants for 2020–2021.

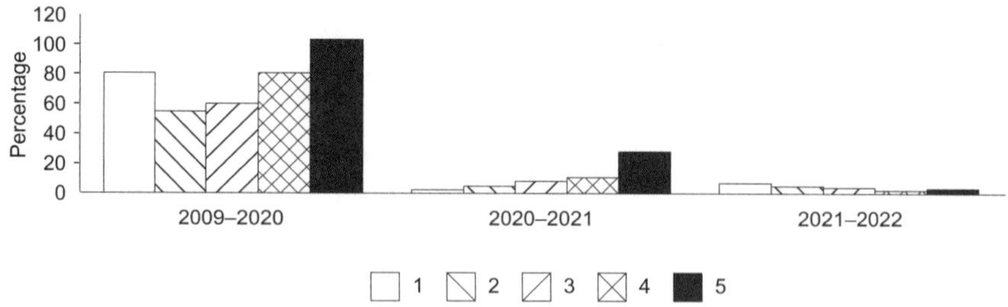


**Fig. 4.5 Changes in reported distributions (Schedule D) by group and year of colleges in groups 1–5**

much lower rate of increase the following year, which was an unusually negative year for investments. We group these two critical years, 2020–21 and 2021–22, in table 4.3 and present results for them separately in figures 4.4 and 4.5. By contrast, colleges in Group 1 had little change in 2020–21 but a substantial increase of 7.1 percent in Schedule D distributions in 2021–22. These findings suggest that the colleges in Group 5 respond quickly whereas colleges in Group 1 respond slowly but fairly decisively to changes in economic conditions.

## 4.5 Spending Rules and Their Properties

In this section, we provide a brief accounting-based overview of the relationship of the moving average and hybrid rules as a precursor to using them to simulate and estimate the spending rules that we observe in the IRS 990 tax data. We examine the impact on distributions from the endowment of an additional inflow of revenue, as a way of comparing the properties of these alternative rules. We conclude that in fact they are very similar, and when we turn to simulating and estimating the actual rules from the IRS data, it is difficult to distinguish them with any precision. At the same time, we demonstrate later that both rules are to some extent misleading on the contributions of the endowment to spending, because they do not take into account reinvestments in the endowment through funds functioning as endowment, which may be offsetting the impact of the gross distributions resulting from the rules on actual spending.

### 4.5.1 Accounting Properties of Spending Rules

Endowment spending rules provide specific guidance about the dispersion of revenues over time. Sedlacek and Jarvis (2010) identify four categories of these rules based on institutional responses to the NACUBO survey: about 75 percent report a *Moving Average Rule* that applies a target annual spending rate to the average of past endowment levels (usually on a quarterly basis for a three-year period). Sedlacek and Jarvis further observe 12 to 15 percent of institutions with largest endowment levels use a *Hybrid Rule* based on a weighted sum of recent endowment level and previous year's endowment spending.

### 4.5.2 Basic Framework and Spending Rules

We define $\mathbf{X}_t$ as the endowment level, $\mathbf{R}_t$ as revenue or inflows to the endowment, and $\mathbf{S}_t$ as spending or distributions from the endowment in year (or period) ***t*** and assume initially that there is no inflation and no return on endowment investments. The endowment changes over time according to the accounting rule (i.e. "*The Law of Motion*")

(1) $$\mathbf{X}_{t+1} = \mathbf{X}_t + \mathbf{R}_t - \mathbf{S}_t.$$

#### *4.5.2.1 Simple Proportional Spending Rule*

The simplest spending rule sets a yearly endowment payout as a fixed proportion of current endowment based on payout rate $\boldsymbol{\alpha}$, which is often 0.05 for non-profit organizations. We begin discussion with this rule—which is simpler than the rules used by most institutions in our sample—because its properties are so clear.

(2) $$\mathbf{S}_t = \alpha \mathbf{X}_t$$

Using (1) to substitute for $\mathbf{X}_t$ and then using (2) to substitute for $\mathbf{S}_{t-1}$ as a function of $\mathbf{X}_{t-1}$ gives

(3) $$\mathbf{S}_t = \alpha(\mathbf{X}_{t-1} + \mathbf{R}_{t-1} - \mathbf{S}_{t-1})$$

(4) $$\mathbf{S}_t = \alpha(\mathbf{X}_{t-1} + \mathbf{R}_{t-1} - \alpha\mathbf{X}_{t-1}) = \alpha(1 - \alpha)\mathbf{X}_{t-1} + \alpha\mathbf{R}_{t-1}$$

Iterating this pair of steps, we can replace $\mathbf{X}_{t-1}$ with linear terms for $\mathbf{X}_{t-2}$ and $\mathbf{R}_{t-2}$ and then gradually expand the expression to include further terms for past revenues with the result that $\mathbf{S}_t$ is ultimately a weighted sum of past revenues where those weights form a geometric series.

(5) $$\mathbf{S}_t = \alpha\mathbf{R}_{t-1} + \alpha(\mathbf{1} - \alpha)\mathbf{R}_{t-2} + \alpha(\mathbf{1} - \alpha)^2\, \mathbf{R}_{t-3} + \ldots$$

If we assume that the college's endowment was initiated with at time 0 with revenue $\mathbf{R}_0$, then we can express $\mathbf{S}_t$ in summation form as a weighted sum of revenues $\mathbf{R}_j$ from periods 0 to t – 1.

(6) $$\mathbf{S}_t = \sum_{j=0}^{t-1} \alpha(\mathbf{1} - \alpha)^j \mathbf{R}_{t-j-1}.$$

Equation (6) also shows that revenue in period **t** first influences endowment spending at period **t + 1**. In each subsequent period, proportion α of the remaining value of revenue $\mathbf{R}_t$ is designated for payout but that remaining value declines over time. Specifically, each additional dollar of revenue in period ***t*** yields additional payout $\alpha(\mathbf{1} - \alpha)^{k-1}$ in period **k**.[4]

4. That is, the dispersion of revenue $\mathbf{R}_t$ follows a geometric series forward from period **t + 1** with initial value $\alpha\mathbf{R}_t$ and multiplier (1 – α) so by the geometric series rule, the eventual sum of revenue payouts over time is $\alpha R_t / [1 - (1 - \alpha)] = R_t$.

Following similar logic, the hybrid spending rules discussed below can also be expressed as weighted linear sums of past revenue values. We explain the relationship of the rules and the minor mechanical differences between them in supplemental notes available from the authors. For expositional simplicity, we focus on the hybrid rule in the main text; our simulated reconstructions from the 990 data are also slightly more accurate for the hybrid than for the moving average spending rule.

*4.5.2.2 Hybrid Spending Rule*

Sedlacek and Jarvis (2010) explain that hybrid spending was introduced by Stanford and is known interchangeably as the Stanford and Yale rules depending on the weights. Yale University currently describes this policy on its website as follows:

> *The payout under the Spending Policy is equal to 80 percent of the prior year's spending plus 20 percent of the long-term spending rate applied to the previous year's beginning endowment market value, with the sum adjusted for inflation.* Yale University (2023)

One important element of Yale's policy is that spending in a given year is a function of lagged values of both the endowment level and spending, so that revenues in year $\mathbf{t}$ influence the endowment level in year $\mathbf{t+1}$ but do not affect endowment spending until year $\mathbf{t+2}$. With this in mind, an endowment spending rule of this form is defined by parameters $\boldsymbol{\alpha}$ and $\beta$ where $\alpha$ represents the targeted long-term spending rate (once again, this is commonly set to 0.05) and $\beta$ is the proportional weight on the endowment level. That is,

$$\mathbf{S_t} = \beta(\alpha\mathbf{X_{t-1}}) + (1-\beta)\mathbf{S_{t-1}}. \tag{7}$$

In period $\mathbf{t+1}$, revenue $\mathbf{R_t}$ in period $\mathbf{t}$ affects the endowment value but not the spending level. Starting in period $\mathbf{t+2}$, those revenues $\mathbf{R_t}$ in period $\mathbf{t}$ influence both the spending level and the endowment level, so the effect of each increase in revenue on future spending gradually increases over an initial phase-in period. Figure 4.5 compares payout rates over time for different values of $\beta$, the weight for the endowment level, holding fixed the target payout rate $\alpha = .05$ and excluding the effects of compound interest and inflation to simplify initial discussion.

We highlight several features of the spending patterns that are evident in figure 4.6.

- Increasing $\beta$ shifts the distribution or payout of revenue from year 0 earlier in time because new revenues have an immediate effect on endowment level and only a gradual effect on spending levels.
- The payout of revenues from year 0 are always less than the target payout rate $\alpha = .05$ with maximum payout increasing in $\beta$.

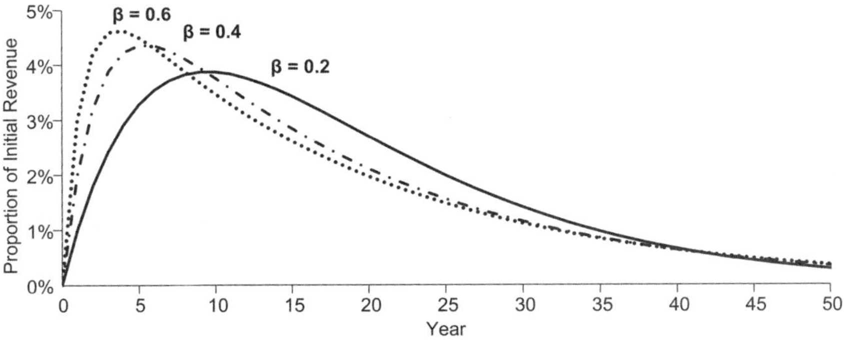


**Fig. 4.6 Spending of endowment revenue over time with a hybrid rule**

- Yearly payouts initially increase and reach a maximum value between years 5 and 10.
- Yearly payouts for lower values of β eventually catch up and surpass payouts for higher values of β.

Amherst uses a variant of the hybrid rule that relies on a moving average of past endowments.

> *the . . . spending rule . . . combines a three-year smoothed historical endowment value (30 percent) with a modest increase (inflation) in last year's spending value (70 percent).*

This formulation combines properties of the moving average and hybrid rules and thereby reduces the influence of recent changes in the endowment. As Ehrenberg (2009) summarizes,

> *wide fluctuation in endowment values may suggest the need to base spending on a longer period of endowment values to provide less variability in the flow of spending. . . . The downside of basing spending rules on longer historical periods is that during prolonged upswings in market valuations (such as that experienced during most of the past 20 years), spending as a share of the current value of the endowment will fall below the target percentage share.*

Figure 4.7 shows how the distribution of revenues is affected by investment returns. In this case, we assume a 4 percent annual return on investments; since this is less than the target payout rate, the endowment does not grow forever and new revenues are still dispersed over time.

- As in figure 4.1, spending increases over time and is initially larger for larger values of β.
- The endowment is initially growing because the investment return is initially higher than the effective payout rate for the new revenue.
- The peak payout rate goes above the target rate of 0.05.

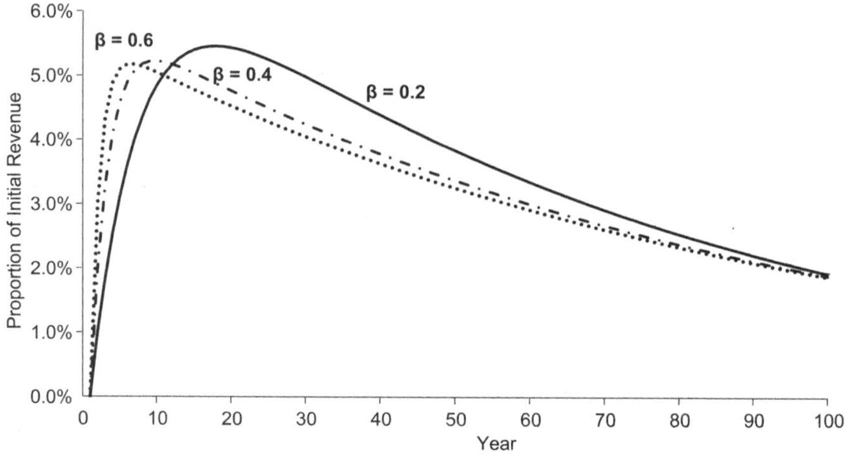


**Fig. 4.7 Spending of new revenue with hybrid rule and investment returns**

- Distribution of new revenues is quite elongated. After 100 years, 35 percent of the initial revenue still remains in the endowment for each of these three weighting schemes.

## 4.6 Spending Rule Simulations

We conducted simulation exercises to attempt to reverse engineer the spending rules of the institutions in the sample using a one-step lagged rule given by (8) for the hybrid model.

$$S_{j,t} = W_E X_{t-1} + W_S S_{t-1} \tag{8}$$

As an initial background step for our simulations, we ran a separate OLS regression for each college (13 observations per college using the first year of data as the baseline values) with spending $\mathbf{S}_t$ as the dependent variable in (9).

$$S_{j,t} = \beta_E X_{t-1} + \beta_S S_{t-1} + \varepsilon_{j,t} \tag{9}$$

We excluded a constant term in these regression specifications, so the OLS model does not incorporate a target spending level or restrict the values of the coefficients or their sums, thereby allowing for average per-year spending levels other than 5 percent of endowment level. We also restricted the coefficients based on the rules $0 \le \hat{\beta}_E \le 0.06$ and $0 \le \hat{\beta}_S \le 1.2$, so that each component contributes a positive amount, but not too large an amount to estimated spending. When these conditions held, which occurred for 80.7 percent of cases with the hybrid rule, we apply the regression coefficients directly as weights so that $W_E = \hat{\beta}_E, W_S = \hat{\beta}_S$. Where the regression coefficients did not meet these conditions, we reverted to a default choice of parameters $W_E = 0.03$, $W_S = 0.4$.[5]

### 4.6.1 Detailed Rules for the Simulations

With the general form of the one-step spending rule equations and the weights for the spending rules in place, we made the following further assumptions to carry out the simulations.

- We assume that college **j** generates the same proportion $\gamma_{j,t}$ of revenue in year **t** as in the observed data for that year. That is, the ratio of the sum of (1) investment earnings and (2) contribution to endowment value at the start of the fiscal year as reported in Schedule D is the same in the simulations as in practice.
- We work in terms of nominal values with no adjustments for inflation.
- We take the actual endowment and spending values as given for the first year (2009) for the hybrid rule since (8) includes one lagged observation.

To carry out the simulation for a given college for the hybrid rule, we used equation (8) to compute spending $\hat{S}_{j,t}$, computed revenue in year **t** as proportion $\gamma_{j,t}$ of the starting endowment in that year ($\hat{R}_{j,t} = \gamma_{j,t}\hat{X}_{j,t}$) and applied the accounting rule for the law of motion (originally listed in equation [1]) to compute simulated endowment for the next year:

$$\hat{X}_{j,t+1} = \hat{X}_{j,t} + \hat{R}_{j,t} - \hat{S}_{j,t}. \tag{10}$$

By iterating this series of steps, applying (10) once for each year, we filled out a complete time series of estimated endowment, revenue, and spending values ($\hat{X}_{j,t}$, $\hat{R}_{j,t}$, $\hat{S}_{j,t}$) for each college **j** and years **t** from 2010 to 2022.

### 4.6.2 Results of the Simulations

Once the simulated spending patterns were generated, we compared the simulated and actual endowment values at the end of the sample period in July 2022 according to the absolute value for the percentage difference between simulated $\hat{X}_{2022}$ and actual final endowment level $X_{2022}$.

$$\text{Error Rate} = \left|\frac{\hat{X}_{2022} - X_{2022}}{X_{2022}}\right|$$

We classify the simulation results into three categories: (1) Error Rate < 5 percent; (2) Error Rate between 5 and 10 percent; (3) Error Rate greater than 10 percent. As shown in table 4.4, our simulations produce error rates of less than 5 percent for more than 70 percent of the colleges and error rates of less than 10 percent in approximately 83 percent of them. Fur-

5. These default parameters correspond to a 5 percent target rule for contributions. For instance, weights of 60 percent on past endowment and 40 percent on past cost with a 5 percent target rule yield a weight of $0.6 * 0.05 = 0.03$ on past endowment.

**Table 4.4** **Accuracy of simulated spending patterns**

| Hybrid Model | ALL | Groups 1 and 2 | Groups 3 to 5 |
|---|---|---|---|
| 0 to 5% Absolute Error | 132 (70.6%) | 34 (73.9%) | 98 (69.5%) |
| 5.1 to 10% Absolute Error | 23 (12.3%) | 7 (15.2%) | 16 (11.3%) |
| 10.1 or more Absolute Error | 32 (17.1%) | 5 (10.9%) | 27 (19.1%) |
| TOTAL | 187 (100%) | 46 | 141 |

ther, the simulations had slightly lower error rates for colleges with larger endowments, with error rates less than 10 percent for nearly 90 percent of the colleges.

Figure 4.8a depicts the simulated and actual distributions or costs for Yale University where these relationships are fairly typical of cases where the simulation produced an error rate less than 5 percent. Here, the simulated values given repeated application of (10) produced results close to but clearly distinct from actual spending, with both periods of underestimating (about 2011 to 2014) and overestimating (about 2015 through 2019) actual reported costs.

Figure 4.8b shows the results for Brown University, where the simulation produces an error rate above 5 percent. In this case, the simulated values include relatively large overestimates of endowment spending at both the beginning and end of the sample period.

As these examples suggest, institutional spending tends to be less predictable than these spending rules suggest. The projected distributions in the simulations are most inaccurate when the hybrid rule cannot reproduce relatively complicated spending patterns of individual colleges. While our method is clearly ad hoc and we are only judging the accuracy of the simulation based on the end result in terms of endowment level, these results suggest that the spending patterns of the colleges are at least reasonably described by a weighted average spending rule. For this reason, we focus attention on the projected weights for the 85 percent of cases where the hybrid rule produces a simulated final endowment within 10 percent of the true value.

Equation (8) ($S_{j,t} = W_E X_{t-1} + W_S S_{t-1}$) for simulations of the hybrid spending rule corresponds to a target spending rate $\alpha$ when $(W_E / \alpha) + W_S = 1$ which means $\alpha = (W_E / 1 - W_S)$. Table 4.5 reports the average weights for simulations of the hybrid rule for the 151 institutions with final projected endowment levels within 10 percent of the actual value.[6] The given average weights in each category correspond to target spending rates between 5.2

6. We exclude four institutions where the simulation used the default parameters listed in footnote 5.

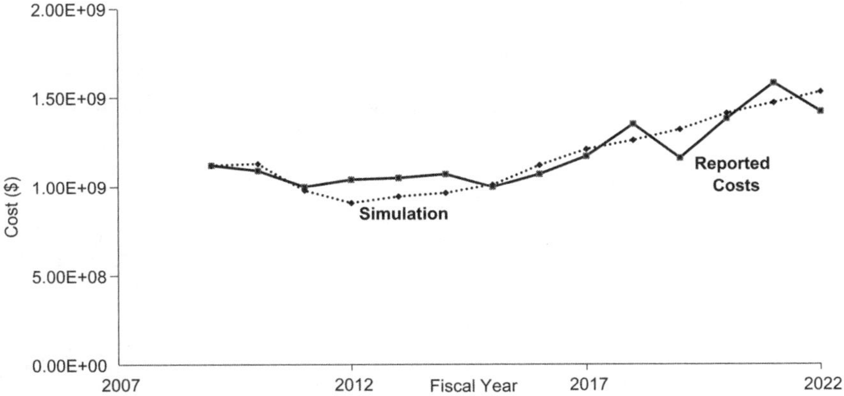


**Fig. 4.8a Simulated and actual spending from the endowment for Yale University**

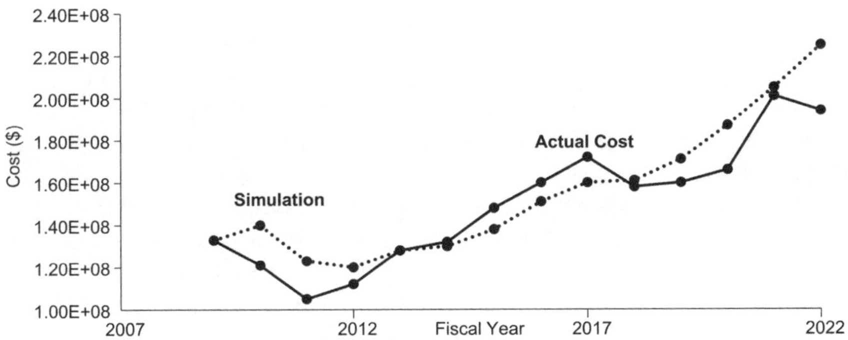


**Fig. 4.8b Simulated and actual spending from the endowment for Brown University**

**Table 4.5 Average weights for successful simulations**

| | All | Group 1 | Group 2 | Group 3 | Group 4 | Group 5 |
|---|---|---|---|---|---|---|
| Endowment | .025 | .028 | .018 | .021 | .025 | .032 |
| Weight | (.015) | (.015) | (.012) | (.014) | (.014) | (.018) |
| Lagged Cost | .546 | .508 | .680 | .628 | .538 | .374 |
| Weight | (.268) | (.273) | (.234) | (.253) | (.254) | (.267) |
| Target Spending* | 5.51% | 5.73% | 5.59% | 5.73% | 5.50% | 5.19% |
| Colleges | 151 | 17 | 20 | 29 | 63 | 22 |

* The standard deviation for each reported value is reported in parentheses. The target spending level is computed at the average weights listed in each column.

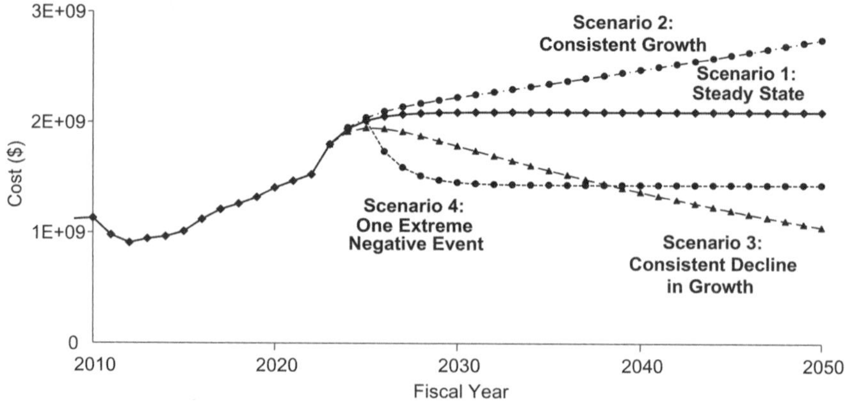


**Fig. 4.9 Projected future endowment expenditures for Yale University**

and 5.7 percent, which seems broadly plausible. Institutions in Groups 1 to 4 are estimated to use average weights of 50 to 65 percent on previous spending, which imposes considerable smoothness on the spending pattern, though not as much as with the 80 percent weight on prior spending from the Yale Rule.

It is notable that the implied target spending rates listed in table 4.5 are somewhat greater than 5 percent even though the descriptive statistics in table 4.2 showed that average spending was close to 5 percent of current endowment levels for each group of colleges. These results are actually consistent with each other in a period of rising endowments since then a spending rule designed for target spending equal to proportion α of recent *past endowment levels* will produce endowment payout of less than that proportion α of the *current endowment level.*

The hybrid rule is conducive to simulations of future endowment paths because it requires so little information and is straightforward to apply. Figure 4.9 projects the results of simulations of four scenarios for the trajectory of the endowment path for Yale University through 2050 using the estimated hybrid rule weights for Yale as described above. Scenarios 1 through 3 assume that Yale receives revenue each year (starting in 2022–23) equal to a fixed proportion of its current endowment, where that proportion is equal to the yearly payout rate in Scenario 1, 6 percent in Scenario 2 (approximately 1 percentage point higher than the yearly payout rate), and 2.5 percent in Scenario 3 (approximately half the yearly payout rate). Scenario 4 makes one adjustment to Scenario 1, assuming a onetime negative event that causes a 25 percent loss of the endowment in investment returns in 2024–25.

As shown in figure 4.9, total distributions stabilize relatively quickly in Scenarios 1 and 4, indicating that the endowment level also stabilizes in

**Table 4.6** **Regression results for predicting current year spending**

| | All | All | Group 1–2 | Group 1–2 | Group 3–5 | Group 3–5 |
|---|---|---|---|---|---|---|
| Balance Lag 3 | .046** | .042** | .045** | .042** | .051** | .051** |
| | (.0005) | (.001) | (.001) | (.002) | (.001) | (.002) |
| Invest Gains | .003* | .003** | .003 | .003 | .008** | .007** |
| | (.001) | (.001) | (.003) | (.002) | (.003) | (.003) |
| Invest Gains | .008** | .010** | .008** | .010** | .002 | .001 |
| Lag 1 | (.001) | (.001) | (.003) | (.003) | (.003) | (.003) |
| Invest Gains | .038** | .030** | .038** | .030** | .030** | .027** |
| Lag 2 | (.003) | (.003) | (.006) | (.005) | (.006) | (.005) |
| Invest Gains | .038** | .037** | .038** | .037** | .020** | .020** |
| Lag 3 | (.002) | (.001) | (.003) | (.003) | (.003) | (.003) |
| Contributions | .017* | .008 | .016 | .008 | −.034** | −.014 |
| | (.008) | (,007) | (.016) | (.015) | (.010) | (.009) |
| Contributions | .114** | .098** | .115** | .010** | .035** | .051** |
| Lag 1 | (.009) | (.008) | (.018) | (.015) | (.011) | (.010) |
| Contributions | .034** | .020** | .032 | .020 | .020 | .037** |
| Lag 2 | (.009) | (.008) | (.019) | (.016) | (.011) | (.010) |
| Contributions | .027** | .001 | .025 | −.000 | .026* | .041** |
| Lag 3 | (.009) | (.008) | (.018) | (.016) | (.012) | (.010) |
| Constant | 0.56M | 8.75M | 4.38M | 30.6M** | 0.02M | −0.39M |
| | (0.66M) | (1.32M) | (3.23M) | (8.4M) | (.024M) | (0.64M) |
| Fixed Effects by Institution | NO | YES | NO | YES | NO | YES |
| R2 | .9839 | .9892 | .9783 | .9867 | .8744 | .9235 |
| Colleges | 187 | 187 | 44 | 44 | 143 | 143 |
| Observations | 2,057 | 2,057 | 506 | 506 | 1,551 | 1,551 |

* = significant at 0.05, ** = significant at 0.01 level.

those cases, though at a much lower level in Scenario 4 than in Scenario 1. By contrast, we project steady increases in Scenario 2 and steady reductions in Scenario 3 for both total distributions and endowment level. These results indicate that the hybrid rule is an especially good match for relatively stable conditions but that it will result in consistent under- or over-spending if the target payout rate is different than the rate of revenue generation.[7]

### 4.6.3 Descriptive Regression Analysis of Spending

Our simulations implicitly give equal weight to contributions and investment returns. To distinguish between these two sources of revenue, we conduct descriptive regressions to predict current spending levels. As shown in table 4.6, investment gains and contributions have estimated positive and

7. These scenarios assume a spending rate equal to the long-term real return on the endowment. We assume no inflation and no change in the long-term spending rule, although a significant change in the expected long-term return as in Scenarios 2 and 3 would lead to a change in the spending rule.

generally significant effects on future endowment spending, but there are apparent distinctions in the effects of these two separate sources of funds.

- Contributions are estimated to have the largest effect in the first year after realization and substantially diminishing effect beyond that to the point where they have no discernible effect in year 3 for the institutions in Groups 1 and 2 (those with highest endowments).
- Investment gains have relatively small initial effect and then growing effect over time, consistent with the properties of one-step spending rules.

## 4.7 Quasi-Endowments and Net Spending

As part of their 990 Schedule D filings, colleges and universities report the division of the endowment into three categories defined by the Financial Accounting Standards Board (FASB): (1) **quasi-endowment**, often known as "**Funds Functioning as Endowment**"; (2) permanent endowment; (3) term or restricted endowment.[8] In essence, quasi-endowments serve as unrestricted funds, as indicated by the instructions for Schedule D from the Internal Revenue Service: "**Board-designated endowments or quasi-endowments** result from an internal designation and are generally not donor-restricted and are classified as net assets without donor restrictions. The governing board has the right to decide at any time to expend such funds."

When a donor makes an endowment gift for a specific purpose, spending rules are designed to protect the real value of the gift and support that activity in perpetuity. The real value of the endowment over time depends on the value of inflows from new gifts, investment returns in excess of the amount needed to maintain the real value of the endowment, and reinvestment of operating surpluses. The board of trustees may choose to designate discretionary funds to the quasi-endowment to take advantage of the higher return on the endowment investments compared to other possible investment options. The quasi-endowment then serves to increase the overall value of the endowment, and the spending it supports, or to save for some specific lumpy expenditure in the future.

Figure 4.10 shows that the average proportion of endowments in the term endowment category approximately doubled from 2008–09 to 2013–14 and then remained fairly steady after that. This increase in the proportion held as term endowments appears to be explained almost entirely by a corresponding decline in the proportion of funds held in the permanent endowment. These changes may be explained at least partly by an initial period of limited donations and solid investment returns in the aftermath of the Great Reces-

8. New donations are classified in the second category as "permanent endowment" but investment earnings on funds in the permanent endowment are typically moved into term endowment.

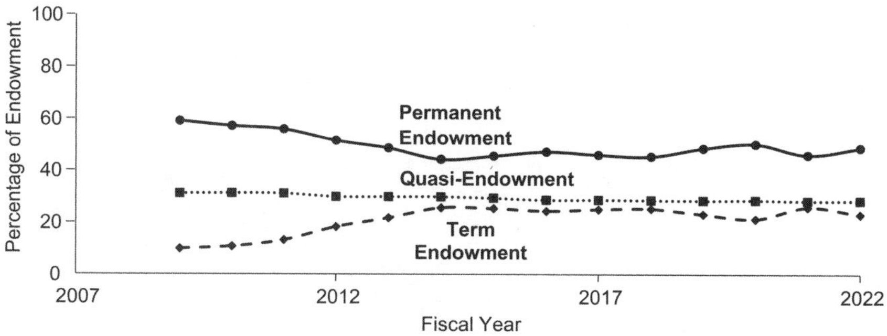


**Fig. 4.10 Average division of endowments by category**

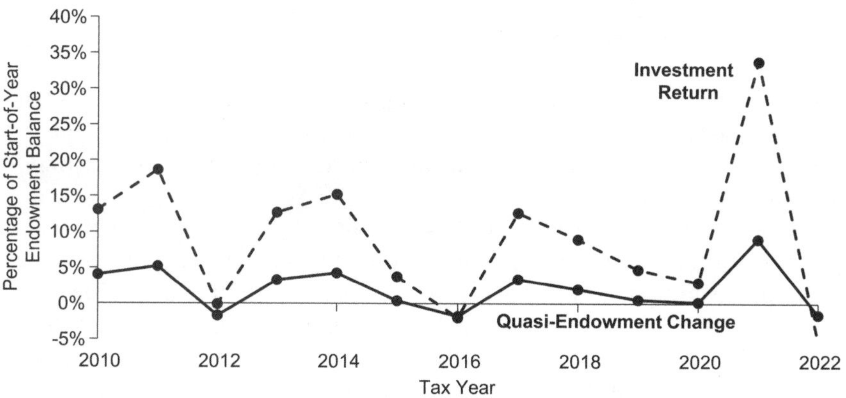


**Fig. 4.11a Investment returns and changes in quasi-endowment value**

sion. It is also interesting to see that the proportion held as quasi-endowment remained relatively close to 30 percent throughout the sample period, which suggests that the spending power of these institutions grew in proportion to the increase in real endowment level.

Figure 4.11a graphs investment returns and the change in quasi-endowment value as a percentage of start-of-year endowment balance. The two curves take quite similar shape, suggesting that quasi-endowment balance moves in the same direction as investment returns, though on a much smaller proportional scale. In the years with the lowest observed investment returns, quasi-endowment values remained relatively flat or experienced modest declines. By contrast, in years with investment returns greater than 10 percent, quasi-endowments levels tended to grow, with typical returns in the sample period of gains of the order of 4 to 5 percent of endowment balance in those years, and much more than that in the unusual year of 2020–21.

Figure 4.11b provides a similar graph of contributions and the change

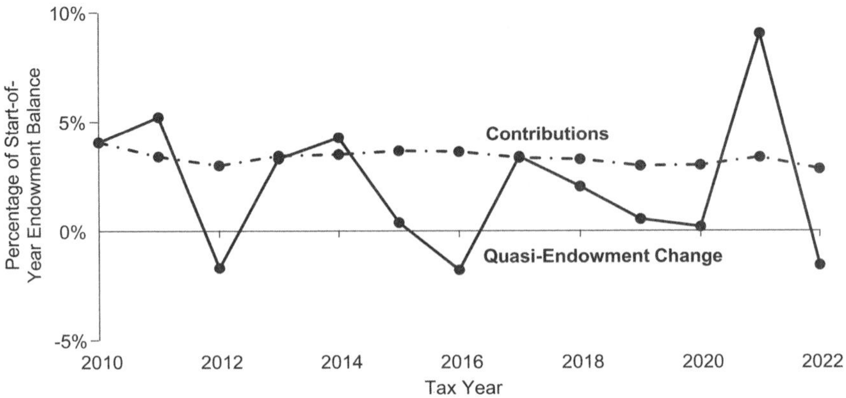


**Fig. 4.11b Contributions and changes in quasi-endowment value**

in quasi-endowment value as a percentage of start-of-year endowment balance. While there is some suggestion of positive correlation between the two values, there is much less variation in contributions than in investment returns on a year-by-year basis.

We represent the values in figures 4.11a and 4.11b as percentages of the endowment balance at the start of the tax year so that these values are in comparable unit. Since increases in the quasi-endowment offset endowment spending, we define "Net Endowment Spending" as the distribution from the endowment as recorded in the 990, minus any reinvestment in the endowment in the form of funds functioning as endowment. Distributions represent funds allocated to support spending, while reinvestment of funds in the endowment as funds functioning represent unrestricted income or revenues that are not spent and instead invested in the endowment. Net endowment spending represents the impact on spending of these two activities.

Figure 4.12 graphs net endowment spending by tax year in the sample period. Ordinary endowment spending (the sum of all expenses reported in Schedule D of the 990 tax return) is fairly consistent at slightly above 5 percent for most years in the sample period. By contrast, net endowment spending varies considerably by year with values near to or less than 0 percent in several years and values near to or above 5 percent in six other years.

As expected, the correlation between investment returns and changes in the quasi-endowment from figure 4.11a carries over to figure 4.12. The five years with lowest net endowment spending rates were each characterized by unusually positive (greater than 10 percent) average investment returns. Similarly, the years with net endowment spending at approximately 5 percent or higher were the ones in the sample period with lowest average investment returns.

Tables 4.7a and 4.7b provide results of descriptive regression specifications with net endowment spending and change in quasi-endowment as the dependent variables and investment returns and contributions as inde-

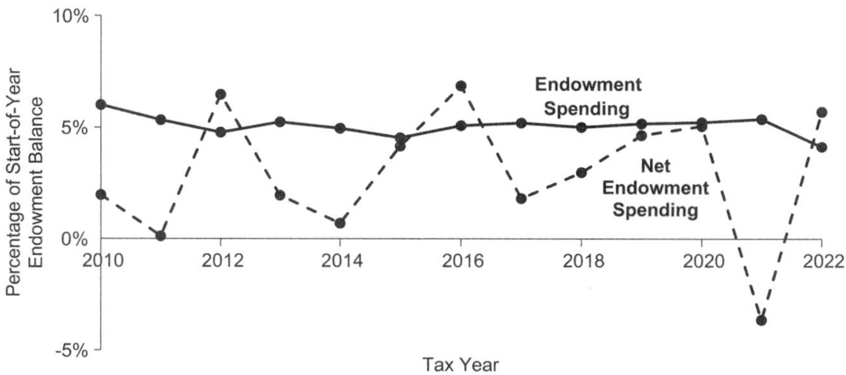


**Fig. 4.12 Endowment and net endowment spending**

pendent variables. Consistent with our observations of figures 4.9a, 4.9b, and 4.10, contemporaneous investment returns and contributions are significant predictors of these dependent variables. Each unit increase in investment returns is predicted to reduce net spending and increase the quasi-endowment by approximately 0.3 units. Similarly, each unit increase in contributions is predicted to reduce net spending and increase the quasi-endowment by approximately 0.4 units.

To some degree, we might view these relationships as mechanical implications of accounting rules because unexpected financial windfalls in a given year necessarily have effects on the balance sheet. From this perspective, perhaps the most interesting question is how universities adjust their future policies in response to current year gains and losses. One common theory of transmission of contributions/investment returns is an initial increase/decrease in the quasi-endowment/net-spending (when the new money could be considered unexpected) followed by a corresponding reversal in subsequent years once the institution identifies a suitable project to spend the full contribution/investment return on. Table 4.7a provides some evidence in favor of this theory as lagged investment returns are predicted to have positive effects on net spending yet lagged contributions have little to no observable effect on net spending. Table 4.7b provides much more mixed evidence with both positive and negative significant effects of lagged investment returns and contributions on current year changes in the quasi-endowment.

Taken together, these results imply that the source of endowment revenue matters for whether institutions engage in strategic behavior with respect to how spending is allocated. The majority of investment gains appear to be strategically managed by institutions so as to provide budgetary flexibility (e.g., a permanent shift to the quasi-endowment). On the other hand, contributions appear to conform more to the transitory theory presented above, with any initial increase in the quasi-endowment spent down in subsequent years.

**Table 4.7a** **Regression results for net spending**

| | All | All | Group 1–2 | Group 1–2 | Group 3–5 | Group 3–5 |
|---|---|---|---|---|---|---|
| Balance Lag 3 | .070** | .021** | .069** | .020 | .074** | .101** |
| | (.003) | (.006) | (.006) | (.013) | (.007) | (.0105) |
| Invest Gains | −.327** | −.303** | −.328** | −.304** | −.330** | −.348** |
| | (.007) | (.008) | (.015) | (.016) | (.018) | (.017) |
| Invest Gains | .038** | .081** | .038* | .082** | −.001 | −.031 |
| Lag 1 | (.008) | (.009) | (.016) | (.019) | (.022) | (.022) |
| Invest Gains | −.018 | −.032 | −.020 | −.034 | −.000 | −.004 |
| Lag 2 | (.016) | (.018) | (.033) | (.036) | (.031) | (.032) |
| Invest Gains | .067** | .063** | .067** | .063** | .022 | .018 |
| Lag 3 | (.009) | (.009) | (.018) | (.018) | (.014) | (.014) |
| Contributions | −.373** | −.393** | −.375** | −.386** | −.553** | −.531** |
| | (.044) | (.048) | (.091) | (.098) | (.045) | (.046) |
| Contributions | −.091 | −.085 | −.106 | −.093 | −.034 | −.062 |
| Lag 1 | (.050) | (.051) | (.103) | (.105) | (.047) | (.047) |
| Contributions | .111* | .071 | .114 | −.080 | .115* | .099 |
| Lag 2 | (.054) | (.054) | (.110) | (.110) | (.055) | (.055) |
| Contributions | −.213** | −.273** | −.229* | −.284** | .029 | .016 |
| Lag 3 | (.052) | (.053) | (.107) | (.108) | (,055) | (.055) |
| Constant | 6.82M | 73.0M** | 21.2M | 238M** | 1.71M | −2.76M |
| | (3.83M) | (9.03M) | (18.8M) | (58.1M) | (0.95M) | (2.29M) |
| Fixed Effects by Institution | NO | YES | NO | YES | NO | YES |
| R2 | .6670 | .7170 | .6570 | .7080 | .4103 | .5449 |
| Colleges | 187 | 187 | 44 | 44 | 143 | 143 |
| Observations | 2,057 | 2,057 | 506 | 506 | 1,551 | 1,551 |

* = significant at 0.05, ** = significant at 0.01 level.

## 4.8 Analysis of IPEDS Spending Data

We utilize IPEDS data to look at specific changes in expenditures by institutions, focusing on four categories (academic support, institutional support, instruction, student support) that were consistently reported in our sample. Webber and Ehrenberg (2010) and Deming and Walters (2017) establish a particular connection between funding for student support and student success in terms of persistence and degree completion, so we focus on that category in our analysis.[9]

9. "Student services" includes admissions, registrar activities, and activities for which the primary purpose is to contribute to students' emotional and physical well-being and to their intellectual, cultural, and social development outside the context of the formal instructional program. Intercollegiate athletics and student health services may also be included except when operated as self-supporting auxiliary enterprises. See "Postsecondary Institution Expenses," National Center for Education Statistics, https://nces.ed.gov/programs/coe/indicator/cue/post secondary-institution-expense.

**Table 4.7b** **Regression results for quasi-endowment change**

| | All | All | Group 1–2 | Group 1–2 | Group 3–5 | Group 3–5 |
|---|---|---|---|---|---|---|
| Balance Lag 3 | −.024** | .021** | −.024** | .022 | −.021** | −.030** |
| | (.003) | (.006) | (.006) | (.012) | (.004) | (.008) |
| Invest Gains | .330** | .307** | .331** | .307** | .273** | .281** |
| | (.007) | (.008) | (.014) | (.015) | (.010) | (.011) |
| Invest Gains | −.030** | −.071** | −.031 | −.072** | −.010 | .004 |
| Lag 1 | (.008) | (.009) | (.016) | (.018) | (.012) | (.013) |
| Invest Gains | .056** | .061** | .058 | .063 | −.054** | −.047* |
| Lag 2 | (.016) | (.017) | (.032) | (.035) | (.020) | (.022) |
| Invest Gains | −.028** | −.026** | −.029 | −.026 | −.002 | .001 |
| Lag 3 | (.008) | (.008) | (.017) | (.017) | (.011) | (.011) |
| Contributions | .391** | .400 | .391** | .394** | .557** | .531** |
| | (.043) | (.046) | (.088) | (.094) | (.037) | (.040) |
| Contributions | .205** | .183** | .220* | .192 | −.062 | −.059 |
| Lag 1 | (.048) | (.049) | (.099) | (.101) | (.038) | (.041) |
| Contributions | −.078 | −.051 | −.082 | −.060 | .071 | .087* |
| Lag 2 | (.051) | (.052) | (.105) | (.106) | (.041) | (.043) |
| Contributions | −.239** | .274** | .254* | .284** | −.014 | .003 |
| Lag 3 | (.050) | (.051) | (.103) | (.104) | (.042) | (.044) |
| Constant | −6.25M | 64.2M** | −16.9M | −208M** | −0.11M | 1.99M |
| | (3.68M) | (8.69M) | (18.1M) | (55.9M) | (0.88M) | (2.73M) |
| Fixed Effects by Institution | NO | YES | NO | YES | NO | YES |
| R2 | .6868 | .7320 | .6714 | | .4850 | .5564 |
| Colleges | 187 | 187 | 44 | 44 | 143 | 143 |
| Observations | 2,057 | 2,057 | 506 | 506 | 1,551 | 1,551 |

* = significant at 0.05, ** = significant at 0.01 level.

Figure 4.13a shows overall increases of 40 to 50 percent in total IPEDS costs (the sum of expenses reported in the four categories listed above) from 2008–09 to 2019–20, with modest decline followed by subsequent increases in the next two years.

Figure 4.13b shows larger proportional increases in spending on student support both during the first 12 years of the sample period and in 2021–22 where spending increased by an average between 12 percent and 18 percent in each of the five groups of colleges. Investment in health and specifically mental health services for students likely contribute to the cost increases observed in student services for 2021–22; a total of 77 percent of institutions reported expansions of mental health service during 2022 in a separate survey.[10]

10. "Colleges Are Investing in Student Mental Health. But 'There's Still a Long Way to Go,' Survey Finds," Eva Surovell, January 18, 2023, *The Chronicle of Higher Education*, https://www.chronicle.com/article/colleges-are-investing-in-student-mental-health-but-theres-still-a-long-way-to-go-survey-finds.

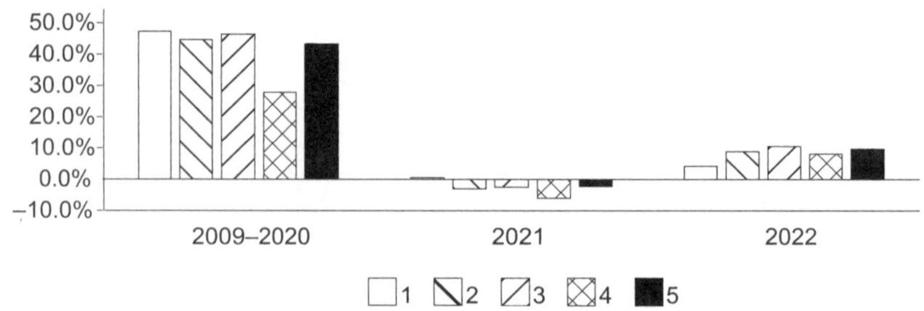


**Fig. 4.13a % increases in IPEDS reported costs by group and year of colleges in groups 1–5**

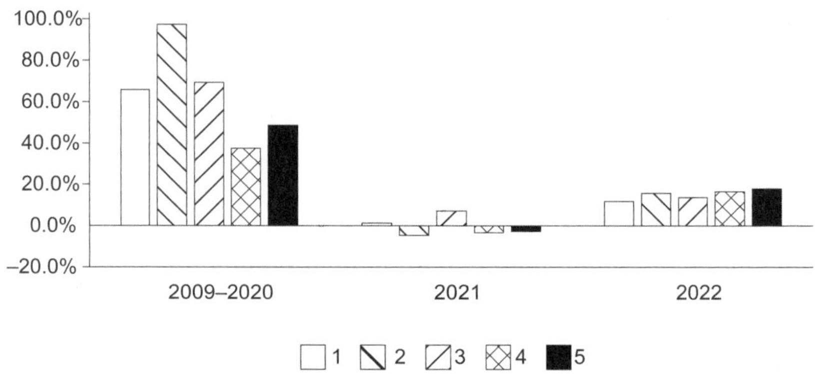


**Fig. 4.13b % change in yearly spending on student support by group and year of colleges in groups 1–5**

To understand the impact of endowments and endowment distributions on spending and savings, more work is needed on the relationship of distributions from the endowment, reinvestment in funds functioning as endowment, and spending in the operating budget on different categories. The IPEDs data reported here, for example, suggest endowment growth exceeded expenditure growth on these categories, but also that endowment growth in 2020–21 might have supported increased spending in 2022.

## 4.9 Discussion and Conclusion

Previous papers by Tobin (1974), Hansmann (1990), Merton (1993), and Hoxby (2015), among others, discussed the conceptual basis for university endowments. Hoxby conceptualizes universities as organizations that promote increases in intellectual capital through research and teaching, using endowments to fund both current and future productive activity. Hoxby further suggests that long periods of real endowment growth may suggest suboptimal spending rules:

*The financial side would only grow persistently as a share of the total portfolio if (a) the returns on future intellectual capital projects were* substantially *higher than those of today's intellectual capital projects and (b) adjustment costs were such that when those future days arrive, the cost of suddenly needing to provide infrastructure and expertise to them would not be exorbitant.*

*Since circumstances (a) and (b) probably do not often arise in conjunction, the model implies that a university should examine itself if its financial market portfolio's share of its total portfolio rises very persistently. It seems most likely that this would occur if the university were not solving its investment problem correctly according to the model.*

From this perspective, the optimal payout rate for endowments should equate the marginal value of present and expected future activities at the university that create intellectual capital, taking all revenue streams into account. Universities have other revenue streams beyond earnings on the endowment, and their optimization of spending over time should depend on all these revenue streams, which would then have implications for optimal real endowment growth.

Ehrenberg (2009) in contrast suggests a rule of thumb for spending that maintains the university's endowment level in real terms over time:

*To provide future generations with protection against inflation, the endowment for a specific funded activity must grow over time by the average rate of inflation faced by the university.*

This prescription protects the activities funded by donors with restrictions but does not really address the optimality of the consistent growth of the university endowments that we study, and especially the growth of quasi-endowments during the sample period. Table 4.8 shows that 80.2 percent of the institutions in our sample and almost all of the initially wealthiest institutions produced endowment growth greater than the cumulative inflation rate of 40.9 percent from 2008–09 to 2021–22. Similarly, Lerner et al. (2008) observed median annual endowment growth rates of 7.4 percent during the 13-year period from 1992 to 2005 when the average annual inflation rate was 2.6 percent; they also identified positive correlation between endowment size and endowment growth, primarily because institutions with the largest

**Table 4.8 Endowment growth relative to inflation**

| Group | Endowment Growth > Inflation | Endowment Growth < Inflation | Total |
|---|---|---|---|
| 1 | 21 (95.5%) | 1 (4.6%) | 22 |
| 2 | 22 (91.7%) | 3 (12.5%) | 24 |
| 3 | 30 (88.2%) | 4 (11.8%) | 34 |
| 4 | 58 (74.4%) | 15 (25.6%) | 78 |
| 5 | 20 (69.0.4%) | 9 (31.0%) | 29 |
| TOTAL | 150 (80.2%) | 37 (19.8%) | 187 |

endowments had superior average returns on investments during those 13 years.[11]

One subtlety in the interpretation of endowment growth is that universities generally report that 70 percent or more of their endowment funds are restricted in their use, which opens the possibility that a university could experience long-lasting endowment growth on paper and yet still face ongoing financial stress. Ehrenberg's rule of thumb accounts for this possibility by stipulating a comparison of the endowment return *for a "**specific funded activity**"* to the inflation rate, implicitly suggesting that contributions may be extraneous to the comparison because they are often targeted for new rather than for existing funded activities.[12]

On the other hand, many restrictions on the endowment direct funds toward uses, such as financial aid, that the university would choose on its own. From the outside, however, it is not easy to determine the degree to which restrictions on endowment spending do or don't align with university priorities. As Baum et al. (2018) conclude, "*The available data do not make it possible to determine to what extent these restrictions in fact constrain the spending decisions of colleges and universities.*"

Our results from table 4.7 in section 4.7 offer a middle ground interpretation since we estimate that 40 percent of each increase in contributions translates into an increase in university spending power as measured by the size of the quasi-endowment. From this perspective, our findings indicate that our sample period was characterized by growth in endowment spending power for both existing and new activities.

A second justification that endowment growth need not be suboptimal is that increased universities may already be overcommitted in their spending plans. Campbell, Stein, and Wu (2024) in this volume estimate that the Harvard Faculty of Arts and Sciences has been running a 21 percent structural budget deficit even with the increased payouts that have resulted from the long-term growth of the endowment. Based on IPEDS reporting, the institutions in our sample have yearly expenses of approximately 35 percent of their endowment values, so they are much more dependent on revenues from other sources than from endowment payouts. Further, the findings of J. Brown et al. (2014) that universities cut expenses beyond

11. Piketty (2014) summarized results from the longer period from 1980 to 2010 and found in his analysis of 850 institutions that "U.S. universities earned an average real return of 8.2 percent on their capital endowments, and all the more so for higher endowments."

12. Ehrenberg observed that the average yearly rate of return on endowment investments over the 40-year period from 1956 to 1997 was 9.8 percent and that inflation as measured by the Higher Education Price Index (HEPI) was 5.2 percent per year for that same period. Allowing for estimated administrative costs of 0.7 percent per year for managing the endowment, Ehrenberg suggested an annual payout rate of 9.8 percent −5.2 percent −0.7 percent = 3.9 percent, quite close to the 4.1 percent median and 4.3 percent mean payout observed for universities during that period of time. One notable feature of this computation is that it implicitly assumes that contributions have negligible value for addressing existing needs.

the level called for by their existing spending rules suggest that the financial situations of these institutions may be surprisingly precarious. The increase in quasi-endowments that we observe may be an optimal response to expectations of declines in future revenue, for example from mean reversion in endowment returns, declines in net tuition revenue given projected student demographics, or even concerns about increases in the recently instituted endowment tax.

To the degree that the growth of university endowments has expanded their spending power, the standard model of sustainable spending (Campbell and Sigalov 2022) calls for a smoothed increase in future spending and incremental expansion of funded activities, as would be suggested by a fixed payout rate for a stable endowment level after adjusting for inflation.[13] From this perspective, the increase in average endowment payout rate from 4.3 percent from the period (1956–1997) observed by Ehrenberg to more than 5 percent per year at present suggests that universities have increased endowment spending given an assessment that their continuing strong investment returns increase the level of spending that is sustainable. The increase in quasi-endowment suggests that the higher spending rate has not led one for one to higher spending, but is in fact a reallocation from restricted to unrestricted endowments, as savings in the budget are reallocated as funds functioning without restrictions. It should be noted that we are not implying a literal reallocation from restricted to unrestricted fundings in a direct accounting sense. Rather, we view this as an implicit reallocation because money is fungible, and administrators have some latitude in deciding how spending is prioritized. For instance, if a department is gifted an endowed professorship at the same time they are owed a tenure-track line due to a recent retirement, it would be easy for a budget-conscious dean to justify substituting the endowed line for the owed line. The department would be at the same level as before the last retirement, and the restricted donation would now take the place of previously unrestricted funding.

This increases the institution's flexibility to respond to future events. The increase in quasi-endowments may be a rational response to the possibility of mean reversion in financial returns with the implication that universities might have to be less optimistic about future financial returns after the ahistorical rise in stock market values in 2020–2021.

An alternative to the guidance of smoothed spending over time is for institutions to proceed with larger investments (that were presumably not previously feasible) with potentially outsize benefit-cost returns in response to long-term increases in endowment level. Given such an unexpected surplus of funds, an institution could consider onetime investments, such as a

13. Campbell and Martin (2023) provide a different perspective on sustainable spending based on the concept from environmental economics of maintaining equal utility levels for individuals in different generations.

new building or the start-up costs for a new academic program or longer-term investments based on discrete increases in endowment payouts. But, as highlighted by figure 4.1 earlier in the paper, increases in spending or commitments to spending in the present and in the near-future implicitly reflect the view that marginal increases in spending will produce greater value now than in the future, constituting a bet that may be uncomfortable for many boards of trustees.

One possible use of endowment funds would be to provide additional financial aid. Baum and Lee (2019) suggest that it is paradoxical that some institutions with outsize endowments practice need-aware admissions, meaning that they have a systematic policy of rejecting some well-qualified students solely on the basis of financial need. Bulman (2022) studies the effects of investment returns on future spending and concludes that plausibly exogenous increases in endowments lead to more spending, but do not appear to increase diversity or the number of low-income students who enroll. Similarly, Baum et al. (2018) find that "*Institutions with high endowments per student do use these resources to lower net prices for students, but not necessarily to enroll greater shares of students with financial need compared to other institutions.*" These authors emphasize that since most institutions with very large endowments are need-blind and offer generous financial aid programs to students who are admitted, it would only make sense to direct additional funds to financial aid in tandem with substantive changes in recruiting and admission practices. If it is optimal to increase spending on need-based aid, it would most likely need to be a sustainable long-term rather than a onetime or short-term increase, which may explain why Bulman (2022) finds that exogenous increases in endowment returns do not lead to observable increases in financial aid.

The cliche "A rising tide lifts all boats" applies both to restricted and unrestricted endowment funds; a period of unusually large investment returns would necessarily open new possibilities for unrestricted spending for any institution that was not initially dramatically underwater. The last two years of our sample period and the nearly two years since the end of our sample period may meet this definition. Our sample data indicated nominal endowment increases averaging 30 percent in 2020–21 in a year with essentially no inflation. Though 2021–22 brought a combination of endowment declines and outsize inflation, both 2022–23 and the first three quarters of 2023–24 have been fertile periods for investments. For example, the S&P 500 increased 17.6 percent in 2022–23 (from 3785 on 6/30/22 to 4450 on 6/23) and another 17.6 percent so far in 2023–24, a year of declining inflation. Based on these figures, it could be common for an institution to increase its endowment by 50 percent in real terms during these four years. A change in endowment status of that size would likely provide a variety of new opportunities and suggest substantive adjustments to existing endowment spending rules. The optimal response will depend on future expectations however of all revenue and expenditure streams, as suggested by Campbell, Stein, and Wu. The increase in quasi-endowments that we observe do suggest that institutions are optimizing over all revenue streams, not just from endowments, and that they are anticipating challenges in the future. Whether this should be considered "hoarding" depends on one's view of the likelihood of these anticipated challenges.

## References


Ang, Andrew, Andrés Ayala, and William N. Goetzmann. 2018. "Investment Beliefs of Endowments." *European Financial Management* 24: 3–33.

Baum, Sandy, Catharine Bond Hill, and Emily Schwartz. 2018. "College and University Endowments: In the Public Interest?" Ithaka Policy Report.

Baum, Sandy, and Victoria Lee. 2019. "The Role of College and University Endowments." Center on Education Data and Policy Research Report.

Blanchett, D, 2014. "Donation Risk and Optimal Endowment Portfolio Allocations." *Journal of Portfolio Management* 41: 109–20.

Brown, David, and Dan Scholz. 2019. "Discount Rates and Asset Returns: Implications for Endowment Strategies." Working Paper.

Brown, Jeffrey R., Stephen G. Dimmock, Jun-Koo Kang, and Scott J. Weisbenner. 2014. "How University Endowments Respond to Financial Market Shocks: Evidence and Implications." *American Economic Review* 104(3): 931–62.

Brown, Keith, and Cristian Tiu. 2013. "The Interaction of Spending Policies, Asset Allocation Strategies, and Investment Performance at University Endowment Funds." In *How the Financial Crisis and Great Recession Affected Higher Education*, edited by Jeffrey R. Brown and Caroline M. Hoxby. Chicago: University of Chicago Press.

Bulman, George. 2022. "The Effect of College and University Endowments on Financial Aid, Admissions, and Student Composition." NBER Working Paper No. 30404. Cambridge, MA: National Bureau of Economic Research.

Campbell, John, and Ian Martin. 2023. "Sustainability in a Risky World." Working Paper.

Campbell, John, and Roman Sigalov. 2022. "Portfolio Choice with Sustainable Spending: A Model of Reaching for Yield." *Journal of Financial Economics* 143: 188–206.

Campbell, John Y., Jeremy C. Stein, and Alex A. Wu. 2025. "Economic Budgeting for Endowment-Dependent Universities." In *Financing Institutions of Higher Education*, edited by John Y. Campbell and Kaye Husbands Fealing. National Bureau of Economic Research Conference Report. This volume. Chicago: University of Chicago Press.

Cejnek, Georg, Richard Franz, and Neal M. Stoughton. 2023. "Portfolio Choice with Endogenous Donations—Modeling University Endowments." Working Paper.

Cejnek, Georg, Richard Franz, Otto Randl, and Neal M. Stoughton, 2014. "A Survey of University Endowment Management Research." *Journal of Investment Management* 12: 90–117.

Chambers, David, Elroy Dimson, and Charikleia Kaffe, 2020. "Seventy-Five Years of Investing for Future Generations." *Financial Analysts Journal* 76: 5–21.

Dahiya, Sandeep, and David Yermack. 2021. "Investment Returns and Distribution Policies of Non-Profit Endowment Funds." Working Paper.
Dimmock, Stephen G. 2012. "Background Risk and University Endowment Funds." *Review of Economics and Statistics* 94: 789–99.
Dybvig, Philip, and Zhenjiang Qin. 2021. "How to Squander your Endowment: Pitfalls and Remedies." Working Paper.
Deming, David, and Christopher Walters. 2017. "The Impact of Price Caps and Spending Cuts on U.S. Postsecondary Attainment," NBER Working Paper No. 23736. Cambridge, MA: National Bureau of Economic Research.
Ehrenberg, Ronald G. 2000. *Tuition Rising*. Harvard University Press.
Ehrenberg, Ronald G. 2009. "Demystifying Endowments." TIAA-CREF Institute Advancing Higher Education Working Paper.
Filosa, Tracy. 2023. *The Role of the Endowment in the Dynamic College and University Business Model*. Cambridge Associates. Presentation, NBER Conference, Financing Higher Education, Spring.
Gilbert, Thomas, and Christopher Hrdlicka. 2015. "Why Are University Endowments Large and Risky?" *Review of Financial Studies* 28: 2643–2686.
Grawe, Nathan D. 2018. *Demographics and the Demand for Higher Education*. Johns Hopkins Press.
Halem, Zachery, Andrew Lo, Egor Matveyev, and Sarah Quraishi. 2022. "The Effects of Spending Rules and Asset Allocation on Nonprofit Endowments." *Journal of Portfolio Management* 49: 44.
Hansmann, Henry. 1990. "Why Do Universities Have Endowments?" *Journal of Legal Studies* 19(1): 3–42.
Hoxby, Caroline M. 2015. "Endowment Management Based on a Positive Model of the University." In *How the Financial Crisis and Great Recession Affected Higher Education*, edited by Jeffrey R. Brown and Caroline M. Hoxby. Chicago: University of Chicago Press.
IRS. Form 990 data, including Schedule D.
Lerner, Josh, Antoinette Schoar, and Jialan Wang. 2008. "Secrets of the Academy: The Drivers of University Endowment Success." NBER Working Paper No. w14341, Available at SSRN: https://ssrn.com/abstract=1271374.
Lo, Andrew, Egor Matveyev, and Stefan Zeume. 2019. "The Risk, Reward, and Asset Allocation of Nonprofit Endowment Funds." Working Paper.
Merton, Robert. 1993. "Optimal Investment Strategies for University Endowment Funds." In *Studies of Supply and Demand in Higher Education*, edited by Charles T. Clotfelter and Michael Rothschild. University of Chicago Press.
National Center for Education Statistics (NCES). Annual publication. Integrated Postsecondary Education Data System, Complete Data Files. U.S. Department of Education. https://nces.ed.gov/ipeds/datacenter/DataFiles.aspx.
Piketty, Thomas. 2014. *Capital in the 21st Century*. Harvard University Press.
Sedlacek, Verne O., and William F. Jarvis. 2010. "Endowment Spending: Building a Stronger Policy Framework," Commonfund Institute Report. https://eric.ed.gov/?id=ED559301.
Stein, Jeremy. 2023. "Economic Budgeting for Universities." Presentation at NBER Financing Higher Education Conference, February 3, 2023.
Tobin, James. 1974. "What Is Permanent Endowment Income?" *American Economic Review Papers and Proceedings* 64(2): 427–32.
Webber, Douglas A. 2018. "Higher Ed, Lower Spending: As States Cut Back, Where Has the Money Gone?" *Education Next* 18(3): 72–78. https://www.educationnext.org/higher-ed-lower-spending-as-states-cut-back-where-has-money-gone/.
Webber, Douglas A., and Ronald Ehrenberg G., 2010. "Do Expenditures Other than

Instructional Expenditures Affect Graduation and Persistence Rates in American Higher Education." *Economics of Education Review* 29(6): 947–58.
Yale University. 2023. "2202 Endowment Spending and Distributions." It's Your Yale. Yale University.

## Comment Jeffrey R. Brown

It is a privilege to have the opportunity to discuss a paper by an incredibly talented set of authors on a topic that is of both intellectual and practical interest. This paper by Avery, Ehrenberg, Hill, and Webber certainly qualifies on all counts. They study endowment spending during the academic years 2008–09 through 2021–22 using Schedule D from the informational IRS Form 990. The authors do a nice job of explaining their data source's relative advantages (e.g., possibly less measurement error due to official tax filings) and disadvantages (e.g., exclusion of public institutions) over data used in prior studies (e.g., NACUBO).

In the early part of the paper, the authors clearly explain how endowments and quasi-endowments work and the constraints managers face. The authors also provide useful summary statistics of endowment growth over their sample. The authors take a slightly different approach from prior research in that they estimate payout functions rather than examine empirical deviations from stated payout rules (as done, for example, in Brown et al. 2014). Using a simple empirical model and limited assumptions, they approximate spending rules for 80 percent of the sample. Among the important results of this paper are that endowments grew considerably over the period of study, with growth rates exceeding that of the spending of the universities they support. The authors discuss the extent to which their findings could be consistent with various models of endowments.

Rather than provide a detailed critique of their data and methods, I am going to invoke the discussant's prerogative to speak more broadly about the topic. Part of my motivation is there is still important work to be done: there are still many unanswered questions about how endowments should and do operate, and this ought to be of special interest to those of us employed by universities that partly rely on endowments for funding.

A useful place to start evaluating the behavior of university endowments is to examine their mission statements, since these presumably are highly

Jeffrey R. Brown is the Larry Gies Family Chair in Business and Professor of Finance at the University of Illinois Urbana-Champaign, and a research associate of the National Bureau of Economic Research.
For acknowledgments, sources of research support, and disclosure of the author's material financial relationships, if any, please see https://www.nber.org/books-and-chapters/financing-institutions-higher-education/comment-endowment-spending-rules-brown.

correlated with what economists would characterize as the objective function of an endowment. There is a noticeable similarity across a range of public and private institutions. For example, the foundation supporting the University of Illinois (where I serve as a dean) says it exists "to advance the interests and welfare of the University." Yale University's massive endowment has a mission that is stated as "to best serve the university's mission and ensure its longevity." The mission of Harvard's endowment is "to support the educational and research goals of the University." Many other mission statements read similarly.

This focus on supporting, serving, or advancing the university suggests that to understand how to strategically manage an endowment, one should focus on the objective function of the university that the endowment serves. It turns out, however, that this is not so easy. There is no consensus in the literature on how to model what it is that universities seek to optimize, with possibilities ranging from expanding educational access to maximizing the prestige of the university, among other possibilities. Of course, universities can differ from one another in their relative priorities (e.g., consider a large public land-grant research university versus a small, elite liberal arts college). Even within the same institution, leaders might simultaneously pursue multiple objectives, such as expanding knowledge through research, delivering high-quality education, and creating innovative solutions to societal problems. These objectives can be difficult to measure. For example, rankings are widely considered a highly flawed measure of prestige, and research is measured by most universities based on expenditures rather than on the social value created. Additionally, different parts of the university often pursue very different objectives: the head of a research institute in the sciences might prioritize external research funding, a dean might emphasize academic program success, a department chair in social sciences might care about publications in a small set of elite journals, and an athletic director might care about football wins and losses. The relative priority of these objectives can vary in importance over time and under different leadership regimes. And, of course, there are a myriad of constraints—funding, legal, regulatory, political, societal, and so on—that make it difficult to characterize optimal behavior of a university.

I will assert from casual observation (and without formal evidence) that there exists considerable heterogeneity in the "effective" objective functions of universities. This heterogeneity makes it difficult to make precise predictions about how university endowments "ought" to behave with respect to their two key decisions: (i) how to allocate their portfolio; and (ii) how to pay out income from the endowment to the university over time.

So, what is a researcher to do? One approach is to observe how universities manage payouts from their endowments over time and through different economic environments to see what we can infer about what they value.

This paper is in that spirit, and it supports what earlier papers have also shown: that most endowments use some form of "smoothing" mechanism to determine how much to pay out to a university each year. This paper uses a flexible empirical model that captures both moving average rules (i.e., a target that calculates payouts to some number of years of prior endowment values) and hybrid rules (i.e., rules that take into account past endowment values but also current endowment spending) and estimates the parameters for each private university in their sample.

The predominance of smoothing functions shown by this and prior papers means that payouts are less volatile than the returns on the endowment's portfolio. Such smoothing makes intuitive sense insofar as the university is making long-term commitments based on expected payouts. For example, if a sub-account of an endowment is dedicated to funding a faculty position with a steady stream of expenses, it is reasonable that the university may want to have a lower-volatility revenue stream to fund it over time.

But are these smoothing rules really optimal? In my view, the preponderance of the evidence suggests that although they may be simple and convenient, they are unlikely to be optimal. Let us take the idea that universities desire stable revenue streams to support long-term commitments. If one narrowly frames the expenditure needs and thinks only in terms of a particular endowment sub-account funding a particular expenditure, then one might expect to see more "asset-liability matching," i.e., investing in a portfolio that de-risks the income used to fund the expenditure, such as by investing primarily in fixed income instruments. This is akin to an insurance company investing primarily in fixed income instruments to back annuity liabilities. Yet this is not what we observe: most university endowments have portfolios that are heavily invested in public and private equity, and many follow the Yale example of being extremely heavily invested in alternative asset classes. These alternative investments have high expected returns, but they also carry elevated risk, especially when one defines risk as the ability to match the desired payout stream.

One could also take a broader view of investing, which recognizes that the university's endowment is only one part of its overall revenue portfolio. Universities also receive funding from tuition, federal research grants, gifts, contracts, and public funds for state institutions, among many other sources. From the perspective of a university's larger portfolio of revenue, one might want to invest the endowment in a manner that considers the covariances of endowment returns with the variability of other sources. For example, federal research funding varies with changes in presidential and congressional leadership. Tuition, although set by the institution, can be subject to macroeconomic conditions and political or social pressures. Alumni giving varies with economic conditions (see, for example, Brown et al. 2015). Athletic ticket and sponsorship revenue vary with team performance. And for public institutions, state budget appropriations are subject to political uncertainty. If one recognizes that income from the university endowment is only one part of an overall revenue portfolio, one might expect endowments to choose investments that partially hedge some of these other risks. Yet we observe little of using endowment investments to hedge other risks.

What is going on? Mission statements aside, it may be that endowments are not actually optimizing in pursuit of the objective function of the university. The likely reason is that principal-agent problems abound. As mentioned earlier, university objective functions are often difficult to measure, university and foundation presidents may have limited time horizons, foundations have their own boards who might have interests that do not perfectly align with the university's, it may be easier to communicate to donors in terms of return performance of the endowment than to communicate in terms of how well the endowment took into account covariances with other revenue streams, and so on. University and endowment presidents have an incentive to care about the growth of the endowment *per se*, as this is an easy metric to which to point as evidence of success. (Indeed, a simple search of news articles and press releases about presidents and chancellors stepping down often point to their success at growing the endowment as a key accomplishment.)

Indeed, this was one of the insights of the Brown et al. (2014) paper, in which we showed that universities have an asymmetric response to positive versus negative endowment shocks. In the face of significant negative shocks, endowments often reduce their subsequent payout amount by even more than their own smoothing formula would have indicated. We went on to show that this behavior was concentrated among the subset of universities for which the endowment was within 10 percent of its value when the current president took office. This is consistent with a model in which university presidents are rewarded for endowment growth and thus are willing to take a deeper hit to their operational budget to maintain the value of the endowment, a phenomenon we called "endowment hoarding." Notably, the current paper is unable to further test this hoarding hypothesis in the face of negative shocks because the only negative returns in their sample occurred in the first and last period of their data, suggesting that future work might be appropriate to support or refute this hypothesis.

Overall, I still view the behavior of university endowments to be somewhat of a puzzle, both in terms of how they allocate their portfolios and in terms of how they choose their payout rules. More research is needed on this topic, as our understanding is still limited, especially in comparison to how important these questions are to many of the institutions that employ academic economists! I welcome this additional work on the topic, and I genuinely hope that it spurs additional research going forward by these authors and others.

## References

Brown, Jeffrey R., Stephen G. Dimmock, Jun-Koo Kang, and Scott J. Weisbenner. 2014. "How University Endowments Respond to Financial Market Shocks: Evidence and Implications." *American Economic Review* 104(3): 931–62.

Brown, Jeffrey R., Stephen G. Dimmock, and Scott J. Weisbenner. 2015. "The Supply of and Demand for Charitable Donations to Higher Education." In *How the Financial Crisis and Great Recession Affected Higher Education*, edited by Jeffrey R. Brown and Caroline M. Hoxby. Chicago: University of Chicago Press.

# 5

# Economic Budgeting for Endowment-Dependent Universities

John Y. Campbell, Jeremy C. Stein, and Alex A. Wu

## 5.1 Introduction

Universities with substantial endowments are fortunate to have financial assets that generate capital income to support research and teaching activities that would otherwise be unaffordable. Instead of relying entirely on tuition, state subventions, or sponsored research funding, these universities can spend endowment distributions to bridge the gap between external funds and the costs of their operations.

A standard view of endowment spending is that it must be sustainable in the sense that it is expected to be no smaller in the future than it is in the present. As James Tobin put it in a famous 1974 article, "The trustees of an endowed institution are the guardians of the future against the claims of the present. Their task is to preserve equity among generations. The trustees of an endowed university like my own assume the institution to be immortal.

John Y. Campbell is the Morton L. and Carole S. Olshan Professor of Economics at Harvard University, and a research associate of the National Bureau of Economic Research.

Jeremy C. Stein is the Moise Y. Safra Professor of Economics at Harvard University, and a research associate of the National Bureau of Economic Research.

Alex A. Wu is a PhD student at Harvard University studying Business Economics.

This paper was presented at the NBER Conference on the Financing of Higher Education, funded by the Alfred P. Sloan Foundation, on April 4–5, 2024, in Cambridge, Massachusetts. We are grateful to Jay Herlihy, Scott Jordan, Susan Duda, and the financial staff of the Harvard Faculty of Arts and Sciences for their consistent support of this project, and to Antoinette Schoar for her discussion at the conference. For acknowledgments, sources of research support, and disclosure of the authors' material financial relationships, if any, please see https://www.nber.org/books-and-chapters/financing-institutions-higher-education/economic-budgeting-endowment-dependent-universities.

They want to know, therefore, the rate of consumption from endowment which can be sustained indefinitely."[1]

Whether or not this sustainable spending policy is followed, it is an inescapable truth that spending more from the endowment today reduces the resources available to be spent tomorrow. Richer academic discussions of endowment management such as Hansmann (1990) and Campbell (2012), and formal models such as Gilbert and Hrdlicka (2015), Dybvig and Qin (2021), and Campbell and Sigalov (2022) capture this intertemporal trade-off.

Although the intertemporal constraints on endowment spending are easily understood by economists, they are harder for some other observers to grasp. Some members of the university community and some outside observers interpret the endowment as if it were a discretionary fund, available to spend on new activities, which will be refilled if depleted.[2] From this point of view, having a large endowment is a sign that a university has failed to make good use of its donors' generosity and is simply hoarding cash without using it for the good of the university community or society.

Such a perspective naturally leads to calls for universities to spend more aggressively. As Derek Bok, former president of Harvard, put it in a recent article in the *Chronicle of Higher Education*, "Although large endowments were a blessing for the universities that possessed them, they brought disadvantages as well. Among liberals, such accumulations of wealth led to demands on these universities to use their money to achieve social goals."[3] Pressures of this sort do not come only from the left; several Republican senators have advocated taxing large endowments to give universities an incentive to run them down.[4]

1. Or, as Harvard University puts it on its website, "Many endowments, including Harvard's, are structured to exist in perpetuity, meaning that the institution must continue to rely on the endowment's earnings forever. Because of this, our endowment is not only for today's generation, but is for all future generations of Harvard students and scholars. Guided by this principle of intergenerational equity, Harvard's endowment is carefully managed in order to ensure that future generations will enjoy its benefits just as much as the current one." See "Supporting Our Mission," Harvard University, accessed February 6, 2024, https://www.harvard.edu/about/endowment/.

2. In other words, the distinction between wealth and the income from wealth is ignored. Consistent with this, the value of large endowments is sometimes compared with national incomes as a rhetorical device to emphasize the wealth of universities. Writing for CBS Moneywatch, Aimee Picchi recently wrote, "Harvard's endowment, at more than $50 billion, is the biggest among U.S. universities and is larger than the GDP of more than 120 nations, including countries such as Tunisia, Bahrain, and Iceland." (See "How rich is Harvard? It's bigger than the economies of 120 nations," by Aimee Picchi, *CBS News MoneyWatch*, December 12, 2023 https://www.cbsnews.com/news/harvard-endowment-2023-harvard-president-salary/.)

3. Derek Bok, "Why Americans Love to Hate Harvard," *Chronicle of Higher Education*, January 4, 2024.

4. Large endowments began to pay an excise tax on endowment income in 2017, and the One Big Beautiful Bill Act of 2025 increased the top tax rate to 8 percent in 2026. Proposals for even more aggressive taxation of large endowments were made during the Biden administration by Senators Tom Cotton and J. D. Vance, among others.

Even within a university, standard budgeting procedures foster this attitude. It is common for university budgeting processes to consider one year at a time, and to treat endowment distributions within that year as a source of income that is discretionary—at least to the university's trustees if not to the administrators working on the budget. Within a setup like this, a budget deficit can always be "solved" by increasing the endowment distribution. A long-run consequence of higher endowment spending today, which is lower endowment spending in the future, is obscured by this procedure. The one-year budgeting framework fosters a similar attitude toward debt since proceeds from new debt issues are treated as income while repayment of debt is treated as an expense. Yet debt issuance simply moves resources from one year to another but does not change the present value of the resources available to the university over the long term.

Harvard's Faculty of Arts and Sciences (FAS) employs two of the authors of this paper, John Campbell and Jeremy Stein. In 2021, Claudine Gay, then Dean of the FAS, asked Stein to co-chair a faculty study group to develop a better understanding of the FAS financial position and explore strategic options for the management of the FAS. Within this larger effort, Campbell chaired a working group to develop an economic budgeting framework that would address the deficiencies of standard year-by-year budgeting.[5] The goal was to think about university finances like economists rather than accountants, and to present the university's budget constraint in an intertemporal context.

This paper explains the framework the working group developed, and illustrates it with actual numbers that describe the FAS in fiscal year 2023. We are grateful for the consistent support of FAS financial staff in refining the framework and providing us with the updated data we show here.

The remainder of the paper is organized as follows. In section 5.2, we describe the traditional accounting-based approach to budgeting that has been used by the FAS for many years, and examine some of the potential drawbacks of relying too heavily on such an approach for decision-making. In section 5.3, we introduce our alternative economic approach based on the intertemporal budget constraint, and walk through a specific application using recent FAS numbers. In section 5.4, we put this approach through its paces, doing a number of sensitivity analyses that help to illustrate the key drivers of long-term financial health for the FAS. In section 5.5, we explore the implications of our economic budgeting framework for the Harvard endowment—more specifically, we ask how the endowment's risk tolerance should be shaped by what we learn from the economic budgeting exercise. Finally, section 5.6 concludes.

5. The other members of the working group were Stephen Blyth, then Professor of the Practice of Statistics, Jay Herlihy, then FAS Associate Dean for Finance, and Thomas Hollister, then Harvard University Chief Financial Officer and Vice President for Finance. We are grateful for their contributions to this analysis.

**Table 5.1** **Harvard FAS budget for fiscal year 2023**

| Item | FY23 Amount ($m) |
|---|---|
| Tuition and Fees | 449.2 |
| Tuition Discount | −303.7 |
| **Net Tuition** | **145.5** |
| Net Continuing Ed and Exec Fees | 201.4 |
| **Total Student Income** | **346.9** |
| Federal Sponsored Programs | 143.1 |
| Non-Federal Sponsored Programs | 63.0 |
| **Total Sponsored Support** | **206.0** |
| Current Use Gifts | 153.0 |
| Net Endowment Distribution | 834.9 |
| Other Revenue | 83.0 |
| **Total Operating Revenue** | **1623.8** |
| Faculty Salaries and Wages | 209.5 |
| Other Salaries and Wages | 346.9 |
| **Total Salaries and Wages** | **556.5** |
| Benefits | 150.0 |
| Scholarships excl. discounts | 85.2 |
| Supplies and Equipment | 71.3 |
| Space and Occupancy excl. interest | 202.7 |
| Interest | 50.2 |
| Depreciation | 128.1 |
| Other Expenses | 317.1 |
| **Total Operating Expenses** | **1561.0** |
| **GAAP Operating Profit** | **62.8** |

## 5.2 A Traditional GAAP Approach to Budgeting

The usefulness of our explicitly intertemporal approach can be motivated by first reviewing a more traditional approach to university budgets. To make this discussion concrete, we describe the methods that have been used for years at Harvard FAS, but we suspect that similar methods are common in other university settings.

Table 5.1 shows a simplified representation of the Harvard FAS budget for the fiscal year 2023, prepared according to generally accepted accounting principles (GAAP). This budget adds together a number of sources of "operating revenue," then subtracts various items that are deemed "operating expenses," to arrive at a net GAAP budget surplus or deficit. And importantly for management purposes, running a GAAP surplus—or at least avoiding a significant GAAP deficit—has long been considered an important metric of financial health for the FAS. Indeed it is not an exaggeration to say that in past years, targeting this metric, i.e., aiming to balance the budget in GAAP terms, has been a primary goal of FAS financial management.

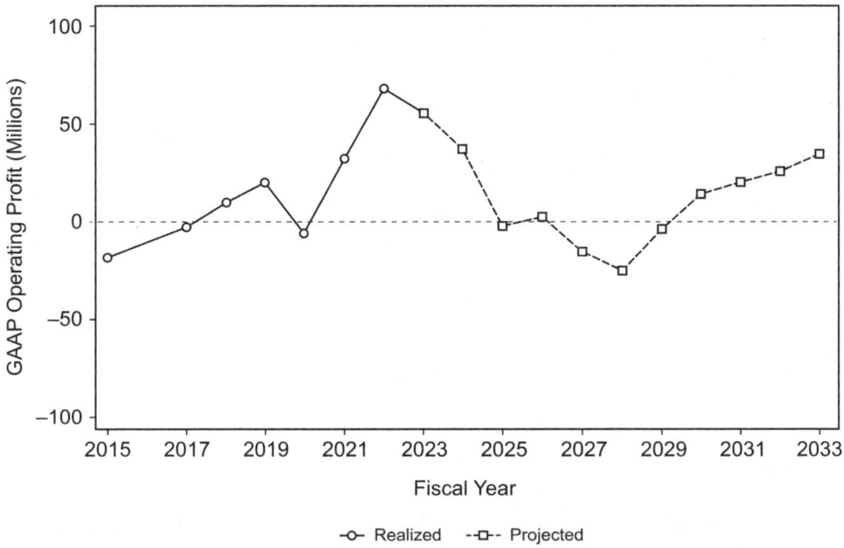


**Fig. 5.1 Harvard FAS GAAP operating profit**

Figure 5.1 shows that according to this GAAP budget-balance metric, Harvard FAS generally looks to be in solid shape. Since 2017, the budget measured this way has either been in surplus or quite close to it—even in the pandemic year of 2020—and forecasts for the next few years are generally encouraging even though there are a few years of modest anticipated deficits later in this decade.

However, from the perspective of an economist interested in the university's intertemporal budget constraint, this GAAP surplus/deficit construct is misleading in several ways. First, it mixes financial flows with the real-side revenues and expenses that reflect the physical economics of the university. Most obviously, the distribution from the endowment is treated as a form of revenue. But of course, increasing the payout from the endowment does not improve the university's long-run financial position in the same way that, for instance, increased tuition income does. Rather, it just represents a transfer of a portion of a fixed pool of resources from the future to the present. Similarly, the proceeds of new debt issuance are treated as revenue while interest and principal payments on existing debt are treated as an expense. This confuses matters, because it suggests that borrowing more or delaying the repayment of debt would improve the university's financial position. Again, this is not correct, because these actions simply increase the debt payments that must be made in the future.

A second drawback of the GAAP approach is that it treats depreciation as an expense, even though depreciation—which depends on a somewhat arbitrary accounting judgment—does not represent a cash outflow in any sense. The other side of this accounting treatment is that annual capital expenditures on plant and equipment are *not* directly captured in the GAAP presentation, even though these do represent real dollar outflows. To be clear, one would not want to load all of a given year's capital expenditures into that year's budget, especially if management decisions are heavily influenced by the goal of attaining budget balance on a year-by-year basis. Doing so would run the risk of encouraging deferrals of needed maintenance and upkeep, deferrals that might be highly uneconomic over the longer run.

This brings us to the third issue with the GAAP approach, namely that an excessive focus on current budgets—or even on budgets a few years into the future—is inherently myopic, and potentially at odds with optimal long-term stewardship of the university's financial position. This point is underscored by the pressures that can arise from such an approach when there is a large transitory shock, such as occurred when the COVID-19 pandemic put a major dent in tuition revenues. From the perspective of a single annual budget cycle, this shortfall was so big that maintaining budget balance would have required drastic cutbacks in other areas. But given that the shortfall was expected to be transitory, a rational approach to budgeting would suggest a significant degree of intertemporal smoothing of the shock—i.e., allowing a deficit to emerge temporarily, to be offset by a series of small surpluses in the future.[6]

The first drawback of single-year GAAP accounting appears to be recognized by credit rating agencies in their procedures for rating universities. Moody's, for example, calculates revenue using average endowment payout rates for the higher education sector rather than actual payout rates, while S&P Global lowers the credit rating of universities with endowment payout rates above 6 percent.[7] These procedures implicitly recognize that high endowment spending lowers future resources, but they retain a focus on current university budgets so they may inappropriately penalize universities that use endowment spending to smooth temporary shocks. We instead advocate an intertemporal approach that departs more radically from standard GAAP accounting.

6. And indeed, in the particular case of the pandemic, the need for this sort of smoothing was well recognized by university leadership, who allowed for bigger draws from the endowment at the height of the pandemic. For example, the endowment share of FAS operating revenue increased from 50 percent in FY19 to 53 percent in FY20 and 54 percent in FY21. Note, however, that given that such endowment draws are counted as revenues, the underlying operating deficit created by this smoothing policy does not fully show through in the conventional budgeting framework.

7. Moody's Investors Service, "Higher Education Methodology," August 24, 2021, available online at https://ratings.moodys.com/api/rmc-documents/72158. S&P Global, "Criteria | Governments | General: Global Not-For-Profit Education Providers," April 24, 2023, available online at https://www.spglobal.com/ratings/en/research/articles/230424-criteria-governments-general-global-not-for-profit-education-providers-12585765.

## 5.3 An Intertemporal Approach to Budgeting

The intertemporal approach to budgeting developed by our working group can be understood by analogy to the planning problem of a retired household. In this example, the household has a given level of accumulated wealth, and uses this wealth to fund a sequence of consumption expenditures into the indefinite future. The intertemporal budget constraint is then simply the requirement that the present value of the planned consumption expenditures, discounted at an appropriate discount rate, not exceed the current level of wealth. Similarly, for a university, there is a sequence of anticipated net expenditures, in this case given by spending on salaries and benefits, supplies and equipment, capital expenditures and the like, less income from net tuition revenue, government research sponsorship, and other fees. One can take the present value of these net expenditures, compare it to the current value of the endowment (adjusted for debt and anticipated future philanthropy), and ask whether the university is on track to satisfying its long-run budget constraint.

Crucially, this approach does two things differently from the conventional budgeting method. First, it does not rely on accounting judgments, in that accounting depreciation never shows up in the analysis; rather, actual cash outlays on capital spending are captured in the year they are expected to occur. Second, it fully separates real and financial flows. The real operating economics of the university are captured in the present value of the net expenditures, which do not include anything having to do with debt issuance, interest expense, or endowment payouts. And financial resources are fully captured by the current value of the endowment in excess of debt obligations. There is no need to ever explicitly model borrowing and lending decisions, or the timing of endowment payouts, since these purely financial choices do not change the present value of the university's underlying wealth—only how it is distributed over time.

Framing things this way has several advantages. It makes clear that the size of the endowment must be compared with the sequence of obligations that the endowment is expected to support. It removes the temptation to think that financial engineering of various sorts can solve fundamental economic problems, and instead focuses attention on the real-side decisions that university leadership must make—decisions about revenue generation (e.g., policies regarding tuition-setting), operating costs such as headcount, salaries, and benefits, and the path of capital expenditures. And it makes transparent how alternative assumptions about each of these affects financial sustainability. In so doing, it can highlight the most important drivers of intertemporal budget balance, and clarify the policies and combinations of policies that are likely to be most effective in achieving budget balance.

In order to implement our approach, we need to make a series of modeling

Table 5.2 Modeling assumptions

| | |
|---|---|
| Inflation Rate | 2% |
| Real Growth Rate Assumptions | |
| Compensation (FY28 & Beyond) | 1% |
| Def'd Maint (FY28 & Beyond) | 1% |
| Student Inc (FY28 & Beyond) | 1% |
| Sponsored Rev (FY28 & Beyond) | 0% |
| Other Income (FY28 & Beyond) | 0% |
| Nominal Discount Rate—Scenario 1 | 7% |
| Nominal Discount Rate—Scenario 2 | 6% |

assumptions. To generate real-side operating cashflows, we rely on the FAS multi-year financial plan for fiscal years 2024 through 2028, which projects line-item spending and revenues in granular detail. Because we need to forecast these cash flows over an infinite horizon, we then make simple constant growth rate assumptions for the years that extend beyond the FAS planning horizon. Working in nominal-dollar terms, we assume an inflation rate of 2 percent, based on the premise that the Federal Reserve will roughly hit its inflation target over time. For a base case, we then assume, consistent with past history, that there will be real growth in compensation, maintenance costs, and net tuition; we set real growth for each of these at 1 percent. Other sources of income, such as sponsored research and other fees, are assumed to be constant in real terms.

To discount these cash flows, in the base case we use a nominal discount rate of 7 percent. Given our 2 percent inflation assumption, this corresponds to assuming a 5 percent real discount rate. We choose this value because it is consistent with Harvard's long-term endowment payout rate of 5 percent. In order to be able to sustain a payout rate of 5 percent without depleting the endowment in real terms, it must be that the endowment is able to earn a 5 percent real rate of return in expectation. If that is in fact the case, then it makes sense to use a 5 percent real discount rate to present-value the operating cash flows.

Of course, there is no guarantee that a 5 percent expected rate of return on the endowment can actually be achieved without taking undue levels of risk in the current market environment, so it is going to be critically important to stress-test this assumption. As we will see, given that the FAS is highly endowment-dependent, relatively small changes in the assumed rate of return on the endowment have large consequences for financial sustainability. Indeed, this is one of the most important conclusions of our analysis. With this observation in mind, we also work with an alternative scenario in which the real return on the endowment is 4 percent, corresponding to a nominal discount rate of 6 percent.

Table 5.2 summarizes these modeling assumptions. Table 5.3 gives a high-level overview of our analysis, and table 5.4 provides more line-item detail.

**Table 5.3** **Model overview**

| Present Value of Income and Wealth ($b) | | Present Value of Expenses ($b) | |
|---|---|---|---|
| Operating Revenues | 16.07 | Operating Costs | 36.23 |
| Endowment less Debt | 17.69 | Capital Expenditures | 8.28 |
| Future Philanthropy | 4.21 | | |
| Total | 37.97 | | 44.51 |
| Present Value Shortfall ($b) | −6.54 | | |
| Annualized Structural Deficit ($m) | −327 | | |

Note: All figures are present values of forecasted future cash flows in billions, except for the Annualized Structural Deficit, which annualizes the Present Value Shortfall and is in millions.

Let us begin by focusing on the first column of table 5.4, which corresponds to the base-case assumption of a 7 percent nominal discount rate. With this assumption, the present value of all revenues—which are driven primarily by net tuition revenues (net of financial aid) and by sponsored research funding—add up to $16.07 billion. While this is a large number, it is far less than the present value of all operating costs, almost two-thirds of which are for compensation and benefits, and which total $36.23 billion. In addition, the present value of planned capital expenditures is $8.28 billion. Putting it all together, the net present value of all operating and capital cash flows in the base case is −$28.44 billion (16.07 − 36.23 − 8.28 = −28.44). In other words, in keeping with the household analogy, the FAS has present-value obligations of $28.44 billion to fund its future stream of planned consumption. This large number arises because tuition and other revenue, substantial as they are, are not nearly enough to cover anticipated expenditures on personnel, research support, and the physical plant.

How do these obligations compare to the wealth available to support them? In column (1) of table 5.4, we see that the FAS share of Harvard's endowment stands at $17.84 billion. This value needs to be adjusted in a few ways in order to present a more complete picture of total wealth. There are some unspent endowment distributions which must be added back, and some existing debt that the FAS owes which reduces net wealth. Finally, the FAS has an important off-balance sheet asset, namely future philanthropy, which is expected to bring in a present value of $4.21 billion.[8] Putting it all together, the total on- and off-balance sheet wealth of the FAS is estimated to be $21.9 billion.

With these numbers in hand, it is now straightforward to assess the overall financial balance of the FAS. With present-value obligations of $28.44 bil-

8. In modeling future philanthropy, it is important to only count *budget-relieving* gifts, i.e., gifts that come without a requirement to commensurately increase expenditures, by, e.g., launching a new center that would not have been otherwise launched under the baseline plan.

**Table 5.4** **Detailed model**

| | Net Present Value of Cash Flows ($b) | | Projected Cash Flows ($m) | | | | |
|---|---|---|---|---|---|---|---|
| | Scenario 1 | Scenario 2 | | | | | |
| | 7.0% | 6.0% | FY24 | FY25 | FY26 | FY27 | FY28 |
| Cash Flows from Operations | | | | | | | |
| Revenues | | | | | | | |
| —Student Income (net of Financial Aid) | 9.52 | 12.67 | 360 | 367 | 380 | 406 | 427 |
| —Sponsored Revenue | 4.09 | 5.10 | 199 | 204 | 209 | 214 | 219 |
| —Other Income | 2.47 | 3.08 | 113 | 120 | 125 | 129 | 133 |
| Operating Revenues Total | 16.07 | 20.84 | 672 | 692 | 715 | 749 | 779 |
| Costs | | | | | | | |
| —Compensation & Benefits | **(21.00)** | **(27.96)** | **(758)** | **(811)** | **(854)** | **(898)** | **(944)** |
| —Operating Space Costs | **(4.69)** | **(5.84)** | **(231)** | **(227)** | **(236)** | **(245)** | **(251)** |
| —Other Costs | **(10.55)** | **(13.16)** | **(480)** | **(505)** | **(525)** | **(546)** | **(570)** |
| Operating Costs Total | **(36.23)** | **(46.96)** | **(1,469)** | **(1,543)** | **(1,615)** | **(1,689)** | **(1,765)** |
| NET OPERATING CASH FLOWS | **(20.16)** | **(26.13)** | **(797)** | **(852)** | **(901)** | **(939)** | **(986)** |
| Cash Flows from Capital Expenditures | | | | | | | |
| Total Capital Expenditures | **(8.28)** | **(9.99)** | **(451)** | **(492)** | **(648)** | **(743)** | **(788)** |
| OPERATING & CAPITAL CASH FLOWS | **(28.44)** | **(36.11)** | **(1,248)** | **(1,343)** | **(1,549)** | **(1,682)** | **(1,774)** |

| | | | | | | | |
|---|---|---|---|---|---|---|---|
| Existing Wealth | | | | | | | |
| Endowment Market Value | 17.84 | 17.84 | | | | | |
| Unspent Endowment Distributions | 1.02 | 1.02 | | | | | |
| Market Value of FAS Debt | **(1.17)** | **(1.17)** | | | | | |
| TOTAL EXISTING WEALTH | 17.69 | 17.69 | | | | | |
| Cash Flows from Future Philanthropy | | | | | | | |
| Current Use Gifts | 1.87 | 2.34 | 71 | 73 | 73 | 90 | 104 |
| House Renewal Gifts | 0.003 | 0.003 | 1 | 1 | 1 | 0 | 0 |
| Budget-Relieving Endowment Gifts | 2.34 | 2.93 | 123 | 115 | 130 | 132 | 141 |
| TOTAL PHILANTHROPY | 4.21 | 5.27 | 194 | 188 | 203 | 222 | 245 |
| TOTAL EXISTING WEALTH & PHILANTHROPY | 21.90 | 22.96 | 169 | 175 | 190 | 207 | 195 |
| Present Value Shortfall | **(6.54)** | **(13.15)** | | | | | |
| Annualized Structural Deficit ($m) | **(327)** | **(526)** | | | | | |

Note: The present value columns are in billions, while the year-by-year projections and the annualized structural deficit are in millions. Negative numbers appear with parentheses in bold.

lion, and total wealth of $21.9 billion, the FAS faces an estimated present-value shortfall of $6.54 billion. To translate this value into something that is more easily interpreted, one can annualize it by multiplying by the real discount rate of 5 percent, yielding an annualized structural deficit of $327 million. In other words, given our assumptions, in order to achieve what we would consider to be long-run structural budget balance, the FAS would have to generate an additional $327 million per year in real terms (i.e., growing by 2 percent per year in nominal terms) through some combination of revenue increases or cost-cutting measures. This figure can be compared to FY 2023 total operating costs of $1.56 billion to get a sense of magnitude; one might thus say that in our base case, the FAS has a structural budget deficit of something like 21 percent. Given how inflexible much of the cost structure is in the short-to-medium run, this is a meaningful number.

Thus, a first conclusion that emerges from our work is that this economic approach to university budgeting can, depending on the circumstances at hand, yield quite different conclusions than the traditional GAAP-based approach. Recall that in figure 5.1, the GAAP-based approach painted a considerably rosier picture of the FAS financial position, forecasting several years of budgetary surpluses.

To be clear, the $327 million estimate of the structural budget deficit in our base case is just that—an estimate. And it is subject to very significant modeling uncertainty, given how difficult it is to make anything like accurate forecasts of either revenues or costs so far out into the future. Rather than thinking of it as a decisive final answer, we believe it is more pragmatically useful as a point of departure for a discussion of the drivers of long-run fiscal sustainability and the levers university leadership has at its disposal as it pursues this goal. To illustrate this point, we turn next to a series of scenario analyses.

## 5.4 Scenario Analyses and Interpretation

As noted above, one of the most important uncertainties in our analysis has to do with the expected return on the endowment, which shows up in our framework as the rate used to discount FAS operating income and expenditures. Column (2) keeps everything else the same as in column (1), but changes the nominal discount rate to 6 percent, which now maps into assuming a 4 percent real rate of return on the endowment as opposed to the 5 percent in the base case. As can be seen, this makes a dramatic difference to our results: the present value of the budget shortfall jumps from $6.54 billion to $13.15 billion, and the corresponding annualized structural deficit goes from $327 million to $526 million: over one-third of the $1.56 billion currently budgeted for annual spending. A proportional structural deficit of this magnitude looks daunting indeed. Simply put, even a mod-

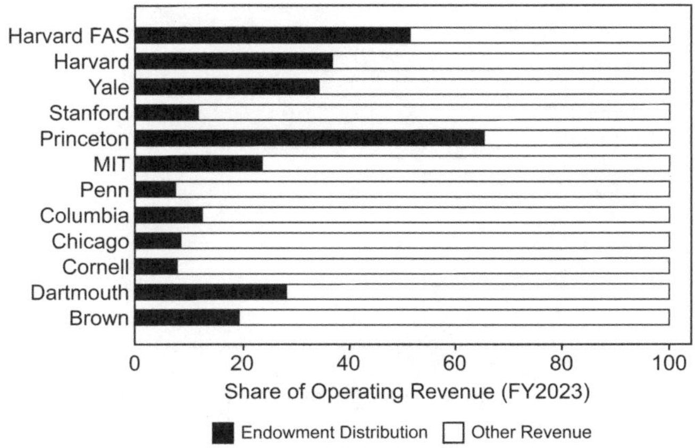


**Fig. 5.2 Endowment dependence of Harvard FAS, Harvard University, and peers**

estly lower return on the endowment fundamentally changes the long-run financial sustainability of the FAS.

This strong sensitivity to endowment returns reflects the relatively high level of endowment dependence of the FAS. This is illustrated in figure 5.2, which displays a simple measure of endowment dependence—namely, the fraction of the current annual budget covered by payout from the endowment—for the FAS, for Harvard University as a whole, and for ten of Harvard's peers: Yale, Stanford, Princeton, MIT, Penn, Columbia, Chicago, Cornell, Dartmouth, and Brown. Other than Princeton, the FAS, with an endowment dependence of 51 percent in fiscal year 2023, sits at the top of the pack on this metric, well higher than most of its leading peers. Also of note is that the FAS is considerably more endowment-dependent than Harvard as a whole. Several of Harvard's other schools, notably Harvard Business School, generate more than 80 percent of their income from non-endowment sources, such as tuition, executive programs, and publishing, and so are less vulnerable to variation in endowment returns.

Moreover, the comparison with Princeton in particular may actually understate the relative exposure of the FAS to its endowment performance. This is because, as figure 5.3 shows, Princeton's endowment on a per-student basis is more than double that of Harvard. So while Princeton is relying on its endowment for a significant fraction of its current spending, figure 5.3 suggests that that current level of spending is extremely generous on a per-student basis. Which in turn implies that all else equal, it might be less painful for Princeton to cut back on spending in a world with subdued endowment returns.

This discussion naturally raises the question of what levers university leadership might use to restore financial balance, if indeed endowment per-

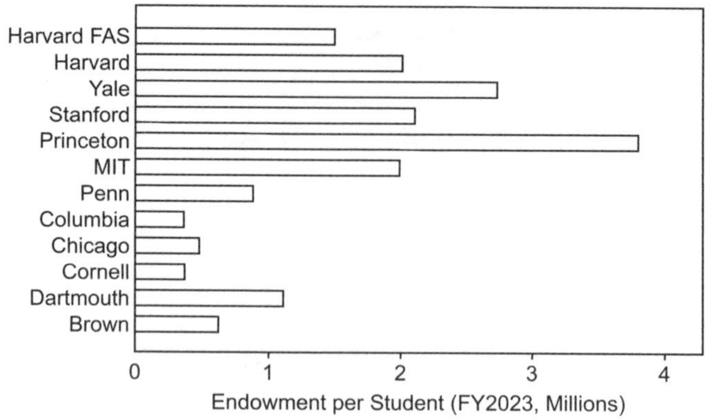


**Fig. 5.3 Endowment per student of Harvard FAS, Harvard University, and peers**

formance does disappoint and the structural deficit widens accordingly. Our framework is perhaps most useful in this regard, i.e., in helping to identify which levers have the most noteworthy first-order effects. For example, given that employee compensation is the single largest item on the cost side of the ledger, one might ask what adjustment to the growth of compensation is needed to achieve a given improvement in the structural deficit.

A simple calculation based on the model in column (1) of table 5.4 yields the following conclusion: suppose that compensation is untouched between now and FY 28, but thereafter grows at only 0.5 percent in real terms as opposed to the base-case value of 1.0 percent; this step-down could reflect either a slower growth of head count, a more gradual trajectory of pay increases for existing employees, or some combination of the two. It turns out that this relatively modest change, even when implemented with a delay of a few years, is nevertheless quite powerful: it cuts the present value of the budget shortfall by $2.2 billion, and the annualized structural deficit by $112 million.

One caveat about this use of our framework is that it can be abused if university leaders succumb to the temptation to assume unrealistic cost control measures in distant future years. Just as it is all too easy for governments to set ambitious targets for carbon emissions reduction in the 2030s and 2040s while doing little or nothing in the 2020s, similarly the growth rates assumed in our analysis can be manipulated to obscure a university's long-run financial problems. Realism in the assumptions is absolutely critical for the validity of our analysis.

## 5.5 Implications for Endowment Risk Tolerance

In addition to being useful for budgeting and planning purposes, the methodology we have proposed here can also be of help in thinking about certain issues related to the management of a university's endowment. Two of us (Campbell and Stein) have served on the board of Harvard Management Company (HMC, the university's endowment manager). From 2019 to 2022 Stein chaired a sub-committee of the board that sought to create a framework for determining the appropriate level of risk for the endowment portfolio. The sub-committee was formed as a response to the observation that HMC had apparently been taking moderately less risk—i.e., had a modestly lower model-based estimate of the standard deviation of its returns—than some of its leading peers. The question then posed to the sub-committee was whether HMC should increase its portfolio risk profile so as to come into closer conformity with these peers.

The primary insight that drove the sub-committee's work was the idea that it cannot make sense to think about the appropriate level of risk of the endowment in a vacuum, divorced from the underlying operating economics of the university. The two need to be analyzed in an integrated fashion.[9] In particular, if a university—or, as in the case of the FAS, a decentralized unit of the university—is heavily endowment-dependent, and thus would be forced to cut back sharply on crucial strategic investments in the event of a series of lower-tail return realizations, this should lead it to prefer a more conservative investment portfolio for the endowment, all else being equal. The logic is similar to the argument for target date funds that reduce their risk exposure as their investors approach retirement and become more dependent on capital income relative to labor income.

Our framework can be used to quantify the impact of investment risk on the university's financial position, by calculating how the present value shortfall changes when the endowment return is better or worse than expected. Table 5.5 illustrates how the deficit varies with the growth of the endowment's real value under our baseline scenario. The base case in the table is zero real growth, which is achieved if the endowment earns the assumed 5 percent real return and distributes 5 percent of its value. Assuming the endowment return has an annual standard deviation of 15 percent, then over a one-year horizon, a one standard deviation lower return of −10 percent, which leads the real value of the endowment to decline by 15 percent net of the 5 percent payout, increases the annualized deficit from $327 million to $461 million. On the other hand a one standard deviation higher return of 20 percent, which increases the real value of the endowment by 15 percent, shrinks the annualized deficit to $193 million. This result highlights the exposure of the FAS to financial market risks, particularly in the short run when the university's operating decisions are relatively fixed. The university's

9. This lesson was hammered home at Harvard by events during the global financial crisis in 2008–09, when interest rate swaps, put in place as part of a financing strategy for campus expansion, incurred large losses that amplified the risk exposure of the endowment. In response the Harvard Corporation formed a finance committee to provide integrated oversight of the financial activities of HMC and the university.

**Table 5.5 Effect of endowment growth on the budget deficit**

| Endowment Growth | Present Value Surplus/Deficit ($b) | Annualized Structural Surplus/ Deficit ($m) | Deficit Growth vs. Baseline |
|---|---|---|---|
| −35% | −12.79 | −639 | 95% |
| −30% | −11.89 | −595 | 82% |
| −25% | −11.00 | −550 | 68% |
| −20% | −10.11 | −505 | 55% |
| −15% | −9.22 | −461 | 41% |
| −10% | −8.33 | −416 | 27% |
| −5% | −7.43 | −372 | 14% |
| 0% | −6.54 | −327 | 0% |
| 5% | −5.65 | −282 | −14% |
| 10% | −4.76 | −238 | −27% |
| 15% | −3.87 | −193 | −41% |
| 20% | −2.97 | −149 | −55% |
| 25% | −2.08 | −104 | −68% |
| 30% | −1.19 | −59 | −82% |
| 35% | −0.30 | −15 | −95% |

Note: Endowment growth is the growth of the endowment's real value under the baseline scenario.

ability to make spending adjustments grows over a longer time horizon, but risk also grows with the square root of the time horizon. Over a five-year horizon, a one standard deviation lower return increases the deficit to $626 million while a one standard deviation higher return lowers the deficit to $28 million.

This analysis illustrates the fact that, over the long run, the university's adjustments in spending must have the same volatility, and more generally the same systematic risk exposures, as the returns on the endowment. At the analytical level, this is what justifies our assumption that net operating cash flows can be discounted at the endowment's rate of return. The operations of an endowment-dependent university look very different in this regard from the operations of a pension fund, which must meet fixed liabilities using a financial portfolio together with backstop guarantees from pension plan sponsors (corporations or state and local governments). Novy-Marx and Rauh (2011) have cogently criticized the accounting rules that allow public pensions to discount their liabilities using the expected returns on their assets, arguing that guaranteed liabilities should be discounted at the riskless interest rate. This criticism does not apply to our analysis because a university's spending plans are variable rather than fixed.

The implication of this for a university's management is that flexibility in spending is vital if the university is dependent on the payouts from a risky endowment. This flexibility need not be instantaneous—our framework allows for gradual adjustment to satisfy the intertemporal budget

**Table 5.6** **Endowment risk-return trade-off**

| Nominal Expected Return | Standard Deviation of Return | Change in Mean Annualized Structural Deficit ($m) | Change in Effect of −1SD Return on Annualized Structural Deficit ($m) |
|---|---|---|---|
| 5% | 11% | 436 | −75 |
| 6% | 13% | 199 | −41 |
| 7% | 15% | 0 | 0 |
| 8% | 17% | −184 | 48 |
| 9% | 19% | −360 | 103 |
| 10% | 21% | −533 | 166 |

Note: The calculation assumes a Sharpe ratio of 0.46. The standard deviation of returns is rounded to the nearest percentage point. Changes in the mean and standard deviation of the annualized structural deficit as the level of risk varies are calculated relative to the baseline scenario of 7 percent nominal expected returns.

constraint—but it has to exist at some horizon. Put another way, a university must align its endowment risk-taking with its ability to adjust its spending plans to financial market conditions.

We can use our framework to explore the trade-off between expected return and risk at the level of the university's economic budget. Assuming a fixed Sharpe ratio for the endowment, a higher expected return will lower the deficit in the baseline scenario (as shown in table 5.4 and the previous analysis) but increase the risk, in the sense that a one standard deviation lower return on the endowment will lead to a larger increase in the structural deficit. Table 5.6 presents the relationship between expected returns and risk under the assumption that the endowment can achieve a relatively attractive Sharpe ratio of 0.46. In the baseline scenario of a 7 percent nominal rate of return, the annualized structural deficit is $327 million and a one standard deviation lower return leads to a $134 million increase in the deficit. If the endowment takes on more risk and increases its expected return to 8 percent, the university's mean annualized structural deficit decreases by $184 million, but the effect of a one standard deviation lower return on the deficit increases by $48 million. Endowment risk-taking brings rewards, if the Sharpe ratio can be maintained at a high level, but once again we see that risk-taking must be accompanied by operating flexibility.

With these insights in mind, the economic budgeting framework developed above wound up playing a key role in the sub-committee's deliberations, and ultimately in its recommendations to the Harvard Corporation, who had to approve any change in the endowment's risk target. Beyond the specific decision at hand, using the budgeting framework as a device to provoke a conversation across these two different functions—university strategic planning and endowment management—proved to be a valuable way to help leadership come to an integrated understanding of the university's overall economic model.

## 5.6 Conclusion

We believe an economic approach to university budgeting has important advantages. First, by relating the university's endowment and debt to the present value of its net operating expenditures, it shows that an apparently large endowment may already be fully utilized supporting those expenditures and may not be available to underwrite expensive new ventures. A university that appears to be "rich," in the vernacular sense that it can afford luxuries, may in fact be merely "endowment-dependent."

Second, the economic approach focuses the attention of university leaders on long-run strategic solutions to financial problems, rather than short-term fixes that use financial engineering to balance single-year accounting budgets by borrowing from the future.

Third, the approach highlights the fact that financial market conditions have a huge impact on endowment-dependent universities. If the level of real interest rates declines, for example, the return on the endowment will decline unless the university's endowment manager takes more risk. Accepting a low return worsens the university's structural budget deficit and requires painful measures to raise operating revenues or lower expenses. Taking more risk improves the current budget position but requires increased flexibility in the event that disappointing returns are realized in risky financial markets. These are tough choices, but university leaders need to face them squarely and an economic budgeting framework helps them do this.

## References

Bok, Derek. 2024. "Why Americans Love to Hate Harvard." *Chronicle of Higher Education*, January 4.

Campbell, John Y. 2012. "Investing and Spending: The Twin Challenges of University Endowment Management." In *Forum Futures 2012*, 32–40. Cambridge, MA: Forum for the Future of Higher Education.

Campbell, John Y., and Roman Sigalov. 2022. "Portfolio Choice with Sustainable Spending: A Model of Reaching for Yield." *Journal of Financial Economics* 143: 188–206.

Dybvig, Philip H., and Zhenjiang Qin. 2021. "How to Squander Your Endowment: Pitfalls and Remedies." Unpublished paper, SSRN 3939984.

Gilbert, Thomas, and Christopher Hrdlicka. 2015. "Why Are University Endowments Large and Risky?" *Review of Financial Studies* 28: 2643–2686.

Hansmann, Henry. 1990. "Why Do Universities Have Endowments?" *Journal of Legal Studies* 19: 3–42.

Novy-Marx, Robert, and Joshua Rauh. 2011. "Public Pension Promises: How Big Are They and What Are They Worth?" *Journal of Finance* 66: 1211–1249.

Tobin, James. 1974. "What Is Permanent Endowment Income?" *American Economic Review Papers and Proceedings* 64: 427–32.

## Comment Antoinette Schoar

The paper by Campbell, Stein and Wu (2024) tackles an important and timely topic that is still largely understudied: How do universities conduct their (annual) budgeting and to what extent does annual budgeting that follows GAP accounting distort the optimal spending and capital allocation out of their endowments? This topic is especially urgent in a time when many universities are accused of not providing enough contribution to the common good or of hoarding their endowment rather than spending from it.

The authors observe that many universities resort to annual budgeting, which treats distributions out of the endowment as discretionary income and encourages short-termism. The authors show how this approach does not correspond to what they define as an optimal policy and that it obfuscates potential, longer-term funding shortfalls. Using data from Havard's Faculty of Arts and Sciences (FAS), the authors compare the approach used by FAS to a hypothetical intertemporal budgeting framework that takes into account the trade-off of between spending today versus that forgone by the future.

The authors highlight two main insights. First, the current approach encourages short-termism on a number of dimensions: (1) the mixing of financial flows and real-side revenues makes borrowing to cover current expenses deceptively attractive; (2) treating depreciation as an expense risks deferring maintenance and upkeep in order to suppress current capital expenditures; and (3) the need to balance the book annually heavily distorts other spending in the face of large, transitory shocks.

I would also add to the benefits of the intertemporal budgeting approach that it allows decision-makers to model how (some) expenses or investments can affect future revenue streams. For example, spending on university infrastructure might attract more tuition-paying students, or faculty who bring in more grant money, among other benefits. Looking at the example of MIT, the university used endowment money to facilitate a transition into novel subfields of biotech and nanotech. But of course, the usefulness of this approach depends on how realistic the assumptions and projections are.

One might worry that such longer-horizon modeling as proposed in the paper might increase the complexity and go beyond the modeling sophistication of a typical university administration might have. Separately, I suspect

Antoinette Schoar is the Stewart C. Myers-Horn Family Professor of Finance and Entrepreneurship at the MIT Sloan School of Management, and a research associate and codirector of the Corporate Finance Program at the National Bureau of Economic Research.

I thank Egor Matveyev for generously providing the data and calculations for tables 5C.1 and 5C.2 of this note. For acknowledgments, sources of research support, and disclosure of the author's material financial relationships, if any, please see https://www.nber.org/books-and-chapters/financing-institutions-higher-education/comment-economic-budgeting-endowment-dependent-universities-schoar.

**Table 5C.1 University endowment sizes and returns**

| Endowment size | Number of universities | Average annual return | Average std. deviation of returns |
|---|---|---|---|
| >1B | 54 | 6.12% | 10.27% |
| [100M,1B] | 260 | 5.10% | 10.23% |
| [10M,100M] | 583 | 4.92% | 9.28% |
| <10M | 372 | 3.41% | 6.20% |

Note: Data for this table are sourced from Lo et al. (2021).

that by providing university administrators with more levers to build in optimistic assumptions, for example, about the expected returns on the endowment, or the ability of the university to smooth future expenses, the scheme has the potential to further obfuscate true budget shortfalls in the future.

The second main insight is an emphasis on the interdependence between the level of investment risk taken in the endowment and the underlying operating economics of the university: To balance the budget in the long run, universities' adjustments in spending must have the same volatility or systematic risk exposure as the investment returns on the endowment. If there are expenses that cannot be scaled with the return on the endowment, they should be discounted with a lower discount factor to reflect the fact that these are compulsory expenses in the future. Alternatively, the university has to be willing to make painful adjustments to its budget, or staffing level, in the future, in a bad realization of endowment returns. The authors also suggest that endowment-dependent universities should opt for lower-risk investment strategies.

To what extent do universities follow the principles that are laid out in the paper? Using data from the paper by Lo et al. (2021) on nonprofit endowments, we can see in table 5C.1 that endowments with more than a billion dollar in assets had higher annual returns on average than those in lower size brackets, e.g., 6.12 percent for endowments with above $1 billion compared to 3.41 percent for endowments with less than $10 million. Interestingly, we also see that the standard deviation of returns also increases with endowment size, with one exception. The very largest endowments with assets above $1B do not have higher volatility than the next size bracket. The explanation for this surprising statistic might be that these largest funds heavily invest in private equity and other alternative assets that are not mark-to-market. Thus, the numbers might not reflect the full volatility of their underlying assets.

Maybe more importantly in the context of the current discussion, table 5C.2, again relying on data from Lo et al. (2021), shows that more endowment dependent universities had higher past returns with only minimally high standard deviations, even holding constant the size of the endowment. Since the level of endowment dependence is a choice of the university,

**Table 5C.2** **University endowment sizes, dependence and returns**

| Endowment size | Endowment dependence | Average annual return | Average std. deviation of returns |
|---|---|---|---|
| >1B | High | 6.68% | 10.64% |
| >1B | Low | 5.99% | 10.19% |
| [100M,1B] | High | 5.19% | 10.36% |
| [100M,1B] | Low | 4.96% | 9.97% |

Note: Endowment dependence is defined as the fraction of total expenses covered by the endowment fund. "High" and "low" are defined as above and below the median, respectively, within the subsamples of endowments with over $1B AUM and [100M, 1B] AUM. Data for this table are sourced from Lo et al. (2021).

one can speculate that universities with higher returns felt more confident that they would be able to generate high future returns. Thus, they were more willing to lean on their endowments for current expenses.

This raises an important issue about the interaction between the budgeting function and university governance. In an ideal world, universities are well governed and they efficiently trade off the utility of future generations against that of today's students and faculty. Having more transparent budgeting should only have positive effects. However, anyone who has stepped foot into a university (or any big institution, for that matter) knows that organizations are difficult to govern given their sometimes decentralized structures and multi-faceted constituencies, who often have varying or opposing objectives. For example, making trade-offs between investments in different research areas and cutting back staff who are unproductive can be very difficult, especially since returns from many academic activities are intangible and therefore hard to measure. In these situations, it is often easier to keep spending for the sake of harmony, even when that is known to be unsustainable in the long run.

In such a second (or even third) best world, one might argue that a budget crisis is a welcome chance to force universities to tighten their budget and bring back some discipline to the budgeting process. However, the question is how budget discipline will be applied in these situations. If indeed a crisis leads university leaders to cut unnecessary slack and unproductive activities, a budget crisis induced by short-termist budgeting might serve as a second-best governance mechanism. If, in contrast, a budget crisis shifts bargaining power to the already entrenched and unproductive parties, it might have exactly the opposite effect. To answer this question, we would like to know who the most vulnerable stakeholders are in a crisis, and whether improved governance actually emerges in the resolution of budget crises.

While much more research is needed on this topic, some suggestive evidence is provided in Brown et al. (2014) published in the *American Economic Review*. This paper examines how universities respond to financial shocks to their endowments by adjusting their annual payout and staff employment.

The authors find that a year with a −10 percent endowment return leads to an 8.2 percent reduction in payouts as a means of budget smoothing. Remarkably, there is a stark asymmetry in the response to positive versus negative shocks. In former cases, universities leave their payouts unchanged, rather than increase them, pointing to potential endowment hoarding. This finding is surprising as it is in contradiction with most of universities' written payout policies which would imply much smoother payouts from year to year.

In addition, the paper shows starkly different cuts across personnel employed in different parts of a university. A 10 percent negative endowment shock leads to a 5.1 percent decline in employment of support staff, such as secretaries, which is the biggest concurrent reduction among all categories employed. The next largest reduction is in tenure track faculty with a nearly 5 percent reduction in the year following the return shock. In contrast, university administrators are largely unaffected, which paves way for the suspicion that a tighter connection to the leadership acts as a protective cushion in times of crises. While, of course, there might be compelling organizational reasons why university administrators are exempted from staffing cuts in a crisis, it at least raises the possibility that closeness to the decision power becomes useful in a crisis. Similarly, it appears short-termist to disproportionally cut faculty positions during a crisis given that they provide the core of the university's services and intellectual outputs. While far from being the final word, this evidence raises the question of whether indeed universities use budget crises to impose better governance on the operations. It weakens any argument that year-to-year budgeting can have unintended positive governance consequences, and it further supports the intertemporal budgeting framework laid out in this paper.

To conclude, the paper, "Economic Budgeting for Endowment-Dependent Universities," provides a profoundly useful framework to help university administrators move from a myopic planning and budgeting process to an intertemporal approach. Overall, this paper brings much needed rational thinking into an important yet sometimes politically difficult subject. I hope that these insights will be useful for university leaders and will help them to think more sophisticatedly about their budgeting choices.

## References

Brown, Jeffrey R., Stephen G Dimmock, Jun-Koo Kang, and Scott J Weisbenner. 2014. "How University Endowments Respond to Financial Market Shocks: Evidence and Implications." *American Economic Review* 104(3): 931–62.

Lo, Andrew W., Egor Matveyev, and Stefan Zeume. 2021. "The Risk, Reward, and Asset Allocation of Nonprofit Endowment Funds." Unpublished Working Paper.

6

# The Role of Debt in Financing Higher Education

Matteo Binfarè and Kyle E. Zimmerschied

In 2020, US four-year public and private not-for-profit universities had more than $265 billion in long-term debt outstanding alone. While much media and academic attention has been focused on the student loan crisis (Mueller and Yannelis 2022, 2019) from the student perspective, considerably less work has addressed the feedback effects stemming from the uptake of debt by universities themselves. For example, in 2020, the average university paid approximately $1,000 per student per year in interest expenses, whereas the average in-state tuition for in-state students at public universities was $10,000 per year.

The optimal use of debt financing is particularly important for universities in their role to facilitate the development of human capital. They have a unique governance structure as nonprofits, with no ability to issue equity in themselves and a lack of an explicit residual claimant. Underinvestment by universities implies an inefficient supply of human capital development, while overinvestment in debt has perverse impacts on the uptake of human capital, overburdening students with debt. This leads to an inefficient allocation of human capital (Chakrabarti et al. 2023; Hampole 2022).

In this paper, we examine universities' debt issuances, the cost of debt,

Matteo Binfarè is an assistant professor in the Finance Department at the Robert J. Trulaske, Sr. College of Business, University of Missouri.

Kyle E. Zimmerschied is an assistant professor in the Finance Department at the Sam M. Walton College of Business, University of Arkansas.

We thank Daniel Bergstresser (discussant), John Campbell, Kaye Husbands Fealing, Fotis Grigoris, Phillip Levine, Jim Poterba, Jeremy Stein, and participants at the 2024 NBER Financing and Higher Education Conference for helpful comments and suggestions. All errors are our own. For acknowledgments, sources of research support, and disclosure of the authors' material financial relationships, if any, please see https://www.nber.org/books-and-chapters/financing-institutions-higher-education/role-debt-financing-higher-education.

leverage, and use of debt across US four-year public and private not-for-profit universities. We provide descriptive trends and institutional details to aid the practitioner's understanding of the intersection of debt and higher education *across* time, and also examine more fine-grained variation *within* time, location, and bond features to understand the behavior of universities and impact of external factors like state support. Our main empirical analysis focuses on three main results connected to the cost of debt *across* universities, changes in leverage *within* a university over time, and changes following increasing leverage *within* a university. To the extent that universities might use alternative sources of explicit leverage (e.g., bank debt) or implicit leverage through public-private partnerships (P3s), our results provide a lower bound of the true use of leverage by universities.[1]

Descriptively, we show that university issuances have increased from about $3 billion in 1985 to a peak of nearly $60 billion in 2019.[2] Historically, almost all issuances were tax exempt, but there has been a notable increase in taxable debt, especially following the Great Recession. Overall, leverage levels for public universities have increased since 2001, coinciding with a decline in state support, but private universities have experienced a decline in leverage. We document that the excess return of university issuances in excess of the risk-free rate has increased by about 1 percent following the breakdown of the municipal bond insurance market from the Great Recession.

First, we document that public universities have a lower cost of debt issuances than their private university counterparts. Descriptively this gap is about 45 basis points and this gap remains statistically and economically significant as we include bond controls, university controls, and tighter fixed effects, declining to about 18 basis points. For the average public university issuer, we estimate a savings of about $2.8 million in interest expense payments over the lifetime of a bond relative to a comparable private university issuer. We find that underlying state economic conditions explain variation in a university's issuance yield which provides some evidence that the presence of an implicit governmental stakeholder for public universities (the state government) might make their debt less risky than an equivalent private university.

Second, we find that changes in governmental support explain variation in leverage for primarily public universities. Public universities are more heavily reliant on state support than their private university counterparts (40 percent versus 5 percent as a proportion of total revenue) which leads

1. For context, between 1997 and 2015, higher education P3s were completed in 35 states with about $13 billion in total bond issuances issued by the P3 entities (P3 Resource Center 2018). See "A Guide to Higher Ed Public-Private Partnerships," Brailsford & Dunlavey, https://p3resourcecenter.com/wp-content/uploads/2018/07/A-Guide-to-Higher-Ed-Public-Private-Partnerships.pdf for more information on the history and growth of P3s.

2. In recent years, four-year universities accounted for 6 percent of total municipal issuances (Lord Abbett 2024).

public universities to be vulnerable to declines in state funding stemming from state-level operating crises. We find that public universities experience statistically significant increases in their future leverage following contemporaneous drops in state support as universities attempt to smooth operating crises or attract new students. These declines in state support were particularly sizable from 2008 to 2012 as state governments cut funding to public universities in the aftermath of the Great Recession.

Third, we examine the effects of these increases in leverage, and we find that increases in cost are driven by university spending on quality expenses which consist of student services and auxiliary expenses. We find no detectable increase in academic expenses or the quality of education as most issuance proceeds appear to be invested in physical infrastructure serviced directly by student revenues such as dormitories. These increases in leverage are linked to subsequent increases in tuition for only in-state students which reflects their more inelastic demand in comparison to out-of-state students. To further strengthen inference of this result, we show these increases in leverage are not necessary to accommodate more students. We find a null result for increases in total enrollment which supports the fact that debt issuances are undertaken to attract more out-of-state students who are more profitable for institutions.

Our findings have several implications. First, the increasing use of taxable debt by universities due to its increasing flexibility in its use cases suggests that policymakers might consider a closer regulatory examination of tax-exemption use cases. The modern university has increasingly shifted away from tax-exempt debt due to its limited use cases that restrict for-profit industry collaborations, advanced refinancing, and the smoothing of operating crises, while some of these use cases seem in alignment to helping the modern university serve its stakeholders. Second, the breakdown of the municipal bond insurance market following the Great Recession has led to increases in the average issuance yield net of the risk-free rate by about 1 percent as many insurers permanently left this market. In light of the dependence of universities on this market and the large proportion of segmented retail investors, our results provide motivation for further study of this market to assure that universities have access to the capital they need at reasonable costs. Third, the impact of declining state support on public university debt suggests the importance of state governments providing more consistent funding to their in-state universities to assure certain student cohorts do not disproportionately share the burden of budget declines.

Related Literature. Our paper contributes to the literature on the impact of state support on increasing student loan debt borne by students (Chakrabarti et al. 2023; Chakrabarti et al. 2020). Similar to the prior literature, we document that increasing costs are borne disproportionately by specific student cohorts. However, our results provide additional context for this mechanism by documenting that these universities take on additional debt to smooth these operating crises and this cost is borne primarily by *in-state* students rather than *out-of-state* students. Our paper is also broadly related to the literature examining the investment decisions of non-profits, namely hospitals (Adelino et al. 2015; Wedig et al. 1989), which have increasingly focused on improving the *appearance* of quality—a more observable aspect—than the *underlying* quality (Goldman and Romley 2008; Goldman et al. 2010). In the context of the municipal bond market in higher education, Dougal et al. (2019) find that historically Black colleges and universities (HBCUs) pay higher underwriting fees and gross spreads, consistent with racial discrimination.

Our main empirical result is most closely connected to Jacob et al. (2018), which finds that students value consumption amenities using data on the enrollment decisions of US students. Similar to Jacob et al. (2018), we document that universities have increased expenditures on amenity-related expenses and contribute an understanding that these expenditures stem from municipal bond issuances rather than endowment spending or gifts. Related to the capital structure decision of universities, Rosen and Sappington (2016) examine the leverage decision of universities as a function of cash flow uncertainty and find evidence supporting the pecking order theory of capital structure in which firms use internal financing before issuing debt or equity (Myers and Majluf 1984). Our paper contributes to this literature by examining specific cash-flow determinants of university leverage and heterogeneous differences in the cost of debt for US *public* and *private* four-year universities.

## 6.1 Institutional Details

Higher education institutions, including both four-year public and private colleges, frequently turn to the municipal market to fund a variety of projects. These projects range from constructing new research facilities to building campus dormitories and parking garages for students and staff. Given that nonprofit organizations like colleges and universities lack shareholders and cannot issue equity, municipal debt serves as a significant source of external financing for them.

**Taxable versus Tax-Exempt Bonds.** Historically, US colleges have heavily relied on tax-exempt municipal debt issuances. This type of debt provides tax-exempt interest for all investors at the federal level and typically at the state level for in-state investors. Public colleges often issue tax-exempt bonds directly. However, in some cases, state law restricts this, prompting government entities or the state itself to issue bonds on behalf of the university (e.g., state of Wisconsin). Conversely, private universities typically utilize conduit issuers, such as state or local governmental entities or nonprofit organizations, to issue tax-exempt debt. These conduit issuers offer a pathway for universities to access the tax-exempt bond market. For instance, Harvard University might have revenue bonds issued by the Massachusetts Development Finance Agency.[3] In addition to tax-exempt debt, higher education institutions might opt for taxable debt. These bonds might be issued for projects or activities that do not qualify for tax-exempt status under federal tax laws and offer university issuers greater flexibility in the use of proceeds. For example, if bond proceeds are used for a project generating unrelated business income, the interest on those bonds might become taxable. Universities might also issue taxable debt to partner with a for-profit corporation or to refinance a bond as advanced refunding requires issuing taxable debt following the Tax Cuts and Jobs Act of 2017. The yield-to-maturity on tax-exempt bonds is typically lower than that of taxable debt, as investors do not pay taxes on interest income of tax-exempt issuances. Ultimately, the decision to issue taxable or tax-exempt bonds hinges on factors like the nature of the project, investor demand, and tax considerations.

**Security Features.** Municipal debt issued by colleges can take one of two forms: general obligation bonds (GO) and revenue bonds. GO bonds are backed by the full faith, credit, and taxing power of the issuing municipality or governmental entity, which in this context refers to the college or university. However, as colleges do not collect tax receipts, they cannot issue GO bonds in their pure form. Nevertheless, some states do issue GO bonds specifically designated for higher education facilities at certain institutions. Most universities, private and public alike, issue revenue bonds. These bonds are issued to fund specific revenue-generating projects or facilities such as dormitories, parking garages, athletic facilities, or student centers. Repayment of revenue bonds is typically supported by the revenue generated by the project being financed. For instance, if a university issues revenue bonds to construct a new dormitory, the bond's repayment would primarily rely on the income generated by the dormitory. Revenue bonds do rely, in general, on various sources of repayment, such as tuition and fees, or revenues from an auxiliary facility (e.g., student rec center).

**Credit Ratings.** Most higher education issuers and their respective issuances undergo evaluation by credit rating agencies such as Moody's, Fitch, and Standard & Poor's. These agencies provide credit ratings for higher education institutions, including colleges and universities, assessing their capability to fulfill financial obligations. Such evaluations are critical as they impact borrowing costs, access to capital markets, and overall financial flexibility of the organizations. Various factors contribute to determining the credit rating of a higher education institution, encompassing revenue sources (such as tuition, state support, and private gifts), liquidity, existing leverage, enrollment trends, market strength, and reputation. Credit rat-

3. See figure 6A.1 for a summary of issuer frequency for public and private universities.

ing agencies utilize a blend of qualitative and quantitative metrics in this evaluation process. For instance, Harvard University holds a AAA rating from S&P, the highest achievable credit rating. In contrast, S&P rates the University of Missouri System at AA+, which stands two notches below the AAA rating. In the case of public universities, fluctuations in state appropriations and state credit risk often influence credit ratings. Conversely, for private universities which lack that source of financing, credit agencies tend to focus more on factors like revenue concentration and market power in shaping student demand and revenues from tuition.

**Credit Enhancement.** Credit enhancement techniques are often used by higher education issuers to improve their credit rating and thus lower borrowing costs. The main types of credit enhancement strategies are (1) bond insurance; (2) letters of credit (LOCs); and (3) other guarantees. Bond insurance refers to the purchase of an insurance policy on the bonds and thus a transfer of credit risk from the borrower to the insurer, which would make interest payments if the borrower fails to do so. Bond insurance was fairly common before the 2008 financial crisis but has since declined in usage. Examples of insurers are AGM, formerly known as Financial Security Assurance, and Build America Mutual (BAM). Institutions can secure LOCs from banks or financial institutions, which serve as a guarantee to repay bondholders in case of default. This backing by a financially stable entity enhances the credit quality of the bonds, potentially resulting in lower interest rates. Finally, guarantees can take many forms, but the most common ones are state guarantees using reserve funds (e.g., Colorado Intercept Program).

## 6.2 Data and Measurement

### 6.2.1 Debt Issuances

Our issuance level data consists of municipal bond issuances and US higher education institutions reporting to the Integrated Postsecondary Education Data System (IPEDS). We begin by downloading all municipal bond issuances from Refinitiv's SDC Platinum with the main use of proceeds denoted as "Higher Education" paying a fixed coupon rate which returns 18,689 issuances. We then obtain a unique list of municipal bond issuers and beneficiaries of proceeds (in cases where conduit authorities issue debt on behalf of higher education institutions), and hand-match these with the universe of IPEDS reporting organizations. We match by a bond's beneficiary which returns 9,766 linked issuances and then by a bond's issuer which results in 15,353 linked issuances. Restricting our sample to bond issuances from academic years 1985–2022 by US four-year public and non-profit universities with non-missing yield and other key bond features leaves us with

9,473 bond issuances used in our issuance analysis.[4] In some of our robustness tests, we adjust bond yields to account for differences in marginal tax rates at the federal and state level. Following Schwert (2017), we compute tax-equivalent yields as:

$$y_{i,t}^{\text{taxable}} = \frac{y_{i,t}^{\text{tax-exempt}}}{(1 - \tau_t^{\text{fed}})(1 - \tau_{s,t}^{\text{state}})}. \tag{1}$$

### 6.2.2 University Financial and Operating Data

Our data on the financial position and operations of US four-year public and private not-for-profit universities comes from IPEDS, which began collecting data on US higher education institutions annually from 1985 to 2022.[5] We merge this data, which include relevant university controls from 1985 to 2022, into our issuance panel. This panel consists of universities *conditional* on having a debt issuance in a given year. Additionally, we construct a university-year panel data that covers all university-year observations *regardless* of their debt issuance decision to examine changes in leverage within a university over time and how proceeds are used. Due to many balance sheet measures being recorded starting in 2001 to IPEDS, we restrict our analysis in this setting to data from 2001 to 2022.

### 6.2.3 State Economic Conditions and Credit Rating Data

We also bring in state economic condition data to understand how a university's home state affects a university's debt issuance behavior. We obtain state economic data from the Philadelphia Federal Reserve Bank based on its coincident index (a measure of economic activity) and unemployment rates. Additionally, to control for underlying state distress risk, we obtain data from S&P global on ratings changes at the state level.[6]

### 6.2.4 Summary Statistics

Table 6.1 provides a breakdown of summary statistics across our bond issuance sample. Panel A shows that the average issuance yield of university bonds is 4.67 percent. However, the data mask a significant degree of variation. While the median issuance yield-to-maturity is 4.70 percent, yields can range from as low as 1.25 percent to as high as 8.30 percent. This suggests that some universities issue debt with lower yields due to better underlying fundamentals (e.g., cross-sectional variation) or more advantageous timing during periods of lower aggregate yields. When we adjust tax-exempt yields

4. The main sample attrition is due to restricting our sample analysis to four-year public and non-profit universities.

5. We thank Urban Institute for providing direct access to this data.

6. We obtain this data from S&P Global, "History of US State Ratings," https://www.spglobal.com/ratings/en/research/articles/190319-history-of-u-s-state-ratings-2185306.

**Table 6.1 Issuance panel: descriptive statistics**

*Panel A: Bond Characteristics*

| | N | Mean | SD | Min | p25 | Median | p75 | Max |
|---|---|---|---|---|---|---|---|---|
| *Yield Measures* | | | | | | | | |
| Issuance Yield | 9473 | 4.67 | 1.51 | 1.25 | 3.61 | 4.70 | 5.60 | 8.30 |
| Issuance Yield Tax-Adjusted | 9266 | 6.08 | 2.18 | 1.52 | 4.59 | 5.85 | 7.29 | 11.43 |
| Issuance Yield Less Risk Free Rate | 9473 | 0.04 | 1.08 | −2.09 | −0.75 | −0.01 | 0.77 | 3.27 |
| Issuance Yield Tax-Adjusted Less Risk Free Rate | 9266 | 1.41 | 0.90 | −0.61 | 0.83 | 1.32 | 1.92 | 4.50 |
| *Bond Characteristics* | | | | | | | | |
| Years to Maturity | 9473 | 21.26 | 8.58 | 0.98 | 16.00 | 21.17 | 29.62 | 37.97 |
| Issue Amount | 9473 | 67.62 | 110.95 | 1.25 | 11.94 | 27.80 | 70.00 | 702.28 |
| Gross Spread | 6704 | 7.49 | 4.78 | 0.00 | 4.13 | 6.18 | 9.98 | 22.50 |
| Negotiated Bid | 9473 | 0.79 | 0.40 | 0.00 | 1.00 | 1.00 | 1.00 | 1.00 |
| Callable Issue | 9473 | 0.85 | 0.35 | 0.00 | 1.00 | 1.00 | 1.00 | 1.00 |
| Refinancing or Refunding Flag | 9473 | 0.44 | 0.50 | 0.00 | 0.00 | 0.00 | 1.00 | 1.00 |
| Tax-Exempt | 9473 | 0.88 | 0.33 | 0.00 | 1.00 | 1.00 | 1.00 | 1.00 |
| Sinking Fund | 9473 | 0.54 | 0.50 | 0.00 | 0.00 | 1.00 | 1.00 | 1.00 |
| Revenue Bond | 9473 | 0.94 | 0.23 | 0.00 | 1.00 | 1.00 | 1.00 | 1.00 |
| Insured | 9473 | 0.26 | 0.44 | 0.00 | 0.00 | 0.00 | 1.00 | 1.00 |
| *Bond Ratings* | | | | | | | | |
| Ratings Combined Underlying | 9473 | 3.32 | 2.75 | 0.00 | 0.00 | 5.00 | 6.00 | 7.00 |
| Ratings Combined | 9473 | 4.71 | 2.58 | 0.00 | 4.00 | 6.00 | 7.00 | 7.00 |
| AAA Rated Underlying | 9473 | 0.04 | 0.21 | 0.00 | 0.00 | 0.00 | 0.00 | 1.00 |
| AA Rated Underlying | 9473 | 0.27 | 0.44 | 0.00 | 0.00 | 0.00 | 1.00 | 1.00 |
| Below AA Rated Underlying | 9473 | 0.29 | 0.45 | 0.00 | 0.00 | 0.00 | 1.00 | 1.00 |
| Unrated Underlying | 9473 | 0.39 | 0.49 | 0.00 | 0.00 | 0.00 | 1.00 | 1.00 |

| | | | | | | | | |
|---|---|---|---|---|---|---|---|---|
| *Panel B: Issuer Characteristics* | | | | | | | | |
| *University Type* | | | | | | | | |
| Public | 9473 | 0.62 | 0.49 | 0.00 | 0.00 | 1.00 | 1.00 | 1.00 |
| NCAA Division I | 9473 | 0.63 | 0.48 | 0.00 | 0.00 | 1.00 | 1.00 | 1.00 |
| R1 | 9473 | 0.41 | 0.49 | 0.00 | 0.00 | 0.00 | 1.00 | 1.00 |
| System | 9473 | 0.35 | 0.48 | 0.00 | 0.00 | 0.00 | 1.00 | 1.00 |
| HBCU | 9473 | 0.02 | 0.14 | 0.00 | 0.00 | 0.00 | 0.00 | 1.00 |
| Land Grant | 9473 | 0.20 | 0.40 | 0.00 | 0.00 | 0.00 | 0.00 | 1.00 |
| Hospital | 9473 | 0.13 | 0.34 | 0.00 | 0.00 | 0.00 | 0.00 | 1.00 |
| *University Prestige* | | | | | | | | |
| Total Enrollment | 9013 | 16.79 | 13.72 | 0.71 | 4.38 | 12.95 | 26.54 | 53.29 |
| Proportion Admitted to Applied | 5936 | 0.66 | 0.21 | 0.04 | 0.55 | 0.70 | 0.81 | 1.00 |
| Average SAT | 5147 | 11.57 | 1.33 | 8.60 | 10.65 | 11.45 | 12.35 | 14.90 |
| *Panel C: Issuer Financial Characteristics* | | | | | | | | |
| *Balance Sheet* | | | | | | | | |
| Assets | 6672 | 1.86 | 3.13 | 0.03 | 0.27 | 0.73 | 2.05 | 19.71 |
| Liabilities | 6672 | 0.67 | 1.08 | 0.01 | 0.09 | 0.26 | 0.81 | 6.86 |
| Long-Term Debt | 5925 | 0.37 | 0.50 | 0.00 | 0.07 | 0.17 | 0.46 | 2.82 |
| Value of Endowment | 6961 | 0.66 | 1.57 | 0.00 | 0.03 | 0.14 | 0.58 | 10.81 |
| *Leverage Ratios* | | | | | | | | |
| Long-Term Debt/Assets | 5918 | 0.25 | 0.12 | 0.00 | 0.16 | 0.23 | 0.33 | 0.60 |
| Liabilities/Assets | 6672 | 0.40 | 0.19 | 0.09 | 0.27 | 0.37 | 0.48 | 1.09 |
| Endowment/Assets | 5301 | 0.29 | 0.20 | 0.00 | 0.13 | 0.26 | 0.41 | 0.87 |
| *Revenue Concentration* | | | | | | | | |
| HHI Non-Financial Income | 9325 | 0.40 | 0.15 | 0.21 | 0.29 | 0.36 | 0.48 | 1.00 |
| HHI Revenue | 9218 | 0.38 | 0.15 | 0.17 | 0.27 | 0.33 | 0.45 | 1.00 |

Note: This table presents the summary statistics for the sample of bond issuances and the underlying university issuer. Panel A describes the characteristics of the bond issuance including its yield, features, and ratings. Panel B describes the characteristics of the university issuer including its type and prestige. Panel C contains information regarding the university issuer's financial condition based on its balance sheet, leverage, and revenue concentration.

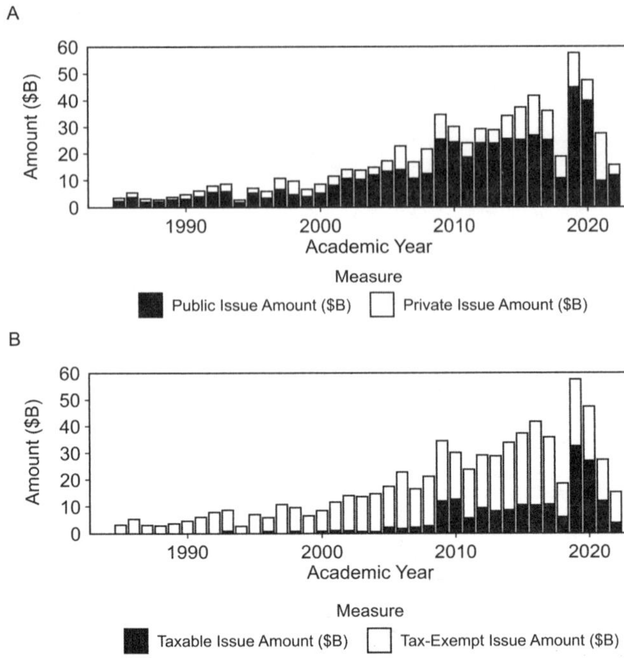


**Fig. 6.1 Issuance and taxable amounts**

Note: This figure shows the issuance amounts of debt by year across public and private universities in Panel A and taxable versus tax-exempt debt in Panel B.

using Equation 1, the average tax-adjusted rate is comparable to a taxable bond offering a 6.08 percent yield. The average bond has a maturity of nearly 22 years and a composite issue amount of $67.22 million, indicating these bond issuances are economically large. About 88 percent of bonds are taxable while 39 percent of university issuers are unrated, implying that their debt might carry a large risk premium without the use of insurance or credit enhancement.

Figure 6.1 shows that there has been significant growth in the use of debt by universities since 1985. In 1985, debt issuance amounts across all universities totaled about $3 billion which increased to over $50 billion in 2019. These issuances have steadily increased with Panel A showing that much of these debt issuances are carried by public universities. Panel B documents an increasing use of taxable debt in recent years which spiked following the Great Recession of 2008 and around the onset of COVID-19 in 2020. The spike in taxable debt following the Great Recession was partially driven by the Build America Bonds which offered subsidized borrowing costs for taxable debt and expired in 2010.[7] Figure 6A.2 provides evidence the more

7. See "Why the surge in taxable municipal bonds?" Lorena Hernandez Barcena and David Wessel, Brookings Institution, December 21, 2020, https://www.brookings.edu/articles/why-the-surge-in-taxable-municipal-bonds/.

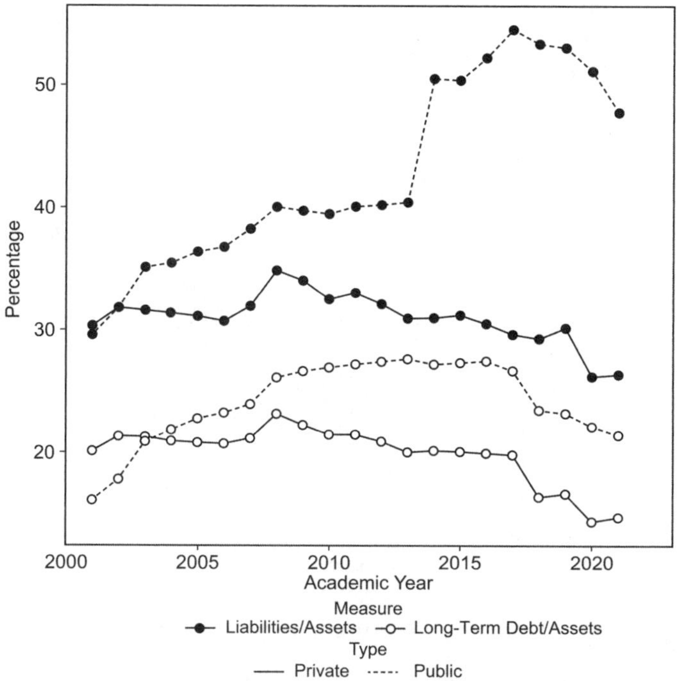


**Fig. 6.2 Leverage measures across private and public universities**

Note: This figure shows measures of leverage across public and private universities in the IPEDS sample. The red lines show the ratio of liabilities scaled by assets for private (solid line) and public (dashed line), and the blue lines show the ratio of long-term debt by assets for private (solid line) and public (dashed line) universities.

recent increase in taxable debt appears to be driven by tightening margins for US universities, especially for public universities, while the low interest rate environment has also contributed.

Panel B of table 6.1 provides a breakdown of the characteristics of the average university issuer. On average, these university issuers are part of large, growing institutions rather than small, financially distressed universities. About 62 percent of university issuers are public universities and more than 40 percent are R1 doctoral designated schools. The average university issuer has nearly 17,000 students and has an admittance rate of 66 percent. Panel C of table 6.1 shows that the average university has assets of $1.86 billion with its endowment about 30 percent of its asset base. Long-term debt is also a significant factor in these universities as it comprises 25 percent of a firm's asset base while total liabilities are 40 percent. Figure 6.2 shows the change in time-varying leverage for universities from 2001 to 2022. Public universities have experienced increases in leverage defined either as *Liabilities/Assets* or *Long-Term Debt/Assets* while the leverage of private universities has actually declined. For public universities this increase in leverage is

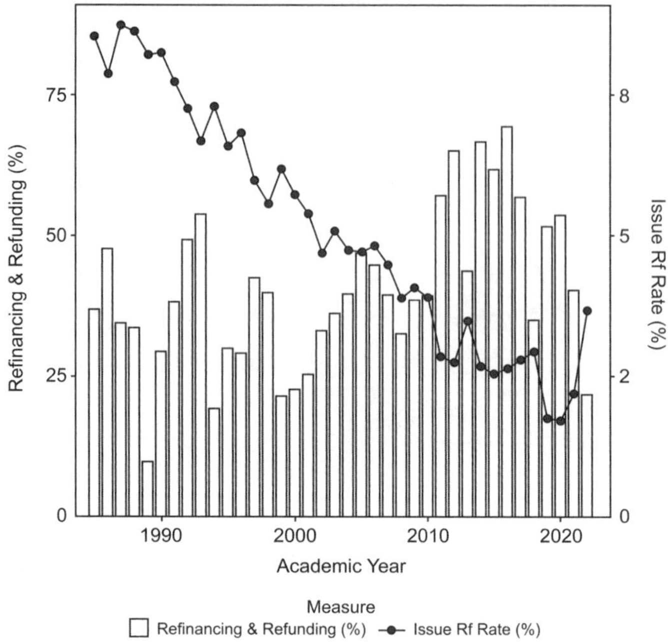


**Fig. 6.3 Refinancing and refunding issuances versus risk-free rate**

Note: This figure shows the average proportion of debt issuances used to refinance or refund existing issuances within a given academic year versus the risk-free rate of the issuing maturity length.

observed primarily until 2013 before gradually declining. The increase in *Liabilities*/*Assets* for public universities in 2014 reflects net pension liabilities shifting onto the balance sheet for public universities.[8]

While the large increases in annual issuance amounts shown in Panel A of figure 6.1 and small changes in leverage in Panel B of figure 6.2 appear to be in contrast, much of these issuances result in no changes in university leverage as they stem from a university refinancing previously issued debt. Figure 6.3 plots the proportion of issuances within each academic year and shows an increasing propensity of universities to refinance debt during declining interest rate environments. The risk-free rate has declined from close to 9 percent in 1985 to nearly 0 percent in 2020 which coincided with an increase in issuances for the purpose of refinancing from about 30 percent in the late 1980s to around 60 percent in the late 2010s.

8. See "The State Pension Funding Gap: 2014, New accounting rules help provide a clearer picture" Issue Brief, Pew Charitable Trusts, August 24, 2016, https://www.pewtrusts.org/en/research-and-analysis/issue-briefs/2016/08/the-state-pension-funding-gap-2014, for more information.

Table 6.2 displays summary statistics across university issuer types to better understand variation in the cost of debt, use of debt, and financial structure across universities. Panel A of table 6.2 shows that across issuer types, public universities have the lowest issuance yields of 4.50 percent which is about 50 basis points less than private universities. It is possible that this descriptive difference exists simply as a result of public universities being more likely to issue insured debt or to modify other debt features to lower their cost of debt, so we return to this pattern in our empirical analysis. We find that historically Black colleges and universities (HBCUs) have the highest gross spread or fee charged by the underwriter to sell the debt issuance which is consistent with Dougal et al. (2019).

Universities with hospitals have the largest issuance sizes with an average amount of nearly $150 million reflecting the large investment necessary to maintain and grow health-care infrastructure. We find that public universities are the most likely to purchase insurance and do so 31 percent of the time while R1 doctoral universities have the highest underlying issuer rating. Panel B of table 6.2 shows the leverage ratio of *Liabilities/Assets* or *Long-Term Debt/Assets* is much smoother across university types than the scaled endowment base of *Endowment/Assets,* as private universities have nearly double the proportion of scaled endowment assets as public universities (0.40 vs. 0.23).

Panel C of table 6.2 documents significant heterogeneity in the revenue sources across university types. Public universities rely primarily on state support (40 percent), net tuition revenue (20 percent), and other auxiliary revenue sources (19 percent). In contrast, the average private university has almost no reliance on state support (5 percent) while instead relying on net tuition revenue (32 percent), financial revenue (23 percent), and other revenue (18 percent).[9] Additionally, private universities have the largest revenue concentration based on the Herfindahl-Hirschman Index (HHI), while R1 doctoral universities have the most diversified revenue sources.

Figure 6.4 displays the time-varying average yields across private and public issuers over time. Overall, this descriptive difference in yields across private and public university issuers is quite stable over time with this gap of about 45 basis points based on the issue yield. The figure also shows a secular increase in the excess issuance net the risk-free rate which was below zero for the period preceding 2008 but has risen to about 1 percent afterwards. To understand this gap, Panel A of figure 6.5 shows the underlying ratings of the issuing universities over time. After 2000, an increasing number of universities have transitioned from being unrated with the largest increase occurring within the *Below AA Rated* and *AA Rated* groups, but there has

9. Figure 6A.3 shows the full unconditional breakdown of revenues and expenses across public and private universities. Figure 6A.4 and figure 6A.5 show the time-varying composition of revenues and expenses by university type, respectively.

**Table 6.2** **Issuance panel: descriptive statistics by university type**

| University Type:<br>% of Observations: | Public<br>62% | Private<br>38% | HBCU<br>2% | R1<br>41% | System<br>35% | Hospital<br>13% | NCAA D1<br>63% |
|---|---|---|---|---|---|---|---|
| *Panel A: Bond Characteristics* | | | | | | | |
| *Yield Measures* | | | | | | | |
| Issuance Yield | 4.50 | 4.96 | 5.00 | 4.57 | 4.57 | 4.57 | 4.58 |
| Issuance Yield Tax-Adjusted | 5.81 | 6.52 | 6.40 | 5.90 | 5.90 | 5.88 | 5.92 |
| Issuance Yield Less Risk Free Rate | −0.03 | 0.15 | 0.18 | −0.17 | −0.05 | −0.12 | −0.07 |
| Issuance Yield Tax-Adjusted Less Risk Free Rate | 1.26 | 1.66 | 1.60 | 1.14 | 1.25 | 1.19 | 1.25 |
| *Bond Characteristics* | | | | | | | |
| Gross Spread | 7.12 | 8.04 | 8.20 | 6.38 | 6.94 | 6.67 | 6.93 |
| Years to Maturity | 20.47 | 22.53 | 22.06 | 20.69 | 20.83 | 20.68 | 20.92 |
| Issue Amount | 76.09 | 53.97 | 32.69 | 107.02 | 96.60 | 154.64 | 83.37 |
| Negotiated Bid | 0.71 | 0.93 | 0.89 | 0.73 | 0.73 | 0.78 | 0.73 |
| Callable Issue | 0.84 | 0.87 | 0.85 | 0.83 | 0.85 | 0.80 | 0.85 |
| Refinancing or Refunding Flag | 0.42 | 0.45 | 0.46 | 0.43 | 0.41 | 0.40 | 0.43 |
| Tax-Exempt | 0.86 | 0.91 | 0.88 | 0.85 | 0.84 | 0.83 | 0.86 |
| Sinking Fund | 0.50 | 0.59 | 0.60 | 0.48 | 0.51 | 0.48 | 0.51 |
| Revenue Bond | 0.93 | 0.96 | 0.98 | 0.91 | 0.94 | 0.86 | 0.93 |
| Insured | 0.31 | 0.17 | 0.46 | 0.24 | 0.29 | 0.20 | 0.29 |
| *Bond Ratings* | | | | | | | |
| Rating Underlying | 3.64 | 2.80 | 2.14 | 4.18 | 3.81 | 3.92 | 3.81 |
| Rating Combined | 5.25 | 3.85 | 4.72 | 5.43 | 5.35 | 4.97 | 5.30 |
| AAA Rated Underlying | 0.04 | 0.06 | 0.01 | 0.09 | 0.05 | 0.07 | 0.06 |
| AA Rated Underlying | 0.36 | 0.13 | 0.11 | 0.46 | 0.42 | 0.44 | 0.36 |
| Below AA Rated Underlying | 0.25 | 0.35 | 0.30 | 0.17 | 0.19 | 0.16 | 0.26 |
| Unrated Underlying | 0.35 | 0.46 | 0.58 | 0.29 | 0.34 | 0.33 | 0.33 |

| | | | | | | | |
|---|---|---|---|---|---|---|---|
| *Panel B: Issuer Characteristics* | | | | | | | |
| *Balance Sheet Measures* | | | | | | | |
| Assets | 1.96 | 1.73 | 0.30 | 4.03 | 2.07 | 5.78 | 2.56 |
| Liabilities | 0.79 | 0.51 | 0.13 | 1.42 | 0.81 | 2.15 | 0.93 |
| Interest Expense | 17.08 | 12.21 | 3.04 | 30.31 | 18.96 | 48.76 | 20.03 |
| Long-Term Debt | 0.40 | 0.31 | 0.08 | 0.72 | 0.41 | 1.07 | 0.48 |
| Value of Endowment | 0.60 | 0.79 | 0.05 | 1.34 | 0.70 | 1.76 | 0.85 |
| Long-Term Debt/Assets | 0.26 | 0.23 | 0.28 | 0.23 | 0.24 | 0.22 | 0.24 |
| Liabilities/Assets | 0.45 | 0.33 | 0.46 | 0.39 | 0.43 | 0.40 | 0.41 |
| Endowment/Assets | 0.23 | 0.40 | 0.14 | 0.34 | 0.25 | 0.34 | 0.28 |
| *University Prestige* | | | | | | | |
| Total Enrollment | 23.02 | 6.26 | 5.15 | 28.49 | 25.11 | 26.99 | 23.37 |
| Proportion Admitted to Applied | 0.70 | 0.58 | 0.58 | 0.62 | 0.67 | 0.52 | 0.66 |
| Average SAT | 11.34 | 11.98 | 9.10 | 12.24 | 11.57 | 12.49 | 11.70 |
| *Panel C: Scaled Revenues (% Total Revenues)* | | | | | | | |
| % State Revenue | 0.40 | 0.05 | 0.35 | 0.31 | 0.40 | 0.23 | 0.33 |
| % Federal Revenue | 0.14 | 0.09 | 0.25 | 0.16 | 0.15 | 0.14 | 0.14 |
| % Net Tuition Revenue | 0.19 | 0.32 | 0.17 | 0.17 | 0.18 | 0.13 | 0.21 |
| % Gift Revenue | 0.05 | 0.13 | 0.07 | 0.08 | 0.06 | 0.07 | 0.07 |
| % Other Revenue | 0.20 | 0.18 | 0.13 | 0.25 | 0.20 | 0.40 | 0.21 |
| % Financial Revenue | 0.02 | 0.23 | 0.03 | 0.03 | 0.02 | 0.04 | 0.04 |
| *Revenue Concentration* | | | | | | | |
| HHI Revenue | 0.36 | 0.43 | 0.35 | 0.34 | 0.36 | 0.36 | 0.36 |

Note: This table presents the summary statistics for the sample of bond issuances and the underlying university issuer across university types. Values displayed in the table coincide with the mean value for the respective university type. Panel A describes the characteristics of the bond issuance including its yield, features, and ratings. Panel B describes the characteristics of the university issuer including its balance sheet, leverage, and prestige. Panel C contains information regarding the university issuer's scaled revenues and revenue concentration.

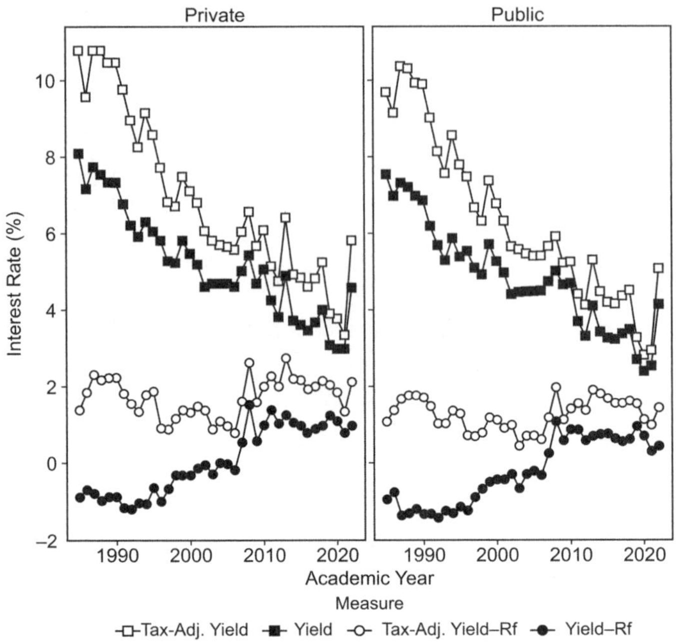


**Fig. 6.4 Bond yield measures at issuance**

Note: This figure shows the average issuance yields for private and public university issuers over time. Yield is the interest rate of the bond at issuance, and Tax-Adj. Yield modifies the yield to account for the exemption from federal and state income taxes for an in-state investor. Tax-Adj. Yield − Rf nets out the risk-free rate based on the maturity-matched, risk-free rate and Yield − Rf nets out the risk-free rate from the issuance yield.

also been an increase in *AAA Rated* issuers. Although the change in underlying ratings does not explain this increase in risk premium, Panel B of figure 6.5 examines whether the underlying rating of the bond itself has changed. The change in bond rating decomposition is quite striking as post-2008, the proportion of *AAA* rated debt issuances has declined from about 50 percent to less than 10 percent. These patterns reflect the breakdown of the municipal bond insurance market in the aftermath of the Great Recession, and figure 6A.6 shows that this decline in *AAA* rated debt is almost perfectly matched by the decline of bonds with insurance.

### 6.2.5 Empirical Methodology

#### *6.2.5.1 Empirical Methodology: Bond Features*

To examine how college and university demographic and financial characteristics affect bond issuance features, we estimate the following empirical specification:

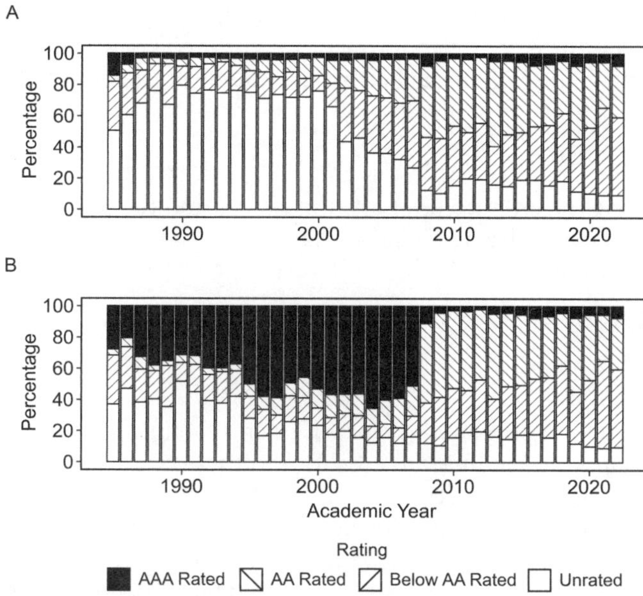


**Fig. 6.5 Rating of underlying issuer versus bond rating**

Note: This figure shows the composition of ratings for the underlying university issuer in Panel A, and Panel B shows the actual rating of the bond issuance.

$$(2) \quad Y_{i,s,t} = \beta_1 \text{Public}_i + \beta_2 \text{School Controls}_{i,t} + \beta_3 \text{Bond Controls}_{i,t} + \lambda_{s,t} + \varepsilon_{i,s,t},$$

where $Y_{i,s,t}$ denotes a bond feature such as the underlying rating, the presence of bond insurance, or the yield to maturity for school $i$ in state $s$ at time $t$. One of the main coefficients of interest is $\beta_1$ which represents the incremental effect of a public versus a private college on a particular bond feature (e.g., yields). School Controls is a vector of financial and demographic features such as revenue concentration, the natural logarithm of total revenue, the natural logarithm of total enrollment, time-average SAT scores, leverage ratios, and the natural logarithm of endowment size. Bond Controls include the natural logarithm of bond maturity, the natural logarithm of bond amount, credit ratings, whether the bond is insured, whether the bond is tax-exempt, whether the bond has a sinking fund provision, whether the bond is callable, and whether the bond is refunding existing debt. $\lambda_{s,t}$ denotes state-by-year fixed effects, which controls for time-varying unobservable characteristics within a state in a given year, such as shocks to the regulatory environment or local economic conditions. In related tests, we also additively include state and year fixed effects to provide inference of the spillovers of underlying, time-varying characteristics of a state's economic conditions (e.g., unemployment rate or credit rate) on a university issuer's bond features. Standard errors are double-clustered at the state and year level.

*6.2.5.2 Empirical Methodology: Leverage Levels and Use of Debt*

To examine the leverage levels of universities and the impact of debt on *future* university characteristics we estimate variations of the following empirical specification:

$$(3) \quad Y_{i,s,t+1} = \beta_1 \text{University Characteristic}_{i,t} + \beta_2 \text{School Controls}_{i,t} + \delta_i + \lambda_{s,t} + \varepsilon_{i,s,t+1},$$

where $Y_{i,s,t+1}$ denotes the leverage level of interest or university characteristic for school $i$ in state $s$ at time $t + 1$. School controls are a vector of financial and demographic features such as the natural logarithm of total revenue, the natural logarithm of total enrollment, and a university's net income margin. $\delta_i$ denotes university fixed effects which controls for time-invariant characteristics of a given university such as its prestige. $\lambda_{s,t}$ denotes state-by-year fixed effects, which control for time-varying unobservable characteristics within a state in a given year, such as shocks to the regulatory environment or local economic conditions. Standard errors are double-clustered at the state and year level.

## 6.3 Main Results

While many of the patterns we have documented reflect secular trends of universities over time (e.g., increasing issuances, tax-exempt issuances, excess issuance yields over the risk-free rate), we proceed to examine variation either within a given year, a given state × year, or a given state × year × bond rating to gain a better understanding across universities' bond features, leverage levels, and the ultimate use of these proceeds.

### 6.3.1 Determinants of Bond Characteristics

Table 6.3 examines variation in the bond features themselves. The results in column (1) show that public universities have similar underlying university credit ratings to private universities, while declines in the 30-year risk-free rate at the time of issuance (within a given year) are associated with an issuer having a higher credit rating. We also find that universities comprised of students with higher SAT scores and with larger size (proxied for by total revenues) have higher credit ratings, while increases in revenue concentration are associated with a school having a lower credit rating. Related to the use of the proceeds, the results in column (2) show that public universities are 7 percent less likely than private universities to refinance their debt. The

**Table 6.3** **Explaining bond features**

| | Und. Rating | Refinance | Insured | Log(Amount) | | Log(Maturity) | |
|---|---|---|---|---|---|---|---|
| | (1) | (2) | (3) | (4) | (5) | (6) | (7) |
| Public | 0.39 | −0.07** | 0.18*** | −0.37* | −0.31 | −0.05 | −0.05 |
| | [0.25] | [0.03] | [0.05] | [0.20] | [0.20] | [0.06] | [0.06] |
| 30-Year $R_f$ Rate | −0.19** | −0.06** | −0.01 | −0.11** | −0.09** | −0.09*** | −0.08*** |
| | [0.08] | [0.03] | [0.01] | [0.04] | [0.04] | [0.03] | [0.03] |
| Average SAT | 0.42*** | 0.02* | 0.04*** | 0.01 | 0.00 | 0.08*** | 0.08*** |
| | [0.07] | [0.01] | [0.02] | [0.04] | [0.04] | [0.03] | [0.02] |
| HHI Revenue | −1.36*** | 0.12* | 0.12 | −0.13 | 0.00 | 0.33** | 0.31** |
| | [0.39] | [0.07] | [0.08] | [0.19] | [0.23] | [0.14] | [0.13] |
| Log(Revenue) | 0.43*** | −0.03 | −0.08*** | 0.28*** | 0.33*** | −0.16*** | −0.18*** |
| | [0.14] | [0.02] | [0.02] | [0.06] | [0.06] | [0.05] | [0.05] |
| Log(Enrollment) | −0.05 | 0.02 | 0.09*** | 0.17** | 0.11 | 0.16*** | 0.16*** |
| | [0.17] | [0.02] | [0.02] | [0.07] | [0.07] | [0.05] | [0.05] |
| Underlying Rating | | 0.01*** | −0.05*** | 0.04*** | 0.03** | 0.06** | 0.07** |
| | | [0.00] | [0.01] | [0.01] | [0.01] | [0.02] | [0.03] |
| State Economic Activity | | | | 0.01* | | −0.00 | |
| | | | | [0.01] | | [0.00] | |
| State Unemployment Rate | | | | 0.01 | | −0.02* | |
| | | | | [0.03] | | [0.01] | |
| State Credit Rating | | | | −0.05** | | −0.05*** | |
| | | | | [0.02] | | [0.01] | |
| Observations | 8320 | 8320 | 8320 | 8240 | 8320 | 8240 | 8320 |
| Adjusted $R^2$ | 0.50 | 0.14 | 0.47 | 0.52 | 0.57 | 0.15 | 0.19 |
| Year & State F.E. | No | No | No | Yes | No | Yes | No |
| Year x State F.E. | Yes | Yes | Yes | No | Yes | No | Yes |
| Issuer Type Controls | Yes | Yes | Yes | Yes | Yes | Yes | Yes |
| Y-mean | 3.30 | 0.44 | 0.27 | 3.39 | 3.37 | 2.89 | 2.88 |

Note: This table presents the OLS regression coefficients from regressing a bond's characteristics on university, financial conditions, and other state characteristics. The dependent variable in column(1) is the underlying rating of the issuer at issuance, (2) is an indicator for whether the issuance is refinancing or refunding a prior issuance, (3) is an indicator for whether the bond issuance is insured, (4) to (5) is the logarithm of the total issuance amount, and (6) to (7) the logarithm of the total maturity. The regressions include *Issuer Type Controls* based on the ultimate issuer of the bond (e.g., university or state issuer). Regressions include variations of state and year and state × year fixed effects. Standard errors are clustered at the state and year level. ***, **, * correspond to statistical significance at the 1 percent, 5 percent, and 10 percent level, respectively.

decision to refinance is strongly connected to a university's prestige and underlying rating while variation in the risk-free rate *within* a given year is also informative. The results in column (3) show that public universities are significantly more likely to issue insured debt in comparison to private universities and comprise a majority of insured debt issuances (18 percent higher relative to the sample average of 27 percent). We find idiosyncratic variation in relationship to size and prestige in the take-up of bond insurance as we find that schools with higher-ability students and larger enrollments are more likely to purchase insurance while schools with larger revenues and higher credit ratings are less likely to purchase insurance at issuance.

State economic conditions are also an important driver for bond issuance decisions. The results in column (4) show that an improvement in state economic activity is associated with larger bond issuances, while improvements in a university's home state's credit rating have opposite effects as they are associated with smaller issuances. Overall, columns (4) and (5) which examine a university's choice of issuance amount find significant evidence for larger universities with higher credit ratings issuing larger bonds. Examining the choice of a bond's maturity, we find that increases in a state's unemployment rating are linked to shorter maturity bond issuances and improvements in a state's credit rating are also connected to shorter maturity issuances. Across the choice of maturity in columns (6) and (7) we find no evidence of differences in maturities across issuances by public and private universities, while improvements in a university issuer's underlying size or credit rating are associated with longer-dated maturity bonds.

### 6.3.2 Determinants of Bond Yields

In table 6.4 we examine how university characteristics affect a school's issuance yield, as the cost of debt for universities is a significant determinant of their level of investment. The results in column (1) show that public universities have an estimated lower cost of debt of about 35 basis points, which is slightly less than the descriptive mean difference of 46 basis points. Column (1) also estimates the impact of the underlying state on a university's issuing yield and finds significant spillovers as improvements in state economic activity and decreases in a state's unemployment rate reduce issuance yields.[10]

The results in column (2) and (3) show that this gap in yields is partially attributable to differences in bond features across university issuer types as the estimated yield for public universities falls in magnitude to about 18 basis points following the inclusion of rating, maturity, issuance amount, and other bond controls along with the inclusion of year × state fixed effects. However, this estimated gap in yields remains both highly statistically significant and economically significant as the average public issuer would save about $2.8 million in interest expense payments over the lifetime of the bond.[11]

The results in column (4) show that this difference in yields across public and private issuers is not driven by differences in an ability to account for a bond's tax status. With the inclusion of an interaction between a univer-

10. We provide evidence of the spillover from a university's home state to its underlying issuances as the university is uniquely constrained to its home state's economic activity that is unique from other businesses. We do not formally disentangle the impact of state economic activity on issuance yields between the supply of credit (reductions in a state's economic activity lead to crowding out due to an increased supply of municipal debt) versus the demand for credit (reductions in credit lead to a reduced demand for tax-exempt bond issuances due to less taxable income to shield).

11. This saving in interest payments is computed as 18 basis points × $76.09 million (mean issue amount for university issuers) × 20.47 years ≈ $2.8 million.

**Table 6.4** **Explaining issuance yields**

| | Yield | | | | | | | |
|---|---|---|---|---|---|---|---|---|
| | (1) | (2) | (3) | (4) | (5) | (6) | (7) | (8) |
| Public | −0.35*** | −0.26*** | −0.18*** | −0.15*** | −0.21*** | −0.28*** | −0.16** | −0.56*** |
| | [0.07] | [0.05] | [0.04] | [0.04] | [0.04] | [0.07] | [0.07] | [0.16] |
| State Economic Activity | −0.01** | | | | | | | |
| | [0.00] | | | | | | | |
| State Unemployment Rate | 0.04** | | | | | | | |
| | [0.02] | | | | | | | |
| Log(Maturity) | | 0.67*** | 0.69*** | 0.69*** | 0.67*** | 0.75*** | 0.77*** | 0.80*** |
| | | [0.06] | [0.05] | [0.05] | [0.05] | [0.08] | [0.09] | [0.11] |
| Log(Issue Amount) | | −0.06*** | −0.08*** | −0.08*** | −0.04*** | −0.02 | −0.02 | −0.05 |
| | | [0.01] | [0.01] | [0.01] | [0.01] | [0.01] | [0.02] | [0.03] |
| Underlying Rating | | | −0.06*** | −0.06*** | −0.04*** | −0.05*** | 0.00 | −0.01 |
| | | | [0.01] | [0.01] | [0.01] | [0.01] | [0.00] | [0.01] |
| Public × Taxable | | | | −0.30*** | | | | |
| | | | | [0.10] | | | | |
| Average SAT | | | | | −0.09*** | −0.10*** | −0.07** | 0.02 |
| | | | | | [0.02] | [0.03] | [0.03] | [0.06] |
| HHI Revenue | | | | | 0.19* | 0.22 | 0.04 | −0.20 |
| | | | | | [0.10] | [0.19] | [0.22] | [0.34] |
| Log(Revenue) | | | | | −0.03 | −0.03 | −0.02 | 0.12* |
| | | | | | [0.02] | [0.03] | [0.02] | [0.06] |
| Long-Term Debt/ Assets | | | | | | 0.27 | 0.36* | 1.34** |
| | | | | | | [0.19] | [0.19] | [0.59] |
| Log(Endowment) | | | | | | −0.02 | 0.00 | −0.17*** |
| | | | | | | [0.02] | [0.01] | [0.05] |
| Observations | 9439 | 9185 | 9185 | 9185 | 8615 | 5051 | 4399 | 2786 |
| Adjusted $R^2$ | 0.68 | 0.78 | 0.84 | 0.84 | 0.85 | 0.75 | 0.80 | 0.84 |
| Year & State F.E. | Yes | No | No | No | No | No | No | No |
| Year × State F.E. | No | Yes | Yes | Yes | Yes | Yes | No | No |
| Year × State × Rating F.E. | No | No | No | No | No | No | Yes | No |
| Year × County × Rating F.E. | No | No | No | No | No | No | No | Yes |
| Issuer Controls | Yes | Yes | Yes | Yes | Yes | Yes | Yes | Yes |
| Bond Controls | No | No | Yes | Yes | Yes | Yes | Yes | Yes |
| Y-mean | 4.67 | 4.65 | 4.65 | 4.65 | 4.66 | 3.90 | 3.88 | 3.84 |

Note: This table presents the OLS regression coefficients from regressing a bond's issuance yield on university, financial conditions, and other state characteristics. The dependent variable in columns (1) to (7) is the yield at issue for a given bond. The regressions include *Issuer Type Controls* based on the ultimate issuer of the bond (e.g., university or state issuer), and *Bond Controls* based on characteristics of the bond (e.g., taxable, sinking fund, insured). Regressions include variations of year and state, state × year, state × year × rating, and county × year × rating fixed effects. Standard errors are clustered at the state and year level. ***, **, * correspond to statistical significance at the 1 percent, 5 percent, and 10 percent level, respectively.

sity's public status and a bond issuance's tax-exempt status (Public × Tax-Exempt), we are able to directly compare public and private issuances *within* the same tax status. The main effect of *Public* now represents the gap in yields between public and private university tax-exempt bonds which is estimated to be 15 basis points lower for public universities while the coefficient on Public × Tax-Exempt of −0.30 estimates that the gap between public and private taxable issuances is 30 basis points lower for an estimated gap of 45 basis points in taxable bonds (15 basis points lower less 30 basis points lower = 45 basis points lower).

The results in columns (5) and (6) show that public universities continue to have a lower cost of debt at issuance than private universities, even when accounting for the quality of a university's students, its revenue concentration, and leverage. In column (7) we tighten our comparison group by comparing bonds issued within the same state, within the same year, and at the same rating level. We continue to find that public universities have a lower cost of debt with an estimated difference in yields of 16 basis points and also find evidence that this model is better accounting for differences in characteristics *across* issuers as *Long-Term Debt/Assets* now has a positive estimated effect on issuance yields which aligns with prior capital structure theory proposing increases in borrowing costs as default risk increases (Modigliani and Miller 1958). Lastly, in column (8) we use an even tighter unit of identification by comparing bonds issued by universities within the same county, within the same year, within the same rating grouping, and we continue to find that public universities have a lower estimated cost of debt than private universities.

### 6.3.3 Variation in University Financial Leverage

In table 6.5, we proceed forward to examining variation in the level of a university's leverage over time *within* the same university. In column (1) we examine a university's future leverage (*Long-Term Debt / Assets*$_{t+1}$) on its composition of revenue sources. We find that declines in governmental revenue support result in increases in a university's future leverage. In column (2) we separate total governmental revenue into its components of state and federal government revenue, and we find that only changes in a university's federal governmental revenue support are statistically significant in explaining variation in a university's subsequent leverage levels. To understand the heterogeneous impact of state and federal revenue support across university type, in column (3) we interact these revenue components with a university's public status. We find that declines in state support are informative in explaining variation in a university's subsequent leverage, but only for public universities with declines in state support leading to increases in future leverage. In contrast, shifts in federal revenue support have no difference in their impact *across* public and private universities, with both experiencing increases in leverage in response to declines in federal government support.

**Table 6.5 Explaining university leverage**

| | Long-Term Debt/Assets$_{t+1}$ | | | Liabilities/Assets$_{t+1}$ | | |
|---|---|---|---|---|---|---|
| | (1) | (2) | (3) | (4) | (5) | (6) |
| % Government Revenue | −0.06** | | | −0.20*** | | |
| | [0.03] | | | [0.07] | | |
| % State Revenue | | −0.10 | 0.03 | | −0.26 | 0.19* |
| | | [0.07] | [0.07] | | [0.15] | [0.10] |
| Public × % State Revenue | | | −0.17* | | | −0.71*** |
| | | | [0.08] | | | [0.21] |
| % Federal Revenue | | −0.05* | −0.06** | | −0.23 | 0.00 |
| | | [0.03] | [0.03] | | [0.13] | [0.08] |
| Public × % Federal Revenue | | | −0.00 | | | −0.90*** |
| | | | [0.08] | | | [0.26] |
| % Net Tuition Revenue | 0.01 | 0.00 | −0.00 | 0.04 | 0.03 | −0.00 |
| | [0.02] | [0.02] | [0.02] | [0.04] | [0.04] | [0.03] |
| % Gift Revenue | −0.03* | −0.03*** | −0.04*** | −0.03 | −0.05* | −0.09*** |
| | [0.01] | [0.01] | [0.01] | [0.03] | [0.02] | [0.02] |
| % Other Revenue | 0.01 | 0.01 | 0.00 | 0.12** | 0.11* | 0.03 |
| | [0.02] | [0.01] | [0.01] | [0.06] | [0.05] | [0.04] |
| % Financial Revenue | −0.01 | −0.01 | −0.02 | −0.03 | −0.04 | −0.07 |
| | [0.01] | [0.01] | [0.01] | [0.04] | [0.04] | [0.04] |
| Observations | 28507 | 28507 | 28507 | 31583 | 31583 | 31583 |
| Adjusted $R^2$ | 0.74 | 0.74 | 0.74 | 0.77 | 0.77 | 0.77 |
| University Controls | Yes | Yes | Yes | Yes | Yes | Yes |
| Year × State F.E. | Yes | Yes | Yes | Yes | Yes | Yes |
| University Fixed Effects | Yes | Yes | Yes | Yes | Yes | Yes |
| Y-mean | 0.22 | 0.22 | 0.22 | 0.36 | 0.36 | 0.36 |

Note: This table presents the OLS regression coefficients from regressing a university's leverage on a university's revenue composition and other university characteristics. The dependent variable in columns (1) to (3) is *Long-Term Debt/Assets*$_{t+1}$ and in columns (4) to (6) is *Liabilities/Assets*$_{t+1}$. The regressions include *University Controls* based on a university's endowment, enrollment, and revenue. Regressions include state × year fixed effects. Standard errors are clustered at the state and year level. ***, **, * correspond to statistical significance at the 1 percent, 5 percent, and 10 percent level, respectively.

As many universities might rely on other liability sources to respond to changes in their revenue concentration, we also examine shifts on a university's leverage, defined more broadly as *Liabilities / Assets*$_{t+1}$ in columns (4) to (6) of table 6.5. The results in column (4) show that declines in total governmental revenue are largely informative of a university's subsequent leverage, with an estimated effect size relative to the mean about two times that of the comparable estimate in column (1). Surprisingly, the decomposition of total governmental revenue into state and federal governmental revenue results in two statistically insignificant effects despite both coefficients being larger in magnitude than the overall effect estimated in column (4). Lastly, in column (6) we interact these components of governmental revenue on a university's public status. Similar to the results in columns (1) to (3) a decline in state revenue precedes large increases in its leverage, but only for public universities, as private universities actually have increases in leverage in response to universities receiving additional state support. In regards to changes in federal revenue, we find that declines in the proportion of federal revenue precede increases in $Liabilities / Assets_{t+1}$ for only public universities but have no impact on private universities.

### 6.3.4 The Effects of Debt on Higher Education

Up to this point, we have shown that declines in state support often precede increased leverage for public universities. These debt issuances might be optimal if they allow universities to smooth operating crises caused by declines in state support to assure that optimal investment is occurring in the development of human capital. In contrast, additional leverage driven by a desire to increase the *appearance* of university educational quality rather than educational quality itself would be less optimal (Goldman and Romley 2008; Goldman et al. 2010; Jacob et al. 2018).

In table 6.6 we examine changes in university behavior that follow increases in a university's ratio of $Long\text{-}Term\ Debt/Assets_t$. Panel A of table 6.6 examines changes in a university's composition of expenses and dormitory capacity following increased leverage. The results in column (1) show that increases in leverage precede increased investment in quality expenses, which include student service expenses and auxiliary expenses. Columns (2) and (3) show that the ratio of quality expenses to academic expenses and quality expenses per student also increases, providing evidence that most of these debt issuances are targeted toward student-related services. The results in column (4) document significant increases in dormitory capacity following these increases in leverage. In summary, these results provide evidence that universities have increasingly used debt as a tool to cater to student demand for increasing amenity quality, with no evidence of spillovers to educational quality.

In Panel B of table 6.6 we examine who bears these increasing costs and whether these increases in leverage are driven by a need to increase infrastructure due to increased student enrollment or a shift in the composition of student enrollment. The results in column (1) find that increases in leverage precede increases in the cost of in-state tuition with the inclusion of controls for a university's composition of revenues, endowment, enrollment, and net income margin. These controls provide some assurance this link is not mechanical—e.g., that a state might reduce its state support which results in a need for a university to shift this operating crisis to its students. Column (2) documents no increase in costs for out-of-state students' tuition costs, which might reflect the fact that these students have more elastic demand than in-state students due to having more choices. The null effect of leverage on a university's subsequent enrollment in column (3) suggests that schools are not taking on additional leverage due to the need to expand operations to accommodate a growing student body. In contrast, the results in column (4) show that the number of out-of-state students increases following leverage

**Table 6.6** **Implications of university leverage**

| | Quality Expense (%)$_{t+1}$ (1) | Quality/ Academic Exp.$_{t+1}$ (2) | Log(Quality Expense/ Enrollment)$_{t+1}$ (3) | Log(Dormitory Capacity)$_{t+1}$ (4) |
|---|---|---|---|---|
| | *Panel A: Quality & Capacity* | | | |
| Long-Term Debt/Assets$_t$ | 0.01* | 0.04* | 0.15*** | 0.23*** |
| | [0.00] | [0.02] | [0.03] | [0.04] |
| Controls | Yes | Yes | Yes | Yes |
| Observations | 28200 | 28200 | 26452 | 25283 |
| Adjusted $R^2$ | 0.90 | 0.85 | 0.91 | 0.97 |
| Year × State F.E. | Yes | Yes | Yes | Yes |
| University Fixed Effects | Yes | Yes | Yes | Yes |
| Y-mean | 0.25 | 0.60 | 8.60 | 6.96 |
| | *Panel B: Cost and Enrollment* | | | |
| | Log(In-State Tuition)$_{t+1}$ (1) | Log(Out-State Tuition)$_{t+1}$ (2) | Log(Enrollment)$_{t+1}$ (3) | Log(Enrollment Out-State)$_{t+1}$ (4) |
| Long-Term Debt/Assets | 0.08*** | 0.01 | 0.01 | 0.18** |
| | [0.03] | [0.02] | [0.01] | [0.06] |
| Controls | Yes | Yes | Yes | Yes |
| Observations | 25871 | 25871 | 26644 | 19574 |
| Adjusted $R^2$ | 0.98 | 0.94 | 1.00 | 0.94 |
| Year × State F.E. | Yes | Yes | Yes | Yes |
| University Fixed Effects | Yes | Yes | Yes | Yes |
| Y-mean | 9.69 | 9.97 | 7.89 | 4.72 |

Note: This table presents the OLS regression coefficients from regressing university characteristics on its leverage. Panel A includes measures of quality and capacity as the dependent variable which include column (1) as the percentage of quality expenses, (2) as the ratio of quality to academic expenses, (3) as the logarithm of the ratio of quality expenses scaled by enrollment, and (4) as the university's dormitory capacity. Panel B includes measures relating to the cost and enrollment as the dependent variable which include column (1) as the logarithm of in-state tuition, (2) as the logarithm of out-state tuition, (3) as the logarithm of enrollment, and (4) as the logarithm of out-state enrollment. The independent variable of interest is *Long-Term Debt/Assets* which represents a university's leverage. The regressions include *Controls* based on a university's endowment, enrollment, revenue, and revenue sources. Regressions include state × year and university fixed effects. Standard errors are clustered at the state and year level. ***, **, * correspond to statistical significance at the 1 percent, 5 percent, and 10 percent level, respectively.

increases which suggests that schools take on additional debt to attract out-of-state students which are more profitable to these universities, especially in periods of declining state appropriations.[12]

12. For example, the University of Alabama's non-resident student base grew from 626 students in 2002 to 2,406 students in 2018. See "UA is 'extreme case' of state schools recruiting out-of-state residents, report finds" Howard Koplowitz, AL.com, March 26, 2019, https://www.al.com/news/2019/03/ua-is-extreme-case-of-state-schools-recruiting-out-of-state-residents-report-finds.html.

### 6.4 Conclusion

Colleges and universities have increasingly relied on debt over the last 35 years to meet an increasing demand for higher education. We document large secular increases in the use of taxable debt as universities desire more flexible uses of financing and the breakdown of the municipal bond insurance market which contributed to an increase in excess municipal bond yields. We find significant heterogeneity in leverage and the cost of debt across public and private universities. Public universities have experienced a 50 percent increase in leverage over the last 20 years due to declines in state support while private universities have experienced a 25 percent decrease in leverage. We find that public universities have a lower cost of debt by about 20 basis points which has also contributed to these differences in leverage across public and private universities. Lastly, in regards to the use of these debt issuances, we document that increases in leverage precede increases in quality-related expenses and dormitory expansions. These quality-related issuances result in increases in cost that are born primarily by in-state students while it seems universities more aggressively recruit out-of-state students.

## Appendix

### Variable Definition

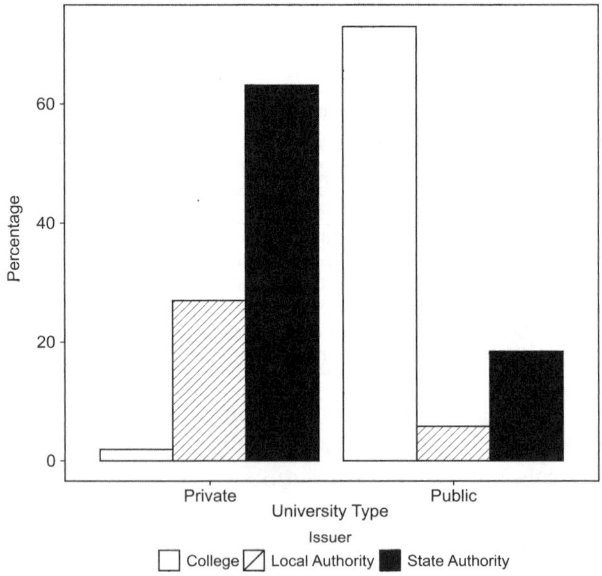


**Fig. 6A.1 Issuer type by university status**

Note: This figure shows the proportion of issuances for private and public university issuers across the three most common issuer types including College, Local Authority, State Authority.

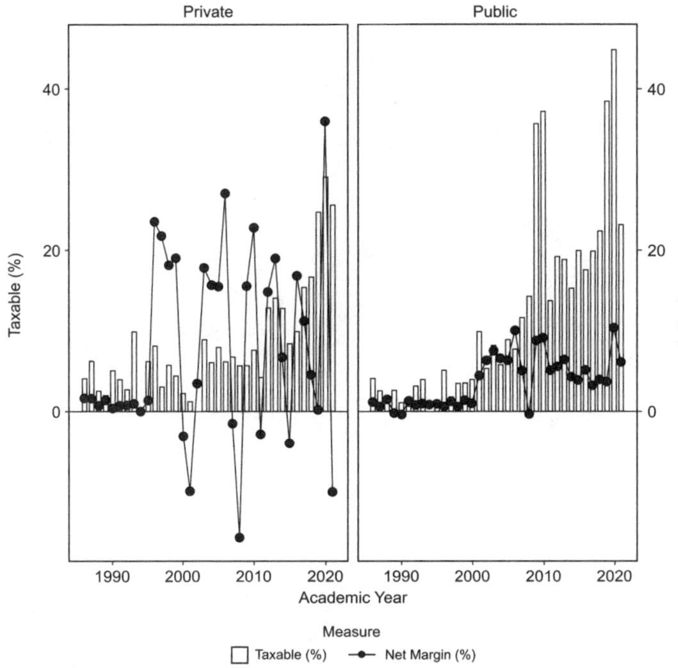


**Fig. 6A.2 Taxable debt issuances across private and public universities**

Note: This figure shows the percent of taxable issuances within a given year across private and public universities versus the average net margin for issuing universities.

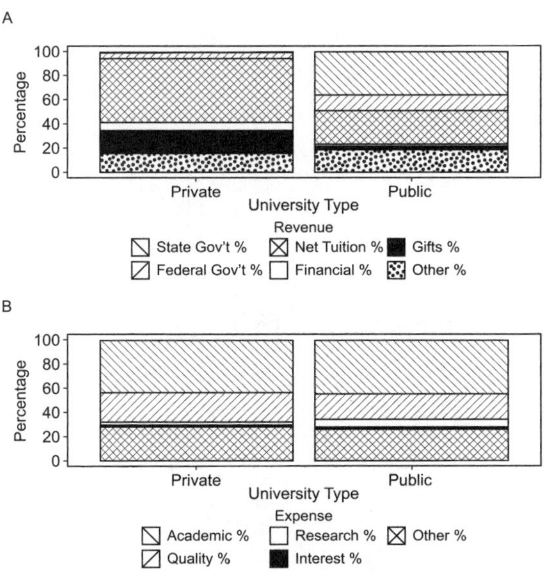


**Fig. 6A.3 Scaled revenues and expenses across private and public universities**

Note: This figure shows the composition of revenues and expense sources across private and public universities in the IPEDS sample. Panel A displays the average breakdown of revenues, and Panel B displays the average breakdown of expenses.

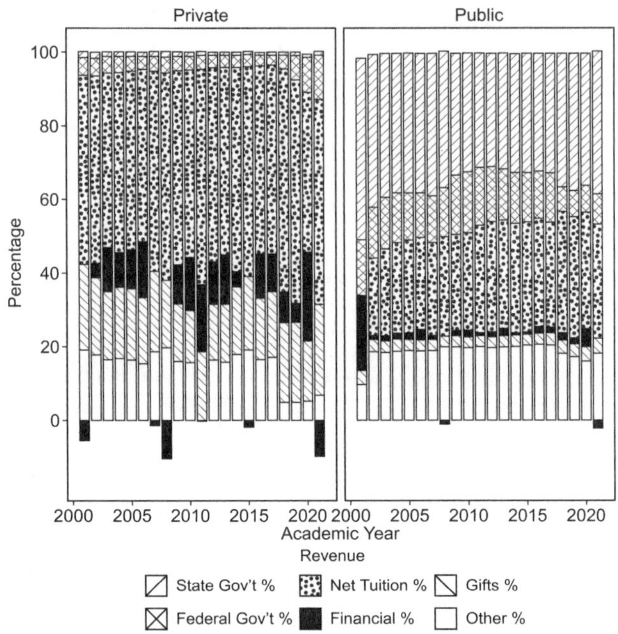


**Fig. 6A.4 Scaled revenues across private and public universities over time**
Note: This figure shows the composition of revenues sources within each year across private and public universities in the IPEDS sample. Due to rounding, not all totals sum to 100%.

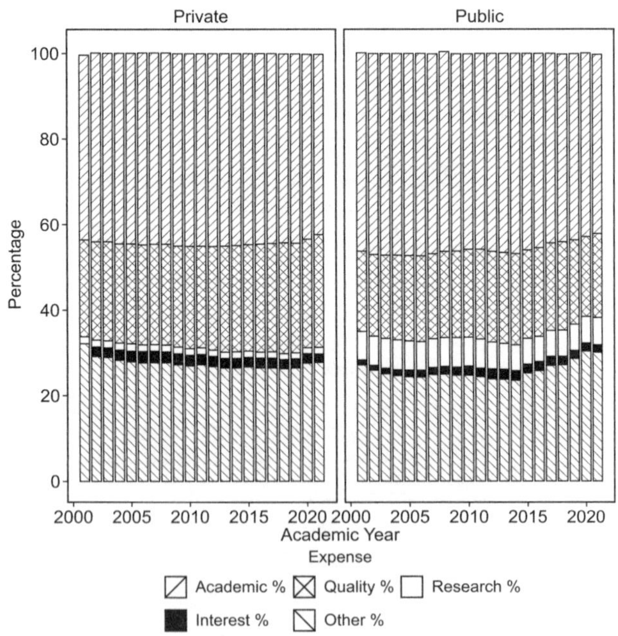


**Fig. 6A.5 Scaled expenses across private and public universities over time**
Note: This figure shows the composition of expense sources within each year across private and public universities in the IPEDS sample. Due to rounding, not all totals sum to 100%.

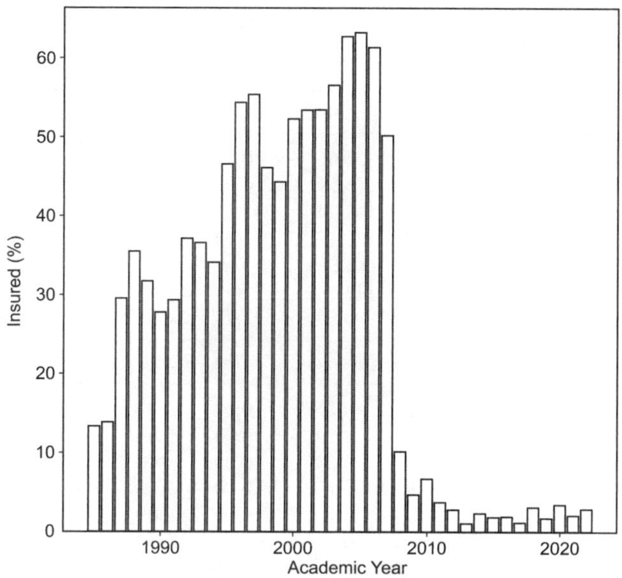


**Fig. 6A.6 Insured issuances over time**

Note: This figure shows the proportion of insured bond issuances over time.

**Table 6A.1** **Issuance panel: absolute and scaled revenues and expenses**

| | N | Mean | SD | Min | p25 | Median | p75 | Max |
|---|---|---|---|---|---|---|---|---|
| | | | | *Panel A: Absolute Revenue* | | | | |
| Federal Appropriations | 9473 | 79.18 | 136.66 | 0.00 | 1.66 | 16.55 | 93.09 | 686.23 |
| State Appropriations | 9473 | 131.63 | 183.91 | 0.00 | 1.12 | 55.45 | 195.63 | 906.59 |
| Net Tuition Revenue | 9473 | 105.29 | 167.74 | −258.24 | 17.61 | 55.61 | 151.71 | 802.97 |
| Gift Revenue | 9473 | 43.80 | 80.17 | 0.00 | 3.23 | 13.16 | 47.39 | 491.81 |
| Other Revenue | 9473 | 194.84 | 463.97 | 0.00 | 7.19 | 28.40 | 162.69 | 2,983.81 |
| Financial Revenue | 9473 | 34.04 | 116.96 | −127.53 | 0.05 | 2.53 | 16.14 | 829.78 |
| Total Revenue | 9325 | 629.74 | 989.89 | 3.23 | 74.63 | 232.70 | 761.96 | 5,621.92 |
| | | | | *Panel B: Scaled Revenues (% Total Revenue)* | | | | |
| % State Revenue | 9325 | 0.27 | 0.25 | 0.00 | 0.01 | 0.25 | 0.42 | 0.88 |
| % Federal Revenue | 9325 | 0.12 | 0.10 | 0.00 | 0.03 | 0.11 | 0.17 | 0.45 |
| % Net Tuition Revenue | 9325 | 0.26 | 0.24 | 0.00 | 0.00 | 0.24 | 0.41 | 0.89 |
| % Gift Revenue | 9325 | 0.09 | 0.10 | 0.00 | 0.03 | 0.06 | 0.11 | 0.50 |
| % Other Revenue | 9325 | 0.20 | 0.15 | 0.00 | 0.09 | 0.16 | 0.24 | 0.75 |
| % Financial Revenue | 9325 | 0.06 | 0.13 | −0.34 | 0.00 | 0.01 | 0.07 | 0.67 |
| | | | | *Panel C: Absolute Expenses* | | | | |
| Academic Expense | 9473 | 236.37 | 332.82 | 0.00 | 36.76 | 107.79 | 295.98 | 1,801.58 |
| Quality Expense | 9473 | 96.15 | 119.12 | 0.00 | 18.94 | 49.00 | 127.56 | 638.21 |
| Research Expense | 9473 | 103.34 | 182.37 | 0.00 | 0.43 | 12.66 | 132.99 | 908.81 |
| Interest Expense | 5966 | 15.11 | 22.52 | 0.02 | 2.42 | 6.40 | 17.43 | 134.08 |
| Total Other Expense | 9213 | 202.73 | 429.39 | 2.77 | 18.38 | 56.22 | 169.88 | 2,677.47 |
| Total Expenses | 9213 | 656.32 | 986.77 | 12.27 | 84.36 | 254.32 | 802.99 | 5,548.78 |
| | | | | *Panel D: Scaled Expenses (% Total Expenses)* | | | | |
| % Academic Expense | 9213 | 0.42 | 0.10 | 0.15 | 0.36 | 0.42 | 0.49 | 0.64 |
| % Quality Expense | 9213 | 0.21 | 0.09 | 0.04 | 0.15 | 0.20 | 0.27 | 0.43 |
| % Research Expense | 9213 | 0.09 | 0.10 | 0.00 | 0.01 | 0.05 | 0.16 | 0.37 |
| % Interest Expense | 5947 | 0.02 | 0.02 | 0.00 | 0.01 | 0.02 | 0.03 | 0.09 |
| % Total Other Expense | 9213 | 0.26 | 0.13 | 0.07 | 0.17 | 0.23 | 0.33 | 0.69 |

Note: This table presents the summary statistics for the sample of bond issuances and the underlying university issuer. Panel A displays the composition of total revenues, Panel B displays the composition of revenues as a percentage of total revenues. Panel C displays the composition of total expenses, Panel B displays the composition of revenue as a percentage of total expenses.

**Table 6A.2 IPEDS sample descriptive statistics**

| | N | Mean | SD | Min | p25 | Median | p75 | Max |
|---|---|---|---|---|---|---|---|---|
| | | | *Panel A: Income Statement and Balance Sheet Items* | | | | | |
| Total Revenue | 72002 | 124.09 | 316.96 | 0.06 | 5.17 | 25.66 | 85.80 | 2,229.73 |
| Total Expenses | 70035 | 135.18 | 329.99 | 0.44 | 10.48 | 32.12 | 94.75 | 2,287.29 |
| Net Income | 70024 | 9.65 | 36.90 | −46.31 | −0.13 | 0.55 | 5.21 | 269.17 |
| % Net Income | 70023 | 0.04 | 0.19 | −0.93 | −0.01 | 0.03 | 0.11 | 0.58 |
| Assets | 46697 | 0.41 | 1.03 | 0.00 | 0.03 | 0.10 | 0.30 | 7.46 |
| Liabilities | 46585 | 0.14 | 0.36 | 0.00 | 0.01 | 0.03 | 0.10 | 2.42 |
| Long-Term Debt | 36917 | 0.09 | 0.20 | 0.00 | 0.01 | 0.02 | 0.08 | 1.29 |
| Value of Endowment | 40453 | 0.14 | 0.41 | 0.00 | 0.01 | 0.02 | 0.07 | 3.08 |
| Endowment/Assets | 30023 | 0.29 | 0.21 | 0.00 | 0.11 | 0.24 | 0.43 | 0.85 |
| Liabilities/Assets | 46584 | 0.34 | 0.24 | 0.01 | 0.18 | 0.30 | 0.45 | 1.36 |
| Long-Term Debt/Assets | 35393 | 0.22 | 0.17 | 0.00 | 0.10 | 0.19 | 0.30 | 0.84 |
| | | | *Panel B: Revenue Sources* | | | | | |
| Total Gov't Appropriations | 84033 | 30.73 | 90.35 | 0.00 | 0.00 | 0.84 | 9.48 | 593.83 |
| State Appropriations | 84033 | 21.08 | 60.05 | 0.00 | 0.00 | 0.06 | 6.37 | 385.06 |
| Federal Appropriations | 84033 | 12.43 | 43.46 | 0.00 | 0.00 | 0.52 | 3.52 | 312.90 |
| Net Tuition Revenue | 84033 | 23.19 | 55.08 | −80.47 | 0.13 | 6.57 | 24.83 | 336.43 |
| Gift Revenue | 84033 | 8.12 | 23.55 | 0.00 | 0.13 | 1.42 | 5.02 | 175.49 |
| Other Revenue | 84033 | 25.23 | 95.05 | 0.00 | 0.07 | 1.30 | 8.92 | 736.70 |
| Financial Revenue | 84033 | 5.26 | 22.33 | −21.27 | 0.00 | 0.12 | 1.65 | 172.72 |
| Total Revenue | 72002 | 124.09 | 316.96 | 0.06 | 5.17 | 25.66 | 85.80 | 2,229.73 |
| *Scaled Revenues* | | | | | | | | |
| % Government Revenue | 72001 | 0.26 | 0.31 | 0.00 | 0.01 | 0.09 | 0.47 | 0.98 |
| % State Revenue | 72001 | 0.17 | 0.26 | 0.00 | 0.00 | 0.01 | 0.30 | 0.91 |
| % Federal Revenue | 72001 | 0.10 | 0.13 | 0.00 | 0.01 | 0.05 | 0.15 | 0.68 |
| % Net Tuition Revenue | 72001 | 0.31 | 0.30 | 0.00 | 0.00 | 0.26 | 0.55 | 1.00 |
| % Gift Revenue | 72001 | 0.18 | 0.21 | 0.00 | 0.03 | 0.10 | 0.26 | 0.92 |
| % Other Revenue | 72001 | 0.17 | 0.19 | 0.00 | 0.05 | 0.12 | 0.22 | 1.00 |
| % Financial Revenue | 72001 | 0.07 | 0.15 | −0.40 | 0.00 | 0.01 | 0.09 | 0.69 |
| | | | *Panel C: Expense Sources* | | | | | |
| Academic Expense | 84033 | 43.07 | 99.42 | 0.00 | 1.42 | 9.07 | 34.19 | 661.84 |
| Quality Expense | 84033 | 18.12 | 37.76 | 0.00 | 0.49 | 4.87 | 17.19 | 244.62 |
| Research Expense | 84033 | 12.66 | 50.79 | 0.00 | 0.00 | 0.00 | 0.63 | 362.21 |
| Interest Expense | 35227 | 3.88 | 8.56 | 0.00 | 0.20 | 0.95 | 3.25 | 55.89 |
| Total Other Expense | 70035 | 40.71 | 122.91 | 0.10 | 3.41 | 8.64 | 22.96 | 946.01 |
| Total Expenses | 70035 | 135.18 | 329.99 | 0.44 | 10.48 | 32.12 | 94.75 | 2,287.29 |
| *Scaled Expenses* | | | | | | | | |
| % Academic Expense | 70035 | 0.42 | 0.12 | 0.13 | 0.34 | 0.42 | 0.50 | 0.78 |
| % Quality Expense | 70035 | 0.21 | 0.11 | 0.00 | 0.14 | 0.21 | 0.29 | 0.47 |
| % Research Expense | 70035 | 0.03 | 0.06 | 0.00 | 0.00 | 0.00 | 0.02 | 0.30 |
| % Interest Expense | 34715 | 0.02 | 0.02 | 0.00 | 0.01 | 0.02 | 0.03 | 0.10 |
| % Total Other Expense | 70035 | 0.32 | 0.15 | 0.06 | 0.20 | 0.30 | 0.43 | 0.77 |

Note: This table presents the summary statistics for the IPEDS sample. Panel A displays the financial characteristics of universities from the balance sheet and income statement. Panel B displays the composition of absolute revenue and scaled revenue, and Panel C displays the composition of absolute expenses and scaled expenses.

**Table 6A.3 IPEDS panel: descriptive statistics by university type**

| | Public 26% | Private 74% | HBCU 4% | R1 7% | System 26% | Hospital 4% | NCAA D1 16% |
|---|---|---|---|---|---|---|---|
| | *Panel A: Revenue Sources* | | | | | | |
| % Government Revenue | 0.59 | 0.13 | 0.51 | 0.44 | 0.49 | 0.30 | 0.44 |
| % State Revenue | 0.50 | 0.04 | 0.26 | 0.30 | 0.41 | 0.20 | 0.33 |
| % Federal Revenue | 0.14 | 0.09 | 0.28 | 0.17 | 0.12 | 0.12 | 0.13 |
| % Net Tuition Revenue | 0.16 | 0.37 | 0.18 | 0.15 | 0.21 | 0.15 | 0.22 |
| % Gift Revenue | 0.04 | 0.24 | 0.12 | 0.09 | 0.08 | 0.07 | 0.08 |
| % Other Revenue | 0.15 | 0.18 | 0.13 | 0.24 | 0.16 | 0.41 | 0.18 |
| % Financial Revenue | 0.01 | 0.09 | 0.03 | 0.06 | 0.02 | 0.04 | 0.05 |
| | *Panel B: Academic vs. Amenities* | | | | | | |
| Government Revenue Per FTE | 15.29 | 2.79 | 12.10 | 15.35 | 13.89 | 42.63 | 8.14 |
| Federal Revenue Per FTE | 4.95 | 2.27 | 7.70 | 9.19 | 4.33 | 17.30 | 3.94 |
| State Revenue Per FTE | 11.68 | 0.56 | 5.00 | 6.89 | 10.72 | 28.73 | 4.82 |
| Academic Expenses Per FTE | 11.66 | 10.02 | 9.06 | 18.30 | 12.13 | 35.92 | 11.34 |
| Quality Expenses Per FTE | 3.79 | 4.80 | 4.60 | 6.62 | 3.89 | 6.69 | 5.26 |
| % Academic Expense | 0.44 | 0.42 | 0.35 | 0.38 | 0.44 | 0.33 | 0.42 |
| % Quality Expense | 0.19 | 0.22 | 0.22 | 0.15 | 0.19 | 0.09 | 0.21 |
| | *Panel C: University Characteristics* | | | | | | |
| Tuition Growth | 0.06 | 0.05 | 0.05 | 0.06 | 0.06 | 0.06 | 0.06 |
| Enrollment Growth | 0.01 | 0.02 | 0.01 | 0.01 | 0.02 | 0.01 | 0.01 |
| Endowment Growth | 0.17 | 0.10 | 0.13 | 0.14 | 0.16 | 0.14 | 0.15 |
| Total Enrollment | 10.88 | 2.08 | 2.93 | 22.08 | 8.47 | 12.79 | 15.12 |
| Percent Enrollment In-State | 0.82 | 0.58 | 0.64 | 0.61 | 0.80 | 0.60 | 0.69 |
| Assets | 0.71 | 0.32 | 0.17 | 3.23 | 0.52 | 2.50 | 1.41 |
| Liabilities | 0.30 | 0.09 | 0.06 | 1.09 | 0.22 | 0.90 | 0.51 |
| Long-Term Debt | 0.17 | 0.07 | 0.04 | 0.59 | 0.12 | 0.50 | 0.28 |
| Value of Endowment | 0.15 | 0.14 | 0.03 | 0.87 | 0.12 | 0.68 | 0.37 |
| Endowment/Assets | 0.16 | 0.35 | 0.18 | 0.35 | 0.19 | 0.29 | 0.26 |
| Liabilities/Assets | 0.46 | 0.31 | 0.38 | 0.37 | 0.43 | 0.40 | 0.39 |
| Long-Term Debt/Assets | 0.25 | 0.20 | 0.23 | 0.21 | 0.24 | 0.19 | 0.23 |
| % Net Income | 0.03 | 0.04 | 0.04 | 0.05 | 0.03 | 0.04 | 0.05 |
| | *Panel D: Student Characteristics* | | | | | | |
| In State Tuition and Fees | 5.17 | 16.90 | 7.17 | 12.89 | 7.00 | 12.64 | 11.77 |
| Proportion Admitted to Applied | 0.69 | 0.67 | 0.57 | 0.55 | 0.69 | 0.53 | 0.64 |
| Average SAT | 10.65 | 10.98 | 8.98 | 12.50 | 10.60 | 12.45 | 11.39 |
| Repayment Rate | 0.60 | 0.63 | 0.27 | 0.73 | 0.60 | 0.73 | 0.65 |
| Default Rate | 0.05 | 0.04 | 0.12 | 0.03 | 0.05 | 0.02 | 0.04 |
| Completion Rate | 0.46 | 0.56 | 0.34 | 0.70 | 0.46 | 0.70 | 0.59 |

Note: This table presents the summary statistics for IPEDS sample across university types. Panel A displays the composition of scaled revenues, and Panel B displays the government revenues per full-time enrolled student and mix of academic versus quality expenses. Panel C displays information across the university's financial and other characteristics, and Panel D displays information regarding a university's student base.

**Table 6A.4** **Explaining university issuer choice**

| | Direct Issuer | | Local Gov't Issuer | | State Issuer | |
|---|---|---|---|---|---|---|
| | (1) | (2) | (3) | (4) | (5) | (6) |
| Public | 0.62*** | 0.57*** | −0.14** | −0.07 | −0.41*** | −0.45*** |
| | [0.07] | [0.08] | [0.07] | [0.07] | [0.09] | [0.08] |
| Tax-Exempt | −0.04* | −0.04 | −0.03** | −0.03*** | 0.08*** | 0.07** |
| | [0.02] | [0.02] | [0.01] | [0.01] | [0.03] | [0.03] |
| Insured | 0.01 | 0.01 | −0.02 | −0.01 | 0.03 | 0.03 |
| | [0.03] | [0.03] | [0.03] | [0.02] | [0.03] | [0.03] |
| Underlying Ratings | 0.01 | −0.00 | −0.01*** | −0.01 | 0.01 | 0.01 |
| | [0.00] | [0.00] | [0.00] | [0.00] | [0.01] | [0.01] |
| State Economic Activity | 0.00 | | −0.00 | | 0.00 | |
| | [0.00] | | [0.00] | | [0.00] | |
| State Unemployment Rate | −0.00 | | 0.01 | | −0.01 | |
| | [0.01] | | [0.01] | | [0.01] | |
| State Credit Rating | 0.00 | | −0.01 | | 0.01 | |
| | [0.00] | | [0.01] | | [0.01] | |
| Average SAT | | 0.03*** | | −0.01** | | −0.01 |
| | | [0.01] | | [0.00] | | [0.01] |
| Log(Enrollment) | | 0.05** | | −0.05** | | 0.02 |
| | | [0.02] | | [0.02] | | [0.03] |
| HHI Revenue | | 0.06 | | −0.07 | | 0.03 |
| | | [0.09] | | [0.07] | | [0.06] |
| Observations | 9073 | 8320 | 9073 | 8320 | 9073 | 8320 |
| Adjusted $R^2$ | 0.65 | 0.69 | 0.34 | 0.38 | 0.42 | 0.47 |
| Year & State F.E. | Yes | No | Yes | No | Yes | No |
| Year × State F.E. | No | Yes | No | Yes | No | Yes |
| Y-mean | 0.46 | 0.47 | 0.14 | 0.14 | 0.35 | 0.35 |

Note: This table presents the OLS regression coefficients from regressing a university's choice of issuer on university and other state characteristics. The dependent variable in columns (1) and (2) is whether a university directly issues its own debt, columns (3) and (4) is whether a university uses a local government issuer to issue its debt, and columns (5) and (6) is whether a university uses a state authority to issue its debt. Regressions include variations of state and year and state × year fixed effects. Standard errors are clustered at the state and year level. ***, **, * correspond to statistical significance at the 1 percent, 5 percent, and 10 percent level, respectively.

## References

Adelino, M., K. Lewellen, and A. Sundaram. 2015. "Investment Decisions of Non-profit Firms: Evidence from Hospitals." *Journal of Finance* 70(4): 1583–1628.

Chakrabarti, R., V. Fos, A. Liberman, and C. Yannelis. 2023. "Tuition, Debt, and Human Capital." *Review of Financial Studies* 36(4): 1667–1702.

Chakrabarti, R., N. Gorton, and M. F. Lovenheim. 2020. "State Investment in Higher Education: Effects on Human Capital Formation, Student Debt, and Long-term Financial Outcomes of Students." Technical Report. Cambridge, MA: National Bureau of Economic Research.

Dougal, C., P. Gao, W. J. Mayew, and C. A. Parsons. 2019. "What's in a (School)

Name? Racial Discrimination in Higher Education Bond Markets." *Journal of Financial Economics* 134(3): 570–90.
Goldman, D., and J. A. Romley. 2008. "Hospitals as Hotels: The Role of Patient Amenities in Hospital Demand." Technical Report. Cambridge, MA: National Bureau of Economic Research.
Goldman, D. P., M. Vaiana, and J. A. Romley. 2010. "The Emerging Importance of Patient Amenities in Hospital Care." *New England Journal of Medicine* 363(23): 2185.
Hampole, M. V. 2022. "Financial Frictions and Human Capital Investments." Working Paper.
Jacob, B., B. McCall, and K. Stange. 2018. "College as Country Club: Do Colleges Cater to Students' Preferences for Consumption?" *Journal of Labor Economics* 36(2): 309–48.
Lord Abbett. 2024. Privatized Student Housing: A Guide for Municipal Bond Investors. Accessed: 2024–06–17.
Modigliani, F., and M. H. Miller. 1958. "The Cost of Capital, Corporation Finance and the Theory of Investment." *American Economic Review* 48(3): 261–97.
Mueller, H., and C. Yannelis. 2022. "Increasing Enrollment in Income-Driven Student Loan Repayment Plans: Evidence from the Navient Field Experiment." *Journal of Finance* 77(1): 367–402.
Mueller, H. M., and C. Yannelis. 2019. "The Rise in Student Loan Defaults." *Journal of Financial Economics* 131(1): 1–19.
Myers, S. C., and N. S. Majluf. 1984. "Corporate Financing and Investment Decisions When Firms Have Information That Investors Do Not Have." *Journal of Financial Economics* 13(2): 187–221.
P3 Resource Center. 2018. "A Guide to Higher Ed Public-Private Partnerships." Washington, DC: Brailsford & Dunlavey. Accessed June 17, 2024.
Rosen, H. S., and A. J. Sappington. 2016. "To Borrow or not to Borrow? An Analysis of University Leverage Decisions." *Research in Economics* 70(1): 170–85.
Schwert, M. 2017. "Municipal Bond Liquidity and Default Risk." *Journal of Finance* 72(4): 1683–1722.
Wedig, G. J., M. Hassan, and F. A. Sloan. 1989. "Hospital Investment Decisions and the Cost of Capital." *Journal of Business* 517–37.

## Comment Daniel Bergstresser

Binfarè and Zimmerschied have written a very useful paper that presents new data on the use of debt by colleges and universities in the United States. American colleges and universities do a great deal of borrowing in debt markets, and understanding the nature, purposes, and consequences of this debt issuance is an important part of understanding higher education.

Taking a step back from a narrow focus on debt issuance, the financial and

Daniel Bergstresser is the Chair of the Undergraduate Business Program and an associate professor at the Brandeis International Business School.

For acknowledgments, sources of research support, and disclosure of the author's material financial relationships, if any, please see https://www.nber.org/books-and-chapters/financing-institutions-higher-education/comment-role-debt-financing-higher-education-bergstresser.

business landscape for American higher education has been and is likely to remain challenging. College and university enrollment peaked at 21 million in 2010 and has been in decline since then. Government funding for higher education has not kept pace with inflation since the global financial crisis of 2007–2009. Although colleges and universities have been closing for almost as long as they have been opening, these economic pressures are real and predictions of an increasing pace of school closures are not difficult to find.

Turning to the authors' work on higher education debt, they point out that American institutions had more than $265 billion in debt outstanding in 2020, and that they issued more than $50 billion in debt during 2019. To give these numbers context, degree-granting postsecondary institutions spent a total of $702 billion during the 2020–2021 year. Public institutions spent $450 billion of that total, private nonprofit institutions spent $239 billion, and for-profit institutions spent $14 billion.[1] The aggregate amount of debt is smaller than the total size of university endowments, which at the end of 2021 was about $927 billion.[2] These endowments are often encumbered, however; a dollar in an endowment is frequently matched by a specific obligation to endowment income for a particular purpose. Borrowing by higher education institutions is also smaller in aggregate than student borrowing, which now amounts in total to about $1.6 trillion.[3]

The authors document some useful facts about the higher education debt market, in particular the pace and composition of issuance over recent decades. Higher education institutions can often borrow in the tax-exempt market, a market of bonds issued by a very diverse collection of issuers that includes states, cities, counties, hospitals, transportation systems, hospitals, and other entities responsible for different types of infrastructure investment. Colleges and universities have recently been issuing large quantities of taxable bonds as well; the taxable issuance gives issuers flexibility to structure bonds and use bond proceeds in ways that fall outside of the boundaries required by the IRS for tax exemption. Documenting the increasing pace of taxable bond issuance is a useful contribution.

The authors also show that a large amount of this issuance activity has been the issuance of bonds that are used to refinance existing debt. This development follows naturally from the overall downward trend in interest rates during most of this period, which the authors document. Higher education debt, like other municipal debt, frequently is "callable" by issuers, meaning that issuers have the right to repurchase the debt from investors at a pre-specified price. This callability and certain market-specific nuances

1. "Fast Facts," Expenditures, National Center for Education Statistics, https://nces.ed.gov/fastfacts/display.asp?id=75.

2. "Fast Facts," Endowments, National Center for Education Statistics, https://nces.ed.gov/fastfacts/display.asp?id=73.

3. Household Debt and Credit Report, (Q4 2024), Center for Microeconomic Data, Federal Reserve Bank of New York, https://www.newyorkfed.org/microeconomics/hhdc.

have been a focus of recent academic work on the municipal bond market. This literature has often found evidence that issuers frequently appear to behave suboptimally when it comes to structuring and exercising the various options that can be embedded in the debt that they issue.

The main contributions of the authors in this paper include showing that public universities borrow at lower yields than private universities. Perhaps unsurprisingly, they also show that more heavily indebted universities appear to borrow at higher yields (table 6.4). The authors also show that borrowing is lower at universities that receive more government revenue (table 6.5). Increases in debt appear to precede expansions in dormitory capacity and expansions in the enrollment of out-of-state students (table 6.6).

Although the paper's approach is primarily descriptive, presenting correlations that might be open to a variety of causal interpretations, these results seem quite consistent with the authors' overall narrative: higher education institutions are using debt to finance the purchase and construction of facilities such as dormitories. The authors refer to this type of infrastructure as "amenities," making a distinction between these types of facilities and expenses that are directly linked to educational efforts. This is consistent with previous work (see Jacob et al. 2018) that has shown that these types of amenities can have a significant influence on student's decisions about which college to attend.

I think that using debt to finance the acquisition of infrastructure like dormitories can achieve various objectives. As anyone with a home mortgage knows, debt is an extremely useful tool—it helps institutions and households use assets without needing to save up in advance the cash to purchase them. Using debt to finance dorm construction is similar in many ways to households accessing the home mortgage market while avoiding unsecured borrowing: it is easier to borrow if that borrowing is collateralized by assets that can be seized by a creditor and redeployed elsewhere in the event that the borrower defaults. Some of the trends that we have seen in higher education infrastructure investment, for example the trend toward high-amenity and apartment-style housing, can be explained by the greater ease that creditors would have seizing higher-amenity collateral and reallocating it toward other uses. Given the demographic trends and the challenging picture for higher education, building flexible infrastructure—dormitories that could convert to old-folks' homes–provides some diversification for the investors.

One wrinkle in analyzing debt is that arrangements with the economic substance of debt comes in various forms. Borrowing can be explicitly memorialized with a bond. This institutional arrangement makes debt tradeable from investor to investor, and bond market debt is the focus of this paper. Borrowing can come in other forms, though. Both nonprofits and for-profits borrow from their employees in the form of pension and retirement health care arrangements. These arrangements are promises to deliver value to employees later, and they can have much of the same economic substance of debt, with the wrinkle that the borrowing is from employees. Understanding the aggregate debt burden of the higher education sector requires understanding both bond market debt and also pension and other retirement promises, a fact that is apparent in figure 6.2 of the authors' paper.

Institutions can also write contracts with third-party providers of infrastructure, committing to make payments in exchange for the future availability of infrastructure such as dorms, parking lots, or classroom or office space. These contracts, of which "public-private partnerships" or "P3s" are an example that is becoming more common in higher education and among other traditional municipal bond market issuers, can have much of the same economic substance as debt. They commit institutions to future payments, as debt does, but these arrangements have different labeling and often have different contractual and organizational implications. Uncertainty about future developments in higher education and other pressures may accelerate the use of these types of arrangements, which can allow more flexibility than the traditional "borrow money in the bond market and use the proceeds to build a dormitory" model. But supervising the negotiation and renegotiation of these arrangements may pose new challenges, in particular given their complexity and given that the arrangements can commit institutions to payments or other obligations that stretch beyond administrators' career horizons.

Institutions, regardless of their form, have "operating leverage" as well as financial leverage. An example of operating leverage would be the salary of a tenured faculty member. This faculty member's salary and benefits are something like interest payments, because unless the institution defaults or declares a state of financial exigency, these payments must be made. Understanding the interaction between operating leverage and financial leverage, and understanding the interaction between the higher education labor market and higher education borrowing, will be important. In the for-profit bond market, scholars (for example Matsa 2010) have argued that high leverage can be a strategic choice for issuers in the context of difficult negotiations with employees. If employees are well organized and enjoy bargaining advantages, committing to high debt service payments can be a way for debt issuers to "tie their hands" in future bargaining with employees.

Overall this paper is a useful and timely contribution to our understanding of ongoing trends in higher education. The authors' narrative, backed up by the evidence that they present, is that the race to recruit students in a challenging environment is driving debt-financed infrastructure investment. Our ongoing challenging and very uncertain times may also spur financial and organizational innovations that make it very important to pay careful attention to the wide range of arrangements and commitments that can have the economic substance of traditional bond-market debt.

## References

Jacob, B., B. McCall, and K. Stange. 2018. "College as Country Club: Do Colleges Cater to Students' Preferences for Consumption?" *Journal of Labor Economics* 36(2): 309–48.

Matsa, David A. 2010. "Capital Structure as a Strategic Variable: Evidence from Collective Bargaining." *Journal of Finance* 65(3): 1197–1232.

7

# Financing Community Colleges
## Current Landscape and Future Directions

Nikki Edgecombe, Elise Swanson, Thomas Brock,
Maria Cormier, Christopher Avery, and Carmen Huynh

### 7.1 Introduction

Public two-year colleges—better known as community colleges—play a critical and unique role in the US higher education system. There are nearly 1,000 community colleges that together enroll more than 5 million students per academic year (37 percent of US undergraduate college students) (Causey et al. 2023). As open-access institutions, most community colleges embrace a dual mission of preparing students to transfer to four-year colleges or universities and helping students acquire skills needed for

Nikki Edgecombe was a senior research scholar at the Community College Research Center at Teachers College, Columbia University, when this chapter was written. She is now Vice President of Impact at the ECMC Foundation.

Elise Swanson is associate director of research of the Center for Education Policy Research at Harvard Graduate School of Education.

Thomas Brock is director of the Community College Research Center at Teachers College, Columbia University.

Maria Cormier was a senior research associate of the Community College Research Center at Teachers College, Columbia University.

Christopher Avery is the Roy E. Larsen Professor of Public Policy at Harvard Kennedy School, and a research associate of the National Bureau of Economic Research.

Carmen Huynh was a research assistant at the Community College Research Center at Teachers College, Columbia University when this chapter was written.

We would like to thank Isaac McFarlin Jr. for comments on an earlier draft of this chapter and Paul Bisagni and Doug Slater from the Community College Research Center for editorial support. This research is supported by funding from the Gates Foundation, Ascendium Education Group, the Institute of Education Sciences at the US Department of Education (Grant R305X220022 and Grant R305X220018), and Lumina Foundation. For acknowledgments, sources of research support, and disclosure of the authors material financial relationships, if any, please see https://www.nber.org/books-and-chapters/financing-institutions-higher-education/financing-community-colleges-current-landscape-and-future-directions. The views expressed herein are those of the authors and do not necessarily reflect the views of the funders or the National Bureau of Economic Research.

employment. Consistent with this mission, community colleges serve more part-time and older students as well as more low-income, racially minoritized, and first-generation college students than do four-year institutions. Research linking education to earnings finds positive returns to earning a community college credential (Belfield and Bailey 2017). Yet for all their virtues, community colleges struggle with low completion rates and achievement gaps between demographic groups.

Community colleges are attractive to many students because they are close to home and relatively low in cost.[1] In 2021–22, they charged an average of $4,000 for tuition and fees, compared to an average of $9,700 for public four-year institutions and $38,800 for private nonprofit four-year institutions (National Center for Education Statistics 2023b). With relatively low tuition revenue per student, community colleges depend heavily on funds from state and local governments to deliver instruction, provide student services, and carry out other core functions. Accounting for all sources of funding, community colleges spent approximately $21,000 per full-time equivalent (FTE) student in 2020–21. By comparison, public four-year colleges spent approximately $39,000 per FTE student, and private nonprofit four-year institutions spent about $51,000 per FTE student (National Center for Education Statistics 2023a). The differences in FTE spending across sectors may be explained in part by differences in institutional missions, including a much heavier emphasis on research (and the infrastructure to support it) at four-year institutions. Nonetheless, community college students may have additional academic and nonacademic support needs (Kolbe and Baker 2019).

Government funding for higher education has eroded over time, making it harder for community colleges and public four-year institutions to fund their operations. Baum and Johnson (2015) report a decline of approximately 25 percent in state appropriations in real terms on an FTE student basis from 2000–2001 to 2014–2015, and funding declines have continued since then (Mitchell et al. 2019). While some public four-year colleges have been able to compensate for state funding reductions by increasing tuition revenue (Bound et al. 2019), community colleges are more constrained in their ability to set tuition levels and cannot rely on increasing the proportion of students paying out-of-state tuition. Community colleges also cannot depend on maintaining steady enrollments, particularly as local employment rates go up or down, as the relationship between enrollment and the economy tends to be countercyclical (Betts and McFarland 1995). This means that community colleges experience the greatest demand for instruction and services precisely when tax revenues are falling and when state and local government budgets are under the most strain.

1. In their chapter of this volume, Acton et al. (2024) show how young people's sensitivity to distance varies across populations such that institutional closures would likely have larger negative impacts on Black, Hispanic, and economically disadvantaged populations.

The onset of the COVID-19 pandemic precipitated a sudden economic downturn paired with steep enrollment declines in community colleges—the reverse of the usual countercyclical pattern. From fall 2019 to fall 2021, community college enrollments dropped by more than 15 percent, and revenue from tuition and fees fell sharply as well (National Student Clearinghouse Research Center 2024). The fiscal consequences for community colleges would have been devastating if not for swift federal intervention through the Coronavirus Aid, Relief, and Economic Security (CARES) Act and subsequent legislation, through which Congress appropriated nearly $25 billion for community colleges as part of the Higher Education Emergency Relief (HEER) Fund (Daniels Sarica et al. 2024). This infusion more than compensated for lost revenue from tuition and fees at community colleges, amounting to an increase of $1,700 per FTE student in 2021–22 compared to 2018–19 (Belfield et al. 2024b). HEER funding lasted approximately three years before the program ended in June 2023.

With the worst of the pandemic now behind them—and HEER funding no longer available—community colleges face three major challenges to their funding. First, they must continue to operate in an environment in which their ability to raise revenue is constrained by how much students can afford to pay and what state and local governments are willing to spend. Second, they must adapt to factors that are outside their control, including labor market conditions and the projected decline in high school graduates after 2025 (Irwin et al. 2024). Third, they must respond to pressure to improve student outcomes. This is especially true in states that have adopted performance-based funding models in which some institutional funding is tied to the outcomes they produce, such as the number of students graduating within a given time frame or finding employment post-graduation. Given the importance of community colleges in ensuring access to higher education—particularly for groups that are underrepresented in higher education as a whole—it is critical for researchers and policymakers to understand current funding models and what financing strategies may be better suited to promoting equitable student success.

This chapter addresses these issues and proceeds as follows. Section 7.2 lays a foundation with a more detailed review of the mission of community colleges, the students they serve, and the outcomes they produce. Section 7.3 summarizes key results from past literature on higher education finance and the relationship between financing and institutional performance. Section 7.4 presents a comparative analysis of the funding models in six states—California, Michigan, New York, Ohio, Tennessee, and Texas—to illustrate different approaches to generating revenue and incentivizing outcomes. Section 7.5 examines HEER funding for community colleges in the focal states and analyzes results from an institutional survey and interviews to understand how college leaders used federal funds to weather the pandemic and what their choices reveal about their fiscal needs and priorities. Section 7.6, the conclusion, builds on these results to discuss the outlook for community college finance as well as policy and research implications.

## 7.2 Community College Mission, Students, and Performance[2]

Community colleges were introduced in the early 20th century in fast-growing states in the Midwest and on the West Coast that did not have the concentration of private colleges and universities found on the East Coast. Junior colleges, as they were then known, were designed to make it easier for students to complete the first two years of college at low cost to students and taxpayers. They were publicly financed and often operated as extensions of high school. The University of Chicago and other four-year institutions championed the junior college model so that they could place more emphasis on research and professional training rather than on providing general education to entering students (Thelin 2004; Wood 1987).

In the second half of the 20th century, the role of community colleges expanded to encompass vocational or workforce training. Initially, this came in response to the country's need to find productive work for soldiers returning from World War II and to complete the shift from a wartime to a peacetime economy. The Presidential Commission on Higher Education, created by Harry S. Truman in 1946, identified the need for postsecondary institutions that would offer adult education, apprentice-style vocational preparation, and terminal programs that did not require advanced study. The Commission, credited with introducing the term *community college* into the lexicon, called for federal funding to help address regional and local demands for higher education and vocational training. Neither the Truman administration nor Congress was inclined to act on the Commission's recommendations, but history suggests that the report influenced higher education leaders and the development of state higher education systems (Gilbert and Heller 2010; Reuben and Perkins 2007; Thelin 2004).

Today, most community colleges offer programs aimed at students with a wide variety of interests and personal goals. With two years of full-time study, students may earn an associate of arts (AA) or associate of science (AS) degree that prepares them to enter a four-year institution as college juniors. Students may also earn an associate of applied science (AAS) degree—generally considered a terminal two-year degree—in fields such as business, nursing, information technology, and mechanical engineering. For students interested in shorter-term programs and certificates, community colleges offer an array of credit and noncredit programs that can help them learn English or occupational and life skills.

The community college mission continues to evolve. In many parts of the country, community colleges now partner with local school districts to offer

2. Portions of this section are adapted from Brock, Mateo, and Ray (2025).

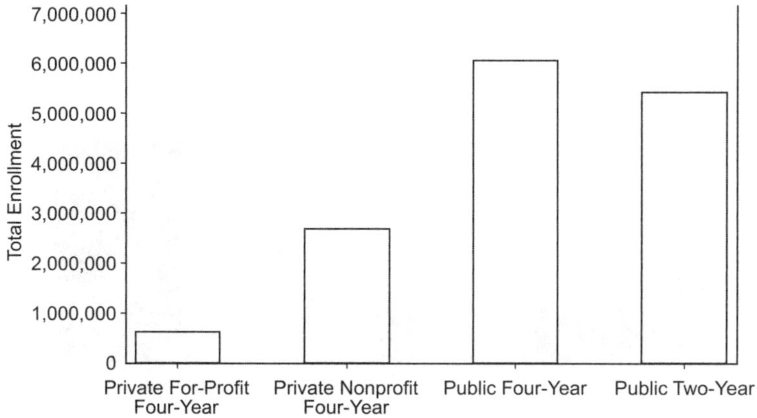


**Fig. 7.1 Total enrollment by sector (fall 2022)**
Source: Causey et al. (2023). "Public Two-Year" includes CCB-granting institutions.

dual enrollment programs, in which high school students earn high school and college credits simultaneously. Dual enrollment has grown markedly over the past 10 years and accounts for one out of every five community college students in the nation (Fink and Jenkins 2023). In roughly half the states, community colleges have also started to offer bachelor's degrees. These credentials, known as the community college baccalaureate (CCB), are usually limited to a few high-demand fields such as nursing and are offered in rural areas that are underserved by four-year institutions (Soler 2019). Some states, such as Florida and Washington, now offer the CCB at urban and rural community colleges.

The emergence of the CCB has complicated the traditional definition of a community college as a public two-year institution. The National Center for Education Statistics classifies CCB-granting institutions as four-year public institutions, even though the CCB usually accounts for a small fraction of the degrees awarded by the colleges. The American Association of Community Colleges (AACC) and the Community College Research Center (CCRC) argue that CCB-granting institutions should remain classified as public two-year institutions so long as they are primarily associate-degree-granting institutions (Fink and Jenkins 2020), and we follow that convention here.

### 7.2.1 Student Characteristics

Figure 7.1 shows the total enrollment in public two-year, public four-year, and private nonprofit four-year institutions in fall 2022, using data from the National Student Clearinghouse Research Center (Causey et al. 2023). In fall 2022, public two-year colleges enrolled approximately 5.4 million students at 983 institutions, or 37 percent of all undergraduate students in

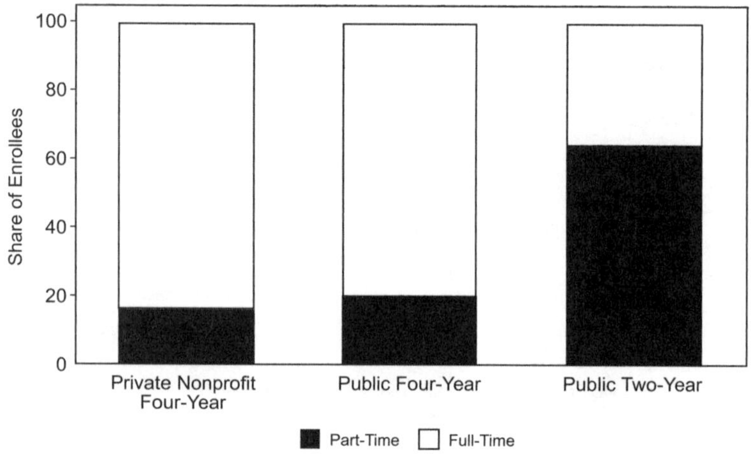


**Fig. 7.2 Share of enrollment by sector by full- and part-time status**
Source: Causey et al. (2023). "Public Two-Year" includes CCB-granting institutions.

the United States. Public four-year institutions enrolled just over 6 million undergraduates (41 percent), and private nonprofit four-year institutions enrolled close to 2.7 million (18 percent). Private for-profit four-year institutions, many of which deliver instruction online, accounted for a little more than 600,000 undergraduates (4 percent).

Figure 7.2 compares undergraduate enrollment in the three major sectors of higher education by full-time/part-time status (for simplicity, we exclude enrollments at private for-profit colleges). The difference in enrollment status across higher education sectors is striking: At public two-year institutions, most students attend part-time (64 percent), whereas at public and private non-profit four-year institutions, most students attend full-time (80 percent and 77 percent, respectively).

Figure 7.3 compares the age distribution of students across the three major sectors of higher education. One difference that stands out is that students attending public two-year institutions are often older than students attending four-year institutions. Slightly more than one-third of students attending community college are over 24 years old, compared to 17 percent of undergraduates at public four-year institutions and 24 percent of undergraduates at private nonprofit colleges and universities. This means that community college students are often working or raising families while they go to college and likely have different needs for support than do traditional-age college students.

Figure 7.4 presents undergraduate enrollments by race/ethnicity. Compared to four-year institutions—public or private—community colleges enroll a higher percentage of Hispanic students (24 percent versus 16 percent or 12 percent at public four-year or private four-year institutions, respec-

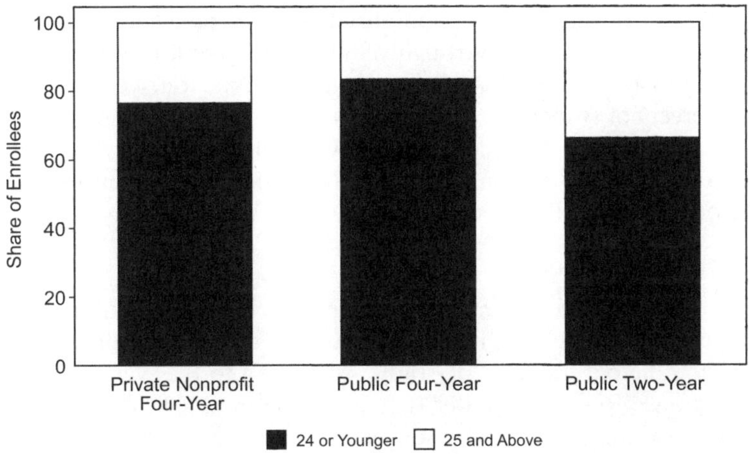


**Fig. 7.3 Share of student enrollments by sector and age**
Source: Causey et al. (2023). "Public Two-Year" includes CCB-granting institutions.

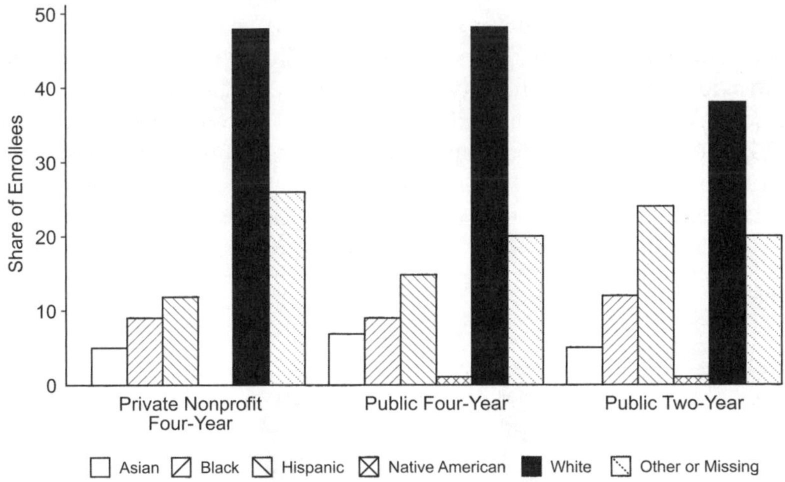


**Fig. 7.4 Student race/ethnicity by sector**
Source: Causey et al. (2023). "Public Two-Year" includes CCB-granting institutions.

tively) and fewer White students (38 percent versus 48 percent). Public two-year institutions also serve proportionally more Black and Native American students and fewer Asian students than their four-year counterparts.

There is no systematic reporting by colleges and universities on the household incomes of their students, but an analysis of data from the US Census Bureau affirms the important role community colleges play in serving low-income students. Fifty-seven percent of undergraduates attending public two-year institutions are from households with income below 200 percent of federal poverty guidelines (roughly $60,000 per year for a family of four), compared to 46 percent of students attending public four-year institutions and 42 percent of students attending private four-year institutions. The Census data also show that students from low-income families are more likely to attend open-access or minimally selective institutions than more selective public or private institutions (Fountain 2019).

### 7.2.2 Student Outcomes

Figure 7.5 presents six-year completion rates by higher education sector and highlights the fact that many students who attend community colleges do not complete a program of study. According to the National Student Clearinghouse Research Center (Lee and Shapiro 2023), only 43 percent of degree-seeking students who started at a community college in fall 2017 earned a credential from *any* institution within six years, compared to 67 percent of students who began at a public four-year institution and 78 percent of students who began at private four-year institutions. Only a small fraction of community college students transfer to a four-year institution and just 16 percent earn a bachelor's degree within six years of entering college. Analysis of student transfer in the Ohio public higher education system found evidence of a "community college penalty," meaning that bachelor's-degree-seeking students who initially enrolled at a community college were less likely to achieve this goal than similar students who began at a four-year institution after controlling for student demographics, parental income, and standardized test scores upon entering college (Long and Kurlaender 2009).

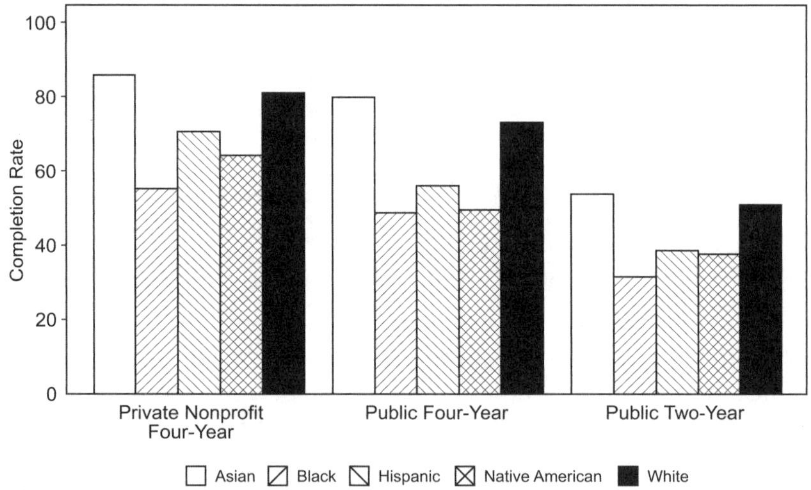


**Fig. 7.5 Six-year completion rates by sector**
Source: Lee and Shapiro (2023). "Public Two-Year" includes CCB-granting institutions.

There are also disparities by race and ethnicity across all higher education sectors. In community colleges, 32 percent of Black students earned credentials within six years, compared to 54 percent of Asian students and 51 percent of White students. Lower income, Black, and older students transfer and complete a bachelor's degree at lower rates than students overall (11 percent, 9 percent, and 9 percent, respectively) (Velasco et al. 2024). Finally, there are gaps by gender and age group. Male students at community colleges are less likely to earn credentials than female students (41 percent versus 47 percent), and students who begin college when they are older (over age 24) are less likely to earn credentials than those who begin college when they are age 20 or younger (35 percent versus 46 percent) (Lee and Shapiro 2023).

There is clear evidence of the positive association between educational attainment and earnings (US Bureau of Labor Statistics 2023), and a few studies have tried to ascertain the causal effect of community college attendance on economic outcomes. Using data from the National Longitudinal Survey of Youth and controlling for students' prior academic performance and family background, Kane and Rouse (1995) found that the average two-year college student earned about 5 percent more than a high school graduate for every year of college attended. Belfield and Bailey (2017) drew on large-scale administrative data from eight states and used an individual fixed-effects model to assess the value added of a community college education. They found that completing an associate degree yielded on average $4,640 to $7,160 per annum (2014 dollars) compared to entering college but not earning an award; for community college certificates, they found modest returns that generally faded within a few years post-college. Using administrative data from Texas, Mountjoy (2022) employed an instrumental variables approach that combined distance from home to (1) nearest four-year college and (2) nearest community college. He found significant value added for two-year entrants who otherwise would not have attended college but negative impacts on students diverted from immediate four-year entry.

Finally, there is some evidence that community colleges may increase intergenerational income mobility. Chetty et al. (2017) examined education and income tax records for 30 million individuals between 1999 and 2013 and found examples of community colleges and mid-tier public universities that were more successful in moving students from the bottom income quintile to the top income quintile than the nation's most selective colleges and universities. Two institutions that outperformed all others were the City University of New York (CUNY)—which includes two- and four-year colleges—and Glendale Community College, near Los Angeles. The authors called for more research to identify the policies and practices that led to these outcomes and concluded that channeling more funding to institutions like these may offer a scalable strategy to increase upward mobility for larger numbers of students.

Given these positive impacts community colleges can have on individual and social welfare, it is important to understand how they are supported through public investments as well as the institutional incentives created by these funding structures.

## 7.3 Community College Revenues and Funding Models

The multidimensional and evolving mission of community colleges can make funding the sector a complex and varied process. Nationally, about half of all funding for community colleges comes from state appropriations, whereas federal investments generally represent a small source (about 5 percent to 15 percent) of their revenue (Ward et al. 2020). Community colleges also receive funding directly from students in the form of tuition and fees; nationally, tuition and fees represented about 21 percent of total revenue for community colleges in 2022 (Belfield et al. 2024a). This is down from a high of 31 percent in 2013 and 28 percent in 2019 before the pandemic (Belfield et al. 2024a). In 2018, community colleges in 29 states were at least partially funded through local appropriations, but in 21 states no community colleges received local revenue, up from 12 states in 2007 (Ortagus et al. 2022; Tollefson 2009).

The revenue profiles that result from these sources of funding vary across states. For example, in 2019, community colleges in Hawaii, Wyoming, and Wisconsin received the largest share of their revenue—65 percent, 47 percent, and 36 percent, respectively—from state appropriations. By contrast, community colleges in Arizona and Vermont received 5 percent and 20 percent, respectively, from state appropriations (Belfield et al. 2024a). Tuition also varies substantially across states, with students in Vermont community colleges paying roughly six times as much in tuition as students in California community colleges ($8,660 versus $1,440, respectively, in 2023–2024) (Ma and Pender 2023).

Prior research suggests that state appropriations for higher education affect student outcomes. Using quasi-experimental designs, researchers have demonstrated that increases in state investments in higher education lead to greater enrollments and completions in the two- and four-year sectors (Bound et al. 2019; Chakrabarti et al. 2020; Deming and Walters 2018). Despite this evidence, some states have been shifting away from investments in higher education, particularly in terms of general operating funding, and often reduce higher education funding first in tight budget years (Bound et al. 2019; Cummings et al. 2021; Delaney and Doyle 2011).

In certain contexts, these reductions in appropriations can be offset by increased local revenues or student tuition and fees, but institutions' ability to raise these funds varies widely (Bound et al. 2019; McFarlin et al. 2017; Webber 2017). Local revenues are generally derived from property taxes, but community colleges in a small number of states generate local funding from sales taxes and utility fees (Education Commission of the States 2021). Research has documented how reliance on local revenue can increase inequities in funding across institutions within a state, to the disservice in particular of institutions in rural communities and institutions serving larger shares of low-income students (Ortagus et al. 2022). Similarly, tuition increases have larger negative impacts on enrollments in community colleges than in four-year institutions and among students from lower income families than among students from more economically advantaged families (Kane 1995), depressing an important channel for equitable access to postsecondary education and economic mobility. Pragmatically, tuition and fees are also capped in some states, cutting off this avenue for institutions to supplement state funding. For example, in California, community colleges are explicitly restricted from raising tuition above a statewide limit ($46 per credit hour).

The sources of institutional funds are a critical feature of community college finance, as are the restrictions on how those funds may be expended. Categorical funds are restricted to specific programs or budget line items, such as special programs for specific student populations or technological infrastructure costs. In contrast, flexible revenue in institutional general funds can be used for a variety of institutional functions, allowing colleges to respond more nimbly to changing student needs and priorities. General funding establishes consistent institutional incentives through the allocation mechanisms of state funding formulas and is where we focus our attention below.

### 7.3.1 State Funding Formulas

State support for community colleges reflects the public benefits generated by college attainment, including economic growth, reduced reliance on social assistance programs, improved health outcomes, and civic participation (Bloom et al. 2007; Ma et al. 2016; Ma et al. 2019; Oreopoulos and Salvanes 2011). As noted earlier, community colleges first emerged as extensions of the secondary educational system; these origins have influenced funding policies as well, with certain aspects of community college funding formulas more closely resembling K-12 district funding formulas than appropriations to four-year universities (Mullin and Honeyman 2008). The ways that states determine how appropriated funds are distributed to community colleges and the extent to which policymakers attempt to shape institutional actions reflect the principal–agent dynamic between state governments and community colleges (Lane and Kivisto 2008).

A number of typologies have been proposed to describe funding models. Recently, Lingo et al. (2023) bucketed community college funding formulas into three categories: (1) traditional (also referred to as base or incremental) models, wherein institutions experience similar changes in allocations regardless of institutional characteristics (i.e., location), inputs (i.e., enrollments), or outputs (i.e., completions); (2) incentive (also referred to as performance- or outcomes-based) models, wherein funding is tied to institutional inputs or outputs; and (3) hybrid models, wherein funding is jointly determined by some base amount as well as institutional inputs or outputs. Across these categories, states can introduce additional features into their funding models, including stabilization (or hold-harmless) provisions that maintain institutional funding for a period of time in the face of declining enrollments to smooth out atypical fluctuations in enrollment or that allow institutions to adapt in the face of costs that are fixed in the short run but variable over the long run.

Baum and Cohn (2023) conclude that traditional funding models often lead to inequities in funding across community colleges within a state because they do not adequately account for differences in enrollment and local funding. To this end, incentive and hybrid models may include equity components, which weight the funded factors (such as enrollment or student outcomes) by student characteristics (such as low-income status), institutional characteristics (such as rurality), and program characteristics (for instance, programs aligned with high-wage or high-growth fields) (Kelchen et al. 2023). Nationally, there is variation in funding models across the two- and four-year college sectors. Incentive and particularly hybrid models are more common in the community college sector, while traditional models are more common for four-year colleges and universities (Kelchen et al. 2023). Equity components are slightly more common in the two-year sector but have been increasing in prevalence in both sectors since about 2020 (Kelchen et al. 2023). The number of systems tying funding for two-year colleges to base allocations, student enrollments, and student outcomes rose from 2 to 17 between 2004 and 2020 (Lingo et al. 2023). Between 2004 and 2020, 26 systems added an equity component (Kelchen et al. 2023). Over the same time period, the prevalence of traditional models decreased as hybrid models increased (Lingo et al. 2023).

While blunt, funding formulas are the key mechanism by which states invest in community colleges and incentivize them to improve performance. Viewed through the principal–agent framework, these shifts indicate that states initially considered their contracts with community colleges as means to expand opportunity and access to higher education for students, first by providing general funding for community colleges and then by explicitly incentivizing greater student enrollments. Over time, that focus has shifted to include a stronger emphasis on student outcomes, often in response to popular opposition to taxes and questions about the value of higher education (Dougherty et al. 2014). However, the evidence to date suggests that performance-based funding has at best a tenuous relationship with improved student outcomes and likely has unintended consequences on equitable student access and institutional funding (Kelchen et al. 2024; Ortagus et al. 2020; Ortagus et al. 2021a; Ortagus et al. 2021b; Tandberg and Hillman 2014).

Equity components represent a desire both to mitigate disparities in educational opportunities and outcomes across student populations and to tighten the connection between community colleges and the labor market. Some equity components based on institutional characteristics, such as rurality, seek to address community colleges' high fixed costs in the budget model. Often referred to as stabilization funds, this mechanism helps address the challenges some colleges have in achieving economies of scale, as well as the economic constraints in particular localities. The variability in institutional contexts and the dynamics of funding and costs illustrate the complexity of community college finance and the challenge of incentivizing institutional behavior statewide via a single funding formula.

While the typologies of funding models are useful for understanding broad themes in community college finance, they can also obscure important nuances of specific allocation mechanisms within funding formulas that shape institutional resources and behavior. For example, enrollment-based and outcomes-based models are grouped together as incentive models (Lingo et al. 2023), but the ways in which institutions respond to try to increase enrollment—and the extent to which they can increase enrollment given the often constrained geography of community college service areas—are quite different from the strategies typically deployed to improve student degree completion. Similarly, when thinking about outcomes-based models, institutions may invest resources differently depending on whether the measured outcomes are connected more tightly to enrollment (e.g., early momentum metrics such as the number of students completing an initial transfer-level English or math course) or to outcomes of institutional and student actions (i.e., credential completion) and the relative weight placed on those outcomes. For these reasons, we focus on specific allocation mechanisms of funding formulas rather than a broad-level categorization of models in this chapter.

Persistently low community college attainment suggests that the dominant funding approaches are not working well. Is there *enough* public money going to community colleges? Do existing funding formulas *distribute* money within states in ways that help all community colleges strengthen their performance? How should community colleges *deploy* the funding they receive so that they generate improved and more equitable outcomes? Researchers have turned to other potential frameworks to answer these questions and better understand the ways public investment in community colleges can promote student success.

### 7.3.2 Adequacy and Equity in Community College Funding

Shaped by a series of state and federal judicial rulings, K-12 funding is often discussed in terms of adequacy and equity (Hanushek and Lindseth 2009; Odden 2000; Romano and Palmer 2023). In this framing, funding adequacy is defined as providing educational organizations with the financial resources needed to ensure students are equipped with basic literacy and numeracy skills, as enumerated in certain state constitutional provisions or as interpreted by the courts (for example, the Rose standards in Kentucky enumerating specific skills and knowledge students should acquire via a public education). A national adequacy study for K-12 education found that the average cost of an adequate education in 2004–05 was just over $9,600 (over $14,000 in 2022 dollars), with state estimates ranging from about $11,000 to about $20,000 when converted to 2022 dollars (Odden et al. 2010). These estimates represent the average K-12 student, not accounting for additional services that may be needed for certain populations or the cost of workforce training programs that require specialized equipment and facilities.

Some scholars have argued that an approach based on funding adequacy may be useful for designing community college finance (Baker and Levin 2017; The Century Foundation 2019; Kahlenberg 2015; Kolbe and Baker 2019; Melguizo et al. 2017; Romano and Palmer 2023). The translation of such a framework is complicated by at least three challenges. First, there is no set of agreed-upon common measures of a "successful" community college education. Should measures be based on students completing a degree within 150 percent of expected completion, prior students meeting some income threshold after completion, students earning a particular score on a yet-to-be-developed common assessment, or something else? Without a defined outcome, the costs of producing that outcome cannot be estimated (Carnevale et al. 2018; Romano and Palmer 2023). Second, even if there were an agreed-upon set of outcomes to be measured, state constitutional education clauses apply to a compulsory K-12 education, not to higher education, meaning there is no imperative for states to ensure community college students reach those outcomes (Melguizo et al. 2017). In theory, students who make the voluntary choice to enroll in community college are highly motivated, but they may have higher concentrations of disadvantage than the average K-12 student, and that could make the provision of an adequate community college education for them especially costly. Third, determining whether adequate funding is provided requires an estimated cost function for community colleges to produce the desired outcome, including cost estimates of the inputs that lead to student success (The Century Foundation 2019).

One approach to determining adequate funding levels for community colleges is to estimate total costs for a combination of inputs deemed sufficient to support the progression of students to complete a degree and (perhaps) navigate a subsequent transition into the workforce. An obvious challenge for this approach is determining the constellation of inputs to consider, as community college students bring many strengths but may confront an array of barriers to completing a degree and attaining an appropriate job, including basic needs insecurities (Wood and Harris 2022); a lack of trusting relationships with instructors, advisors, and administrators (Stanton-Salazar

1997); unmet financial need (Dynarski and Scott-Clayton 2006; Dynarski et al. 2013); and labor market frictions (Wood and Harris 2022).

Goolsbee et al. (2019) applied this general approach to estimate the cost of increasing the share of working-age Americans with a college degree or equivalent credential to 65 percent by 2030, which they estimated to equal the "expected share of jobs requiring advanced skills in that year" (p. 19). They proceeded in two stages. First, they computed that additional funding of $11.9 billion per year would equalize funding for community college and public four-year college students on a per-FTE basis. Next, they used funding elasticity estimates from Deming and Walters (2018) to conclude that an additional $10.1 billion per year would be required to enable substantially more students to meet the desired goal in terms of degree completion.

To assess adequate funding levels for community colleges, we can also look at the costs associated with interventions that successfully improve community college student degree completion. The guided pathways model utilizes system-level reforms to provide additional structure and support for students (Bailey et al. 2015), but such reforms require considerable institutional will to implement at scale and require additional resources. Belfield (2020) found that guided pathways implementation costs approximately $7.1 million a year, or $450 per student, for a typical institution enrolling 4,000 FTE students. This represents 12 percent of the typical college's annual budget. The City University of New York (CUNY) developed a comprehensive model called the Accelerated Study in Associate Programs (ASAP) for students who agree to attend community college full-time. It offers financial support (in the form of a last-dollar scholarship as well as subsidizing or covering transportation costs) in addition to intensive advising, block scheduling, and a multi-semester success seminar. An initial experimental evaluation of ASAP found that it nearly doubled degree completion rates, but with a relatively high net cost per student of $16,284 over three years (Scrivener et al. 2015). More recent experimental studies of ASAP have found that a scaled-down version of the program still produces significant positive results (Azurdia and Galkin 2020; Miller and Weiss 2022).

Another approach to determining adequate funding for a community college education is to estimate a cost function based on past budget data. In the context of the early 2000s California system, researchers estimated a cost of $9,200 per FTE student—about 84 percent higher than the $5,000 typically spent on a per-FTE basis at the time[3] (The Century Foundation 2019). A more recent cost analysis from the Texas community college system suggests $10,385–$11,998 per student would represent adequate funding, with funding needs increasing from that range based on student characteristics—for example, the estimated cost for a first-generation student is almost $15,000 (Levin et al. 2022).

As with funding adequacy, funding equity is challenging to translate to

3. In current dollars, the cost estimated at $9,200 in 2003 is about $15,700.

the community college context. Equity in K-12 finance redresses variation in the available tax base across school districts and directs additional funding toward students with more costly educational needs. In the K-12 context, state and federal funding often counter disparities in local funding and direct more funding toward learners based on need (Chingos and Blagg 2017; Education Commission of the States, n.d.). In the community college context, certain features of state funding formulas can perpetuate resource inequities across institutions by, for example, providing similar funding to institutions regardless of differences in their local funding and in the characteristics of their students (Kelchen et al. 2024; Shaw et al. 2023). State funding formulas can also function progressively by including equity components based on institutional (e.g., rurality), programmatic (e.g., programs aligned with high-demand fields), and student characteristics (e.g., adult students). Scholars (e.g., Melguizo et al. 2017) have proposed methods by which states can assess their funding formulas to determine the extent to which they promote both equitable funding and efficient operations among community colleges.

## 7.4 Comparative State Case Studies of Finance Policy and Funding Models

This analysis delves deeper into the variation in state finance policy and funding formulas for community colleges in six states: California, Michigan, New York, Ohio, Tennessee, and Texas. It contributes to the scholarship first by expanding the number of states for which we have case studies of funding models. We build on recent multi-state analyses (Baum and Cohn 2023; Shaw et al. 2023), adding three states (Michigan, New York, and Tennessee). These case studies are also useful context for analyses presented later in this chapter, where we compare absolute levels of HEER funding received and HEER funding as a percentage of total revenue.

The states included in our comparative analysis collectively enroll about half of all community college students nationally. Each has a unique historical and political context that has shaped higher education policy in the state, its funding model and allocation mechanisms, and state and institutional priorities. In California, for example, voter-enacted referenda, such as Proposition 13 and Proposition 98, constrain state revenue generation and budget allocations in ways that affect community college funding.[4] California also caps tuition that community college students can be charged, meaning

4. Proposition 13 placed limits on property tax increases, meaning local education agencies are more reliant on state allocations from revenue generated via income, capital gains, sales, corporate, and other taxes that have more variable year-to-year revenues (Baker et al. 2023). Proposition 98 guarantees a minimum annual funding level for K-14 education, including community colleges, but the proportion of Proposition 98 spending allocated to community colleges versus K-12 schooling is not guaranteed (Kaplan and Saucedo 2024), and in times of budget contractions, the state may be more likely to shrink spending on community colleges to preserve funding for the K-12 sector (Delaney and Doyle 2011).

institutions cannot turn to tuition increases in times of budget shortfalls. In Texas, state appropriations comprise a smaller share of community college revenues than in California, with more coming from local taxes and tuition on average. Property values, decisions about whether to levy taxes, and tax rates differ across Texas community college service areas, leading to wide variability in the share of revenue from local sources. Tuition is set locally and therefore can also vary. Texas has a strong focus on the workforce development function of community colleges and has categorical funding streams dedicated to occupational training in high-demand fields.

Community colleges in these states also vary in size and governance structures. Some states, such as Michigan and Ohio, do not have a statewide community college system, while others, such as California and Tennessee, operate with broadly decentralized statewide systems. Three of these states were already under study in a project led by the Community College Research Center (CCRC, n.d.). More recently, state leaders in each signaled an interest in questions of finance, agreeing to participate in a survey conducted by the Accelerating Recovery in Community Colleges (ARCC) Network that asked community colleges how they used HEER funds during the pandemic.[5]

### 7.4.1 Community College Revenue

Total revenue per FTE student in 2019–20 varies across our six focal states, from a low of $15,704 in Tennessee to a high of $22,986 in Michigan (in 2024 dollars). This compares to total revenue per FTE student nationally of $19,497.[6] The sources of funding also vary by state, as shown in figure 7.6. We use 2019 data for these comparisons because they exclude federal pandemic relief funding and thus reflect a more typical revenue profile of each state than that of the last few years.

Among the states in our sample, Tennessee (52 percent) derives the most revenue from the state, followed by California (43 percent) and Ohio (39 percent).[7] Texas (22 percent), under the funding model in place in 2019, and Michigan (22 percent) have the lowest proportion of state funding. Local funding varies across states as well, with community colleges in Texas receiving the most local funding (36 percent) and colleges in Tennessee receiving the least (1 percent). Tuition and fees, which nationally make

5. The resulting study (ARCC Network, n.d.) includes federal data analysis paired with the results of a survey of college relief spending and will inform pandemic recovery efforts and help policymakers plan for future public health or other emergencies.

6. These figures are from a 2024 analysis conducted by CCRC using IPEDS data. A public Tableau dashboard includes national and state-level data and reports revenues in 2024 dollars; see "Aftershocks: How the Pandemic Affected Community College Finances," Community College Research Center, February 14, 2024, https://ccrc.tc.columbia.edu/easyblog/aftershocks-how-pandemic-affected-community-college-finances.html.

7. Data from Ohio for this analysis excludes Eastern Gateway Community College (EGCC). EGCC, which will close in October 2024, has been the subject of investigation and monitoring by the US Department of Education related to a free college program that significantly increased the college's online enrollment and use of federal financial aid.

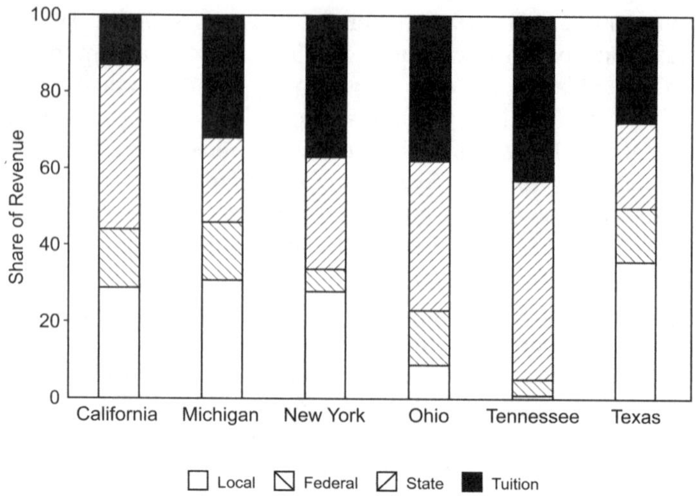


**Fig. 7.6 Proportion of funding per FTE Student by Source and State (2019)**
Source: IPEDS. In Ohio, Eastern Gateway Community College is excluded from this analysis.

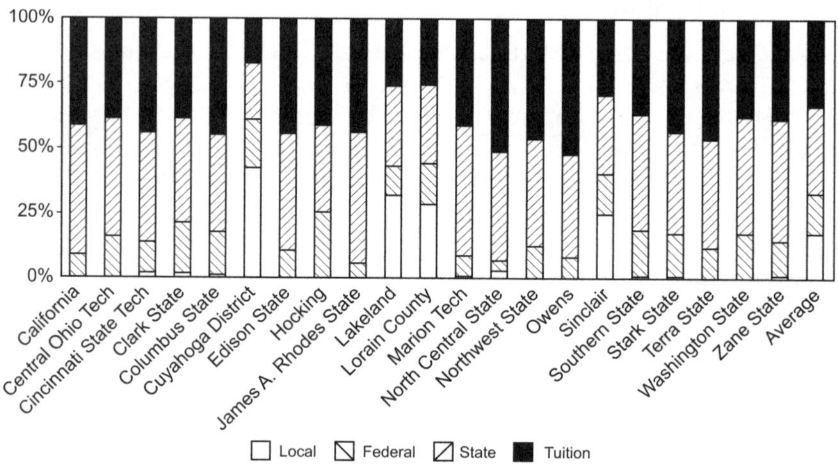


**Fig. 7.7 Distribution of revenue by source in Ohio (2019)**
Source: IPEDS. This analysis excludes Eastern Gateway Community College, including from the statewide average.

up 28 percent of community college revenue in 2019, comprise the highest proportion of total revenues for colleges in Tennessee (43 percent) and the lowest in California (13 percent).

The aggregate state-level revenue distribution can obscure significant variation within states, driven primarily by variation in local funding. Figure 7.7 shows this variation in Ohio as an example. In 2019, Cuyahoga Community

**Table 7.1** **State funding formula allocation mechanisms**

| Allocation Mechanism | Description |
|---|---|
| Base | Institutions receive a similar percentage-point increase/decrease based on prior year's funding |
| Enrollment | Funding at each college is tied to student enrollment levels as measured by head count or FTE student and does not protect base funding levels; funding can vary by degree program |
| Performance | All funding for a college is allocated based on performance metrics as outlined by the state or board |
| Enrollment + Performance | Combination of enrollment and performance mechanisms |
| Base + Enrollment | Combination of base and enrollment mechanisms; typically includes a protected base or stop-loss provision |
| Base + Performance | Combination of base and performance mechanisms; typically a performance-based model that includes stop-loss provisions that protect the majority of current funding |
| Base + Enrollment + Performance | Combination of base, enrollment, and performance mechanisms; typically includes performance metrics and a protected base or a stop-loss provision |

Source: Adapted from Lingo et al. (2021, 2023).

College derived 22 percent of revenue from the state, 42 percent from local sources, and 17 percent from tuition and fees. Marion Technical College, by contrast, received 50 percent of revenue from the state and 41 percent from tuition and fees and received no local funding. Ohio has significant intrastate variation in revenues, in part due to variation in which colleges are allowed to raise revenue from local taxes.

### 7.4.2 Description of State Systems and Funding Models

We compare the underlying allocation mechanisms of the funding formulas in our six focal states. Our typology of allocation mechanisms is based on particular features of the models, such as whether all or part of the state allocations to colleges is determined by multiplying a fixed dollar amount (e.g., $2,000) by FTE enrollment (categorized as "enrollment") or by achieving a particular benchmark or outcome like a specific persistence or graduation rate (categorized as "performance"). Table 7.1 presents more information about funding formula allocation mechanisms.

We used a two-step process to classify the funding models for each of these six states. First, we used primary data collected during the course of CCRC's project on community college finance as well as IPEDS data and information from secondary sources (e.g., policy documents and existing research) to produce preliminary descriptions of funding and allocation mechanisms in each state. Second, we refined these descriptions based on interviews with policymakers in each state. Our resulting state-level summaries include general information about the community college sector, enrollment data (including changes that occurred during the pandemic), a description of system and institutional governance, and a description of the funding model.

**California.** There are 116 community colleges in 73 districts in California. These colleges enrolled approximately 2.2 million students (912,691 FTE students) in 2019, with community colleges receiving on average $18,878 in total revenue per FTE student. From 2019 to 2022, community college enrollment declined by 19 percent. Community college students comprised roughly 45 percent of undergraduates in California in 2021. California uses a participatory governance structure whereby a state board of governors sets policy that is administered through the California Community Colleges Chancellor's Office. California's Student-Centered Funding Formula (SCFF) went into effect in 2018 and combines enrollment and supplemental performance mechanisms (Linden 2022). Districts' share of state funding collected through Proposition 98 (funds from state and local taxes that go to K-12 and community colleges) is distributed based on overall enrollment (70 percent, on average, of a district's apportionment), count of enrollees receiving financial aid and undocumented students (i.e., students deemed to have socioeconomic need) (20 percent), and count of students achieving nine specified success outcomes (10 percent), including completion of a certificate or associate degree and transfer to a four-year institution. The inclusion of supplemental funding for enrolling financial aid recipients was designed to increase college access and the take-up of federal and state aid (Linden 2022). The supplemental funding associated with student outcomes is higher when those outcomes are achieved by financial aid recipients. The original SCFF legislation included a three-year hold-harmless provision that was extended through the pandemic. It instituted a funding floor to smooth the transition between the old formula and SCFF and to protect colleges from revenue losses. The hold-harmless provision is now slated to expire in 2025.

**Michigan.** There are 31 community colleges in Michigan. These colleges enrolled approximately 249,160 students (113,355 FTE students) in 2019, accounting for about 49 percent of undergraduate enrollments in the state (MI School Data, n.d.). On average, Michigan community colleges received $22,986 in total revenue per FTE student in 2019. Between 2019 and 2022, community college enrollment declined 13 percent. There is no centralized governance structure for Michigan's community colleges. A newly created state agency, the Michigan Department of Lifelong Education, Advancement, and Potential (MiLEAP), works with the Department of Education to set and provide policy guidance. The Michigan Community College Association serves a coordinating and advocacy function for the sector, including on matters of finance. Each community college is governed by elected trustees. The community college funding formula comprises a mix of allocation mechanisms, including a base funding component (30 percent), funding for contact hours weighted for health and technology/industrial fields (30 percent), performance metrics (30 percent), funding for administrative costs (5 percent), and local strategic value (5 percent) (Zielak 2022). Base funding allocations were set several decades ago and have remained consistent since. There are three evenly weighted performance metrics: number of degree and certificate completions, six-year completion rates, and completion improvement measured over six years.

**New York.** There are two community college systems in New York. The State University of New York (SUNY) system has 30 community colleges and enrolled 266,872 students (or 165,331 FTE students) in 2019. Community college students comprised 50 percent of total SUNY undergraduate enrollments in fall 2023 (State University of New York 2024). SUNY's community colleges are decentralized, and each college is governed by a board of trustees appointed by the governor or local sponsors. The City University of New York (CUNY) system has 7 community colleges and enrolled approximately 126,023 students (72,106 FTE students) in 2019. Community college students were roughly 34 percent of all CUNY undergraduates in fall 2022. The CUNY colleges report to a single board of trustees, with some members appointed by the governor and others by the mayor. From 2019 to 2022, statewide community college enrollment (including both SUNY and CUNY) declined 24 percent, the largest enrollment drop in our sample. Total revenue per FTE student in New York (SUNY and CUNY) was $21,716 in 2019.

While some of their funding sources are distinct, SUNY and CUNY have similar funding models. The state share of the model is calculated based on the lesser of (1) two-fifths (40 percent) of the net operating budget or net operating costs of the college, or (2) the amount for funded full-time enrollments (estimated or actual FTE students multiplied by a state-determined amount) in eligible programs plus up to half of rental costs for space. Additionally, community colleges rely on local sponsors (e.g., New York City for CUNY) to contribute funding for baseline operating costs and programmatic budget priorities. In recent years, community college funding levels have been bolstered by a funding floor (or maintenance-of-effort mechanism), whereby the state approves FTE student funding amounts as a percentage of funding from the previous year. This maintenance-of-effort mechanism has stabilized community college funding amounts amid enrollment declines that accelerated during the pandemic.

**Ohio.** There are 23 community colleges in Ohio. These community colleges enrolled 229,976[8] students (or 99,011 FTE students) in 2019, comprising 25 percent of total undergraduate enrollments in the state (Ohio Department of Higher Education 2024). Statewide, total revenue per FTE student was $15,839 in 2019. Between 2019 and 2022, enrollment declined about 12 percent. As in Michigan, there is no formal community college

8. Enrollment figures for Ohio exclude Eastern Gateway Community College.

system in Ohio. Instead, the colleges are overseen by the Ohio Department of Higher Education and rely on the Ohio Association of Community Colleges for statewide organization and advocacy efforts. Ohio's State Share of Instruction (SSI) model is performance based and funds community colleges through three outcome measures: course completion (which constitutes 50 percent of funding), success points (25 percent), and completion milestones (25 percent). Course completion is determined by multiplying an average statewide cost-based calculation by the number of FTE students who pass a course. Success points include credit-hour benchmarks earned in 12-credit increments and completion of college-level English and math courses within 30 credit hours. Completion milestones include the number of associate degree and certificate completions and transfers with 12 or more credit hours (Ohio Board of Regents 2020). The SSI model uses a proportional distribution method for each set of outcomes, whereby institutions receive a proportional share of funding for the total earned across each outcome plus an additional amount for outcomes achieved by students who qualify for equity and access categories. Notably, the largest performance measure, course completion, is correlated with enrollment.

**Tennessee.** There are 13 community colleges in Tennessee. These colleges enrolled 114,690 students (56,894 FTE students) in 2019, or roughly 22 percent of undergraduate enrollment in the state (Tennessee Higher Education Commission [THEC] 2021). The total revenue per FTE student in Tennessee in 2019 was $15,704. From 2019 to 2022, community college enrollment declined 18 percent. The Tennessee Board of Regents (TBR) is the governing board for community colleges and approves new programs, budgets, and tuition, among other items. Tennessee's funding formula is performance based: The state collects performance data from its community colleges, counts each outcome at each institution, and attaches premiums and weights to the counted outcomes (including rewards for achieving certain outcomes overall and among specific populations of students) (Quittmeyer and Veach 2023). The outcomes are first compared to the institution's average outcomes from the previous three years to determine the degree of improvement or decline and are then compared to other institutions in the state. Finally, community colleges are awarded points based on student outcomes (i.e., performance points), and higher scoring institutions receive greater funding.

Tennessee assigns roughly 80 percent of performance points to institutions for achieving specific student outcomes (Quittmeyer and Veach 2023). Outcomes in the formula include student progression (i.e., accumulating 12, 24, or 36 credit hours), credential completion, and efficiency measures. Outcome data, which are collected by the THEC, are weighted for specific student characteristics, including being an adult learner, low income, and academically underprepared. When a student with one of the characteristics achieves one of the outcomes, the state awards the college an 80 percent premium. This premium is applied to the underlying outcome count. For example, if 100 students graduate, all of whom are low income, the model acts as though 180 students graduated. The premium rises to 100 percent if the student has two of the specified characteristics (e.g., a low-income adult learner) and to 120 percent if the student has all three characteristics. Additional points are awarded for fixed costs (e.g., facility upkeep) and quality assurance (i.e., additional funding to institutions that meet certain quality standards such as student assessment scores). These categories account for the remaining 20 percent of the state's allocation formula.

**Texas.** There are 50 community colleges (and an additional 10-campus technical college system) in Texas. The community colleges enrolled 1,088,133 students (419,817 FTE students) in 2019, or roughly 40 percent of the state's undergraduate enrollment. From 2019 to 2022, community college enrollment declined 3 percent, the smallest drop for these years in our sample. The Texas Higher Education Coordinating Board (THECB) regulates the state's community colleges and coordinates the locally elected boards of trustees that govern each community college district. Texas has a new funding model that was approved by the state legislature in 2023. Under House Bill 8 (HB 8), the new model allocates what is called performance tier funding (PTF) based on the attainment of specified outcomes, including the number of credentials earned (with an emphasis on high-demand occupations), four-year transfer outcomes, and dual credit outcomes (Texas Higher Education Coordinating Board 2024). The funding received for the PTF is weighted for student populations of interest, including Pell-eligible students (25 percent), academically disadvantaged students (25 percent), and adult learners age 25 and older (50 percent). Additionally, select community college districts are eligible for base tier funding, which ensures institutions with relatively low local revenue (as a result of lower taxable property values) can cover the costs of core operations.[9] For the 2024 fiscal year, 23 of the 50 community colleges are eligible for base tier funding. Baum and Cohn (2023) suggest that these targeted funds are intended to promote educational success for students "facing educational barriers" (p. 28) as well as those attending smaller colleges and rural institutions. In 2019, prior to the introduction of the new performance-based funding model, total revenue per FTE student in Texas was $16,800.

### 7.4.3 Comparative Analysis of State Funding Models

The states in our analysis vary by funding model and allocation mechanisms. While Ohio, Tennessee, and Texas all have performance-based models, the performance metrics and how much funding is allocated to each are

9. Additional funding is determined as the difference between instruction and operations (I&O) and local property tax amounts. If local property taxes exceed I&O amounts, the college does not receive base aid.

**Table 7.2** **Features of state community college funding formulas**

| | | CA | MI | NY | OH | TN | TX |
|---|---|---|---|---|---|---|---|
| **Funding Allocation Mechanism** | Base | | | | | | |
| | Base + Performance | | | | | | |
| | Base + Enrollment + Performance | | | | | | |
| | Enrollment | | | | | | |
| | Performance | | | | | | |
| | Performance + Enrollment | | | | | | |
| **Equity Components** | Equity-Focused Performance Measures | | | | | | |
| | Equity-Focused Enrollment Measures | | | | | | |
| | Institutional Stabilization Measures | | | | | | |
| **Other Components** | Prioritization of In-Demand Fields | | | | | | |

different. California rewards community colleges with additional money for enrolling financial aid recipients and undocumented students and provides modest incentives for improved student outcomes. New York's model has two funding allocation mechanisms: One is based on colleges' costs, while the other is based on enrollment. Colleges receive funding based on which mechanism generates a lower state share (or, in other words, which calculation costs the state less money). Michigan's funding model has a multitude of components, including base funding, enrollment, and performance mechanisms. Table 7.2 organizes our focal states by funding allocation mechanism.

As noted, there is significant variation in the underlying allocation mechanisms by state, even among similar models. For example, Ohio and Tennessee both use a performance-based model, but the particulars of each model are quite different. In Ohio, 100 percent of funding is performance based, and the largest portion of funding comes from performance on the outcome of course completion. By contrast, in Tennessee, 80 percent of funding is based on student outcomes, with all outcomes weighted for student populations of interest. Some of this variation appears to be driven by characteristics of and priorities of the state. In Michigan, the contact hours outcome measure is weighted toward programs that can prepare students for jobs in growing industries and potentially offset long-term job losses in manufacturing (Zielak 2022).

Enrollment-related metrics directly or indirectly account for a considerable portion of state revenue for five of six states (Texas is the exception). The funding models in California, Michigan, and New York include per-FTE-student or per-contact-hour components. Ohio's model rewards enrollment indirectly by allocating the majority of performance funding to course completion, an outcome strongly correlated with enrollment. Though these models are quite different, they are all sensitive to fluctuations in enrollment. This finding is consistent with those of Shaw et al. (2023), who examined the importance of enrollment in the funding models of California, Ohio, and Texas community colleges. Given accelerated enrollment declines during the pandemic and the weak demographic outlook for future cohorts, community colleges in states with models that rely on enrollment may encounter financial challenges.

With the financial outlook for the sector deteriorating (Belfield et al. 2024a), the importance of stabilization and equalization funding features will grow. These model features aim to create more parity and/or equity across institutions within a state and may be more generous to smaller colleges or colleges with more concentrated student needs. The new model in Texas, for example, provides supplemental funding to colleges whose ability to fund core operations is impaired by a lack of local funding or other factors. California's model also has an equalization feature that pools state and local funding and then redistributes it primarily based on enrollment.

## 7.5 Effects of the Pandemic on Community Colleges' Financial Condition

The wide-ranging effects of the pandemic compounded the sector-wide enrollment losses experienced by community colleges in the wake of the Great Recession. As local institutions, community colleges were on the front lines assisting the individuals and communities disproportionately impacted by the devastating health and economic consequences of COVID-19 (Brock and Diwa 2021). They did this work with unprecedented financial support from the federal government. While researchers have only begun to examine the effects of these investments on student experiences and outcomes, we can document what community colleges received and disbursed relative to pre-pandemic revenue and expenditure trends. We also draw on institutional survey data and interviews with institutional leaders to identify lessons they will carry forward even as institutions face uncertain financial conditions.

### 7.5.1 Higher Education Emergency Relief Funding

The Higher Education Emergency Relief Fund allocated approximately \$25 billion to public two-year colleges for direct student aid and institutional aid. The first round of HEER funding weighted FTE Pell recipients

**Table 7.3** **Comparison of HEER Funding**

| | CA | MI | NY | OH | TN | TX | Total |
|---|---|---|---|---|---|---|---|
| Total HEER Funding Awarded | $4.402B | $695.7M | $1.433B | $542.2M | $458.1M | $2.584B | $10.115B |
| HEER Funding Awarded per FTE | $11,060 | $14,993 | $10,762 | $11,097 | $10,115 | $12,919 | $11,603 |
| Student Aid per FTE | $6,120 | $8,280 | $5,654 | $6,085 | $5,490 | $6,838 | $6,294 |
| Institutional Aid per FTE | $4,396 | $6,004 | $4,147 | $4,568 | $4,060 | $4,955 | $4,564 |
| Other Aid per FTE | $544 | $709 | $960 | $444 | $564 | $1,126 | $745 |

Note. FTE student enrollment data is from IPEDS and from fall 2020. Other aid (bottom row), awarded in addition to the HEER student and institutional aid funding allocations, was provided to colleges deemed to have substantial needs because they met certain criteria for enrolling underserved student populations by income or racial/ethnic categories, such as Historically Black Colleges and Universities (HBCUs), Minority Serving Institutions (MSIs), or Tribally Controlled Colleges and Universities (TCCUs).

heavily; the second and third rounds of funding also weighted Pell recipient head count (as opposed to FTE students) and included fully online students. Student aid was disbursed directly to students by the colleges to cover expenses related to food, housing, course materials, technology, health care, and childcare. Colleges could use institutional aid to defray costs associated with the pandemic, such as lost revenue, technology enhancements, and staff training. Colleges could also use institutional aid to supplement the direct student aid.

The states in our sample received a total of $10.1 billion in HEER funding, or roughly 40 percent of all HEER funding distributed. On average, the colleges in our sample received $9.9 million in HEER funds for emergency cash aid to students and $13.6 million for operating expenses at the institution. On a per-FTE-student basis, this translated to an average of $11,793 for our sample, with per-FTE-student funding ranging from $10,115 in New York to $14,993 in Michigan. This cross-state variation in total per-FTE funding was likely due to the criteria the federal government used to determine institutional allocations. In Michigan, for example, 70 percent of students were part-time and 39 percent of students were Pell eligible in 2020. This is comparable to California, where the same percentage of students were part-time, but substantially fewer were Pell eligible (25 percent).[10] The differences between these eligibility criteria likely contributed to the difference of nearly $4,000 per FTE student in total HEER funding awarded in these two states and may also have contributed to differences in the amount of federal relief funding received by community colleges within states.

10. Pell Grant awards consider Expected Family Contribution (EFC, now the Student Aid Index) and the cost of attendance. Because community college tuition in California is relatively low, many California students either do not apply or do not qualify.

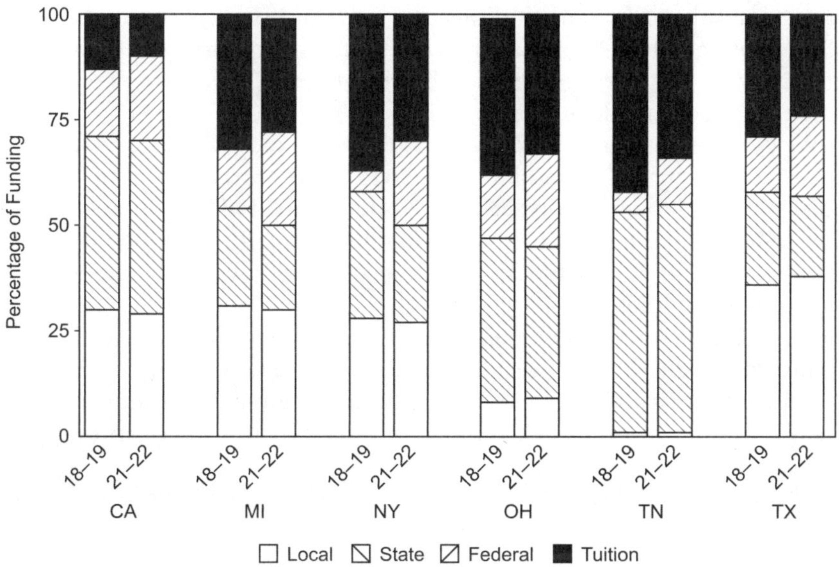


**Fig. 7.8 Change in percentage of funding per FTE student by source pre- and during pandemic**
Source: IPEDS. Eastern Gateway Community College in Ohio is excluded from this analysis.

Figure 7.8 presents average revenue per FTE student by source as a share of total revenue pre-pandemic and during the pandemic for the states in our sample. All of the states saw both a decline in tuition revenue and an increase in federal funding from 2018–2019 to 2021–2022. (Data from 2022 are the most recent currently available in IPEDS.) The percentage-point increase in federal funding was highest in New York (15 ppt). State and local funding per FTE student was generally stable in our sample, consistent with national trends, due in part to declines in enrollment (Belfield et al. 2024b).

A recent ARCC Network analysis found that HEER funding was substantial and more than made up for the drop in tuition revenue community colleges experienced at the start of the pandemic due to lower enrollment. With the addition of HEER funding, total revenue per FTE student was up 21 percent nationally. That represents an additional $1,700 (on a per-student basis) net of lost tuition revenue (Belfield et al. 2024b).

### 7.5.2 Spending During the Pandemic

Community colleges have high fixed costs that may limit their ability to reallocate money quickly and respond to emerging challenges—such as those of a global pandemic. HEER funding provided institutions more spending flexibility by allowing them to allocate funds toward a broadly defined set of institutional investments (Daniels Sarica et al. 2024). These funds not only enabled institutions to cover high fixed costs but also presented community college leaders with a onetime opportunity to identify and implement strategies to reduce barriers to enrollment and persistence and promote equitable outcomes.

We draw on institutional survey and college stakeholder interview data collected in summer 2023 as part of the ARCC Network analysis of federal relief efforts (Daniels Sarica et al. 2024; Klempin et al. 2024) to examine how colleges used institutional aid, what groups of students they targeted for assistance, and what types of assistance they felt were most important to retaining and helping students advance. Survey data include responses from administrators and/or staff at 170 community colleges across the six focal states (or 64 percent of all community colleges in these states). We also include analysis from interviews with college administrators, staff, and faculty conducted between 2021 and 2023 as part of CCRC's project on community college finance.

When asked to indicate their priorities if future federal funding were made available, colleges' top three survey responses were additional student aid (71 percent), mental health services (49 percent), and technology hardware (35 percent). Consistent with these survey responses, our interview data suggested three priority areas for the use of HEER funds as we describe below.

1. *Offsetting Lost Tuition.* According to survey data, the biggest use of institutional aid was to make up for lost revenue associated with enrollment declines: Institutions reported allocating about $4.9 million per college for these purposes. However, many colleges also used institutional aid to supplement the emergency aid to students ($2.5 million on average per college), provide tuition discounts ($1.4 million), and give tuition reimbursements ($791,000). Community college leaders additionally discussed using HEER funding for retention initiatives intended to help students persist (e.g., emergency funding, free/subsidized textbooks, and debt forgiveness for students with prior postsecondary experiences).

2. *Providing Support for Basic Needs of Students.* Community colleges applied institutional aid toward expanding basic needs support so that students could engage with the educational activities of the college. Over a third of institutions (36 percent) reported spending HEER funds on food assistance, and 17 percent used aid for housing assistance. Close to half (46 percent) used HEER funds for mental health services. A recurring theme of the interviews with college administrators was the importance of creating a "culture of caring" by providing comprehensive services on community college campuses, especially as the pandemic exposed existing student vulnerabilities. Through pandemic-related funds, colleges were able to augment their delivery of basic needs services. Several reported that they centralized basic needs services within a single location, and some colleges hired additional staff to support basic needs initiatives. Prior to the pandemic, basic

needs services were generally funded through a mixture of local and philanthropic dollars with some support from federal funding (e.g., Perkins). With HEER funding, these programs were expanded. However, HEER funding had to be spent by June 2023, and now these programs may be in jeopardy. Indeed, in the survey, 55 percent of institutions reported worrying about reducing basic needs services because of the end of HEER funding.

3. *Investing in Technology Infrastructure.* The sudden shift to fully online courses and student services at the start of the pandemic was costly for community colleges. HEER funds made it possible for community colleges to invest in the technology and training required to make this transition. Approximately 88 percent of the institutions in our sample of six states reported using HEER funding to buy and upgrade technology. Additionally, 78 percent of colleges used aid for distance learning supplies, and 71 percent used aid for high-speed internet. When combined with technology hardware and distance learning supplies, colleges in our sample states allocated roughly 15 percent of their total institutional aid toward technology-related expenses. Nearly every college leader interviewed described using HEER dollars to accelerate technology adoption. These investments took three forms: (1) providing equipment, such as WiFi hotspots and loaner laptops, to students; (2) investing in training for faculty to teach online, including training in learning management systems; and (3) equipping classrooms with the technology required for hybrid and HyFlex course modalities.[11] The adjustments to teaching and learning made possible by HEER funding not only helped maintain instruction during the height of the pandemic but also built community colleges' capacity to continue to offer students a mix of course modality options that make course taking more feasible.

## 7.6 Discussion and Conclusion

The community college sector faces headwinds, including longer-term trends of declining enrollments and public disinvestment, wherein less revenue may come from state and local governments and more from students and families (in the form of tuition and fees). Graduation rates remain low, and disparities in those rates by race/ethnicity and income persist. Research has generated rigorous evidence on policies, practices, and programs that improve student outcomes. However, these interventions can be costly and necessitate more funding to implement at scale. The analysis in this chapter sought to understand the extent to which existing community college funding policies and formulas could enable the types of changes required to improve institutional performance and student outcomes. It also aimed to learn from the federal government's unprecedented investment in com-

11. HyFlex courses allow students to attend in person or online and require video and audio capabilities in the classroom.

munity colleges during the pandemic. We delved into these topics in six states whose community colleges collectively enroll about half of all students in the sector.

Although state appropriations make up the largest share of community college revenue nationally, there is significant variation across states. The state is thus a more influential funding entity in some places compared to others. Variation is also evident in the funding models states use. The states in this analysis generally allocated their share of funding in multiple ways, based on a fixed amount per student enrolled, achievement of specified outcomes, increase or decrease to previous year's funding, and other approaches. Though the funding models frequently combine different allocation mechanisms, most of them are tied directly or indirectly to enrollment. While community college enrollments have rebounded somewhat in the last two years, these gains have not offset the sharp declines of the first two years of the pandemic, much less the prior decade of enrollment erosion. As discussed elsewhere in this volume, the so-called demographic cliff portends future higher education declines in both enrollment and state and tuition revenues, particularly for community colleges (Vigdor 2024).

In addition to the enrollment challenges facing community colleges, institutions are facing a reality of heightened student need across multiple dimensions. Given trends in K-12 achievement (Fahle et al. 2024), students whose K-12 schooling was interrupted by the pandemic may enter college less academically prepared than past cohorts. Both traditional-age and older students may experience food and housing insecurity, transportation disruptions, high childcare costs, and a range of other basic needs. Additionally, the need for mental health support also increased in the wake of the pandemic (Elharake et al. 2023), straining institutional resources. HEER funding provided temporary respite, plugging budget holes caused by declining enrollment and allowing community colleges to invest in academic supports and basic needs and mental health services. But these needs will persist. Even students who do not face severe challenges require high-quality academic advising and instructional support, which can be costly. Both funding models and community college business models will need to adapt to address these changing realities and enable community colleges to serve their students more effectively.

A broader audience has begun to acknowledge these challenging conditions and take action to better understand and address them. Scholars and advocates have focused on scrutinizing existing funding policies and models and identifying opportunities to make them more equitable and effective. Several states have embarked on reviews of their community college funding models, and Texas has completely redesigned its funding model. Notably, Texas policymakers recognized the importance of stabilizing funding mechanisms by providing supplemental funding to colleges whose ability to fund core operations is impaired by a lack of local funding or other factors. In doing so, they aimed to create more parity and/or equity across institutions within the state, particularly for colleges with more concentrated student needs. The increasing prevalence of equity components in state funding formulas is another emerging policy trend, but more work is needed to understand how states can best design their funding formulas to promote greater access to and success in higher education for low-income and racially minoritized students.

Academic scholarship can play a key role in helping the community college sector adapt to its current circumstances by addressing three central policy questions.

*1. What strategies and practices effectively serve diverse community college students with a range of academic and nonacademic needs, and what are the costs of scaling these approaches?*

A key goal of community colleges is to support students through credential completion so they accrue benefits in the labor market. While this goal has been elusive for large shares of community college students, there is a growing body of evidence on effective policies and practices that can improve student outcomes in community colleges. A number of discrete interventions in areas such as developmental education (Bickerstaff et al. 2022) and advising (Karp et al. 2021) have been rigorously evaluated and demonstrated effectiveness. Some comprehensive reforms, such as ASAP, show large positive impacts on completion in rigorous evaluations (Miller and Weiss 2022), and others, such as guided pathways, show promise in states and colleges that fully implement the model (Jenkins et al. 2024). Importantly, many of these evaluations include cost studies, which provide useful information on the resource requirements and costs of these reforms for institutions. This type of scholarship must continue to grow, as it has the potential to inform the work of policymakers responsible for state finance policy and of advocates who aim to make community college funding more effective and equitable.

*2. How can public higher education finance policy incentivize and support community colleges to innovate and implement evidence-based practices without undermining local autonomy?*

Policymakers face a conundrum. As the body of evidence on effective policies and practices in community colleges grows, there is an opportunity to make state finance policy more prescriptive and to direct colleges to invest in proven and promising approaches. Prescriptive finance policies, however, would be incredibly unpopular and run counter to the autonomy institutional leaders need to deploy available financial resources in service of their strategic priorities and the needs of their communities. This suggests that redesigns to funding models will need to incorporate strong upfront financial incentives for colleges to take up evidence-based approaches; the models will also need to subsidize robust implementation support. The tenets underlying tiered-evidence grantmaking, which has been used by federal agencies like the US Department of Education and the National Science Foundation for nearly a decade, might provide inspiration to state policymakers (US GAO 2016). This approach provides larger sums of money to applicants pursuing programs with more evidence of effectiveness and smaller amounts to applicants pursuing less tested innovations. Any tiered funding approach would need to consider potential implications for less-resourced community colleges to maintain core operations while investing in the institutional capacities required to effectively adopt and implement evidence-based programs.

*3. How can local, state, and federal policymakers work collaboratively to invest in community college students and their success?*

Reforms of state finance systems can help community colleges only to a limited degree if they do not also result in substantial increases in overall funding levels for public higher education. An expanded role of the federal government in community college funding could help. The federal government is likely the only source of the level of investment called for by Goolsbee et al. (2019) to yield dramatic increases in the proportion of adults with college degrees or certificates. Prior to the pandemic, federal funding generally accounted for less than one-sixth of total community college revenue, with much of it designated for student financial aid. Federal funding increased to 20 percent during the pandemic due to HEER funding, but state and local funding has always accounted for most community college revenue (Belfield et al. 2024b).

The HEER funding program illustrated how federal funding could be aligned with student and institutional needs. The HEER funding formula ensured that institutions enrolling large numbers of low-income students received substantially more funding than institutions serving fewer low-income students by weighting enrollments by Pell Grant receipt. Congress further appropriated HEER funding for institutions that enrolled underserved student populations, such as Historically Black Colleges and Universities and Tribally Controlled Colleges and Universities. Together, these provisions reflect the ability of the federal government to provide equitable funding based on student characteristics across institutions and states.

Community colleges provide affordable, accessible pathways to higher education for millions of students each year and are critical to state and national goals to enhance postsecondary attainment and economic growth. Yet, many institutions are routinely under-resourced and struggle to deliver on their mission. State funding continues to offer a powerful lever that could be used to shape institutional decision-making and performance and promote both improved and more equitable student outcomes. Federal funding can augment state funding in ways that give institutions flexibility to address student needs and adopt evidence-based practices. We believe that significant improvements are unlikely without significant new investment. Some states are moving in this direction. Similarly, some community colleges are implementing reforms designed to increase graduation rates, improve labor market outcomes, and eliminate disparities in these outcomes by income, race, and ethnicity.

## References

Accelerating Recovery in Community Colleges Network. n.d. *Community Colleges' Spending of Federal Recovery Funds.* https://ccrc.tc.columbia.edu/arccnetwork/projects/spending-of-federal-recovery-funds/.

Acton, R., K. Cortes, and C. Morales. 2024. "Distance to Opportunity: Higher Education Deserts and College Enrollment Choices." Presented at the 2024 NBER Financing Higher Education conference. https://conference.nber.org/conf_papers/f191190.pdf.

Azurdia, G., and K. Galkin. 2020. "An Eight-Year Cost Analysis from a Randomized Controlled Trial of CUNY's Accelerated Study in Associate Programs." Working Paper, MDRC, July. https://www.mdrc.org/sites/default/files/ASAP_Cost_Working_Paper_final.pdf.

Bailey, T., S. Jaggars, and D. Jenkins. 2015. *Redesigning America's Community Colleges: A Clearer Path to Student Success*. Harvard University Press. https://doi.org/10.4159/9780674425934.

Baker, B., M. Di Carlo, and Z. Oberfield. 2023. *The Source Code: Revenue Composition and the Adequacy, Equity, and Stability of K-12 School Spending.* The Albert Shanker Institute, April. https://files.eric.ed.gov/fulltext/ED629096.pdf.

Baker, B., and J. Levin. 2017. "Estimating the Real Cost of Community College." The Century Foundation, October 23. https://production-tcf.imgix.net/app/uploads/2017/10/02113912/estimating-the-real-cost-of-community-college.pdf.

Baum, S., and M. Johnson. 2015. *Student Debt: Who Borrows Most? What Lies Ahead?* Urban Institute, April 20. https://www.urban.org/research/publication/student-debt-who-borrows-most-what-lies-ahead.

Baum, S., and J. Cohn. 2023. *Variation in Community College Funding Levels: A Focus on Equity*. Urban Institute, December 5. https://www.urban.org/research/publication/variation-community-college-funding-levels.

Belfield, C., and T. Bailey. 2017. *The Labor Market Returns to Sub-Baccalaureate College: A Review.* Center for Analysis of Postsecondary Education and Employment, March. https://capseecenter.org/labor-market-returns-sub-baccalaureate-college-review.

Belfield, C. 2020. "The Economics of Guided Pathways: Cost, Funding, and Value." CCRC Working Paper 123. New York, NY: Community College Research Center. https://www.ibhe.org/assets/files/Technical/2023/Jan/5/CCRC_economics-guided-pathways-cost-funding-value.pdf.

Belfield, C., T. Brock, J. Fink, and D. Jenkins. 2024a. *Aftershocks: How the Pandemic Affected Community College Finances.* The Mixed Methods Blog, February 14. Community College Research Center. https://ccrc.tc.columbia.edu/easyblog/aftershocks-how-pandemic-affected-community-college-finances.html.

Belfield, C., T. Brock, J. Fink, and D. Jenkins. 2024b. *How HEER Funding Rescued Community Colleges from the Pandemic.* Accelerating Recovery in Community

Colleges Network Brief, March. Community College Research Center. https://ccrc.tc.columbia.edu/media/k2/attachments/how-heer-funding-rescued-community-colleges-pandemic.pdf.

Betts, J. R., and L. L. McFarland. 1995. "Safe Port in a Storm: The Impact of Labor Market Conditions on Community College Enrollments." *Journal of Human Resources* 39(4): 741–65.

Bickerstaff, S., K. Beal, J. Raufman, E. B. Lewy and A. Slaughter. 2022. *Five Principles for Reforming Developmental Education: A Review of the Evidence.* Center for the Analysis of Postsecondary Readiness.

Bloom, D. E., M. Hartley, and H. Rosovsky. 2007. "Beyond Private Gain: The Public Benefits of Higher Education." In *International Handbook of Higher Education*, edited by J. J. F. Forest and P. G. Altbach, 293–308. Springer International Handbooks of Education. https://doi.org/10.1007/978-1-4020-4012-2_15.

Bound, J., B. Braga, G. Khanna, and S. Turner. 2019. "Public Universities: The Supply Side of Building a Skilled Workforce." NBER Working Paper No. 25945. Cambridge, MA: National Bureau of Economic Research. https://www.nber.org/papers/w25945.

Brock, T., and C. Diwa. 2021. "Catastrophe or Catalyst? Reflections on COVID's Impact on Community Colleges." *Journal of Postsecondary Student Success* 1(2): 2–17. https://doi.org/10.33009/fsop_jpss129901.

Brock, T., A. Mateo, and A. Ray. 2025. "Community Colleges: History, Performance, and Paths to Improvement." *Handbook of Education*, 1565–86. American Educational Research Association.

Carnevale, A., A. Gulish, and J. Strohl. 2018. *Educational Adequacy in the Twenty-First Century*. The Century Foundation, May 2. https://production-tcf.imgix.net/app/uploads/2018/04/01160741/TCF_EducationalAdequacyReport.pdf.

Causey, J., J. Cohen, S. Lee, M. Ryu, and D. Shapiro. 2023. *Current Term Enrollment Estimates Expanded Edition: Fall 2022*. National Student Clearinghouse Research Center.

The Century Foundation. 2019. *Recommendations for Providing Community Colleges with the Resources They Need.* The Century Foundation, April 25. https://tcf.org/content/report/recommendations-providing-community-colleges-resources-need/.

Chakrabarti, R., N. Gorton, and M. Lovenheim. 2020. "State Investment in Higher Education: Effects on Human Capital Formation, Student Debt, and Long-Term Financial Outcomes of Students." NBER Working Paper No. 27885. Cambridge, MA: National Bureau of Economic Research. https://www.nber.org/papers/w27885.

Chetty, R., J. N. Friedman, E. Saez, N. Turner, and D. Yagan. 2017. "Mobility Report Cards: The Role of Colleges in Intergenerational Mobility." NBER Working Paper No. 23618. Cambridge, MA: National Bureau of Economic Research. https://www.nber.org/papers/w23618.

Chingos, M., and K. Blagg. 2017. *Do Poor Kids Get Their Fair Share of School Funding?* Urban Institute, May. https://www.urban.org/sites/default/files/publication/90586/school_funding_brief_1.pdf.

Community College Research Center. n.d. *Paving the Way to Equitable, Adequate, and Effective Community College Funding*. https://ccrc.tc.columbia.edu/research-project/equitable-community-college-funding.html.

Cummings, K., S. Laderman, J. Lee, D. Tandberg, and D. Weeden. 2021. *Investigating the Impacts of State Higher Education Appropriations and Financial Aid.* State Higher Education Executive Officers Association, May. https://sheeo.org/wp-content/uploads/2021/05/SHEEO_ImpactAppropationsFinancialAid.pdf.

Daniels Sarica, H., T. Monahan, and M. Anderson. 2024. *An Analysis of Fed-*

*eral Pandemic Relief Funding at Community Colleges.* Accelerating Recovery in Community Colleges Network. Community College Research Center, February. https://ccrc.tc.columbia.edu/media/k2/attachments/analysis-federal-pandemic-relief-funding-community-colleges.pdf.

Delaney, J., and W. Doyle. 2011. "State Spending on Higher Education: Testing the Balance Wheel over Time." *Journal of Education Finance* 36(4): 343–68. https://www.jstor.org/stable/23018116.

Deming, D., and C. Walters. 2018. "The Impact of State Budget Cuts on US Postsecondary Attainment." https://scholar.harvard.edu/files/ddeming/files/dw_feb2018.pdf.

Dougherty, K., S. Jones, H. Lahr, R. Natow, L. Pheatt, and V. Reddy. 2014. "Performance Funding for Higher Education: Forms, Origins, Impacts, and Futures." *Annals of the American Academy* 655 (Sept): 163–84.

Dynarski, S. M., and J. E. Scott-Clayton. 2006. "The Cost of Complexity in Federal Student Aid: Lessons from Optimal Tax Theory and Behavioral Economics." *National Tax Journal* 59(2): 319–56.

Dynarski, S., J. Scott-Clayton, and M. Wiederspan. 2013. "Simplifying Tax Incentives and Aid for College: Progress and Prospects." *Tax Policy and the Economy* 27(1): 161–202.

Education Commission of the States. n.d. *State Information Request—School Finance Equalization.* Education Commission of the States. https://www.ecs.org/wp-content/uploads/State-Information-Request_-School-Finance-Equalization.pdf.

Education Commission of the States. 2021. *State Information Request—Local Funding for Community Colleges.* Education Commission of the States, December 6. https://www.ecs.org/wp-content/uploads/State-Information-Request_Local-Funding-for-Community-Colleges.pdf.

Elharake, J. A., F. Akbar, A. A. Malik, W. Gilliam, and S. Omer. 2023. "Mental Health Impact of COVID-19 among Children and College Students: A Systematic Review." *Child Psychiatry & Human Development* 54: 913–25. https://doi.org/10.1007/s10578-021-01297-1.

Fahle, E., T. J. Kane, S. F. Reardon, and D. O. Staiger. 2024. *The First Year of Pandemic Recovery: A District-Level Analysis.* Education Recovery Scorecard. January. https://educationrecoveryscorecard.org/wp-content/uploads/2024/01/ERS-Report-Final-1.31.pdf.

Fink, J., and D. Jenkins. 2020. "Shifting sectors: How a Commonly Used Federal Datapoint Undercounts over a Million Community College Students." *Community College Research Center, Mixed Methods Blog*, April 30. https://ccrc.tc.columbia.edu/easyblog/shifting-sectors-community-colleges-undercounting.html.

Fink, J., and D. Jenkins. 2023. *Rethinking Dual Enrollment as an Equitable On-Ramp to a Career-Path College Degree Program after High School.* Community College Research Center, October. https://ccrc.tc.columbia.edu/media/k2/attachments/revamping-dual-enrollment-equitable-college-degree-paths_1.pdf.

Fountain, J. H. 2019. *The Postsecondary Undergraduate Population: Student Income and Demographics.* CRS Report R45686. Congressional Research Service. https://sgp.fas.org/crs/misc/R45686.pdf.

Gilbert, C., and D. E. Heller. 2010. *The Truman Commission and Its Impact on Federal Higher Education Policy from 1947 to 2010* [Conference session]. Association for the Study of Higher Education Annual Conference, November 17–20, Indianapolis, IN, United States. https://edwp.educ.msu.edu/te/wp-content/uploads/sites/3/2012/03/ASHE_2010_Gilbert_Heller.pdf.

Goolsbee, A., G. Hubbard, and A. Ganz. 2019. *A Policy Agenda to Develop Human Capital for the Modern Economy.* Aspen Institute Working Paper, February 4. https://www.aspeninstitute.org/longform/expanding-economic-opportunity-for-more-americans/a-policy-agenda-to-develop-human-capital-for-the-modern-economy/.

Hanushek, E., and A. Lindseth. 2009. *Schoolhouses, Courthouses, and Statehouses.* Princeton University Press.

Irwin, V., T. M. Bailey, R. Panditharatna, and A. Sadeghi. 2024. Projections of Education Statistics to 2030 (NCES 2024–034). US Department of Education, Washington, DC: National Center for Education Statistics. Retrieved June 13, 2024, from https://nces.ed.gov/programs/pes/.

Jenkins, D., H. Lahr, and T. Brock. 2024. *Lessons from Two Major Evaluations of Guided Pathways.* CCRC Research Brief. Community College Research Center. https://ccrc.tc.columbia.edu/publications/lessons-two-major-evaluations-guided-pathways.html.

Kahlenberg, R. 2015. *How Higher Education Funding Shortchanges Community Colleges.* The Century Foundation, May 28. https://tcf.org/content/report/how-higher-education-funding-shortchanges-community-colleges/.

Kane, T. J. 1995. "Rising Public College Tuition and College Entry: How Well Do Public Subsidies Promote Access to College?" NBER Working Paper No. 5164. Cambridge, MA: National Bureau of Economic Research. https://www.nber.org/system/files/working_papers/w5164/w5164.pdf.

Kane, T. J., and C. E. Rouse. 1995. "Labor Market Returns to Two- and Four-Year Colleges: Is a Credit a Credit and Do Degrees Matter?" *American Economic Review* 85(3): 600–614. https://www.jstor.org/stable/2118190.

Kaplan, J., and E. Saucedo. 2024. *What Is Proposition 98 and How Does the State Budget Shortfall Affect It?* California Budget & Policy Center, February. https://calbudgetcenter.org/resources/what-is-proposition-98-and-how-does-the-state-budget-shortfall-affect-it/.

Karp, M., S. Ackerson, I. Cheng, E. Cocatre-Zilgien, S. Costelloe, B. Freeman, S. Lemire, D. Linderman, B. McFarlane, S. Moulton, J. O'Shea, A. Porowski, and L. Richburg-Hayes. 2021. *Effective Advising for Postsecondary Students: A Practice Guide for Educators.* National Center for Education Evaluation and Regional Assistance (NCEE), Institute of Education Sciences, US Department of Education. https://ies.ed.gov/ncee/wwc/Docs/PracticeGuide/WWC-practice-guide-advising-full-text-revised2.pdf.

Kelchen, R., M. Lingo, D. Baker, K. Rosinger, J. Ortagus, and J. Wu. 2023. *A Typology and Landscape of State Funding Formulas for Public Colleges and Universities from 2004 to 2020.* InformEd States Higher Education Policy Initiative, April. https://static1.squarespace.com/static/5d9f9fae6a122515ee074363/t/65806fa9bb51333f6f90475b/1702916010095/ISPaper_TypologyandLandscapeofStateFundingFormulas_PublicCollegesandUniversities_2004-2020.pdf.

Kelchen, R., J. Ortagus, K. Rosinger, D. Baker, and M. Lingo. 2024. "The Relationships Between State Higher Education Funding Strategies and College Access and Success." *Educational Researcher* 53(2): 100–110. https://doi.org/10.3102/0013189X231208964.

Klempin, S. C., S. Griffin, T. J. Monahan, M. N. Anderson, and T. Brock. 2024. *Pandemic Relief Spending and Recovery Strategies: Findings from a Survey of Community Colleges in Six States.* Accelerating Recovery in Community Colleges Network and Community College Research Center.

Kolbe, T., and B. D. Baker. 2019. "Fiscal Equity and America's Community Colleges." *Journal of Higher Education* 90(1): 111–49.

Lane, J. E., and J. A. Kivisto. 2008. "Interests, Information, and Incentives in Higher Education: Principal-Agent Theory and Its Potential Applications to the Study of Higher Education Governance." In *Higher Education: Handbook of Theory and Research*, edited by J. C. Smart, 141–79. https://doi.org/10.1007/978-1-4020-6959-8_5.

Lee, S., and D. Shapiro. 2023. "Completing College: National and State Report with Longitudinal Data Dashboard on Six- and Eight-Year Completion Rates." National Student Clearinghouse Research Center. November. https://nscresearchcenter.org/wp-content/uploads/Completions_Report_2023.pdf.

Legislative Analyst's Office. 2023. *The 2023–24 Budget: California Community Colleges.* Legislative Analyst's Office. California State Legislature. https://lao.ca.gov/reports/2023/4695/CCC-Budget-022223.pdf.

Levin, J., B. Baker, J. Lee, D. Atchison, and R. Kelchen. 2022. *An Examination of the Costs of Texas Community Colleges.* Institute of Education Sciences. https://ies.ed.gov/ncee/rel/regions/southwest/pdf/REL_2023142.pdf.

Linden, R. 2022. "Understanding the Student-Centered Funding Formula: A Primer on California Community College Finance." UC Davis Wheelhouse. https://education.ucdavis.edu/community-college-finance.

Lingo, M., R. Kelchen, K. Rosinger, D. Baker, J. Ortagus, and J. Wu. 2023. *The Landscape of State Funding Formulas for Public Colleges and Universities (Revised)*. InformEd States Higher Education Policy Initiative, April. https://static1.squarespace.com/static/5d9f9fae6a122515ee074363/t/6446df7a981da30ef202a70c/1682366330568/ISBrief_TheLandscapeofStateFundingFormulas_PublicCollegesUniversities_April2023.pdf.

Lingo, M., R. Kelchen, K. Rosinger, D. Baker, J. Ortagus, and J. Wu. 2021. *The Landscape of State Funding Formulas for Public Colleges and Universities.* Policy Brief. InformEd States Higher Education Policy Initiative.

Long, B. T., and M. Kurlaender. 2009. "Do Community Colleges Provide a Viable Pathway to a Baccalaureate Degree?" *Educational Evaluation and Policy Analysis* 31(1): 30–53. https://doi.org/10.3102/0162373708327756.

Ma, J., and M. Pender. 2023. *Trends in College Pricing and Student Aid 2023*. College Board. https://research.collegeboard.org/media/pdf/Trends%20Report%202023%20Updated.pdf.

Ma, J., M. Pender, and M. Welch. 2016. *Education Pays 2016: The Benefits of Higher Education for Individuals and Society*. College Board. https://files.eric.ed.gov/fulltext/ED572548.pdf.

Ma, J., M. Pender, and M. Welch. 2019. *Education Pays 2019: The Benefits of Higher Education for Individuals and Society*. College Board. https://research.collegeboard.org/media/pdf/education-pays-2019-full-report.pdf.

McFarlin, I., P. Martorell, and B. McCall. 2017. *Do Public Subsidies Improve College Attainment and Labor Market Outcomes? Evidence from Community College Taxing District Expansions*. Working Paper. https://drive.google.com/file/d/1kRioM16sZe5fuGUdGCcb9REqZZdCrRCq/view.

Melguizo, T., K. Witham, K. Fong, and E. Chi. 2017. "Understanding the Relationship between Equity and Efficiency: Towards a Concept of Funding Adequacy for Community Colleges." *Journal of Education Finance* 43(2): 195–216. http://www.jstor.org/stable/45093659.

MI School Data. n.d. *Community College Data.* Center for Educational Performance and Information. Michigan Department of Education. Michigan Data Hub. Michigan.gov. https://www.mischooldata.org/community-college-data/.

Miller, C., and M. J. Weiss. 2022. "Increasing Community College Graduation Rates: A Synthesis of Findings on the ASAP Model from Six Colleges across Two States."

*Educational Evaluation and Policy Analysis* 44(2): 210–33. https://doi.org/10.3102/01623737211036726.

Mitchell, M., M. Leachman, and M. Saenz. 2019. *State Higher Education Funding Cuts Have Pushed Costs to Students, Worsened Inequality*. Center on Budget and Policy Priorities, October 24. https://www.cbpp.org/sites/default/files/atoms/files/10-24-19sfp.pdf.

Mountjoy, Jack. 2022. "Community Colleges and Upward Mobility." *American Economic Review* 112(8): 2580–2630. http://doi.org/10.1257/aer.20181756.

Mullin, C. M., and D. S. Honeyman. 2008. "The Funding of Community Colleges: Formulas & Governance." *Community College Journal of Research and Practice* 32(7): 512–24, https://doi.org/10.1080/10668920701382518.

National Center for Education Statistics. 2023a. Postsecondary Institution Expenses. *Condition of Education*. US Department of Education, Institute of Education Sciences. Retrieved June 13, 2024, from https://nces.ed.gov/programs/coe/indicator/cue.

National Center for Education Statistics. 2023b. Price of Attending an Undergraduate Institution. *Condition of Education*. US Department of Education, Institute of Education Sciences. Retrieved August 4, 2023, from https://nces.ed.gov/programs/coe/indicator/cua.

National Student Clearinghouse Research Center. 2024. *Current Term Enrollment Estimates: Fall 2023, exp. ed.* National Student Clearinghouse Research Center. https://nscresearchcenter.org/current-term-enrollment-estimates/.

Odden, A. 2000. "The New School Finance: Providing Adequacy and Improving Equity." *Journal of Education Finance* 25(4): 467–87. http://www.jstor.org/stable/40691077.

Odden, A., L. Picus, and M. Goetz. 2010. "A 50-State Strategy to Achieve School Finance Adequacy." *Educational Policy* 24(4): 628–54. doi: 10.1177/0895904809335107.

Ohio Board of Regents. 2020. Ohio Higher Education SSI Funding Formula. https://highered.ohio.gov/data-reports/hei-system/hei-data-submission/hei-ssi-info.

Ohio Department of Higher Education. 2024. *Enrollment.* Ohio Department of Higher Education. https://highered.ohio.gov/data-reports/key-topic-areas/dr-enrollment.

Oreopoulos, P., and K. Salvanes. 2011. "Priceless: The Nonpecuniary Benefits of Schooling." *Journal of Economic Perspectives* 25(1): 159–84. https://pubs.aeaweb.org/doi/pdfplus/10.1257/jep.25.1.159.

Ortagus, J. C., R. Kelchen, K. Rosinger, and N. Voorhees. 2020. "Performance-Based Funding in American Higher Education: A Systematic Synthesis of the Intended and Unintended Consequences." *Educational Evaluation and Policy Analysis* 42(4): 520–50. https://doi.org/10.3102/0162373720953128.

Ortagus, J., D. Baker, K. Rosinger, R. Kelchen, O. Morales, and M. Lingo. 2022. *The Revenue Implications of Community Colleges' Reliance on Local Funding.* InformEd States Higher Education Policy Initiative, August. https://static1.squarespace.com/static/5d9f9fae6a122515ee074363/t/639a4d24d478053d45f601f9/1671056677780/ISPaper_RevImplicationsofCCCollegesRelianceLocalFunding.pdf.

Ortagus, J., R. Kelchen, K. Rosinger, G. Chu, and M. Lingo. 2021a. *The Unequal Impacts of Performance-Based Funding on Institutional Resources in Higher Education.* InformEd States Higher Education Policy Initiative, November. https://static1.squarespace.com/static/5d9f9fae6a122515ee074363/t/619e68d8ce6b7b31807b116a/1637771480975/InformEdStates_Brief_PBFandInstitutionalResources.pdf.

Ortagus, J., K. Rosinger, R. Kelchen, N. Voorhees, and G. Chu. 2021b. *A National*

*Analysis of the Impact of Performance-Based Funding on Completion Outcomes among Underserved Students.* InformEd States Higher Education Policy Initiative.

Quittmeyer, R., and M. Veach. 2023. Outcomes Based Funding Formula Update. Legislative Brief. Tennessee Comptroller of the Treasury, September. https://comptroller.tn.gov/content/dam/cot/orea/advanced-search/2023/OBF2023Update.pdf.

Reuben, J. A., and L. Perkins. 2007. "Introduction: Commemorating the Sixtieth Anniversary of the President's Commission report, Higher Education for Democracy." *History of Education Quarterly* 47(3): 265–76. https://doi.org/10.1111/j.1748-5959.2007.00100.x.

Romano, R., and J. Palmer. 2023. "Funding Adequacy and the Community College." *New Directions for Community Colleges* 2023(203): 165–72. https://doi-org.ezp-prod1.hul.harvard.edu/10.1002/cc.20595.

Scrivener, S., M. Weiss, A. Ratledge, T. Rudd, C. Sommo, and H. Fresques. 2015. *Doubling Graduation Rates: Three-Year Effects of CUNY's Accelerated Study in Associate Programs (ASAP) for Developmental Education Students.* MDRC. February. https://www.mdrc.org/sites/default/files/doubling_graduation_rates_fr.pdf.

Shaw, K., L. Asher, and S. Murphy. 2023. *Mapping Community College Finance Systems to Develop Equitable and Effective Finance Policy.* HCM Strategists, March. https://ccrc.tc.columbia.edu/media/k2/attachments/mapping-community-college-finance-systems-develop-equitable-effective-policy.pdf.

Soler, M. C. 2019. *Updating the National Landscape: State Adoption of Community College Baccalaureate Degrees.* New Baccalaureate Series, Data Note 3, November 18. University of Washington, Community College Research Initiatives. https://www.washington.edu/ccri/2019/11/18/datanote3-ccb/.

Stanton-Salazar, R. 1997. "A Social Capital Framework for Understanding the Socialization of Racial Minority Children and Youths." *Harvard Educational Review* 67(1): 1–41. https://doi.org/10.17763/haer.67.1.140676g74018u73k.

State University of New York. 2024. *SUNY Fast Facts.* State University of New York. https://www.suny.edu/about/fast-facts/.

Tandberg, D., and N. Hillman. 2014. "State Higher Education Performance Funding: Data, Outcomes, and Policy Implications." *Journal of Education Finance* 39(3): 222–43.

Tennessee Higher Education Commission. 2021. *Tennessee Higher Education Fact Book 2020–2021.* Tennessee Higher Education. Tennessee Student Assistance Corporation. https://www.tn.gov/content/dam/tn/thec/bureau/research/other-research/factbook/Fact%20Book%202020-2021_Full%20Draft_Suppressed.pdf.

Texas Higher Education Coordinating Board. 2024. *Community College Formula Funding Model—Fiscal Year 2025.* Texas Higher Education Coordinating Board. https://reportcenter.highered.texas.gov/reports/fiscal/community-college-formula-funding-model-fiscal-year-2025/.

Thelin, J. R. 2004. *A History of American Higher Education.* Johns Hopkins University Press.

Tollefson, T. A. 2009. "Community College Governance, Funding, and Accountability: A Century of Issues and Trends." *Community College Journal of Research and Practice* 33(3–4): 386–402. https://doi.org/10.1080/10668920802580481.

US Bureau of Labor Statistics. 2023. *Earnings and Unemployment Rates by Educational Attainment, 2022.* https://www.bls.gov/emp/chart-unemployment-earnings-education.htm

US Government Accountability Office. 2016. *Tiered Evidence Grants.* GAO-16–818. September 21. https://www.gao.gov/products/gao-16-818.

Velasco, T., J. Fink, D. Jenkins, and M. Bedoya. 2024. *Tracking Transfer: Community College Effectiveness in Broadening Bachelor's Degree Attainment.* Community College Research Center. https://ccrc.tc.columbia.edu/media/k2/attachments/tracking-transfer-community-college-effectiveness.pdf.

Vigdor, J. 2024. "The Ebbing Tide: How Will Higher Education Adapt to Demographic Change?" Presented at the 2024 NBER Financing Higher Education conference. https://conference.nber.org/conf_papers/f191185.pdf.

Ward, J. D., E. D. Pisacreta, B. Weintraut, and M. Kurzweil. 2020. "An Overview of State Higher Education Funding Approaches: Lessons and Recommendations." Ithaka S+R. December 10. https://doi.org/10.18665/sr.314511.

Webber, D. A. 2017. "State Divestment and Tuition at Public Institutions." *Economics of Education Review* 60: 1–4. https://doi.org/10.1016/j.econedurev.2017.07.007.

Wood, S. H. 1987. *The People's Legacy: A History of Joliet Junior College 1901–1984.* Joliet Junior College Foundation. https://archive.org/stream/peopleslegacy his00susa/peopleslegacyhis00susa_djvu.txt.

Wood, J. L., and F. Harris. 2022. "Differences in Self-Reported GPA for Students Experiencing Insecurities." *Community College Journal of Research and Practice* 46(4): 288–91. https://doi.org/10.1080/10668926.2020.1835746.

Workgroup on CTE Cost Analysis. 2023. *Incremental Costs in Career and Technical Education.* American Institutes for Research, Career and Technical Education Research Network.

Zielak, P. 2022. State of Michigan House Fiscal Agency. Fiscal Brief, November 15. https://www.house.mi.gov/hfa/PDF/Alpha/Fiscal_Brief_CC_Performance%20Funding_Formula_FY23_Nov15.pdf.

8

# Distance to Opportunity
## Higher Education Deserts and College Enrollment Choices

Riley Acton, Kalena E. Cortes, and Camila Morales

## 8.1 Introduction

In the United States, the economic returns to attending college and completing a postsecondary degree are substantial and tend to increase over one's lifetime (Deming 2023). For students from low-income and minority backgrounds, in particular, colleges are catalysts of economic mobility that provide substantial value-added in earnings post-graduation (Chetty et al. 2020). Empirical evidence indicates that attending college, whether an elite institution or a public four-year university, boosts earnings for low-income students by 8 to 20 percent (Dale and Krueger 2002, 2014; Smith et al. 2020; Zimmerman 2014). On average, returns to college also tend to be positive

Riley Acton is the Frank H. Jellinek Jr. Endowed Assistant Professor in the Department of Economics at Miami University.

Kalena E. Cortes holds the Verlin and Howard Kruse '52 Founders Professorship at Texas A&M University's Bush School of Government and Public Service, and is a research associate of the National Bureau of Economic Research.

Camila Morales is an assistant professor of economics at the University of Texas at Dallas.

We thank Rachel Baker, Zachary Bleemer, John Campbell, Celeste Carruthers, Joshua Goodman, Scott Imberman, Kaye Husbands Fealing, Michael Lovenheim, James Poterba, Lori Taylor, and seminar and conference participants at Texas A&M University, University of Pennsylvania, the Association for Education Finance and Policy (AEFP) 2024 Annual Conference, and the NBER's Financing Higher Education Spring 2024 conference for their helpful comments and suggestions. We are especially grateful to Lois Miller for providing data capturing the driving time between each Texas high school and college campuses. Institutional support was provided by Miami University, University of Texas at Dallas, Texas A&M University, and Stanford University. This research uses data from the UT Dallas Education Research Center (ERC). The conclusions discussed in this paper do not reflect the opinions or official positions of the ERC, Texas Education Agency, the Texas Higher Education Coordinating Board, or the State of Texas. For acknowledgments, sources of research support, and disclosure of the authors' material financial relationships, if any, please see https://www.nber.org/books-and-chapters/financing-institutions-higher-education/distance-opportunity-higher-education-deserts-and-college-enrollment-choices.

and large for minority students, though there is evidence of substantial heterogeneity in earnings premia across college quality and majors (Andrews et al. 2016).

Despite significant returns, meaningful disparities in college enrollment and completion persist across socioeconomic and racial groups (Cahalan et al. 2021; Reber and Smith 2023). For instance, as of 2019, 78 percent of 18- to 24-year-olds from high-income households were enrolled in college, while only 48 percent of those from low-income households were. Similarly, in the same year, 62 percent of White and 84 percent of Asian young adults were enrolled in college, while only 57 percent of Black and Hispanic 18- to 24-year-olds were (Cahalan et al. 2021). Furthermore, when they do enroll in college, low-income and underrepresented minority (URM) students are disproportionately more likely to enroll in open-access, public, two-year institutions (i.e., community colleges), as opposed to more selective, four-year institutions. These disparities in college enrollment and institutional choice result in large, persistent gaps in bachelor's degree completion rates across racial groups. As of 2022, 45 percent of White young adults aged 25 to 29 held a bachelor's degree, compared to just 28 percent of Black and 25 percent of Hispanic young adults (Reber and Smith 2023).

Consequently, higher education scholars have explored the myriad of determinants that contribute to the persistent gap in college-going and attainment among low-income and URM students compared to their higher-income and non-URM peers. A large body of literature considers *demand-side* determinants, such as credit constraints, lower levels of academic preparedness, and informational barriers (for comprehensive literature reviews, see, for example, Dynarski, Nurshatayeva, et al. 2022; Dynarski, Page, et al. 2022). A parallel line of research has also investigated *supply-side* determinants, such as institutional capacity constraints, admissions policies, and public-sector funding (see, for example, Bound and Turner 2007; Fu 2014; Bulman and Cunha 2021; Deming and Walters 2017; Black, Cortes, and Lincove 2015, 2016; Cortes and Lincove 2016, 2019). Building on this prior body of work, our study integrates the role of both supply- and demand-side determinants through the lens of college proximity by investigating the extent to which racial and socioeconomic disparities in college-going can be explained by differences in students' *geographic access* to colleges, as well as differences in students' *sensitivity to distance*.

It is well documented that colleges and universities in the United States are unevenly distributed across space (Hillman 2016; Hillman and Weichman 2016), leaving many Americans without local access to higher education. Approximately 3.8 million Americans live in a commuting zone with *no* colleges, while an additional 11.2 million live in a commuting zone with only one college option. The statistics are even starker when considering access to public colleges and universities, which most students attend: 16.5 million (5 percent) Americans across 41 states live in a commuting zone without a public, two-year college (i.e., a community college) and 35.3 million (11 percent) across 45 states live in a commuting zone without a public, four-year college.[1] Moreover, a large body of literature spanning different contexts and cohorts consistently shows that geographic distance affects whether and where students apply to and attend college (Card 1995; Long 2004; Alm and Winters 2009; Turley 2009; Doyle and Skinner 2016; Skinner 2019; Cortes and Lincove 2019; Black et al. 2020; Fu et al. 2022; Morales and Cortes 2022), particularly for students considering attending community colleges (Rouse 1995; Mountjoy 2022).[2]

However, existing work has largely not considered how these relationships vary across racial and socioeconomic groups, nor how changes in the spatial distribution of colleges may affect racial and socioeconomic gaps in postsecondary enrollment and attainment; closing those gaps is a stated priority for state policymakers (Harnisch and Laderman 2023). State policymakers' desire to increase college enrollment and attainment for low-income and URM students is also evident in the structure of various policies, including those governing higher education financing, particularly in the two-year sector. As of 2020, 30 states have implemented an outcomes-based funding scheme to distribute funds to community colleges, by which institutions are rewarded for making progress toward student success such as persistence, transfers to four-year institutions, and degree attainment (Li 2021). Considering that minority and low-income students are more likely to interact with the two-year sector, improving outcomes for community college students is likely to have a disproportionate impact on these students and the possibility of addressing equity gaps. Consequently, our study informs the ongoing policy discussions on effective funding models for community colleges as the geographic diffusion of two-year institutions to their nearest four-year universities will moderate how successful outcomes-based funding mechanisms are, and how they may differentially impact students of various racial and ethnic backgrounds.

We leverage rich, student-level, administrative data from Texas to descriptively (a) document disparities in geographic access to public postsecondary institutions, including two-year community colleges and four-year universities,[3] by race and socioeconomic status; (b) estimate how access to

1. Authors' calculations from 2019 Integrated Postsecondary Education Data System (IPEDS) college location data and US Census Bureau population estimates. In Texas, the setting for this paper, 5.3 percent of the population lives in a commuting zone without a public two-year college and 7.7 percent lives in a commuting zone without a public four-year college.

2. Students may be particularly sensitive to distance in the community college setting because community colleges in 38 states offer lower tuition rates to students who live in their local taxing areas or "districts." Denning (2017) and Acton (2021) show that living in a taxing district increases community college enrollment, in Texas and Michigan, respectively, even after holding distance to a community college campus constant.

3. Throughout the text, we use the phrases *community colleges* or *two-year community colleges* or *two-year colleges* to refer to Texas's public community and technical colleges. We use the phrases *four-year colleges* or *four-year universities* or *universities* to refer to the state's public

nearby public postsecondary institutions relates to students' college enrollment choices across racial and socioeconomic groups; and lastly, (c) simulate how changes in geographic access to these postsecondary institutions or sensitivity to distance would affect the number and the characteristics of students enrolling in two-year and four-year colleges in Texas. Texas is an ideal state in which to conduct this analysis because it is large, racially and socioeconomically diverse, and has the nation's largest, and one of the most racially diverse, rural populations (US Census Bureau 2022), many of whom live far distances from colleges and universities. Moreover, the state maintains a robust longitudinal data system where we can link students' K–12 academic records with their postsecondary education outcomes, including enrollment, course-taking behavior, transfer, and degree completion. Although our results should not be interpreted as causal, this rich data set allows us to account for some confounding factors through student- and school-level controls.

We first document that while there are over 200 public two-year colleges and university campuses in Texas, geographic access to these institutions differs dramatically across the state. Students living in the "Texas Triangle" region surrounding Dallas, Houston, and Austin/San Antonio have access to many more nearby *local* postsecondary institutions than students in the south and west areas of the state. Given the demographic differences between these areas, these disparities in local postsecondary access also appear along racial lines: White and Hispanic students tend to face more limited local college choice sets than their Black and Asian peers, in part because they tend to live in more rural areas, where local college access is most limited.

Next, we show that students are sensitive to how far they must travel to reach a college or university campus. Overall, students are less likely to attend two-year colleges—and less likely to attend any public colleges (two-year or four-year) overall—when they live farther from a two-year college. They are also less likely to attend a four-year college when they live farther from one, but in general, distance to a four-year college does not affect whether a student attends any public college overall. However, these effects are quite different across racial groups and socioeconomic status. Conditional on a student's distance to the nearest four-year institution, White and non-disadvantaged students respond to living far from a two-year college primarily by enrolling in four-year colleges, whereas Black and Hispanic, and economically disadvantaged students primarily respond by not enrolling in any type of college. As a result, when White, non-disadvantaged students live in a "community college desert"—30 miles or more from the

universities, as defined by the THECB: see data on public and independent institutions at http://www.txhighereddata.org/Interactive/Institutions.cfm. All of Texas's public four-year institutions have *university* in their names, though they differ substantially in their research and graduate degree production (see Acton 2022 for more information on the distinction between colleges and universities.)

nearest public two-year college—they are no less likely to enroll in a four-year college than comparable peers who do not live in a desert. But when Black, Hispanic, and disadvantaged students do, they are 6–12 percentage points less likely to attend a four-year college in Texas.

Finally, we conduct a series of decomposition and simulation exercises to inform public policy efforts to increase college enrollment and completion, especially among underrepresented groups. In general, results from the decomposition analyses indicate that differences in students' sensitivity to distance, rather than differences in distance to colleges, is a larger contributor to observed four-year college enrollment gaps across groups. Importantly, differences in *how students respond* to distance to two-year colleges contribute to nearly 12 percent of the four-year college enrollment gap between URM and non-URM students. We further show that the closure of campuses in predominantly Hispanic regions of Texas would have a large effect on Hispanic college enrollment rates, both because these students tend to be more sensitive to distance than their White peers, *and* because they tend to have fewer nearby college options available to them than other underrepresented groups, such as Black students. As a corollary, constructing or expanding campuses in Hispanic regions that currently lack them could be an effective way to increase enrollment rates.

Together, our results contribute to the existing literature on geographic access to public postsecondary institutions along three important dimensions. First, we collect location information for *all* campuses of community college systems—as opposed to only the main campuses that are commonly reported in federal databases—to accurately assess students' access to all public local college options. Doing so is important to understand the true college choice sets students face when deciding whether and where to enroll in postsecondary institutions, and to reduce measurement error in measures of geographic accessibility to those institutions.

Second, we estimate the heterogeneous effects of distance to both two-year and four-year colleges on enrollment outcomes across different racial and socioeconomic groups. In doing so, we document important differences in how URM and economically disadvantaged students respond to distance, compared to their White and non-disadvantaged peers. Specifically, we show that local access to two-year colleges tends to increase—or *democratize* (Rouse 1995)—overall postsecondary enrollment for URM and disadvantaged students, whereas it tends to *divert* enrollment from four-year colleges for White and non-disadvantaged students. As a result, we may expect different enrollment responses to the closure or opening of new college campuses, depending on the characteristics of the local student population.

Lastly, we directly provide simulations that can inform potential state and local policy initiatives related to the opening, closing, merging, or conversion of college campuses. These simulations are timely as states seek to address various challenges currently facing higher education. For example, states with declining populations and high school cohort sizes have increasingly considered merging or consolidating public colleges (Gardner 2021; Gretzinger 2024), which may disparately impact geographic access to college across demographic groups. Meanwhile, other states, such as Kentucky (Blake 2024) and the University of California system (Waxmann 2024), are considering opening new colleges or "elevating" community colleges to public four-year college status, which also stand to change students' local college choice sets. Our simulations can provide predictions of how these policy changes will impact college-going behavior, not only overall but also across demographic groups.

## 8.2 Prior Literature on College Proximity and Student Outcomes

Understanding the causes and consequences of schooling decisions has long been a question of interest for many scholars. In 1995, David Card proposed using college proximity as an instrument for completed education to estimate the returns to schooling (Card 1995). He found that growing up in a county with a four-year college increased educational attainment by approximately 0.32 years and earnings by 4.5 percent, implying a return to education of 12–14 percent per year. Since Card's pioneering work, several other authors have used the local availability of colleges as an instrument to estimate the labor market returns to education (Kling 2001; Cameron and Taber 2004; Carneiro and Lee 2009; Carneiro et al. 2011; Doyle and Skinner 2016), or to explore the impact of education on other long-run outcomes, such as health (Currie and Moretti 2003, and, more recently, Fletcher and Noghanibehambari 2024 and Cowan and Tefft 2023). Researchers interested in understanding community college enrollment choices, specifically, have used distance to both two-year and four-year colleges as instruments to study the effects of beginning one's postsecondary career at a community college. Rouse (1995) posited that enrollment at community colleges may increase or decrease educational attainment, as they can "democratize" opportunity by providing educational access to students who otherwise would not have enrolled in postsecondary education, but may also "divert" students away from attending four-year colleges, potentially reducing their years of completed education. She finds that students who are diverted from four-year colleges to community colleges complete fewer years of schooling, but overall, community colleges increase educational attainment. Subsequent research (e.g., Long and Kurlaender 2009; Mountjoy 2022) supports this democratization vs. diversion framework, which we also adopt in this paper to understand how proximity to two-year and four-year public colleges in Texas impacts students from different racial groups and of different socioeconomic status (SES).

We focus on distance because a large body of work across a variety of contexts (see, for example, Alm and Winters 2009; Turley 2009; Hirschl and Smith 2020) indicates that distance plays a large role in determining where students will apply to and enroll in college, with some evidence indicating that lower-income students value attending a college close to home more than their high-income peers (Fu et al. 2022).[4] In addition, research exploiting college openings or expansions finds that increased local access to colleges generally increases college-going, educational attainment, and improves longer-run outcomes. For example, Lapid (2018) finds that the construction of new public universities in California increased four-year college attendance for students from local high schools, with larger effects for URM students. In a historical setting, Connolly (2023) finds that the massive expansion of US two-year public colleges between 1920 and 1980 increased educational attainment for children in nearby towns and improved long-run health outcomes.[5]

Most closely related to our work, Miller (2023) finds that the openings of new branch campuses of community colleges in Texas increased community college enrollment among local high school graduates but reduced enrollment in four-year colleges, generating little overall increase in educational attainment. Our research differs from Miller's in that she studies openings that, on average, changed the driving time to a local community college by approximately 10 minutes, whereas we study the relationship between distance and college-going across all students, including those who live very far from any college campus. In doing so, we contribute to an emerging literature on higher education deserts (Hillman 2016; Klasik et al. 2018) and provide some of the first evidence on how living in a higher education desert affects college enrollment choices, particularly across race and SES.

## 8.3 Data Sources and Overview of Texas Higher Education Landscape

### 8.3.1 Administrative Records from Texas K-12 and Higher Education Sectors

Our analysis leverages longitudinal, student-level records from the Texas Education Agency (TEA) and the Texas Higher Education Coordinating Board (THECB), which we access through the Education Research Center at the University of Texas at Dallas. The TEA records on K–12 school enrollment and high school graduation allow access to student demographic characteristics (e.g., sex, race and ethnicity, immigrant status, economic disadvantage status) and academic background information (e.g., special education and Limited English Proficiency status, and enrollment in gifted

4. There is some evidence that students have become less sensitive to distance over time (Hoxby 1997; Long 2004; Skinner 2019), but it remains an important determinant of college choices.

5. Frenette (2009) and Nimier-David (2023) similarly study the expansion of college campuses in Canada and France, respectively.

and career and technical education programs), as well as standardized test scores in math and reading at the end of eighth grade.[6] We link these data with THECB records that contain information on student enrollment in all of Texas's public two-year and four-year postsecondary institutions. Throughout our analysis, we define a student as enrolling in a public two-year or four-year institution if they do so within 12 months of their high school graduation date.

Our analytic sample consists of five high school graduation cohorts (2013–2017) whom we observe in the higher education enrollment records from 2014–2018.[7] Panel A of table 8.1 provides summary statistics on these students, measured in their final year of high school. Our sample is diverse across race and socioeconomic status: 47 percent of students are classified as economically disadvantaged, meaning they are eligible for free and/or reduced-price lunch or other public assistance programs. Forty-eight percent are Hispanic, 33 percent are White, 13 percent are Black, and 4.3 percent are Asian. Black and Hispanic students are more likely to be economically disadvantaged, while Hispanic and Asian students are more likely to be immigrants and identified as Limited English Proficiency. On average, White and Asian students have higher eighth grade test scores than Black and Hispanic students, and non-disadvantaged students have higher test scores than economically disadvantaged students.

Panel B of table 8.1 provides college enrollment rates for our analysis sample, both overall and by student subgroup. Overall, 53.2 percent of students enroll in a Texas public postsecondary institution within one year of high school graduation, with 39.4 percent of students enrolling in public two-year colleges and 21.4 percent of students enrolling in public four-year universities.[8] Mirroring national data, Black, Hispanic, and economically disadvantaged students in Texas enroll in college at lower rates than their White, Asian, and non-disadvantaged peers. These disparities in enrollment are particularly stark in the four-year sector, where only 21.8 percent of Black and 16.9 percent of Hispanic students enroll within one year of high school graduation, compared to 25.2 percent of White and 40.6 percent of Asian students. Similarly, only 15.6 percent of economically disadvantaged students enroll in a four-year college within one year of high school graduation, whereas 26.6 percent of non-disadvantaged students do.

6. We do not observe eighth grade test scores for approximately 11 percent of students. For these students, we impute their test scores to be the mean of their high school and graduation cohort and include a binary variable indicating whether we have imputed their math and/or reading test scores in our regression specifications.

7. Enrollment in a postsecondary institution is captured during the first year following high school graduation. Therefore, dual enrollment is not accounted for in our analysis.

8. Students who enroll in both a two-year and four-year college within one year of high school graduation (e.g., who transfer from a two-year college to a four-year university, or vice versa, after one semester) are counted in both enrollment rates. Thus, the overall college enrollment rate is less than the summation of the two-year and four-year enrollment rates.

**Table 8.1** **Summary statistics by student and high school characteristics**

| | All (1) | White (2) | Black (3) | Hispanic (4) | Asian (5) | Econ. Dis. (6) | Not Econ. Dis. (7) | Urban (8) | Suburban (9) | Town/Rural (10) |
|---|---|---|---|---|---|---|---|---|---|---|
| *Panel A: Student Characteristics* | | | | | | | | | | |
| Economic Disadvantage | 0.473 | 0.187 | 0.595 | 0.661 | 0.310 | 1.000 | 0.000 | 0.541 | 0.412 | 0.449 |
| Non-Hispanic White | 0.332 | 1.000 | 0.000 | 0.000 | 0.000 | 0.131 | 0.512 | 0.217 | 0.349 | 0.473 |
| Non-Hispanic Black | 0.127 | 0.000 | 1.000 | 0.000 | 0.000 | 0.159 | 0.097 | 0.139 | 0.147 | 0.085 |
| Hispanic | 0.477 | 0.000 | 0.000 | 1.000 | 0.000 | 0.667 | 0.307 | 0.578 | 0.418 | 0.405 |
| Non-Hispanic Asian | 0.043 | 0.000 | 0.000 | 0.000 | 1.000 | 0.028 | 0.056 | 0.047 | 0.061 | 0.015 |
| Non-Hispanic Other | 0.021 | 0.000 | 0.000 | 0.000 | 0.000 | 0.015 | 0.027 | 0.019 | 0.025 | 0.022 |
| 8th Grade Reading Score | 0.114 | 0.247 | 0.022 | 0.030 | 0.233 | 0.003 | 0.213 | 0.071 | 0.150 | 0.132 |
| 8th Grade Math Score | 0.059 | 0.194 | −0.103 | −0.011 | 0.242 | −0.034 | 0.142 | 0.015 | 0.087 | 0.089 |
| *Panel B: College Enrollment* | | | | | | | | | | |
| Public Two-Year Enrollment | 0.394 | 0.435 | 0.344 | 0.383 | 0.357 | 0.356 | 0.428 | 0.361 | 0.390 | 0.445 |
| Public Four-Year Enrollment | 0.214 | 0.252 | 0.218 | 0.169 | 0.406 | 0.156 | 0.266 | 0.215 | 0.220 | 0.207 |
| Any Public Enrollment | 0.532 | 0.585 | 0.511 | 0.489 | 0.646 | 0.461 | 0.595 | 0.509 | 0.541 | 0.552 |
| *Panel C: High School Characteristics* | | | | | | | | | | |
| Total Enrollment | 1,886 | 1,751 | 1,979 | 1,905 | 2,417 | 1,789 | 1,973 | 2,019 | 2,369 | 1,142 |
| City | 0.392 | 0.256 | 0.431 | 0.475 | 0.435 | 0.448 | 0.341 | 1.000 | 0.000 | 0.000 |
| Suburb | 0.326 | 0.343 | 0.379 | 0.286 | 0.465 | 0.284 | 0.364 | 0.000 | 1.000 | 0.000 |
| Town/Rural | 0.282 | 0.402 | 0.190 | 0.239 | 0.100 | 0.268 | 0.295 | 0.000 | 0.000 | 1.000 |
| Student-Teacher Ratio | 15.63 | 15.22 | 15.87 | 15.74 | 16.72 | 15.46 | 15.77 | 16.34 | 16.42 | 13.72 |
| Charter | 0.039 | 0.021 | 0.047 | 0.050 | 0.029 | 0.055 | 0.025 | 0.076 | 0.019 | 0.011 |
| Magnet | 0.062 | 0.024 | 0.113 | 0.078 | 0.051 | 0.085 | 0.042 | 0.147 | 0.014 | 0.001 |
| Title I | 0.737 | 0.556 | 0.823 | 0.865 | 0.514 | 0.896 | 0.594 | 0.775 | 0.629 | 0.809 |
| Observations | 1,563,036 | 518,984 | 197,844 | 745,834 | 66,787 | 739,326 | 823,710 | 612,667 | 509,801 | 440,568 |

Note: Variables are summarized over our sample of 2013–2017 Texas high school graduates, as measured in their final year of high school. The number of observations shown in columns (2)–(5) do not add up to the number in column (1) because we exclude the "Other race/ethnicity" column (N = 33,587). Please refer to table 8A.1 for the summary statistics related to this category.

### 8.3.2 Locations and Characteristics of Texas High Schools

We merge our student-level sample with characteristics of Texas high schools from the National Center for Education Statistics (NCES) Common Core of Data (CCD). Within the CCD, we observe a high school's latitude and longitude, urbanicity, overall student enrollment, student-teacher ratio, and indicators for whether a school is a charter school, magnet school, and/or eligible for Title I funding. In addition, we construct school-by-cohort averages of the demographic variables described in section 8.3.1. Panel C of table 8.1 provides information on the high schools our students attend. The typical student in our sample attends a high school that enrolls just under 1,900 students, with a student-teacher ratio of 15.6. Thirty-nine percent of students attend a high school in a city, while 33 percent attend one in a suburb, and 28 percent attend one in a town or rural area. On average, urban and suburban schools are larger than rural ones, and suburban students tend to be less disadvantaged and higher-performing in eighth grade than both their urban and rural peers.

### 8.3.3 Locations and Characteristics of Texas College Campuses

To create measures of distance between all Texas high schools and their nearest postsecondary higher education institutions, we obtain information on the locations of all public and private, not-for-profit colleges in both the two-year and four-year sectors from several data sources.[9] First, we collected the latitudes and longitudes of all colleges reported in the Integrated Postsecondary Education System (IPEDS). IPEDS is a comprehensive survey carried out annually by the National Center for Education Statistics under the US Department of Education. This system collects data from all colleges, universities, technical, and vocational institutions involved in federal student financial aid programs. However, institutions often report their data under one primary campus location, rather than disaggregating across campus sites. For example, Houston Community College reports one latitude and longitude to IPEDS, despite having 21 unique campus locations across the Houston metropolitan area. As such, we supplement the IPEDS data with individual campus locations from other sources: (a) the Texas Higher Education Coordinating Board (THECB); (b) the American Association of Community Colleges (AACC) website; and (c) the Texas Association of Community Colleges (TACC) website.

These additional sources along with IPEDS enabled us to obtain the pre-

9. Some community colleges in Texas do award bachelor's degrees, but before a policy change in 2017, fewer than 500 per year were awarded across the state (compared to 80,000 per year or more associate degrees awarded): see Degree Dashboard, THECB DataBridge, June 19, 2024. https://databridge.highered.texas.gov/degree-dashboard/. Thus, for the time frame of our analysis, the primary educational purpose of Texas's community colleges was to offer two-year degrees and certificates and provide transfer pathways to four-year universities.

cise locations of all two- and four-year postsecondary institution campuses in Texas. Figure 8A.1 shows the locations of campuses when we only use IPEDS data (Panel A) versus when we use the supplementary sources (Panel B). In the two-year sector, we obtain the locations of 87 additional community college campuses from our supplementary sources, more than doubling the number of two-year college campuses in the state from 82 to 169.

Leveraging latitude and longitude data spanning the universe of two- and four-year campuses in Texas, we computed the distance in miles from each high school to all college campuses within the state. This enabled us to determine the distance to the nearest institution of higher education by sector. Unsurprisingly, distance in miles corresponds strongly to driving times—an alternative distance measure employed in the literature (e.g., Miller 2023). As shown in figure 8A.2, the correlation between distance and driving times to two- and four-year colleges is remarkably high, with correlation coefficients of 0.96 and 0.98, respectively.

### 8.3.4 Texas Higher Education Landscape

The public postsecondary educational landscape in Texas is notable for several features. First, enrollment in public higher education institutions in the state corresponds to nearly 10 percent of total fall enrollment in degree-granting postsecondary institutions nationwide (National Center for Education Statistics 2023). Second, over the past decade, the state's demographic landscape has changed rapidly, with more racially and ethnically diverse students graduating from high school. In 2004, Texas became a majority-minority state, with the growth rate of Hispanic, Black, and Asian populations overtaking the growth rate of non-Hispanic Whites. Third, the 254 counties in the state are represented by ten state-defined higher education regions: High Plains (region 1), Northwest (region 2), Metroplex (region 3), Upper East (region 4), Southeast (region 5), Gulf Coast (region 6), Central Texas (region 7), South Texas (region 8), West Texas (region 9), and Upper Rio Grande (region 10). Fourth, there are six distinct public university systems: University of Houston, University of North Texas, University of Texas, Texas A&M University, Texas State University, and Texas Tech University. In total, there are 37 public universities in the state, two of which are Historically Black Colleges and Universities (HBCUs) and 25 of which are Hispanic Serving Institutions (HSI). In addition, there are 50 community college districts serving 249 counties in the state, most of which contain multiple campuses[10] and a public, two-year technical college system (Texas State Technical College) with ten campuses throughout the state.

10. Each community college district has a state-defined geographic area, known as a service area, that the college is intended to serve (Baker et al. 2023). These service areas typically constitute a collection of counties, though in some instances they only cover a portion of a given county. As of 2021, there are only five Texas counties that do not belong to any community college service area.

Together, these institutions provide a broad set of postsecondary opportunities for college-bound Texans.

## 8.4 Geographic Access to College and University Campuses

We begin our analysis by documenting the geographic dispersion of college and university campuses in Texas with respect to a variety of county-level demographic characteristics to illustrate the spatial patterns of access to higher education and the demographic groups that are predominantly impacted by disparities in access. We first construct several maps overlaying the location of all public two-year colleges and all public and private, not-for-profit four-year universities in Texas on county demographic characteristics, which we obtained from the US Census. Specifically, we plot the locations of colleges over county-level quartiles of the share of the youth (aged 5–24) population that is White, Black, Hispanic, and Asian, as well as the child poverty rate and the share of households with broadband internet access.

Figure 8.1 presents these maps. Colleges and universities in Texas are highly concentrated around the "Texas Triangle"—the area formed by the state's largest metropolitan areas of Dallas-Fort Worth, Houston, San Antonio, and Austin, which has experienced some of the nation's largest population and employment growth over the past 40 years (Thompson and Hines 2023). Compared to the state as a whole, these areas tend to have larger Black and Asian populations, lower rates of child poverty, and more households with broadband internet, representing a higher degree of urbanization. In contrast, the southern and western areas of the state—which have far fewer postsecondary options—are heavily Hispanic, have higher rates of child poverty, and are more rural, with less broadband internet access.

Figure 8A.3 further illustrates the disparities in local college access across the regions of Texas. First, we plot the average number of institutions within 30 and 60 miles of a high school, by region. The average high school in Texas has approximately 6.9 public two-year colleges and 1.3 public four-year colleges within a 30-mile radius. However, in the Central (Austin/San Antonio), Metroplex (Dallas-Fort Worth), and Gulf Coast (Houston) regions, an average high school has 8.6 public two-year, 1.9 public four-year, and 3 private four-year colleges within a 30-mile radius. Elsewhere in the state, such as West Texas, an average high school has fewer than 1 college *of any type* within a 30-mile radius and fewer than 3 colleges of *any type* within a 60-mile radius. As a result, students in southern and western areas of the state have to travel much farther to reach a postsecondary institution. For example, in the Central, Metroplex, and Gulf Coast regions, the average distance from a high school to the nearest two-year college is 9 miles and the distance to the nearest four-year college is 15.6 miles. In contrast, in West Texas, the

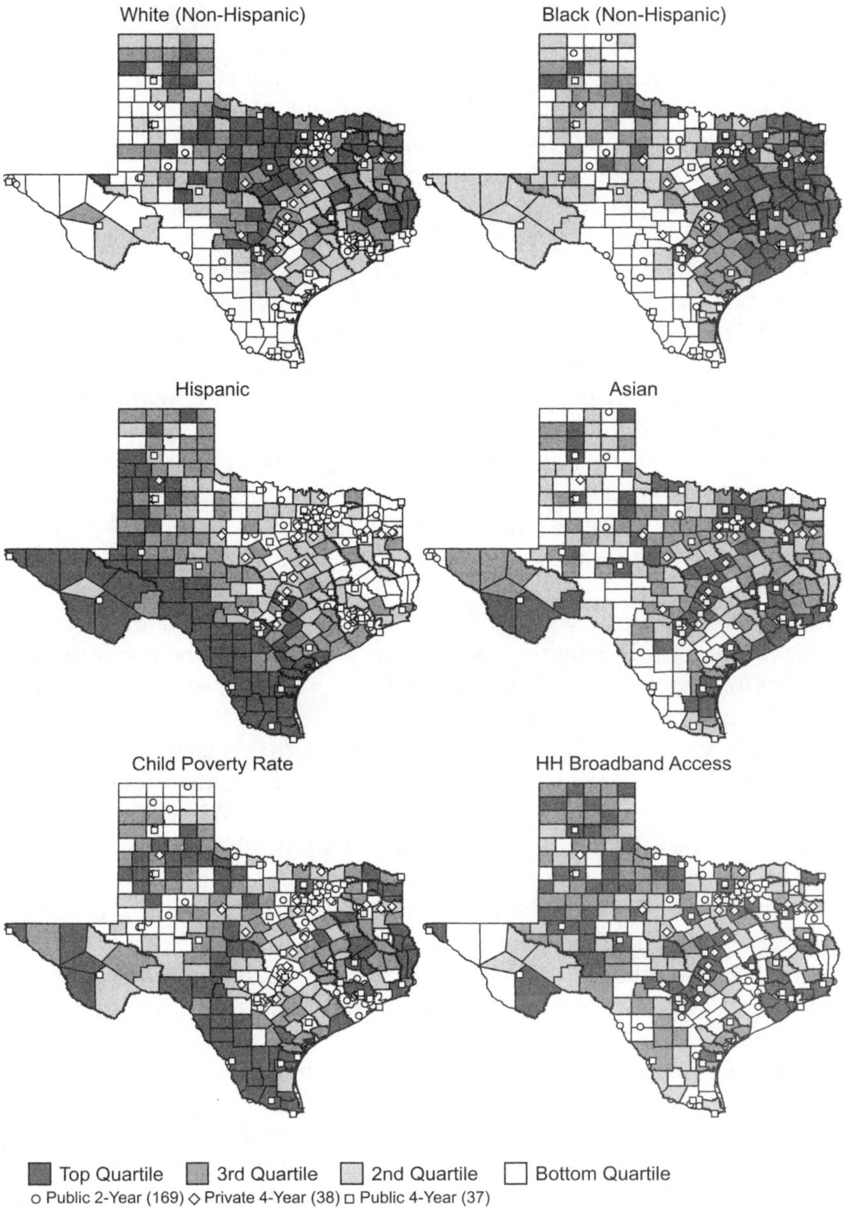


**Fig. 8.1 Spatial distribution of Texas higher education institutions**

Note: This figure plots the location of each public two-year, public four-year, and private four-year postsecondary institution campus in Texas. Each subfigure overlays the locations on various county characteristics, which we measure in quartiles.

average distance to the nearest two-year college is 31 miles and the average distance to the nearest four-year college is 39.3 miles.

Next, table 8.2 presents descriptive statistics summarizing the distance to the nearest college by sector across racial and ethnic groups, economic disadvantage status, and school urbanicity status. The average student in our sample lives 7.3 miles from the nearest public two-year college and 17.3 miles from the nearest public four-year university.[11] These distances are similar for economically disadvantaged and non-disadvantaged students but vary across racial groups. Asian students tend to live closest to postsecondary options (4.6 miles to two-year, 13.6 miles to four-year), followed by Black students (5.5 miles to two-year, 14.7 miles to four-year), and then Hispanic (6.6 miles to two-year, 16.2 miles to four-year) and White students (9.2 miles to two-year, 20.8 to four-year). As a result, fewer White and Hispanic students live within 30 or 60 miles of a public institution—of any type—than Black and Asian students. In addition, Hispanic students, on average, live much farther from the state's flagship institutions (University of Texas, in Austin, and Texas A&M University, in College Station)—176.3 miles, compared to 151 miles for White students, 119 miles for Black students, and 117 miles for Asian students.

Figure 8.2 further shows the differences in students' proximate colleges, by student subgroup, by counting the number of public two-year and four-year colleges located within 30 (Panel A) or 60 (Panel B) miles of a student's high school. Across the two panels, we consistently see that White and Hispanic students have fewer colleges located near them than Black or Asian students. These racial differences in geographical accessibility of colleges and universities can be explained, in part, by the fact that White and Hispanic students are more likely to live in rural areas than Black and Asian students, and these areas tend to be located much farther from colleges than suburban and urban areas. For instance, only 88 percent of students attending a rural high school have a public, two-year college located within 30 miles of their high school, whereas *all* students in suburban and urban areas do. Even more striking, only 61 percent of students attending a rural high school have a public, four-year college located within 30 miles of their high school, whereas 96 percent of urban and 99 percent of suburban students do. These disparities in geographic access to public four-year colleges could explain why a lower share of students from rural high schools attend Texas public four-year colleges (20.7 percent) than students from urban (21.5 percent) and suburban (22 percent) schools, despite having similar tests scores and economic disadvantage status as suburban schools. In the next section, we

11. Throughout the text, we use the phrase lives to refer to how far away a student's high school is from a public postsecondary institution. Data from the National Household Travel Survey indicate that the median high school student in Texas lives 15 minutes away from school. Driving times are comparable for those in urban vs. rural areas (Federal Highway Administration 2017).

**Table 8.2** **Summary statistics by college distance characteristics**

| | All (1) | White (2) | Black (3) | Hispanic (4) | Asian (5) | Econ. Dis. (6) | Not Econ. Dis. (7) | Urban (8) | Suburban (9) | Town/ Rural (10) |
|---|---|---|---|---|---|---|---|---|---|---|
| *Panel A: Distance to Nearest Colleges* | | | | | | | | | | |
| Any Public | 6.608 | 8.474 | 5.007 | 5.944 | 4.246 | 6.329 | 6.858 | 3.213 | 4.513 | 13.75 |
| Public Two-Year | 7.278 | 9.213 | 5.484 | 6.646 | 4.621 | 7.004 | 7.523 | 3.782 | 4.583 | 15.26 |
| Public Four-Year | 17.46 | 20.79 | 14.67 | 16.19 | 13.63 | 16.84 | 18.01 | 10.31 | 14.36 | 30.99 |
| Public Flagship | 151.2 | 133.3 | 118.9 | 176.3 | 117.4 | 165.2 | 138.7 | 168.6 | 131.5 | 149.9 |
| *Panel B: College Presence within 30 Miles* | | | | | | | | | | |
| Any Public | 0.972 | 0.962 | 0.988 | 0.972 | 0.996 | 0.971 | 0.973 | 1.000 | 1.000 | 0.901 |
| Public Two-Year | 0.966 | 0.953 | 0.982 | 0.968 | 0.995 | 0.965 | 0.967 | 1.000 | 1.000 | 0.879 |
| Public Four-Year | 0.868 | 0.802 | 0.915 | 0.892 | 0.969 | 0.870 | 0.865 | 0.956 | 0.987 | 0.607 |
| Public Flagship | 0.067 | 0.086 | 0.053 | 0.056 | 0.080 | 0.051 | 0.082 | 0.081 | 0.044 | 0.075 |
| *Panel C: College Presence within 60 Miles* | | | | | | | | | | |
| Any Public | 0.997 | 0.998 | 1.000 | 0.997 | 1.000 | 0.997 | 0.998 | 1.000 | 1.000 | 0.991 |
| Public Two-Year | 0.996 | 0.997 | 1.000 | 0.995 | 0.999 | 0.996 | 0.997 | 1.000 | 1.000 | 0.987 |
| Public Four-Year | 0.972 | 0.968 | 0.990 | 0.968 | 0.995 | 0.971 | 0.974 | 0.990 | 1.000 | 0.916 |
| Public Flagship | 0.136 | 0.189 | 0.119 | 0.101 | 0.134 | 0.096 | 0.171 | 0.123 | 0.104 | 0.190 |
| Observations | 1,563,036 | 518,984 | 197,844 | 745,834 | 66,787 | 739,326 | 823,710 | 612,667 | 509,801 | 440,568 |

Note: Variables are summarized over our sample of 2013–2017 Texas high school graduates, as measured in their final year of high school. Distances are calculated using the latitude and longitude of a student's high school. The number of observations shown in columns (2)–(5) do not add up to the number in column (1) because we exclude the "Other race/ethnicity" column (N = 33,587). Please refer to table 8A.1 for the summary statistics related to this category.

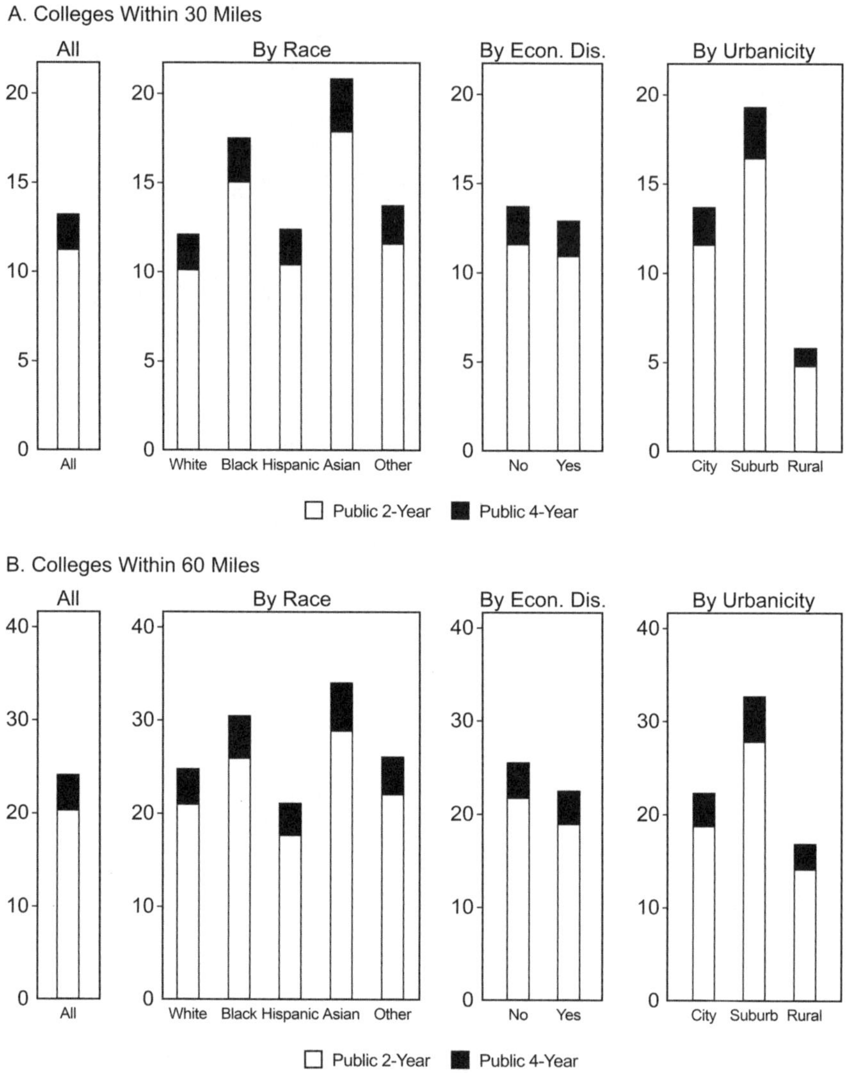


**Fig. 8.2 Number of proximate colleges by demographic characteristics**

Note: These figures summarize the number of public two-year and public four-year college campuses within 30 (Panel A) or 60 (Panel B) miles of a student's high school, averaged over all students and all students of a particular demographic group.

begin to explore the effects of distance to public postsecondary institutions on students' college enrollment choices by race and socioeconomic status.

## 8.5 Access to Postsecondary Institutions and College Enrollment Choices

In this section, we investigate the relationship between the likelihood of enrolling in a Texas public college, generally and by sector (i.e., two-year and four-year colleges), and a student's geographic access to college campuses. We estimate regression models of the following form:

$$(1) \qquad Enroll_{ist} = \alpha + \boldsymbol{Distance}_s\Gamma + \boldsymbol{X}_{it}\Pi + \boldsymbol{Z}_{st}\Phi + \lambda_t + \epsilon_{ist}$$

where $Enroll_{ist}$ is a binary enrollment indicator of interest (e.g., 1 if a student enrolls in a public institution, 0 otherwise) for student $i$, who graduated from high school $s$, in year $t$. Specifically, we consider enrollment in any Texas public institution of higher education, as well as, separately, enrollment in two-year vs. four-year colleges. The vector $\boldsymbol{Distance}_s$ contains measures of the distance between high school $s$ and various college options, such as distance to the nearest two-year and four-year colleges.

While our regressions should *not* be interpreted as the causal effects of distance on postsecondary choices—as distance to college is not randomly assigned across students—we account for some confounding factors that may drive outcome differences across students facing disparities in distance to postsecondary schools by controlling for student- and school-level factors represented in vectors $\boldsymbol{X}_{it}$ and $\boldsymbol{Z}_{st}$, respectively. Some of the individual-level characteristics include sex, race and ethnicity, economic disadvantage, Limited English Proficiency status, and academic performance in reading and math captured by students' end-of-grade assessments in eighth grade. Similarly, some of the school-level factors correspond to school-wide characteristics of the student population (race/ethnicity and economic disadvantage), as well as measures of resources, such as the student-teacher ratio and a school's eligibility for Title I funding. In supplemental specifications, we further control for estimated neighborhood poverty levels surrounding high school campuses and demographic characteristics of school districts (e.g., average household income, percentage of adults with a college degree, etc.) obtained from the American Community Survey (ACS). Finally, $\lambda_t$ are year fixed effects that account for secular trends in the likelihood of college enrollment over time.

We estimate several regressions following the functional form described in equation (1), where we vary the distance measures captured by the vector $\boldsymbol{Distance}_s$. We assess the relationship between the likelihood of college enrollment and the linear distance to the nearest public two-year and four-year colleges, as well as non-linear effects established by binning the distance to the nearest colleges in 5-mile intervals, and the effects of living in a college "desert"—which we define as living more than 30 miles from a public two-year and/or four-year college. Lastly, to further examine the extent to which students' sensitivity to distance varies across demographic groups and socioeconomic status, we also estimate equation (1) separately by students' race/ethnicity and economic disadvantage status.

### 8.5.1 Linear Effects of Distance on College Enrollment Choices

Table 8.3 shows the linear effects of distance to a student's nearest two-year and four-year public institution on the likelihood that they enroll in a Texas public two-year college (Panel A), Texas public four-year university (Panel B), or any Texas public postsecondary institution (Panel C). We iteratively add student demographic controls, student test scores, and school-level control variables across the table columns.

Panel A shows that the farther a student lives from a public two-year college, the *less* likely they are to attend a public two-year college. Meanwhile, the farther they live from a public four-year university, the *more* likely they are to enroll in a public two-year option. These effects persist and are highly statistically significant across specifications, including those that account for additional neighborhood-level and school district demographic characteristics (columns 5–6), indicating that the correlations we observe between distance and enrollment outcomes are largely not driven by differences in observable characteristics between students who live close to versus far away from college campuses. In our preferred specification, shown in column (4), living 10 miles farther from a public two-year college is associated with a 2.4 percentage point reduction in the probability of enrolling in a Texas public two-year college, whereas living 10 miles farther from a public four-year college is associated with a 1.3 percentage point increase in the probability of enrolling in public two-year colleges—or about half the effect of the two-year distance measure.

Panel B shows a similar effect for public four-year college enrollment: the farther a student lives from a public four-year college, the *less* likely they are to enroll in a public four-year college, but the farther they live from a public two-year college, the *more* likely they are to enroll in a public four-year. However, these effects are smaller than those on the two-year college margin, suggesting that distance matters more for two-year college enrollment than four-year college enrollment. In our preferred specification in column (4), we find that an increase in distance to a public four-year college of 10 miles is associated with a 0.5 percentage point reduction in the probability of enrollment in public four-year colleges—about a quarter of the size of the "own-distance" effect for two-year colleges. This effect is also only significant at the 10 percent level. Meanwhile, living 10 miles farther from a public two-year college is associated with a 1.5 percentage point increase in the probability of enrollment in a public four-year college.

Finally, Panel C shows the effects of distance to a student's nearest public two-year and four-year institutions on overall enrollment in the Texas public

**Table 8.3** **Linear effects of distance on enrollment choices**

| | No Controls (1) | + Dem. Char. (2) | + Test Scores (3) | + School Char. (4) | + NCES Poverty (5) | + District ACS (6) |
|---|---|---|---|---|---|---|
| | | | *Panel A: Public Two-Year Enrollment* | | | |
| Distance to Nearest | −0.006 | −0.012*** | −0.012*** | −0.024*** | −0.025*** | −0.026*** |
| Two-Year (10 miles) | (0.004) | (0.004) | (0.004) | (0.004) | (0.004) | (0.003) |
| Distance to Nearest | 0.020*** | 0.018*** | 0.017*** | 0.013*** | 0.012*** | 0.008*** |
| Four-Year (10 miles) | (0.003) | (0.003) | (0.003) | (0.003) | (0.003) | (0.003) |
| | | | *Panel B: Public Four-Year Enrollment* | | | |
| Distance to Nearest | 0.011*** | 0.011*** | 0.011*** | 0.015*** | 0.015*** | 0.016*** |
| Two-Year (10 miles) | (0.003) | (0.003) | (0.003) | (0.002) | (0.002) | (0.002) |
| Distance to Nearest | −0.008*** | −0.008** | −0.008** | −0.005* | −0.005* | −0.003* |
| Four-Year (10 miles) | (0.003) | (0.003) | (0.003) | (0.002) | (0.002) | (0.002) |
| | | | *Panel C: Any Public Enrollment* | | | |
| Distance to Nearest | −0.003 | −0.007** | −0.007** | −0.010*** | −0.011*** | −0.010*** |
| Two-Year (10 miles) | (0.003) | (0.003) | (0.004) | (0.003) | (0.003) | (0.003) |
| Distance to Nearest | 0.007*** | 0.006** | 0.005** | 0.006*** | 0.005*** | 0.004* |
| Four-Year (10 miles) | (0.003) | (0.003) | (0.003) | (0.002) | (0.002) | (0.002) |

Note: All specifications include year fixed effects (2013–2017). Demographic student-level controls: economic disadvantage, race and ethnicity, at-risk for dropout, gifted, immigrant status, Limited English Proficient (LEP) status, sex, special education, Career and Technical Education (CTE) enrollment (all measured in last year of high school). Test score controls: eighth grade reading test score (standardized) and eighth grade math test score (standardized). High school-level controls: total enrollment, % of each race and ethnicity, % economic disadvantage, % at-risk for dropout, % gifted, % immigrant, % LEP, % special education, % CTE enrollment, city/suburb/rural, student/teacher ratio, charter dummy, magnet dummy, and Title I dummy. NCES poverty control: Estimated school neighborhood income-to-poverty ratio. School district ACS controls: % single-mother households, % non-English-speaking, % foreign-born, mean family income, % of households receiving SNAP benefits, % of children living below poverty line, % of adults with at least H.S. diploma, % of adults with at least bachelor's degree, mean travel time to work, % of workers in professional occupations. Columns (1)—(5) include 1,563,036 student observations, column (6) includes 1,556,381 student observations, column (7) contains 1,550,751 student observations, and column (8) contains 1,501,790 student observations. Standard errors shown in parentheses are clustered at the school district level. $*p < 0.10$, $**p < 0.05$, $***p < 0.010$.

higher education system. These effects are a summation of the *own-distance effect* and the *substitution effect* for each distance measure. For example, the public two-year distance effect on overall enrollment is a summation of its effect on public two-year college enrollment and its effect on public four-year college enrollment. Across specifications, we find that living farther from a public two-year college is associated with a reduced likelihood of enrolling in Texas public institutions—meaning, the own-distance effect is larger than the substitution effect into four-year colleges. In contrast, we see little effect of four-year distance on overall Texas public enrollment, suggesting that the own-distance and substitution effects for four-year college distance tend to offset one another. Put differently, we find that attending a high school that is far from public four-year universities affects *where* students attend college but not *whether* they do, whereas attending a high school that is far from a public two-year college affects whether students enroll in college at all.

Table 8.4 then repeats the specifications in column (4) across racial groups and economic disadvantage status. Looking across groups in Panel A, we see broadly similar reductions in public two-year college enrollment as students attend high schools farther away from two-year colleges. The only exception to this pattern is Asian students, who do not significantly differ in their two-year college enrollment across our distance measure. In Panel B, we see that, across groups, students are less likely to attend public four-year colleges when their distance to these colleges increases, whereas they are more likely to attend public four-year colleges as their distance to two-year colleges increases. However, this effect is much larger for White and non-disadvantaged students than for Black, Hispanic, and economically disadvantaged students. In Panel C, we see the net effect of these disparate responses: attending a high school that is far away from public two-year colleges reduces overall college enrollment for all groups, but to a larger extent for Black, Hispanic, and economically disadvantaged students. That is, White and non-disadvantaged students are more likely to respond to living far from public two-year colleges by substituting toward four-year colleges, whereas Black and Hispanic and economically disadvantaged students are more likely to forgo college enrollment altogether.

### 8.5.2 Non-Linear Effects of Distance on College Enrollment Choices

While our previous results suggest that college enrollment decisions are responsive to the distance to a student's nearest public two-year or four-year institution, it is not obvious that we should expect these responses to be linear. For example, if a college that is 5 or 10 miles away can be easily accessed via public transportation, but a college that is 15 miles away cannot be, we may expect a non-linear response between these distances. We consider these potential non-linear responses by re-estimating equation (1) with our distance measures binned in 5-mile intervals.

Figure 8.3 considers the non-linear effects of distance for White, Black, and Hispanic students separately. First, in Panel A, we consider how living

**Table 8.4** **Linear Effects of distance on enrollment choices by race and economic disadvantage status**

| | All (1) | White (2) | Black (3) | Hispanic (4) | Asian (5) | Not Econ. Dis. (6) | Econ. Dis. (7) |
|---|---|---|---|---|---|---|---|
| | | | Panel A: Public Two-Year Enrollment | | | | |
| Distance to Nearest | −0.024*** | −0.028*** | −0.022*** | −0.022*** | −0.008 | −0.025*** | −0.023*** |
| Two-Year (10 miles) | (0.004) | (0.004) | (0.005) | (0.004) | (0.012) | (0.004) | (0.004) |
| Distance to Nearest | 0.013*** | 0.014*** | 0.013*** | 0.012*** | 0.003 | 0.013*** | 0.013*** |
| Four-Year (10 miles) | (0.003) | (0.004) | (0.004) | (0.002) | (0.008) | (0.003) | (0.002) |
| Observations | 1,556,381 | 517,147 | 196,661 | 742,704 | 66,442 | 820,649 | 735,732 |
| | | | *Panel B: Public Four-Year Enrollment* | | | | |
| Distance to Nearest | 0.015*** | 0.025*** | 0.010*** | 0.009*** | 0.014 | 0.020*** | 0.010*** |
| Two-Year (10 miles) | (0.002) | (0.002) | (0.004) | (0.003) | (0.009) | (0.003) | (0.002) |
| Distance to Nearest | −0.005* | −0.005** | −0.003 | −0.004 | −0.008 | −0.004 | −0.005** |
| Four-Year (10 miles) | (0.002) | (0.002) | (0.003) | (0.003) | (0.005) | (0.003) | (0.002) |
| Observations | 1,556,381 | 517,147 | 196,661 | 742,704 | 66,442 | 820,649 | 735,732 |
| | | | *Panel C: Any Public Enrollment* | | | | |
| Distance to Nearest | −0.010*** | −0.008*** | −0.011** | −0.012** | 0.002 | −0.008** | −0.012** |
| Two-Year (10 miles) | (0.003) | (0.003) | (0.005) | (0.005) | (0.011) | (0.003) | (0.005) |
| Distance to Nearest | 0.006*** | 0.007*** | 0.011*** | 0.005*** | −0.004 | 0.005** | 0.007*** |
| Four-Year (10 miles) | (0.002) | (0.003) | (0.003) | (0.002) | (0.006) | (0.003) | (0.002) |
| Observations | 1,556,381 | 517,147 | 196,661 | 742,704 | 66,442 | 820,649 | 735,732 |

Note: All regressions shown in columns (1)–(7) control for year fixed effects (2013–2017), demographic student-level characteristics, eighth grade test scores, and high school level characteristics. See note in table 8.3 for a detailed description of these controls. Standard errors shown in parentheses are clustered at the school district level. *$p < 0.10$, **$p < 0.05$, ***$p < 0.010$.

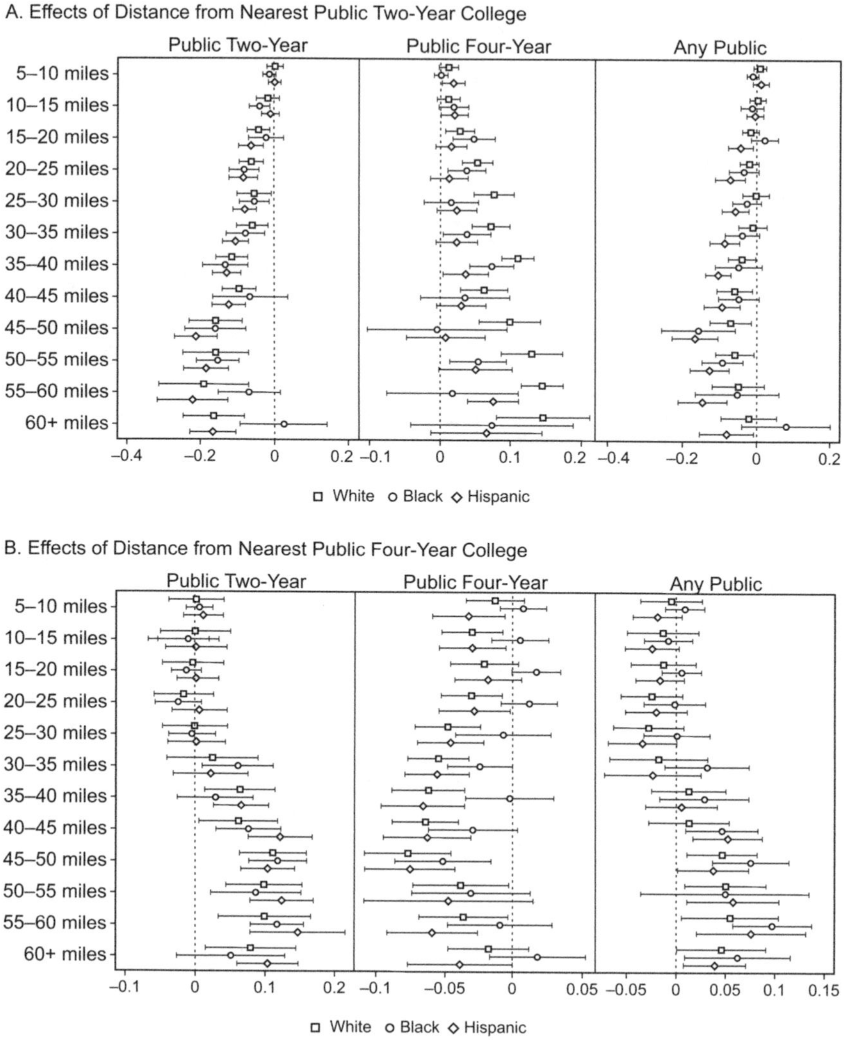


**Fig. 8.3 Non-linear effects of distance on enrollment by race and ethnicity**

Note: These figures plot the estimated coefficients from equation (1), where we measure distance to public two-year and four-year colleges in five-mile intervals. Each regression controls for student demographic characteristics, eighth grade test scores, school-level characteristics, and cohort indicators. Standard errors are clustered at the school district level, and we present 95 percent confidence intervals.

farther from a public two-year college—relative to living within five miles of one—affects the likelihood that a student enrolls in a public two-year college, public four-year college, or any public college.[12] For all three groups,

12. Throughout this analysis, we control for the distance to a student's nearest public four-year college in analogous five-mile bins. Similarly, when we consider the effects of four-year

we see that students are less likely to attend a public two-year college when they live more than 10 miles from the nearest one and that this response increases with distance, particularly at distances of 30 miles or more. We then see that students are more likely to attend four-year colleges when they live more than 10 miles from a public two-year college—but, as we saw in table 8.4, this effect is larger for White students than for non-White students. Combined, these effects produce a larger decrease in any public college enrollment for Black and Hispanic students when they live more than 10 miles from the nearest public two-year college, though the magnitude of the effect increases for all groups as distance increases. In Panel B, we see that White and Hispanic students are more responsive to four-year college distance than Black students. However, for all groups, substitution toward two-year colleges only occurs when students live more than 30 miles from the nearest public four-year college.

Figure 8.4 then considers the non-linear effects of distance for economically disadvantaged and non-disadvantaged students. In Panel A, we see that economically disadvantaged and non-disadvantaged students are both less likely to attend public two-year colleges when they live farther from them, but this effect begins at smaller distances for disadvantaged students. In addition, disadvantaged students are less likely to substitute toward four-year colleges when they live far from two-year colleges, resulting in a larger overall decline in public college enrollment for disadvantaged students when they live farther from two-year colleges. However, in Panel B, we see that disadvantaged and non-disadvantaged students respond similarly to living farther from public four-year colleges.

### 8.5.3 Effects of Living in College Deserts

In both figures 8.3 and 8.4, students appear particularly responsive to living 30 or more miles from a postsecondary institution. We now formally estimate how living this distance away from an institution affects students' enrollment choices by replacing our distance variable in equation (1) with an indicator for living 30 miles or more from a public two-year or four-year college—which we refer to as living in a two-year or four-year college desert, respectively.[13] We then add interaction terms between this indicator and a student's URM and/or economic disadvantage status to assess how students' responses vary across both race and socioeconomic status.[14]

Table 8.5 presents these results for public two-year college deserts. Recall, from table 8.2, that while all urban and suburban students have access to a public two-year college within 30 miles, over 12 percent of rural students do

college distance on students' enrollment outcomes in Panel B, we control for the distance to a student's nearest public two-year college in five-mile bins.

13. In these specifications, we continue to control for the distance to a student's nearest four-year college (or two-year, in table 8.6) in five-mile bins.

14. For the purposes of this analysis, we define URM students as Black, Hispanic, and "other" students. Non-URM students are White and Asian students.

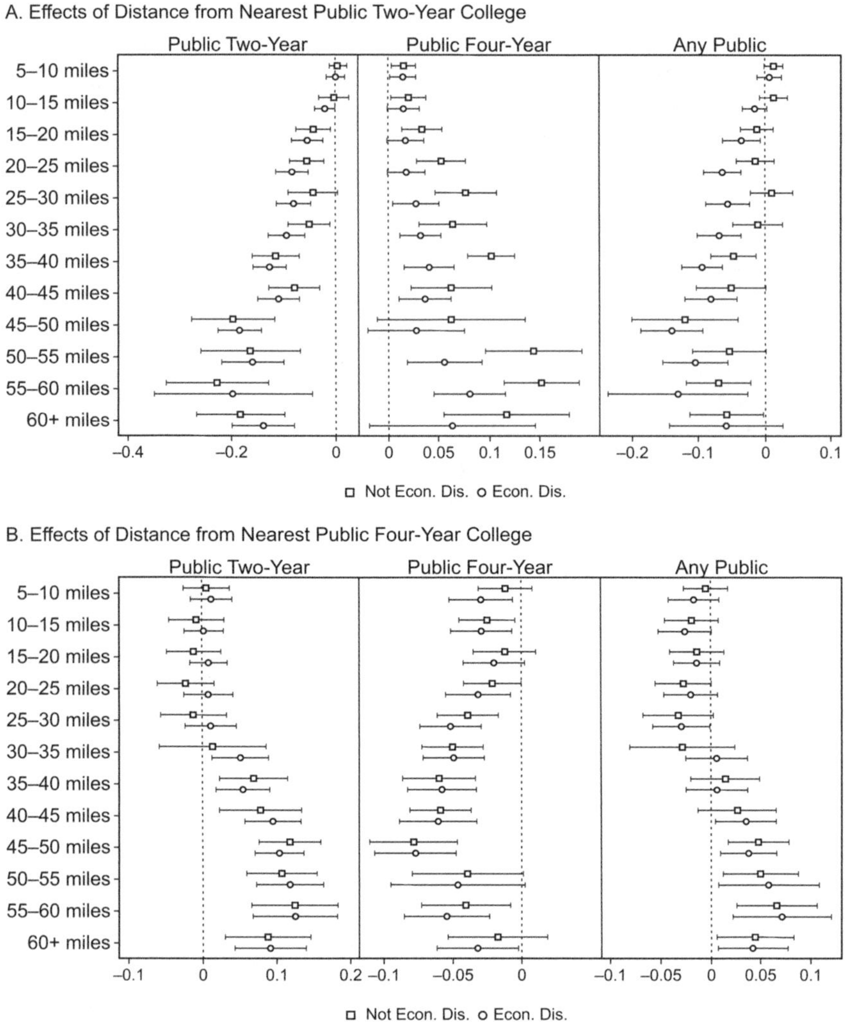


**Fig. 8.4 Non-linear effects of distance on enrollment by economic disadvantage status**

Note: These figures plot the estimated coefficients from equation (1), where we measure distance to public two-year and four-year colleges in five-mile intervals. Each regression controls for student demographic characteristics, eighth grade test scores, school-level characteristics, and cohort indicators. Standard errors are clustered at the school district level, and we present 95 percent confidence intervals.

**Table 8.5** **Effects of living in a community college desert on enrollment choices**

| | (1) | (2) | (3) | (4) |
|---|---|---|---|---|
| *Panel A: Public Two-Year Enrollment* | | | | |
| Community College (CC) Desert | −0.099*** | −0.058*** | −0.056*** | −0.037** |
| | (0.012) | (0.015) | (0.015) | (0.016) |
| CC Desert × URM Status | | −0.079*** | | −0.054*** |
| | | (0.012) | | (0.012) |
| CC Desert × Econ. Dis. Status | | | −0.088*** | −0.069*** |
| | | | (0.011) | (0.011) |
| *Panel B: Public Four-Year Enrollment* | | | | |
| Community College (CC) Desert | 0.044*** | 0.069*** | 0.065*** | 0.078*** |
| | (0.008) | (0.009) | (0.010) | (0.010) |
| CC Desert × URM Status | | −0.048*** | | −0.037*** |
| | | (0.009) | | (0.010) |
| CC Desert × Econ. Dis. Status | | | −0.043*** | −0.030*** |
| | | | (0.008) | (0.008) |
| *Panel C: Any Public Enrollment* | | | | |
| Community College (CC) Desert | −0.061*** | −0.020* | −0.022* | −0.001 |
| | (0.010) | (0.011) | (0.012) | (0.012) |
| CC Desert × URM Status | | −0.079*** | | −0.058*** |
| | | (0.011) | | (0.011) |
| CC Desert × Econ. Dis. Status | | | −0.080*** | −0.060*** |
| | | | (0.010) | (0.010) |

Note: Students are classified as living in a "community college desert" if there is no public two-year college within 30 miles of their high school. Underrepresented Minority (URM) students include all Black, Hispanic, and "Other race/ethnicity" students. All regressions shown in columns (1)–(4) control for year fixed effects (2013–2017), demographic student-level characteristics, eighth grade test scores, and high school-level characteristics. See note in table 8.3 for a detailed description of these controls. In these specifications, we continue to control for the distance to a student's nearest four-year college in five-mile bins. Columns (1)–(4) include 1,556,381 student observations. Standard errors shown in parentheses are clustered at the school district level. *$p < 0.10$, **$p < 0.05$, ***$p < 0.010$.

not. In Panel A, we see that, overall, living farther than 30 miles from a public two-year college is associated with a 9.9 percentage point reduction in the probability of attending one. However, this effect is 5–8 percentage points larger for URM students and 7–9 percentage points larger for economically disadvantaged students. In Panel B, we more clearly see that non-URM and non-disadvantaged students substitute toward four-year colleges at higher rates when they live far from public two-year colleges. Overall, living 30 or more miles from a public two-year college is associated with a 4.4 percentage point increase in the likelihood of attending a public four-year college, but this effect is about 8 percentage points for non-URM, non-disadvantaged students. Finally, in Panel C, we see that for non-URM, non-disadvantaged students, living in a public two-year college desert has a small to negligible

**Table 8.6** **Effects of living in a four-year college desert on enrollment choices**

| | (1) | (2) | (3) | (4) |
|---|---|---|---|---|
| *Panel A: Public Two-Year Enrollment* | | | | |
| Four-Year College Desert | 0.077*** | 0.093*** | 0.108*** | 0.110*** |
| | (0.015) | (0.019) | (0.022) | (0.023) |
| Four-Year Desert × URM Status | | −0.032*** | | −0.007 |
| | | (0.012) | | (0.009) |
| Four-Year Desert × Econ. Dis. Status | | | −0.069*** | −0.066*** |
| | | | (0.016) | (0.014) |
| *Panel B: Public Four-Year Enrollment* | | | | |
| Four-Year College Desert | −0.029*** | −0.017*** | −0.021*** | −0.015** |
| | (0.007) | (0.007) | (0.007) | (0.007) |
| Four-Year Desert × URM Status | | −0.022*** | | −0.018** |
| | | (0.008) | | (0.008) |
| Four-Year Desert × Econ. Dis. Status | | | −0.017*** | −0.011** |
| | | | (0.006) | (0.005) |
| *Panel C: Any Public Enrollment* | | | | |
| Four-Year College Desert | 0.040*** | 0.056*** | 0.062*** | 0.067*** |
| | (0.011) | (0.014) | (0.017) | (0.017) |
| Four-Year Desert × URM Status | | −0.032*** | | −0.015* |
| | | (0.010) | | (0.008) |
| Four-Year Desert × Econ. Dis. Status | | | −0.051*** | −0.045*** |
| | | | (0.013) | (0.012) |

Note: Students are classified as living in a four-year college desert if there is no public four-year college within 30 miles of their high school. Underrepresented Minority (URM) students include all Black, Hispanic, and "Other race/ethnicity" students. All regressions shown in columns (1)–(4) control for year fixed effects (2013–2017), demographic student-level characteristics, eighth grade test scores, and high school-level characteristics. See note in table 8.3 for a detailed description of these controls. In these specifications, we continue to control for the distance to a student's nearest two-year college in five-mile bins. Columns (1)–(4) include 1,556,381 student observations. Standard errors shown in parentheses are clustered at the school district level. $*p < 0.10$, $**p < 0.05$, $***p < 0.010$.

effect on overall college enrollment, but for URM and economically disadvantaged students, it is associated with a decrease in the likelihood of college enrollment by up to 12 percentage points.

Table 8.6 then repeats the specifications from table 8.5 for public four-year college distance. In Panel A, we see that living more than 30 miles from a public four-year college is associated with an increased likelihood of enrolling in public two-year colleges of 7.7 percentage points, though this effect is smaller for economically disadvantaged students. Panel B then shows that, as expected, living more than 30 miles from a public four-year college is associated with a reduced likelihood of attending a public four-year by 2.9 percentage points. On net, we see in Panel C that, conditional on distance to two-year colleges, students who live in a four-year college desert are more likely to enroll in a Texas public college overall (because they are more likely to attend a two-year college), but this effect is smaller for URM and, particularly, economically disadvantaged students.

In summary, our results reveal how both supply-side (i.e., geographic access to colleges) and demand-side determinants (i.e., sensitivity to distance) can contribute to the college enrollment gap for low-income and URM students. Our analysis indicates that (1) students are sensitive to the distance they must travel to reach a college campus; (2) the distance a student must travel to reach a two-year college affects both whether and where a student attends college, whereas the distance a student must travel to reach a four-year college primarily affects where a student will enroll (and to a lesser extent than the two-year distance); and (3) White and non-disadvantaged students respond to living far from two-year colleges by enrolling in four-year colleges, whereas Black and Hispanic and economically disadvantaged students primarily respond by forgoing college enrollment. In the next section, we use these results to conduct simulations of enrollment responses to hypothetical policy changes.

## 8.6 Policy Simulations

In the final section, we engage in a series of policy simulation exercises that enable us to make predictions involving changes in the likelihood of postsecondary enrollment by racial group and economic disadvantage status, as well as changes in the college enrollment gap between groups of students. We conduct these analyses under counterfactual policy scenarios that systematically increase or decrease students' distance to college. We note that these estimates assume our regression results reflect a causal relationship between distance and college-going, which we believe is plausible given the stability of our coefficients when we condition on a rich set of observable characteristics. However, we caution that to the extent to which our results reflect unobserved differences in college-going propensity between students who live far from colleges versus close to colleges, our simulations will generally *overstate* the effect of changes in distances on changes in college enrollment.

### 8.6.1 Oaxaca-Blinder Decomposition

Drawing upon the Oaxaca-Blinder decomposition approach (Blinder 1973; Oaxaca 1973), we begin by assessing the extent to which observed gaps in mean college enrollment rates between non-URM and URM students can be attributed to differences between observed and unobserved factors. Specifically, we use an alternative decomposition approach proposed by Neumark (1988) which uses common coefficients estimated from a pooled regression of non-URM and URM students.[15] We highlight the role of distance to postsecondary institutions as our key observed components, among various other demographic, academic, and school-level controls. Specifically, we estimate the following:

$$(2)\quad (\overline{Enroll}^1 - \overline{Enroll}^0) = (\bar{D}^1 - \bar{D}^0)\hat{\Gamma}^P + (\bar{X}^1 - \bar{X}^0)\hat{\Pi}^P + \bar{D}^1(\hat{\Gamma}^1 - \hat{\Gamma}^P) + \bar{D}^0(\hat{\Gamma}^P - \hat{\Gamma}^0) + \bar{X}^1(\hat{\Pi}^1 - \hat{\Pi}^P) + \bar{X}^0(\hat{\Pi}^P - \hat{\Pi}^0)$$

where $\overline{Enroll}^d$ indicates the average postsecondary enrollment rate for group $d$, which takes on the value of 1 for the group of URM (or economically disadvantaged) students and 0 otherwise. $\bar{D}$ denotes a measure of the average distance to various college options and $\bar{X}$ is a row vector of all remaining observable characteristics, including demographic variables, academic background, and school-level controls. Lastly, $\hat{\Gamma}$ and $\hat{\Pi}$ are the coefficients obtained from regressions of the form described in equation (1) estimated for the subset of students for a given group, $d$, as well as estimates from a pooled regression of students across all subgroups, $p$. Estimates of the first term isolate how much of the enrollment gap is explained by differences in distance to college options between URM and non-URM (or economically disadvantaged and non-disadvantaged) students, while estimates of the third and fourth terms describe the extent to which the enrollment gap can be attributed to differences across students' sensitivity to distance.

We conduct decomposition exercises for three sets of outcomes: enrollment in two-year public colleges, enrollment in four-year public colleges, and enrollment in any public institution in Texas. Moreover, we separately analyze differences by students' race and ethnicity as well as economic disadvantage status. Results from the decomposition analyses are shown in table 8.7.

As reported in column 1 of Panel C, there is a 9.6 percentage point disparity in the college enrollment rates between non-URM and URM students in Texas. This gap is largely attributed to differences in observable characteristics, which contribute to 6.4 percentage points of the observed difference. However, the role of the distance components specifically, both in the explained and unexplained proportions, is notably small compared to other observed characteristics such as demographic factors. Indeed, the decomposition results suggest that if URM students faced the same average distance to four-year institutions as their non-URM peers, the enrollment gap would only narrow by 0.2 percentage points. Conversely, differences in access to two-year colleges widen the overall college enrollment gap, which is consistent with our finding that some URM students, namely Black students,

15. This approach, however, has been shown to systematically underestimate the unexplained portion particularly in instances when there is "high power of the covariates in explaining group membership" (Elder et al. 2010).

**Table 8.7 Oaxaca-Blinder decomposition**

| | | Characteristics | | Coefficients | |
|---|---|---|---|---|---|
| | Difference | Distance to Nearest Two-Year | Distance to Nearest Four-Year | Distance to Nearest Two-Year | Distance to Nearest Four-Year |
| *Panel A: Public Two-Year Enrollment* | | | | | |
| Non-URM v. URM | 0.051*** | −0.006*** | 0.005*** | −0.003 | 0.002 |
| | (0.007) | (0.001) | (0.002) | (0.004) | (0.005) |
| White v. Hispanic | 0.052*** | −0.006*** | 0.006*** | −0.004 | 0.003 |
| | (0.007) | (0.001) | (0.002) | (0.004) | (0.006) |
| White v. Black | 0.092*** | −0.010*** | 0.008*** | −0.003 | 0.002 |
| | (0.008) | (0.002) | (0.003) | (0.003) | (0.005) |
| By Econ. Dis. Status | 0.072*** | −0.001 | 0.001 | −0.001 | −0.001 |
| | (0.007) | (0.001) | (0.001) | (0.003) | (0.004) |
| *Panel B: Public Four-Year Enrollment* | | | | | |
| Non-URM v. URM | 0.089*** | 0.003*** | −0.002* | 0.011*** | −0.001 |
| | (0.006) | (0.001) | (0.001) | (0.002) | (0.005) |
| White v. Hispanic | 0.084*** | 0.004*** | −0.002* | 0.013*** | −0.001 |
| | (0.007) | (0.001) | (0.001) | (0.003) | (0.005) |
| White v. Black | 0.035*** | 0.009*** | −0.003** | 0.008*** | −0.003 |
| | (0.007) | (0.001) | (0.001) | (0.002) | (0.004) |
| By Econ. Dis. Status | 0.110*** | 0.001 | −0.001 | 0.008*** | 0.000 |
| | (0.005) | (0.000) | (0.000) | (0.002) | (0.003) |
| Panel C: Any Public Enrollment | | | | | |
| Non-URM v. URM | 0.096*** | −0.002*** | 0.002** | 0.003 | 0.002 |
| | (0.007) | (0.001) | (0.001) | (0.004) | (0.005) |
| White v. Hispanic | 0.095*** | −0.003*** | 0.003** | 0.003 | 0.003 |
| | (0.008) | (0.001) | (0.001) | (0.004) | (0.005) |
| White v. Black | 0.074*** | −0.003** | 0.005*** | 0.001 | −0.006 |
| | (0.008) | (0.001) | (0.002) | (0.003) | (0.004) |
| By Econ. Dis. Status | 0.133*** | −0.001 | 0.001 | 0.003 | −0.003 |
| | (0.007) | (0.000) | (0.000) | (0.004) | (0.004) |

Note: Regressions control for year fixed effects (2013–2017), demographic student-level characteristics, eighth grade test scores, and high school-level characteristics. See note in table 8.3 for a detail description of these controls. Standard errors shown in parentheses are clustered at the school district level. $*p < 0.10$, $**p < 0.05$, $***p < 0.010$.

have access to multiple institutions of both types within a short distance given that a nontrivial share of them reside near large urban areas. Lastly, we find that differences in the coefficients associated with the distance measures explain small and insignificant shares of the overall college enrollment gap. We observe a similar pattern with respect to differences in community college enrollment, as reported in Panel A: sensitivity to distance is not a statistically significant factor contributing to observed disparities in two-year college enrollment rates.

By contrast, in the context of enrollment rates at four-year colleges specifically, differences in how URM and non-URM students respond to living far away from two-year institutions explain a sizable proportion of the observed gap. As reported in Panel B of table 8.7, on average, there is an 8.9 percentage point difference in the four-year college enrollment rates between these student groups. Results from the decomposition analyses indicate a 12.4 percent reduction in this gap if URM students' sensitivity to distance from a two-year institution was that of their non-URM peers.[16] In other words, if URM students substituted going to four-year universities at the same marginal rate as their non-URM counterparts, the four-year college enrollment gap would close by more than 12 percent. By contrast, differences in the observed distances account for only 3.4 percent of the gap. Furthermore, we find notable differences in the relative contribution of sensitivity to distance when considering the four-year enrollment gap across specific pair-wise comparisons, such as White vs. Hispanic and White vs. Black enrollment. We find it to be most salient among Hispanic students in comparison to White students. The decomposition results examining the factors contributing to the four-year college enrollment gaps between these groups attribute nearly 16 percent of the discrepancy to differences in how Hispanic and White students substitute going to four-year colleges when faced with long distances to two-year institutions, whereas differences in the geographic access to community colleges between these groups contribute to 5 percent of the gap.[17]

Finally, we also decompose differences in college-going rates by students' economic disadvantage status. Overall, the findings mirror the patterns observed across student race and ethnicity. As shown in Panel C of table 8.7, there is a large college enrollment gap between low- and high-income students: 13.3 percentage points. This difference can be attributed to both explained and unexplained factors by roughly equal proportions, with demographic characteristics contributing to a greater extent relative to distance to postsecondary institutions of any type. With respect to enrollment in four-year universities, in particular, we again observe that differences in the sensitivity to distance to two-year colleges play an important role in explaining the gap. Our findings suggest a 7.3 percent reduction in the four-year college enrollment gap if low-income students responded to living far from two-year colleges by enrolling in four-year universities at the same marginal rate as higher-income peers.

16. Differences in sensitivity to distance between URM and non-URM students contribute 0.011 of the 0.089 gap in the four-year college enrollment rate. Hence, 12.4 percent of this gap (0.011/0.089) is attributed to variation in how students respond to living farther away from two-year colleges.

17. For Black students, differences in the sensitivity to distance and geographic access to college contribute a larger share of the observed gap (which is smaller than the White/Hispanic gap), though in roughly the same proportions: approximately 23 to 25 percent.

### 8.6.2 Simulated College Enrollment Under Campus Closures

Our second simulation approach involves predicting the change in college enrollment rates across demographic groups following the closure of each two-year and four-year college campus in the state, one at a time. As noted in our introduction, several states have closed or merged college campuses in recent years as a response to declining populations and/or financial challenges. Our analyses provide important policy recommendations to the state of Texas if they were to engage in these policy decisions. Specifically, we can identify college closures that would have the largest (or smallest) effect on overall college enrollment, enrollment across college sectors, and enrollment across race and socioeconomic status.

We conduct our analysis in two steps. First, we re-estimate the minimum distance from each high school to the nearest public two-year and public four-year institution following the hypothetical closure of each campus. Using these hypothetical distances, we predict the expected change in college enrollment for each student in our sample using the estimated coefficients from equation (1) capturing sensitivity to distance, $\hat{\Gamma}$. Specifically, we calculate the following:

$$\frac{\partial Enroll}{\partial \widetilde{(\boldsymbol{Distance})}_{st|J-j}} = \hat{\Gamma}\ \widetilde{\boldsymbol{Distance}}_{st|J-j} \tag{3}$$

where $\widetilde{\boldsymbol{Distance}}_{st|J-j}$ corresponds to the distance between a given high school to the nearest two-year and four-year institution calculated from a subset of colleges, namely $\{J-j\}$ where $J$ denotes the universe of postsecondary campuses in Texas and $j$ indicates a single campus. We evaluate equation (3) separately by student race and ethnicity, and also by economic disadvantaged status, for each simulated campus closure, using the linear estimates we present in table 8.4. We then average our effects over all students in a given racial or socioeconomic group.

Figure 8.5 presents the change in statewide college enrollment rates, by race and ethnicity (Panel A) and economic disadvantage status (Panel B), for the 10 two-year campus closures that we estimate would have the largest effect on overall two-year college enrollment. We predict that the closure of Angelina College in east Texas would have the largest effect on two-year enrollment, with larger effects for White and Black students, who make up the majority of students in the local area.[18] However, we predict that White students would substitute toward four-year colleges at a higher rate than Black students, generating larger overall reductions in college enrollment for Black students.

18. The 5- to 24-year-old population in Angelina County, where Angelina College is located, is approximately 50 percent White and 18 percent Black.

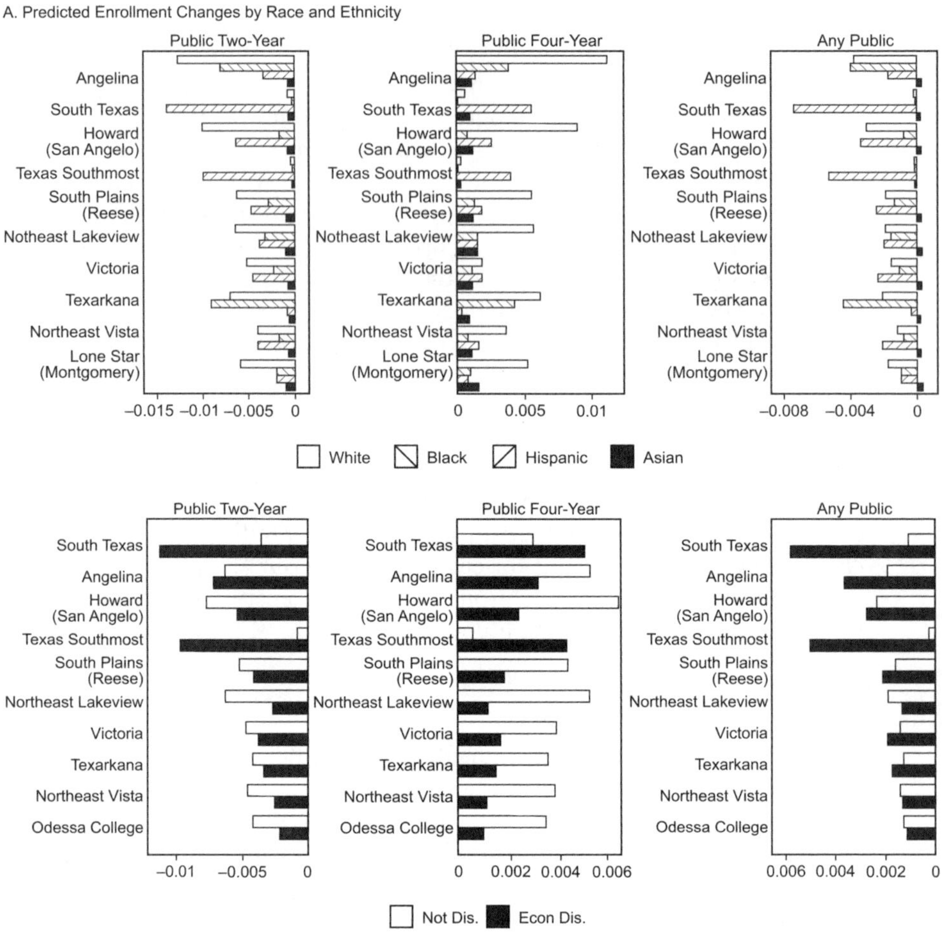


**Fig. 8.5 Predicted enrollment changes of two-year college campus closures**

Note: These figures plot the estimated statewide changes in college enrollment rates, across race (Panel A) and economic disadvantage status (Panel B) if each listed two-year college campus were to close. Details of the exercise are provided in section 8.6.2.

These substitution patterns are also relevant for understanding what we predict would happen if two-year colleges in predominantly Hispanic regions were to close. For example, we predict the largest overall reductions in overall public college enrollment to occur if South Texas College, in the Rio Grande Valley, or Texas Southmost College, in the Gulf Coast, were to close. This is because these colleges serve largely Hispanic populations, who respond strongly to distance to two-year colleges, but substitute toward four-year colleges at low rates.[19] We would also see the largest reductions in overall college enrollment for economically disadvantaged students under these closures due to a similarly large own-distance response, and smaller substitution effect, for the large number of disadvantaged students these colleges tend to serve.

Figure 8.6 repeats our analysis for the closure of four-year college campuses. Here, we predict that four-year college enrollment would decrease dramatically for Hispanic students and economically disadvantaged students if UT-El Paso or UT-Rio Grande Valley were to close. However, if this were to happen, we would expect to see a large increase in two-year college enrollment for these students, generating an overall increase in enrollment in Texas public colleges. Outside of these particular closures, we would not expect to see large changes in college enrollment—in the four-year sector or overall—due to the closure of four-year campuses, in part because students tend to be less sensitive to four-year college distance and in part, because Texas's four-year campuses tend to be clustered around the Texas triangle. Thus, if one campus were to close, the distance to the nearest four-year campus would change minimally for many students.

## 8.7 Discussion and Concluding Remarks

Access to higher education is often seen as a pathway to social mobility in the United States (Chetty et al. 2020). However, due to the strikingly uneven distribution of both two- and four-year public colleges across space, many students across the nation, particularly low-income and rural students, find that attending college is simply not an option for them. To understand all of the determinants that contribute to the ongoing disparities in postsecondary access among students in the United States, scholars and policymakers must also take into account not only the locations of institutions but also how students respond to those locations. Thus, our paper contributes to the growing literature on geographic access to colleges with several important insights. First, we confirm prior work by finding that students' college choices are influenced by the distance they must travel to reach a college or university campus. However, to our knowledge, we are the first to document that the relationship between distance and attendance varies significantly across racial and ethnic lines, and socioeconomic groups as well. When considering a student's proximity to the nearest two-year public institution, White and non-economically disadvantaged students tend to enroll in four-year colleges when they live far away from two-year colleges. In contrast, we

19. South Texas College is located in Hidalgo County, whose 5- to 24-year-old population is 96 percent Hispanic, and Texas Southmost College is located in Cameron County, whose 5- to 24-year-old population is 95 percent Hispanic.

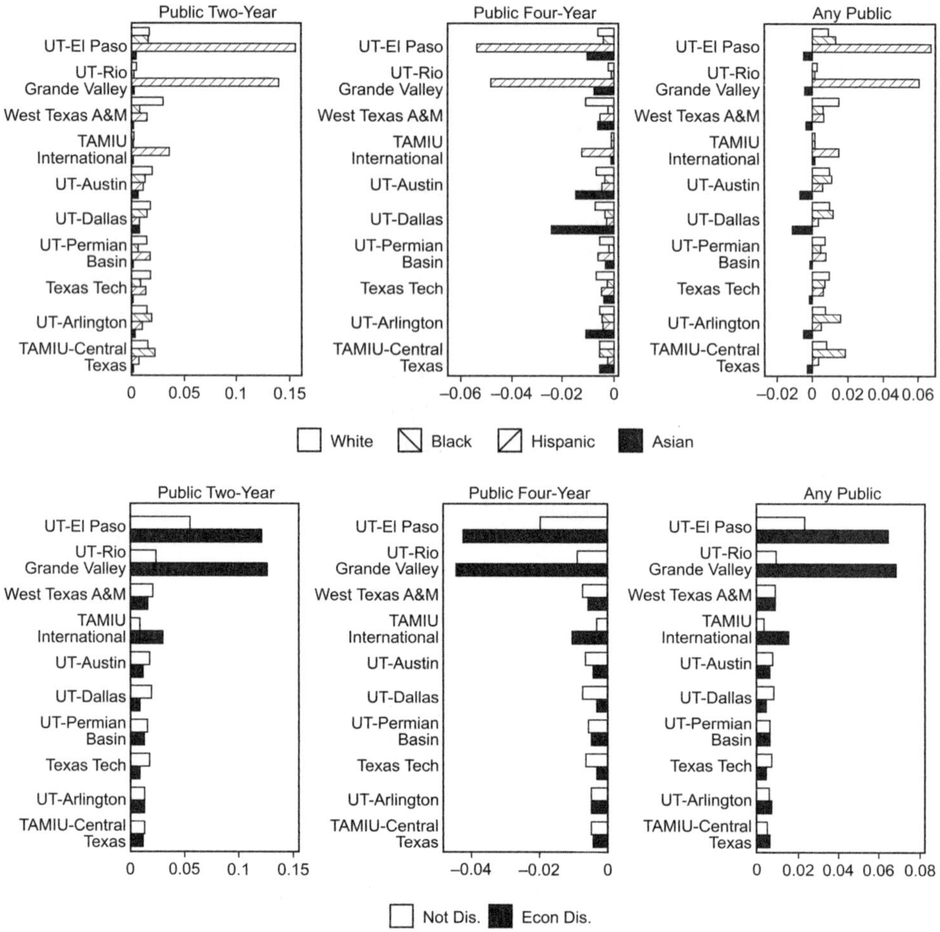


**Fig. 8.6 Predicted enrollment changes of four-year college campus closures**

Note: These figures plot the estimated statewide changes in college enrollment rates, across race (Panel A) and economic disadvantage status (Panel B) if each listed four-year college campus were to close. Details of the exercise are provided in section 8.6.2.

observe this "substitution" toward four-year colleges at a much lower rate for Black, Hispanic, and economically disadvantaged students, and they are more likely to forgo college enrollment altogether when they live far from two-year colleges. Our results are particularly striking for students who live in "community college deserts"—we find that White and non-disadvantaged students who live in a desert are no less likely to attend college overall, compared to similar peers who do not live in such areas. However, Black,

Hispanic, and economically disadvantaged students who live in these deserts are 6–12 percentage points less likely to attend college overall.

The findings from our regression results, as well as our various policy simulations, could help guide state and local policy initiatives regarding the potential *opening*, *closing*, *merging*, or *conversion* of college campuses, and how these policy initiatives could impact who enrolls in the US higher education system. These simulations are particularly salient as institutions across the nation grapple with various challenges confronting the higher education sector, such as states experiencing declining college enrollments and colleges facing budget cuts. Our simulations offer insights into how the closing of colleges might impact college enrollment, not just overall but also among underrepresented demographic groups, which the higher education sector has struggled to recruit, retain, and graduate.

Lastly, taken all together, our findings tie back to the seminal work of Rouse (1995), where she finds that community colleges have the potential to *democratize* postsecondary education access by drawing in students who would otherwise not attend college, or to *divert* students away from four-year colleges. We add new nuance to our understanding of these democratization and diversion effects. Specifically, we find that geographic access to community colleges democratizes enrollment for many of the groups that have traditionally been underrepresented in US higher education (Black, Hispanic, and low-income students) but may divert enrollment for White and non-disadvantaged students. As a result, renewed investment in community colleges in racially diverse and low-income areas has the potential to broaden participation in the US higher education system and to further social mobility goals.

# Appendix

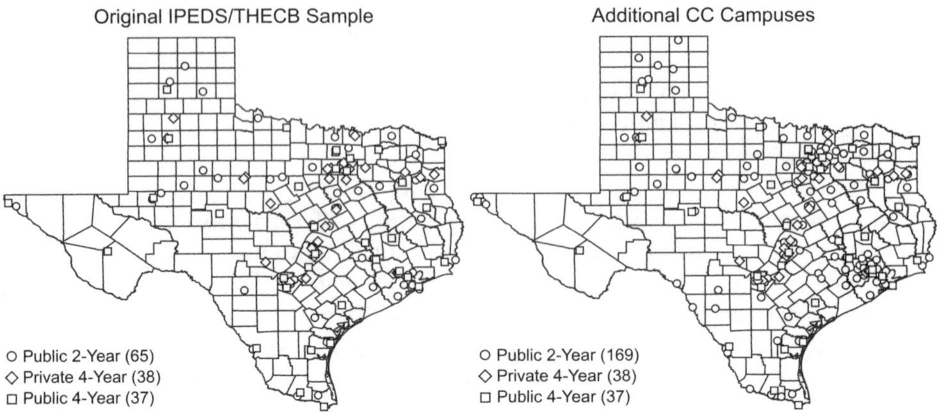


**Fig. 8A.1 Additional community college campuses**

Note: These figures show the locations of public two-year, public four-year, and private four-year college campuses in Texas. The figure on the left only uses geographic information in the Integrated Postsecondary Education System (IPEDS), while the panel on the right uses additional supplementary sources described in the text.

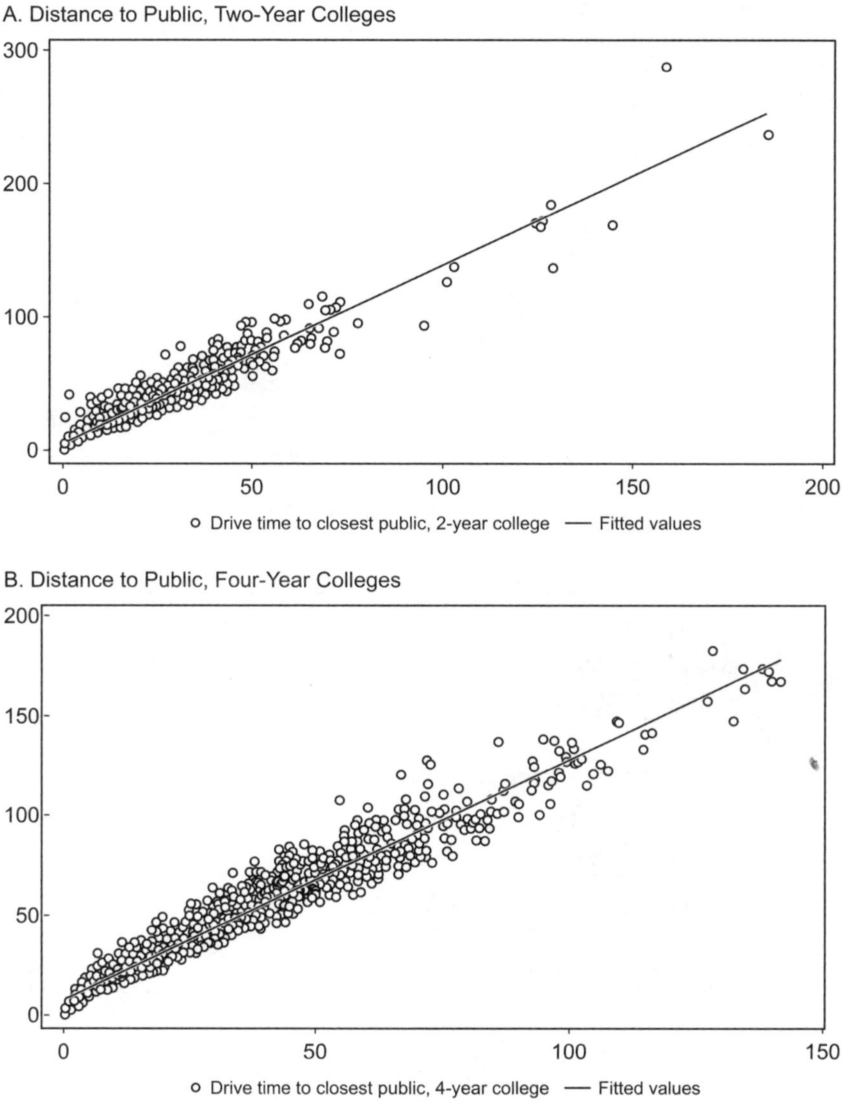


**Fig. 8A.2 Correlation between linear distance and driving time**

Note: These figures show the distance from each Texas high school to its nearest public two-year (Panel A) and public four-year (Panel B) college campus, measured in miles on the x-axis and driving time in minutes on the y-axis. The correlation in Panel A is 0.964 and the correlation in Panel B is 0.975. See Miller (2023) for details on the calculation of driving times.

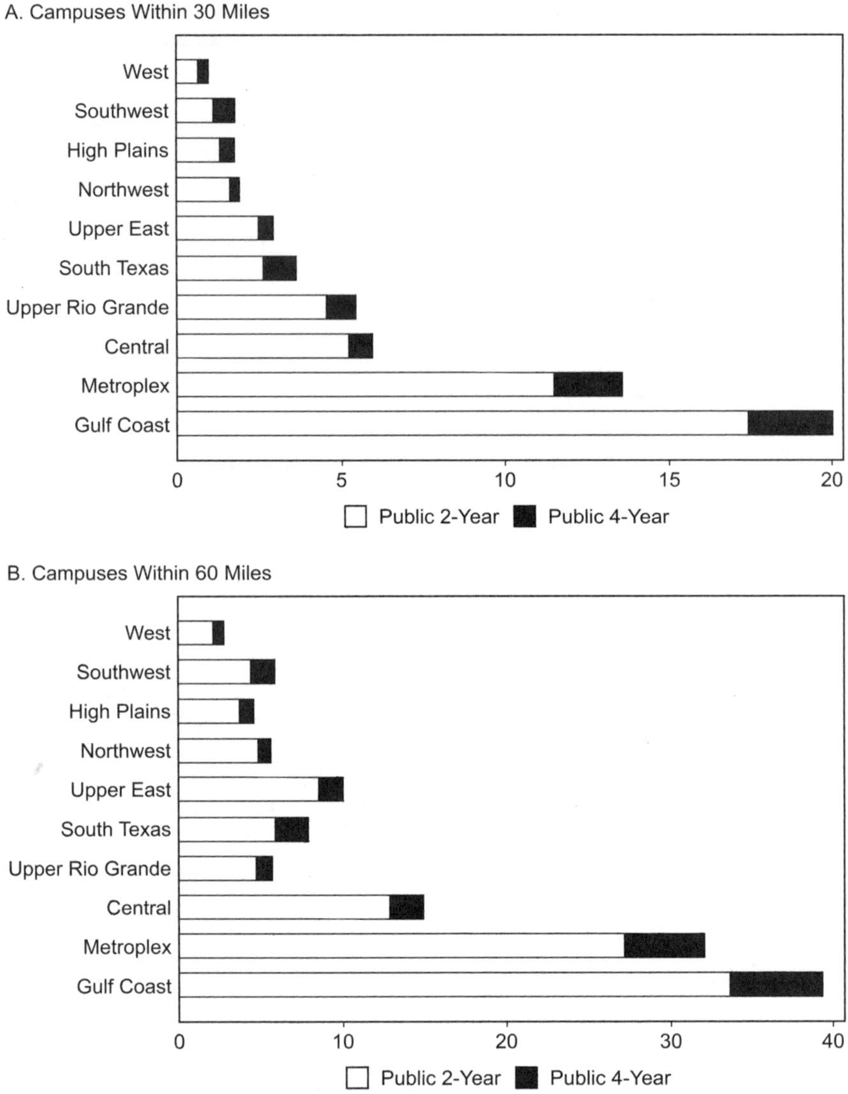


**Fig. 8A.3 Higher education access by Texas region**

Note: These figures summarize the number of public two-year and four-year college campuses within 30 (Panel A) or 60 (Panel B) miles of Texas high schools, averaged over high schools in each Texas higher education region.

**Table 8A.1** **Summary statistics**

| | All (1) | White (2) | Black (3) | Hispanic (4) | Asian (5) | Other (6) | Econ. Dis. (7) | Not Econ. Dis. (8) | Urban (9) | Suburban (10) | Town/Rural (11) |
|---|---|---|---|---|---|---|---|---|---|---|---|
| *Panel A: Student Characteristics* | | | | | | | | | | | |
| Economic Disadvantage | 0.473 | 0.187 | 0.595 | 0.661 | 0.310 | 0.329 | 1.000 | 0.000 | 0.541 | 0.412 | 0.449 |
| Non-Hispanic White | 0.332 | 1.000 | 0.000 | 0.000 | 0.000 | 0.000 | 0.131 | 0.512 | 0.217 | 0.349 | 0.473 |
| Non-Hispanic Black | 0.127 | 0.000 | 1.000 | 0.000 | 0.000 | 0.000 | 0.159 | 0.097 | 0.139 | 0.147 | 0.085 |
| Hispanic | 0.477 | 0.000 | 0.000 | 1.000 | 0.000 | 0.000 | 0.667 | 0.307 | 0.578 | 0.418 | 0.405 |
| Non-Hispanic Asian | 0.043 | 0.000 | 0.000 | 0.000 | 1.000 | 0.000 | 0.028 | 0.056 | 0.047 | 0.061 | 0.015 |
| Non-Hispanic Other | 0.021 | 0.000 | 0.000 | 0.000 | 0.000 | 1.000 | 0.015 | 0.027 | 0.019 | 0.025 | 0.022 |
| Underrepresented Minority (URM) | 0.625 | 0.000 | 1.000 | 1.000 | 0.000 | 1.000 | 0.841 | 0.432 | 0.736 | 0.590 | 0.512 |
| At-Risk for Dropout | 0.426 | 0.275 | 0.524 | 0.526 | 0.236 | 0.340 | 0.558 | 0.307 | 0.476 | 0.399 | 0.387 |
| Gifted | 0.098 | 0.130 | 0.050 | 0.078 | 0.202 | 0.114 | 0.065 | 0.127 | 0.108 | 0.095 | 0.086 |
| Immigrant | 0.009 | 0.002 | 0.005 | 0.011 | 0.046 | 0.004 | 0.012 | 0.006 | 0.011 | 0.009 | 0.005 |
| Limited English Proficient (LEP) | 0.057 | 0.005 | 0.009 | 0.103 | 0.109 | 0.014 | 0.096 | 0.022 | 0.077 | 0.052 | 0.034 |
| Male | 0.501 | 0.507 | 0.495 | 0.497 | 0.512 | 0.491 | 0.492 | 0.508 | 0.494 | 0.502 | 0.508 |
| Special Education | 0.081 | 0.075 | 0.123 | 0.079 | 0.025 | 0.074 | 0.102 | 0.061 | 0.081 | 0.072 | 0.090 |
| Career & Technical Education (CTE) | 0.782 | 0.771 | 0.780 | 0.802 | 0.667 | 0.759 | 0.805 | 0.762 | 0.748 | 0.756 | 0.860 |
| Early College High School | 0.055 | 0.014 | 0.025 | 0.094 | 0.020 | 0.016 | 0.092 | 0.023 | 0.071 | 0.047 | 0.040 |
| 8th Grade Reading Score | 0.114 | 0.247 | 0.022 | 0.030 | 0.233 | 0.222 | 0.003 | 0.213 | 0.071 | 0.150 | 0.132 |
| 8th Grade Math Score | 0.059 | 0.194 | −0.103 | −0.011 | 0.242 | 0.105 | −0.034 | 0.142 | 0.015 | 0.087 | 0.089 |
| Observations | 1,563,036 | 518,984 | 197,844 | 745,834 | 66,787 | 33,587 | 739,326 | 823,710 | 612,667 | 509,801 | 440,568 |

(*continued*)

**Table 8A.1 (cont.)**

| | All (1) | White (2) | Black (3) | Hispanic (4) | Asian (5) | Other (6) | Econ. Dis. (7) | Not Econ. Dis. (8) | Urban (9) | Suburban (10) | Town/Rural (11) |
|---|---|---|---|---|---|---|---|---|---|---|---|
| *Panel B: High School Characteristics* | | | | | | | | | | | |
| Total enrollment | 1,886 | 1,751 | 1,979 | 1,905 | 2,417 | 1,946 | 1,789 | 1,973 | 2,019 | 2,369 | 1,142 |
| Percent White | 0.332 | 0.541 | 0.248 | 0.202 | 0.356 | 0.433 | 0.223 | 0.430 | 0.217 | 0.349 | 0.473 |
| Percent Black | 0.127 | 0.095 | 0.298 | 0.101 | 0.153 | 0.135 | 0.138 | 0.116 | 0.139 | 0.147 | 0.085 |
| Percent Hispanic | 0.477 | 0.291 | 0.379 | 0.653 | 0.322 | 0.338 | 0.593 | 0.374 | 0.578 | 0.418 | 0.405 |
| Percent Asian | 0.043 | 0.046 | 0.051 | 0.029 | 0.141 | 0.055 | 0.030 | 0.054 | 0.047 | 0.061 | 0.015 |
| Percent Other | 0.021 | 0.028 | 0.023 | 0.015 | 0.028 | 0.038 | 0.017 | 0.026 | 0.019 | 0.025 | 0.022 |
| Percent Economic Disadvantage | 0.473 | 0.317 | 0.516 | 0.587 | 0.332 | 0.363 | 0.606 | 0.354 | 0.541 | 0.412 | 0.449 |
| Percent At-risk | 0.426 | 0.340 | 0.468 | 0.485 | 0.325 | 0.375 | 0.493 | 0.365 | 0.476 | 0.399 | 0.387 |
| Percent Gifted | 0.098 | 0.100 | 0.090 | 0.096 | 0.124 | 0.098 | 0.092 | 0.103 | 0.108 | 0.095 | 0.086 |
| Percent Immigrant | 0.009 | 0.007 | 0.009 | 0.010 | 0.014 | 0.008 | 0.009 | 0.008 | 0.011 | 0.009 | 0.005 |
| Percent LEP | 0.057 | 0.027 | 0.054 | 0.080 | 0.046 | 0.037 | 0.078 | 0.038 | 0.077 | 0.052 | 0.034 |
| Percent Special Education | 0.081 | 0.079 | 0.087 | 0.082 | 0.064 | 0.080 | 0.086 | 0.076 | 0.081 | 0.072 | 0.090 |
| Percent CTE | 0.782 | 0.781 | 0.771 | 0.792 | 0.720 | 0.766 | 0.795 | 0.771 | 0.748 | 0.756 | 0.860 |
| Percent Early College High School | 0.068 | 0.031 | 0.038 | 0.103 | 0.030 | 0.034 | 0.100 | 0.038 | 0.079 | 0.075 | 0.044 |
| City | 0.392 | 0.256 | 0.431 | 0.475 | 0.435 | 0.338 | 0.448 | 0.341 | 1.000 | 0.000 | 0.000 |
| Suburb | 0.326 | 0.343 | 0.379 | 0.286 | 0.465 | 0.375 | 0.284 | 0.364 | 0.000 | 1.000 | 0.000 |
| Town/Rural | 0.282 | 0.402 | 0.190 | 0.239 | 0.100 | 0.286 | 0.268 | 0.295 | 0.000 | 0.000 | 1.000 |
| Student-Teacher Ratio | 15.63 | 15.22 | 15.87 | 15.74 | 16.72 | 15.67 | 15.46 | 15.77 | 16.34 | 16.42 | 13.72 |
| Charter | 0.039 | 0.021 | 0.047 | 0.050 | 0.029 | 0.027 | 0.055 | 0.025 | 0.076 | 0.019 | 0.011 |
| Magnet | 0.062 | 0.024 | 0.113 | 0.078 | 0.051 | 0.043 | 0.085 | 0.042 | 0.147 | 0.014 | 0.001 |
| Title I | 0.737 | 0.556 | 0.823 | 0.865 | 0.514 | 0.618 | 0.896 | 0.594 | 0.775 | 0.629 | 0.809 |
| Observations | 1,563,036 | 518,984 | 197,844 | 745,834 | 66,787 | 33,587 | 739,326 | 823,710 | 612,667 | 509,801 | 440,568 |

| | | | | | | | | | | | |
|---|---|---|---|---|---|---|---|---|---|---|---|
| *Panel C: College Enrollment* | | | | | | | | | | | |
| Public Two-Year Enrollment | 0.394 | 0.435 | 0.344 | 0.383 | 0.357 | 0.387 | 0.356 | 0.428 | 0.361 | 0.390 | 0.445 |
| Public Four-Year Enrollment | 0.214 | 0.252 | 0.218 | 0.169 | 0.406 | 0.231 | 0.156 | 0.266 | 0.215 | 0.220 | 0.207 |
| Any Public Enrollment | 0.532 | 0.585 | 0.511 | 0.489 | 0.646 | 0.543 | 0.461 | 0.595 | 0.509 | 0.541 | 0.552 |
| *Panel D: Distance to Nearest Colleges* | | | | | | | | | | | |
| Any Public | 6.608 | 8.474 | 5.007 | 5.944 | 4.246 | 6.662 | 6.329 | 6.858 | 3.213 | 4.513 | 13.75 |
| Public 2-Year | 7.278 | 9.213 | 5.484 | 6.646 | 4.621 | 7.247 | 7.004 | 7.523 | 3.782 | 4.583 | 15.26 |
| Public 4-Year | 17.46 | 20.79 | 14.67 | 16.19 | 13.63 | 18.06 | 16.84 | 18.01 | 10.31 | 14.36 | 30.99 |
| Public Flagship | 151.2 | 133.3 | 118.9 | 176.3 | 117.4 | 128.2 | 165.2 | 138.7 | 168.6 | 131.5 | 149.9 |
| *Panel E: College Presence in 30 Miles* | | | | | | | | | | | |
| Any Public | 0.972 | 0.962 | 0.988 | 0.972 | 0.996 | 0.977 | 0.971 | 0.973 | 1.000 | 1.000 | 0.901 |
| Public 2-Year | 0.966 | 0.953 | 0.982 | 0.968 | 0.995 | 0.971 | 0.965 | 0.967 | 1.000 | 1.000 | 0.879 |
| Public 4-Year | 0.868 | 0.802 | 0.915 | 0.892 | 0.969 | 0.863 | 0.870 | 0.865 | 0.956 | 0.987 | 0.607 |
| Public Flagship | 0.067 | 0.086 | 0.053 | 0.056 | 0.080 | 0.092 | 0.051 | 0.082 | 0.081 | 0.044 | 0.075 |
| *Panel F: College Presence in 60 Miles* | | | | | | | | | | | |
| Any Public | 0.997 | 0.998 | 1.000 | 0.997 | 1.000 | 0.999 | 0.997 | 0.998 | 1.000 | 1.000 | 0.991 |
| Public 2-Year | 0.996 | 0.997 | 1.000 | 0.995 | 0.999 | 0.999 | 0.996 | 0.997 | 1.000 | 1.000 | 0.987 |
| Public 4-Year | 0.972 | 0.968 | 0.990 | 0.968 | 0.995 | 0.976 | 0.971 | 0.974 | 0.990 | 1.000 | 0.916 |
| Public Flagship | 0.136 | 0.189 | 0.119 | 0.101 | 0.134 | 0.199 | 0.096 | 0.171 | 0.123 | 0.104 | 0.190 |
| Observations | 1,563,036 | 518,984 | 197,844 | 745,834 | 66,787 | 33,587 | 739,326 | 823,710 | 612,667 | 509,801 | 440,568 |

Note: As in table 8.1, variables are summarized over our sample of 2013–2017 Texas high school graduates, as measured in their final year of high school. Distances are calculated using the latitude and longitude of a student's high school.

## References

Acton, Riley. 2021. "Effects of Reduced Community College Tuition on College Choices and Degree Completion." *Education Finance and Policy* 16(3): 388–417.

Acton, Riley K. 2022. "Is a Name Change a Game Change? The Impact of College-to-University Conversions." *Economics of Education Review* 88: 102240.

Alm, James, and John V. Winters. 2009. "Distance and Intrastate College Student Migration." *Economics of Education Review* 28(6): 728–38.

Andrews, R. J., J. Li, and M. F. Lovenheim. 2016. "Quantile Treatment Effects of College Quality on Earnings." *Journal of Human Resources* 51(1): 200–238.

Baker, Dominique J., Bethany Edwards, Spencer FX Lambert, and Grace Randall. 2023. "Defining the "Community" in Community College: A National Overview and Implications for Racial Imbalance in Texas." *American Educational Research Journal* 60(3): 588–620.

Black, Sandra E., Kalena E. Cortes, and Jane A. Lincove. 2020. "Apply Yourself: Racial and Ethnic Differences in College Application." *Education Finance and Policy* 15(2): 209–40. Spring.

Black, Sandra E., Kalena E. Cortes, and Jane Arnold Lincove. 2015. "Academic Undermatching of High-Achieving Minority Students: Evidence from Race-Neutral and Holistic Admissions Policies." *American Economic Review* 105(5): 604–10. May.

Black, Sandra E., Kalena E. Cortes, and Jane A. Lincove, 2016. "Efficacy vs. Equity: What Happens When States Tinker with College Admissions in a Race-Blind Era?" *Educational Evaluation and Policy Analysis* 38(2): 336–363.

Blake, Jessica. 2024. "Kentucky Explores Creating New College in 'Postsecondary Desert.'" *Inside Higher Ed.*. Accessed March 2024.

Blinder, A. S. 1973. "Wage Discrimination: Reduced Form and Structural Estimates." *Journal of Human Resources* 8(4): 436–55.

Bound, J., and S. Turner. 2007. "Cohort Crowding: How Resources Affect Collegiate Attainment." *Journal of Public Economics* 91(5–6): 877–99.

Bulman, G., and J. Cunha. 2021. "Factors Shaping College Investment and Enrollment Gaps." Chap. 12 in *The Routledge Handbook of the Economics of Education*, edited by Brian P. McCall, 309–42. London: Routledge.

Cahalan, Margaret W., Marisha Addison, Nicole Brunt, Pooja R. Patel, and Laura W. Perna. 2021. "Indicators of Higher Education Equity in the United States: 2021 Historical Trend Report." *Pell Institute for the Study of Opportunity in Higher Education.*

Card, David. 1995. "Using Geographic Variation in College Proximity to Estimate the Return to Schooling." In *Aspects of Labour Market Behavior: Essays in Honour of John Vanderkamp*, edited by Louis Christofides, E. Kenneth Grant, and Robert Swindinsky, 201–22. Toronto: University of Toronto Press.

Cameron, Stephen V., and Christopher Taber. 2004. "Estimation of Educational Borrowing constraints Using Returns to Schooling." *Journal of Political Economy* 112(1): 132–82.

Carneiro, Pedro, and Sokbae Lee. 2009. "Estimating Distributions of Potential Outcomes Using Local Instrumental Variables with an Application to Changes in College Enrollment and Wage Inequality." *Journal of Econometrics* 149(2): 191–208.

Carneiro, Pedro, James J. Heckman, and Edward J. Vytlacil. 2011. "Estimating Marginal Returns to Education." *American Economic Review* 101(6): 2754–2781.

Chetty, Raj, John N. Friedman, Emmanuel Saez, Nicholas Turner, and Danny Yagan. 2020. "Income Segregation and Intergenerational Mobility across Colleges in the United States." *Quarterly Journal of Economics* 135(3): 1567–1633.

Connolly, Kevin. 2023. "How Does Access to College Affect Long-Term Life Outcomes? Evidence from U.S. Openings of Two-Year Public Colleges." Unpublished Manuscript.

Cortes, Kalena E., and Jane Arnold Lincove. 2016. "Can Admissions Percent Plans Lead to Better Collegiate Fit for Minority Students?" *American Economic Review* 106(5): 348–54.

Cortes, Kalena E. and Jane A. Lincove. 2019. "Match or Mismatch? Automatic Admissions and College Preferences of Low- and High-Income Students." *Educational Evaluation and Policy Analysis* 41(1): 98–123.

Cowan, Benjamin, and Nathan Tefft. 2023. "College Access and Adult Health." Forthcoming in *American Journal of Health Economics*.

Currie, Janet, and Enrico Moretti. 2003. "Mother's Education and the Intergenerational Transmission of Human Capital: Evidence from College Openings." *Quarterly Journal of Economics* 118(4): 1495–1532.

Dale, S. B., and A. B. Krueger. 2002. "Estimating the Payoff to Attending a More Selective College: An Application of Selection on Observables and Unobservables." *Quarterly Journal of Economics* 117(4): 1491–1527.

Dale, S. B., and A. B. Krueger. 2014. "Estimating the Return to College Selectivity over the Career Using Administrative Earnings Data." *Journal of Human Resources* 49(2): 323–58.

Deming, David J. 2023. "Why Do Wages Grow Faster for Educated Workers?" NBER Working Paper No. 31373. Cambridge, MA: National Bureau of Economic Research.

Deming, D. J., and C. R. Walters. 2017. "The Impact of Price Caps and Spending Cuts on US Postsecondary Attainment." NBER Working Paper No. 23736. Cambridge, MA: National Bureau of Economic Research.

Denning, Jeffrey T. 2017. "College on the Cheap: Consequences of Community College Tuition Reductions." *American Economic Journal: Economic Policy* 9(2): 155–88.

Doyle, William R., and Benjamin T. Skinner. 2016. "Estimating the Education-Earnings Equation Using Geographic Variation." *Economics of Education Review* 53: 254–67.

Dynarski, Susan, Aizat Nurshatayeva, Lindsay C. Page, and Judith Scott-Clayton. 2022. "Addressing Non-Financial Barriers to College Access and Success: Evidence and Policy Implications." NBER Working Paper No. 30054. Cambridge, MA: National Bureau of Economic Research.

Dynarski, Susan, Lindsay C. Page, and Judith Scott-Clayton. 2022. "College Costs, Financial Aid, and Student Decisions." NBER Working Paper No. 30275. Cambridge, MA: National Bureau of Economic Research.

Elder, Todd E., John H. Goddeeris, and Steven J. Haider. 2010. "Unexplained Gaps and Oaxaca–Blinder Decompositions." *Labour Economics* 17(1): 284–90.

Federal Highway Administration. 2017. National Household Travel Survey. US Department of Transportation. Retrieved from https://nhts.ornl.gov/ May 2024.

Fletcher, Jason, and Hamid Noghanibehambari. 2024. "The Effects of Education on Mortality: Evidence Using College Expansions." *Health Economics* 33(3): 541–75.

Frenette, Marc. 2009. "Do Universities Benefit Local Youth? Evidence from the Creation of New Universities."" *Economics of Education Review* 28(3): 318–28.

Fu, C. 2014. "Equilibrium Tuition, Applications, Admissions, and Enrollment in the College Market." *Journal of Political Economy* 122(2): 225–81.

Fu, Chao, Junjie Guo, Adam J. Smith, and Alan Sorensen. 2022. "Students' Heterogeneous Preferences and the Uneven Spatial Distribution of Colleges." *Journal of Monetary Economics* 129: 49–64.

Gardner, Lee. 2021. "More States Turn to Public-College Mergers, but Easy Fixes May Remain Elusive." *Chronicle of Higher Education*. February 24.

Gretzinger, Erin. 2024. "Wisconsin Is Closing Another 2-Year Campus but Hopes It's Found a Solution to Its Biggest Challenges." *Chronicle of Higher Education* 70(15).

Harnisch, Tom and Sophia Laderman. 2023. "State Priorities for Higher Education in 2023: Survey of SHEEOs." *State Higher Education Executive Officers* Association.

Hillman, Nicholas. 2016. "Geography of College Opportunity: The Case of Education Deserts." *American Education Research Journal* 53(4): 987–1021.

Hillman, Nicholas, and Taylor Weichman. 2016. *Education Deserts: The Continued Significance of "Place" in the Twenty-First Century*. American Council on Education Center for Policy Research and Strategy.

Hirschl, Noah, and Christian Michael Smith. 2020. "Well-Placed: The Geography of Opportunity and High School Effects on College Attendance." *Research in Higher Education* 61(5): 567–87.

Hoxby, Caroline M. 1997. "How the Changing Market Structure of US Higher Education Explains College Tuition." NBER Working Paper No. 6323. Cambridge, MA: National Bureau of Economic Research.

Klasik, Daniel, Kristin Blagg, and Zachary Pekor. 2018. "Out of the Education Desert: How Limited Local College Options Are Associated with Inequity in Postsecondary Opportunities." *Social Sciences* 7(9): 165.

Kling, Jeffrey R. 2001. "Interpreting Instrumental Variables Estimates of the Returns to Schooling." *Journal of Business & Economic Statistics* 19(3): 358–64.

Lapid, Patrick. 2018. "Expanding College Access: The Impact of New Universities on Local Enrollment." Unpublished Manuscript.

Li, A.Y. 2021. "Four Decades of Performance Funding and Counting." In *Higher Education: Handbook of Theory and Research*, edited by L. W. Perna. Higher Education: Handbook of Theory and Research, vol. 36, 1–64. Springer, Cham.

Long, Bridget Terry. 2004. "How Have College Decisions Changed Over Time? An Application of the Conditional Logistic Choice Model." *Journal of Econometrics* 121(1–2): 271–96.

Long, Bridget Terry, and Michal Kurlaender. 2009. "Do Community Colleges Provide a Viable Pathway to a Baccalaureate Degree?" *Educational Evaluation and Policy Analysis* 31(1): 30–53.

Miller, Lois. 2023. "Small Distances that Matter: Effects of Local Community College Openings on Enrollment and Degree Completion." Unpublished Manuscript.

Morales, Camila, and Kalena E. Cortes. 2022. "A Profile of Community College Students in Texas." Texas Commission on Community College Finance, Texas Higher Education Coordinating Board.

Mountjoy, Jack. 2022. "Community Colleges and Upward Mobility." *American Economic Review* 112(8): 2580–2630.

National Center for Education Statistics. 2023. Table 304.15: Total fall enrollment in degree-granting postsecondary institutions, by control and level of institution: 2000 through 2022. In *Digest of Education Statistics*. US Department of Education. Retrieved from https://nces.ed.gov/programs/digest/d23/tables/dt23_304.15.asp.

Neumark, David. 1988. "Employers' Discriminatory Behavior and the Estimation of Wage Discrimination." *Journal of Human Resources* 23(3): 279–95.

Nimier-David, Elio. 2023. "Local Human Capital and Firm Creation: Evidence from the Massification of Higher Education in France." Unpublished Manuscript.

Oaxaca, Ronald. 1973. "Male-Female Wage Differentials in Urban Labor Markets." *International Economic Review* 14(3): 693–709.
Reber, Sarah, and Ember Smith. 2023. "College Enrollment Disparities, Understanding the Role of Academic Preparation." The Brookings Institution.
Rouse, Cecilia Elena. 1995. "Democratization or Diversion? The Effect of Community Colleges on Educational Attainment." *Journal of Business & Economic Statistics* 13(2): 217–24.
Skinner, Benjamin T. 2019. "Choosing College in the 2000s: An Updated Analysis Using the Conditional Logistic Choice Model." *Research in Higher Education* 60: 153–83.
Smith, J., J. Goodman, and M. Hurwitz. 2020. "The Economic Impact of Access to Public Four-Year Colleges." NBER Working Paper No. 27177. Cambridge, MA: National Bureau of Economic Research.
Thompson, Jesse, and Keighton Hines. 2023. "State Output Remains Distinctly Texan, While Jobs Mix Increasingly Resembles the U.S." Federal Reserve Bank of Dallas. https://www.dallasfed.org/research/swe/2023/swe2313.
Turley, Ruth N. López. 2009. "College Proximity: Mapping Access to Opportunity." *Sociology of Education* 82(2): 126–46.
US Census Bureau. 2022. "Nation's Urban and Rural Populations Shift Following 2020 Census." https://www.census.gov/newsroom/press-releases/2022/urban-rural-populations.html.
Waxmann, Laura. 2024. "University of California Considers S.F. for Expansion in Wake of Mayor Breed's Plea." *San Francisco Chronicle*, January 13.
Zimmerman, S. D. 2014. "The Returns to College Admission for Academically Marginal Students." *Journal of Labor Economics* 32(4): 711–54.

## **Comment** Zachary Bleemer

Lower-income Americans are persistently and increasingly less likely to enroll in college than their higher-testing high school peers (Bailey and Dynarski 2011). Male children of parents from the top parental income tercile are about twice as likely to go to college as children from the bottom parental income tercile, a gap that first appeared in the late 1990s and is larger than that of any period in the past 100 years other than the decades immediately following World War Two (Bleemer and Quincy 2025). These gaps parallel enrollment gaps by race, with White and especially Asian enrollment outpacing Black and Hispanic enrollment. What explains this growing stratification on the extensive margin of college enrollment?

One set of candidate explanations may have been changes on the supply

Zachary Bleemer is an assistant professor of economics at Princeton University and a faculty research fellow of the National Bureau of Economic Research.

For acknowledgments, sources of research support, and disclosure of the author's material financial relationships, if any, please see https://www.nber.org/books-and-chapters/financing-institutions-higher-education/comment-distance-opportunity-higher-education-deserts-and-college-enrollment-choices-bleemer.

side of higher education. First, could today's large gap in college-going by parental income be the result of the high cost of college education? Goldin and Katz (1999) show that enrollment at relatively lower-cost public universities persistently rose throughout the 20th century, rising from 25 to 70 percent by the 1970s, implying that lower-cost public enrollment is no less popular in this period of poor lower-income collegiate enrollment. While tuition costs at private and public universities have risen in recent decades, the rise in real four-year college costs (including tuition, fees, room, and board) predates the growing parental income gap in college enrollment by at least 15 years, and real average community college costs didn't start rising until the Great Recession of the late 2000s (Bleemer and Quincy 2025). Trends in college costs thus seem to be an unlikely explanation for lower-income students' failure to keep up with their higher-income peers' rising college enrollment.

A second candidate supply-side explanation is the rise of "meritocratic" admissions policies—like rising reliance on standardized tests and other measures of academic preparation and the steady phase-out of race-based affirmative action since the late 1990s—which might differentially limit college access to lower-income students (e.g., Arrow et al. 2000; Markovits 2019; Bleemer 2022, 2023). However, Hoxby (2009) shows that the distribution of university selectivity hardly shifted rightward in the 1990s and 2000s, and not at all among universities with below-median test scores; lower-income students have maintained broad access to four-year public colleges and universities in recent decades. Supply-side policies appear unlikely to explain recent differential changes in college enrollment by parental income.

On the demand side, a series of studies have hypothesized that information frictions may play an important role in explaining differences in college enrollment by parental income (Hoxby and Turner 2013; Bleemer and Zafar 2018), though a recent large-scale information experiment conducted by the College Board found little evidence that information provision could close the observed gap (Gurantz et al. 2021). Instead, a series of studies originating with Card (1993) has hypothesized the role of a complementary demand-side explanation for the enrollment gap: differences in distances to the nearest college or university, which themselves may cause differential frictions arising from information, cost, or norms that lead lower-income students to be less likely to go to college, especially with regard to community college (see, e.g., Rouse 1995; Mountjoy 2022).

Acton et al. (2025) join this tradition by proposing to explain racial differences in college-going by both differences in the distribution of distance-to-college between racial groups and differences in the responsiveness of college-going to distance-to-college by racial group. The striking descriptive statistics shown in the first three panels of figure 8.1 prefigure their findings: Texas's four-year universities are much more likely be located in regions of the state with large White population shares, and the visual evidence suggests that the state's community colleges are often relatively distant from the regions where the population shares of Black and especially Hispanic residents are highest.

The study's centerpiece is a decomposition estimating the contributions of distance-to-college to racial enrollment gaps. Figure 8.3a provides evidence that members of all races who live far from any community college are less likely to enroll at such an institution, but while most of the difference in White and higher-income two-year enrollment is replaced by higher four-year enrollment, Black and Hispanic students and lower-income students appear more likely to forgo higher education altogether. Using these estimates to simulate public college enrollment responses to community college closures, the authors find suggestive evidence that certain community college closures in south Texas would lead to substantial declines in Hispanic college enrollment. The authors conclude that about 16 percent of the racial (SES) gap in four-year college enrollment—and 8 percent of the SES gap—can be explained by distances to community college, largely due to different enrollment elasticities to distance rather than differences in average distances across racial group, but that distance explains none of the gap in overall college enrollment.

While the study's abstract highlights distance's small observational contribution to the four-year racial enrollment gap, the study's more surprising finding is that there are no meaningful differences in the average distance that Black, Hispanic, and White Texans live from public community colleges. Indeed, neither differences in distance-to-college nor differences in the elasticity of college-going to distance explain a meaningful portion of the 10 percentage point gap in college-going by race (or the 13 percentage point gap by SES), at least taking the presented observational relationships as causal.

Future work could consider a number of interesting extensions of the presented results. The first would be to validate (or invalidate) the presented observational estimates of race- and SES-specific college-going elasticities to distance using quasi-experimental variation in either residential or college location. This would identify the causal race-specific relationship between college-going and distance. A number of recent studies have exploited new college openings as one viable source of such variation. For example, Lapid (2018) shows that the construction of UC Merced and three new California State University campuses led to substantial disproportionate increases in college enrollment from high schools near those campuses. Connolly (2023) documents substantial variation in the opening year of US community colleges and leverages their staggered timing to estimate the health effects of educational attainment. Most recently, Nimier-David (2023) studies the educational and local labor market effects of staggered late-20th-century expansions of a series of French universities, documenting substantial increases in collegiate human capital in the local labor market.

Future researchers could extend these designs to validate the selection-on-observables design implemented in the present study. Potential examples in the Texas context may be the many openings and closures of for-profit institutions across Texas in the 2000s and 2010s and the merger of UT Pan American and UT Brownsville in 2015.

A second potential avenue for future work would be to study the geographic determinants of college major choice in the United States. There is very substantial variation in the relative labor market return to different college majors, with some majors offering a larger *causal* return (relative to a lower-paying major like elementary education) than the overall wage difference between college-goers and non-college high school graduates (Card 1999; Altonji et al. 2016; Kirkeboen et al. 2016; Bleemer and Mehta 2022). Since the late 1990s, Black and Hispanic students have become steadily less likely to earn high-value college majors like engineering and economics, with the largest declines at selective public universities (Bleemer and Mehta, 2021, 2023). A similar gap has grown between the college majors earned by students from lower-and higher-income families (Startz 2024; Bleemer and Quincy 2025). Future work could estimate parallel distance regressions to those put forward in this study focusing on engineering schools, two- and four-year nursing programs, and other high-return fields, and then employ the results to measure the contribution of distance or the distance elasticity to the existing gaps in college major attainment between groups.

Finally, the estimates provided in this study could become more policy relevant with an extension that considers the expected effects of expansions to Texas's community college system. Where could colleges be opened in order to maximize future enrollment in the state? Is there viable legislation or local action that could found new vocational programs or other two-year institutions? This would be especially interesting with regard to new engineering and nursing programs at existing universities. It would also be valuable to use these estimates to enhance the cost-benefit analysis of new community college construction relative to university expansion, perhaps leveraging variation between schools in their excess student capacity.

In conclusion, this study provides a useful contribution to the literatures considering the supply-side determinants of college enrollment inequities and the ramifications of constructing new or branched colleges and universities.

## References

Acton, Riley, Kalena Cortes, and Camila Morales. 2025. "Distance to Opportunity: Higher Education Deserts and College Enrollment Choices." NBER Manuscript. This volume.

Altonji, Joseph, Peter Arcidiacono, and Arnaud Maurel. 2016. "The Analysis of

Field Choice in College and Graduate School: Determinants and Wage Effects." *Handbook of the Economics of Education* 5: 305–96.
Arrow, Kenneth, Samuel Bowles, and Steven Durlauf. 2000. *Meritocracy and Economic Inequality*. Princeton, NJ: Princeton University Press.
Bailey, Martha, and Susan Dynarski. 2011. "Inequality in Post-Secondary Education." In *Whither Opportunity*, edited by Greg Duncan and Richard Murnane, 117–32. New York: Russell Sage Foundation.
Bleemer, Zachary. 2022. "Affirmative Action, Mismatch, and Economic Mobility after California's Proposition 209." *Quarterly Journal of Economics* 137(1): 115–60.
———. 2023. "Affirmative Action and Its Race-Neutral Alternatives." *Journal of Public Economics* 220: 104839.
Bleemer, Zachary, and Aashish Mehta. 2021. "College Major Restrictions and Student Stratification." *Center for Studies in Higher Education Research Paper* 21 (14).
———. 2022. "Will Studying Economics Make You Rich? A Regression Discontinuity Analysis of the Returns to College Major." *American Economic Journal: Applied Economics* 14(2): 1–22.
———. 2023. *Restricted Access to Lucrative College Majors Harms Underrepresented Students Most*. Washington, DC: Brookings Institution.
Bleemer, Zachary, and Sarah Quincy. 2025. "Changes in the College Mobility Pipeline Since 1900." NBER Working Paper No. 33797. Cambridge, MA: National Bureau of Economic Research.
Bleemer, Zachary, and Basit Zafar. 2018. "Intended College Attendance: Evidence from an Experiment on College Returns and Costs." *Journal of Public Economics* 157: 184–211.
Card, David. 1993. "Using Geographic Variation in College Proximity to Estimate the Return to Schooling." In *Aspects of Labour Economics: Essays in Honour of John Vanderkamp*, edited by Louis Christofides, E. Kenneth Grant, and Robert Swindinsky, 201–22. Toronto: University of Toronto Press.
———. 1999. "The Causal Effect of Education on Earnings." *Handbook of Labor Economics* 3: 1801–1863.
Connolly, Kevin. 2023. "How Does Access to College Affect Long-Term Life Outcomes? Evidence from U.S. Openings of Two-Year Public Colleges." Manuscript.
Goldin, Claudia, and Lawrence Katz. 1999. "The Shaping of Higher Education: The Formative Years in the United States, 1890 to 1940." *Journal of Economic Perspectives* 13(1): 37–62.
Gurantz, Oded, Jessica Howell, Michael Hurwitz, Cassandra Larson, Matea Pender, and Brooke White. 2021. "A National-Level Informational Experiment to Promote Enrollment in Selective Colleges." *Journal of Policy Analysis and Management* 40(2): 453–79.
Hoxby, Caroline, and Sarah Turner. 2013. "Expanding College Opportunity for High-Achieving, Low-Income Students." *SIEPR Working Paper* 12(14).
Hoxby, Caroline M. 2009. "The Changing Selectivity of American Colleges." *Journal of Economic Perspectives* 23(4): 95–118.
Kirkeboen, Lars, Edwin Leuven, and Magne Mogstad. 2016. "Field of Study, Earnings, and Self-Selection." *Quarterly Journal of Economics* 131(3): 1057–1111.
Lapid, Patrick. 2018. "Expanding College Access: The Impact of New Universities on Local Enrollment." Manuscript.
Markovits, Daniel. 2019. *The Meritocracy Trap*. New York: Penguin Press.
Mountjoy, Jack. 2022. "Community Colleges and Upward Mobility." *American Economic Review* 112(8): 2580–630.

Nimier-David, Elio. 2023. "Local Human Capital and Firm Creation: Evidence from the Massification of Higher Education in France." Manuscript.

Rouse, Cecilia. 1995. "Democratization or Diversion? The Effect of Community Colleges on Educational Attainment." *Journal of Business & Economic Statistics* 13(2): 217–24.

Startz, Dick. 2024. *Economic Inequalities Among College Graduates Are Linked to College Major Choice*. Washington, DC: Brookings Institution.

9

# Examining the Effects of Tuition Reset Policies on Enrollment and Institutional Finances at Minority Serving Institutions

James Dean Ward, Daniel Corral, and Catharine Hill

The advertised cost of providing a postsecondary education has increased faster than public support for higher education (Webber 2017). These changes have shifted the burden of paying for college from the federal government and state to students and families, through the reduced purchasing power of Pell Grants and direct appropriations comprising smaller shares of institutional revenues. This financial repositioning has disproportionately impacted historically underserved groups, such as racially minoritized students, economically disadvantaged students, and first-generation college students. Further, public divestment in higher education has resulted in steadily increasing tuition at public colleges and universities and ballooning student debt. Again, this shift in the burden of paying for college has reduced access for some students by creating an unaffordable price tag and, thus, has dissuaded a non-negligible share of students from enrolling at certain institutions due to their perceptions of the price. Put another way, some students experience "sticker shock" when they see high published tuition and fees, regardless of what the net price may be for a student after they receive financial aid, which prevents them from applying and enrolling

James Dean Ward is currently vice president of research at Strada Education Foundation, and was the principal of policy and economic research on the Educational Transformation team at Ithaka S+R when this chapter was written.

Daniel Corral is an assistant professor of higher education in the Department of Leadership, Higher and Adult Education at the Ontario Institute for Studies in Education at the University of Toronto.

Catharine Hill is managing director of Ithaka S+R.

For acknowledgments, sources of research support, and disclosure of the authors material financial relationships, if any, please see https://www.nber.org/books-and-chapters/financing-institutions-higher-education/examining-effects-tuition-reset-policies-enrollment-and-institutional-finances-minority-serving.

(Levine et al. 2022). As Levine (2022) notes, "Perceived costs are one of the most important factors influencing where students apply" (366). This phenomenon is particularly salient among Black, Hispanic, and lower-income students (Grodsky and Jones 2007; Nienhusser and Oshio 2017).

Minority Serving Institutions (MSIs) have historically played a unique role in the postsecondary sector and continue to serve a broad mission of expanding access and opportunity for racially minoritized individuals. While each MSI differs in its origin, they collectively seek to educate large concentrations of underrepresented students, often through their relatively affordable price tag. However, MSIs are not immune to the broader context of austerity and have also had to respond by increasing their sticker price to varying degrees, by institutional sector. For instance, the in-state sticker price increased for both public and private MSIs between 2017 and 2021 between 17 percent and 18 percent, respectively (authors' calculations using data from "The MSI Data Project," Nguyen et al. 2023). When sticker shock impacts enrollments, it hampers MSIs' ability to fulfill their missions in two ways. First, it reduces the pool of students who apply and enroll at MSIs, thus, potentially reducing the number of students receiving benefits from an MSI education. Second, low enrollments reduce revenues and put a financial strain on institutions, limiting their ability to serve enrolled students effectively.

To counter this sticker shock, an increasing number of institutions have "reset" tuition, or cut sticker prices by at least 5 percent (Lapovsky 2015, 2019). This is a relatively recent tuition-setting approach. Its corresponding research has documented its purported effects primarily in the private, not-for-profit sector (Corral and Ward 2024; Ward and Corral 2023). However, there needs to be more evidence concerning the effectiveness of this practice, especially across MSIs which vary in their financial strength and resilience (Edwards et al. 2023; Williams and Davis 2019). Additionally, the limited research on tuition resets suggests that their effectiveness is significantly impacted by institutional context and that there is heterogeneity in effects across reset sizes (Corral and Ward 2024). As such, examining the effectiveness of tuition resets for increasing enrollments and improving institutional financial stability at MSIs is important given their unique mission and position within the postsecondary sector. Given the inequities within the postsecondary system, we expect our findings to provide MSI leaders with useful starting evidence to help them serve their target populations more effectively and reduce systemic inequities.

This chapter aims to fulfill three goals. First, we provide a brief historical overview and policy context of MSIs. This background serves as the basis to further understand their financial conditions, including relevant sources of funding and a discussion of historical inequities. The second goal is to provide a background and a review of research on tuition reset approaches. That section will inform our final aim and the empirical and descriptive portion of our chapter: examining institutional enrollment and financial outcomes of MSIs that have reset tuition. We conclude with a discussion of our findings, limitations, and potential recommendations for institutional leaders and other stakeholders.

## 9.1 Historical Overview of MSIs

MSIs are postsecondary institutions that enroll and educate significant shares of students of color and economically disadvantaged students. However, these institutions differ in their origins and contemporary missions. Various reauthorizations of the Higher Education Act of 1965 (HEA) created the various MSI monikers as they continue to expand and grow (Castro Samayoa 2022). There are 11 active and different MSI classifications according to the Department of Education (ED) as we illustrate in table 9.1. Each of these classifications refers to ED funding programs for which institutions may be eligible, thus, allowing a college or university to achieve the MSI distinction (Dortch 2023; Hegji 2017). MSIs generally fall into two distinct categories: 1) institutions created with the explicit mission of serving certain student populations, and 2) colleges and universities that meet a specific enrollment threshold for students from particular racial groups, along with meeting other student-related enrollment and financial requirements (see table 9.1; Nguyen et al. 2023). To exemplify the former, higher education leaders recognized Historically Black Colleges and Universities (HBCUs) and Tribal Colleges and Universities (TCUs), also known as Tribally Controlled Colleges and Universities, in direct response to the historical and systemic racial discrimination experienced by Black and Indigenous people (Gasman et al. 2015). The proceeding paragraphs provide a brief historical overview of these distinct types of institutions.

### 9.1.1 HBCUs

The federal government formally recognizes HBCUs as postsecondary institutions established before 1964 with the intention of providing access to higher education for African Americans and Black people. The majority of HBCUs were founded after the Civil War and during the Reconstruction era, with Cheyney University serving as the first HBCU. This period in history saw a significant push toward educating freed slaves, with the support of religious missionary organizations, philanthropic foundations, and the Freedmen's Bureau (Gasman 2008). While funding from various sources was crucial in their development, relying on these entities proved to be unsustainable (Gasman 2008). The turn of the 20th century also saw increased philanthropic support for these institutions from well-known industrialists of the time (e.g., Rockefeller and Carnegie). Moreover, the Second Morrill Act of 1890 required states to establish land-grant colleges (Agricultural and Mechanical Institutions) for Black students if their existing land-grant

**Table 9.1 Description of MSI types and criteria**

| Mission-Based MSI | Primary Student Enrollment Criteria | Legislation & HEA Federal Program Names | Purpose of Funding Program & Other Criteria | # of Eligible Institutions in 2023[a] |
|---|---|---|---|---|
| Historically Black College and University (HBCU) | None | Title III, Part B & F, Strengthening Historically Black Colleges and Universities Program | Assists HBCUs in "strengthening their academic, administrative, and fiscal capabilities" | 101 |
| | None | Title III, Part D, Historically Black College and University Capital Financing Program | Provides HBCUs with loans to improve infrastructure | 101 |
| Historically Black Colleges and Universities Graduate Institutions (HBGI) | None | Title III, Part B, Strengthening Historically Black Graduate Institutions Program | Authorizes grants to HBCUs with graduate programs to improve "academic, administrative, and fiscal capabilities" | 24 |
| Historically Black Colleges and Universities Masters Institutions (HBCU Masters) | None | Title VII, Part A, Master's Degree Programs at Historically Black Colleges and Universities | Support HBCUs in improving graduate STEM education | 18 |
| Tribal College and University (TCU) | None | Title III, Part A & F, Strengthening American Indian Tribally Controlled Colleges and Universities (TCCUs) program | Provides funds to enhance academic quality, institutional management, and financial stability | 35 |
| | | Tribally Controlled College or University Assistance Act (TCCUAA) of 1978[b] | Provides the majority of institutional funding for TCUs based on the number of Indigenous FTE students ($8,000) | 35 |
| **Enrollment-Based MSI** | **Primary Student Enrollment Criteria** | **HEA Federal Program** | | **# of Eligible Institutions in 2023[a]** |
| Hispanic Serving Institution (HSI) | 25% Hispanic student undergraduate enrollment | Title V, Part A, Developing Hispanic-Serving Institutions Program | Provides general capacity-building grants to expand educational opportunities for Hispanic students | 539 |

| | | | | |
|---|---|---|---|---|
| HSI—STEM | 25% Hispanic student undergraduate enrollment | Title III, Part F, HSI STEM and Articulation Programs | Offers grants with two separate aims: 1) Increase the number of Hispanics in STEM via improving academic quality and capacity, and 2) Develop transfer pathways and articulation agreements between two-year and four-year institutions | — |
| HSI—Promoting Postbaccalaureate Opportunities for Hispanic Americans Program (PPOHA) | 25% of undergraduate enrollment identify as Hispanic | Title V, Part B, Promoting Postbaccalaureate Opportunities for Hispanic Americans Program | Provide grants to increase postbaccalaureate opportunities for Hispanics and expand postbaccalaureate academic offerings | — |
| Predominantly Black Institution | 40% of undergraduate enrollment identify as Black | Title III, Part A & F, Strengthening Predominantly Black Institutions | Offers grants with specific purposes, such as enhancing institutional capacity, expanding educational opportunities, and financial stability | 65 |
| PBI—Master's Degree Programs[c] | 40% of undergraduate enrollment identify as Black | Title VII, Part A, Master's Degree Programs at Predominantly Black Institutions | Provide grants to establish Master's degree programs at PBIs (with a focus on STEM) | 5 |
| Asian American and Native American Pacific Islander-Serving Institutions (AANAPISI) | 10% of undergraduate enrollment identify as Asian American and Pacific Islander | Title III, Part A & F, Strengthening AANAPISIs program | Offer grants to improve AANAPISI's ability to serve Asian Americans and Native American Pacific Islanders and low-income individuals | 207 |
| Alaska Native and Native Hawaiian-Serving Institutions (ANNHIs) | 20% of undergraduate enrollment identify as Alaska Native | Title III, Part A & F, Strengthening (ANNHIs) program | Provide grants to support Alaska Natives or Native Hawaiians. | 16 |
| Native American-Serving Nontribal Institutions | 10% of undergraduate enrollment identify as Indigenous | Title III, Part A & F, Strengthening NASNTIs program | Offer grants to support | 32 |

Note. Adapted from Hegji (2017), Dortch (2023); Nguyen et al. (2023); and Rutgers Center for MSIs (2023).

[a] Based on the Rutgers Center for MSIs (2023) eligibility list.

[b] The TCCUAA is not an MSI funding program from the HEA but does provide considerable base funding for TCUs. The US Bureau of Indian Affairs administers it.

[c] The federal government last funded this program in 2014 and we therefore consider it inactive.

colleges were segregated, which led to the establishment of several public HBCUs. The Second Morrill Act also provided significant federal funding for public HBCUs. Throughout the 20th century, HBCUs expanded their academic offerings and played a critical role in providing higher education to Black students, especially in the Jim Crow South where segregation laws prevented them from attending Predominantly White Institutions (PWIs). As of 2023, there were 101 HBCUs located in 19 states (Rutgers Center for Minority Serving Institutions 2023). There are 51 public HBCUS and 50 private HBCUs.

Stakeholders often laud HBCUs for their outsized contribution in enrolling and educating Black and other racially minoritized students. And for good reason; they are thought of as institutions doing more with less (Edwards et al. 2023; Gasman et al. 2017). As described in more detail below, HBCUs face decades of financial inequities while still producing proportionally greater outcomes in several domains. For example, despite comprising 3 percent of all postsecondary institutions, about 40 percent of Black students apply to at least one HBCU, and HBCUs enroll 10 percent of all Black college students (Edwards et al. 2023). Furthermore, HBCUs collectively have a disproportionate impact on the production of Black STEM degrees and serve as an important pathway to our country's professional class. To illustrate, in 2018, HBCUs produced nearly 14 percent of all Black bachelor's degrees (National Center for Science and Engineering Statistics 2021). Finally, there is growing positive economic evidence for Black students attending HBCUs. Using a robust administrative data set that linked college applications, college enrollment, and financial outcomes, Edwards and colleagues (2023) found that Black students who enrolled in an HBCU experienced a household income around age 30 that is 5 percent higher compared to otherwise similar Black students who do not enroll in an HBCU but applied.[1] Thus, HBCUs offer a considerable contribution in terms of access and success. Nevertheless, as we describe later, HBCUs' financial stability continues to be a contentious issue despite being eligible for and receiving mandatory federal funding; HBCUs continue to receive inequitable funding relative to their PWI counterparts along with private HBCUs continuing to rely heavily on student tuition dollars.

### 9.1.2 TCUs

TCUs are institutions the federal government recognized beginning in 1965 that are critical to the development and sustainability of Indigenous communities. Tribal governments officially charter TCUs, and these institutions serve many purposes (American Indian Higher Education Consortium 2022). The broad aims of TCUs are to (1) preserve and promote Indigenous

1. The analytic sample includes applicants that did not enroll in any college who comprise roughly 10 percent of the study group.

culture, language, and traditions; (2) provide career and technical education; and (3) offer access to postsecondary education that many rural communities would not otherwise have. Diné College (formerly Navajo Community College) was the first Tribal college officially created in 1968. Both the Civil Rights movement and the Self-Determination movement starting in the 1960s helped ignite the recognition and eventual growth of these institutions as ways to counteract the historical and vile discrimination, including forced assimilation, Indigenous folks experienced (Marroquín 2019). The Self-Determination movement promoted a focus among Indigenous people in developing and self-governing their own educational institutions (Gasman 2008). Accordingly, the 1970s and 1980s experienced an increase in the number of TCUs, primarily two-year institutions (Johnson et al. 2006, cited in Gasman 2008). As of 2022, there are 35 fully accredited TCUs located across 15 states (American Indian Higher Education Consortium 2022).

### 9.1.3 Enrollment-Based MSIs

The second category of MSIs we referenced earlier refers to enrollment-based MSIs. The federal government recognizes this cadre of institutions as colleges and universities that enroll a specific share of racially minoritized students, along with meeting other criteria, often related to student enrollment targets and finance. This group broadly consists of Alaska Native and Native Hawaiian Serving Institutions (ANNHSI), Native American-Serving Nontribal Institutions (NASNTI), Predominantly Black Institutions (PBIs), Hispanic Serving Institutions (HSIs), and Asian American and Native American Pacific Islander-Serving Institutions (AANAPSIs), each with their own unique enrollment threshold and histories. For instance, PBIs differ from HBCUs as they tend to be institutions created post-1964 and Black students must represent at least 40 percent of their student body, along with enrolling at least 1,000 undergraduates. In addition to these specific enrollment specifications, there is also a requirement that relates to institutions enrolling a certain fraction of students needing financial assistance. HSIs, for example, must have 25 percent of their undergraduate enrollment comprised of Hispanic students, *and* 50 percent of students must show financial need. Table 9.1 includes a list summarizing MSI types and their notable criteria. Note that institutions can meet the requirements of several MSIs, although they can only hold one federal MSI grant at a time (Yang and Masulit 2017). According to the Center for Minority Serving Institutions at Rutgers University (2023), there were 848 MSI-eligible institutions.

It is important to note that while these postsecondary institutions enroll and educate high concentrations of racially minoritized students and historically underrepresented students, this does not necessarily suggest they effectively serve students. On the one hand, the growing number of enrollment-based MSIs may reflect the demographic realities of a growing and diverse America. This may be the case with the appreciable increase in the number of HSIs. One study documents that the number of HSIs has increased by nearly 200 percent since 1995, from 189 to 559 in 2021 (Marin and Aguilar-Smith 2023). On the other hand, there is also a growing strand of literature challenging the assumption of an institution's "servingness." Questioning an institution's servingness refers to the notion that simply because an institution matches federal criteria for funding, it may not represent the institution's intrinsic motivation and/or ability to serve specific student populations or promote equitable academic outcomes (Garcia 2017; Nguyen et al. 2023). Some scholars posit that institutions may purposefully target specific demographic enrollments to attain an MSI status and the accompanying funding or meet the criteria by happenstance rather than with purposeful intentionality. On the contrary, institutions may not be in the appropriate position to support students despite gaining MSI status. As a result, while the MSI category offers researchers a useful heuristic to think about and analyze institutions educating great shares of marginalized students, researchers must also be aware that an institution's intention may not reflect an institution's commitment and capacity to serve racially minoritized students.

## 9.2 Financing MSIs

Public and private not-for-profit colleges and universities receive funding from a variety of sources. Two primary sources of income include (1) federal and state appropriations, and (2) tuition and fees (Smith 2019). This section discusses these primary sources of income at MSIs.

### 9.2.1 MSI Federal Funding Programs

The MSI designation is a result of institutions meeting the eligibility criteria for, applying, and ultimately securing institution-specific funding programs. Therefore, the distinction confers significant financial benefits. These financial resources are a way to address historic inequities by race and ethnicity through building institutional capacity with support from the federal government. Currently, the federal government provides financial resources to MSIs through the HEA's 11 grants program under Title V (see table 9.1).

The application process for an eligible MSI is intricate and requires thorough documentation to prove that the institution meets the necessary criteria the federal government requires for funding. The application process involves submitting extensive data on student demographics, financial aid, and the proposed academic program(s). However, potential issues can arise in this process. First, the bureaucratic nature of the application process can be daunting, particularly for smaller institutions that may need more resources to manage complex paperwork and data submission. Aguilar (2021) interviewed institutional administrators working at HSIs to understand their experiences in applying for Title V funding. She interviewed both unsuccessful and successful applicants. Successful Title V grantees, for instance, were able to hire outside grant writers who had previous experience in securing ED grants. Some participants noted they also had difficulty navigating the request for proposals (RFPs) as the federal government creates these documents filled with technical jargon that many administrators were not familiar with. What is more, Aguilar (2021) noted that successful HSIs had institutional research offices that were agile enough to respond to ED's unpredictable and short-windowed RFPs. For context, in FY 2020, the Title V Developing HSI Program opened on December 27, 2019, and closed on February 23, 2020, allowing less than two months for institutions to apply. These issues highlight the need for a more streamlined and transparent application process and ongoing support for institutions to fulfill their role as MSIs effectively.

While the 11 grant programs formally designate an institution as an MSI, they are not the only form of funding MSIs receive from the government. A large share of federal funding for MSIs is given indirectly through student aid programs (e.g., Pell Grant program and Work Study program; Williams and Davis 2019). Nevertheless, the latest government report on these programs suggests that in FY 2023, the MSI funding programs awarded approximately $1.293 billion (Dortch 2023) We now briefly describe each federal funding program.

The federal government authorizes most of the funds to MSIs via their "Strengthening Institutions Program" (SIP) which is denoted as Title III-A and Title III-F of the HEA. SIP serves as the foundation for outlining some criteria for MSIs to be eligible for a particular program. According to Dortch (2023), to qualify for Title III-A and Title III-F programs, institutions must meet three criteria:

- Have relatively low educational and general expenditures
- 50 percent of undergraduate students receive need-based financial assistance
- Is an accredited and authorized two- or four-year college or university located in the United States or its associated jurisdictions.

Institutions may request a waiver if they fail to meet one or several of these requirements. An eligible institution is thus eligible to receive institution-specific SIP funding (described below). For instance, all enrollment-based institutions plus TCUs receive funds through Title III-A and Title III-F. HSIs receive capacity-building grants instead through Title V while also receiving STEM-specific funds from Title III-F. HBCUs, on the other hand, receive funds through other sections of Title III.

As mentioned previously, building institutional capacity is the chief motive for these federal funds. Some funding programs offer general capacity-building grants, while others focus on supporting specific disciplines and programs, like STEM and increasing access to graduate education. For example, an eligible HSI may be entitled to apply to one of three different types of federal funding opportunities: (1) the Developing Hispanic-Serving Institutions Program; (2) Hispanic-Serving Institutions—Science, Technology, Engineering, or Mathematics and Articulation Programs; or (3) Promoting Postbaccalaureate Opportunities for Hispanic Americans Program. In an effort to understand the types of programs funded through these specific programs, Boland (2018) conducted a content analysis of enrollment-based MSIs that applied for Title III and V grants. He found that the abstracts of the funded program proposals generally focused on initiatives such as tutoring and advising centers, remedial courses, technology and data improvements, and faculty and staff professional development. These programs were generally described as efforts to improve course completion, student retention, transfer, and/or graduation.

While some of these MSI Funding Programs are guaranteed through legislation, others are non-compulsory. According to Hegji (2017), the MSI "programs are typically funded through annual discretionary appropriations, but additional annual mandatory appropriation" (Summary section). In fact, over 80 percent of funds appropriated to MSIs are discretionary funding. The distinction between discretionary and mandatory appropriations in MSI funding is crucial because it impacts the stability, predictability, and planning capabilities of these institutions. Discretionary funds, subject to annual budget negotiations, can fluctuate, affecting the ability of MSIs to plan long-term initiatives. Mandatory funds, on the other hand, provide a more ostensibly predictable stream of funding, allowing for more secure and sustained programming, staffing, and resources to support their educational missions and the communities they serve. Despite efforts by the Trump administration to curtail funding for MSIs, both mandatory and discretionary funds tend to be stable year over year (Castro Samayoa 2022).

#### *9.2.1.1 Additional TCU Federal Funding*

TCUs receive federal funding from sources other than the Strengthening Institutions Program. The federal government also provides funds for TCUs through the Tribally Controlled College or University Assistance Act (TCCUAA) of 1978, which the US Bureau of Indian Affairs administers. Through the TCCUAA, the federal government authorizes a set amount of money per Indigenous student at TCUS, with the latest figures suggesting each institution receives $8,000 per student (Nelson and Frye 2016; Postsecondary National Policy Institute [PNPI] 2022). However, TCUs rarely receive the authorized amount from the federal government, leading some to claim that TCUs remain perpetually underfunded (Nelson and Frye 2016). While these per-student subsidies serve as the base budget for TCUs, it is important to note that TCUs do not receive federal funds for non-Indigenous students, who make up an appreciable share of the TCU student body—roughly one in five students (21 percent) in 2022 (PNPI 2022).

## 9.2.2 State Funding

State appropriations represent a meaningful share of revenue at public colleges, but that share has decreased over time (Li 2017). Typically states provide funding for colleges and universities to pay for university operations, but they also provide appropriations for research and financial aid grants. However, state support for universities has declined over time, particularly around 2008. The decline in state higher education also comes at a time when costs for Medicaid and K-12 schools are increasing (Smith 2019). These competing priorities for limited resources may crowd out higher education funding. As previous research has shown, higher education is often the first area to reduce funding during periods of austerity and the last area to have funding restored (Delaney and Doyle 2011; Gándara et al. 2023). Moreover, political partisanship may exacerbate cuts to higher education and do so in a way that disproportionately impacts institutions serving larger shares of historically underserved students (Taylor et al. 2020, 2023). While public colleges rely quite a bit on states for funding, private colleges receive a smaller share from states.

### *9.2.2.1 Performance-Based Funding*

The framework states use to appropriate money to public colleges has changed in recent decades, with potentially severe consequences for MSIs. It has long been the norm that public colleges and universities receive state funding based on a combination of the number of enrolled students and the prior year's appropriation (Layzell 2007; Ortagus et al., "A National Analysis," 2023). However, over the past three decades, most states have adopted or redesigned performance-based funding (PBF, also known as outcomes-based funding) models that base appropriations on measurable outputs. Examples of measurable outcomes include the number of degrees awarded, retention rates, and job placement rates. While states sanction outcomes-based funding under the rubric of efficiency and accountability, the literature supporting this approach is thin. This is particularly the case when outputs are difficult to measure, tasks are complex, and/or organizations do not have the organizational or human capacity to support efforts (Hillman and Corral 2018).

Thus, it may come as no surprise that research examining whether and to what extent MSIs might be disadvantaged by such pay-for-play regimes has produced concerning results (Li et al. 2018; Hillman and Corral 2018; Ortagus et al., "Unequal Impacts," 2023). For instance, Hillman and Corral (2018) explore to what extent the adoption of PBF models was associated with changes in state appropriations for MSIs in PBF states compared to MSIs in non-PBF states. They found that such policies were associated with about a $763 per full-time or equivalent (FTE) student decline in funding. Furthermore, Ortagus and colleagues ("Unequal Impacts," 2023) explored whether the design and dosage of PBF affected state funding for HBCUs and four-year universities that serve high concentrations of racially minoritized students. They found that states with high-dosage PBF policies (states that apportion greater than 10 percent of their funding via outcomes metrics) had large and negative effects on these institutions. HBCUs received 23.5 percent less state money, which translates to about $2,215 less per FTE student. Institutions that serve above-average shares of students of color experienced a loss of about $905 per FTE student. However, states that incorporate "equity premiums"—financial bonuses to institutions that promote access and success for underserved students—into their PBF models might counteract the potential negative consequences of paying for performance (Gándara and Rutherford 2018). In sum, the state higher education landscape appears to be steadily headed toward a future that puts money on the table for student and institutional outcomes regardless of whether an institution has the capacity to act upon them.

#### *9.2.2.2 Inequitable State Funding at HBCUs and TCUs*

**HBCUs.** Although there has been ongoing support at the federal level to support HBCUs financially, there are significant inequities at the state level for public HBCUs. These inequities date back to the Second Morrill Act of 1890 as states were required to have equal levels of funds between land-grant colleges founded through the First Morrill Act of 1862 (US Department of Education 2023). These inequities have also been highlighted in the Supreme Court case of *United States v. Fordice* (1992), which had effects on the way states must dismantle de jure segregated higher education systems, including increasing funding for HBCUs.

However, inequitable funding is still present at HBCUs. For instance, in September 2023, US Secretary of Education Miguel Cardona and US Secretary of Agriculture Thomas Vilsack highlighted existing inequities. They sent letters to 16 governors highlighting that there is an aggregate funding disparity between public land-grant HBCUs and their non-HBCU land-grant counterparts totaling over $12 billion. Calculating these disparities between 1987 and 2020 using IPEDS data, the secretaries present a disparity range from $172 million to $2.1 billion. They recommend states appropriate additional funds to these institutions, while also suggesting rectifying the situation through private donor gifts, which may or may not be feasible at certain institutions.

**TCUs.** Tribal Colleges also operate in a distinct state funding environment relative to other MSIs. Both two- and four-year TCUs have quite distinct revenue streams relative to their non-TCU counterparts. According to Nelson and Frye (2016), roughly 70 percent of TCUs' revenue come from federal sources. The next biggest revenue streams are local appropriations and net tuition and fees. The smallest share of funding TCUs receive is less

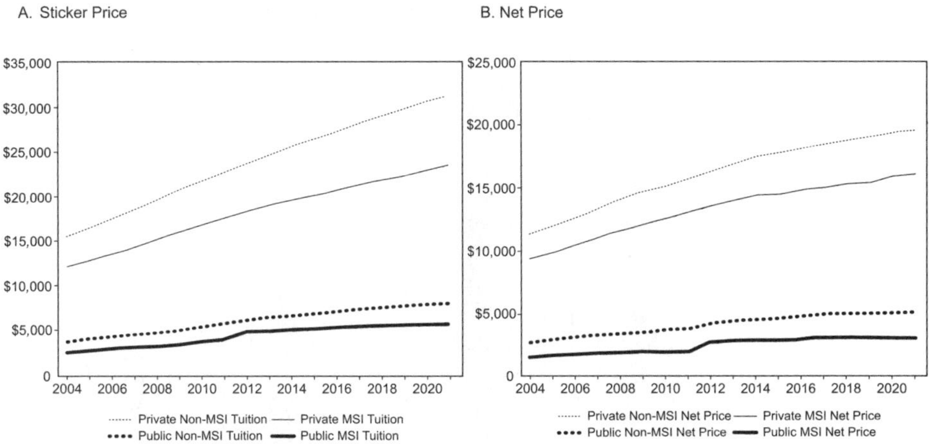


**Fig. 9.1 Average sticker price and net price, by MSI status and control**

than 3 percent from the state. This low number is due to how the federal government recognizes Indigenous colleges as tribally chartered institutions, as opposed to state postsecondary institutions (Nelson and Frye 2016). As a result, "states have no obligation to fund the operations of TCUs and in most cases do not—not even for their non-Native state residents that attend TCUs" (Nelson and Frye 2016, 3–4). This is worrisome given that TCUs do enroll an appreciable number of non-Indigenous students annually but are not provided the corresponding funds to help educate them.

### 9.2.3 Tuition and Fees

Tuition and fees typically comprise a meaningful share of revenue for postsecondary institutions, which vary by public and private status. For context, figure 9.1 shows the average sticker price from 2004 through 2021 for public and private MSIs and non-MSIs as well as the average estimated net price over this period. The gap in both sticker price and net price between public and private institutions has grown over time. Moreover, the gap between MSIs and non-MSIs has grown, more so among private institutions. The lower sticker and net prices of MSIs likely reflect organizational missions and the populations served by these institutions. As described above, some MSI designations explicitly include serving lower-income students, and all MSIs serve groups of students who have been historically excluded from higher education. The lower prices reflect a purposeful expansion of access to these groups.

Both public and private colleges and universities have different financial structures and student demographics, which can influence their tuition strategies and dependency. Public institutions receive an appreciable share

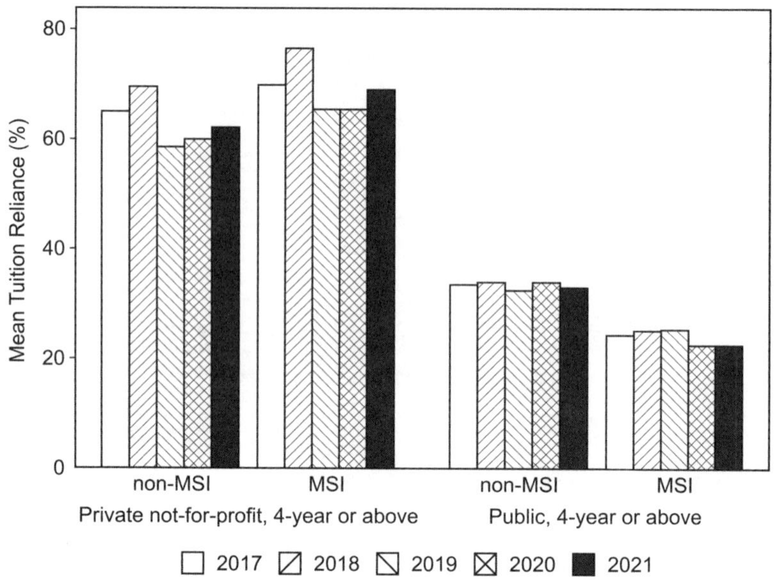


**Fig. 9.2 Mean share of tuition reliance by sector and MSI-status**
Data source: The MSI Data Project (Nguyen et al. 2023).

of state funding, which can alleviate some reliance on tuition. However, as noted previously, this support has been declining over the years, increasing the tuition burden on students and families (Delaney and Doyle 2011; Gándara et al. 2023). Private institutions, on the other hand, rely more heavily on tuition and fees due to receiving a smaller share of state funding. Private institutions often have larger endowments and resources to support financial aid programs and scholarships, but endowment sizes vary significantly between MSIs and non-MSIs.

Figure 9.2 represents mean tuition reliance (tuition and fees as a fraction of core revenues) between 2017 and 2021, separated by private and public status and MSI and non-MSI status. Privates rely more on tuition than publics. We also see private MSIs relying more on tuition than their private non-MSI counterparts. Tuition revenue, on the other hand, is around 30 percent for public non-MSIs, while the share of tuition revenue is lower for public MSIs. Dependence on tuition and fees as a major revenue source comes with risks, especially during an economic downturn or demographic shifts that lead to declining enrollment. Institutions must navigate these challenges by developing robust financial strategies, such as diversifying revenue streams, enhancing recruitment and retention efforts, and advocating for increased governmental and philanthropic support, to ensure financial stability and fulfill their educational mission. One potential avenue is the adoption of a tuition reset.

## 9.3 Tuition Reset Background and Evidence

A tuition reset is a strategy for setting tuition among postsecondary institutions. While there is no formal definition, the literature has coalesced around defining the notion as a reduction in sticker price by at least 5 percent (Lapovsky 2015, 2019). Recent research has also focused on this approach within the private, not-for-profit sector (Corral and Ward 2024; Ward and Corral 2023). For instance, tuition resets have been common in recent years as 63 private baccalaureate-granting colleges have instituted one between 2012 and 2018 (Ward and Corral 2023). Before discussing the current state of research on tuition resets, we compare this contemporary tuition-setting strategy with the well-established approach of tuition discounting (Hillman 2012).

### 9.3.1 Relation to Tuition Discounting

Institutions typically award financial aid to students after accepting them. These financial aid awards include federal student aid (e.g., Pell Grants, Direct Student Loans, and Federal Work Study); institutional aid (e.g., need-based grants and merit-based scholarships); and students' expected contributions through earned income during the academic year and summer. Researchers often refer to institutional aid as tuition discounting (Hillman 2012). More than 90 percent of first-year students at private colleges and universities receive a discount averaging a 56 percent reduction in sticker price (NACUBO 2023). Institutions may draw from endowment funds or use other philanthropic donations to cover these grants and scholarships. Colleges and universities essentially forgo tuition revenue from students when they discount tuition. Although nearly all students at private nonprofit institutions receive a discount, the individual awards vary. Colleges use these discounts to meet certain organizational goals such as increasing opportunities to lower-income students via need-based grants or prestige striving via merit-based awards that help an institution improve metrics used for rankings or advertising (Grodsky and Kalogrides 2008; Lucido 2014; Weisbrod et al. 2008). As a result, there is a trade-off between increased efficiency in the pricing process and a social inefficiency of charging each student what they can afford to pay. This can have equity implications if institutions are unable to effectively lower the price for lower-income students to an affordable level.

### 9.3.2 Background on Tuition Resets

A tuition reset, on the other hand, shifts this discounting practice, at least partially, from a back-end to a front-end process. Rather than reducing tuition via institutional awards after an institution has accepted a student, a reset reduces the published sticker price before a student opens an application. Tuition resetting is thus a clear shift from the "high-tuition, high-aid" model of postsecondary pricing as a way to improve perceived affordability from the perspective of the student (Turner 2018). As such, a tuition reset has the potential added benefit of streamlining the financial aid process by reducing the amount of individual awards that need to be calculated and balanced. Of course, the efficiency benefits of this streamlining depend on the size of the reset and how much of the discounting process institutions shift to the front end.

*9.3.2.1 Theoretical Perspectives on How Students Perceive College Pricing*

How might students perceive tuition resets? Cheslock and Riggs (2021) provide a framework that offers two relevant perspectives to understand the psychological aspects that inform student and family decision-making in the context of higher education pricing. As they note, "Prices can potentially also convey information about the quality of the institution and the value placed upon the student by the institution" (Cheslock and Riggs 2021, 759). The first relevant perspective is the price-quality heuristic. This notion suggests that given the wide variation in characteristics among colleges and universities, students might derive inferences about institutional quality based on ancillary factors, such as listed price. As a result, students who have the least amount of information about higher education might be likely to rely on price as a proxy for quality. In this instance, prices decreasing might lead to decreased demand leading potential matriculants, thus considering higher education as a "Veblen Good." The second relevant perspective in Cheslock and Riggs' (2021) framework is the silver lining principle. This idea relates to the way students may interpret a "transaction that includes gains and losses," similar to an institutional aid award (763). The interpretation of gains and losses center on how a student integrates them and evaluates the result. Cheslock and Riggs (2021) provide the example of a student confronted with a sticker price the student receives. For instance, if a student receives financial aid, they might either see it as reducing the overall cost of attending the institution or as a separate gain. This principle suggests that students might view colleges differently depending on how they perceive the relationship between tuition costs and financial aid.

In light of the insights put forth by Cheslock and Riggs (2021), it becomes evident that students' perceptions of a tuition reset in higher education are inherently complex. To summarize, students may interpret a tuition reset through two primary lenses. First, employing the price-quality heuristic, students might see a reduction in tuition as signaling a decline in institutional quality, particularly if they correlate higher tuition with better education. Conversely, drawing from the silver lining principle, students may evaluate a tuition reset in terms of gains and losses. On the one hand, for some students, a tuition reset could be seen as a welcome relief, reducing the overall financial burden. On the other hand, it might be perceived as a loss, especially if they equate higher tuition with prestige. Thus, the way students perceive a tuition reset depends on their individual perspectives, which are shaped by their background and postsecondary preparation.

### *9.3.2.2 Empirical Research on Tuition Resets*

What effects do resets have on institutional finances? Previous research on these approaches has focused on the private sector, where institutions frame and promote sticker price reductions in a particular way, often lauding an increase in institutional affordability (Corral and Ward 2024). The research on private not-for-profit institutions implementing a tuition reset studies the policies using institution-level data and a difference-in-differences design (Corral and Ward 2024; Ward and Corral 2023). One study confirms that when institutions reset tuition they shift the discounting process from the back end to the front end and reduce institutional aid expenditures (Ward and Corral 2023). This shift is roughly offsetting as per-student net-tuition revenue remains steady following a discount. Importantly, this shift has the potential to hamstring institutions' ability to engage in price discrimination (Levine 2022). There is mixed evidence on the efficacy of a reset in increasing enrollment among private universities. On average, resets do not appear to increase overall enrollment, but institutional context and the size of the reset appear to create wide variation in the effectiveness, particularly when resets are as steep as 20 percent or 30 percent (Corral and Ward 2024). This variation transfers to the overall revenue effects of resets and their ability to improve an institution's financial outlook. An important unknown factor is how resets impact applications and yield. Even if there are no strong enrollment effects, these pricing approaches may have spillover benefits that help colleges improve stability through increased student demand as measured by increased applicants or yield rates.

There is other emerging research focusing on price reductions as well, primarily in the community college and public four-year sector (Acton 2021; Denning 2017; Klasik et al. 2024). For example, Denning (2017) studied how some community college districts in Texas, which are supported by local property taxes, shifted their tuition structure thus creating boundaries that provide in-district versus out-of-district tuition. Using a difference-in-differences approach, Denning found a $1,000 decrease in tuition was associated with a 5.1 percentage point increase in immediate enrollment. Acton (2021), studying similar changes in tuition boundaries in the community college context, found a lower estimate of about 3.5 percentage points when tuition decreased by $1,000. Acton (2021) further found students' persistence and likelihood of transferring to a four-year college also increased. This finding suggests potential effects beyond enrollment and on improving student success. Finally, Klasik et al. (2024) provide novel evidence on sticker price reductions in the public four-year sector by studying North Carolina Promise, a state-level policy that slashed tuition for all students attending one of the three colleges in the University of North Carolina System. Using a synthetic control design, Klasik and colleagues (2024) found no significant increase among first-year students but did find an increase in transfer students and among Hispanic students at one institution. Thus, the research on cuts in sticker price across the board for students even before considering applying offers mixed evidence.

Why might students considering MSIs behave differently in response to tuition resets? MSIs have historically served students who need more financial resources. Research shows that lower-income students are more price-sensitive and experience higher levels of sticker shock (Grodsky and Jones 2007; Nienhusser and Oshio 2017). However, MSIs are already an attractive option for students of color as they are often located in areas already serving racially diverse demographics and earn a federal distinction of serving great shares of students of color. Furthermore, MSIs may use tuition resets strategically, not only to enhance their competitive positioning in the higher education market but also to align with their institutional missions of serving underrepresented students and fostering diversity. The historical and cultural ethos of these institutions plays a crucial role in how prospective students and families perceive tuition resets and can influence the regional and community-specific strategies employed to meet enrollment and diversity objectives. Based on the enrollment and financial histories of MSIs, previous research on tuition resets, and the underlying theory driving perceptions of institutional pricing, we anticipate student enrollment at these institutions should increase following a reset.

## 9.4 Research Design

### 9.4.1 Data, Sample, and Measures

We rely on data collected from the Institutional Postsecondary Educational Data System (IPEDS) to estimate the relationship between a tuition reset and institutional outcomes. IPEDS gathers information from all US postsecondary institutions that participate in federal financial aid programs. The data include information on institutional enrollment and finance. We compiled a panel data set from 2003 through 2021 of 2,966 public and private institutions. In addition to IPEDS data, we leverage MSI classification data compiled by Nguyen et al. (2023). As described above, HBCU and TCU status remain constant over time due to their statutory designation. Other MSIs can toggle in and out of their designations depending on enrollment demographics and satisfying financial requirements. We classify an institution as an MSI, generally, if it holds this designation in 2021. We also include an indicator in our data whether an MSI is a statutorily identified one (i.e., TCU or HBCU) or one achieved through a formula (see table 9.1 for an overview of these designations). This indicator reflects the heterogeneity across MSIs and allows us to account for different institutional motivations.

An institution's total revenue is a function of enrollment, sticker price, and institutional aid or discounts. In this study we seek to assess the relationship of a tuition reset with each of these elements in order to present a complete understanding of the benefits or drawbacks of a reset. Table 9.2 describes our key outcomes of interest, which include the average number of undergraduate enrollment applications, fall undergraduate full-time equivalent (FTE) enrollment, Pell enrollment, tuition allowances per FTE, tuition revenue per FTE, and total tuition revenue. Pell enrollment is only available from 2010 forward, and our models reflect this shorter sample period. We use a log transformation of outcome variables in our models. Table 9.2 also includes state revenue per FTE, a control which is likely related to enrollment and our finance variables, as well as the percentage of adults with a bachelor's degree or higher in an institution's state and the state unemployment rate, which serve as time varying covariates that may influence the demand for higher education. In order to better understand potential differences across treatment and control institutions and types of MSI, we also examine three-year rolling averages of changes in enrollment and the amount of institutional aid given to students.

Table 9.2 provides means separately for institutions that enacted a reset and those that did not. It also presents means across the following subgroups: non-MSIs, MSIs, public MSIs, private, formula-driven MSIs, and statutorily designated MSIs. There are substantial differences in institutional characteristics between reset and non-reset institutions generally and across the subgroups. These differences likely reflect the underlying causes of a reset and the fact that many institutions are motivated to reset tuition in an effort to increase student demand and improve financial outlooks. As seen in table 9.2, although reset and non-reset institutions are similarly sized, those engaging in resets receive fewer applications, suggesting lower student demand. The notable exceptions are at private MSIs and HBCUs and TCUs.

To identify treatment institutions, we calculate year-over-year percent changes in reported tuition. Institutions with a decrease of more than 5 percent were identified as having a tuition reset, aligned with definitions used in previous research (Corral and Ward 2024; Lapovsky 2015, 2019; Ward and Corral 2023). We remove institutions that reset tuition multiple times during the study period as these institutions are likely to be unique cases that should be analyzed separately. This results in a final sample of 574 treated institutions. We consider an institution to have a reset until the tuition level returns to the pre-reduction amount. Figure 9.3 shows the distribution of reset lengths. More than half of resets last three years or less, although some institutions maintain a lower tuition level for an extended period of time.

There is also significant variation in the timing and size of resets across institutions. Other than a spike among MSIs in 2008, the distribution of resets is relatively constant across sample years, as shown in figure 9.4. This distribution of timing factors into our estimation strategy, as described below. Figure 9.5 shows the variation in reset size is similar among MSIs and non-MSIs. Roughly 55 percent of resets are more than a 15 percent

**Table 9.2** **Descriptive statistics of analytic sample, by MSI status**

| | All Institutions | | Non-MSIs | | MSIs | | Public MSIs | | Private MSIs | | Formula-Driven MSIs | | Statutory MSIs | |
|---|---|---|---|---|---|---|---|---|---|---|---|---|---|---|
| | Reset | Non-Reset | Reset | Non-Reset | Reset | Non-Reset | Reset | Non-Reset | Reset | Non-Reset | Reset | Non-Reset | Reset | Non-Reset |
| Number of Applications | 3,982 | 6,003 | 3,831 | 5,924 | 4,463 | 6,342 | 5,335 | 10,108 | 2,910 | 2,499 | 4,349 | 6,702 | 4,833 | 4,775 |
| Fall FTE | 6,171 | 5,988 | 5,598 | 5,732 | 7,716 | 7,068 | 10,292 | 11,199 | 2,199 | 2,729 | 9,313 | 8,311 | 3,294 | 2,764 |
| Number of Pell Recipients | 2,044 | 1,700 | 1,640 | 1,422 | 3,092 | 2,744 | 3,979 | 4,219 | 1,048 | 1,140 | 3,481 | 3,095 | 1,923 | 1,489 |
| Total Tuition Revenue | 42,800,000 | 64,000,000 | 47,300,000 | 68,700,000 | 31,100,000 | 44,400,000 | 35,500,000 | 58,000,000 | 21,600,000 | 30,000,000 | 36,200,000 | 52,100,000 | 16,900,000 | 17,800,000 |
| Tuition Rev. per FTE | 8,639 | 11,553 | 9,916 | 12,528 | 5,286 | 7,483 | 3,298 | 4,380 | 9,544 | 10,769 | 5,157 | 7,549 | 5,675 | 7,254 |
| Avg. Inst. Aid Award | 4,128 | 5,776 | 4,678 | 6,338 | 2,684 | 3,431 | 1,871 | 1,950 | 4,426 | 5,000 | 2,634 | 3,617 | 2,842 | 2,789 |
| State Funding per FTE | 2,998 | 3,501 | 2,268 | 3,246 | 4,915 | 4,566 | 7,046 | 7,665 | 350 | 1,284 | 4,528 | 4,163 | 5,994 | 5,956 |
| Rolling Avg. Enrl. Change | 0.97% | 0.82% | 1.10% | 0.86% | 0.60% | 0.69% | 0.89% | 0.97% | −0.04% | 0.40% | 0.70% | 0.84% | −0.01% | 0.16% |
| Rolling Avg. Aid Award | 4,009 | 5,538 | 4,565 | 6,083 | 2,586 | 3,286 | 1,787 | 1,870 | 4,359 | 4,802 | 2,512 | 3,455 | 2,802 | 2,701 |
| State BA Attainment Rate | 29.80% | 30.34% | 29.85% | 30.52% | 29.67% | 29.53% | 30.13% | 29.52% | 28.58% | 29.53% | 29.67% | 30.30% | 29.72% | 27.03% |
| State Unemployment Rate | 5.95% | 6.02% | 5.94% | 6.01% | 5.98% | 6.08% | 5.90% | 6.02% | 6.17% | 6.14% | 6.01% | 6.12% | 5.92% | 5.93% |

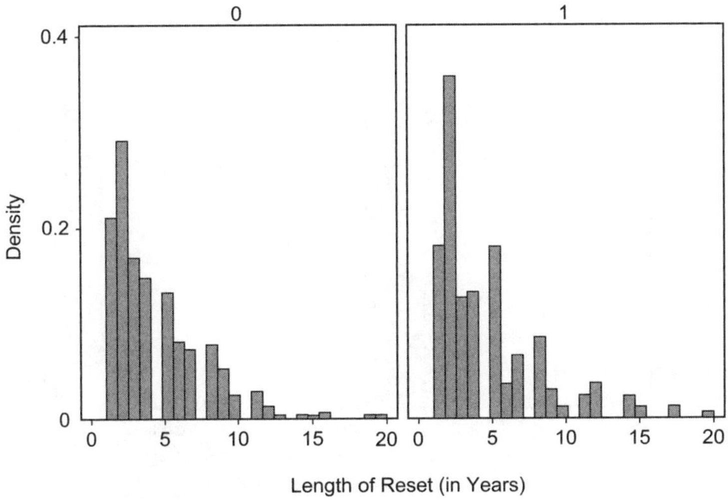


**Fig. 9.3 Length of tuition resets, by MSI status**

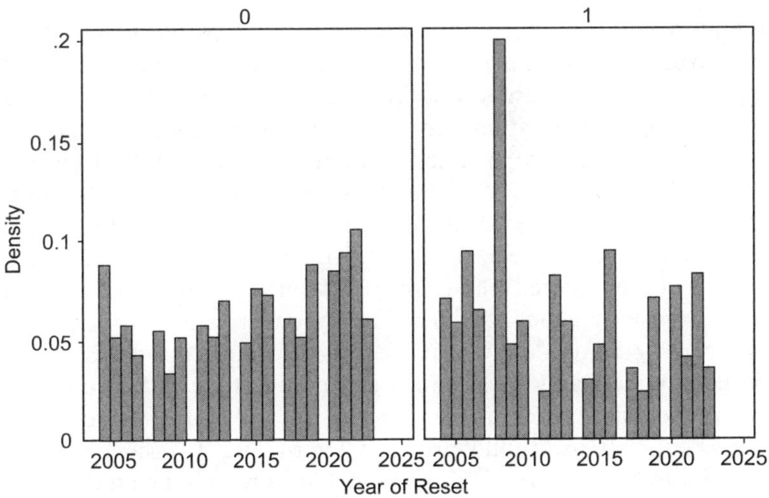


**Fig. 9.4 Distribution of tuition resets across sample years, by MSI status**

reduction in tuition. We explore the relationship between dosage and outcomes in our analysis.

## 9.4.2 Analytic Technique

To estimate the relationship between tuition resets and our outcomes of interest, we use a difference-in-differences (DiD) approach. Recent advances in econometrics methods suggest staggered treatment adoption and the abil-

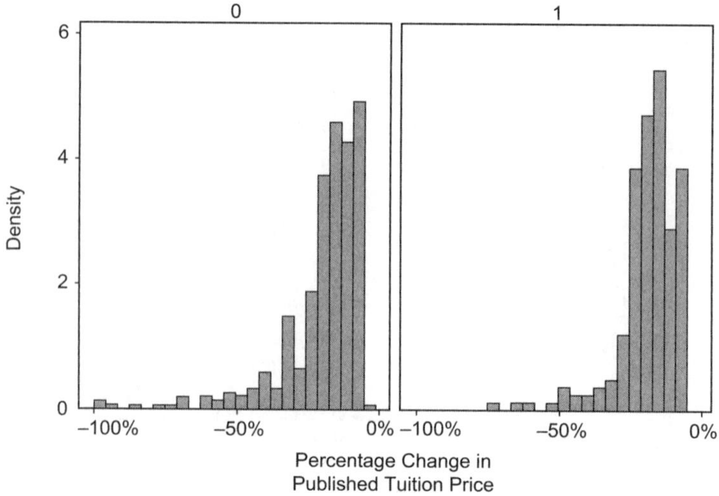


**Fig. 9.5 Distribution of tuition reset sizes, by MSI status**

ity of units to move between treated and control groups may bias traditional two-way fixed-effects estimates (Baker et al. 2022; Goodman-Bacon 2021; Wing et al. 2024). To address issues related to staggered adoption of resets and the ability of the treatment to switch on and off, we use the approach developed by de Chaisemartin and D'Haultfœuille (dCDH) (de Chaisemartin and D'Haultfœuille 2020, 2023). This approach enables us to estimate the instantaneous average treatment effect on the treated (ATT) at the time a reset occurs as well as the dynamic ATTs over specified periods. Given the immediacy of the expected relationship between a reset and our outcomes of interest, the instantaneous ATT is helpful for understanding organizational shifts occurring alongside a tuition reset, and the longer-term dynamic ATT allows us to understand the sustainability of the strategy. Because institutions that reset tuition likely accompany these actions with press releases and marketing efforts (Corral and Ward 2024; Lapovsky 2019), these institutions may benefit to some degree from press materials remaining on the internet or lingering in students', parents', or school counselors' minds after tuition levels have returned to normal rates.

In estimating the DiD model using dCDH's approach, we identify all nontreated institutions during the sample period and create a set of matched control institutions based on a logit model using the variables from table 9.2 to estimate propensity scores of the likelihood of enacting a reset. We restrict the sample of control institutions to account for the aforementioned institutional motivations for lowering sticker prices. Figure 9.6 presents kernel density plots of propensity scores for analytic sample which closely track across the subsamples of institutions.

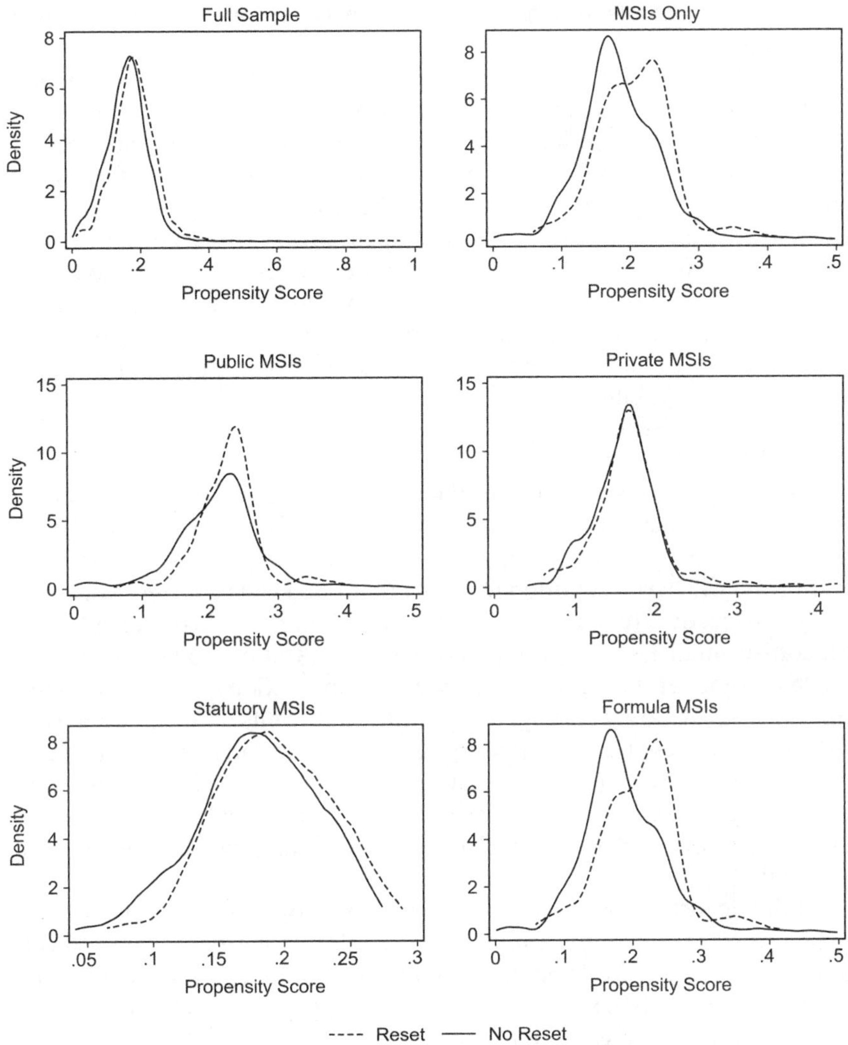


**Fig. 9.6 Kernel density plots of matched sample propensity scores**

We analyze the relationship between resets and institutional outcomes among all public and private nonprofit institutions as a reference point and then examine the relationship exclusively among MSIs and several subsamples. We examine how the relationship varies between public and private MSIs given the differences in sticker price and discounting strategies across the sectors. We also examine how the relationship differs between MSIs that are formula driven and those defined by statutes. Because formula-driven MSIs may have incentives to shift enrollment patterns, including among

Pell recipients, resets may be a strategic device to earn or maintain their MSI status.

As a robustness check to our findings, we also specify event study models using approaches developed by Sun and Abraham (2021) and Borusyak et al. (2022), which are included in the appendix. We also examine how outcomes vary at schools enacting larger resets given that previous research suggests reset dosage impacts enrollments across different student populations (Corral and Ward 2024). Given students are imperfect consumers and may be more likely to respond to the absolute size of the reset than percentage discounts, we use a $5,000 threshold to examine the effects of larger resets. To maintain our comparison group of never-treated institutions, we eliminate institutions with resets smaller than $5,000 from the sample when estimating dosage effects.

### 9.4.3 Limitations

Among private institutions, tuition resets are designed and implemented by institutions themselves. As such, the "treatment" is endogenous and institutional leaders consider the financial impact of such a decision. Often, an institution will have net tuition revenue targets and will package aid accordingly. Prospective students may negotiate their financial aid package. Simultaneously, financial aid administrators balance tuition dollars secured as students sign enrollment contracts with the institution's pool of available financial aid dollars for unsigned students or students accepted off a waitlist. Our estimates of the relationship between a reset and financial outcomes do not constitute a causal relationship. Instead, we use the DiD approach to understand the relationship between resets and financial aid expenditures and tuition revenue to inform a broader understanding of organizational strategy.

At public institutions, tuition resets may be exogenously decided by system leadership, a state governing board, or the legislature, however, this is not always the case. We do not have comprehensive data on whether these are externally mandated so we are hesitant to make any causal claims regarding financial outcomes measured in this study.

Enrollments represent student demand; however, institutions have the ability to constrain this demand through the admissions process. As discussed above, the sticker price of an institution impacts the likelihood of applying, especially for certain groups of institutions, but merely applying does not ensure admission or enrollment. Since many institutions enacting a reset are intending to increase enrollments (Corral and Ward 2024; Lapovsky 2019) and the reset is exogenous to potential applicants, there is a greater likelihood that enrollment effects may be causal. However, we caution a causal interpretation because of the limitations of enrollment as a measure of student demand and the likelihood that an institution enacting a reset may also be implementing other marketing strategies simultaneously.

We do estimate the effect on the number of applicants, which is likely a better estimate of demand. However, we cannot disaggregate applications by students' income to assess differential effects on demand from lower-income students.

## 9.5 Findings

We present our findings through several event study graphs. Figure 9.7 shows the estimated dynamic effects for enrollment-related outcomes across the full set of institutions and the MSI-only sub-sample. Panel A shows the estimated effect of a reset (of at least 5 percent) on the number of applications. We find little effects of a reset on the number of applicants, although there may be a negative impact in the longer term. This downward trend appears more pronounced at MSIs than among the full sample of institutions. Importantly, these findings suggest a reset does not induce higher levels of student demand, as measured by the number of applications. Panels B and C show the relationship between a reset and fall enrollment and Pell enrollment, respectively. Among the full sample of institutions, point estimates are small but positive over time, although standard errors remain large. No relationships with either enrollment outcome are shown among MSIs.

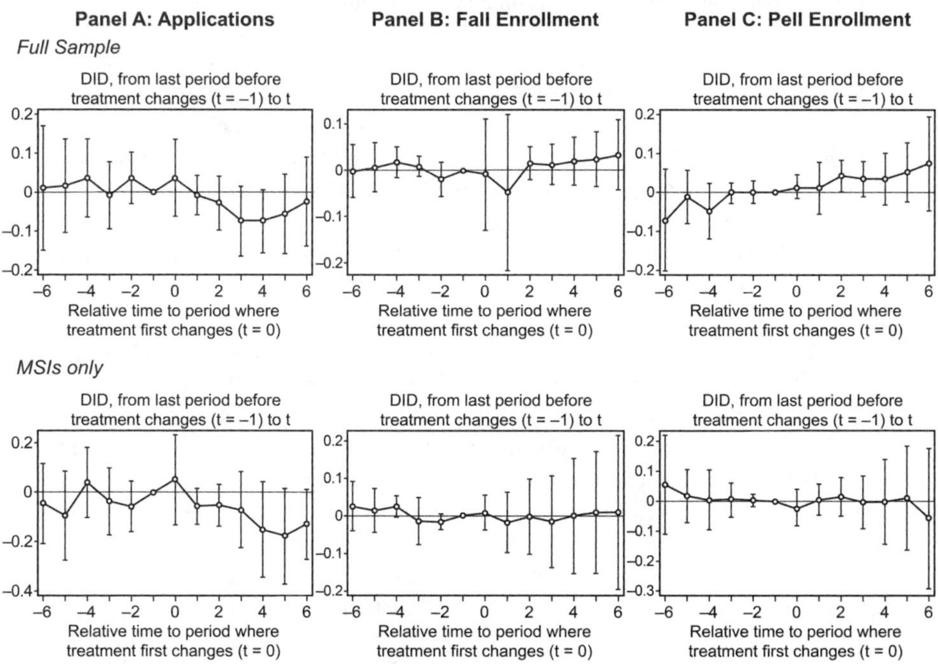


**Fig. 9.7 Dynamic treatment effects on enrollment outcomes**

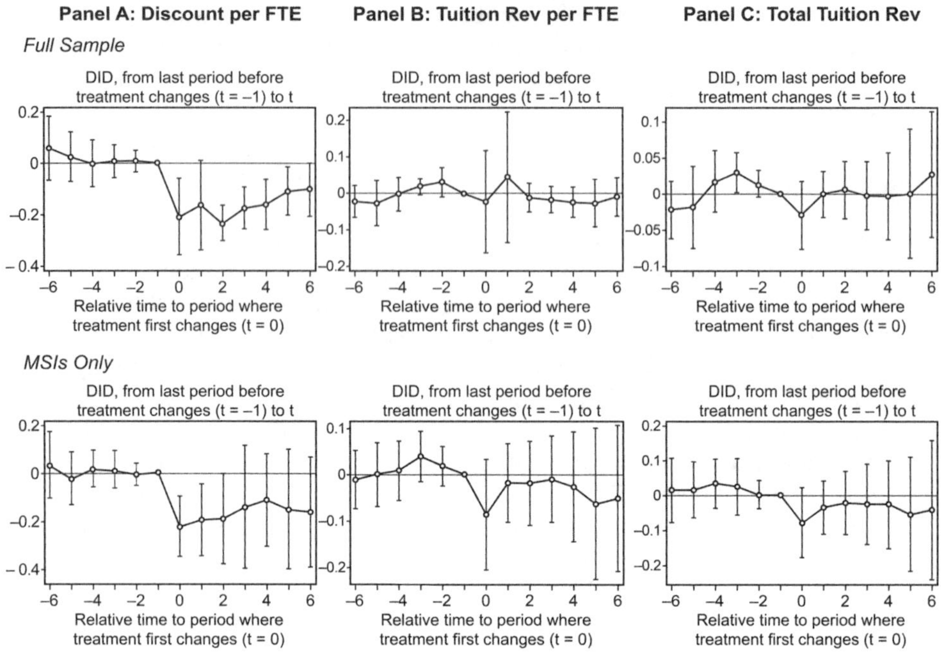


**Fig. 9.8 Dynamic treatment effects on finance outcomes**

Figure 9.8 provides dynamic estimates of the relationship between tuition resets and institutions' financial outcomes. Panel A shows changes in per-FTE institutional aid (i.e., discount) expenditures. On average, a reset is associated with a 20 percent reduction in institutional aid expenditures. Given the average size of a reset is 19.1 percent, this suggests a near one-to-one trade-off by shifting tuition discounts from the financial aid process on the back end of the admissions cycle to a reduced sticker price on the front end of the application process. In both the full sample and among MSIs, this effect fades somewhat over time, likely accompanying the rise in tuition back toward its pre-reset price. Panels B and C of figure 9.8 show the net tuition revenue on a per-student basis and in absolute terms, respectively. Among both the full sample of institutions and the sub-sample of MSIs, resets do not appear to be associated with substantial shifts in tuition revenue patterns. These findings call into question the effectiveness of a reset to create demand which could result in increased tuition revenue.

Although institutions may be mission driven, they must operate within fiscal constraints. As institutions have become increasingly reliant on tuition revenue, the effect of any policy on tuition revenue is critical for institutional viability. Total revenue is a function of enrollment, sticker price, and institutional aid and thus a culmination of the treatment and other reported outcomes. As shown in Panel C of figure 9.7, after an initial decrease in total tuition revenue, most institutions appear to recover and may have positive tuition revenue with the exception of public MSIs.

### 9.5.1 Subgroup Variation

Figure 9.9 shows application and enrollment effects of four subgroups of MSIs: public institutions, private institutions, statutory MSIs (i.e., HBCUs and TCUs), and formula-driven MSIs. As shown in Panel A, we find that resets are associated with decreases in the number of applicants across all subgroups, however standard errors remain large, which is likely due to the smaller sample sizes. Point estimates are most negative among private and statutory MSIs, approaching nearly 50 percent decrease in the number of applicants during prolonged resets.

Despite the apparent negative associations between resets and applications, enrollments following a reset differ across subgroups. At public MSIs, overall and Pell enrollments trend downward, but these enrollment patterns are reverse at private MSIs. While standard errors remain large across both groups and both outcomes, we do see the point estimates to be more extreme among Pell enrollment in both groups reaching 20 percent decreases and increases, respectively, for longer resets. There is some evidence that Pell enrollments increase in the long-run at statutory MSIs, however, enrollment estimates pre-treatment trends across the statutory and formula-driven subgroups do not follow similar trends relative to the comparison group.

Figure 9.10 shows stark differences in changes in institutional aid across public and private MSIs. Public institutions do not appear to substantially adjust aid expenditures while private MSIs reduce aid expenditures by more than 50 percent, an association that persists over time. These differences are important given that public and private MSIs have similar average discount rates (18 percent and 21 percent, respectively). Differences in institutional aid responses may reflect the origins of reset policies. Private institutions autonomously determine their tuition price and thus a reset is part of a larger conversation about financial and enrollment strategies. Public institutions may implement a reset in a similar way but can also have one externally imposed on them from the system or state level. If a reset is externally determined, a public institution may not have planned to adjust institutional aid expenditures. Alternatively, public institutions may face restrictions on changing institutional aid expenditures or have mission-oriented earmarked spending on institutional aid to provide access to in-state students which would contribute to the null findings among public MSIs.

At private MSIs, the decreases in aid translate to relatively stable per-FTE tuition revenue. We observe an upward trend in total revenue, which tracks with the upward trends in total enrollment at private MSIs. The relatively steady levels of institutional aid at public MSIs coupled with a reset appear to yield decreases in per-FTE and total tuition revenue. The small point

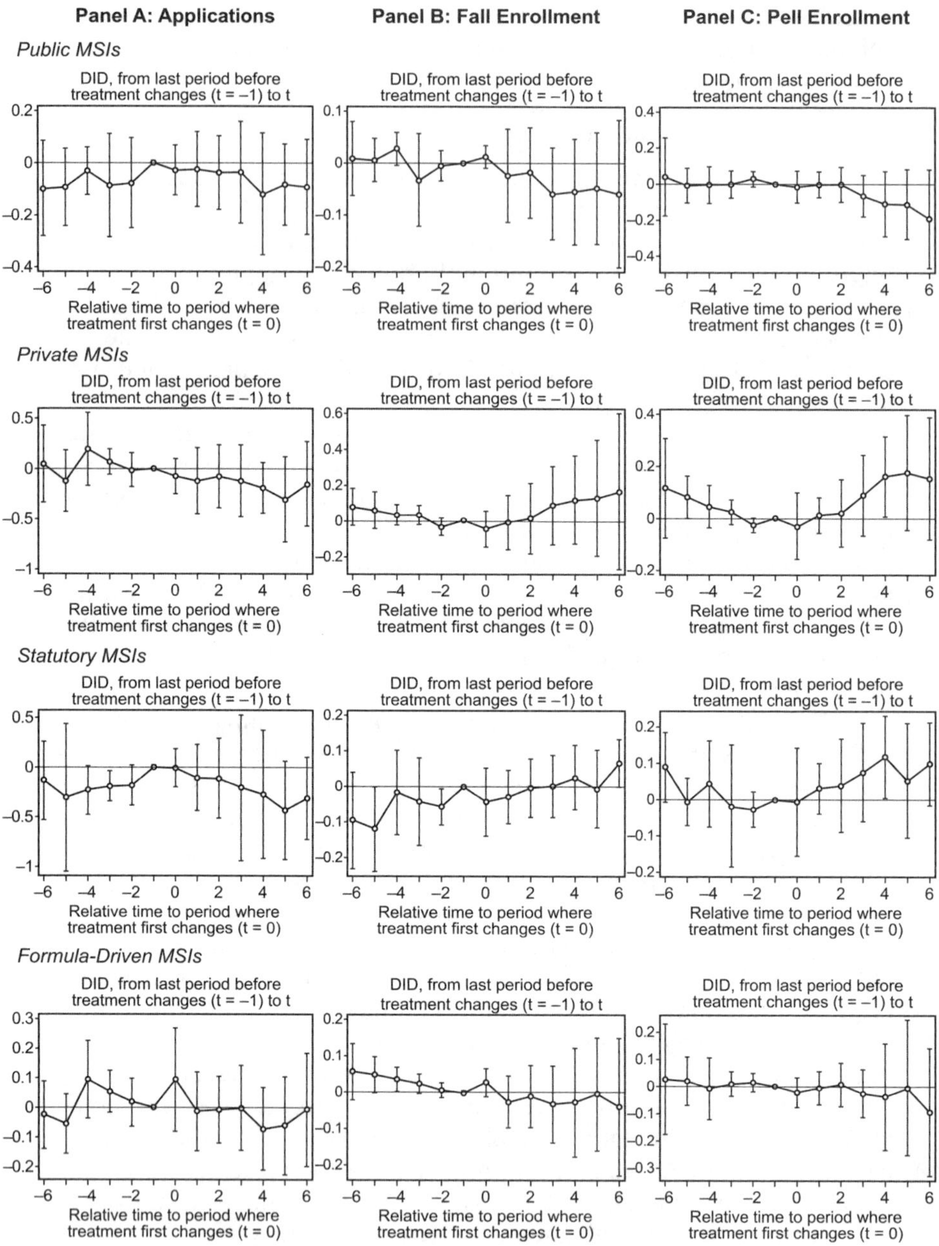


**Fig. 9.9 Dynamic treatment effects on enrollment outcomes, MSI subgroups**

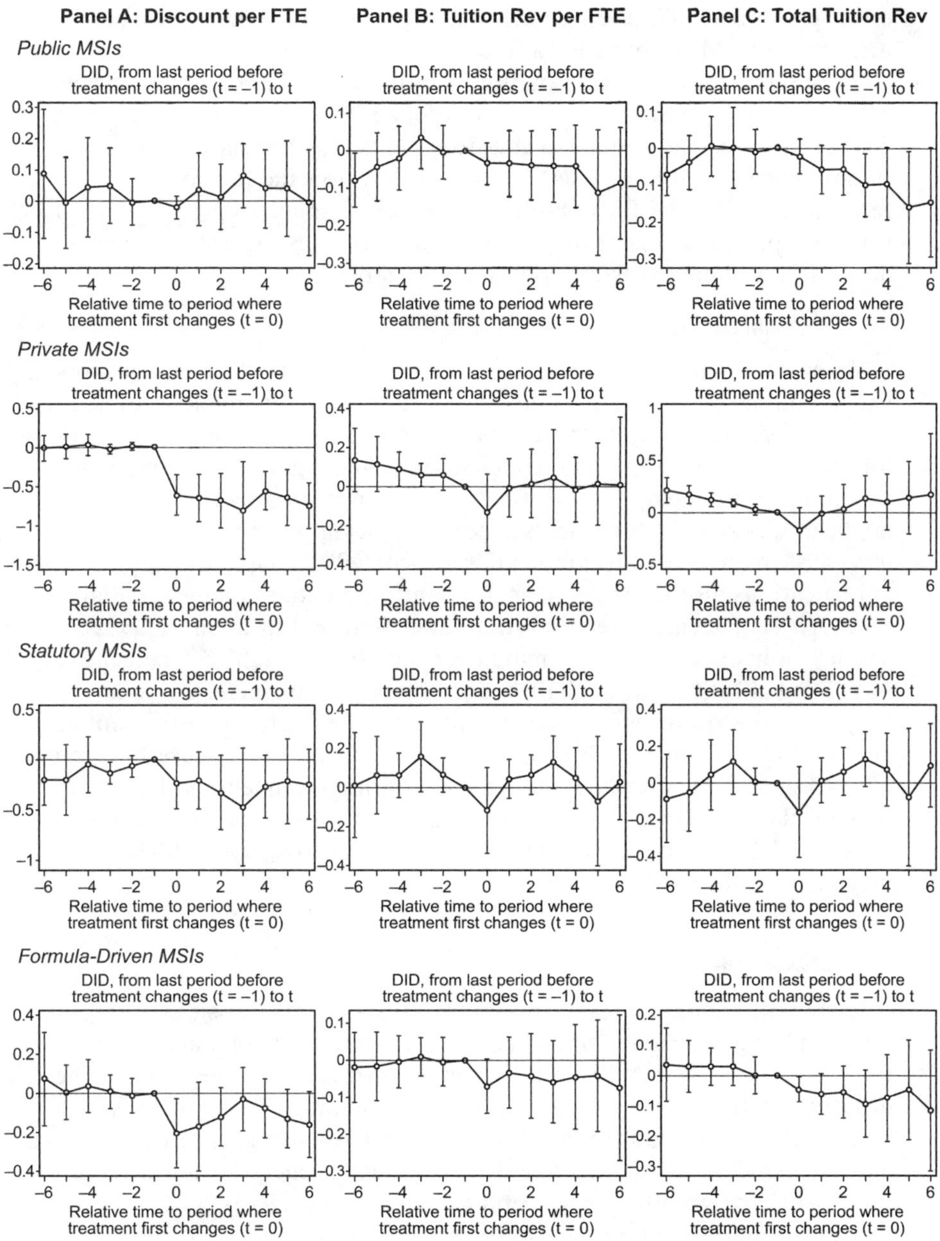


**Fig. 9.10 Dynamic treatment effects on finance outcomes, MSI subgroups**

estimates for per-FTE revenue likely reflect the observed decreases in enrollment at public MSIs following a reset.

We observe decreases in discounting at both statutory and formula-driven MSIs, although point estimates for statutory MSIs dip substantially lower. These larger decreases in aid at statutory MSIs may translate to increased tuition revenue, but these effects do not persist over the full six-year post-reset time period. At formula-driven MSIs, the smaller decreases in aid lead to apparent decreases in revenue; point estimates suggest a 10 percent decrease, but standard errors continue to be large.

### 9.5.2 Dosage Effects

We examine our six outcomes following larger resets of $5,000 or more to examine variation driven by dosage effects. Due to the smaller sample of institutions engaging in larger resets, we only estimate these relationships for the full sample and all MSIs pooled. As seen in figure 9.11, larger resets do not appear related to student demand, as measured by the number of applicants. However, enrollments in both samples appear to increase following a large reset, especially among lower-income Pell recipients.

Institutions also decrease their discounting practices following a large reset. These decreases are substantial and persistent at about 60 percent among all institutions and ranging over time from roughly 75 percent to 40 percent at MSIs. Although these decreases in aid are large, they may not fully offset the lost revenue associated with the reset. In both the full sample and among MSIs per-FTE tuition revenue appears to decrease between 10 percent and 20 percent. However, total tuition revenue in both samples remains flat following a reset. This is particularly striking given the downward trend in total tuition revenue prior to the reset, suggesting this strategy may help stabilize institutional revenues.

## 9.6 Discussion

Our findings suggest that, on average, MSIs experience similar enrollment and financial outcomes as non-MSIs, although resets may be positively associated with Pell enrollments at non-MSIs to a greater extent. The negative relationship between a reset and the number of applicants may indicate that higher education is a Veblen Good, where higher prices induce more demand, or a "Chivas Regal" effect. Such a phenomenon has been documented at wealthy, low-acceptance institutions (Kirp 2004), but the dominant discourse about postsecondary education more broadly centers on unaffordability and how students are price sensitive (Dynarski et al. 2022; Goldrick-Rab 2016). Importantly, we cannot disaggregate applicants by income using IPEDS data. It is possible that reductions in applications are driven by higher-income students and that the extent to which college is a Veblen Good is directly proportional to a student's financial well-being.

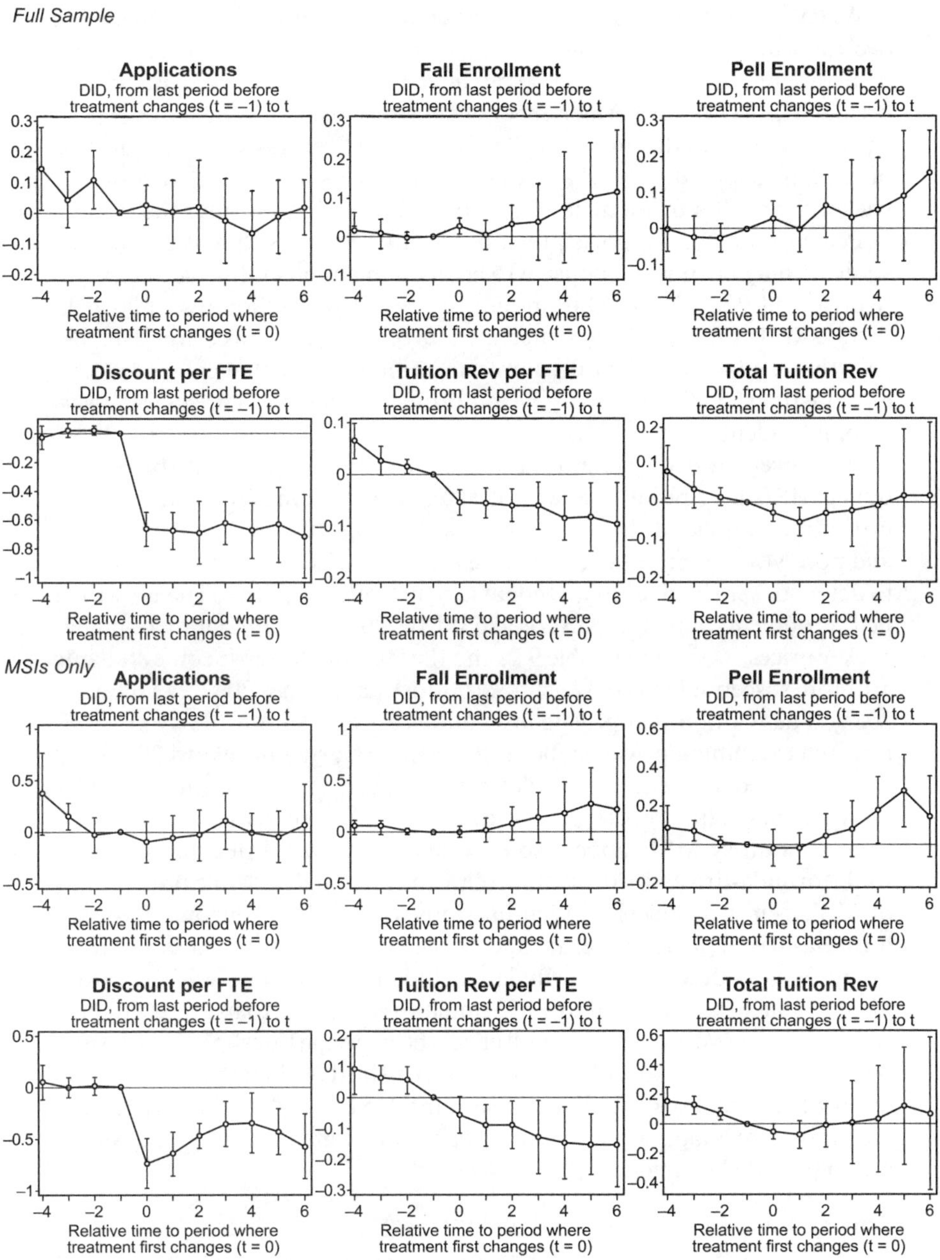


**Fig. 9.11 Dynamic treatment effects of large resets**

When we disaggregate MSIs into different subgroups, we continue to see decreases in applicants following a reset, however we find important enrollment differences. We find a sharp split in Pell enrollment between public and private MSIs with the former experiencing decreases and the latter experiencing increases. Although enrollment is neither exclusively an indicator of student demand, due to an admissions process, nor exclusively tied to sticker price, due to financial aid and back-end discounting, the growth in Pell enrollments supports previous research findings that lower-income students may be most responsive to changes in actual and perceived prices (Corral and Ward 2024). Our findings suggest that a tuition reset may help private MSIs fulfill income-related aspects of their missions. Moreover, the growth in Pell in both the full sample and among MSIs that enacted a reset of more than $5,000 reinforces the importance of perceived prices for lower-income students.

Our observed decrease in total enrollment and among Pell students at public MSIs may point to a lack of efficacy of tuition resets among these institutions. Public MSIs, which have lower average tuition than their private and non-MSI counterparts, may have a sticker price that is sufficiently low to deter sticker shock even if students are net-price sensitive. The growth in Pell enrollments at private MSIs is likely driven by the combination of higher sticker prices, as shown in table 9.2, and the fact that lower-income students are more susceptible to sticker shock (Grodsky and Jones 2007; Levine et al. 2023). These findings at private institutions are also supported by previous research examining private colleges in general (Corral and Ward 2024).

We also find differences in enrollment trends across statutory and formula-driven MSIs. While both groups' overall enrollment remained relatively stable, statutory MSIs appear to experience a growth in Pell enrollments while formula-driven MSIs' Pell enrollments remain flat. While both groups of MSIs generally have it in their missions to serve lower-income students, formula-driven MSIs have an added incentive to enroll these students because many designation formulae include lower-income student enrollment. As such, we expected to see formula-driven MSIs to use resets to pursue this group. We may observe null effects because the threshold is easily met by these institutions considering roughly one-third of their students already receive Pell (see table 9.2) or because some MSI designations only require a certain percentage to receive need-based aid which is a more expansive group than Pell recipients.

### 9.6.1 Implications for Institutional Finance

The overwhelming majority of institutions lack an abundance of alumni with deep pockets or a sizable endowment from which to draw funds. Instead, institutions are operating on tight budgets where every enrolled student and their net tuition revenue are critical for meeting organizational revenue goals (Lucido 2014). Simultaneously, the shifting burden of postsecondary costs to students and their families coupled with rising costs of colleges have created more price-sensitive students and put college out of the financial reach of many students. In the face of declining enrollments and increased opacity in college pricing, many institutions have turned to tuition resets as a marketing tool and a way to communicate to students that their institution is affordable.

Total tuition revenue, an important component of institutional revenue especially among private MSIs, is a function of total enrollment, sticker price, and institutional aid. As sticker price decreases, as in the case of a tuition reset, it is expected that institutional aid will also decrease in order to keep net tuition revenue per FTE constant. Of course, if an institution can increase its enrollment with a low marginal cost for each additional student, it is possible that a decrease in sticker price does not necessitate an equivalent decrease in institutional aid to grow total tuition revenue.

Our findings in figure 9.8 suggest that, on average, a tuition reset does not substantially improve an institution's total tuition revenue or tuition revenue per FTE. This is due to large decreases in institutional aid and relatively null enrollment effects. However, these outcomes differ between public and private MSIs. We observe private MSIs experiencing some growth in fall enrollment and total tuition revenue. These effects appear to be strongest when resets are prolonged, suggesting a reset is not a quick fix to the revenue equation. Nevertheless, private MSIs that reset tuition appear to benefit financially in the long term.

Public MSIs, however, show a downward trajectory in total tuition revenue. These institutions experience decreases in enrollment, especially in the longer term, and do not appear to change institutional aid expenditures substantially. The steady per FTE discounts may be due to public institutions' lack of discretion in some public dollars earmarked for institutional aid. Additionally, tuition revenue comprises a smaller share of total revenue thus making the pass through of decreases in sticker price to decreases in institutional aid less important for the organization's bottom line. However, public institutions do experience decreased total tuition revenue, a decrease which grows in magnitude over time.

Tuition resets, especially larger and more prolonged resets, represent a shift away from a high tuition/high aid model toward a low tuition/low aid model. Both public and private institutions have moved toward the high tuition/high aid model over the past several years, although the shift has been more pronounced among private institutions. As such, we expect a reset to be more impactful in this sector. Private institutions using this model generally charge each student a different net price after various types of aid are included to discount the sticker price. The high tuition/high aid models allows enrollment managers at private institutions to strategically use aid to advance institutional goals which may include significant need-based aid to improve affordability for lower-income students, targeted grants that reduce the price and increase enrollment of historically underserved populations, or specialty awards to bolster academic, athletic, or other extracurricular accomplishments at the institution. Resetting tuition and moving toward a low tuition/low aid model likely places constraints on an institution's ability to use aid to recruit certain groups of students.

Some scholars have pointed out that restricting tuition prices may harm lower-income students as institutional aid budgets will not grow sufficiently to make college affordable for those with higher demonstrated financial need (Levine 2022). Moreover, they argue that cutting sticker prices may harm lower-income students. Our findings suggest that private MSIs, which have higher sticker prices, increase Pell enrollments following a reset and larger cuts to the sticker price generally are followed by increases in Pell enrollments. Moreover, larger resets are associated with decreases in per-FTE tuition revenue which suggests a substantial change in pricing model may translate to lower net prices for students. Previous research has also indicated that while all students at private institutions experience a decrease in net price following a reset, the decrease is smallest for the highest-income students and the net price for lower-income students remains lower than middle- and upper-income students (Corral and Ward 2024). Although IPEDS data do not allow for a student-by-student examination of net price, our findings that Pell enrollments grow suggest that resets may be a useful tool for lowering sticker shock and bringing more transparency to the college pricing process for this group.

Finally, tuition resets do not appear to bring increased financial stability to institutions. Although a reset may have positive effects on students, especially lower-income students, the null or negative relationships between resets and tuition revenue suggests there are no financial revenue gains for institutions using this approach. There may be improved administrative efficiencies that result in lower costs for the institution, and we encourage future research to examine this. While the benefits to students are an important outcome, if these institutions are engaging in resets as a strategy to combat poor financial outlooks, then resets do not appear to be a feasible solution for their problems.

## 9.7 Conclusion

In many ways MSIs are fundamentally different than their non-MSIs. These institutions have distinct missions, experience different trends in and shocks to demand, receive mission-aligned federal funding, but have also been historically neglected through other funding mechanisms. As a result of this unique position, many MSIs are facing financial constraints that may jeopardize their ability to fulfill their mission or remain solvent. Both MSIs and non-MSIs have engaged in tuition reset policies in an effort to counter flagging enrollment, induce demand for the institution, and improve the organization's financial outlook. In this study, we build upon prior research to understand how students and institutions respond to decreases in sticker prices at MSIs.

Our findings suggest tuition resets may not induce demand, on average, as intended. Enrollment changes are likely driven by organizational strategy, and we find a divergence between public and private MSIs. These strategies do not appear to be linked to improved financial outcomes for institutions. Taken together, our findings suggest that private MSIs may use resets to grow enrollment and possibly increase overall tuition revenue. They appear to do this while also increasing access to lower-income students, although our findings cannot disaggregate if the reset hampers the institution's ability to meet these students' financial needs. Resets may be a viable option for some institutions, but context and individual strategy likely play a pivotal role in the success of such a strategy.

Our findings, and those from previous scholarship, suggest additional avenues for future research. We believe it is important to better understand the factors related to and preceding the adoption of a reset policy. These antecedents of the policy may provide useful ways to further disaggregate estimates of the effects of resets and give important context that influences the success of such a strategy. Additionally, it is important to further explore the effects among public institutions and identify if enrollment and finance outcomes differ when institutions devise the reset strategy themselves as opposed to its being externally mandated. Finally, we suggest that future research explore students' responses and perceptions of a reset to better understand when and if resets can be an effective tool for institutions.

# Appendix

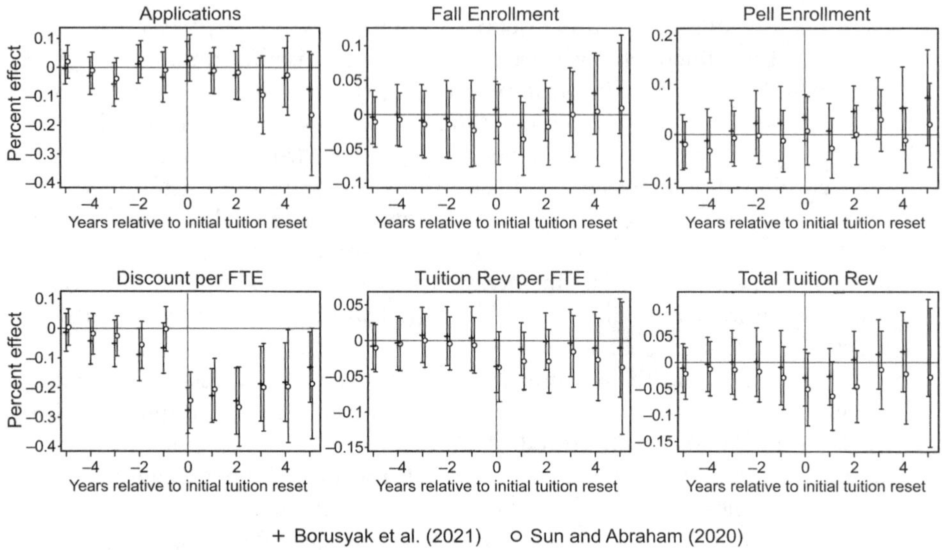


**Fig. 9A.1 Robustness checks for full sample**

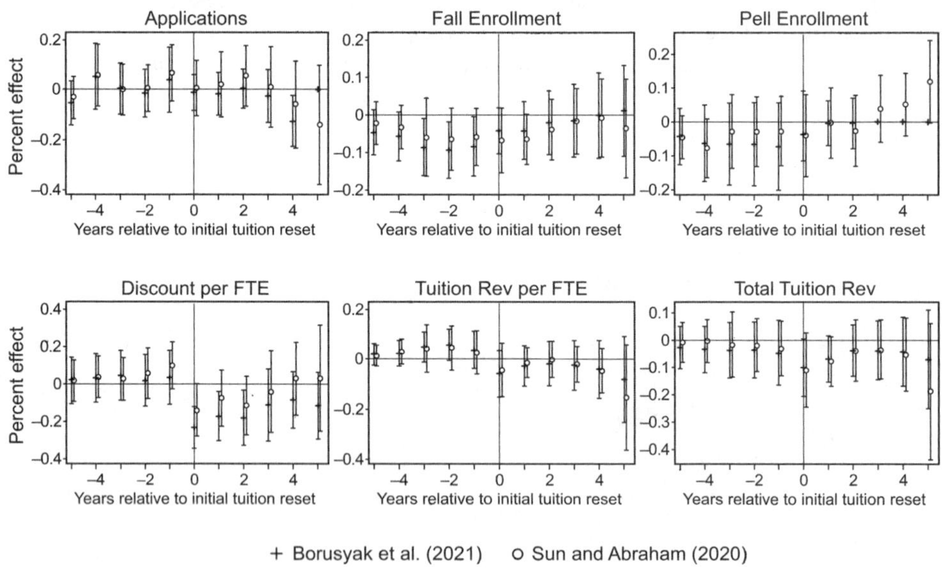


**Fig. 9A.2 Robustness checks for MSI Subsample**

## References


Acton, R. 2021. "Effects of Reduced Community College Tuition on College Choices and Degree Completion." *Education Finance and Policy* 16(3): 388–417. https://doi.org/10.1162/edfp_a_00313.

Aguilar, S. 2021. *Sources of Inequity of the Title V Program: A Critical Qualitative Study of Institutional Agents' Understanding of Hispanic-Serving Institutions' Grant-Seeking Competitiveness.* PhD diss., Michigan State University. https://www.proquest.com/docview/2559455654/abstract/A00FCCA8832F46A9PQ/1.

American Indian Higher Education Consortium. 2022. *Tribal Colleges & Universities*. https://www.aihec.org/tribal-colleges-universities/.

Baker, A. C., D. F. Larcker, and C. C. Y. Wang. 2022. "How Much Should We Trust Staggered Difference-in-Differences Estimates?" *Journal of Financial Economics* 144(2): 370–95. https://doi.org/10.1016/j.jfineco.2022.01.004.

Boland, W. 2018. "The Higher Education Act and Minority Serving Institutions: Toward a Typology of Title III and V Funded Programs." *Education Sciences* 8(1): 33. https://doi.org/10.3390/educsci8010033.

Borusyak, Kirill, Peter Hull, and Xavier Jaravel. 2022. "Quasi-experimental shift-share research designs." *Review of Economic Studies* 89(1): 181–213.

Callaway, B., and P. H. C. Sant'Anna. 2021. "Difference-in-Differences with Multiple Time Periods." *Journal of Econometrics* 225(2): 200–230. https://doi.org/10.1016/j.jeconom.2020.12.001.

Castro Samayoa, A. 2022. "Minority-Serving Institutions: Current Policies and Future Actions." In *Civil Rights and Federal Higher Education*, edited by N. W. Hillman and G. Orfield, 127–42. Harvard Education Press.

Cheslock, J. J., and S. O. Riggs. 2021. "Psychology, market pressures, and pricing decisions in higher education: The case of the US private sector." *Higher Education* 81(4): 757–774.

Corral, D., and J. D. Ward. 2024. "Calibrating Costs: Do Tuition Reset Policies Affect Diverse Student Enrollment at Private Baccalaureate Colleges?" *Review of Higher Education* 47(2): 189–215.

de Chaisemartin, C., and X. D'Haultfœuille. 2020. "Two-Way Fixed Effects Estimators with Heterogeneous Treatment Effects." *American Economic Review* 110(9): 2964–2996. https://doi.org/10.1257/aer.20181169.

de Chaisemartin, C., and X. D'Haultfœuille. 2023. "Two-Way Fixed Effects and Differences-in-Differences with Heterogeneous Treatment Effects: A Survey." *Econometrics Journal* 26(3): C1–C30. https://doi.org/10.1093/ectj/utac017.

Delaney, J. A., and W. R. Doyle. 2011. "State Spending on Higher Education: Testing the Balance Wheel over Time." *Journal of Education Finance* 36(4): 343–68.

Denning, J. T. 2017. "College on the Cheap: Consequences of Community College Tuition Reductions." *American Economic Journal: Economic Policy* 9(2): 155–88.

Dortch, C. 2023. *Programs for Minority-Serving Institutions under the Higher Education Act*. Congressional Research Service.

Edwards, A., J. Ortagus, J. Smith, and A. Smythe. 2023. *HBCU Enrollment and Longer-Term Outcomes*. EdWorkingPaper: 23–883. Annenberg Institute at Brown University. https://doi.org/10.26300/4xqa-cs32.

Gándara, D., M. S. Billings, P. G. Rubin, and L. Hammond. 2023. "One of the Weakest Budget Players in the State": State Funding of Higher Education at the Onset of the COVID-19 Pandemic." *Educational Evaluation and Policy Analysis*, 01623737231168812.

Gándara, D., and A. Rutherford. 2018. "Mitigating Unintended Impacts? The Effects

of Premiums for Underserved Populations in Performance-Funding Policies for Higher Education." *Research in Higher Education* 59(6): 681–703. https://doi.org/10.1007/s11162-017-9483-x.
Gasman, M. 2008. "Minority-Serving Institutions: A Historical Backdrop." In *Understanding Minority-Serving Institutions*, edited by M. Gasman, B. Baez, and C. S. V. Turner, 18–27. State University of New York Press.
Gasman, M., T.-H. Nguyen, and C. F. Conrad. 2015. "Lives Intertwined: A Primer on the History and Emergence of Minority Serving Institutions." *Journal of Diversity in Higher Education* 8(2): 120–38. https://doi.org/10.1037/a0038386.
Gasman, M., T.-H. Nguyen, A. C. Samayoa, and D. Corral. 2017. "Minority Serving Institutions: A Data-Driven Student Landscape in the Outcomes-Based Funding Universe." *Berkeley Review of Education* 7(1): 5–24.
Garcia, G. A. 2017. "Defined by Outcomes or Culture? Constructing an Organizational Identity for Hispanic-Serving Institutions." *American Educational Research Journal* 54(1S): 111S-134S. https://doi.org/10.3102/0002831216669779.
Goldrick-Rab, Sara. 2016. *Paying the Price*. University of Chicago Press.
Goodman-Bacon, A. 2021. "Difference-in-Differences with Variation in Treatment Timing." *Journal of Econometrics* 225(2): 254–77. https://doi.org/10.1016/j.jeconom.2021.03.014.
Grodsky, E., and M. T. Jones. 2007. "Real and Imagined Barriers to College Entry: Perceptions of Cost." *Social Science Research* 36(2): 745–66. https://doi.org/10.1016/j.ssresearch.2006.05.001.
Grodsky, E., and D. Kalogrides. 2008. "The Declining Significance of Race in College Admissions Decisions." *American Journal of Education* 115(1): 1–33. https://doi.org/10.1086/590673.
Hegji, A. 2017. *Programs for Minority Serving Institutions under the Higher Education Act*. Congressional Research Service. https://files.eric.ed.gov/fulltext/ED597886.pdf.
Hillman, N. W. 2012. "Tuition Discounting for Revenue Management." *Research in Higher Education* 53(3): 263–81. https://doi.org/10.2307/41475391.
Hillman, N. W., and D. Corral. 2018. "The Equity Implications of Paying for Performance in Higher Education." *American Behavioral Scientist* 61(14): 1757–1772. https://doi.org/10.1177/0002764217744834.
Kirp, David L. 2004. *Shakespeare, Einstein, and the Bottom Line: The Marketing of Higher Education*. Harvard University Press.
Klasik, D., Z. William, R. E. Worsham, and M. G. Springer. 2024. "Do Students Respond to Sticker-Price Reductions? Evidence from the North Carolina Promise." EdWorkingPaper No. 24–918. Annenberg Institute at Brown University. https://edworkingpapers.com/ai24-918.
Lapovsky, L. 2015. "Tuition Reset: An Analysis of Eight Colleges That Addressed the Escalating Price of Higher Education." https://lapovsky.com/wp-content/uploads/2015/11/TuitionReset.pdf.
Lapovsky, L. 2019. "Do Price Resets Work?" https://lapovsky.com/wp-content/uploads/2010/07/Do-Price-Resets-Work-.pdf.
Layzell, D. T. 2007. "State Higher Education Funding Models: An Assessment of Current and Emerging Approaches." *Journal of Education Finance* 33(1): 1–19.
Levine, P. B. 2022. *A Problem of Fit: How the Complexity of College Pricing Hurts Students—and Universities*. The University of Chicago Press.
Levine, P. B., J. Ma, and L. C. Russell. 2023. "Do College Applicants Respond to Changes in Sticker Prices Even When They Don't Matter?" *Education Finance and Policy* 18(3): 365–94. https://doi.org/10.1162/edfp_a_00372.
Li, A. Y. 2017. "Dramatic Declines in Higher Education Appropriations: State Con-

ditions for Budget Punctuations." *Research in Higher Education* 58(4): 395–429. https://doi.org/10.1007/s11162-016-9432-0.

Li, A. Y., D. Gándara, and A. Assalone. 2018. "Equity or Disparity: Do Performance Funding Policies Disadvantage 2-Year Minority-Serving Institutions?" *Community College Review* 46(3): 288–315. https://doi.org/10.1177/0091552118778776.

Lucido, J. A. 2014. "How Admission Decisions Get Made." In *Handbook of Strategic Enrollment Management*, edited by D. Hossler and B. Bontrager, 147–73. Jossey-Bass.

Marin, P., and S. Aguilar-Smith. 2023. "The Evolving Portrayal of Hispanic-Serving Institutions? A Systematic Review of More Than 20 Years of Research." *Journal of Hispanic Higher Education* 22(4): 446–59. https://doi.org/10.1177/15381927221137691.

Marroquín, C. 2019. "Tribal colleges and universities: A testament of resilience and nation building." Center for Minority Serving Institutions.

National Association of College and University Business Officers (NACUBO). 2023. 2022 Tuition Discounting Study. https://www.nacubo.org/Research/2021/NACUBO-Tuition-Discounting-Study.

Nelson, C. A., and J. R. Frye. 2016. *Tribal College and University Funding: Tribal Sovereignty at the Intersection of Federal, State, and Local Funding*. American Council on Education. https://www.acenet.edu/Documents/Tribal-College-and-University-Funding.pdf.

National Center for Science and Engineering Statistics. 2021. *Table 5–4: Bachelor's Degrees Awarded by All Institutions and by HBCUs to Black U.S. Citizens and Permanent Residents, by Field: 2008–18*. https://ncses.nsf.gov/pubs/nsf21321/data-tables.

Nguyen, M. H., J. J. Ramirez, and S. Laderman. 2023. "What Counts as a Minority-Serving Institution? Toward the Utilization of a Standardized and Uniform Definition and Typology." *Educational Researcher* 52(3): 174–79. https://doi.org/10.3102/0013189X221105861.

Nienhusser, H. K., and T. Oshio. 2017. "High School Students' Accuracy in Estimating the Cost of College: A Proposed Methodological Approach and Differences among Racial/Ethnic Groups and College Financial-Related Factors." *Research in Higher Education* 58(7): 723–45. https://doi.org/10.1007/s11162-017-9447-1.

Ortagus, J. C., K. Rosinger, R. Kelchen, N. Voorhees, G. Chu, and H. Allchin. 2023. "A national analysis of the impact of performance-based funding on completion outcomes among underserved students." *Review of Higher Education* 46(4): 415–452. 10.1353/rhe.2023.a900568.

Ortagus, J. C., K. O. Rosinger, R. Kelchen, G. Chu, and M. Lingo. 2023. "The Unequal Impacts of Performance-Based Funding on Institutional Resources in Higher Education." *Research in Higher Education* 64(5): 705–39. https://doi.org/10.1007/s11162-022-09719-2.

Postsecondary National Policy Institute. 2022. *Tribal Colleges and Universities Primer*. Postsecondary National Policy Institute.

Rutgers Center for MSIs. 2023. List of Minority Serving Institutions 2023. Rutgers University. https://cmsi.gse.rutgers.edu/sites/default/files/2023%20CMSI%20MSI%20List.pdf.

Smith, D. O. 2019. *University Finances: Accounting and Budgeting Principles for Higher Education*. Johns Hopkins Press.

Sun, L., and S. Abraham. 2021. "Estimating Dynamic Treatment Effects in Event Studies with Heterogeneous Treatment Effects." *Journal of Econometrics* 225(2): 175–99. https://doi.org/10.1016/j.jeconom.2020.09.006.

Taylor, B. J., B. Cantwell, K. Watts, and O. Wood. 2020. "Partisanship, White Racial

Resentment, and State Support for Higher Education." *Journal of Higher Education* 91(6): 858–87. https://doi.org/10.1080/00221546.2019.1706016.
Taylor, B. J., K. Kunkle, and K. Watts. 2023. "Democratic Backsliding and the Balance Wheel Hypothesis: Partisanship and State Funding for Higher Education in the United States." *Higher Education Policy* 36(4): 781–803.
Turner, S. 2018. "The Evolution of the High Tuition, High Aid Debate." *Change: The Magazine of Higher Learning* 50(3–4): 142–48. https://doi.org/10.1080/00091383.2018.1509652.
US Department of Education. 2023. "Secretaries of Education, Agriculture Call on Governors to Equitably Fund Land-Grant HBCUs." https://www.ed.gov/news/press-releases/secretaries-education-agriculture-call-governors-equitably-fund-land-grant-hbcus.
Ward, J. D., and D. Corral. 2023. "Resetting Prices: Estimating the Effect of Tuition Reset Policies on Institutional Finances and Enrollment." *Research in Higher Education* 64(6): 862–92.
Webber, D. A. 2017. "State Divestment and Tuition at Public Institutions." *Economics of Education Review* 60: 1–4. https://doi.org/10.1016/j.econedurev.2017.07.007.
Weisbrod, B. A., J. P. Ballou, and E. D. Asch. 2008. *Mission and Money: Understanding the University*. Cambridge University Press. https://doi.org/10.1017/CBO9780511511011.
Williams, K. L., and B. L. Davis. 2019. *Public and Private Investments and Divestments in Historically Black Colleges and Universities*. American Council on Education. https://www.acenet.edu/Documents/Public-and-Private-Investments-and-Divestments-in-HBCUs.pdf.
Wing, C., M. Yozwiak, A. Hollingsworth, S. Freedman, and K. Simon. 2024. "Designing Difference-In-Difference Studies with Staggered Treatment Adoption: Key Concepts and Practical Guidelines." *Annual Review of Public Health* 45. https://doi.org/10.1146/annurev-publhealth-061022-050825.
Yang, J., and M. Masulit. 2017. "The Problematic Challenges Faced by Dual Designation at California State Universities." In *Educational Challenges at Minority Serving Institutions*, edited by M. Gasman, A. Castro Samayoa, W. C. Boland, and P. Esmieu, 52–62. Routledge.

# **Comment** Bridget Long

## Introduction

First, I want to commend the organizers of this book for focusing on an important, but relatively overlooked, set of research questions. The higher education sector plays a meaningful role in the economy at both the individual level and in shaping the well-being of communities and the nation at large. Yet, colleges and universities, most of which are non-profit in the

Bridget Long is a Harvard University Distinguished Service Professor and the Saris Professor of Education and Economics at the Harvard Graduate School of Education, and a research associate of the National Bureau of Economic Research.

For acknowledgments, sources of research support, and disclosure of the author's material financial relationships, if any, please see https://www.nber.org/books-and-chapters/financing-institutions-higher-education/comment-examining-effects-tuition-reset-policies-enrollment-and-institutional-finances-minority.

United States, function in ways that differ distinctly from the traditional for-profit firms and organizations that are the focus of most study in economics. By seeking to investigate the financial circumstances, pressures, and strategies of higher education institutions, this book expands our understanding of this important segment of society.

I was especially delighted to see a focus on minority-serving institutions (MSIs), including Historically Black Colleges and Universities (HBCUs), Tribal Colleges and Universities (TCUs), and Enrollment-Based MSIs. To varying degrees, these colleges and universities have the distinct mission to serve specific student populations, and within this category, the HBCUs have a history of offering access to underserved students and producing Black college graduates, especially in STEM and professional fields, at disproportionately higher levels than their share of the postsecondary market. In recent years, MSIs have received increasing attention given their historic and potentially future role in serving students. At the federal level, the government allocated more than $16 billion in funding to HBCUs from fiscal years 2021 to 2024, a dramatic increase over previous years.[1] As noted by the authors, these institutions warrant further study, and hopefully, this paper will be one of many to take a closer look at this part of higher education.

While I applaud the paper's attention on MSIs, my comments focus on several issues that have important implications for how one might approach the task of estimating the impact of tuition reset policies. The first point is to note that many of the characteristics of MSIs that the authors highlight are not unique to these institutions, which leads to questions about the degree to which this study reflects the specific experience of MSIs as opposed to something broader or defined differently. I then remark on the incredible diversity of MSIs. Many differences between MSIs are pointed out by the authors, but there are additional distinctions that are meaningful when considering the impact of a tuition policy change; they should be taken into account when designing the analytical strategy. Finally, I elaborate on the factors that drive an institution's tuition-setting behavior, which should also be incorporated into the analysis so that the researchers are better able to isolate the effects of being an MSI.

## What Is Distinctive About an MSI?

The paper begins with a historical overview and discussion of the policy context for MSIs, and the authors highlight important features that make MSIs unique, which I would summarize into four main points. First, these institutions focus on race, with either a historical race-based purpose or by

1. Source: White House statement May 16, 2024. "FACT SHEET: Biden-Harris Administration Announces Record Over $16 Billion in Support for Historically Black Colleges and Universities (HBCUs)." Accessed September 4, 2024 at https://www.whitehouse.gov/briefing-room/statements-releases/2024/05/16/fact-sheet-biden-harris-administration-announces-record-over-16-billion-in-support-for-historically-black-colleges-and-universities-hbcus/.

meeting an enrollment threshold for a racial group. Second, the authors emphasize that MSIs have a distinct mission as "they collectively seek to educate large concentrations of underrepresented students . . ." (3). The focus on this mission could result in decision-making and reforms that prioritize student access and success. The third distinction is that these institutions receive special federal funding, and a fourth feature is that MSIs, HBCUs in particular, have had outsize success in producing graduates in fields such as engineering, medicine, and law.

Looking closely at the indicators the authors use to define how MSIs are unique, it is clear that the sample constructed in the paper contains institutions that vary in how closely they fit the MSI description. For example, there are reasons to question whether all MSIs are committed to the stated mission. The authors are forthcoming that enrollment-based MSIs may not actually perceive themselves as having a special mission related to race, though it is important to note that the vast majority of the sample the authors label as MSIs fall into this enrollment-based category. In 2023, according to their data, there were 539 Hispanic Serving Institutions (HSIs) and 65 Predominantly Black Institutions relative to only 101 HBCUs and 35 TCUs (i.e., the categories of institutions that were created with an explicit race-based purpose). This suggests that the study's results are largely driven by the behavior of a set of institutions for whom their missions are unknown. We do not know whether these schools truly embrace their distinctive role through their priorities or actions, which is partly what motivated the focus of the paper and assertion that these institutions are unique. At a more basic level, as shown in table 9.2, "statutory" versus "formula-driven" MSIs differ in their characteristics and state locations, which prompts questions about how they might differ from institutions with an explicit race-based purpose.

It is also the case that many non-MSIs exhibit the features termed as "unique" in the paper. First, as described by the authors, obtaining the MSI designation for enrollment-based institutions is cumbersome—it requires completing complex forms and submitting extensive data. Some applicants are not successful, and some who would qualify based on demographics do not apply. Due to the bureaucratic process, there are institutions defined as non-MSIs that are actually quite similar to colleges with the MSI designation. Putting aside the focus on race, there are also many predominantly White institutions (PWIs) that emphasize the mission of creating access and supporting success for underserved students. Examples range from the University of Massachusetts Boston to Western Governors University[2] to basically all community colleges.

Finally, while the eligibility for special federal funding is truly unique to MSIs, these funds have traditionally been relatively small, so it is not clear

2. WGU states: "Our mission is to change lives for the better by creating pathways to opportunity." It is the largest, non-profit online university.

that MSIs have reaped large benefits relative to institutions without the special designation. Additionally, the authors note that public MSIs receive comparatively less in state funding than their PWI counterparts, and so the federal aid may just help to address inequities in the public sector and not actually result in serving as additional funds. For these two reasons, the financial circumstances of many MSIs are not that distinctive from some non-MSIs. Numerous institutions are struggling financially, so many of the concerns of MSIs discussed in the paper also apply more broadly for all higher education institutions and especially schools with fewer resources.

Altogether, these observations call into question what the group of institutions defined as MSIs in the paper truly represent. As defined in the paper, it includes some schools that may not see themselves as "minority serving" while excluding some that fit that definition. I would urge more focused attention on the statutory MSIs, which may best fit the "unique" qualities emphasized by the authors. Additionally, it is worth looking within the group of formula-driving MSIs to distinguish between those that might truly fulfill the distinct role the authors seek versus those that only technically fit the description. For example, schools with especially large proportions of minority students (as opposed to barely making the federal cutoff) are more likely to truly see themselves as MSIs. The length of time an institution has the MSI label may also matter (i.e., getting the designation 20 years versus only 3 years ago). Such efforts could help the study focus more clearly on institutions that truly embody the MSI distinction.

## The Diversity of MSIs

As noted above, there is a great deal of variation within the group of MSIs highlighted in the paper. Even if one were to refine the definition to focus only on one type of MSI, such as HBCUs, this would still be an incredibly diverse group of colleges and universities. To illustrate some of the variation, I focused on four HBCUs—Howard University, Spelman College, Southern University, and Cheyney University—using College Rover, an online college search tool. The schools range in selectivity, with Howard and Spelman accepting only 35 and 51 percent, respectively, and Cheyney accepting 74 percent. They also vary in the percentage of their students with the Pell Grant, a proxy for being from a low-income family. Howard and Spelman are at 43 percent Pell, while Southern is at 80 percent Pell. Howard also stands out in terms of instructional expenditures ($18,570) versus Spelman ($13,439), Cheyney ($9,890), and Southern ($5,336).

There is also tremendous variation in the available financial resources of HBCUs. Looking at 2021, Howard and Spelman have endowments that exceed most American colleges ($806 and $571 million, respectively), while Southern's endowment was only $12.0 million and Cheyney had $1.7 million. These gaps are likely to grow, as Spelman received a $100 million donation in January 2024, and Howard has also received several large gifts recently. Meanwhile, the news headlines suggest that 1 in 10 HBCUs were found to be "financially fragile" before the pandemic strained the resources of all colleges and universities.

Taking a broader view of all HBCUs, which are defined by their historical purpose to serve African Americans, it is clear that they vary in their level of racial diversity. According to IPEDS data (the source used by the authors), the student bodies at public four-year HBCUs were 8.0 percent White and 3.0 percent international. Meanwhile, public two-year HBCUs were only 45.0 percent Black, with White students making up 34.3 percent of the student body and Hispanic students making up 14.7 percent.

Such differences and even the racial diversity found within HBCUs prompts the question of whether "MSI" is a meaningful category to use to analyze higher education finances. My answer continues to be an emphatic "yes," but these observations about the range of characteristics of MSIs should be recognized and discussed as part of the motivation for studying them. Their diversity should also influence how such research is approached. MSIs are not monolithic; they exhibit the incredible diversity found throughout American higher education. As such, the MSI label does not mean the institutions have similar circumstances and student bodies, and studies of their behavior and impact should consider the specific resources, student bodies, and competition different kinds of MSIs face. Grouping MSIs together without attention to these differences could mask important behavior and trends. Additionally, the variation within MSIs could be useful in developing empirical strategies that exploit such differences to estimate effects.

## What Drives an Institution's Tuition Policy

The attention the paper gives to special categories of colleges and universities sheds light on aspects of higher education that are often ignored. Still, given the focus of the paper on tuition resets, much more could be said about the specific financial circumstances of the institutions being studied and how these details relate to tuition policy. Regardless of their missions or student body composition, tuition decisions and their effects will be driven by these other institutional factors, but little attention is given to these specifics. For example, the paper refers to the general financial concerns among MSIs, but given the diversity of these institutions (as discussed above), the colleges and universities in the sample do not face the same pressures or constraints. This is at least partly due to differences in funding sources, which range from federal and state appropriations to charitable gifts and endowment returns. They also differ in the freedom they have to alter—or reset—their tuition, due to the legislative oversight some public colleges and universities must contend with.

The enrollment context of each institution also matters when considering tuition policies and the impact of a reset. Students vary considerably in terms of their achievement levels, family resources, preferences, and needs, and different institutions attract different kinds of students. Moreover, as colleges and universities seek to enroll students, each institution must also take into account its competitive environment and the alternatives potential students might be considering. For instance, some MSIs attract more academically competitive students, draw applications from across the country, and are in direct competition with other selective MSIs and PWIs; facing such competitors influences their decisions and student reactions. At the other end of the spectrum, there are MSIs that have open admissions, draw primarily from local populations, and are being compared to the alternative of not attending any college. Many institutions are somewhere in the middle, exercising minimum standards for admissions and drawing applicants regionally.

The details about an institution's financial circumstances, potential student population, and competitive environment help to determine an institution's decisions about their list tuition price and a host of other things, such as financial aid awards, which are likely to be very important in determining future enrollment. Unfortunately, the paper does little to explore these specifics and consider how variation in institutional finances and the admissions context might result in a tuition reset having very different effects. There is acknowledgment that students' perception of a tuition reset is complex, with some equating price with quality and judging a tuition reduction as a negative while others may see a tuition cut as positively addressing concerns about affordability. The authors are correct in noting that a student's perception is likely related to their background and academic standing, though this important fact is not incorporated into the design of the study.

In summary, the analysis treats all institutions similarly, aside from their MSI designation and sector, and the paper does little to consider how the effects of a tuition reset might relate to the types of students the institution attracts or their specific competitive (or non-competitive) environment. If one considers how this study might be approached if MSI status were not the focus, it is highly unlikely given the current state of the research literature that one would include selective and non-selective institutions in the same model. It is also unlikely that a study would group public and private institutions together given the differences in subsidies and governance that strongly impact the setting of tuition. This study would be strengthened by accounting for these kinds of factors in the research design and empirical strategy. Stated another way, future research should try to better account for other important differences between institutions so that the analysis can get closer to estimating an "apples to apples" comparison that varies only in terms of MSI status.

P

# Panel Discussion

P1

# The Finances of a Public Flagship University

Benjamin E. Hermalin

A common claim is that public flagship universities are public in name only; that they are not especially dependent on state funding. After all, as an example, just 14 percent of the University of California, Berkeley's budget comes from the state of California.[1] Although not trivial, such a percentage nevertheless suggests that Berkeley's fortunes should be fairly independent of the state's: the vicissitudes of state funding should have only a marginal effect on Berkeley's budget. Yet, as this essay will make clear, such a view is far too rosy and Berkeley far more dependent on the state than 14 percent might suggest.

A caveat upfront: this is a case study of a single university. That is important insofar as institutions of higher education are exceedingly heterogeneous; indeed, there are non-trivial differences even among the ten campuses of the UC system. Consequently, one is cautioned against ascribing too much generality to what follows. That being said, from conversations with my counterparts at other public universities, I believe what follows does offer lessons beyond Berkeley.

Benjamin E. Hermalin is Executive Vice Chancellor and Provost, Schneider Distinguished Professor of Finance, and Distinguished Professor of Economics at the University of California, Berkeley, a research member of the European Corporate Governance Institute (ECGI), and a member of the board of directors of the National Bureau of Economic Research.

The author thanks John Campbell, Rita d'Escoto, Dan Feitelberg, Chris Stanich, and Chris Yetter for helpful comments. The views and opinions expressed are the author's and do not necessarily reflect those of the University of California. For acknowledgments, sources of research support, and disclosure of the author's material financial relationships, if any, please see https://www.nber.org/books-and-chapters/financing-institutions-higher-education/panel-discussion-finances-public-flagship-university.

1. Unless stated otherwise, financial figures are for the 2022–23 academic year (FY 23). Financial data for UC Berkeley can be found at https://controller.berkeley.edu/accounting-and-controls/financial-reporting/uc-berkeley-financial-reports-unaudited.

To understand why Berkeley is more dependent on state funding than that 14 percent figure might suggest, we need to peel back the onion of funding to get to the revenues truly available to support the campus's educational mission. First, nearly a quarter of Berkeley's overall $3.5 billion budget consists of grants and contracts. That funding, while vital for sustaining the campus's research enterprise, including graduate student training, is highly restricted; for the most part, these aren't funds that can be used to support classroom instruction, pay most salaries, or otherwise fund the campus's operations.[2] Similarly, other revenues, such as those generated by auxiliaries (e.g., housing and dining), are part of the $3.5 billion, but, as auxiliaries are largely self-sustaining—or, in some instances require subsidies from the campus—they don't contribute financially to the educational mission. When one finishes peeling the onion, central campus resources—the "*central ledger*"—is slightly more than $1.7 billion. The central ledger pays the salary and benefits of nearly all permanent faculty,[3] funds much of instruction (even beyond the cost of permanent faculty),[4] largely funds academic support units (e.g., the library), and pays utilities, as well as most of the campus's administrative costs. Central ledger funds are, thus, critical to Berkeley's operation. Consequently, as state support ($520 million in FY 23) represents 30 percent of the central ledger's funding, it is clear that Berkeley's dependence on state funding is far greater than the 14 percent figure quoted above.[5]

While the 30 percent figure begins to explain why ups and downs in state funding can have a meaningful effect on Berkeley, it can't be the whole story: after all, if fluctuations in state funding are not too great, then the campus can presumably ensure itself against shocks by building up reserves in years of relatively generous state funding as a buffer against leaner years. The problem with that presumption is that there have simply been too many lean years. Indeed, the history of state funding this century has largely been one

2. Berkeley's $840 million in grants & contracts includes $147 million in indirect cost recovery, which is available to the central administration. The rest ($693 million) is a pass through to pay for research activities.

3. Permanent faculty is essentially synonymous with tenured and tenure-track faculty. To be precise, they are Senate faculty in the Professor and Teaching Professor series. At last census, Berkeley had 1,594 individuals in those series with a full-time-equivalent (FTE) number of 1,570. Except for 68 individuals funded from philanthropic sources or revenues from certain master's programs, these faculty are all funded from the central ledger.

4. Instructional costs consist principally of compensation, including benefits, for lecturers, teaching assistants, and readers. There are some other, relatively minor, costs. The central ledger funds instruction mainly via a yearly determined allocation based largely on estimated need. For FY 25, that allocation exceeds $85 million. There are additional channels through which the central ledger funds instruction. Instructional costs not covered by the central ledger are covered by the schools and colleges using, *inter alia*, revenue from certain master's programs, annual giving directed to them, and certain endowment payouts.

5. Even the 30 percent figure doesn't fully reflect Berkeley's dependence on the state: historically, most of its buildings have been state funded, either directly or from state bond measures. I discuss capital issues more below.

of disinvestment: in *nominal* terms, state funding early in this century was not much lower than funding now ($451 million in 2004 vs. $520 million in 2023); in real terms, however, this represents a tremendous cut—in 2023 dollars, state funding in 2004 was $727.5 million.[6] Sadly, this 28.5 percent reduction in funding, in real terms, over the last 20 years actually *understates* the impact of state disinvestment: in this same period, Berkeley—in response to political pressure—expanded the size of its student body from 30,318 student FTE to 38,902 student FTE. Consequently, when viewed on a per student FTE basis,[7] the real reduction in state funding in this period is 44 percent—a massive disinvestment.

Growing the student body might seem to represent a welcome addition in tuition income. Unfortunately, while it increased tuition revenue, that expansion also increased costs. Accurately calculating the *economic* cost of educating a student is a challenging exercise.[8] Accurate calculations are not, however, necessary to conclude that an *in-state* student's tuition ($11,928 in FY 23) falls far short of any reasonable cost estimate of educating that student, even without accounting for the UC-mandated assessment on tuition dollars to support financial aid ("return to aid"). Evidence does suggest that the tuition paid by a non-California resident probably exceeds the cost of educating them; however, non-residents make up a small (never more than 24 percent) fraction of the undergraduate population. Moreover, due to political pressures to educate more California residents, that fraction (now 22 percent) is shrinking and must be brought to no more than 18 percent within a few years. Overall, *net* tuition, as of 2023, was $786 million, representing 46 percent of the $1.7 billion central ledger budget.

As the largest component of the central ledger, tuition warrants a few words. Owing to political pressures, UC tuition was held flat in nominal terms for much of this century: there was only one year (FY 18) between FY 12 and FY 22 in which tuition was increased (and, then, only by 2.5 percent). This has put further financial pressure on Berkeley. Recently, the UC system adopted a cohort tuition model in which the tuition rate of the entering class is increased by the rate of inflation (CPI) or 5 percent, whichever is less, over the rate paid by the previous class. Once the tuition rate is set for a class, it remains fixed for that class's time at Berkeley. While, in steady state and if the inflation rate is low and stable, tuition income will *almost* grow at the same rate as Berkeley's costs—tuition increases reflect the CPI, not HEPI[9]—

6. Inflation calculated using the Minneapolis Federal Reserve Bank's cpi calculator (https://www.minneapolisfed.org/about-us/monetary-policy/inflation-calculator). As a rule, the cpi understates the inflation rate for higher education, the higher education price index (HEPI) being arguably better.

7. A student taking a full load counts as one FTE. Less than a full load is a partial FTE.

8. One can readily calculate an average cost per student; that being said, such a measure is sensitive to how the numerator is calculated, which is more art than science. Berkeley's "official" average cost estimate is $33,000 ("Campus Budget Update," March 22, 2023).

9. Recall footnote 6.

during the phase-in period or periods of increasing inflation, tuition income grows at a rate far less than inflation.[10]

That 76 percent of Berkeley's sources of core funding have failed to keep pace with inflation—markedly so—for much of this century immediately explains why Berkeley has faced significant financial challenges nearly all of this century. Before addressing how Berkeley has coped with these challenges, let me touch on a few additional financial pressures beyond simple inflation. One is the growing cost of regulatory compliance:[11] higher education, especially public higher education, is one of the most regulated industries in America.[12] While I am unaware of any quantification of these costs overall, it's clear, extrapolating from specific examples, that these costs are in the tens of millions annually.[13] However, increased funding to offset the costs of new regulations is almost never provided. Another driver is that, in keeping with its mission to be an instrument of social mobility, Berkeley seeks to draw from a broader range of socioeconomic strata; expanded access brings its own costs in terms of increased financial aid and other support services. One last cost driver to mention is the rising cost of faculty.[14] While, to an extent, faculty salary growth tracks inflation and, thus, is part of the already discussed challenges of funding failing to keep pace with inflation, there are reasons to suspect that the competition for top faculty has been

10. To gain insight into the logic of cohort tuition, assume, for convenience, that each class is the same size, which we can normalize to 1 without loss of generality. Assume inflation is stable, so there is a constant rate of inflation, $i$. Let $r_t$ be the tuition rate of cohort $t$, which, given the normalization, is also tuition income from that cohort. Let $T_t$ be total tuition income at $t$; i.e., $T_t = \Sigma_{j=0}^{3} r_{r-j}$ (as a further convenience assume each cohort graduates in four years). Just prior to the start of cohort tuition, time 0, we have $r_0 = \cdots = r_{-3}$ and, thus $T_0 = 4r_0$. In the first year of cohort tuition, $T_1 = r_1 + 3r_0 = (1 + i)r_0 + 3r_0 = ir_0 + T_0$: the growth rate in tuition income is, thus, $i / 4$ (recall $r_0 = T_0 / 4$); so the campus continues to fall behind inflation. In steady state, $r_{t-j} = (1 + i)^{\tau - j} r_{t-\tau}$ (the tuition rate in any year can be found by compound inflating of any past year), so we have

$$T_t = \Sigma_{j=0}^{3}(1 + i)^{3-j} r_{t-3} = \Sigma_{j=0}^{3}(1 + i)^{4-j} r_{t-4} = (1 + i)\Sigma_{j=0}^{3}(1 + i)^{3-j} r_{t-4}$$

$$= (1 + i)T_{t-1};$$

hence, the rate of increase of $T_t$ over $T_{t-1}$ is $i$—the growth in tuition income matches the inflation rate. This analysis is readily adapted to show why a spike in inflation (i.e., from $i$ to $i + \Delta$) would not be immediately reflected in full in the growth of tuition income.

11. My noting the growing cost of regulatory compliance should not be read as my suggesting that these compliance measures are intrinsically bad or inappropriate. Many measures help ensure that Berkeley is living up to its goals around access, equity, inclusion, and belonging. My purpose in discussing them is only to note that they are a cost driver.

12. For an interesting take on these issues see Guard and Jacobsen (2024), which, as one measure of the challenges, notes between a two and threefold increase in legal cases involving higher education from the beginning of the century to now (p. 7, figure 1.1).

13. As just one example, new sports facilities at Berkeley to meet Title IX requirements will exceed \$80 million. (This should not, in any way, be read to indicate opposition to Berkeley meeting its Title IX obligations.)

14. In noting rising faculty costs, I'm in no way seeking to blame the faculty for Berkeley's financial challenges. Attracting and retaining the world's best faculty is simply a cost of Berkeley's fulfilling its mission of providing access to excellence.

more heated than inflation over much of the relevant period. Consistent with that supposition, average full professor salaries at Berkeley rose 48 percent, in nominal terms, from 2012 to 2022, but only 30 percentage points of that can be accounted for by cost-of-living increases provided by the university; the remaining 18 percentage points reflect other drivers, arguably including competition.[15] Related evidence is that, in *real* terms, average full professor salaries at Berkeley increased by 14.4 percent, an increase similar to a number of its main competitors (but interestingly not all).[16] Adding to this is the fact that California has become an increasingly expensive place to live relative to the rest of the country.[17] It is not surprising, therefore, that, among the top ten highest-paying public universities in the country, UC campuses occupy eight spots.[18] As a sense of the financial implication, it is notable that if Berkeley's average *full* professor salary were that of the University of Michigan in FY 22, it would have paid $46.7 million less in compensation.[19]

So how has Berkeley coped with these funding challenges? To an extent, it has cultivated other sources of revenue—although not enough to fully offset the real cuts in state funding and tuition. These other sources include philanthropy, improved financial return from intellectual property (IP),[20] new

15. Sources: The 48 percent number from the *Chronicle of Higher Education* website www.chronicle.com/article/explore-faculty-salaries-at-3-500-colleges-2012-20, and the 30 percentage points from comparing salary-scale tables for 2012 and 2022 (increases to those in percentage terms vary slightly across the different steps but cluster tightly around 30 percent). That 30 percent is essentially the cumulative cost-of-living increases from 2012 to 2022 (there are some technical nuances, not worth elaborating on here). While it is true that professors at Berkeley also get *merit*-based pay increases, which correspond to advancements in step, in a steady state with a fixed distribution across steps (i.e., one in which those moving into a step annually simply replace those moving out, where moving in encompasses both progression up the scales and hiring and moving out encompasses both progression and leaving the university), those merit increases can't raise *average* compensation. Of course, reality isn't a steady state with a fixed distribution, but the variance from that hypothetical state is too minor to explain much of the residual 18 percentage points.

16. From FY 12 to FY 24, Berkeley's five top rivals for faculty have been Chicago, Harvard, Princeton, Stanford, and Yale (based on head-to-head retention cases). Of those, Stanford and Yale had similar real increases (10.2 percent and 11.2 percent, respectively), Princeton was somewhat higher (20.4 percent). Surprisingly, Harvard's increase was just 1.9 percent and Chicago had a 2.2 percent real decrease. Source: *Chronicle of Higher Education* website www.chronicle.com/article/explore-faculty-salaries-at-3-500-colleges-2012-20. It is also worth noting that, of Berkeley's top ten competitors, eight currently pay higher average salaries to their full professors than Berkeley (source: *Chronicle of Higher Education*, 2023, p. 60).

17. From 2001 to 2023, the *California* consumer price index rose 82 percent (source: https://www.cdfa.ca.gov/AHFSS/cabb/docs/202406_notice_Feb_California_Consumer_Price_Index_1955-2024.pdf), the national cpi only 72 percent (source: Minneapolis Fed).

18. Source: *Chronicle of Higher Education* (2023), p. 60, "Highest Average Pay for Full Professors, 2021-22." Among the publics, UCLA is first, Berkeley second.

19. The difference in average salaries (source: ibid.) multiplied by 1.359, to account for the FY 22 composite benefit rate, then multiplied by the number of *full* professors at Berkeley.

20. Berkeley has always received royalty income from the patents resulting from research done on the campus. Recently, it has sought to capture a greater fraction of the wealth its IP creates via investing in new firms and creating incubators (e.g., the Bakar Bioenginuity Hub). The campus also has eight shared-carryforward venture capital funds.

high-fee master's programs,[21] and investment income earned on reserves.[22] Of those, only the last goes completely to the central ledger; much of the income from the others flows to the various academic units.[23] The precise accounting for these revenue sources on the central ledger is complex; that being said, a ballpark estimate is they contribute well over $200 million annually. At first blush, that would seem to cover the $207.5 million in real cuts in state funding since 2004; however, not all that $200+ million is new (i.e., some of that funding existed in 2004), to say nothing about the revenue lost to stagnant tuition.

Let me say a bit more about philanthropy. Berkeley's raising $7.37 billion in its recent capital campaign,[24] while impressive, has a more limited impact on its finances than might at first be evident. True, were all $7.37 billion unrestricted endowment, then the central ledger would be better off by roughly $295 million to $350 million annually.[25] However, only a trivial fraction of the funds raised went to unrestricted endowment—no more than a few million;[26] indeed, only $1.5 billion (20 percent of total) went into the endowment at all. To be sure, even restricted funds can be budget relieving: the campaign raised, e.g., funds for 42 new Senate FTE. Additionally, some of the funds that went directly to decanal units will help support instruction (recall footnotes 4 and 23).[27] Still, philanthropic funding—while absolutely critical—is not as fungible as other funding vis-à-vis the center and is, therefore, a less-than-perfect substitute *currently* for lost state funding and the forgone tuition increases from FY 12 to FY 22;[28] long term, it will hopefully prove to be a key part of the solution to state disinvestment, but it is not fully there yet.[29]

21. UC campuses can create Self-Supporting Graduate Professional Degree Programs (SSGPDPS), principally professional master's programs, for which "market" tuition may be charged. The majority of Berkeley's 21 SSGPDPS were created in the past decade or so.

22. The UC system provides a number of investment vehicles—essentially different mutual funds—in which campuses can invest reserves, both central reserves and unit-level reserves.

23. Although this, too, can be budget-relieving for the center insofar as it lessens the funding demands of the academic units on the center.

24. The Light the Way Campaign, which ran 2014 to 2023.

25. Berkeley has two endowments, one run by the University of California, Berkeley Foundation (UCBF), the other by the UC Regents. Currently, the former has a payout rate of 4 percent, the latter 4.75 percent; the numbers in the text are $7.37 billion times those payout rates.

26. A report for the Light the Way Campaign suggests that 0.3 percent of the $1.75 billion that was unrestricted in use went to endowment, so $5.25 million.

27. $5.62 billion (76 percent) of the money raised (or pledged) is restricted in use. Of the remainder that is not restricted in use, 94 percent has restrictions in terms of *user* (i.e., who controls use).

28. Philanthropy is, of course, valuable even when it doesn't add to the central ledger: it has allowed Berkeley to create new programs and build buildings that it otherwise wouldn't have been able to do. Additionally, philanthropy has funded research and other endeavors that are too "high risk" or otherwise not viewed favorably by government agencies.

29. Erasing the $207.5 million cut in state funding requires an *unrestricted* endowment of between $4.37 and $5.19 billion; Berkeley's current endowments are ~$7 billion combined, almost all restricted (see, also, footnote 25).

Berkeley has also coped on the cost-side of the ledger. Here it's less a tale of stop doing and more a tale of *not* doing. Universities are notoriously bad at stopping things. This reflects many forces: a reverence for tradition, shared governance, and an ability of aggrieved parties to mobilize protest campaigns.[30] Not surprisingly, stopping programs, closing centers, and the like have been rare events. Even when something ends, its resources are more likely to be redeployed than returned to the center. So Berkeley's "cost-side" strategy has largely been one of *not* doing. For example, the aforementioned 28 percent growth in student FTE was not matched by a growth in Senate FTE; indeed, its head count of Senate faculty increased by only five from 2004 to 2022.[31] Another significant not-doing is with regard to deferred maintenance: while estimates vary widely, the amount of deferred maintenance at Berkeley could exceed $5 billion. Not doing maintenance—kicking that cost can down the road—is a way to avoid making painful and controversial cuts to operations. Moreover, for the first decade or so of this century, this strategy wasn't wholly crazy insofar as the state did provide dedicated allocations for new buildings and seismic retrofits.[32] In the last decade, however, there has been considerably less state funding for those purposes.[33] Hence, there is a sense that we're fast running out of road down which to kick the deferred-maintenance can.

A further word on capital: as observed earlier, historically, the state was the principal funder of buildings (recall footnote 5). While the state has not wholly abandoned building—a state-funded classroom building is currently under construction—the campus has become more reliant on philanthropic support for new building and, to a limited extent, for retrofitting existing buildings. The campus has also used public-private partnerships (P3s). Yet, capital projects remain a major challenge: state funding is anemic (recall footnote 33); P3s require a revenue stream for the private partner;[34] and the development office describes fundraising for buildings as the hardest dollars to raise. Another issue is that philanthropists tend to favor buildings that will host new endeavors, exhibiting less—but by no means no—appetite for classrooms and facilities for existing endeavors. Moreover, while philanthropists have supported retrofitting buildings for new endeavors, they

30. See Rosenberg (2023) for an interesting take on resistance to change in higher education. Also see Getz and Siegfried (1991) for how those pressures might explain rising costs.

31. The head count jumped significantly, by 42, in 2023 due to additional *non*-state-funded positions, a campus decision to be slightly more expansive in authorizing state-funded lines, and a drop in separations. Even then, the 2023 head count is only 3 percent over 2004.

32. Although funding for seismic retrofits is intended to bring old buildings closer to ever more stringent seismic-related building codes, such retrofits often afforded opportunities to address other maintenance needs.

33. The last state general obligation bond measure that included UC was passed in 2008.

34. A revenue stream is readily identified when the building is directly revenue generating (e.g., a dorm). Another way to generate revenue is for the campus to lease the building or a portion of it. Such leasing arrangements are not, conceptually at least, that different from borrowing and, indeed, such leases factor into the campus's overall debt capacity.

have essentially no desire to refurbish buildings for existing uses. While a small portion of the operating budget does go to deferred maintenance, the pressure to kick the can down the road—as discussed above—has proved difficult to resist. To an extent, the campus can commit not to kick the can by borrowing—debt payments effectively being mandated spending—however, the campus's debt capacity is rather limited.

So how does Berkeley solve its financial challenges? If I knew the answer, I would have far fewer sleepless nights. State *re*investment in the UC is not imminent. Nor will pressures to enroll principally California residents at a relatively low rate of tuition abate anytime soon. If Berkeley can sustain the momentum it has in philanthropy (bringing in over $1 billion in a number of recent years), then this will help tremendously, especially if giving can be steered more toward core activities and/or capital needs. Capturing more of the value its IP generates will also prove important to Berkeley. At the same time, it is difficult to see that Berkeley can overcome its financial challenges unless, one, it actually stops doing things that are less central to its teaching and research mission; and, two, it figures out how to do things differently. No university is a paragon of efficiency, but Berkeley often seems remarkably inefficient (i.e., to be operating well inside the production frontier). But getting to the frontier is not enough: Berkeley needs a better production technology—as, I suspect, do most universities: while Baumol's (1967) cost disease is a debated explanation for why higher education costs have historically outpaced the rest of the economy,[35] it is nonetheless hard to see how Berkeley will be able to afford what it currently does unless it can improve its productivity via technology, such as artificial intelligence (AI). Indeed, the logic of Baumol's cost disease being what it is, if AI leads to productivity gains in other sectors, but not higher education, then higher education's relative cost problem will only get worse.

Despite all this, Berkeley remains the #1 public university in the world. I do not expect that to change anytime soon: in part, because I don't foresee Berkeley deviating from its steadfast commitment to recruit and retain the best faculty; and, in part, because I don't see that other *public* universities are in significantly better financial shape given that state disinvestment has been a widespread phenomenon (see, e.g., Bound et al. 2019). To be sure, the University of California has some challenges vis-à-vis other state universities—higher cost of living, limited capacity to enroll non-resident students, and seismically related deferred maintenance being especially notable—but California also offers myriad advantages. A larger question is whether Berkeley will continue to be able to hold its own against elite *private*

35. For a discussion of the competing hypotheses for the rising cost of higher education, including Baumol's cost disease, see Getz and Siegfried (1991). Archibald and Feldman (2008) offer some evidence in favor of Baumol's cost disease as an explanation.

universities; although there is no evidence so far that Berkeley is slipping.[36] This may reflect, as Campbell et al. in this volume suggest, that even the elite privates are not without financial challenges.

## References

Archibald, Robert B., and David H. Feldman. 2008. "Explaining Increases in Higher Education Costs." *Journal of Higher Education* 79(3): 268–95.

Baumol, William J. 1967. "Macroeconomics of Unbalanced Growth: The Anatomy of Urban Crisis." *American Economic Review* 57(3): 415–26.

Bound, John, Breno Braga, Gaurav Khanna, and Sarah Turner. 2019. "Public Universities: The Supply Side of Building a Skilled Workforce." *RSF: The Russell Sage Foundation Journal of the Social Sciences* 5(5): 43–66.

Campbell, John Y., Jeremy C. Stein, and Alex A. Wu. 2025. "Economic Budgeting for Endowment-Dependent Universities." In *Financing Institutions of Higher Education*, edited by John Y. Campbell and Kaye Husbands Fealing. Chicago: University of Chicago Press. This volume.

*The Chronicle of Higher Education*. 2023. *The Almanac of Higher Education*, 2023–2024. August 18.

Getz, Malcolm, and John J. Siegfried. 1991. "Cost Inflation." In *Economic Challenges in Higher Education*, edited by Charles T. Clotfelter, Ronald G. Ehrenberg, Malcolm Getz, and John J. Siegfried. Chicago: University of Chicago Press.

Guard, Louis H., and Joyce P. Jacobsen. 2024. *All the Campus Lawyers: Litigation, Regulation, and the New Era of Higher Education*. Cambridge, MA: Harvard University Press.

Rosenberg, Brian. 2023. *Whatever It Is, I'm Against it*. Cambridge, MA: Harvard Education Press.

36. Except for Harvard and Stanford, Berkeley has a winning average against top privates in retention battles, ranging from 67 percent to 100 percent in head-to-head competitions.

P2

# Strategy-Centered Leadership and Financial Management Is Needed in Research Universities

Robert A. Brown

## Bowen's Law and University Finances and Budget

Most not-for-profit universities are guided by the prophetic statement of economist Howard Bowen that "each institution endeavors to fulfill its own purpose within the constraints set by the social milieu and the competition of other colleges and universities" (Bowen 1980). Bowen described in his 1980 book on financing higher education that universities spend all the funds available on their mission, creating the simple axiom of university budgets known as the Revenue Theory of Cost or Bowen's Law. Simply, these universities use measures of success other than the bottom line, compelling them to spend all available funds. And there is almost never enough money to satisfy demand, especially when everyone measures success differently.

University push for excellence driven by Bowen's law has been interpreted by many as uncontrolled spending. This hypothesis is not supported by analysis (Clotfelter 1996). The difficulty of identifying a single contributor is complicated by the inability of most of higher education, especially in residential settings, to see cost reductions from deploying technology; universities suffer *cost disease*, a term coined by Baumol and Bowen to describe the inability of an industry to increase productivity with scale or automation (Baumol and Bowen 1965). Unless the university has such a large endow-

Robert A. Brown is President Emeritus and Professor of Computing & Data Sciences at Boston University.

These remarks are an expanded version of the editorial (Brown 2024a). For acknowledgments, sources of research support, and disclosure of the author's material financial relationships, if any, please see https://www.nber.org/books-and-chapters/financing-institutions-higher-education/panel-discussion-strategy-centered-leadership-and-financial-management-needed-research-universities.

ment that it alone can support the demand for funding, increasing tuition becomes an inevitable source.

Nowhere is the tension between resources and expenditures more acute than in our research universities, the less than 100 institutions out of the more than 2,600 four-year colleges and universities in the United States that emphasize scholarship, research, and new inventions as well as undergraduate and graduate education. In terms of quality and productivity, our system of research universities is the envy of the world and is uniquely composed of both state-supported and private universities. As an example of their shared importance, in 2022 the academic research enterprise totaled almost $100 billion supported by government, foundations, and the universities themselves with 57 universities—38 state supported and 19 privates—each spending more than half a billion dollars annually.

This research enterprise was created three-quarters of a century ago at the end of World War II by a covenant between universities and the federal government.[1] From the beginning, both the government and institutions shared in funding the endeavor. However, today the agreement is showing wear and tear, as the balance has shifted toward the universities. As I documented in a recent Op-Ed, the university contribution to the total expenditure has increased to 25 percent of the total, up from 20 percent only 12 years ago (Brown 2024b). The increasing investments in research put most private universities in the unenviable position of having to subsidize research from tuition revenue, trading off student access and the quality of undergraduate and professional education with the cost of establishing the academic environment that attracts the most talented and sought-after research faculty.

## Why Leadership and the Financial Management System Matter

Here is where the connection between leadership and financing and budgeting matters most. In a world of pressures on tuition and access, the cost demands for quality education, and the competition for faculty talent, it is not enough for a university to either attempt to create competitive quality organically or to delegate the strategy to the schools and their deans. Research universities and others must have a university-wide strategic vision for their institution and connect this vision with financial planning and budgeting. The ability to accomplish this depends on the leadership model and the financial management system. The president must own the strategy and work with the board and academic and administrative leadership to develop, implement and measure progress against the plan, and make course corrections as circumstances change.

This is where there has been a divergence in university leadership models

1. The establishment of the mechanisms for federally sponsored research are well described in Cole (2016).

over the last 50 years. With the development of Responsibility Centered Management (referred to as RCM) in the 1970s, universities began moving away from centralized budgeting systems, devolving financial management from the central leadership to a decentralized model giving authority to the deans—moving Bowen's law down in the organization (Whalen 1991). The development of RCM, apparently spearheaded by budget offices, relieved the provost and the president of making the myriad of negative budget decisions that occur in a centralized system, and promised to drive fiscal accountability and entrepreneurship into academic units at a time of budget austerity.

RCM also resolved another growing problem, managing the increasing revenues and expenses associated with medical schools and their clinical enterprises, which could dwarf the budget of the rest of the university. RCM essentially cut them loose from the university's budget, tethering them to their clinical and research revenues.

But RCM profoundly changed the university's leadership structure, reducing it to a loosely federated set of academic schools—a holding company. Leadership of these universities has been described by many fine presidents. James Duderstadt, the longtime president of the University of Michigan, an RCM institution, wrote:

> Today the comprehensive university is managed effectively as a federation. The university administration sets some general rules and regulations, acts as an arbiter, raises money for the enterprise and tries—with limited success—to keep activities roughly coordinated. But rarely does the university find strong vision or leadership from the top. (Duderstadt 2007)

This style of university financial organization and leadership is not well suited to the challenges facing research universities today. Consider the following five questions:

1. Undergraduate education today is more interconnected between traditional disciplines than ever, with new interdisciplinary degrees and minors increasingly important. Does our financial management system make it seamless for our students to take advantage of such opportunities?
2. Most of the grand research challenges facing society that must be the focus of our research and scholarship do not fit neatly in traditional disciplines. What system is best for supporting these initiatives?
3. Given resource constraints, it will be difficult for a research university to compete effectively in every area. How will decisions be made about where to put resources? Which system supports such a process most effectively?
4. Just as students are interested in moving between disciplines, many of the most interesting new faculty members defy simple classification. New hiring and appointments processes may be needed to attract and retain this talent (Brown 2024c). Which system best supports these changes?

5. Universities must develop campus-wide strategies for online education. University-wide organizations will reduce redundancy and lead to a more coherent brand. Can this be accomplished in a decentralized system?

These challenges were not considered when RCM was developed in the 1970s. For example, interdisciplinary research and teaching were not then the norm. In fact, the extensive scholarship on interdisciplinarity barely mentions the influence of the budgeting system and leadership model on the success of such efforts. In my experience these systems matter dramatically. The writing on RCM by financial administrators assumes that these efforts can be funded by taxing schools using the same approach used for core efforts, such as student health services or central IT services. I have yet to meet a dean who thinks taxes are good business, especially to fund academic initiatives that they don't sponsor. RCM was simply not designed to promote all-university strategies. This is a major limitation at a time when research universities need to have individualized strategies to thrive.

Jonathan Cole, the longtime provost of Columbia, an RCM institution, wrote about the need for change by referring to RCM:

> This budgetary system worked reasonably well at many exceptional universities during "the age of disciplinary siloes" or the era of the "multiversity." The open question is whether this form of budgeting has become sufficiently dysfunctional and a drag on the growth of collaboration and the eventual discoveries that come from them. (Cole 2016)

## Strategy-Centered Management

What is the alternative? Another approach to financial management is needed, built on the design principle that *the financial management strategy should mirror the strategy of the university*. The president and provost are at the center of the process, pushing the strategy forward with dogged determination, but having the agility to pivot as required to adapt to market forces. This has been Boston University's approach for 18 years leading to both the growth of the institution and our ability to adapt to extreme challenges like the Great Recession and the COVID-19 pandemic.

Our system has central control of revenues and expenses across the university and focuses on generating annual reserves from operations—a margin—that is strategically reinvested according to our plans. The system is a hybrid, with schools, other academic units, and strategically important initiatives having budgets set by the provost. These budgets are *not* based on revenue sharing for what we refer to as core academic programs, although we closely track these numbers. These budgets are augmented by revenue sharing on non-core activities, usually special educational programs. I refer to such a system as Strategy-Centered Management, or SCM; a diagram of SCM is shown in figure 2P.1.

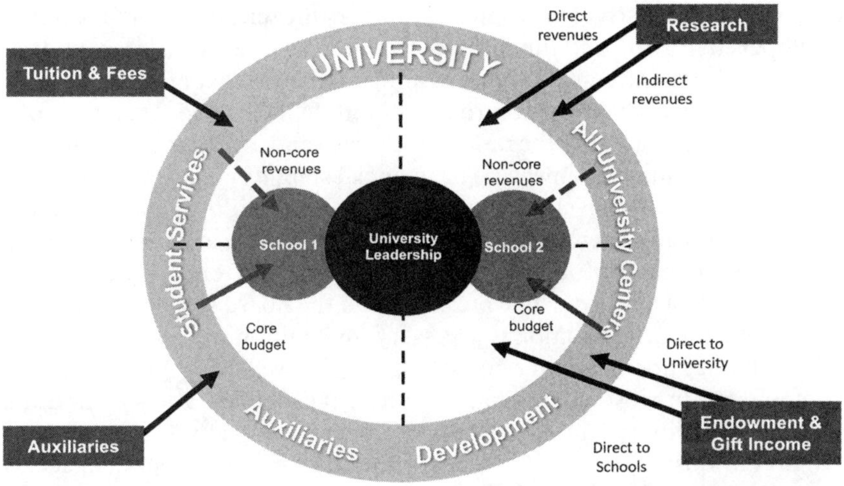


**Fig. 2P.1 Schematic diagram of Strategy-Centered Management (SCM) showing schools encapsulated in all university services with all revenues staying at the university level, except those explicitly designated to either an academic unit (designated endowment income and tuition sharing in non-core programs) or principal investigator for research.**

In SCM all activities associated with undergraduate education are considered core along with the core graduate programs in the professional schools. Everything to do with research also is a core activity; this is key to controlling the increasing university contribution to this part of the enterprise. No budgeting system is purely centralized (or decentralized) and SCM can be modified to account for RCM-like units. Like others with major medical schools where the faculty is funded mostly from clinical revenues and external research, our medical school (as well as the schools of public health and dental medicine) operates on an RCM-like model. Another important distinction at Boston University is that faculty in these three schools are not offered tenure. The combination of the differences in budgeting and faculty appointments makes collaboration between the medical school and the rest of the university more difficult than it should be.

Even so, by any number of metrics SCM has achieved its objectives at BU. As a university with a relatively small endowment (contributing 3–4 percent of our annual operating budget), generating reserves for re-investment has been key. As an example, our free cash flow margin for the five years 2017–2021 averaged 8.4 percent, tied for first place among a list of 16 private university peers who averaged only 2.5 percent for the same period. This difference is dramatic, especially since a large portion of these reserves are held centrally in SCM to be deployed strategically. From cash, we built a student center in 2012, constructed an interdisciplinary life science research building that opened in 2018, and funded over a million square feet of renovation.

For a private university our bond rating matters as it controls our access to debt markets. The fiscal controls built into SCM helped strengthen our balance sheet. As a result, the ratio of total cash and investments to adjusted net debt—an important measure of financial stability—increased from 0.7 in 2004 to 2.3 in 2022. This improvement was a result of net asset growth that has averaged 13 percent for the last five years. These improvements have been reflected in our Moody's bond rating moving up from A3 (negative) in 2004 to AA3 (stable) now. The president and the board sleep better today.

A strong financial position is necessary for a vibrant research university, but the money doesn't matter unless you spend it well. SCM gives the president and the provost, collaborating with the academic leadership and the board, the ability to strategically direct the university in ways that matter. Notably at Boston University we have focused on expanding student access through increased undergraduate need-based financial aid, more than doubling our aid budget over the last decade (an over $200 million increase) to the point where we now meet full need of domestic students and have eliminated loans from financial aid packages for Pell Grant students, who now compose over 25 percent of our domestic student body. A similar increase in the number of underrepresented students has followed.

SCM also enables educational flexibility for undergraduates, who can move among the 12 schools and colleges offering undergraduate degrees. There are no "internal transfers" associated with students taking classes across school boundaries. SCM also was key to the implementation of our new general education system, the BUHub, which engages faculty across our campus. Persistent gains and losses in enrollment are handled by the provost through the annual budgeting process.

Perhaps the biggest advantage of SCM over decentralized systems is in faculty hiring, where the centralized resources can be allocated for increasing start-up costs needed to compete for excellent faculty in areas of strategic focus. Keeping these resources centrally also is key to driving conversations about research priorities across the schools, which otherwise would not be possible. In our case, the discussion about the importance of data science and artificial intelligence led to the creation of a novel academic unit, the Faculty of Computing & Data Sciences (CDS), composed both of faculty with sole appointments in CDS and others jointly appointed with another school or college. I believe this kind of interconnected hiring will be key to future-proofing faculty hiring.

## Postscript

Strongly engaged and transparent leadership is required for SCM to work well. When it does and is combined with a robust fundraising effort you can create the flywheel that Jim Collins refers to in his classic management book, *Good to Great* (Collins 2001). It is a system that, year after year, generates the resources needed to implement the strategy of the university. Even the creators of RCM recognized the power of centralized systems; Curry, Laws, and Strauss said:

> When base allocations are appropriately managed, the model putatively puts a very large steering wheel in the hands of senior leadership: the sum of all unrestricted funds. The ability to steer the university toward central priorities is apparently maximized and the funding of interdisciplinary activities is relatively simple. (Curry et al. 2013)

These are the tools needed to create a cohesive, strategically directed research university that will endure in the decades ahead.

## References

Baumol, W. J., and W. G. Bowen. 1965. "On the Performing Arts: The Anatomy of an Urban Crisis." *American Economic Review* 57: 415–26.

Bowen, H. R. 1980. *The Cost of Higher Education*. Jossey-Bass.

Brown, R. A. 2024a. "The Case for a More Strategic Financial Management System." *Inside Higher Ed*, January 11.

Brown, R. A. 2024b. "The Uncertain Future of Private Research Universities." *Inside Higher Education*, June 7.

Brown, R. A. 2024c. "University Hiring Must Be Centrally Organized Around Interdisciplinarity." *Times Higher Education*, January 30.

Clotfelter, C. T. 1996. *Buying the Best: Cost Escalation in Elite Higher Education*. Princeton University Press.

Cole, J. R. 2016. *Toward a More Perfect University*. PublicAffairs.

Collins, J. 2001. *Good to Great*. Harper Business.

Curry, J. R., A. L. Laws, and J. C. Strauss. 2013. *Responsibility Center Management: A Guide to Balancing Academic Entrepreneurship with Fiscal Responsibility*. NACUBO.

Duderstadt, J. 2007. "Fixing the Fragmented University: A View from the Bridge." In *Fixing the Fragmented University*, edited by J. B. Burke. Jossey-Bass.

National Science Foundation (NSF). 2022. *Higher Education Research and Development (HERD) Survey*. https://www.nsf.gov/statistics/srvyherd/.

Whalen, E. 1991. *Responsibility Center Budgeting*. Indiana University Press.

P3

# Financial Management Challenges in Higher Education

Lisa M. Lynch

The composition of employment in higher education today in the United States is undergoing significant change as colleges and universities attempt to bend the cost curve, respond to enrollment declines at both the undergraduate and graduate levels, and recruit staff amid the strongest labor market since the 1960s. In addition, private sector colleges and universities have faced a surge in adjunct faculty and student-worker union organizing after two important National Labor Relations Board (NLRB) rulings in the last 10 years. In 2014, the NLRB ruled that full-time adjunct or contingent faculty in private colleges and universities are not managerial employees and, therefore, have the right to organize.[1] The second ruling by the NLRB in 2016, involving graduate student workers at Columbia University,[2] held that student workers are considered statutory employees covered by the National Labor Relations Act and have the right to organize.

In the following comments I describe in further detail changes in the

Lisa M. Lynch is the Maurice B. Hexter Professor of Social and Economic Policy at the Heller School for Social Policy and Management at Brandeis University, former Provost and Executive Vice President of Academic Affairs at Brandeis University, and a research associate of the National Bureau of Economic Research.

For acknowledgments, sources of research support, and disclosure of the author's material financial relationships, if any, please see https://www.nber.org/books-and-chapters/financing-institutions-higher-education/panel-discussion-financial-management-challenges-higher-education.

1. For more detail see "Big Union Win," Scott Jaschik, *Inside Higher Ed*, January 1, 2015, https://www.insidehighered.com/news/2015/01/02/nlrb-ruling-shifts-legal-ground-faculty-unions-private-colleges.

2. See Decision on Review and Order, by Chairman Pearce and Members Miscimarra, Hirozawa, and McFerran, Case 02-RC-143012, The Trustees of Columbia University in the City of New York and Graduate Workers of Columbia-GWC, UAW. August 23, 2016. https://studentbenefits.provost.columbia.edu/sites/default/files/content/NLRB%20Decision.pdf.

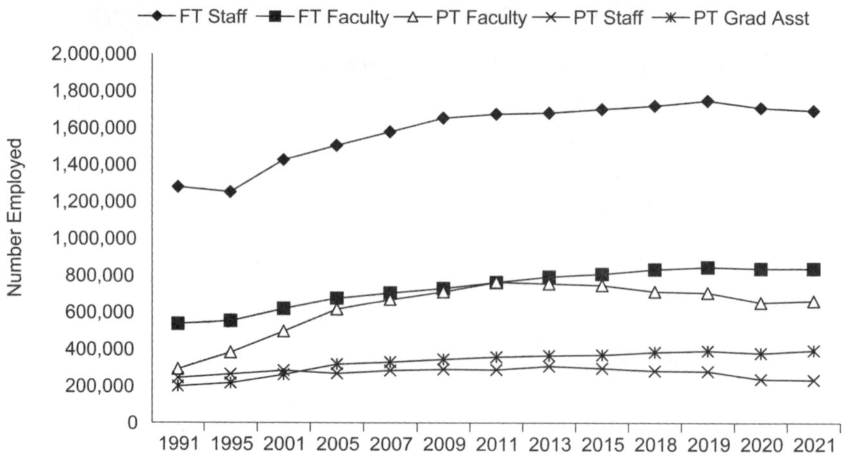


**Fig. 3P.1 Employment trends faculty and staff by full-time and part-time status 1991–2021**

Source: National Center for Education Statistics, Education Digest 2022 and 2023 Table 314.20.

composition of the labor market in higher education over the past 30 years, a few ways in which colleges and universities have responded to demands to reduce personnel costs even in the face of low unemployment, and finally recent trends in faculty and student unionization.

*Employment Composition*. In 2022 there were almost 3.9 million employees in over 3,500 degree-granting higher education institutions in the United States, representing 2.5 percent of the total US workforce. About 1.5 million higher education employees were faculty, and 2 million were staff. Of the faculty, 842,407 were full-time, and 665,234 were part-time.[3] Among staff, the largest categories of employees by occupation were office and administrative support (~370,000), student and campus services (~224,000), management (~280,000), and librarians and instructional support staff (~214,000).[4]

Figure 3P.1 shows some changes in employment in higher education for full and part-time faculty and full and part-time staff from 1991–2021. Focusing on staff first one can see in figure 3P.1 that full-time staff, shown in the top line, represent almost 45 percent of all employees in higher education. Their employment increased steadily through the late 1990s and early 2000s, dropped with COVID-19, and only returned to pre-COVID levels in 2022. Part-time staff make up a little more than 10 percent of all staff, and

3. National Center for Education Statistics, Education Digest 2023 Table 314.20.

4. "Total Number of Employees at U.S. Colleges by occupation," UNIVSTATS, https://www.univstats.com/staffs/ as accessed July 16, 2024.

their numbers have been declining since 2013. Note that staff employed by a third-party contractor are not included here—e.g., dining, custodial, and bookstore. Many colleges and universities, in an effort to reduce expenses, have been outsourcing these categories of employees and others, such as HR, legal, and online program management, over the past decades. Therefore, the actual number of people providing services for colleges and universities is considerably higher than the 3.9 million number cited above.

There has been considerable discussion of how colleges and universities have tried to reduce costs by replacing full-time tenured and tenure-track faculty with part-time contingent or contract faculty. As seen in figure 3P.1, part-time faculty hiring increased sharply from 1991–2011, and by 2011, 50 percent of all faculty were full-time (which may include full-time contract faculty), and 50 percent were part-time. However, the number of part-time faculty fell by almost 100,000 between 2011 and 2022. By 2022 56 percent of all faculty were full-time and 44 percent were part-time. There has also been a slow but steady increase in the number of part-time paid graduate assistants since 1995—now just under 400,000.

These trends raise several questions. For example, are part-time contract faculty becoming full-time contract faculty or full-time tenured and tenure track faculty? Are some part-time contract faculty being replaced by part-time grad students? The American Association of University Professors, AAUP, sheds some light on these questions with their analysis of changes in the academic labor market.[5] Using data on nonmedical instructional faculty in degree-granting nonprofit institutions, they find that full-time contract faculty now represent 20 percent of all faculty, whereas, in the early 1990s, they were around 14 percent. In addition, they find that "about 24 percent of faculty members in US colleges and universities held full-time tenured appointments in fall 2021, compared with about 39 percent in fall 1987, . . . and the number of graduate student employees increased 44 percent from fall 2002 to fall 2021, compared with a 19 percent increase among both full-time and part-time faculty."[6] This suggests that colleges and universities have tried to reduce costs and increase flexibility by reducing tenured and tenure track positions and replacing these jobs with contingent faculty and graduate student workers. Goolsbee and Syverson (2023) argue that four-year colleges and universities have significant monopsony power over their tenure-track faculty[7] and conclude that monopsony power has contributed to this trend toward non-tenure-track faculty hiring in the United States.

5. "Data Snapshot: Tenure and Contingency in US Higher Education," Glenn Colby, American Association of University Professors, https://www.aaup.org/article/data-snapshot-tenure-and-contingency-us-higher-education.

6. Ibid.

7. This is not to say that many a provost has understandably complained about the high cost of recruiting and retaining superstar tenured faculty. But these are more the exceptions in elite research universities rather than the norm for faculty hiring.

Further examination of the data in figure 3P.1 raises the question of how these changes in the composition of faculty and graduate student assistants may have contributed to the increased organizing efforts on behalf of contract faculty and graduate students. In addition, how do these trends vary by public versus private nonprofit versus private for-profit institutions, small versus large institutions, and research-intensive universities versus community colleges? These are all questions that merit further study.

COVID-19 has further impacted the trends in the composition of faculty. In a survey done in October 2020 of 1,122 professors by the *Chronicle of Higher Education*,[8] 73 percent of tenured professors said they had moved up their retirement date. Almost half said they planned to retire within two years or less. In comparison, in 2019, when this question was asked to faculty, only 20 percent said they would retire within two years. With mandatory retirement eliminated for faculty in 1994, many colleges and universities have tried, with mixed success, to introduce various retirement plans to encourage faculty to transition into retirement. An irony with these programs from a financial point of view is that it may well be the case that a long-serving tenured faculty member who retires is paid not that much more, and in some cases less, than what a new tenured track faculty might cost.

As tenured faculty retire, this should result in the hiring and advancement of women and faculty of color. However, the data in figure 3P.1 and from the AAUP suggest that retired faculty are more likely to be replaced by fixed-term contract faculty than by tenure track or tenured faculty. In the face of a marked decrease in the number of students graduating from high school in the United States (the enrollment cliff of 2025), a "hot" labor market that is luring more high school graduates to skip college and directly enter the labor force, and a perception that "college doesn't pay," it should be no surprise that colleges and universities are reluctant to commit to lifetime employment for faculty as colleges and universities struggle to balance declining revenues with rising costs.

*Impact of a "Hot" Labor Market*. While there is some evidence that universities have monopsony power over tenure-track faculty, colleges and universities need to recruit and retain many non-faculty staff positions from a more competitive labor market. With the national labor market experiencing one of the longest stretches of low unemployment in more than 60 years, college administrators have struggled to fill open staff positions and retain key personnel while at the same time managing financial pressures to lower the overall cost of attendance. The College and University Professional Association for Human Resources, CUPA-HR, conducts regular surveys of the higher ed labor market and finds in its 2023–24 survey on wages that

8. "On the Verge of Burnout: Covid-19's Impact on Faculty Well-Being and Career Plans." Research Brief, Fidelity Investments and *The Chronicle of Higher Education*, 2020. https://connect.chronicle.com/rs/931-EKA-218/images/Covid%26FacultyCareerPaths_Fidelity_ResearchBrief_v3%20%281%29.pdf.

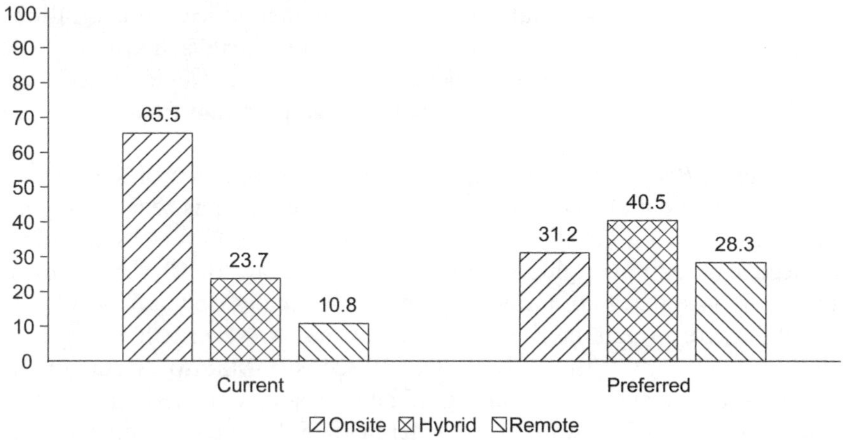


**Fig. 3P.2 Employee preference for remote or hybrid work (percent)**
Source: CUPA-HR 2023 Employee Retention Survey. https://www.cupahr.org/surveys/employee-retention-survey/ accessed July 13, 2024.

"staff (generally non-exempt employees) received the highest increase in pay in comparison to other workforce areas . . . [while] tenure-track faculty continued to receive the lowest pay increases (and were the only group of employees whose raise did not surpass inflation)."[9] In addition, in the 2023 CUPA-HR employee retention survey,[10] they found that one-third of higher education employees are very likely or likely to look for new employment opportunities in the next year. For full-time, exempt staff, turnover has increased from a low of 7.9 percent in 2020–21 to 14.3 percent in 2022–23. Turnover for full-time, non-exempt staff increased from 9.4 percent to 15.2 percent during this same period.

The impact of COVID-19 and a hot labor market has also contributed to marked changes in where staff would like to conduct their work. In responses to the 2023 CUPA-HR employee retention survey, almost 70 percent of non-faculty employees said they would prefer to work either in hybrid mode or fully remote. The only categories of employees for whom less than 50 percent indicated that most duties could be done remotely were librarians, health and wellness staff, and facilities staff. Figure 3P.2 shows a marked difference between where employees report they work (in-person, hybrid, or fully remote) versus where they would like to work. Providing more flexibility in work location may be one way for colleges and universities to lower payroll

9. "Workforce Pay Increases," College and University Professional Association for Human Resources, accessed July 20, 2024. https://www.cupahr.org/surveys/workforce-data/workforce-pay-increases/.

10. "The CUPA-HR 2023 Higher Education Employee Retention Survey," Jacqueline Bichsel, Melissa Fuesting, Diana Tubbs, and Jennifer Schneider, September 2023. https://www.cupahr.org/surveys/research-briefs/higher-ed-employee-retention-survey-findings-september-2023/.

costs, but it is a fundamental change in how higher education institutions create their on-campus community. Yet in high-cost cities, hybrid or fully remote work may be a way for colleges and universities to hire outside the local labor market and not have to pay a wage premium for higher local costs of living.

*Collective Bargaining in Higher Education.* The last area of substantial change and financial consequences in higher education has been the significant increase in unionization of faculty and students over the past decade.[11] Collective bargaining rights are protected by state law for academic professionals in 34 states, but in those 34 states, historically, only a handful provide collective bargaining rights to student workers. Nevertheless, graduate teaching assistants at the University of Wisconsin–Madison secured their first union contract in 1970, and graduate assistants at the University of Michigan won their first union contract in 1975. For faculty and graduate assistants at private colleges and universities, their right to organize is regulated by the National Labor Relations Act (NLRA) and overseen by the five-member National Labor Relations Board, NLRB. Each of the members of NLRB is appointed by the president, with the approval of the Senate, for a term of five years. In 1972, in a decision involving Adelphi University, the NLRB ruled that graduate teaching and research assistants were primarily students and, therefore, not able to unionize. In a landmark 1980 decision, *NLRB v. Yeshiva University*, the US Supreme Court narrowed the protections of the act to non-tenure track employees, including graduate students, unless the institution otherwise agreed to recognize the bargaining unit or the tenured track faculty members did not hold "managerial authority." In 2000, the NLRB reversed its prior decisions in a case involving New York University and ruled that graduate student assistants were employees. The NLRB then backtracked four years later in a case involving Brown University when it decided that graduate student workers were not employees. This is why the 2016 decision by the NLRB to rule that student workers were employees again has been so important for the current surge in student unionization. This back and forth in NLRB decisions also means that university administrators have taken different approaches in how they have engaged with unionization campaigns on their campuses—some try to slow-walk the process in the hope that there will be yet another reversal of opinion by the NLRB while other institutions move forward with the recognition vote and first contract negotiation in a timelier way.

As detailed by Berry and Savarese (2012) in their 2012 Directory of US Faculty Contracts and Bargaining Agents in Institutions of Higher Education and Sproul, there were just over 430,000 faculty and graduate student assistants unionized in 2012, including 42 percent of all public two-year college faculty members unionized, 25 percent of all public four-year fac-

11. For a recent review, see Clemons 2024.

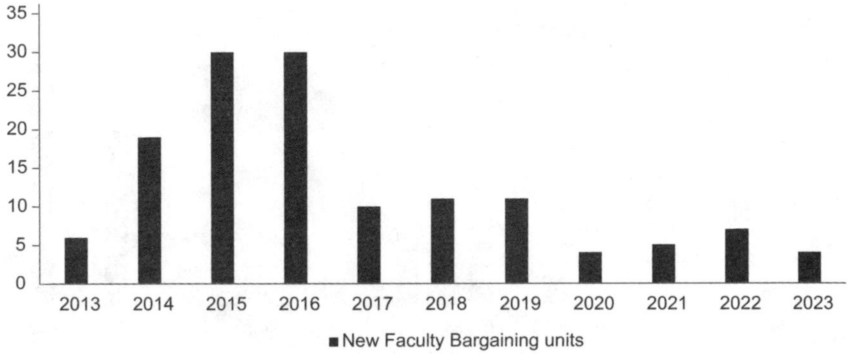


**Fig. 3P.3a Trends in faculty collective bargaining units since 2012**
Source: *The State of the Unions 2023.* Special feature by Herbert et al. (2023), 10. https://slu.cuny.edu/wp-content/uploads/2023/08/Union-Density-2023.pdf. The black boxes in the bar graph are the number of new units each year. Data for 2023 are just through June 30.

ulty members unionized, but just 7 percent of faculty members at private four-year institutions unionized. Starting from this base in 2012 using data collected by the National Center for the Study of Collective Bargaining in Higher Education and the Professions[12] and summarized by Herbert et al. (2023), one can see in figures 3P.3a and 3P.3b the marked increase in the number of new collective bargaining units for both faculty and graduate students that have followed the NLRB 2014 decision that impacted contract faculty and the 2016 decision that impacted graduate student workers. These two figures show the new bargaining units added each year in the bar graphs. Between 2013 and 2023, 137 faculty collective bargaining units won recognition, representing more than 42,000 faculty. The total number of faculty bargaining units by June 30, 2023, is 786. In 2024, data not included in figure 3P.3a, NYU's full-time contract faculty voted to unionize after the university agreed to remain neutral during the election, becoming the largest union of full-time contract faculty at a private college or university with close to 1,000 faculty in the bargaining unit. University administrators may have hoped that replacing tenured and tenure-track faculty with full-time contract faculty would provide more flexibility, but this increased precarity is most certainly an important factor in the rising unionization of both full and part-time contract faculty.

Figure 3P.3b shows the dramatic uptick that began in 2022 in student bargaining units. Just between 2022 and half of 2023, unions won 30 new student-worker collective bargaining units, representing a total of 35,655 workers. As detailed by Herbert et al. (2023), most of the new student collec-

12. National Center for the Study of Collective Bargaining in Higher Education and the Professions, https://www.hunter.cuny.edu/ncscbhep/.

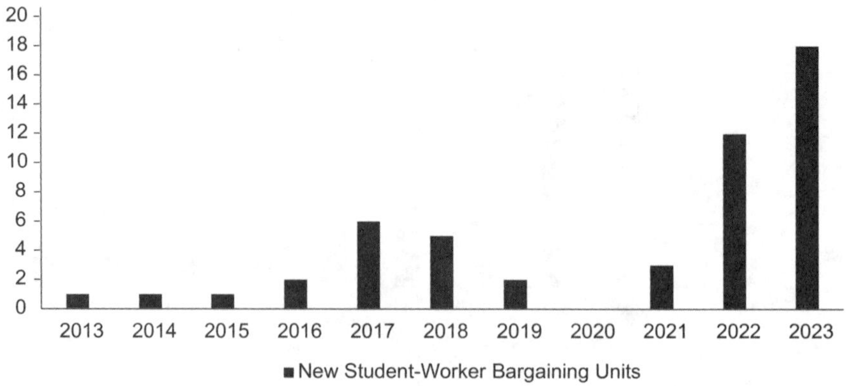


**Fig. 3P.3b Trends in student-worker collective bargaining units since 2012**
Source: From *The State of the Unions 2023.* Special feature by Herbert et al. (2023), 7. https://slu.cuny.edu/wp-content/uploads/2023/08/Union-Density-2023.pdf. The black boxes in the bar graph are the number of new units each year. Data for 2023 are just through June 30.

tive bargaining units have involved graduate student workers, who comprise 62 percent (19) of the new units. However, as also discussed in Herbert et al. (2023), the growth in the number of undergraduate bargaining units is a notable new development in higher education collective bargaining. Prior to 2022, there were hardly any undergraduate unions despite the large number of undergraduates who work on campuses as resident advisors, tutors, dining hall staff, library staff, and more. However, in 2022–2023, many new undergraduate student-worker unions were established on campuses across the country, including the Service Employees International Union (SEIU), which successfully organized a campaign for 20,000 undergraduate student employees at California State University.[13] This is the largest undergraduate student union in the country, and it will be interesting to watch the negotiation dynamics and features of their first collective bargaining agreement.

Student work by undergraduates and graduate students has always been a feature of higher education institutions, so why is there a surge in unionization now? Certainly, the NLRB decision of 2016 has played an important role, but other contributing factors likely include the rising costs of higher education, student debt, and workplace conditions, including discrimination, bullying, sexual harassment, and workplace safety. This presents a unique challenge to higher education administrators as they provide an environment that supports the student as both a learner who pays tuition and an employee earning wages.

The next frontier in union organizing in higher education is student-athletes. In response to an election petition by Dartmouth College basket-

13. This new bargaining unit is not included in figure 3P.3b.

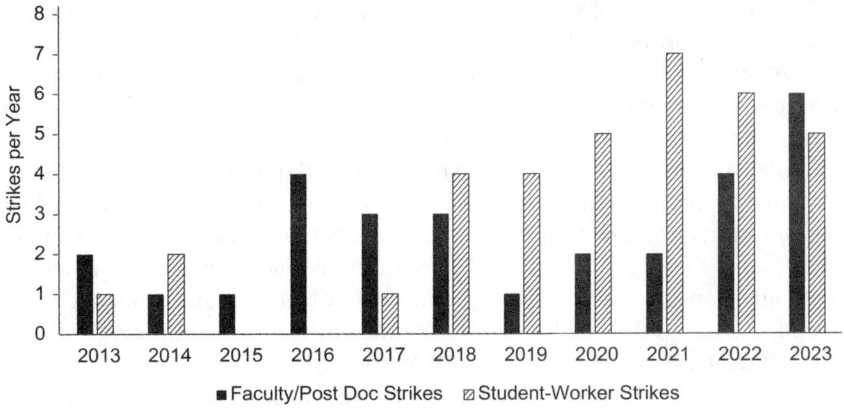


**Fig. 3P.4 Strike activity since 2012**

Source: From *The State of the Unions 2023*. Special feature by Herbert et al. (2023), 11. https://slu.cuny.edu/wp-content/uploads/2023/08/Union-Density-2023.pdf. Data for 2023 are just through June 30.

ball players in September 2023 to form a union, the Boston regional NLRB[14] concluded that the basketball players met the definition of an employee because they performed work that benefited the college, the college exercised significant control over the players' work, and the work was performed in exchange for compensation. The form of compensation was valuable equipment and apparel, tickets to games, lodging, and meals, along with the benefits of the college's peak performance program. After the basketball players voted 13–2 to join the union in 2024, Dartmouth asked for a full review by the NLRB board of the decision. The college said, "If the full NLRB refuses to overturn the regional director's decision, Dartmouth's only remaining option to challenge this legal error is to engage in a technical refusal to bargain, an unprecedented step in our long history of labor negotiations. . . . This will likely result in SEIU Local 560 filing an unfair labor practice charge with the NLRB, which we would appeal. This is the only lever Dartmouth has to get this matter reviewed by a federal court."[15]

Finally, figure 3P.4 presents some data on the number of faculty and student strikes since 2012. There have been several high-profile strikes including the November 2022 strike of six weeks involving some 48,000 academic researchers, postdocs, and student workers in the University of California system, 1,800 adjunct faculty at the New School in New York City, and the 2023 strike at Rutgers University of over 9,000 tenured and tenure-track faculty, contingent faculty, postdoctoral scholars, and graduate assistants.

14. For more details, see "US Labor Official Says Dartmouth Basketball Players Are School Employees, Sets Stage for Union Vote," Jimmy Golen and Ralph{ns}D. Russo, February 6, 2024, https://www.wbur.org/news/2024/02/06/dartmouth-basketball-union-nlrb.

15. Ibid.

After the University of California strike, wages increased 55 to 80 percent for academic employees and 25 to 80 percent for graduate-student researchers.[16] At Rutgers, post-strike salary increases were 33 percent for graduate student workers, 44 percent for adjunct faculty,[17] and 28 percent for postdocs. At the New School, its president and senior administrators had to respond to angry parents who threatened to file lawsuits against the university and withhold tuition and angry faculty who felt prior norms of work were violated when the university demanded proof of work effort and suspended pay of striking adjunct faculty.[18] Even as colleges and universities eventually reach an agreement on wage and working conditions for faculty and students, there are likely additional hidden costs they face in terms of employee morale, alumni relations, and faculty and student retention.

As we consider the financial challenges facing colleges and universities, including the baby bust, declining student enrollments, student debt, the rise of remote learning, and shrinking/shifting sources of funding for research, it is also important to consider how employment decisions made by colleges and universities can both help and exacerbate these challenges.

## References

Berry, Joe, and Michelle Savarese. 2012. *Directory of U.S. Faculty Contracts and Bargaining Agents in Institutions of Higher Education*. September. https://www.hunter.cuny.edu/ncscbhep/assets/files/NCSCBHEP%202012%20Directory%208-15-12%20RC2.pdf 201.

Clemons, Andrea. 2024. "Analyzing the Upward Trend in Academic Unionization: Drivers and Influences." *Journal of Collective Bargaining in the Academy* 15: article 5.

Goolsbee, Austan, and Chad Syverson. 2023. "Monopsony Power in Higher Education: A Tale of Two Tracks." *Journal of Labor Economics* 41(S1): S257–S290.

Herbert, William, Jacob Apkarian, and Joseph van der Naald. 2023. "Union Organizing and Strikes in Higher Education: The 2022–2023 Upsurge in Historical Context" Special feature in *The State of the Unions 2023: A Profile of Organized Labor in New York City, New York State, and the United States*, edited by Ruth Milkman and Joseph van der Naald. https://slu.cuny.edu/wp-content/uploads/2023/08/Union-Density-2023.pdf.

16. UAW 2865 & SRU Contracts, Student Researchers United-UAW, https://www.fairucnow.org/uaw2865-sru-contracts/.

17. As reported in "Striking Faculty and Grad Students Secured Big Pay Raises This Academic Year," by Emma Hall and Zachary Schermele, *Chronicle of Higher Education*, June 6, 2023. https://www.chronicle.com/article/striking-faculty-and-grad-students-won-big-pay-raises-this-academic-year.

18. "'An Extraordinarily Hostile Move': New School Threatens to Withhold Pay in Adjunct Strike," by Katherine Mangan, *Chronicle of Higher Education*, December 7, 2022. https://www.chronicle.com/article/an-extraordinarily-hostile-move-new-school-threatens-to-withhold-pay-in-adjunct-strike.

# Subject Index

Page numbers followed by "f" or "t" refer to figures or tables, respectively.